European Corporate Law

European Company Law Series

VOLUME 5

Editor

Steef Bartman, professor of company law at Leiden University in The Netherlands and lawyer at DLA Piper. The editorial board, made up of leading company law experts from around Europe, ensures that each book is topical, well-written and practical.

Introduction

The European Company Law Series is closely linked to the bimonthly journal European Company Law, also published by Kluwer Law International.

Contents/Subjects

The series covers subjects of company law in a broad sense, including insolvency, co-determination and securities law. Topical issues such as merger control, corporate governance, and piercing the corporate veil have been covered.

Objective of Series

Analysis of topical or complex subjects in European company law.

Readership

Academics; regulators; practitioners.

The titles published in this series are listed at the end of this volume.

European Corporate Law

Third Edition

Adriaan F.M. Dorresteijn
Christoph Teichmann
Erik Werlauff
Tiago Monteiro
Nadia Pocher

Wolters Kluwer

Published by:
Kluwer Law International B.V.
PO Box 316
2400 AH Alphen aan den Rijn
The Netherlands
Website: www.wolterskluwerlr.com

Sold and distributed in North, Central and South America by:
Wolters Kluwer Legal & Regulatory U.S.
7201 McKinney Circle
Frederick, MD 21704
United States of America
Email: customer.service@wolterskluwer.com

Sold and distributed in all other countries by:
Quadrant
Rockwood House
Haywards Heath
West Sussex
RH16 3DH
United Kingdom
Email: international-customerservice@wolterskluwer.com

ISBN 978-90-411-8593-8

e-Book: ISBN 978-90-411-8594-5
web-PDF: ISBN 978-90-411-8595-2

Table of Contents

Preface xiii

List of Abbreviations xvii

CHAPTER 1
Introduction 1

CHAPTER 2
Business Organizations Within the European Union 9
I Introduction 9
A Civil and Commercial Law 10
B Legal Personality 11
C Principal Forms of Business Organization 12
II Partnerships 15
A Civil Partnerships and 'Silent' Commercial Partnerships 16
B General Partnerships in the UK 18
C Continental General Partnerships 20
D Limited Partnerships 24
III Companies 26
A Private Companies 26
B Public or Stock Companies 27
IV Hybrid Forms 28
A LPs with Shares 29
V Business Organizations under EU Law 30
VI Impact of the EU 31
VII The Right of Establishment 33

CHAPTER 3
The Harmonization Programme Within Europe 43
I Introduction 43

A The Legal Basis of European Legislation 44
B European Legal Instruments 46
1 Directives 46
2 Regulations 51
3 Recommendations and Opinions 51
4 Judicial Decisions 52
II Company Law Directives 54
A Disclosure, Validity of Obligations and Nullity of the Company [First Directive] 54
1 Disclosure 55
2 Validity of Obligations 58
3 Nullity of the Company 61
B Formation and Capital of Public Limited Liability Companies [Second Directive] 62
1 Information 64
2 Minimum Capital 64
3 The Maintenance of the Capital 66
4 Alteration of the Capital 68
5 Concluding Remarks 69
C Mergers and Divisions of Limited Liability Companies 70
D Domestic Mergers of Public Limited Liability Companies [Third Directive] 70
1 Merger by Acquisition 71
2 Merger by Formation of a New Company 71
3 Applicable Rules 72
E Divisions of Public Limited Liability Companies [Sixth Directive] 74
F Cross-Border Mergers of Limited Liability Companies [Tenth Directive] 76
1 Introduction and Scope 76
2 The Essential Provisions 79
3 Perspectives 81
G Financial Statements 82
1 Scope of Directive 2013/34 84
2 General Principles 87
3 Special Reports and Publication 87
4 Perspectives 88
H Statutory Audits [Eighth Directive] 88
I Branches: Disclosure Requirements [Eleventh Directive] 91
J Single-Member Private Limited Liability Companies [Twelfth Directive] 93
K Takeover Bids [Thirteenth Directive] 95
L Proposal for a Directive on the Transfer of the Registered Office [Fourteenth Directive] 98

III Shareholders' Rights Directive 102
IV Capital Markets 108

CHAPTER 4
Business Organizations under European Union Law 115
I Introduction 115
II European Economic Interest Grouping 116
A Formation and Publication 118
B Structure 121
C Involvement of Employees 122
D Perspectives of the EEIG 123
III European Company 124
A Applicable Law 126
B Formation and Publication 127
C The Law Applicable to Formation 131
D Widening the Range of Participating Companies 132
E Registered Office and Head Office 133
F Capital 135
G Structure: One-Tier or Two-Tier Board 135
H Structure: General Meeting 138
I Financial Statements, Winding Up and Liquidation 139
J Involvement of Employees 140
K Perspectives of the SE 144
IV Other European Business Organizations 146
A European Cooperative Society 147
B Single-Member Private Limited Liability Company (SUP) 148

CHAPTER 5
Formation and Financing of Companies 153
I Introduction 153
II Public Companies 153
A Formation Procedure 153
1 Registration 159
B Substantive Requirements 160
1 Capital 162
C Pre-incorporation Transactions 165
III Private Companies 168
A Formation Procedure 168
1 Registration 168
B Substantive Requirements 169
1 Capital 170
C Pre-incorporation Contracts 173
IV Financing of Companies 174
A Share Capital 174
B Loan Capital 174

C Securitization 177
D Covered Bonds 179
E Off-Balance-Sheet Arrangements 179

CHAPTER 6
The Management and Control of Companies under National Law 183
I Introduction 183
II France: The SARL 185
A The Basic Management Structure 185
B Control of the Managers 186
C The Role of the Members 187
III France: The SA 188
A The Alternative Structures 188
B The Unitary Board Structure 189
C The Two-Tier Structure 192
D Directors' Liability 193
E The Role of the Members 194
IV France: The SAS 195
V Germany: The GMBH 196
A The Management Structure 196
B Shareholder Meetings 198
VI Germany: The AG 198
A The Two-Tier Board System 198
B The Management Board 199
C The Supervisory Board 200
D The Role of the Shareholders 201
VII Poland: The SP.ZO.O. 202
A The Management Structure 202
B The Role of the Members 204
VIII Poland: The SA 204
A The Management Structure 204
B The Role of the Shareholders 205
IX Spain: The SA and the SRL 206
A Management and Representation 206
B The Role of the Members 208
X Belgium: The NV/SA 211
A The Management Structure 211
B Directors' Liability to the Company 213
C The Role of the Shareholders 214
D Representation by the Directors 215
XI Belgium: The BVBA/SPRL 215
XII The Netherlands: The NV and the BV 216
A The Management Structure 216
B The Structure Regime 218

C The Duties of Directors 220
D The Role of the Shareholders 221
XIII The UK: Public and Private Companies 223
A The General Management Structure 223
B The Directors: Their Appointment, Dismissal and Powers 224
C The Duties of Directors 226
D The Members in General Meeting 229
XIV Italy: The SPA 231
A Board Models 231
1 The Traditional System 232
2 The Two-Tier System 235
3 The One-Tier System 236
B Liability of Directors 237
C The General Meeting 239
XV Italy: The SRL 241
A The Role of the Members 241
B The Management and Control Structure 242
C *Società a Responsabilità Limitata Semplificata* (SRLS) 243

CHAPTER 7
Involvement of Employees 245
I Introduction 245
II Information and Consultation: The EWC, the SE and the SCE 249
III Information and Consultation: Other Directives 255
IV Employee Involvement Within Member States 259
A Belgium 260
B France 261
C Germany 263
D The Netherlands 265
E Poland 266
F Spain 267
G The UK 268
H Italy 269

CHAPTER 8
Cross-Border Cooperation and Acquisitions 273
I Introduction 273
II Cross-Border Cooperation 274
A Strategic Cooperation 274
B The Cross-Border Dimension 276
C Joint Ventures 278
III Acquisitions 280
A Methods of Acquisition 280
B Acquisition of Assets 282
C Acquisition of Shares 283

IV Takeover Defences 284
A The Board Neutrality Rule 284
B Information about Takeover Defences 284
C The Breakthrough Rule 285
D Takeover Defences: Conclusion 287
V Cross-Border Mergers of Companies 288
VI Protection of Rights of Employees 291
VII Merger Control 294
A The Treaty Provisions 294
B The Merger Regulation 296
1 The First Phase 298
2 The Second Phase 300
3 Joint Ventures 301

CHAPTER 9
Financial Statements and Related Reports 303
I Introduction 303
II The IAS/IFRS 305
III General Principles 308
IV Balance Sheet 310
V Profit and Loss Account 314
VI Notes on the Annual Financial Statements 315
VII The Management Report 316
VIII Publication of the Annual Financial Statements 318
IX Reports to Be Published by Listed Companies 320
X Consolidated Financial Reports 322
A Exclusion of Individual Undertakings 324
B Contents of Consolidated Financial Statements 325
XI Audit 327

CHAPTER 10
Groups 329
I Introduction 329
II The Law of Groups in Germany 333
A Enterprise Agreements 334
B Groups Involving Private Companies 336
III EU Group Law 338
A The Formation of Groups 342
B The Functioning of Groups 344
IV Groups Operating Across Borders 346
V Laws of the Member States 347
A Group Concepts 348
B Piercing the Corporate Veil 350
VI Concluding Remarks 355

Bibliography 357

Table of ECJ Cases 361

Index 363

Preface

Since the publication of the first edition of this book, more than twenty years ago, many changes have taken place in the area of European corporate law. In hindsight, one can say that the first edition was dealing with a somewhat rudimentary version of European corporate law. Since then, we have seen major developments, such as the introduction of the European Company, rules on cross-border mergers and employee involvement. The Court of Justice of the European Union (EU) has interpreted the right of establishment in a progressive way, thereby facilitating relocation of companies and other legal entities within the EU. The financial crisis of 2008 and its aftermath gave rise to extensive EU regulation on banks and other financial institutions. The EU rules on accounting, strongly influenced by international accounting standards as they are, have been modernized. They now also contain non-financial reporting obligations with a view of sustainability and other social responsibility concerns.

That is not to say that all initiatives of the European Commission were successful. Among the thwarted proposals are draft directives on the board structure of companies under national law and on a legal framework for groups of companies as well as, more recently, the draft Statute for the European Private Company. But, as the third edition of this book illustrates, these are minor setbacks in view of what has been achieved and what is to be expected, because it is necessary for the functioning of the internal market in a globalized and digitalized economy.

Notwithstanding these developments, at the national level, diversity is still the keyword for those who try to understand corporate laws within the EU (and the EEA).[1] Accordingly, the book contains sections on some key elements of the company laws of a number of Member States of which Italy is included for the first time. The characteristics of national company laws and political incentives remain, of course, a slackening combination to those who are convinced that acceleration of harmonization within the EU is the way to go. Seen from a distance, however, differences in national company laws are often related to details the importance of which should not be overrated. Significantly, in relation to the core issue of duties and liabilities of directors,

1. The European Economic Area (EEA) Agreement provides for the inclusion of EU legislation covering the free movement of goods, services, persons and capital.

Member States differ not so much in regard to substantive rules as they do in relation to judicial enforcement.[2] And as is shown in the work of Kraakman, Armour and their co-authors in *The Anatomy of Corporate Law*, even when observed from a global viewpoint, companies and corporations have a number of basic features in common.[3]

At the completion of the third edition, a few words must be spent on Brexit. The UK have voted to leave the EU and the negotiations procedure has been triggered by the UK government's notification as stated in Article 50 of the Treaty on European Union. It is envisaged by the government that on the day the UK leaves the EU, 'all EU laws which are directly applicable in the UK and all laws which have been made in the UK in order to implement our obligations as a member of the EU are converted into domestic law (...)'.[4] Brexit requires the EU to react to the UK leaving and, simultaneously, with the issue how the EU should proceed.[5] The effects of Brexit, in regard of the topics dealt with by this book, can only be assessed years from now. Therefore, the UK is still featured in this book in the same way as in the previous edition but that might change with the fourth edition of this book.

This book is primarily designed for those at university or others in legal practice who wish to acquire a better understanding of corporate law within the EU and its common characteristics as well as some of the similarities and differences between the various national legal systems. Therefore, we aim at describing some of the main issues of corporate law at the level of the EU as well as at the national level. The latter, of course, cannot be done in a comprehensive way because it would not only represent a task far greater than we could have coped with but it would also be disproportionate to the aims of the book.[6] Even the laws of the restricted number of Member States we have included will be, out of necessity, dealt with in a rather eclectic way. As in the second edition of this book, the laws of Belgium, France, Germany, the Netherlands, Poland, Spain and the UK are taken into account, and in most sections Italy is now included. The selection of countries may be debatable, but the book aims at including examples of continental European legal systems as well as the common law system of the UK, and, where Poland is concerned, an example of the Eastern European Member States.[7]

---

2. *Study on Directors' Duties and Liability*, prepared for the European Commission DG Markt by: Carsten Gerner-Beuerle, Philipp Paech & Edmund Philipp Schuster (Department of Law, London School of Economics), April 2013.
3. Reinier Kraakman et al., *The Anatomy of Corporate Law: A Comparative and Functional Approach*, 3rd edition (Oxford: Oxford University Press, 2017).
4. *Legislating for the United Kingdom's Withdrawal from the European Union*, Department for Exiting the European Union, March 2017, p. 31.
5. Juncker suggests return of powers to shore up post-Brexit EU, *Financial Times* 2 Mar. 2017 https://www.ft.com/content/630c5b6c-fe87-11e6-96f8-3700c5664d30.
6. It would probably lead to 'diminishing returns' in terms of the comparative method, Konrad Zweigert & Hein Kötz, *Introduction to Comparative Law*, 3rd revised edn, (Oxford: Clarendon Press, 1998), 41.
7. In some of the chapters where national law is outlined, a country-by-country pattern is used (notably in Chs 6 and 7), whereas in other parts of the book a topical structure appeared to be the best option. Suggestions for further reading: Nicola de Luca, *European Company Law: Text, Cases and Materials* (Cambridge: Cambridge University Press, 2017), and Stefan Grundmann, *European Company Law*, 2nd edition (Cambridge-Antwerp-Portland: Intersentia, 2011).

We welcome Nadia Pocher as co-author of the book. She has contributed much by updating EU law sections and by writing on Italian law. We are very grateful for the help of Professor Krzysztof Oplustil of Jagiellonian University in Kraków in updating the sections on Polish law. Finally, many thanks are owed to Karina Podkladneva from Ireland for editing all of the texts and, being an advanced law student, for her extremely useful comments on several sections.

June 2017[8]

Dr Adriaan F.M. Dorresteijn, *Utrecht University; AKD Lawyers, Civil-Law Notaries and Tax Lawyers (The Netherlands).*
Tiago Pereira Monteiro, LL.M., *AVM Advogados, Lisbon (Portugal).*
Prof. Dr Christoph Teichmann, *University of Wuerzburg (Germany).*
Prof. Dr Erik Werlauff, *Aalborg University (Denmark).*
Dr Nadia Pocher, *SLF – Studio Legale Fisicaro* and *Centro Studi Europeo Antiriciclaggio e Anticorruzione (Italy).*

8. The book is updated during 2016 and the first five months of 2017.

List of Abbreviations

A.C.	The Law Reports, Appeal Cases
AG	Aktiengesellschaft
AktG	Aktiengesetz
All E.R.	All England Law Reports
APA	Asset Purchase Agreement
ASB	British Accounting Standards Board
B.C.L.C.	Butterworths' Company Law Cases
BERR	Department for Business Enterprise & Regulatory Reform
BetrVG	Betriebsverfassungsgesetz
BGB	Bürgerliches Gesetzbuch
BGBL	Bundesgesetzblatt
BGHZ	Entscheidungen des Bundesgerichtshofes in Zivilsachen
BIICL	British Institute of International Comparative Law
BRRD	Bank Recovery and Resolution Directive
BTA	Business Transfer Agreement
BV	Besloten vennootschap met beperkte aansprakelijkheid
BVBA	Besloten vennootschap met beperkte aansprakelijkheid
BW	Dutch Civil Code
CA 2006	Companies Act 2006
CBM	Cross-Border mergers
CIC	Community Interest Company
CJEU	Court of Justice of the European Union
CLR	Company Law Review Steering Group
COMI	Centre of Main Interests
Com. VA	Commanditaire vennootschap op aandelen
Comm.V	Gewone commanditaire vennootschap

Commission	European Commission
CSR	Corporate Social Responsibility
CV	Commanditaire vennootschap
CVR	Commanditaire vennootschap met rechtspersoonlijkheid
DCC	Dutch Civil Code
DTI	Department of Trade and Industry
EA	European Association
EBA	European Banking Authority
EBOR	European Business Organization Law Review
EC	European Community
ECB	European Central Bank
ECFR	European Company and Financial Law Review
ECGI	European Corporate Governance Institute
ECJ	European Court of Justice (abbreviation previously used for the CJEU)
ECL	European Company Law
ECR	Official reports of cases before the Court of Justice in English
EEC	European Economic Community
EEIG	European Economic Interest Grouping
EIRO	European Industrial Relations Observatory
EIOPA	European Insurance and Occupational Pensions Authority
EMCA	European Model Company Act
EMS	European Mutual Society
EP	European Parliament
ESC	European Securities Committee
ESMA	European Securities and Markets Authority
ESO	Employee Share Ownership
ET	Ley del Estatuto de los Trabajadores
EU	European Union
EUR	Euro
EWC	European Works Council
FASB	Federal Accounting Standard Board (US)
FSAP	Financial Services Action Plan 1999
GAAP	Generally Accepted Accounting Principles (US)
GIE	groupement d' intérêt économique
GmbH	Gesellschaft mit beschränkter Haftung

GmbHG	Gesetz betreffend die Gesellschaften mit beschränkter Haftung
HGB	Handelsgesetzbuch
IAS	International Accounting Standards
IASB	International Accounting Standards Board
IASC	International Accounting Standards Committee
IFRS	International Financial Reporting Standards
IR	Integrated Reporting
InsO	Insolvenzordnung
K.B.	The Law Reports, King's Bench
KG	Kommanditgesellschaft
KgaA	Kommanditgesellschaft auf Aktien
LMA	Loan Market Association
LP	Limited Partnership
LLP	Limited liability partnership
LPA	Limited Partnerships Act
LOI	Letter of Intent
Ltd	Private limited company
MIFID	Markets in financial instruments Directive
MIFIR	Markets in Financial Instruments Regulation
MitbestG	Mitbestimmungsgesetz
MNE	Multinational enterprise
MOMIG	Gesetz zur Modernisierung des GmbH-Rechts und zur Bekämpfung von Missbräuchen
MOU	Memorandum of Understanding
NJ	Nederlandse Jurisprudentie
NJW	Neue Juristische Wochenschrift
NRE	Loi sur les Nouvelles Régulations Économiques
NV	Naamloze vennootschap
OECD	Organisation for Economic Co-operation and Development
OHG	Offene Handelsgesellschaft
OJ	Official Journal of the European Union
OVR	Openbare vennootschap met rechtspersoonlijkheid
PA	Partnership Act
PartG	Partnerschaftsgesellschaft
Plc	Public limited company
RSA	Rappresentanze sindacali aziendali

RIW	Recht der internationalen Wirtschaft
S. Com. por A.	Sociedad comanditaria por acciones
SA	Société anonyme, sociedad anónima, spólka akcyjna
SAPA	Società in accomandita per azioni
SARL	Société a responsabilité limitée
SAS	Société par actions simplifiée
SC	Sociedad regular colective
SCA	Société en commandité par actions
SCE	Societas Cooperativa Europaea (European Cooperative Society)
SCIC	Société coopérative d'intérêt collectif
SCS	Société en commandite simple
SE	Societas Europaea (European Company)
SEAG	SE Ausführungsgesetz
SEC	(extension used for European Commission document reference)
SEC	Sociedad en comandita
SEC	U.S. Securities and Exchange Commission
SI	Statutory Instrument
SKA	Spólka komandytowo-akcynja
SL (or SRL)	Sociedad de responsabilidad limitada
SLNE	Sociedad Limitada Nueva Empresa
SMEs	Small and medium enpterprises
SNC	Société en nom collectif, società in nome collettivo
SOX	Sarbanes-Oxley Act
SPA	Società per azioni, Share purchase agreement
sp. z o.o.	Spólka z ograniczoną odpowiedzialnocią
sp.j.	Spólka jawna
sp.k	Spólka komandytowa
sp.p.	Spólka partnerska
SPE	Societas Privata Europaea (European Private Company)
SPRL	Société privée a responsabilité limitée
SPV	Special purpose vehicle
SRL	Società a responsabilità limitata
SUP	Societas Unius Personae
TEU	Treaty on European Union
TFEU	Treaty on the Functioning of the European Union
VAT	Value-added tax

VOF	Vennootschap onder firma
WOR	Wet op de ondernemingsraden
WvV	Wetboek van Vennootschappen
XBRL	eXtensible Business Reporting Language
ZGR	Zeitschrift für Unternehmens- und Gesellschaftsrecht
ZIP	Zeitschrift für Wirtschaftsrecht

CHAPTER 1

Introduction

1.01 European corporate law, as any corporate law, consists of legal norms relating to certain types of a business organization. In other words, corporate law provides the legal structure of a business enterprise. In general, corporate law includes all incorporated forms of business organizations and thus encompasses more than just company law. For the purposes of this book, corporate law is used in the broader sense.

1.02 Although many business activities are carried out across borders, business organizations are subject to national laws of the Member States. As stated by the European Court of Justice (ECJ) in the *Daily Mail* case regarding companies:

> [It] should be borne in mind that, unlike natural persons, companies are creatures of the law and, in the present state of Community law, creatures of national law. They exist only by virtue of the varying national legislation which determines their incorporation and functioning.[1]

There are, however, exceptions to this principle. The European Union (EU)[2] introduced business organizations that are primarily governed by European law as to their formation and functioning. The most important one is the European Company (Societas Europaea (SE)). Its Statute (2001) prevails over national law, although several issues are still referred to national law, that is, the law of the Member State in which the SE has its registered office.[3] Other business organizations under European

1. *K. v. The Treasury and Commissioners of Inland Revenue, ex parte Daily Mail and General Trust plc* (1989) I All E.R. 328.
2. The abbreviation EU (European Union) will be used even where EC (European Community) would be more appropriate as being one of the communities the EU is built upon. The consolidated version of the Treaty on European Union is published in the OJ 2012, C 326 http://eur-lex.europa.eu/collection/eu-law/treaties.html.
3. Council Regulation (EC) No. 2157/2001 of 8 Oct. 2001 on the Statute for a European company (SE) OJ 2001, L 294.

law are the European Cooperative Society (Societas Cooperativa Europaea (SCE)), which was introduced in 2003, and the European Economic Interest Grouping (EEIG), which dates back to 1985.[4]

1.03 Much older exceptions to the rule that national law governs companies are the 'inter-state enterprises', which are partly disentangled from domestic law. The *'Société européenne pour le financement du materiel ferroviaire'* (Eurofima) was founded in 1956 by a convention among several European countries. According to the convention, this company is subjected to the law of the country in which it is seated (Switzerland), but only insofar as this law does not contravene the convention. The shares of Eurofima are held by the national railways of the contracting states.[5] A similar regime applies to the *Société Internationale de la Moselle.* Subsequent to the 1956 convention between France, Germany, and Luxembourg, it is incorporated under German law, albeit the German government is obliged to safeguard the rights of the shareholders in the event that German company law is changed.[6]

1.04 Notwithstanding these exceptions, the observation made by the court in *Daily Mail* is correct for the majority of companies. Furthermore, even European and international companies, although not primarily based on national law, must be registered in one of the Member States, which adds a national element to them. European corporate law thus encompasses both EU law and all national corporate laws. Nevertheless, for the basic understanding of this area of law, it is not required to study all national corporate laws in detail because business organizations tend to show a fundamentally similar set of legal characteristics.[7] Within the EU, the harmonization programme contributed significantly to this phenomenon.

1.05 Corporate law, approached comparatively, cannot be understood properly without reference to the entrepreneur *pur sang,* the sole trader or the sole proprietor. Similarly, attention has to be paid to the non-corporate forms of business organizations, partnerships or firms. These subjects are dealt with very briefly in this chapter and in Chapter 2. In the section on partnerships, some introductory remarks are made on companies and other incorporated forms of business organizations, which are the main subject of this book. The relevant harmonization programme of the EU is discussed in Chapter 3. As illustrated, corresponding directives and regulations are not

4. Council Regulation (EEC) No. 2137/85 of 25 Jul. 1985 on the EEIG, OJ 1985, L 199 and Council Regulation (EC) No. 1435/2003 of 22 Jul. 2003 on the Statute for a European Cooperative Society (SCE), OJ 2003, L 207.
5. Eurofima (European Company for the Financing of Railroad Rolling Stock) was originally founded for a period of fifty years but in 1984 the members of the Convention approved to extend this period for an additional fifty years, *Eurofima Annual Report 2003*, www.eurofima.org.
6. Moselle Convention of 27 Oct. 1956, *Bundesgesetzblatt* 1956 II, 1838. Georges Ripert, *Droit Commercial,* Tome 1 par Rene Roblot, No. 1724. Ignaz Seidl-Hohenveldern, *Corporations in and under International Law* (Cambridge: Grotius Publications, 1987), 112–114; Christoph Engel, 'Internationale öffentliche Unternehmen', *RabelsZeitschrift* (1995): 495–544, mentions several other examples of international companies based on a treaty between states.
7. Henry Hansmann & Reinier Kraakman, 'What Is Corporate Law', in *The Anatomy of Corporate Law: A Comparative and Functional Approach*, eds Reinier Kraakman et al. (New York: Oxford University Press, 2004), 1.

confined to company law, but can also be found in related areas such as taxation and financial services. Business organizations under Community law are highlighted in Chapter 4. The focus is on the EEIG and the SE, but legislation and proposals concerning other European business organizations are also briefly discussed. Chapters 5 and 6 deal with selected topics regarding companies under their respective national laws; namely, the formation and financing of companies and management structures, including the issue of corporate governance. In Chapter 7, the involvement of employees, being one of the most controversial issues, is discussed. Employee involvement in some of the Member States represents an element of corporate law with a bearing on the decision-making structure. Other Member States traditionally had little experience with employee involvement, but a 2002 directive established a general framework for informing and consulting employees.[8] The dynamics of the business enterprise are highlighted in Chapter 8 on cross-border cooperation and acquisitions, including mergers and takeovers. The annual accounts, also in their consolidated form, are the subject of Chapter 9. Finally, Chapter 10 is a review of the law of groups. With the acknowledgement of groups of companies and other legal entities, the law has certainly been challenged to its limits in dealing with economic reality caused by the fact that a company within the group is both legally independent and simultaneously functions as part of a larger economic entity.

1.06 After this brief survey of the subsequent chapters, it is necessary to return to the principal idea. In general, a business enterprise may be carried on either by a natural person, the sole trader or the sole proprietor, or by a business organization – the latter being any legal entity involving two or more persons, such as a partnership or a private company. This holds even if a single member company carries on the business, because, in that case, two persons are involved: the natural person who is the single member and the company, being a legal person. In the case of the sole trader, the entrepreneur is the owner of the assets belonging to the business and he (or she) personally bears all the risks. There is no legal distinction between his private and business capital. The sole trader sometimes is subject to special rules, depending on the nature of his business. For taxation purposes, he may be obliged to keep books, for instance, in connection with Value Added Tax (VAT). If he is rendering professional services as a lawyer, a physician or an accountant, rules applying to these professions may have an impact on the way the business is organized. Those who are engaged in commercial activities may have an obligation to register at a commercial register, to keep books and to draw up a balance sheet once a year.[9] Nevertheless, the sole trader is the simplest way to carry on a business and its use is widely spread. More than 90% of all enterprises in the Community belong to the micro-class; that is, the self-employed and other enterprises with less than ten employees. Together with the small and

8. Directive 2002/14/EC of 11 Mar. 2002, establishing a general framework for informing and consulting employees in the EC, OJ 2002, L 80.
9. For example, Belgium: Title I and III, Book I Belgian Commercial Code (*Wetboek van Koophandel*) and Articles 1 and 2, *Wet op de boekhouding van de ondernemingen*, retrievable at http://www.ejustice.just.fgov.be and Germany: §§ 1, 2 and 238 German Commercial Code (*Handelsgesetzbuch*), retrievable at http://www.gesetze-im-internet.de.

medium sized enterprises (SMEs: less than 250 employees), they account for more than 99% of all enterprises and the employment of more than 88 million people in the EU.[10] It is likely that sole traders run most of the micro-class enterprises.

1.07 An entrepreneur may seek to cooperate and share the risks of a business enterprise with others for several reasons. Such cooperation is generally considered to be a partnership. The UK Partnership Act (PA) 1890, for example, defines a partnership as the relation that subsists between persons carrying on a business in common with a view of profit.[11] In most Member States, a partnership is a non-incorporated form of a business organization. As outlined in Chapter 2, several continental jurisdictions distinguish between commercial and other partnerships. The former refers to partnerships included in the Commercial Codes, while the latter concerns those partnerships that are ruled by the Civil Codes. Partnerships generally can sue or be sued under their firm name, even where they do not have a legal personality. Chapter 2 contains further details about commercial partnerships.

1.08 The particular branch of a business organization that is set up under foreign law can be regarded, for pragmatic reasons, as yet another non-incorporated business organization. For example, the English branch of a French company or the Dutch branch of a Belgian partnership is not incorporated under the law of the UK or the Netherlands. The EC has taken harmonizing measures regarding disclosure requirements for those branches. They are discussed in Chapter 3.

1.09 Incorporation, in general, means the creation of a corporation; that is, a legal person separate and distinct from its members. The requirements for incorporation may vary according to the different categories of legal persons. As far as companies are concerned, they are incorporated either by registration or by a notarial deed. Generally, registration is a prerequisite for acquiring legal personality, such as for the SE and companies under the national law of several Member States. In several countries, incorporation takes place by a notarial deed, for example, in Belgium, Germany, Italy and Poland, although registration is required before the company actually comes into existence. By contrast, in the Netherlands, legal personality is already acquired upon the completion of a notarial deed, and although registration is obligatory, it is not conditional for the initial existence of the company.[12] Like the SE, the EEIG is incorporated by registration (*see* paragraphs 4.04 and 4.17). It must be noted that, in Germany, this does not result in legal personality for the EEIG, but it has 'the capacity, in its own name, to have rights and obligations of all kinds, to make contracts or

10. European Commission, Annual Report on European SMEs 2013/2014, pp. 10–14. The figures mentioned concern the non-financial business sector.
11. Section 1 *Partnership Act* 1890, retrievable at http://www.legislation.gov.uk.
12. United Kingdom: CA 2006, ss 7–9 and 16; *Polish Commercial Companies Code (Kodeks spółek handlowych)*, 3rd bilingual edition (Warszawa: Wydawnictwo C.H. Beck, 2004), Articles 163 and 306; *Belgian Companies Code* (*Wetboek van Vennootschappen*), Article 2(4), 66 and 68; *Dutch Civil Code* (*Burgerlijk Wetboek*) Book 2, Articles 64 and 175, Articles 2328, 2331 and 2462 *Italian Civil Code (Codice Civile)*.

accomplish other legal acts, and to sue and be sued', as prescribed by the regulation.[13] The issue of formalities and requirements for the incorporation of companies and EEIGs is dealt with in Chapters 4 and 5.

1.10 Registered companies can be classified in several ways: for instance, limited companies, as opposed to unlimited companies. In the UK, a company may be registered as an unlimited company, in which case there is no limit on the liability of its members.[14] In other Member States, members of registered cooperative companies may be liable to contribute to the assets.[15] Managing partners of a German limited partnership with shares (*Kommanditgesellschaft auf Aktien* (KGaA)), as well as its equivalents in other continental Member States, are liable for the obligations of such a partnership, which, in many other respects, resembles a company (*see* paragraph 2.48). Another division is between public companies and private companies. Public companies are companies incorporated as such and subject to stricter requirements than private companies, particularly with regard to capital and company structure. Accordingly, as a rule, only public companies are allowed to be listed on a stock exchange. Private companies are better suited for small or medium-sized enterprises that do not have to call for funding on the capital market.

1.11 The original idea behind the private company is that formation takes place by *intuitu personae* and that a rather concise and flexible statute reflects its personal character, enabling its members to regulate the company's internal affairs. For instance, the first statute in Europe concerning the private company – the 1892 German *GmbHGesetz*, creating the *Gesellschaft mit beschränkter Haftung* (GmbH) – is still valid and consists of less than ninety sections.[16] In comparison, the 1965 German *Aktiengesetz* (AktG) concerning the public company – the *Aktiengesellschaft* (AG) – has more than 400 sections.[17] In French company law, one can find similar differences between the private company – *société à responsabilité limitée* (SARL) – and the public company – *société anonyme* (SA).[18] By way of contrast, in the UK, both types are governed by the same statute, now the Companies Act 2006. Under this Act, a public company is one whose certificate of incorporation states that it is a public company and has been duly registered as such. Requirements for registration include the authorized minimum capital. All other registered companies are private companies to which many provisions of the Companies Act do not apply.[19] Italy and the Netherlands initially regulated

13. Council Regulation (EEC) 2137/85, Article 1(2). According to §1 *EWIV-Ausführungsgesetz* it has the status of the commercial partnership.
14. CA 2006, s. 3.
15. For example, Belgian Companies Code, Article 2(2); Dutch Civil Code, Book 2, Articles 55 and 56.
16. *Gesetz betreffend die Gesellschaften mit beschränkter Haftung* (GmbHG), from 20 Apr. 1892, retrievable at http://www.gesetze-im-internet.de.
17. *Aktiengesetz* (AktG) from 6 Sep. 1965. The second Book, i.e., thirteen sections, concerns the KGaA, which possesses some of the characteristics of both a public company and a limited partnership (*see* paragraph 2.47).
18. French Commercial Code, Articles L223-1–L223-43 (SARL) and L225-1–L225-270 (SA), retrievable at http://www.legifrance.gouv.fr.; Maurice Cozian, Alain Viandier & Florence Deboissy, *Droit des sociétés*, 27e édition (Paris: Litec, 2014), nr. 1251.
19. CA 2006, s. 4.

the private company by copying most of the rules for the pre-existing public company. Recently, they allowed for a more flexible regime for private companies, albeit maintaining a rather voluminous set of rules for this company form.[20] The Polish Commercial Companies Code also shows a tendency to regulate the private company extensively, although it retains certain personal elements such as the right of an individual shareholder to inspect the books and documents of the company.[21]

1.12 In several jurisdictions, the idea to return to the original concept of a restricted and flexible statute for the private company has been put forward, owing to the enhanced freedom of establishment for companies within the EU and the needs of the business community. In some countries, company statutes have been adapted already and new sorts of private companies have been introduced.[22] Freedom of establishment and various categories of public and private companies are further discussed in Chapter 2 and throughout this book, where applicable.

1.13 Finally, companies may also fall into different categories due to factual criteria, such as their size or the type of industry they belong to, but that is beyond the scope of this book. Nevertheless, such facts cannot remain completely overlooked, as they may intertwine with company law. Therefore, the classification of companies shall be expanded slightly. Firstly, companies may be close or open companies. Close companies, also called closely held companies, feature a limited number of shareholders, and the transfer of shares to outsiders is barred, unless all shareholders agree. This, of course, requires contractual arrangements or specific provisions in the articles of the company.[23] Private companies are not, by their very nature, close companies, but they are better suited to be shaped into a close company than public companies. Close companies may be created for several reasons, for example, in order to gain tax benefits or where the partners in a joint venture aim to keep their cooperation exclusive. Secondly, companies with only one shareholder (member) can be seen as a separate category. A company, by its origin, is a vehicle for cooperation, as is shown by its etymology. However, the concept of a general meeting of shareholders has little meaning when all shares are held by one individual or by another company. Separate EU legislation has been enacted to enable such single member companies in all Member States and to subject these companies to specific rules, as seen in Chapter 3.

---

20. Italy: Legislative Decree No. 6 of 17 Jan. 2003 'Riforma organica della disciplina delle società di capitali e società cooperative, in attuazione della legge delega 3 ottobre 2001, n. 366', published in the Official Journal No. 17 on 22 Jan. 2003 (Supplement No. 8). The Netherlands: Wet vereenvoudiging en flexibilisering van 18 juni 2012, Stbl. 2012, 299.

    The introduction of the private company in the Netherlands served to evade disclosure requirements, which were then expected to pertain exclusively to public companies, P. van Schilfgaarde, *Van de NV en de NV*, no. 9 (Deventer: Zestiende druk, 2013). For Belgium: Leon Dabin & Anne Benoit-Moury, *Jura Europae: Company Law Volume II* (loose leaf) (München: Beck, 1964-Belgium), nr. 20.
21. *Polish Commercial Companies Code*, Article 212(1) 3rd bilingual edition (Warszawa: Wydawnictwo C.H. Beck, 2004).
22. 'The Light Vehicle Competition', *European Company Law*, no. 4 (December 2004).
23. Yves Guyon, 'Données juridiques: Essai d'une problématique de la société fermée', in *Propositions pour une société fermée européenne*, sous la direction de Jeanne Boucourechliev (Luxembourg: Office des publications officielles des Communautés européennes, 1997), 37 *et seq.*

Thirdly, companies may belong to a group. Groups are mostly built on share ownership, that is, one company – the parent company – holding the shares of other companies, which are commonly called subsidiaries. Due to shareholdership and other legal and factual bonds, such a group may act as an economic entity (*see* Chapter 10).

CHAPTER 2

Business Organizations Within the European Union

I INTRODUCTION

2.01 The word 'company' means an association of persons who combine for the purpose of a joint activity, commercial or otherwise. In essence, the term 'company law' may be used to cover the legal regulation of all such activities. This is the case in continental legal systems, apart from legal forms like associations. Each country, however, does allow certain specific forms under which joint economic activities may be carried out, and these are generally divided into partnerships and companies. The essential, but not universal, distinction between these two generic forms is that partnerships are based on individual agreements between the partners, whereas companies are organizations that exist independently of their members and depend on capital resources. In other words, the distinction is between partnerships, or personal companies, and capital companies, but all are regarded as companies. In continental languages, the generic term 'company' covers both partnerships and capital companies, such as the French *société*, the Italian *società*, the German *Gesellschaft* and the Polish *spółka*.

2.02 The United Kingdom (UK), on the other hand, deriving its commercial law from a different heritage treats partnerships and companies as entirely different entities for the purpose of legal regulation. Company law is only regarded as applying to two specific types of organizations (public and private limited companies), whereas partnerships are basically regarded as contractual activities. The importance of this different approach is that in most continental systems there is some overlap in the legal regulation of partnerships and companies, whereas there is a complete dichotomy in the UK. Although it is perfectly permissible in the UK for a partnership to use the words '& Co' in its name, it still does not constitute a company within the UK's narrow definition of the word for legal purposes.

A Civil and Commercial Law

2.03 Another difference is that continental legal systems often draw[1] a distinction between civil and commercial law, whereas such a distinction is not made in the UK. In France, for example, Article L210-1 of the Commercial Code states: 'The commercial nature of a company shall be determined by its form or by its objects.' The second sentence adds: 'General partnerships, limited partnerships, limited liability companies and joint-stock companies are trading companies by virtue of their form, irrespective of their objects.' Any such organization that does not comply is therefore of a civil nature, such as the French silent partnership (paragraph 2.18). There are differences between commercial and civil organizations, so this distinction is more than just one of form. For example, in France, commercial organizations must submit themselves to the scrutiny of a special branch of the judiciary (*tribuneaux de commerce*), and, in Germany, the courts have no discretion to waive penalties originating from a contractual agreement if the debtor is a merchant (*Kaufmann*), although they have this option in other cases.[2]

2.04 The methods used by Member States to draw the dividing line between civil and commercial law with regard to business organizations differ slightly. An example of how France makes this distinction is mentioned in the previous paragraph. Another example is Germany, where every person carrying on a commercial business is deemed a merchant (*Kaufmann*). In addition, business is, in any event, a commercial business if its name is registered with the commercial registry.[3] The rules applicable to merchants do apply to general and limited partnerships (LPs) and capital companies alike.[4] In Belgium, the object of a company or a partnership determines its civil or commercial character. Economic reality prevails where the articles of a company state that it has no commercial object, but where the company, in fact, operates for profit.[5] The Spanish Civil Code allows partnerships with civil objects to have the same form as commercial partnerships, in which case the provisions of the Commercial Code apply insofar as they do not contravene those of the Civil Code. By contrast, public and private companies are simply declared commercial by Spanish law.[6] Like other continental countries, Italy used to have a civil code and a commercial code that applied specifically to the merchant (*commerciante*). By the 1942 law reform, the concept of merchant was replaced by the concept of a commercial entrepreneur *(imprenditore commerciale)* and a separate commercial code no longer existed. Entrepreneurs *(imprenditori)* are defined as persons who are professionally engaged in an organized economic activity in order to produce or exchange goods or services.[7]

1. Or used to draw, such as in the Netherlands.
2. Section 348 of the German Commercial Code (*Handelsgesetzbuch or* German Commercial Code) and s. 343 of the German Civil Code (*Bürgerliches Gesetzbuch*, BGB).
3. Sections 1 and 2 German Commercial Code (*Handelsgesetzbuch*, abbreviated HGB).
4. Section 6 German Commercial Code, s. 3 AktG, s. 13(3) GmbHG.
5. Article 3 of the Belgian Companies Code (*Wetboek van Vennootschappen or* WvV).
6. Article 1670 of the Spanish Civil Códe (*Codigo Civil*). Article 2 Capital Companies Act *(Ley de Sociedades de Capital)*, retrievable at https://www.boe.es.
7. Article 2082 Italian Civil Code *(Codice civile)*.

According to Italian law, commercial entrepreneurs are subject to a special legal framework regarding, *inter alia*, registration, accounting, commercial agency and bankruptcy. Small and agricultural entrepreneurs are exempted from part of these rules and the legal framework does not, as a matter of principle, apply to intellectual professionals.[8]

2.05 The common law system in operation in the UK does not have such a distinction. Instead, there is a practical distinction between profit-making and non-profit-making organizations. In fact, a partnership can only be formed 'with a view of profit',[9] and only one form of private company, the company limited by guarantee, is designed for non-profit-making organizations. Thus, whereas an association of lawyers would be regarded as a civil partnership in Belgium or France, it would be a partnership in England in exactly the same way as an association of market traders.

B Legal Personality

2.06 A substantive distinction in the various forms of business organizations available in Europe is between those forms that are given legal personality and those that are not. In all countries, the capital companies have this type of personality conferred by law, whereas partnership forms have either no such personality or a modified form of it. Legal personality in its fullest sense means that the company is a separate and wholly distinct legal person from that of its members. It alone makes contracts and employs people. What follows is an even more important concept of limited liability of those members. A member whose liability is limited by shares is only liable to contribute to the assets up to the amount, if any, unpaid on his shares. Consequently, the company's creditors have recourse to the assets of the company, but not to assets owned by its shareholders or directors. The corollary is that creditors of the shareholders (and the directors), in principle, have no recourse to the assets of the company.[10]

2.07 In its purest form, legal personality may even result in no liability its members at all for the debts of the company or another legal person. This can be seen by reference to the English case of *H. Rayner (Mincing Lane) Ltd v. Department of Trade and Industry* (1990).[11] This case arose out of the collapse of the International Tin Council, which left it owing millions of pounds to a number of banks and traders. A number of Member States formed the council, and the creditors sought to recover their debts from those states. The House of Lords, ruling that the council had a legal personality distinct from its members, stated clearly that being the only legal person, the council had incurred the debts. In addition, because only the party to a contract can

8. Articles 2195, 2083, 2135 Italian Civil Code. G.F. Campobasso, *Diritto Commerciale. 1. Diritto dell'Impresa.* Settima Edizione, UTET Giuridica, Wolters Kluwer Italia S.r.l. 2015 pp. 41–45.
9. Section 1 of the PA 1890, retrievable at http://www.legislation.gov.uk.
10. *See* for the general aspects regarding this asset partitioning, Henry Hansmann & Reinier Kraakman, 'What Is Corporate Law?', in *The Anatomy of Corporate Law: A Comparative and Functional Approach*, ed. Reinier Kraakman et al. (New York: Oxford University Press, second edition 2009), 6–11.
11. *J. H. Rayner (Mincing Lane) Ltd v. Department of Trade and Industry* (1990) 2 A.C 418 (HL).

sue or be sued on it under English law, and that only the council was such a party, there was no liability at all imposed on the Member States. In practice, no business enterprise enjoys such pure legal personality because the law provides that, despite the existence of legal personality, the liability of the members is either unlimited or only limited to some extent, for example, the amount agreed by way of capital contribution. As we shall see, such liability depends on the form of organization chosen, including the civil/commercial and the personal/capital company distinctions referred to previously.

C Principal Forms of Business Organization

2.08 It is possible to characterize the principal forms of business enterprise available in the various countries, bearing in mind the above factors. There are four principal types: general partnerships, LPs, private companies and public or stock companies. Each one is discussed in turn. There are divisions within some of these and not all national forms fit exactly into one mould, particularly some hybrid forms, which are dealt with separately. There has also been a trend to introduce new and modified forms of business organizations into existing legal systems.

2.09 Four factors account for the tendency to introduce new and modified forms. To begin with, countries were urged to limit the joint and several liability of the partners of large firms in professional services who were faced with substantial damages awards. Germany and Poland, for instance, introduced the *Partnerschaftsgesellschaft* (PartG) and the *spólka partnerska* (sp. p.), respectively.[12] These are very similar to general partnerships, but exclude joint and several liability of a partner for negligence concerning professional performance of one of the other partners. In the UK, the *Limited Liability Partnership* (LLP) has been designed for the same purpose, but its use is not limited to certain regulated groups of professionals such as auditors, lawyers and medical doctors. Notwithstanding its name, the LLP is a legal person that has much less in common with the UK partnership than it has with the private company.[13]

2.09a Second, several Member States have undertaken to develop forms of business organizations that suit small and medium-sized enterprises (SMEs) more than the traditional forms. Even the private company is often thought to share too many features with the public company, such as capital requirements and board structure, to effectively function for the benefit of SMEs. Thus, simplified and new types of companies have been introduced which are subject to less formal requirements and

12. Germany: Gesetz vom 25 Jul. 1994 (BGBl. I S. 1744) as amended; many references are made to the regulation of the *Offene Handelsgesellschaft* (OHG). Polish Commercial Companies Code, Articles 86–101.
13. Limited Liability Partnerships Act 2000. Judith Freeman, 'Limited Liability Partnerships in the United Kingdom: Do They Have a Role for Small Firms?', in *The Governance of Close Corporations and Partnerships*, eds Joseph A. McCahery, Theo Raaijmakers & Erik P.M. Vermeulen (Oxford: Oxford University Press, 2004) (McCahery, Raaijmakers & Vermeulen 2004), 293 *et seq.* and Geoffrey Morse, 'Limited Liability Partnerships and Partnership Law Reform in the United Kingdom', in *The Governance of Close Corporations and Partnerships*, eds Joseph A. McCahery, Theo Raaijmakers & Erik P.M. Vermeulen (Oxford: Oxford University Press, 2004), 317 *et seq.*

enjoy more freedom to insert tailor-made provisions into the companies' articles. The enhanced flexibility is offset by the imposition of limitations, such as the prohibition of using the capital market for funding and issuing shares in bearer form.[14] In other words, such companies may not engage in activities where full protection of shareholders, creditors and third parties is necessary. Examples are the *société par actions simplifiée* (SAS), introduced by the French legislator, and the German public company (AG), which has been made accessible for SMEs by abolishing the requirement that at least five persons need to take part in its formation.[15] Similarly, subcategories of the private company have been created, such as the Spanish new enterprise limited liability company (*Sociedad Limitada Nueva Empresa* (SLNE)). The SLNE is a simplified version of the private company with respect to, *inter alia*, its formation procedure and decision-making features.[16] A similar approach has been taken by the German legislator by allowing a *Gesellschaft mit beschränkter Haftung* (GmbH) to be founded without initial capital. Several restrictions apply until the company has built up reserves equal to the level of the statutory minimum capital (*haftungsbeschränkte Unternehmergesellschaft*).[17] Another example of a simplified private company is the Italian *società a responsabilità limitata semplificata* introduced in 2012.[18] It is formed by notarial deed according to a standard template *(Tabella A)* provided by ministerial decree.[19] The capital must be a minimum of EUR 1, but less than EUR 10,000.[20]

2.09b Third, the so-called social enterprises have gained momentum in several European Union (EU) Member States. These enterprises can be discerned from mainstream enterprises in that they have a primary and explicit social purpose. Accordingly, the aim of their economic activities is to benefit society. Social enterprises have limits on distribution of profits and/or assets in order to prioritize the social aim over profit making. In its 2011 Communication Social Business Initiative, the European Commission calls the social economy and social innovation as one of its main concerns and signals 'the growing desire of Europeans for their work, consumption, savings and investments to be more closely attuned to and aligned with "ethical" and "social" principles'.[21]

14. Frank Wooldridge, 'Some New Types of Company and Partnership in France and Germany', *International and Comparitive Corporate Law Journal* 3, no. 2 (2001): 211 *et seq.*
15. Articles L227-1 *et seq.* French Commercial Code and Gesetz für kleine Aktiengesellschaften und zur Deregulierung des Aktienrechts, 2 Aug. 1994.
16. Ley 7/2003, de 1 de abril, de la sociedad limitada Nueva Empresa por la que se modifica la Ley 2/1995, de 23 de marzo, de Sociedades de Responsabilidad Limitada.
17. Section 5a GmbhG, inserted in 2008 by the act to modernize private company law and to curb abuse (*Gesetz zur Modernisierung des GmbH-Rechts und zur Bekämpfung von Missbräuchen (MoMiG)*. 'Renovating the German Private Limited Company', *German Law Journal* 9, no. 9 (2008): Special edition.
18. Article 2463*bis* Italian Civil Code, introduced by Law Decree 1/2012.
19. Decreto Ministero della Giustizia 23/06/2012 n° 138, G.U. 14/08/2012.
20. Article 2463*bis*(3) Italian Civil Code. Serra, L. *Società a responsabilità limitata semplificata*, AltalexPedia, 2013.
21. Brussels, 25.10.2011 COM(2011) 682 final.

For policy objectives, the Commission coined the term 'social enterprise' to cover the following types of businesses:

- those for which the social or societal objective of the common good is the reason for commercial activity, often in the form of a high level of social innovation;
- those where profits are mainly reinvested with the view to achieving a social objective; and
- where the method of organization or ownership system reflects their mission, using democratic or participatory principles, or focusing on social justice.[22]

Several Member States have developed specific legal forms or statutes for social enterprises, such as the French *Société coopérative d'intérêt collectif* (SCIC). Some countries have introduced 'legal statuses' that can be adopted by different types of organizations, provided that they meet pre-defined criteria, such as the Belgian *Vennootschap met sociaal oogmerk*. The UK has adapted the company form to facilitate the *Community Interest Company* (CIC).[23]

2.09c In the fourth place, the European Court of Justice (ECJ) has enhanced the freedom of establishment for companies by three landmark rulings to the effect that no Member State can withhold its citizens from using company forms of other Member States (*see* paragraphs 2.54 *et seq.*). This certainly is another stimulus for legislators to make their business organizations more attractive and flexible.[24] It enforces the trend to deregulate private companies. For instance, it might be expected that several Member States will abandon the mandatory minimum capital for this type of company, thereby copying the traditional position of the UK Ltd. France has skipped this requirement for the *société a responsabilité limitée* (SARL).[25] Similarly, the Dutch legislator has modified the provisions for the *besloten vennootschap met beperkte aansprakelijkheid* (BV) by eliminating most of the capital requirements and by simplifying decision-making rules.[26] Even the UK has taken steps to heighten the attractiveness of its Ltd. The Companies Act 2006 has simplified decision-making for private companies and abolished the requirement to have a company secretary.[27]

---

22. Brussels, 25.10.2011 COM(2011) 682 final, pp. 2–3.
23. *A Map of Social Enterprises and Their Eco-Systems in Europe* (Luxembourg: Publications Office of the European Union, 2015), 51 *et seq.* France: Titre II ter, Loi n° 47-1775; Belgium: Book X, Wetboek van vennootschappen; UK: introduced by the Companies Act 2004. *See* Companies Act 2006, s. 6. Further: A. Argyrou & T. Lambooy, 'An Introduction to Tailor-Made Legislation for Social Enterprises in Europe: A Comparison of Legal Regimes in Belgium, Greece and the UK' [2017], *International and Comparative Corporate Law Journal*, 12(3) (forthcoming).
24. Joseph A. McCahery & Erik P.M. Vermeulen, 'The Evolution of Closely Held Business Forms in Europe', in *The Governance of Close Corporations and Partnerships*, eds Joseph A. McCahery, Theo Raaijmakers & Erik P.M. Vermeulen (Oxford and New York: Oxford University Press, 2004), 191 *et seq.* Also: 'The Light Vehicle Competition', *European Company Law*, no. 4 (December 2004).
25. Article L223-2 French Commercial Code. 'The Light Vehicle Competition', *European Company Law*, no. 4 (December 2004).
26. The new legislation for the BV came into force on 1 Oct. 2012.
27. Explanatory Notes to the Companies Act 2006, 9 and 79.

2.10 As already mentioned in paragraph 2.08, this chapter is structured around the principal forms of a business organization. The starting point is partnerships, followed by companies and hybrid forms. The company forms are addressed again in Chapters 5 *et seq.* Following this classification of national business organizations, the business organizations under EU law are sketched out, although they are presented in more detail in Chapter 4. The EU has had a long-standing impact on national company law because of its harmonization programme. The effects of the harmonization programme are briefly described in this chapter, but are discussed in greater depth in Chapter 3. The final part of this chapter examines the extent to which the freedom of establishment, as guaranteed by the Treaty on the Functioning of the European Union (TFEU), has been accomplished.

II PARTNERSHIPS

2.11 Partnerships are those organizations that do not confer upon their members the privilege of limited liability, whether or not they have legal personality. For that reason alone, they are generally not a popular medium for ordinary commercial transactions. Nor are they suitable for very large organizations, despite very few practical restrictions on size. However, fiscal transparency may motivate enterprises to use general partnerships, especially for joint ventures, because, in such cases, the partners are granted tax deductions for losses endured by the joint venture enterprise. The use of partnerships to avoid mandatory disclosure of annual accounts is no longer possible, since Council Directive 90/605 extended the scope of the Fourth Directive by including partnerships where all members who have unlimited liability are public or private companies, or LPs with shares (*see* paragraph 9.26b). As a rule, partnerships have not been subjected to any EU harmonization programme.

2.12 A common feature of all partnerships is that they are, in essence, personal relationships and, as a result, the assignment of a partner's share is usually restricted without agreement from the other partners. This follows from the partnership's contractual basis. Once agreed upon, as a rule, a contract can only be modified with the consent of each party to the contract and this, of course, also applies to the partnership contract. Partnerships are sometimes characterized as 'the most dangerous' (because of the partners' liability) and the 'most closed' (because it is not possible to transfer a partner's share unless all the other partners agree) of the 'company' forms.[28]

2.13 Partnership law offers the essential attributes for coordinating the economic activity of two or more persons.[29] It provides for a decision-making mechanism comprising both the internal management structure and the authority of partners to

28. Maurice Cozian, Alain Viandier et Florence Deboissy, *Droit des sociétés*, 27e édition (Paris: LexisNexis, 2012), nr. 1204, regarding the société en nom collectif. The term 'companies' is used here in the generic sense, as previously mentioned in paragraph 2.01.
29. Henry Hansmann & Reinier Kraakman, 'The Essential Role of Organizational Law', in *The Governance of Close Corporations and Partnerships*, eds Joseph A. McCahery, Theo Raaijmakers & Erik P.M. Vermeulen (Oxford and New York: Oxford University Press, 2004), 24 *et seq.*

represent the firm. Moreover, partnership law creates a pool of assets to the benefit of the firm's creditors. For classification purposes, it is important to note that these attributes may vary from those that are rather rudimental and weak to more solid and sophisticated features. The law concerning simple partnership forms, such as the silent commercial partnership, confers such 'rudimental' mechanism to the partnership by granting each partner the power to manage the partnership's business, but not the authority to bind other partners by contracting with third parties. More developed types, such as the general partnership, have both elements and, therefore, each of the partners can bind the other partners or the partnership, unless a clause in the partnership contract states otherwise. It must be noted, however, that partnership law, by using default terms, generally leaves substantial freedom for the partners to agree on the internal constitution of the firm. This flexibility enables partnerships to function for a wide spectrum of business enterprises, ranging from family businesses and professional firms, to joint ventures created by transnational enterprises.

2.14 As for the pool of assets, creditors of simple partnership forms are very unlikely to gain access to a lot of it, as the partners may remain the owners of the assets, notwithstanding the fact that the assets are placed at the disposal of the partnership. The pool is then restricted to assets acquired during the term of the partnership's activities and these assets are co-owned only as long as they are not divided. Creditors of the firm can lay claim to these assets. If they are not fully paid, they may also lay claim to a partner's assets, but these must be shared with that partner's creditors. The creditors of a partner may also lay claim to that partner's share of the co-owned assets. In other words, the separation between the simple partnership's assets and the assets of its partners is easily permeable. By contrast, partnership forms enjoying legal personality own the property that is brought into the partnership and only the firm's creditors may lay claim to this property.[30]

2.15 The simple forms of partnership (civil partnership and silent commercial partnership) are dealt with briefly in the next paragraph. Partnerships in the UK are described in paragraphs 2.19–2.23. The continental general partnership and the LP are discussed in paragraphs 2.24–2.34 and 2.35–2.39, respectively.

A Civil Partnerships and 'Silent' Commercial Partnerships

2.16 In the continental countries this book is dealing with, civil partnerships, that is, those that do not have commercial objects as defined by each country, have no legal personality and are regarded, essentially, as a matter of agreement between the partners.[31] They are governed by the civil rather than the commercial codes, although, in some countries, for example, Belgium, they are allowed to take on the commercial

30. Henry Hansmann & Reinier Kraakman, 'Organizational Law as Asset Partitioning', *European Economic Review* 44 (2000) 807 et seq.
31. Note that 'civil partnership' has a different and specific meaning in the UK: The Civil Partnership Act 2004 defines this as a relationship between two people of the same sex ('civil partners'), which is formed when they register as civil partners.

partnership form in order to acquire legal personality.[32] In Spain, the civil partnership has no legal personality as long as it remains silent, but it is regarded as having legal personality if it operates in the name of the partnership.[33]

2.17 More importantly for our purposes, several countries have one or more forms of 'silent' commercial partnerships, which are regarded as a matter of agreement, rather than status, because these partnerships can exist without being registered and without using a firm name. It should be said, however, that these are not the mainstream forms of a general partnership in those countries.

2.18 In France, the *société en participation,* or silent partnership, is a purely private arrangement that does not need to be disclosed to anyone. It has no assets distinct from those of its partners, who retain title to their contributions so that each partner merely makes his assets available to the partnership. Nevertheless, there may be undivided assets held in co-ownership by the partners. It is a very flexible form. It is effectively an agreement between the partners, subject to general rules of contract and a few mandatory provisions for partnerships in general. However, if the silent partnership has commercial character, default rules of a general partnership apply, unless otherwise agreed upon.[34] It is used for business affairs such as joint marketing agreements. Each partner must contract with third parties in his own name. In addition, third parties cannot sue a partner whom they have not dealt with personally, unless he either led them to believe that he was involved in or made a profit from the transaction, or that the existence of the partnership had been voluntarily disclosed to the general public. This is known as a *société en participation ostensible.*[35] The Spanish silent partnership, or *sociedad civil interna,* is similar to the French silent partnership because it is an agreement subject to the general rules of contract. It has no assets and the patrimonial rules of the Civil Code apply.[36] Germany has a slightly different form of silent partnership, the *stille Gesellschaft.*[37] It is designed for an association between an active businessman (the general partner) and a financial backer. In many respects, this type of partnership resembles an LP, in that the undisclosed partner is only liable to his partner for the amount agreed in their contract, but not to third parties. Under Belgian law, there is a similar form of silent partnership known as a *stille handelsvennootschap* or *société en participation.* There are no formal requirements and no separate partnership capital, so, as a result, a creditor can only lay claim to a partner's share. In addition, Belgium has another form of consensual partnership, the *tijdelijke handelsvennootschap* or *association momentanée.* This is a temporary partnership entered into for one or more commercial transactions, which can be wound up automatically at the end of those transactions.[38] In Poland, the civil partnership *(spółka cywilna)* can be

32. They remain civil partnerships as long as their object if of a civil nature, Article 3(2) and (4) Belgian Companies Code.
33. Article 1669 Spanish Civil Code.
34. Articles 1871 and 1871-1 French Civil Code.
35. Article 1872-1 French Civil Code.
36. Articles 1669 and 392 Spanish Civil Code.
37. *See* ss 230–237 German Commercial Code.
38. Articles 2, 47 and 48 Belgian Companies Code.

used for both commercial and non-commercial activities, but, because it requires registration of the partners, it is not a silent form.[39] In the Netherlands, the *maatschap* can function as a silent partnership, but the partners may also use this partnership form to operate under a common name (e.g., in the case of a law firm).[40] The Italian simple partnership, the *società semplice,* is the basic form for cooperation, where the object is not a commercial one. The partnership contract does not have to comply with specific formalities and the partners are basically free to organize their cooperation. Registration is mandatory, but it has no impact on the existence of the partnership.[41]

B General Partnerships in the UK

2.19 Civil partnerships are unknown in England and no partnership is capable of having even a modified legal personality. A partnership is defined simply as 'the relation which subsists between persons carrying on a business in common with a view of profit'.[42] Companies, in the English sense of the word, are excluded from this definition. There are no formal requirements for the formation of an English partnership. As stated earlier, an English partnership arises from an agreement between two or more persons, legal or natural, that they will carry on a business in common with the purpose of creating profit. The agreement may be express, by way of a formal deed, or it may simply be inferred from the course of dealings, in which those involved act as partners, even if they themselves are not aware of the fact that this makes them partners. In general, questions as to whether a partnership exists or not will usually arise where either a creditor wishes to sue the other 'partners' on a contract made by one of them, or there is an internal dispute that requires a partnership obligation to be imposed in order to achieve its accomplishment. In such cases, it should be noted that simply sharing the profits of a business is not a conclusive proof of a partnership, nor is the co-ownership of land.[43] Thus, where X lends money to a partnership or an individual on terms that he is to be repaid out of the profits of the business, he will not be a partner unless he is involved in the business in some way. The real question is whether the transaction is one of a loan or an investment. Similarly, an employee is not a partner, even where he is described as a salaried partner, unless he is involved in the management of the business.

2.20 The essential characteristics that apply to an English partnership are twofold. First, every partner is an agent of his fellow partners in respect of any transaction carried out in the ordinary course of the partnership business.[44] Thus, any act within the ordinary authority of a partner will bind all the other partners. In addition, anyone

39. Katarzyna Michalowska, 'Introduction', in *Polish Commercial Companies Code,* 3rd edition, Bilingual edn, Polish-English (Warszawa: Wydawnictwo C.H. Beck, 2004), XIV.
40. Articles 7A:1655 *et seq.*, Dutch Civil Code.
41. Articles 2251–2290 Italian Civil Code. G.F. Campobasso, *Diritto Commerciale. 2. Diritto delle Società,* Nona Edizione, UTET Giuridica, Wolters Kluwer Italia, p. 56.
42. Section 1 PA 1890.
43. Section 2 PA 1890.
44. Section 5 PA 1890.

who is not actually a partner, but who is represented as such to third parties, for example, a salaried partner, will also have that binding authority.[45] This concept also applies to a partner who is acting outside his ordinary authority, but who has been held out as having additional authority by the other partners.

The second concept is that, as between them, partners are regarded as being in a fiduciary position. This means that they owe each other absolute duties of honesty and disclosure over and above the standard duties of care. Any partner who makes any unauthorized profit from a partnership transaction must account for that amount to the other partners, who need to prove neither fault nor loss. These two concepts are the reason for most disputes concerning the existence or liability of a partnership.

2.21 An English partnership is, as the partnerships mentioned in paragraphs 2.16–2.18, largely a matter of agreement between the partners. The Partnership Act (PA) of 1890 provides a few compulsory provisions, but also includes several implied terms as to management and finance in default. All partners have equal management rights unless there is an agreement to the contrary. If a partnership agreement makes no provision for its duration, it is known as a partnership at will and can be dissolved at any time by a notice issued by one of the partners.[46] This, however, is subject to any contrary intention, which the courts have been quick to find *(Moss v. Elphick* (1910)).[47] If the partnership is deemed not to be at will, mutual consent is required for dissolution, except where the causes mentioned in the PA are involved.[48]

2.22 Although an English partnership is simply a relationship, it does have a name, known as the firm name, under which it can sue and be sued. Although it is subject to the general regime for business names, there are no special requirements for the choice of the firm name. The partners are fully liable for all the debts of the firm. Property that is brought into the partnership by the partners or acquired on account of the firm is known as partnership property. The partners hold it as co-owners, and every partner has the right to have that property applied in payment of partnership debts.[49] In cases of insolvency, where the partners cannot pay the firm's debts or their own, there are two sets of creditors: the personal creditors of each partner and the partnership's creditors. There are also two estates: the partnership's assets and the assets of each individual partner.

All the partners are entitled to share equally in the capital and profits of the business and must contribute equally towards the losses, unless otherwise agreed upon.[50] A partnership is dissolved by termination of the venture, passing of an agreed time period and upon the death or bankruptcy of a partner, unless otherwise agreed. Furthermore, as already mentioned, a partnership for an indefinite period will be dissolved upon notice given by a partner. Finally, the court may order a dissolution.

45. Section 14 PA 1890.
46. Section 26 PA 1890.
47. *Moss v. Elphick* (1910) I K.B. 846.
48. Section 32 PA 1890.
49. Section 20 PA 1890.
50. Section 24 PA 1890.

Dissolution is followed by liquidation of the partnership, resulting in settling the partnership's accounts among the partners.[51]

2.23 In 2003, it was proposed that the PA 1890 be replaced. According to the Law Commission (actually, the Law Commission and the Scottish Law Commission), the act was not devised for larger partnerships and the lack of entity status for partnerships under the law of England and Wales was criticized as being an anomaly. Although a draft bill was attached to the commission's report, no such bill has been introduced to the Parliament. The Law Commission issued a further Joint Consultation Paper on proposals to reform the Limited Partnerships Act (LPA) of 1907. In 2006, the government announced its decision to implement the LP law reforms recommended by the Law Commission, but the recommendations with respect to the general partnership law reform will not be taken forward.[52] Since then, only two of the Law Commission's recommendations were implemented. The Legislative Reform Order 2009 made a certificate of registration conclusive evidence that an LP has been formed at the date shown on the certificate and requires all new LPs to include 'Limited Partnership', 'LP' or equivalent at the end of their names.[53]

C Continental General Partnerships

2.24 The standard form of general partnerships in continental legal systems is different from the English form. The reason for this is that they require some form of registration, and some countries confer legal personality upon the partnership. The French and Belgian *société en nom collectif* (*SNC*)[54] and the Spanish *sociedad regular colectiva* (*SC*)[55] have legal personality, as opposed to the German *Offene Handelsgesellschaft* (*OHG*), the Dutch *vennootschap onder firma* (VOF), the Italian *società in nome collettivo (SNC)* and the Polish *spółka jawna* (*sp.j.*).[56] None of these legal systems, however, confer limited liability upon the partners and so general partnerships are economically transparent in the same manner as a partnership under English law. Legal personality, which goes hand in hand with unlimited liability, is called modified or reduced legal personality. The main difference is restricted to the ownership of partnership property. If the partnership is a legal person, the partnership is the owner of property brought into the partnership, as opposed to co-ownership by

51. Sections 33 *et seq.* PA 1890.
52. *Partnership Law: A Joint Report*, 2003 Law Com No. 283 and Scot Law Com No. 192. The report on limited partnerships included a draft bill. The consultation papers and the report are available from the Law Commission's website, www.lawcom.gov.uk.
53. http://lawcommission.justice.gov.uk/areas/partnership-law.htm, accessed 26 Jan. 2015.
54. In Dutch: *vennootschap onder firma (V.O.F.)* (Belgium). On the 2000 consultation document: Geoffrey Morse, 'Limited Liability Partnerships and Partnership Law Reform in the United Kingdom', 337 *et seq.*
55. Articles 116 and 122 Spanish Commercial Code. The Commercial Code uses frequenly *compañia* but its synonym *sociedad* is also used In the Civil Code *sociedad* is used. The latter is also more frequent in Spanish legal literature, for instance by Uría-Menéndez, *Curso de Derecho Mercantil* Tomo I (Madrid, 1999), (including *derecho de sociedades*).
56. Section 19 German Commercial Code, Article 16 Dutch Commercial Code and Article 24 Polish Commercial Companies Code.

partners of a partnership without legal personality. It should be noted that UK partnerships, which are subject to Scottish law, rather than English law, although identical in every other way to English firms, do have legal personality reflecting the continental influence in that legal system.[57]

2.25 Notwithstanding the differences regarding registration requirements and legal personality, the continental forms of partnerships are similar in many ways to those in the UK. The partnership must operate under a firm name, but, in some countries, an extension to the name, such as *en compagnie*, is mandatory in order to indicate the character of the business organization.[58] In conformity with the basic pattern, the partners of a general partnership have *unlimited liability* and each have a *right of management*, unless there is an agreement to the contrary.[59] As with the execution of any contract, the partners have obligations towards each other to act in accordance with standards of good faith. Obligations towards the partnership include the obligation to contribute to the partnership and to refrain from competing with the partnership, unless agreed otherwise.[60]

2.26 The partners may bind the partnership when *dealing with third parties* within the objects of the partnership, unless the power to do so is limited by the partnership contract. In some jurisdictions, such limitations generally have no effect on third parties (e.g., Germany, Poland, France), whereas elsewhere limitations may be invoked if duly disclosed (e.g., Netherlands).[61]

2.27 In Germany and Poland, a partner's right of representation may be limited by the original partnership contract or by an additional agreement, but this has no effect against third parties. Such limitations mentioned are, for instance, a maximum amount to which a single partner can bind the partnership or the exclusion of real estate transactions by a single partner. The partnership contract may even bar a partner from the right to represent the partnership or determine that he is authorized to represent the partnership only in cooperation with another partner. However, by way of exception, these 'all or nothing' clauses can be relied upon against third parties, if duly disclosed.[62] Basically, this is the same system as is prescribed for companies by the First Directive (*see* paragraph 3.28). Among the most complex forms of a general

57. Section 4(2) PA 1890.
58. Article L221-2 French Commercial Code, Article 126 Spanish Commercial Code, s. 19 German Commercial Code, Article 24 Polish Commercial Companies Code.
59. Articles L221-1 and 3 French Commercial Code, Articles 127 and 129 Spanish Commercial Code, ss 114 and 128 German Commercial Code, Article 1676 Book 7A Dutch Civil Code, Articles 2257, 2258 and 2291 Italian Civil Code, Articles 22 and 39 Polish Commercial Companies Code.
60. For example, s. 112 German Commercial Code, Dutch Supreme Court 19 Oct. NJ 1990, 21 *Koghee v. Akkoca*, Article 136 Spanish Commercial Code, Article 56 Polish Commercial Companies Code, Article 2301 Italian Civil Code.
61. Articles L221-4 and L221-5 French Commercial Code, ss 125 and 126 German Commercial Code, Article 17 Dutch Commercial Code and Article 25 Trade Register Act *(Handelsregisterwet)*, Article 29 Polish Commercial Companies Code, Article 2298 Italian Civil Code.
62. For example, in Poland, Article 30(1) of the Commercial Companies Code allows for deprivation of a partner's right to represent the partnership. According to Polish commentators, such deprivation has effect against third parties if mentioned in the register of entrepreneurs.

partnership is the French SNC. Although there is a presumption of equal management[63] and each partner has wide powers to bind the partnership, in practice the agreement will contain provisions appointing one or more partners, or even third parties, as managers *(gérants)* of the business. In such a case, the management rights of all the other partners are excluded. However, they retain the possibility to remove a non-partner manager by a simple majority decision.[64] The position of the managers is dealt with in detail under French law.[65]

2.28 The *patrimonial regime* of a general partnership depends on it having legal personality in the first place. If so, the partnership owns all assets contributed by the partners or otherwise acquired by the partnership. There are, however, no capital requirements, except for those that may originate from the regulation of specific professions or industries, such as insurance. Even without legal personality, the patrimonial regime of a general partnership may resemble that of a legal person because it can have legal capacity, which may come close to legal personality. For example, the OHG has no legal personality, but it is treated as having legal personality in many respects, especially in relation to third parties, such as its ability to incur obligations, to take legal action or to be sued. Partnership assets are held in the firm's name and all the partners form a community of joint co-owners *(Gesamthandsgemeinschaft)*.[66] Co-owned assets are no longer at the disposal of a single partner, and creditors of the firm may lay claim on this 'pool of assets'.[67] A similar regime applies to the Dutch general partnership *(vennootschap onder firma)*.[68]

2.29 Partnership law generally provides for default rules on the *distribution of profits and losses*. Traditionally, partnership law presumes that the distribution of both profits and losses is made according to the proportion of the capital contributions of the partners. A partner who provides only services, rather than capital, is treated like the capital partner with the lowest capital contribution, unless there is an express agreement to the contrary. This is still the basic rule in France, Belgium, the Netherlands, Italy and Spain. In Spain, however, a partner providing only services is not liable for losses at all, again, unless otherwise agreed upon.[69] In Italy, the position of a partner providing services has to be determined by the court in the case that the partnership contract does not provide for his share of profits and losses.[70] Modern partnership law, such as that of Poland, provides for a different rule: all partners have an equal share of

63. Articles L221-3 *et seq.* French Commercial Code.
64. Article L-221-12 French Commercial Code.
65. Maurice Cozian, Alain Viandier et Florence Deboissy, *Droit des sociétés*, 27e édition (Paris: LexisNexis, 2012), nr. 1217 *et seq.*
66. Section 124 German Commercial Code. The same applies to the Polish general partnership (*sp.j.*), Article 8 Polish Commercial Companies Code.
67. Section 719 German Civil Code.
68. Article 1655 Book 7A Dutch Civil Code and Dutch Supreme Court 17 Dec. 1993, NJ 1994, 301. Under Italian law, partnerships are also deemed to hold assets in the firm's name, G.F. Campobasso, *Diritto Commerciale. 2. Diritto delle Società*, Nona Edizione, UTET Giuridica, Wolters Kluwer Italia S.r.l. 2015; pp. 44–47.
69. Article 1844-1 French Civil Code, Article 30 Belgian Companies Code, Article 1670 Book 7A Dutch Civil Code, Articles 140 and 141 Spanish Commercial Code.
70. Article 2263(2) Italian Civil Code.

profits and losses, unless the partnership agreement prescribes for another distribution arrangement. The German solution has elements of both systems: the capital partners receive a fixed percentage of their contribution before the rest of the profits, if any, are distributed equally. The partners are also equally liable for losses.[71] It is important to note that these are mainly default rules, so the partners are free to choose a distribution that fits the objects of their partnership. However, in several jurisdictions, it is explicitly prohibited to agree in such a way to exclude a partner from profit distribution or to let only one partner receive all the profits ('societas leonina').[72]

2.30 The provisions on the *dissolution of general partnerships* mirror the contractual character, even where a partnership enjoys legal personality. For example, the French SNC is dissolved by causes such as the end of the period for which the partnership has been formed or by other causes envisaged by the drafters of the contract - such causes may equally lead to the dissolution of a company. However, a partnership also may be dissolved upon the dismissal of a manager who is a partner, or upon the bankruptcy or death of a partner. If the participation of one of the partners has become impossible, the personal relationship is supposed to end. If the relationship seriously deteriorates due to a disagreement between the partners which paralyses the firm, the court may decide to dissolve the partnership.[73]

2.31 In many cases, the remaining partners may wish to continue the partnership without the participation of the bankrupt or deceased partner. In such cases, the partnership will continue to exist if the partnership contract provides for it or if the (remaining) partners unanimously decide to carry on its existence.[74]

2.32 In the event that a managing partner is dismissed from the SNC, the dismissed manager may decide to withdraw from the partnership and demand the repayment of his participation, the value of which shall be determined in accordance with the rules set out in the Civil Code.[75]

Other countries have similar provisions concerning the dissolution of general partnerships.[76] In addition, they also provide for the right of each partner to withdraw from the partnership; that is, to terminate the contract, albeit within certain constraints, such as a term that has to be taken into account. It has, in principle, the effect

71. Article 51 Polish Commercial Companies Code, ss 120–122 German Commercial Code.
72. For example, Article 1844-1 French Civil Code, Article 32 Belgian Companies Code Article 2265 Italian Civil Code and, implicitly, Article 51 Polish Commercial Companies Code. Exemption from losses may also be prohibited, e.g., by Article 1844-1 French Civil Code. The term 'societas leonina' refers to one of Fontaine's tales, Maurice Cozian, Alain Viandier, Florence Deboissy, *Droit des sociétés*, 27e édition (Paris: LexisNexis, 2012), nr. 141.
73. Article 1844-7 French Civil Code, Articles L221-12, L221-15 and L221-16 French Commercial Code.
74. Articles L221-12, L221-15 and L221-16 French Commercial Code.
75. Article L221-12 French Commercial Code and Article 1843-4 French Civil Code.
76. Sections 131–133 German Commercial Code, Articles 1680 Spanish Civil Code and 221–224 Spanish Commercial Code, Articles 1683–1686 Book 7A Dutch Civil Code, Articles 58–61 Polish Commercial Companies Code, Articles 39–45 Belgian Companies Code.

that the participation of the withdrawing partner ends, but that the partnership continues to exist (if more than one partner remains and if the partnership contract provides for continuation).[77]

2.33 Upon the death of a partner, his heirs may acquire the rights and obligations of the deceased partner in relation to the partnership. The partnership contract may provide for this situation, for instance, by continuation of the partnership with one of the heirs. Alternatively, where continuation of the partnership is agreed upon excluding the heirs, the latter may be entitled to reimbursement of the share of the deceased partner.[78] Such provisions, however, may conflict with the terms of the will of the deceased partner or with family law provisions. For that reason, the European Commission has recommended that Member States ensure the continuity of the partnership as a going concern in the event of the death of a partner.[79]

2.34 The dissolution must be published in order to inform the creditors of the partnership and is followed by *liquidation of the partnership's assets*. One or more liquidators have to be appointed. As a rule, all partners become liquidators, unless the partnership agreement provides otherwise. Liquidation generally deprives the partnership of its legal capacity in order to take part in any activities other than selling its assets and paying its debts. By its nature, the partnership includes the liability of the partners in the event that the partnership's assets do not bring in sufficient financial means to satisfy the creditors. A surplus will be distributed among the partners. If the partnership is a legal person, it continues to exist until liquidation is completed. Even where the partnership has no legal personality, it must function as an entity until the liquidation procedure is completed.[80]

D Limited Partnerships

2.35 It has been illustrated that the major disadvantage of the general partnership form is that the partners have unlimited liability for the debts of the firm. It is not, therefore, possible to invest in such a firm without assuming such liability. Each country, consequently, has an alternative form of partnership: the LP, which allows some partners to enjoy limited liability for the partnership's debts in the same way as a shareholder of a capital company. The common theme in such partnerships is that there are two types of partners: general partners and limited partners, the latter

77. Sections 131 and 132 German Commercial Code, Article 225 Spanish Commercial Code, Articles 1683 and 1686 Book 7A Dutch Civil Code, Articles 58 and 59 Polish Commercial Companies Code, Articles 39 and 42 Belgian Companies Code, Articles 2272, 2273 and 2284–2290 Italian Civil Code.
78. An example is Article 42 Belgian Companies Code.
79. 94/1069/EC: Commission Recommendation of 7 Dec. 1994 on the transfer of SMEs, OJ 1994, L 385, 31 Dec. 1994. *See also* the *Better Environment for Enterprises* communication by the European Commission to the European Parliament, Brussels 7 Nov. 2002 COM(2002) 610 final.
80. Article 1844-8 French Civil Code, ss 729–740 German Civil Code, Articles 228–237 Spanish Commercial Code, Articles 166 *et seq.* Book 3 Dutch Civil Code, Articles 67–85 Polish Commercial Companies Code. Articles 2275–2280 Italian Civil Code.

enjoying limited liability, but restricted management rights. The general partners have management rights and are called managing partners. Between the general partners, the general partnership rules apply.[81]

2.36 LPs are named and abbreviated as follows:

- France: *société en commandite simple* (SCS).
- Germany: *Kommanditgesellschaft* (KG).
- UK: *limited partnership* (LP).
- Spain: *sociedad en comandita* (SEC).
- The Netherlands: *commanditaire vennootschap* (CV).
- Poland: *spółka komandytowa* (sp.k.).
- Belgium: *gewone commanditaire vennootschap* (Comm.V) or SCS.
- Italy: *società in accomandita semplice* (SAS).

In all countries, except for the UK, these forms contain the Latin word *commenda,* reflecting the medieval origins of the LP.[82]

2.37 All these forms are modifications of the relevant general partnership form. LPs are rarely used in some countries, for example, France and the UK, but are more popular in others, like Germany.[83] The LP may, for instance, be indicated when a partner of a general partnership wishes to retire but the remaining partners cannot reimburse the retiring partner's share. To keep this share at the disposal of the partnership, the retiring partner's status can be changed into that of a limited partner. This way, limited liability can be created without having to adopt the often less flexible structure of a capital company. A capital company could also have unwanted tax consequences, because partnerships are generally regarded as transparent for taxation purposes - that is, taxation is upon the partners and not upon the partnership - whereas companies themselves are subject to taxation.[84]

81. Articles L222-1 *et seq.* French Commercial Code, ss 161 *et seq.* German Commercial Code, ss 1 *et seq.* Limited Partnerships Act 1907, Articles 145–150 Spanish Commercial Code, Article 19 Dutch Commercial Code, Articles 102 *et seq.* Polish Commercial Companies Code, Articles 202 *et seq.* Belgian Companies Code, Articles 2313 and 2318 Italian Civil Code.
82. *See* on the medieval commenda and its even older origins John H. Pryor, 'The Origins of the Commenda Contract', *Speculum* 52, no. 1 (January 1977), 5–37 (via: http://www.jstor.org/stable/2856894).
83. The limited partnership form in the UK was introduced much later than in other countries by the Limited Partnerships Act of 1907 (limited partnership). Limited partnerships are rare in the UK, principally because by the time they were introduced their role had been superseded by the private limited company. For France, Maurice Cozian, Alain Viandier et Florence Deboissy, *Droit des sociétés,* 27e édition (Paris: LexisNexis, 2012), nr. 1250. The popularity of the German Kommanditgesellschaft is partly due to the combination with a private company as a general partner. *See infra,* paragraph 2.46. In Spain such combinations are also (expected to be) popular, Cándido Paz-Ares, 'La Sociedad en Comandita', in *Curso de Derecho Mercantil,* Tomo I ed. Uría-Menéndez (Madrid, 1999), 703–704.
84. On problems of taxation of partnerships in cross-border situations, *see* Peter Essers & Gerard T. Meussen, 'Taxation of Partnerships/Hybrid Entities', in *The Governance of Close Corporations and Partnerships,* eds Joseph A. McCahery, Theo Raaijmakers & Erik P.M. Vermeulen (Oxford and New York: Oxford University Press 2004), 415 *et seq.*

2.38 The limited partner is principally only liable up to the amount of his contributions, which must be in cash or in kind. The agreed contribution of the limited partner cannot be delivered by way of performing services, as this would involve management participation, which is generally forbidden and conflicts with the idea of a determinable amount of the contribution. In order to avoid misleading third parties, it is not permitted to use the name of the limited partner in the name of the partnership. Aside from a few exceptions, violation of this provision may lead to the loss of the limited liability status.[85] However, to properly inform third parties, some details about the limited partner(s) and their contribution must be mentioned in the documents, which the partnership has to file with the commercial registry. National provisions range from requiring publication of the name and the contribution of each of the limited partners,[86] to more global information, such as the total amount of the limited partners' contributions.[87]

2.39 The limited partner may lose his status not only by lending his name to the firm, but also by representing the partnership in dealings with third parties. Strict rules may apply, such as in Belgium, France, the Netherlands and the UK, where the limited partner is not permitted to represent the partnership when dealing with third parties, not even when he is granted a power of attorney by the general partners, without risking his limited liability status.[88] On the other hand, Germany, Poland and Italy permit the limited partner to represent the firm if he has a power of attorney. If he deals with third parties without such a power, he will be personally liable for the transaction, but this will not, as in other jurisdictions, lead to a loss of limited liability for the debts of the partnership.[89]

III COMPANIES

A Private Companies

2.40 Private companies are those forms of business organizations designed for small or medium concerns, which require limited liability and legal personality, but that do not require access to public funding through the general capital markets. Financing comes from contributions by the members themselves or, alternatively, through bank finance. Each country has this type of company, but some, for example, Belgium and France, have severe restrictions on the transferability of the members' interests. They

85. Article L222-6 French Commercial Code, Article 147 Spanish Commercial Code, Article 20 Dutch Commercial Code, Article 104 Polish Commercial Companies Code, Article 207 Belgian Companies Code, s. 6(1) Limited Partnerships Act 1907, Article 2314 Italian Civil Code.
86. Article 1835 French Civil Code, Articles L210-4 and L222-4 French Commercial Code, s. 162 German Commercial Code, s. 8 Limited Partnerships Act, Article 210 *Reglamento del Registro Mercantil* (Spain), Article 110 Polish Commercial Companies Code.
87. Article 10 Dutch Act on the Commercial Registry (*Handelsregisterwet*), Article 69 Belgian Companies Code.
88. Article L 222-6 French Commercial Code, Article 148IV Spanish Commercial Code, Article 207 Belgian Companies Code, s. 6(1) Limited Partnerships Act.
89. Section 170 German Commercial Code and BGHZ 17, 392 *et seq.*, Article 118 Polish Commercial Companies Code, Article 2320 Italian Civil Code.

can, therefore, be regarded as close companies or as capital companies, which retain many of the features of a personal company or partnership. Other countries, such as the UK, Germany and Italy, have no such mandatory restrictions, although many companies adopt some form of restriction on transfers in their charters. The capital requirements in some countries are less rigid in comparison with public companies, and the UK, France and the Netherlands, in fact, do not prescribe a minimum capital at all. In general, the private company forms are very popular and form the vast majority of companies, although the limited liability advantages are often negated by the requirement of the banks for personal guarantees by the members.

2.41 The various national forms of private companies discussed include:

- Belgium: *besloten vennootschap met beperkte aansprakelijkheid or société privée a responsabilité limitée* (BVBA/SPRL).
- France: *société a responsabilité limitée* (SARL).
- Germany: *Gesellschaft mit beschränkter Haftung* (GmbH).
- The Netherlands: *besloten vennootschap met beperkte aansprakelijkheid* (BV).
- Poland: *Spólka z ograniczoną odpowiedzialnocią* (spólka z o.o./sp. z o.o.).
- Spain: *sociedad de responsabilidad limitada* (S.R.L. or S.L.).
- UK: *private limited company* (Ltd).
- Italy: *società a responsabilità limitata* (SRL).

B Public or Stock Companies

2.42 Public or stock companies are available in each Member State. Although there are far fewer of these than private companies, in economic terms they are very significant. These companies are designed for larger enterprises, which have access to all the capital markets for raising finance, in terms of both equity capital from shareholders and loan capital from bondholders. They are genuine capital companies, in that there usually are a large and diverse number of shareholders who, although they, economically speaking, 'own' the company, cannot, in reality, manage or control it. This separation of ownership and control requires complex structures for the governance of such companies.[90] The debate on corporate governance finds its origins here, and corporate scandals, such as the Enron, Ahold and Parmalat scandals, demonstrated the need for appropriate control mechanisms.[91] Because of their economic importance, public companies are also subjected to far greater controls in such areas as mergers and creditor protection. In general, they also have a large number of

90. The consequences of the separation of ownership and control have been researched for the first time by Adolf Berle & Gardiner C. Means, *The Modern Corporation and Private Property*, with a new introduction by Murray L. Weidenbaum & Mark Jensen (New Brunswick/London: Transaction Publishers, 1991). The original publication is from Harcourt, Brace & World, 1932.
91. *The Economist*, 15 Jul. 2002, 'A Guide to Corporate Scandals', *Washington Post*, 14 Oct. 2004, Ahold Settles SEC Fraud Charges. Dutch Grocer Is Not Fined Because of Its Cooperation. *See* furthermore the ECGI (European Corporate Governance Institute) at www.ecgi.org/.

employees and the question of the role of employees in the company has to be addressed. However, this, of course, is not limited to the public company form.

2.43 In legal terms, the common characteristics of public companies include the free transferability of shares and securities (access to public investment requires it), an elaborate system of control and minority shareholder protection, controls on raising and maintaining equity capital, the need to compel disclosure of information to members and to the public, and detailed rules as to the presentation and auditing of accounts. In certain areas, the various national forms of public companies are now very similar because national laws have been harmonized, or, perhaps more accurately, approximated, as the result of the implementation of EU directives. These areas include questions of corporate capacity, share capital, the preparation and auditing of accounts, mergers and divisions and the admission of their securities to the appropriate stock exchanges.

2.44 In other areas, however, they remain very disparate where either no such harmonization has been attempted (e.g., loan capital) or on issues where there has been a failure by various governments to reach an agreement (e.g., the management structure). Each of the national public company forms is regulated by codes or chapters of codes separate to those of the national private companies, with the exception of the UK.

2.45 The various national forms of public or stock companies include:

- Belgium: *naamloze vennootschap/société anonyme* (NV/SA).
- France: *société anonyme* (SA).
- Germany: *Aktiengesellschaft* (AG).
- The Netherlands: *naamloze vennootschap* (NV).
- Poland: *spółka akcyjna* (SA).
- Spain: *sociedad anónima* (SA).
- UK: *public limited company* (plc).
- Italy: *società per azioni* (SPA).

IV HYBRID FORMS

2.46 It is possible for companies having legal personality to be partners in one of the forms of partnership set out previously. Thus in the UK, for example, the general partner in an LP might itself be a limited company – thus, in effect, having complete limited liability. In Germany, for instance, this combination of a company and a partnership has become very popular. This is known as the GmbH & Co. KG. This form has a GmbH as the general partner and individuals as limited partners, who are usually also members of the GmbH. This form is widespread because it combines the advantages of a partnership (such as a simple capital structure) with the limited liability provided by the GmbH and allows the limited partners of the KG to act as directors of the general partner, that is, the GmbH. Moreover, enterprises in the form of a KG are subject to less mandatory rules in comparison with a GmbH. Any problems caused by the fact that the management board of the GmbH is not responsible to the limited partners are usually overcome because they are often also members of the GmbH. Apart from combinations, such as the GmbH & Co. KG, there are some other specific forms available for a business enterprise, which combine elements of companies and partnerships. The main form is a type of LP with shares.

A LPs with Shares

2.47 LPs with shares are, in effect, combinations of partnerships and public companies. They are unknown in the UK, which, as aforementioned, treats the two forms as entirely separate. The continental approach of treating all these forms as types of company allows for such greater flexibility. The French *société en commandité par actions* (SCA) is a good illustration of this and is briefly discussed here.[92] The Commercial Code constitutes the hybrid character of the SCA, where the first provision on the SCA declares that where it is compatible with the special provisions, both the rules on LPs and public limited companies apply to it. Because of its mixed nature, the managing partners cannot assign their shares, except with the consent of all other members, whereas the limited partners (shareholders) have freely transferable shares in the same way as those in an SA. The special provisions, however, render the SCA very flexible compared to the SA. The managing partner(s) can be a legal person, for instance, an SARL, and the articles of the SCA may confer extensive powers to such partner(s), including the exclusive right to appoint and dismiss managers. This, of course, guarantees the general partner(s) a very strong position vis-à-vis the shareholders, who are only partly compensated by the obligation to establish a supervisory board composed of at least three shareholders.[93] The SCA is sometimes used as a listed company and is considered to offer (temporary) protection against a takeover, due to the weak position of its shareholders. In the event that an SA is transformed into an SCA, the shareholders have the right to opt out.[94]

2.48 In Germany, the LP with shares is known as the KGaA,[95] in Spain as the *sociedad comanditaria por acciones* (S. Com. por A.), in Poland as the *Spółka komandytowo-akcyjna* (SKA) and in Italy as the *società in accomandita per azioni* (SAPA).[96] The Spanish version was modernized in 1989 and is primarily a modification of the public company, the *sociedad anónima,* because they are both categorized as *sociedades de capital* and regulated by the same act.[97] The powers of the managing partners are the

92. Articles L226-1 *et seq.* French Commercial Code.
93. Articles L226-2 and L226-4 French Commercial Code.
94. Maurice Cozian, Alain Viandier et Florence Deboissy, *Droit des sociétés*, 27e édition (Paris: LexisNexis, 2012), nr. 955.
95. Sections 278 *et seq.* AktG.
96. Articles 1 Capital Companies Act *(Ley de Sociedades de Capital)* and 169 *et seq.* Spanish Commercial Code, Articles 125 *et seq.* Polish Commercial Companies Code and Articles 2452 *et seq.* Italian Civil Code.
97. The Capital Companies Act *(Ley de Sociedades de Capital).*

same as those of the directors of a public company.[98] In Poland, the position of the general or managing partner(s) is regulated by the provisions on the general partnership, as opposed to other matters, such as the share capital, the supervisory board and the general assembly, which are covered by the provisions for the public or joint-stock company.[99] Like the general partners of the Spanish form, the general partners of an Italian SAPA have the same rights and obligations as directors of the public company.[100] Finally, in Belgium, the *commanditaire vennootschap op aandelen/société en commandite par actions* (Com.VA/SCA) exists. It applies the rules for formation, shares and capital of the NV/SA.[101] In the Netherlands, the LP with shares was abolished in 1971 to prevent the use of this partnership form as an alternative to companies in order to evade harmonized company law.

V BUSINESS ORGANIZATIONS UNDER EU LAW

2.49 The EU legislator has enacted several regulations in order to create legal forms for business organizations under EU law. Primarily, EU law governs such business organizations, which may transfer their registered seat from one Member State to another. By 1985, the first of these business organizations, the European Economic Interest Grouping (EEIG), was introduced. The EEIG aims at enabling cooperation between entrepreneurs and/or enterprises from different Member States. Almost twenty years later, in 2001, the Regulation on the Statute of the European Company, the *Societas Europaea* (SE), was adopted. It took the European institutions almost three decades of debate and negotiations to reach this milestone. The SE is a capital company and is meant to facilitate the restructuring of enterprises at a European level. The third business organization under EU law is the European Cooperative Society, the *Societas Cooperativa Europaea* (SCE), a vehicle for cooperation of natural persons or national cooperative organizations. The SCE regulation, adopted in 2003, applies as of 18 August 2006.[102] The EEIG, the SE and the SCE are dealt with further in Chapter 4. A proposal for a European Private Company, the *Societas Privata Europaea* (SPE), was put forward by the Commission in 2008 but withdrawn in 2014 to be replaced by a proposal for a directive on single-member private limited liability companies, the Societas Unius Personae (SUP). This proposal is also discussed in Chapter 4.

98. Ley de Sociedades de Capital, Article 252.
99. Article 126 Polish Commercial Companies Code.
100. Article 2455 Italian Civil Code. The SAPA is not frequently used: G.F. Campobasso, *Diritto Commerciale. 2. Diritto delle Società*. Nona Edizione, UTET Giuridica, Wolters Kluwer Italia S.r.l. 2015; pp. 548–549.
101. Articles 654 *et seq.* Belgian Companies Code.
102. The European Commission has also launched proposals for a *European Association* (EA) and a *European Mutual Society*.

VI IMPACT OF THE EU

2.50 Whereas developments at the EU level seemed to have come to a halt during most of the 1990s, considerable progress has been made since then.[103] In hindsight, it can be said that the adoption of the Directive on the European Works Council (1994) paved the way for the SE, because it took away the 'employee participation bug', which has infected many proposals in the field of company law to halt their progress.[104] The birth of the SE also brought life to long-pending proposals, such as the Tenth Directive on cross-border mergers. By 2008, it was concluded that the EU harmonization programme yielded a considerable number of directives, ranging from disclosure requirements and annual financial statements to mergers and divisions and takeover bids. The impact of this EU legislation on national company laws is evident and, since then, several directives have been amended and/or simplified.[105] Harmonization has certainly led to modernization of national laws, for instance, in relation to accounting and financial reporting, takeover bids and capital markets. In some cases, it has had a spillover effect, where countries extended implementation of EU legislation beyond the prescribed areas; notably, by further applying provisions of the directive aimed at public companies to private companies. Nevertheless, harmonization has its drawbacks, the most obvious being the risk of 'petrification' of harmonized national law. Drafting and adopting a revised version of a directive may be as burdensome and time consuming as drafting a new one. This is particularly true when directives or amendments are very detailed. Therefore, the European Commission, in its 1985 White Paper on Completing the Internal Market, already featured another approach to lawmaking, in order to minimize harmonization efforts by limiting it to the essentials and relying more on the mutual recognition of national regulations and standards.[106]

2.51 The actual effect of the harmonization programme on the development of corporate law within the EU is difficult to assess. Critics mention the lack of harmonization in core topics, such as the duties of directors and shareholder remedies.[107] Others point out peculiarities of national law that may last even where they should

103. Jan Wouters, 'European Company Law: Quo Vadis?', *Common Market Law Review* 37 (2000): 257–307. For the ups and downs of the harmonization programme, *see also* Christiaan Timmermans, 'First Water van Gerven Lecture', *Company Law as Ius Commune?*, Leuven Centre for a Common Law of Europe, retrievable at the website of the Ius Commune Research School, www.iuscommune.eu. A thorough analysis of the state of harmonization in the 1990s is offered by Richard M. Buxbaum et al. (eds), *European Economic and Business Law, Legal and Economic Analyses on Integration and Harmonization* (Berlin/New York: Walter de Gruyter, 1996).
104. The metaphor is from Wouters, 'European Company Law: Quo Vadis?', *Common Market Law Review* 37 (2000), 263.
105. *See* the 2012 Action Plan for an overview, European Commission, Action Plan: European company law and corporate governance – a modern legal framework for more engaged shareholders and sustainable companies, COM(2012) 740 final, pp. 2–3.
106. This approach was announced in relation to the free movements of goods, COM(85) 310 final, 14 Jun. 1985 White Paper from the Commission to the European Council, *Completing the Internal Market*, 19 *et seq.*
107. Luca Enriques, 'EC Company Law Directives and Regulations: How Trivial Are They?' (May 2005). *ECGI – Law Working Paper* No. 39/2005, http://ssrn.com/abstract=730388.

have been overruled by harmonization. For instance, the contractual origin of companies, which is still clearly visible in the legal system of countries such as France, may be hard to reconcile with the strict limitation of annulment of companies imposed by the First Directive and it may take a long time before legal practice conforms to such harmonization.[108]

2.52 Although the various forms of partnerships and companies under national laws of the EU Member States have many features in common, a number of differences also mark them and each is a purely national form of organization. These two factors have created basic problems that have been brought into focus by the existence and ideals of the EU, in particular the freedom of establishment. The first problem stems from the differences in the national laws and relates to the creation of the single market itself – ideally, in light of the single market, all companies and partnerships operating under various national laws of the Member States should be operating under the same rules. This is expressed by the concept of a level playing field so that, for example, a German AG and a French SA should be subject to the same controls and restrictions. The second problem arises from the fact that purely national forms require registration in and governance by a particular Member State. Thus, for a company that wishes to operate in several Member States, the problem is, in principle, that it cannot move from one Member State to another without being wound up entirely and then set up again in the appropriate form in another Member State.

2.53 The answers to these problems are in different stages of development. In order to solve the level playing field issue, the EU adopted the previously mentioned harmonization programme, which has been successful to a certain point. To compensate, as it were, for the fact that companies are purely national forms, the SE and other business organizations under EU law were introduced in order to facilitate cross-border cooperation and restructuring. Nevertheless, the problem remains partly unresolved for the national entities, except in terms of setting up a branch in another Member State or merging cross-border. The European Commission, in 2004, launched a public consultation on a draft (Fourteenth) Directive on the cross-border transfers of seat, in order to solve this problem.[109] After the consultation, the responsible commissioner concluded in 2007 that there was no need for action at EU level on this issue, *inter alia,* due to the effects of the ECJ judgment in *Sevic [2003],* enabling cross-border mergers (*see* paragraph 3.102). More recently, case law also clarified that the right of establishment entails, to a certain extent, the cross-border conversion of companies (*see* paragraph 2.65a). Notwithstanding these developments, the issue of cross-border

108. Martine Bolzard, 'Incidence des normes européennes sur la liberé de constitution des sociétés en droit francais', *Revue des Sociétés* no. 1 (January/February 2005): 1 *et seq.*; Jean-Victor Louis, 'Ensuring Compliance and Implementation by Member States', in Richard M. Buxbaum et al., *European Economic and Business Law. Legal and Economic Analyses on Integration and Harmonization* (Berlin/New York: Walter de Gruyter, 1996), 1 *et seq.*
109. www.europa.eu.int/comm/internal_market/company/seat-transfer/index_en.htm.

transfers of the registered office returned in the Commission's Action Plan 2012 due to pressure from the EP.[110] A public consultation took place and in September 2013 a feedback statement was published.[111]

2.53a According to the Commission's feedback statement, the consultation focused on gathering data, facts and figures on the transfers of registered offices and their costs, and on possible ways to move forward. Due to the relatively small number of responses (86), no robust data was acquired and it remains unclear how many transfers actually have happened or have been considered. The respondents regarded the search for a favourable tax regime as the main motivation for companies to transfer their registered office abroad, followed by a favourable business climate. Half of the respondents agreed with the statement that the transfer of the registered office should be compulsory along with the transfer of the headquarters (main office); however, the majority of companies among these respondents disagreed with this statement. Other issues at the consultation included the protection of the interests of employees, for which a solution according to the SE legislation was preferred, and minority shareholders, who should be allowed to withdraw in case of a transfer. Finally, respondents summed up specific features the regulation on the transfer of the registered office should have: '(...) the company should not lose its legal personality; the transfer should be fiscally neutral (...); the effectiveness of the transfer (timing) should be clearly defined; the instrument should prevent tax avoidance; a simplified regime for SMEs should be designed; the transfer of a registered office should only be allowed if a real business reason exists.'[112]

VII THE RIGHT OF ESTABLISHMENT

2.54 Regarding the mobility of national companies within the EU, Articles 49 and 54 of the TFEU are relevant. They expressly grant companies the right of secondary establishment in another Member State, for example, through a branch, agency or subsidiary. The ECJ, in *Commission v. France* (1986), seems to have regarded this right as being paramount over national tax considerations.[113] However, the right to primary establishment of companies, as afforded to individuals by Article 49, is not acknowledged fully.

2.55 The right to freedom of establishment within the EU is contained in Article 49 of the TFEU itself. This gives self-employed individuals the right to set up a business in any Member State, including the right to set up a company or partnership. This right of

110. Action Plan: European company law and corporate governance – a modern legal framework for more engaged shareholders and sustainable companies, Strasbourg, 12.12.2012, COM(2012) 740 final. The resolution of the EP on the cross-border transfer of the registered office: OJ 2010/C 87E/02. *See also* the recommendations of the Committee on Legal Affairs of 1 Sep. 2012, European Added Value Assessment, EAVA 3/2012.
111. Summary of responses to the public consultation on Cross-border transfers of registered offices of companies, September 2013 http://ec.europa.eu/internal_market/consultations/2013/seat-transfer/docs/summary-of-responses_en.pdf.
112. Summary of responses, o.c., pp. 7–15.
113. *Commission v. France* (1986), ECR 273.

primary establishment for individuals has been confirmed by the ECJ in the *Reyners* case (1974).[114] Article 49 provides as follows:

> Within the framework of the provisions set out below, restrictions on the freedom of establishment of nationals of a Member State in the territory of another Member State shall be prohibited. Such prohibition shall also apply to restrictions on the setting-up of agencies, branches or subsidiaries by nationals of any Member State established in the territory of any Member State.

Freedom of establishment shall include the right to take up and pursue activities as self-employed persons and to set up and manage undertakings, in particular companies or firms within the meaning of the second paragraph of Article 54, under the conditions laid down for its own nationals by the law of the country where such establishment is effected, subject to the provisions of the chapter relating to capital.

Article 54 then provides as follows:

> Companies or firms formed in accordance with the law of a Member State and having their registered office, central administration or principal place of business within the Union shall, for the purposes of this Chapter, be treated in the same way as natural persons who are nationals of Member States.
>
> 'Companies or firms' means companies or firms constituted under civil or commercial law, including cooperative societies, and other legal persons governed by public or private law, save for those which are non-profit-making.

The question as to whether this provision allows for the primary establishment (i.e., full mobility) of 'companies or firms' will be addressed in the following paragraphs.

2.56 The right to primary establishment would allow a company to be able to move from one Member State to another without having to alter its charter or, at least, its legal personality. Given that a single harmonized system of company law does not yet exist throughout the Union, the solution would require, for example, Belgium to recognize a French incorporated company that chose to move all its offices, management and operations to Belgium as if it were a Belgian company, but without requiring it to actually become a Belgian company.

2.57 Traditionally, two conflicting doctrines of private international law operate within the Union with respect to the recognition of companies. The first, known as the doctrine of incorporation, provides that a foreign company, created in accordance with a foreign legal system and having its registered office in that foreign state, is recognized as such by the host country. Under this principle, a company incorporated and registered, for example, in Spain is regarded as a Spanish company by the UK, even if it is operating, in all senses of the word, only within the UK. This system operates, for example, in the UK and the Netherlands (out of the countries dealt with in this book).[115]

114. Case 2/74, *Reyners v. Belgian State* (1974), ECR 631.
115. According to the *Impact Assessment on the Directive on the Cross-border Transfer of Registered Office*, Commission Staff Working Document, Brussels 12 Dec. 2007 SEC(2007) 1707, 9, the

2.58 The second doctrine, which operates in various forms in other Member States, is that of the *'siege réel'* or real seat. Under this doctrine, the recognition of a company depends on it conforming to the requirements of the country in which it has chosen to locate its real centre of activities or management decision-making. Thus, if the Spanish incorporated and registered company from the previous example moved its real seat of operations to France, it would only be recognized as a corporation there if it complied with French law. Traditionally, Belgium, France, Germany, Poland and Spain used to adhere to the real seat approach. It generally implies that the cross-border transfer of the registered office is not allowed, unless the real seat is simultaneously transferred, but this would result in the winding up of the company. It must be mentioned, however, that Member States differ in the way they apply the real seat doctrine. Germany abandoned the real seat requirement for companies in 2008.[116] In Spanish legal doctrine, it is argued that the incorporation doctrine actually prevails, and the same applies in Poland.[117] In Italy, a mixed approach is installed by the 2003 law reform, requiring that interpretation and application of the provisions regarding foreign companies is to be made in accordance with the principles of the European legal system. Consequently, the real seat approach for foreign companies having their head office and/or principal operations in Italy is derogated for companies under the law of an EU Member State.[118]

2.59 If all Member States adopted the incorporation theory, then movement of companies from one country to another without losing their corporate status in the process would be much easier. The *'siége réel'* system, in effect, requires dissolution and re-formation in the host state. In practice, other differences between the Member States, for example, regarding the role of employees in management of companies, make primary establishment difficult to achieve, despite the wording of Article 54 of the TFEU. Against this background, the ECJ refrained from taking up the question as to which system should prevail in the case of *R v. The Treasury, ex parte the Daily Mail* (1988).[119]

---

incorporation doctrine is followed by nine other Member States, including Denmark, Finland and the Czech Republic. German Courts apply the incorporation doctrine where companies from other EU Member States are concerned, Christoph Teichmann, *European Company Law (ECL)* 5, no. 4 (2008): 189. Furthermore: Luis A. Martinez Giner, Spanish companies and private international law, In: Guglielmo Maisto (red.), *Residence of Companies Under Tax Treaties and EC Law*, EC and International Tax Law Series, IBFD 2009, pp. 753 *et seq.*

116. Eddy Wymeersch, 'The Transfer of the Company's Seat in European Company Law', *ECGI – Law Working Paper* No. 08/2003, March 2003 (www.ssrn.com). *The Impact Assessment on the Directive on the Cross-border Transfer of Registered Office*, 9. Gesetz zur Modernisierung des GmbH-Rechts und zur Bekämpfung von Missbräuchen (MoMiG) which amended s. 4a GmbHG and s. 5 AktG accordingly.
117. Article 17(1) of the Polish International Private Law of 2011 states that a legal person is subject to the law of the state where it has it's seat. In Polish legal doctrine it is assumed that 'seat' means the seat as stated in the articles.
118. The real seat approach flows from the second part of the first paragraph of Article 25 Law No. 218 of 31 May 1995 on the Reform of the Italian System of Private International Law but is now superseded by principles of EU law, according to Article 2507 Italian Civil Code.
119. *R v. The Treasury, ex parte the Daily Mail* (1989) 1 All E.R. 328.

2.60 In the *Daily Mail* case, a UK company wished to transfer all its central management to the Netherlands without losing its status as a UK incorporated company. The practical reason for this was the desire to switch its residence for tax purposes. Under UK law, no company could move its residence for tax purposes without the Treasury's consent, which was refused. The company argued that this consent requirement was contrary to Articles 52 and 58 (now 49 and 54) of the Treaty. In its judgment, the ECJ agreed on the narrow point that the Treaty did preclude a Member State from hindering the movement of one of its companies to another Member State, but it took the view that, because the two countries concerned have the incorporation theory of recognition, there were no problems in recognition. On the broader issue of the general right of establishment, the court was more cautious and was of the opinion that, until the incorporation versus *siège réel* issue was solved by a future convention or legislation, full primary establishment could not be achieved. Such a convention, proposed in 1968 under the old Article 220 (now repealed) of the Treaty, has never been pursued.

2.61 More recent case law, however, shows a fundamental policy switch. Starting with the 1999 *Centros* case, followed by the *Überseering* case (2002) and the *Inspire Art* case (2003), the ECJ removed some of the obstacles to mobility.[120] The interpretation given by these judgments concerning Articles 49 and 54 TFEU (then Articles 43 and 48 of the EC Treaty) can be summarized as follows.

If a company has its registered office in Member State *A* and is formed in accordance with the law of Member State *A*, then Member State *B:*

- *cannot refuse to recognize* that company, even when its entire business is carried on by a branch in Member State *B*, thus evading the (more restrictive) rules for incorporation in Member State *B* (Centros case);
- *cannot deny legal capacity* to that company, even when it is deemed, according to the law of Member State *B*, to have moved its actual centre of administration (its real seat) to that Member State *B;* Member State *B* must *recognize the legal capacity of the company* to be the same as it enjoys under the law of Member State *A* (Überseering case);
- *cannot impose disclosure requirements* on the branch of that company which go beyond the disclosure obligations provided for by the Eleventh Directive (on branches) and
- *cannot impose conditions* on that company provided for in domestic company law relating to minimum capital and director's liability, irrespective of the

120. ECJ, 9 Mar. 1999, Case C-212/97 (*Centros Ltd v. Erhvervs- og Selskabsstyrelsen*), 30 Sep. 2003, 5 Nov. 2002, Case C-208/00 (*Überseering BV v. Nordic Construction Company Baumanagement GmbH* (NCC)), Case C-167/01 (*Kamer van Koophandel en Fabrieken voor Amsterdam v. Inspire Art Ltd*). Kilian Baelz & Teresa Baldwin, 'The End of the Real Seat Theory (Sitztheorie): The European Court of Justice Decision in Ueberseering of 5 Nov. 2002 and its Impact on German and European Company Law', *German Law Journal* 12 (1 Dec. 2002): Private Law (www.germanlawjournal.com).

reasons for which that company was formed in Member State *A* and the fact that it carries on its activities almost exclusively in Member State *B* (Inspire Art case).

2.62 In the *Centros* case, Mr and Mrs Bryde, a Danish couple residing in Denmark, registered a private company named Centros Ltd in England and Wales. The company's registered office was situated in the UK at the home of a friend of Mr Bryde. The Centros' capital was divided into two shares, held by Mr and Mrs Bryde. Mrs Bryde was the director of Centros. During the summer of 1992, Mrs Bryde requested the *Erhvervs- og Selskabsstyrelsen* (the Trade and Companies Board), falling under the Danish Department of Trade, to register a branch of Centros in Denmark. The board refused that registration on the grounds, *inter alia,* that Centros, which does not trade in the UK, was in fact seeking to establish, not a branch, but principal establishment in Denmark, by circumventing the national rules concerning, in particular, the payment of the minimum capital required for Danish private companies. Centros brought an action before the court (*Østre Landsret*) against the refusal of the board to give effect to that registration. Because of the court upholding the arguments of the board, Centros appealed to the Supreme Court (*Højesteret*). The Supreme Court referred questions about the interpretation of the relevant articles of the EC Treaty to the ECJ for a preliminary ruling. This ruling, paraphrased in the previous paragraph, is as follows:

> It is contrary to Articles 52 and 58 of the EC Treaty for a Member State to refuse to register a branch of a company formed in accordance with the law of another Member State in which it has its registered office but in which it conducts no business where the branch is intended to enable the company in question to carry on its entire business in the State in which that branch is to be created, while avoiding the need to form a company there, thus evading application of the rules governing the formation of companies which, in that State, are more restrictive as regards the paying up of a minimum share capital. That interpretation does not, however, prevent the authorities of the Member State concerned from adopting any appropriate measure for preventing or penalising fraud, either in relation to the company itself, if need be in cooperation with the Member State in which it was formed, or in relation to its members, where it has been established that they are in fact attempting, by means of the formation of a company, to evade their obligations towards private or public creditors established in the territory of the Member State concerned.

2.63 The *Überseering* case originated from a conflict between Überseering BV and Nordic Construction Company Baumanagement GmbH (NCC). Überseering, a Dutch private company, acquired a piece of land in Düsseldorf (Germany), which it used for business purposes. By way of a project management contract, Überseering engaged NCC to refurbish a garage and a motel on the site. The contractual obligations were performed, but Überseering claimed that the paintwork was defective. Überseering unsuccessfully sought compensation from NCC for the defective work and it brought an action before the Regional Court *(Landgericht Düsseldorf)*. However, prior to this, two German nationals residing in Düsseldorf had acquired all the shares in Überseering. The *Landgericht* dismissed the action, as did the *Oberlandesgericht* (Higher

Regional Court). It found that Überseering had transferred its actual centre of administration to Düsseldorf once two German nationals acquired its shares. The *Oberlandesgericht* found that, as a company incorporated under Dutch law, Überseering did not have legal capacity in Germany and, consequently, could not bring legal proceedings there. Überseering appealed to the Supreme Court *(Bundesgerichtshof)*, which referred the case to the ECJ for a preliminary ruling. The required ruling, which has been paraphrased in paragraph 2.61, is as follows:

> 1. Where a company formed in accordance with the law of a Member State ('A') in which it has its registered office is deemed, under the law of another Member State ('B'), to have moved its actual centre of administration to Member State B, Articles 43 EC and 48 EC preclude Member State B from denying the company legal capacity and, consequently, the capacity to bring legal proceedings before its national courts for the purpose of enforcing rights under a contract with a company established in Member State B.
>
> 2. Where a company formed in accordance with the law of a Member State ('A') in which it has its registered office exercises its freedom of establishment in another Member State ('B'), Articles 43 EC and 48 EC require Member State B to recognise the legal capacity and, consequently, the capacity to be a party to legal proceedings which the company enjoys under the law of its State of incorporation ('A').

2.63a In the *Inspire Art* case, Inspire Art Ltd, a company governed by the law of England and Wales, requested registration of its branch in the Netherlands. The *Kamer van Koophandel en Fabrieken voor Amsterdam* (Amsterdam Chamber of Commerce and Industry) concluded that Inspire Art was subject to the obligation to record its description as a *formeel buitenlandse vennootschap* (formally foreign company) and to use that description in its business dealings, as provided by the *Wet op de Formeel Buitenlandse Vennootschappen* (Formally Foreign Companies Act). This Statute defined a formally foreign company as a capital company formed under laws other than those of the Netherlands, which carries on its activities entirely, or almost entirely, in the Netherlands and does not have any real connection with the State in which it is registered. Various obligations are imposed on a formally foreign company, concerning, *inter alia*, the company's registration in the commercial register, the minimum share capital and the drawing up and publication of the annual documents. Inspire Art refused to fulfil the registration requirements as a formally foreign company, because such requirements conflict with the freedom of establishment. The case was brought before the Subdistrict Court *(Kantongerecht)*, which referred questions about the applicability of Articles 43 and 48 EC Treaty to the ECJ. It was also questioned whether the requirements imposed by Dutch Law could be justified under Article 46 of the Treaty, due to the alleged involvement of public policy. The ruling by the ECJ, already paraphrased in paragraph 2.61, is as follows:

> 1. It is contrary to Article 2 of the Eleventh Council Directive 89/666/EEC of 21 December 1989 concerning disclosure requirements in respect of branches opened in a Member State by certain types of company governed by the law of another State for national legislation such as the Wet op de Formeel Buitenlandse Vennootschappen (Law on Formally Foreign Companies) of 17 December 1997 to

impose on the branch of a company formed in accordance with the laws of another Member State disclosure obligations not provided for by that directive.

2. It is contrary to Articles 43 EC and 48 EC for national legislation such as the Wet op de Formeel Buitenlandse Vennootschappen to impose on the exercise of freedom of secondary establishment in that State by a company formed in accordance with the law of another Member State certain conditions provided for in domestic company law in respect of company formation relating to minimum capital and directors' liability. The reasons for which the company was formed in that other State, and the fact that it carries on its activities exclusively or almost exclusively in the Member State of establishment, do not deprive it of the right to invoke the freedom of establishment guaranteed by the Treaty, save where the existence of an abuse is established on a case-by-case basis.

2.64 The cases described in the previous paragraphs all concern the same type of situation: a company is formed and registered in accordance with the law of one Member State, while it carries on all or almost all of its activities (its real seat) in another Member State. This situation can only exist where Member States allow domestic companies to migrate their real seat to another country. For obvious reasons, only Member States adhering to the incorporation doctrine will do so. If the host Member State also favours this doctrine, no problem will arise, as long as the company complies with the law of its country of origin. However, even the incorporation doctrine does not always guarantee unprejudiced hospitality. Some host Member States tried to restrict avoidance of their national requirements for private companies, such as a minimum capital, by refusing to register the branch of such a company (*Centros* case) or imposing certain requirements of national law upon registration of such a branch (*Inspire Art*). The ECJ deems these actions to conflict with the freedom of secondary establishment, as guaranteed by the TFEU. If the host country adheres to the real seat doctrine, the problem becomes more fundamental, because, when strictly applied, it prohibits the recognition of a company that does not have its real seat in the country in which it is registered. The host then may deny, for instance, the company's capacity to start legal proceedings, as in the *Überseering* case. According to the ECJ, the TFEU also precludes this. The judgments of the ECJ may have relaxed the (secondary) right of establishment, but still have not eradicated all restrictive policies of the Member States. Member States may continue to prevent their domestic companies from migrating their real seat to another Member State, while retaining their original domestic status *(Cartesio, see* paragraph 2.65) and as discussed later in Chapter 4, even the SE is required to have its real seat in the Member State in which it has its registered office. Nevertheless, the ECJ certainly has stimulated competition for incorporations within the EU, which may be illustrated by the 2008 amendment to the German GmbHG (Limited Liability Companies Act), allowing the GmbH and the AG to have its real seat outside Germany.[121]

121. Gesetz zur Modernisierung des GmbH-Rechts und zur Bekämpfung von Missbräuchen (MoMiG) which amended § 4a GmbHG accordingly. *See also* Teichmann, *European Company Law* 2008, p. 189.

2.65 In 2006, the *Cartesio* case was lodged with the ECJ concerning an LP, which sought to transfer its central administration (real seat) from Hungary to Italy, while remaining registered in Hungary. The Hungarian authorities refused to register the new address of Cartesio on the ground that such a transfer is not possible under Hungarian law. According to Hungarian law, the seat of companies or other legal entities of a commercial nature, such as LPs, shall be the place where the central administration of that entity is situated.[122] The question referred to the ECJ is whether Articles 43 and 48 of the EC Treaty (now 49 and 54 TFEU) preclude national rules that make it impossible for a company constituted under national law to transfer its real seat to another Member State, while retaining its status as a company governed by the law of the state of incorporation.[123] The ECJ repeated elements of the *Daily Mail,* thereby acknowledging the power of a Member State to define the connecting factor required of a company, if it is to be regarded as incorporated under the law of that Member State, and also the connecting factor required if the company is to be subsequently able to maintain that status. Consequently, a Member State has the power of not permitting a company governed by its law to retain that status, if the company moves its seat to the territory of another Member State. Nevertheless, where such a company aims to convert into a form of company that is governed by the law of the host Member State, the law of the Member State of incorporation may not require the winding up or liquidation of that company in preventing it from converting.[124] The ECJ, therefore, classifies this form of relocation to be covered by the right of establishment. As a matter of course, it depends on the law of the host Member State whether such conversion can be effected. It must be noted, however, that the relocation of a company can always be realized indirectly, i.e., through the founding of a subsidiary in the host Member State, thereafter merging the parent company into the subsidiary.[125]

2.66 The ECJ in Case C-378/10 (Vale) had to answer questions relating to facts that are the opposite to *Cartesio*. Vale Costruzioni S.r.l. was incorporated and registered in Rome. Some years later, in 2006, the company discontinued business in Italy and applied to be removed from the Italian register. The company was removed from the register in which it was noted that 'the company had moved to Hungary'. After removal, the director and another person incorporated Vale Építési Kft. and asked the Hungarian commercial court to register this company, together with a statement that Vale Costruzioni S.r.l. was the predecessor in law of the Vale Építési Kft. The commercial court refused to register the company on the grounds that a company incorporated and registered in Italy could not transfer its seat to Hungary and could not be registered as the predecessor in law of the Hungarian company. Upon appeal by Vale Építési Kft., the Hungarian Supreme Court referred preliminary questions to the ECJ as to whether Articles 49 and 54 TFEU preclude legislation or practices of the host Member State that prohibit a company incorporated in another Member State from transferring

122. As set out in the Cartesio judgment, ECJ 16 Dec. 2008, C-210/06, paragraphs 11–19.
123. Case C-210/06 (Cartesio), paragraph 99.
124. Case C-210/06 (Cartesio), paragraphs 112 and 113.
125. Erik Werlauff, 'Relocating a company Within the EU', *European Company Law* 5, no.3 (2008): 136–139.

its seat to the host Member State and continuing to operate under the laws of that Member State.[126] As in previous judgments, the ECJ repeats that companies are creatures of national law and, consequently, a Member State has the power to define the connecting factors required of a company to be regarded as incorporated under its national law and to maintain that status.[127] The ECJ concludes that national legislation enabling companies to convert their legal form, but does not allow companies governed by the law of another Member State to do so, falls within the scope of Articles 49 and 54 of the TFEU. In such a case, companies are treated differently, according to whether the conversion is domestic or of a cross-border nature. Its likely effect is to deter companies having their seat in another Member State from exercising freedom of establishment.[128] Since Hungarian law provides for domestic conversions only, it amounts to an unjustified restriction on the exercise of that freedom and the refusal to register Vale Costruzioni S.r.l. as the predecessor in law of Vale Építési Kft. is incompatible with the said articles of the TFEU.[129] The ECJ acknowledges that cross-border conversions pose specific problems, because such conversions presuppose the consecutive application of two national laws.[130]

126. Judgment of 12 Jul. 2012, C/378-10 (Vale), paragraph 16.
127. Case C/378-10 (Vale), paragraphs 27–29. This is, again, confirmed in the ECJ judgment of 29 Nov. 2011, Case C-371/10 (National Grid Indus).
128. Case C/378-10 (Vale), paragraphs 33 and 36.
129. Case C/378-10 (Vale), paragraphs 52–57.
130. Case C/378-10 (Vale), paragraph 37. Note that the ECJ avoided the issue whether, according to Italian law, Vale Costruzioni S.r.l. actually ceased to exist following its removal from the Italian register and, consequently, before the Hungarian company was incorporated (paragraphs 19–20).

CHAPTER 3

The Harmonization Programme Within Europe

I INTRODUCTION[1]

3.01 The idea that one could speak of European Corporate Law would have remained mainly hypothetical if not for the harmonization programme carried out by the European Union (EU).[2] To grasp the significance of the EU developments, one should observe not only the harmonization of company law of the Member States but also the European legislation with respect to securities regulation, financial services, taxation, social policy and competition, as it often pertains to corporate law or its context. Nonetheless, one should be cautious as not to overestimate what has been achieved. The harmonization programme does not cover all of the important issues of corporate law. Moreover, its actual significance depends on how EU legislative measures are implemented into national law and how their observance is dealt with.[3] Moreover, harmonization is not an end in itself and the same goes for the creation of European business organizations, notably the SE. They serve toward the creation of an internal market – with free movement of goods, persons, services and capital – as a necessary,

1. A much more detailed book on the issues dealt with in this chapter is *European Company Law: Organization, Finance and Capital Markets*, Ius Communitatis Series (Antwerpen/Oxford: Intersentia), 2nd edition 2012, by Stefan Grundmann.
2. It is explained in Ch. 1, n. 2, that 'EU' is used even where 'EC' might be appropriated.
3. Vanessa Edwards, *EC Company Law*, Oxford EC Law Library (Oxford: Clarendon Press, 1999), Ch. 1; Richard M. Buxbaum & Klaus J. Hopt, *Legal Harmonisation and the Business Enterprise* (Berlin/New York: 1988; Volume 4, European University Institute, Integration through Law), 212–218; Werlauff, *EC Company Law: The Common Denominator for Business Undertaking in 12 States* (Denmark: Copenhagen, 1993), 5. *See also* Marcus Lutter, *Europäisches Unternehmensrecht*, vierte, neubearbeitete Auflage (Berlin/New York: 1996), 157–161, Luca Enriques, 'EC Company Law Directives and Regulations: How Trivial Are They?', *University of Pennsylvania Journal of International Law* 27, no. 1 (2006).

but intermediary step in light of the task of the EU to promote, *inter alia*, sustainable development of economic activities, a high level of employment and social protection.[4]

A The Legal Basis of European Legislation

3.02 The legal basis for the EU activities concerning company law is primarily Article 50(2)(g) of the Treaty on the Functioning of the European Union (TFEU). This provision requires the European institutions to reduce the restrictions to the freedom of establishment and to issue directives requiring Member States to amend their laws, in order to comply with the terms of the directive to this effect. According to paragraph (g), the European Parliament (EP) and the Council, by means of directives, have 'to coordinate to the necessary extent the safeguards which, for the protection of the interests of members and others, are required by Member States of companies or firms with a view to making such safeguards equivalent throughout the Community'. The European institutions have always fostered an extensive interpretation as to the scope of this provision and the Commission regards the rights of employees as included among the interests referred to in this article.[5]

3.03 The tasks as set out in Article 50 TFEU function 'to attain freedom of establishment'. That might entail more than equivalence of safeguards for the protection of members, shareholders, employees and creditors throughout the EU. As stated in a 1992 publication by the Commission:

> Gradually, (...) the Community's sights have been set higher, going beyond mobility. The object is to find the legal formulas which permit restructurings between groups from different Member States. The creation of a Community legislative framework for cross-border activities by enterprises and for cooperation between enterprises from different Member States, will make it easier for European enterprises to pool the resources that are available in several Member States and hence be competitive not only in Europe, but also then in the world at large. It is no longer the mere alignment of domestic laws that is being sought, but the creation of a truly European company law.[6]

3.04 Directives based on Article 50 can be adopted by the European Council, according to the ordinary legislative procedure laid down in Article 294 TFEU. As a rule, this procedure allows the Council to act by a qualified majority.[7] Article 50 is also providing the legal basis for legislation with respect to financial services. However, in this area, Article 53 also plays a role, which calls for the mutual recognition of formal qualifications to pursue activities as self-employed persons. To accelerate the

4. Article 3(3) TEU.
5. Karl Gleichmann, *Perspectives on European Company Law*, Forum Internationale (Deventer/Boston: Kluwer Law and Taxation Publishers, 1990), 4, 5 and 7.
6. Commission of the European Communities, *Conditions for Business Cooperation: Public Procurement* (Brussels, 1992) (CO-62-91-003-EN-C), 4.
7. Unanimity may be required if the Commission advises negative on amendments to the proposed directive, Article 294(9). *See* the website of the European Parliament on the complicated co-decision procedure http://www.europarl.europa.eu/aboutparliament/en.

establishment of the internal market, the Single European Act of 1986 added a provision, now Article 114 TFEU, allowing the adoption of measures (directives or other) for the approximation of provisions in Member States 'which have as their object the establishment and functioning of the internal market'. Fiscal provisions, provisions relating to the free movement of persons or the rights and interests of employed persons fall outside the scope of this article. The directive on shareholders' rights in listed companies was enacted on the basis of this article (and Article 50).[8]

3.05 Furthermore, Article 115 TFEU allows for a wide area of discretion for European legislation that may cover the areas exempted from the competence provided by Article 114. It can justify the adoption of any directive 'for the approximation of such laws, regulations or administrative provisions of the Member States as directly affect the establishment or functioning of the internal market'. The restriction put forward by the 'directly affect' demand is mainly symbolic, because the EU institutions avail themselves of the extensive interpretation, which merely requires that measures have to be useful for European integration.[9] Article 115, however, deviates from the ordinary legislative procedure and demands that the Council acts unanimously, thus granting a veto to every Member State.[10] Furthermore, the additional competence granted by Article 153 TFEU should be mentioned. In order to achieve the objectives of the social policy of the EU, as laid down in Article 151, the EP and the Council may adopt, *inter alia*, directives containing minimum requirements. An example is the directive regarding information and consultation of employees, which will be discussed in Chapter 7.

3.06 Finally, attention should be drawn to Article 352 TFEU. This provision grants complementary powers for action to be taken where the Treaties (TEU and TFEU) have not provided the necessary powers to attain one of the objectives set out in the Treaties. Similar to Article 115, it requires unanimous action by the Council, but, unlike Article 115, prior consent of the EP. There are certain limitations, however, for the European institutions to fall back to this 'flexibility clause'.[11] What is now Article 352 has been resorted to, among other things, for the adoption of the regulations constituting the European Economic Interest Grouping (EEIG) and the SE.[12]

8. Directive 2007/36/EC of 11 Jul. 2007 on the exercise of certain rights of shareholders in listed companies, OJ 2007, L 194, at the time the legal basis was Articles 44 and 95 TEC (now Articles 50 and 114 TFEU).
9. K.J. Hopt, 'European Community Legal Harmonisation and the Business Enterprise', in *European Company and Financial Law*, eds K.J. Hopt & E. Wymeersch (Berlin/New York: Walter de Gruyter, 1991), 12.
10. Unless otherwise determined by the TEU, the council shall act by a qualified majority, Article 16(3) TEU.
11. Opinion 2/94 [1996] ECR I-1795 of the ECJ on the accession of the EU to the ECHR. Further: Alan Dashwood et al., *Wyatt & Dashwood's European Union Law* (Oxford and Portland Oregon, 2011), Ch. 5 C.
12. (EEC) 4064/89, OJ 1989, L 395/1 and (EC) No. 2157/2001, OJ 2001, L 294. At the time, the legal basis was Article 308 TEC.

B European Legal Instruments

3.07 The TFEU contains provisions that are directly applicable to the Member States (and individuals), such as to keep from distorting competition within the common market and/or form, which would restrict the freedom of establishment.[13] Further, the treaty empowers its institutions to enact general measures of legislation (secondary legislation), especially directives and regulations. The basic rule articulated in Article 288 states:

> To exercise the Union's competences, the institutions shall adopt regulations, directives, decisions, recommendations and opinions.

Regulations, as a rule, are directly applicable, as opposed to directives, which must be implemented by the Member States before they can have effect. However, upon a Member State's failure to take the appropriate steps, not only the Commission, but also an individual may invoke the directive against the State, though only if it contains clear and unconditional obligations. Thus, in such a case, a directive may have direct effect, creating individual rights that are protected by the national courts against Member States, as was decided in *Van Gend & Loos v. The Netherlands* [1963].[14] An individual cannot invoke direct effect against other individuals or companies.[15]

1 *Directives*

3.08 For the harmonization of company law and its related areas mentioned in paragraph 3.01, with the exception of competition policy, directives are the main legal instruments used. According to Article 288 TFEU, a directive is binding as to the result to be achieved upon each Member State to which it is addressed, leaving the choice of form and methods to the national authorities. According to *Francovich* [1991], Member States can be held liable for non-compliance to implement such obligations.[16] Due to the supremacy of EU law, directives have a so-called blocking effect, because Member States do not have an option of enacting national legal provisions not in accordance with directives under which they are created.[17]

13. Articles 101 and 49 TFEU respectively.
14. Case 26/62 (1963) ECR 1; according to Alan Dashwood et al., *Wyatt & Dashwood's European Union Law* (Oxford and Portland Oregon, 2011), Ch. 8 I, 'It is difficult to overstate the importance of *van Gend en Loos*'.
15. Case 152/84 (1986), ECR 723, *Marshall v. Southampton and South-West Hampshire Area Health Authority*. *See* on the binding force of directives: Sacha Prechal, *Directives in European Community Law. A Study of Directives and Their Enforcement in National Courts* (Oxford: Clarendon Press, 1995), 19 *et seq.*
16. Cases 6/90 and 9/90 (1991) ECR 1-5357. *See* for subsequent case law on the conditions for establishing liability for non-compliance: Alan Dashwood et al., *Wyatt & Dashwood's European Union Law* (Oxford and Portland Oregon 2011), Ch. 9 V C.
17. Case 6/64 [1964] ECR 585 *(Costa/Enel)*. Buxbaum & Hopt, *Legal Harmonisation and the Business Enterprise*, 242.

3.09 As illustrated next, several legislative techniques are reflected in the directives. The early company law directives contained detailed provisions focusing on specific safeguards, such as capital requirements. The gap between diverging national company laws could not always be bridged completely and, thus, alternatives were included and options were left to the Member States, or even to companies, for example, in the 1978 Fourth Directive, 'the Accounts Directive'.[18] Another way to reach a compromise is to set minimum standards, leaving it to the Member States whether or not they want to impose rules that are more stringent ('gold plating'). More recently, directives concentrate not on reaching a harmonized set of national rules, but on removing obstacles to cross-border transactions instead. They tend to be more principle-based, as opposed to rule-based, as illustrated by the 2004 Thirteenth Directive on takeovers.[19] To further the aims of such directives, the Commission may be empowered to adopt implementing measures.[20] A real multilevel approach is followed in the regulation of the financial services sector, including, *inter alia*, the market for securities. Consequently, the directives containing implementing measures (*see* paragraphs 3.103 *et seq.*) follow the directives providing the framework principles.

3.09a In addition, two concepts should be briefly mentioned here. *Codification* in EU law is understood as bringing together a directive or another legislative act and all its amendments in a single new act. This is called vertical codification. Horizontal codification happens when two or more acts covering related subjects are incorporated in a single new act. In both cases, the codification process starts with a consolidated text, a non-official document produced by the Publications Office. On the basis of that text, a new act is prepared and it must pass through the stages of the (accelerated) legislative process.[21] In 2015, the Commission launched a proposal for the codification of acts regarding company law, after no more than ten amendments.[22] *Recasting* also brings together an act with its amendments (vertical) or two or more related acts (horizontal) in a single new act. However, unlike codification, it involves new substantive changes, as amendments are made to the original act or acts during the preparation of the recast text. The subsequent legislative procedure enables the legislative authority to concentrate its attention on the new parts of the legislative proposal.[23] An example is Directive 2012/30/EU on the maintenance and alteration of the capital of public companies, which is the recast of the original Second Council Directive of 1976 and several amendments (paragraph 3.36).

3.09b Regulators often tend to overregulate and the EU legislation is certainly affected by that phenomenon. In its 2016 Communication on better regulation, the

18. (EEC) 78/660, OJ 1978, L 222/11. On the effect of options, *see* Steef M. Bartman, 'The Impact of Optional EU Law Making on National Company Law', *European Corporate Law* 5, no. 6 (December 2008): 271–276.
19. Edwards, *EC Company Law*, 8–10.
20. Directive 2004/25/EC on takeover bids, Preamble (28).
21. Interinstitutional Agreement of 20 Dec. 1994, Accelerated working method for official codification of legislative texts OJ 1996, C 102/2.
22. Brussels, 3.12.2015, COM(2015) 616 final.
23. Interinstitutional Agreement of 28 Nov. 2001 on a more structured recasting technique for legal acts, OJ 2002 C 77/1.

Commission states: 'The European Union has frequently been criticised - often rightly - for producing excessive and badly written regulation (...). Concentrating on measures that are really necessary and not doing things that have only marginal benefits or can be better done at national, regional or local level in Member States, also frees up space and means that collectively the institutions can mobilise more quickly to address new circumstances (...).' The Commission also mentions that reducing the adoption of new rules is necessary: '(...) the number of proposals for regulations and directives made by the Commission for adoption by the European Parliament and the Council (...)has declined from 159 in 2011 to 48 in 2015. Since 2000, the number of directives and regulations adopted by Parliament and the Council (...) has varied annually, with the highest level of legislative output 141 in 2009. In 2015, the first year of the Juncker Commission, 56 pieces of legislation were adopted (...).'[24]

3.10 The First Directive on company law, the 'Disclosure Directive', was adopted in 1968 and provides for the disclosure of certain documents, the validity of obligations entered into by a company and the nullity of the company.[25] Since then, several directives on company law have been adopted, most recently the 2004 Thirteenth Directive on takeover bids, the 2005 Tenth Directive on Cross-Border Mergers (CBM) and the Shareholders' Rights Directive of 2007.[26] Since then, the emphasis has been on amending, recasting and codification of company law directives, as will be seen from paragraph 3.18, where the directives will be discussed. In the medium term, not much new EU legislation in the area of company law is to be expected, perhaps with the exception of long-planned directives to facilitate cross-border transactions, such as divisions (demergers) and the transfer of the registered office.[27]

3.10a Some ambitious proposals by the Commission failed to become directives. In 1972, the Commission proposed a Fifth Directive concerning the structure of the public company. The aim was to prescribe a two-tier structure with employee representation on the supervisory board. Although the Commission went to great lengths to reach a compromise, for instance, by allowing a one-tier structure, the proposal remained controversial.[28] However, over the years, the importance of having a directive harmonizing the board structure has decreased. Firstly, the issues that the draft dealt with are closely related to corporate governance - an intensely debated area with major recent developments (paragraphs 6.01 *et seq.*). Secondly, the introduction of the SE requires Member States to allow for both one-tier and two-tier structures (*see* paragraphs 4.13 *et seq.*). Although this requirement is limited to the SE, it will lead to the same outcome for domestic public companies because Member States will not allow their national

24. Better Regulation: Delivering better results for a stronger Union Brussels 14.9.2016 COM(2016) 615 final, quotes from pp. 2 and 3.
25. (EEC) 68/151, OJ 1968, L 65/8.
26. 2004/109/EC, 2005/56/EC and 2007/36/EC.
27. European Commission. Action Plan 2012 (*Communication from the Commission to the European Parliament, the Council, the European Economic and Social Committee and the Committee of the Regions. Action Plan: European Company law and corporate governance – A Modern Legal Framework for More Engaged Shareholders and Sustainable Companies)* COM (2012) 740 final.
28. On the objections: Marcus Lutter, 'Perspektiven eines europäischen Unternehmensrechts – Versuch einer Summe', *ZGR* 3 (1992).

companies' structure to be less attractive in comparison with the SE. Finally, the European Court of Justice (ECJ) has considerably enhanced the freedom of establishment, thus enabling entrepreneurs to incorporate their businesses under the law of another Member State more easily (*see* paragraphs 2.54 *et seq.*). In the light of this evolution of European company law and the political deadlock regarding the proposed Fifth Directive, it came as no surprise that the draft was withdrawn by the Commission in 2001.[29]

3.10b Another long-standing dispute was sparked by the Commission's plan for the Ninth Directive, containing an encompassing regulation of groups of companies. In reality, there has only been a preliminary draft of such a directive in 1984, whereupon substantial criticism halted it from being proposed to the Council. Subsequently, in 1993, a comparative study on groups of companies in Europe was carried out at the initiative of the Commission in order to survey the development of the group phenomenon within the Member States. Whether EU legislation regarding groups of companies is necessary has been further debated in legal literature. According to the 2003 Company Law Action Plan, the Commission abandoned the idea of the Ninth Directive altogether.[30] Nevertheless, a 'framework rule for groups' was deemed necessary and a corresponding directive was announced for the medium term. Such a rule would allow those concerned with the management of a company belonging to a group to adopt and implement a coordinated group policy. Such a policy, however, would leave the interests of that company's creditors effectively protected and would strike a fair balance of burdens and advantages for that company's shareholders. Notwithstanding the common sense behind this idea, as most companies are part of a group, no progress has been made since 2003. The subject, however, is kept on the agenda by the 2012 Action Plan, albeit labelled as 'recognition of group interest'.[31] Group law is discussed further in Chapter 10.

3.11 Company law is relevant to several areas of law, the first of which to be mentioned here is the regulation of securities and financial markets. The first directive concerning this area dates back to 1979 and regulates conditions for the admission of securities to stock exchange listings.[32] In the 1980s, it was to be followed by directives on the information to be published by companies upon listing and, once listed, on a regular basis and in specific cases such as the acquisition of a major holding.[33] The Commission launched a Financial Services Action Plan (FSAP) in 1999, which led to several new directives representing an encompassing regulation of the area. The financial crisis that began in 2008, invigorated the EU's activities. First, initiatives were

29. Christiaan W.A. Timmermans, *Company Law as Ius Commune*, First Walter van Gerven Lecture (Antwerp/Oxford/New York: Intersentia, 2002), 8.
30. *Modernising Company Law and Enhancing Corporate Governance in the European Union – A Plan to Move Forward*, Brussels, 21.5.2003 COM (2003) 284 final, p. 18.
31. *Action Plan: European Company Law and Corporate Governance – A Modern Legal Framework for More Engaged Shareholders and Sustainable companies*, Strasbourg, 12.12.2012 COM(2012) 740 final, pp. 14–15.
32. (EEC) 79/279 and (EEC) 80/390.
33. 80/390/EEC, 82/121/EEC, 88/627/EEC.

taken to reinforce the corporate governance of banks and other financial institutions. This was followed by the creation of EU supervising authorities, notably the European Securities and Markets Authority (ESMA), and by the wider ambition to set up the Capital Markets Union (CMU). A brief survey of these developments and related directives can be found in paragraphs 3.101 *et seq*. Social policy also has a bearing on company law and the way it functions. The EU has enacted directives dealing, *inter alia*, with information and consultation of employees, the European Works Council (EWC) and the protection of employees' rights, for example, in the event that the undertaking is transferred. These are discussed in Chapter 7 on the involvement of employees and, where relevant, in Chapter 8 on cooperation and acquisitions. The directive supplementing the statute of the SE on the involvement of employees is dealt with in Chapter 4. The last area related to corporate law to be mentioned here is taxation. Several directives generated by the EU tax harmonization programme have a bearing on issues related to corporate law, notably those dealing with harmonizing capital duties, the taxation of mergers, the taxation of a parent company and its subsidiaries, and transfer pricing within groups.[34] To a great extent, taxation is a matter of national law of the Member States and their systems may be rather different.[35] In fact, many corporate transactions are driven by tax considerations and businesses operating cross-border may take advantage of these differences, at times leading to blatant tax avoidance. The Organisation for Economic Co-operation and Development (OECD) has taken a global initiative to curb strategies of businesses exploiting gaps and mismatches in tax rules to artificially shift profits to low or no-tax locations.[36] On their part, the EU Commission, urged by the European Council, launched an Anti-Tax Avoidance Package, which includes enacting a directive that lays down rules against tax avoidance practices (ATA-directive).[37] Furthermore, the Commission aims at providing companies with a single set of corporate tax rules for doing business across the internal market. Therefore, in 2016, two directives are proposed to harmonize the corporate tax base and the consolidated corporate tax base.[38] Notwithstanding its importance for businesses and corporate structures, taxation is not covered in this book.

34. (EEC) 69/335 (as amended) relating to capital duties which will be phased out by 2010, Brussels, 4 Dec. 2006, IP/06/1673; (EEC) 90/434 (as amended) relating to mergers, divisions, transfers of assets and exchanges of shares; (EEC) 90/435 (as amended) relating to the taxation of parent companies and their subsidiaries; (EEC) 90/436 (as amended) relating to the elimination of double taxation in connection with the adjustment of transfers of profits between associated undertakings. For an overview see: www.europa.eu/scadplus/leg/en/s10000.htm.
35. For an overview of the national taxation systems of EU Members States *see Taxation Trends in the European Union*, Eurostat 2015 edition, Luxembourg: Publications Office of the European Union, 2015.
36. OECD, Action Plan on Base Erosion and Profit Shifting, OECD 2013 (downloadable via https://www.oecd.org).
37. Brussels, 28.1.2016 COM(2016) 26 final. Further: http://ec.europa.eu/taxation_customs/taxation/company_tax/anti_tax_avoidance/index_en.htm (accessed August 2016).
38. Proposal for a Council Directive on a Common Corporate Tax Base (CCTB), Strasbourg, 25.10.2016, COM(2016) 685 final and for a Directive on a Common Consolidated Corporate Tax Base (CCCTB), Strasbourg, 25.10.2016 COM(2016) 683 final.

2 *Regulations*

3.12 Regulation is a powerful legal instrument. According to Article 288 TFEU, regulations have general application, because they are binding and directly applicable in all Member States. In principle, they have direct effect and are deemed to be incorporated in the national legal order. Their validity does not depend on national procedures and the courts must safeguard the rights of individuals created by the regulation. It must be admitted, however, that some regulations or parts thereof need implementing rules to be adopted by the Member States in order to ensure effective application. For example, Member States must designate the competent authority to issue the certificate that is required in the event that the SE transfers its registered office to another Member State.[39] In general, regulations serve for the enactment of legal norms that supersede national law and are pre-emptive to national legislation in the concerned area. In the field of corporate law, regulations have been used for several purposes. In the first place, for the creation of business organizations under community law, notably the EEIG and the SE. These are discussed in Chapter 4. Furthermore, Regulation EC 1606/2002 enables the Commission to decide on the applicability of international accounting and reporting standards within the EU, as will be seen in paragraph 3.65 and Chapter 9. Empowering the Commission to enact implementing regulations and other acts is also used in the area of capital markets (3.101 *et seq.*). Finally, regulations play a dominant role in the implementation of the treaty provisions regarding competition. The one most relevant here is the Merger Regulation, which is discussed in Chapter 8.

3 *Recommendations and Opinions*

3.13 Besides directives and regulations, two other legal instruments have been resorted to in the field of corporate law, as provided by the TFEU: recommendations and opinions. Article 288 TFEU provides for recommendations and opinions to be delivered by the European institutions. These instruments have no binding force, but may serve as guidance for the interpretation of national law or Union law. Among the examples is the 1977 recommendation by the Commission, containing a European Code of Conduct relating to transactions in transferable securities, followed by European legislation on insider dealing in 1989.[40] More recently, the Commission enacted a recommendation on the role of non-executive or supervisory directors of listed companies and on the committees of the (supervisory) board (2005/162/EC).[41] In 2009, the Commission issued a recommendation concerning remuneration of directors of listed companies.[42] Opinions can be delivered by several European institutions. Examples include the Commission, who may deliver opinions to Member

39. Articles 69 and 8(8) SE Regulation.
40. Commission recommendation 77/534/EEC, OJ 1977, L 212/37 and L 294/28; (EEC) 89/592, OJ 1989, L 334.
41. 2005/162/EC, OJ 2005, L 52/51.
42. Commission Recommendation 2009/385/EC of 30 Apr. 2009, OJ 2009, L 120/28.

States regarding social policy, and the European Central Bank (ECB), which may submit opinions to other EU institutions and also to national authorities.[43] The last example to be mentioned here is the 2014 Recommendation on a new approach to business failure and insolvency.[44] The Recommendation invited Member States to put in place effective pre-insolvency procedures to help viable debtors to restructure in order to avoid insolvency and to allow a second chance for entrepreneurs in no more than three years after insolvency. After evaluating the effects of recommendation, the Commission in 2016 put forward a proposal for a directive on preventive restructuring.[45]

4 Judicial Decisions

3.14 Important factors to consider are decisions of the Court of Justice of the European Union (CJEU). The CJEU is among the institutions that carry out the tasks entrusted to the Community.[46] Article 19 of the TEU reads that the court 'shall ensure that in the interpretation and application of the Treaties the law is observed'.[47] The CJEU has jurisdiction to give preliminary rulings, at the request of courts or tribunals from Member States, on the interpretation of Union law. Similarly, it rules on actions brought by a Member State, an institution or a natural or legal person (Article 19(3)). The system of preliminary rulings is detailed in Article 267 TFEU. They deal with questions concerning the interpretation of the Treaties and the validity and interpretation of acts of the institutions, bodies, offices or agencies of the Union. Where such a question is raised before a court or tribunal of a Member State, that court or tribunal may request the CJEU to give a ruling thereon. Such court or tribunal is obliged to bring the matter before the Court when there is no judicial remedy under national law.

3.15 The ECJ, the main court of the CJEU,[48] has decided several cases involving company law. Member States have been criticized for failure to implement company law directives. Several preliminary rulings on the interpretation of company law directives have been delivered, notably, in regard of the First, the Second and the Fourth Directives. Furthermore, some cases pertain to the interpretation of the treaty provisions concerning the right of establishment. Among these are the landmark judgments (*Centros, Überseering, Inspire Art, Cartesio and Vale*) dealt with in Chapter

43. TFEU, 159 and Article 132(1).
44. C(2014) 1500 final, 12.3.2014. *See* http://ec.europa.eu/justice/civil/commercial/insolvency/index_en.htm.
45. Proposal for a Directive on preventive restructuring frameworks, second chance and measures to increase the efficiency of restructuring, insolvency and discharge procedures and amending Directive 2012/30/EU, Strasbourg, 22.11.2016 COM(2016) 723 final.
46. Article 13 TEU. Previously, the court was named European Court of Justice (ECJ).
47. According to Article 19 TEU, the CJEU includes the Court of Justice (known as European Court of Justice, abbreviated ECJ), the General Court (previously named Court of First Instance) and specialized courts. The General Court has limited jurisdiction in comparison to the ECJ and its decisions can be appealed to the ECJ (Article 256 TFEU). A specialized court is the Civil Service Tribunal, having jurisdiction over employment disputes between the EU and its civil servants (Council Decision 2004/752/EC, OJ 2004, L 333/7).
48. *See* previous footnote.

2.[49] Finally, a case of significant importance is *Marleasing* [1990].[50] There, the court held that in interpreting the provisions of national law, that implement company law directives, national courts are bound to interpret their law in the light of the text and purpose of the underlying directive. This judgment challenges the tendency of courts and lawyers not to invoke the procedure for preliminary rulings if they are unaware that national provisions refer to Union law.[51]

3.16 Before 2001, the Court's jurisdiction pertained to conventions between Member States, if such conventions provided for it. This was the case with the 1968 Brussels Convention on jurisdiction and the enforcement of judgments in civil and commercial matters.[52] In *Powell Duffryn plc v. Wolfgang Petereit* [1992], the court decided that Article 17 of the Brussels Convention covers a choice of forum clause in a company's articles in relation to disputes between the company and its shareholders.[53] The court held that the relationship between a company and its shareholders, as embodied in the articles, is contractual, qualifying the jurisdiction clause as an agreement under the Brussels Convention. This even applies to shareholders who voted against the adoption of the clause or who acquired their shares afterwards. By becoming and remaining a shareholder, a person consents to adhere to the provisions of the company's articles and the decisions taken by its organs, regardless of his objections to a certain clause or decision. The ruling of the court enables companies to use the choice of forum clause in order to enhance legal predictability and to stimulate concentration of litigation in disputes with its shareholders. Most of the Convention's original field of application is now covered by the Brussels I Regulation (EC) No 44/2001 on jurisdiction and the recognition and enforcement of judgments in civil and commercial matters.[54]

3.17 As is clear from *Marleasing*, decisions of the national courts also have to be taken into account for a thorough assessment of the development of European corporate law. The conduct of the national courts is the decisive factor for the role played by the ECJ, because the national courts can bring a case before the European court based on the preliminary procedure of Article 267 TFEU. In theory, national courts could play an important role in the process of 'integration from below', meaning that case law concerning the interpretation of national corporate law gradually follows a uniform pattern, more or less, within the Community. In reality, hardly any such patterns can be observed and even where company law is harmonized, national courts

49. An overview of ECJ cases involving corporate law issues is attached to Luca Enriques, 'EC Company Law Directives and Regulations: How Trivial are They?' (May 2005). *ECGI – Law Working Paper* No. 39/2005, http://ssrn.com/abstract=730388.
50. Case 106/89, *Marleasing S.A. v. La Comercial International Alimentation S.A.* (1990) ECR4135.
51. Further: Alan Dashwood et al., *Wyatt & Dashwood's European Union Law* (Oxford and Portland Oregon, 2011), Ch. 8 II on the duty of consistent interpretation. Also Buxbaum & Hopt, *Legal Harmonisation and the Business Enterprise*, 269.
52. Most of the Convention's original field of application is now covered by The Council Regulation (EC) No. 44/2001 of 22 Dec. 2000 on jurisdiction and the recognition and enforcement of judgments in civil and commercial matters, OJ 2001, L 12/1.
53. Case 214/89, *Powell Duffryn plc v. Wolfgang Petereit* (1993), *Common Market Law Review*, 406.
54. OJ 2001, L 012.

may be responsible for diverging developments.[55] The EU has taken initiatives to promote that courts of the various Member States discuss their experiences and have established a European Judicial Network in civil and commercial matters.[56]

II COMPANY LAW DIRECTIVES[57]

A Disclosure, Validity of Obligations and Nullity of the Company [First Directive]

3.18 In order to protect the interests of third parties, the First Directive of 1968 (replaced by the consolidating Directive 2009/101/EC)[58] covers issues related to the disclosure of limited liability companies' documents, the validity of obligations that these companies enter into and their nullity. The 2009 Directive is the codified version of a previous critical European legislative act: the First Council Directive, which dates back to 1968 and was based on Article 54 TEEC, (later Article 44(2)(g) TEC and currently Article 50 TFEU). The First Directive is commonly referred to as 'the Disclosure Directive',[59] but actually deals with three different subjects regarding the protection of the interests of third parties: (i) the disclosure of basic documents concerning the company and the persons who are authorized to bind the company; (ii) the restriction of the grounds on which obligations entered into in the name of the company are not valid; (iii) the limitation of cases in which nullity of a company can arise in combination with provisions regarding the retroactive effect of the nullity.

As far as the First Directive is concerned, the implementation by the six Member States at that time revealed no major problems, because the directive generally reflected the solutions already present within their legal systems. For the UK, it was a more comprehensive task to implement this directive, because it had no influence on the drafting of the First Directive, as it had taken place prior to the UK's accession. Some of the directive's provisions, for example, conflicted with the prevailing ultra vires doctrine at the time.[60]

The 2009 codification pursued clarity and rationality. It features the same substantial scope as the original Directive and includes amendments introduced in 2003 in order to simplify and modernize the Directive's disclosure provisions in light of

55. Hopt, 'European Community Legal Harmonisation and the Business Enterprise', 22.
56. 2001/470/EC: Council Decision of 28 May 2001 establishing a European Judicial Network in civil and commercial matters, OJ 2001, L 174. For more information: https://e-justice.europa.eu/content_ejn_in_civil_and_commercial_matters-21-en.do (accessed August 2016).
57. The history and background of most company law directives are extensively described by Edwards, *EC Company Law*.
58. First Council Directive 68/151 of 9 Mar. 1968, OJ 1968, L 65/8, replaced by Directive 2009/101/EC of 16 Sep. 2009, OJ 2009, L 258, 1 Oct. 2009, 11–19, consolidating the amendments to the First Directive.
59. First Council Directive 68/151 of 9 Mar. 1968, OJ 1968, L 65/8.
60. Karl Gleichmann, *Perspectives on European Company Law*, Forum Internationale (Deventer: Kluwer, 1990), 5 and 6. C. Fischer-Zernin, *Der Rechtsangleichungs erflog der Ersten Gesellschaftsrechtlichen Richtlinie der EWG* (Tubingen: I.C.B. Mohz (Paul Siebeck), 1986), 283.

modern communication technologies[61] (Articles 2, 3, 4 and 7), and amendments added by Directive 2012/17/EU to the end of furthering the interconnection of central, commercial and companies registers.[62]

Pursuant to Article 2, in conjunction with Article 1, the directive applies to the laws, regulations and administrative provisions of the Member States relating to private companies, public companies and limited partnerships.

It is important to underline that in December 2015, in line with the 2012 Action Plan on European company law and corporate governance,[63] the European Commission put forward a proposal[64] that pursues a simplification and clarification of European company law by furthering the codification process in a rational way. The plan would encompass merging the First Directive (now Directive 2009/101/EC) with five other company law directives.[65]

1 *Disclosure*

3.19 According to Article 2, the directive requires measures to ensure disclosure of certain documents and particulars, among other things:

- The memorandum of association and the articles ('statutes' according to the directive) and any amendment to those documents.
- The appointment, termination of office and particulars of the persons who are authorized to represent the company in dealings with third parties and in legal proceedings, or who take part in the administration, supervision or control of the company. It must appear from the disclosure whether the persons authorized to represent the company may do so alone or must act jointly.
- The accounting documents (referred to as 'financial statements' starting from 2013) for each financial year, which are required to be published in accordance with, *inter alia*, the Fourth and Seventh Directives (now Directive 2013/34/EU).

61. Directive 2003/58/EC of 15 Jul. 2003 amending Council Directive 68/151/EEC, as regards disclosure requirements in respect of certain types of companies, OJ 2003, L 221, 4 Sep. 2003, 13–16.
62. Directive 2012/17/EU of 13 Jun. 2012 amending Council Directive 89/666/EEC and Directives 2005/56/EC and 2009/101/EC as regards the interconnection of central, commercial and companies registers, OJ 2012, L 156, 16 Jun. 2012, 1-9.
63. European Commission. *Communication from the Commission to the European Parliament, the Council, the European Economic and Social Committee and the Committee of the Regions. Action Plan: European Company law and corporate governance – a modern legal framework for more engaged shareholders and sustainable companies*. COM (2012) 740 final.
64. European Commission. *Proposal for a Directive of the European Parliament and of the Council Relating to Certain Aspects of Company Law (codification).* COM (2015) 616final.
65. The Sixth Council Directive of 17 Dec. 1982, concerning the division of public limited liability companies (82/891/EEC), Eleventh Council Directive of 21 Dec. 1989 concerning disclosure requirements in respect of branches (89/666/EEC), Directive 2005/56/EC on cross-border mergers of limited liability companies, Directive 2009/101/EC regarding disclosure, validity of obligations and nullity of the company, Directive 2011/35/EU concerning mergers of public limited liability companies, Directive 2012/30/EU in respect of the formation of public limited liability companies and the maintenance and alteration of their capital.

- Any transfer of the seat of the company, the winding up of the company and any declaration of nullity of the company by the courts.
- The appointment of liquidators and the termination of the liquidation.
- The striking off the register in Member States where such striking off entails legal consequences.

Other matters must also be disclosed where such requirement is imposed by other directives, such as the Second and Fourth Directives (*see* paragraphs 3.35 and 3.63 *et seq.*).

Pursuant to Article 2a, added by Directive 2012/17/EU, all previously mentioned documents and particulars, with the only exception of accounting documents, are to be entered in the competent register, which, in turn, complies with the system of interconnection of central, commercial and companies' registers. Article 4a, added in 2012, lays down the specifics of the system of interconnection of registers, which is composed of (a) the registers of Member States; (b) the European central platform (that must ensure the domestic systems' interoperability), and (c) the portal serving as the European electronic access point. With reference to the platform, the Commission reserves the right to develop and operate it either by its own means or through a third party, upon the adoption of detailed rules as for, *inter alia*, its supervision, security, protection of data. Article 7a makes specific reference to European legislation concerning data protection and processing. Furthermore, the Commission commits to adopt a series of technical specifications in order to set up the system (Article 4c).[66]

3.20 Article 3(1) requires Member States to have files opened in a register for each of the companies to be registered therein. Furthermore, according to its subparagraph, added by Directive 2012/17/EU, companies must be unequivocally identifiable with reference to the system of interconnection of central, commercial and companies registers by means of a unique identifier. Article 3(2), as amended, obligates Member States to facilitate filing of the above-mentioned documents and particulars by electronic means from 1 January 2007. Furthermore, Member States must ensure that, from that date on, copies are obtainable from the register, by paper or electronic means, at the choice of the applicant. Article 3(4) allows for an exception for paper documents that are filed before 2007, on a date ten years or more before a copy is requested. According to Article 3(5), the disclosure of the filing of the documents and particulars has to be effected by publication in the national gazette appointed for that purpose by the Member State. The publication consists of the full or partial text of the document or contains a reference to the document that has been deposited in the file or entered in the register. The national gazette may be kept in electronic form. The publication in the national gazette may even be replaced with equally effective means entailing, at the very least, a system whereby the information may be accessed through a central electronic platform in chronological order.

66. More information the interconnection of registers: https://e-justice.europa.eu/content_business_registers_at_european_level-105-en.do (accessed August 2016).

3.21 As to the position of the company and third parties, Article 3(6-7) enables third parties, in principle, to resort to what has been published even in cases of discrepancy between the publication and the texts deposited in the file or entered in the register.

Sections 6–7 read as follows:

> 6. The documents and particulars may be relied on by the company as against third parties only after they have been disclosed in accordance with paragraph 4, unless the company proves that the third parties had knowledge thereof.
>
> However, with regard to transactions taking place before the 16th day following the disclosure, the documents and particulars shall not be relied on as against third parties who prove that it was impossible for them to have had knowledge thereof.
>
> 7. Member States shall take the necessary measures to avoid any discrepancy between what is disclosed in accordance with paragraph 5 and what appears in the register or file.
>
> However, in cases of discrepancy, the text disclosed in accordance with paragraph 5 may not be relied on as against third parties; such third parties may nevertheless rely thereon, unless the company proves that they had knowledge of the texts deposited in the file or entered in the register.
>
> Third parties may, moreover, always rely on any documents and particulars in respect of which the disclosure formalities have not yet been completed, save where nondisclosure causes them not to have effect.

According to Article 3a, added by Directive 2017/17/EU, up-to-date and multilingual information has to be made available on the European e-Justice portal, with reference to national provisions that regulate how third parties can rely on particulars and each type of document listed by Article 2, in compliance with Article 3(5), (6) and (7). Basic information, i.e., the name and legal form of the company, its registered office and Member State of registration, and its registration number, must be available free of charge (Article 3c).

Pursuant to Article 3b, the system of interconnection of registers must also allow public access to electronic copies of the documents and particulars listed by Article 2. Member States are tasked to ensure such data is available in a standard message format by electronic means, in compliance with the minimum standards of data transmission security.

Information concerning the opening and termination of any winding-up or insolvency proceedings of the company, and in relation to the striking off of the company from the register (in Member States where it entails legal consequences), must also be made available, free of charge, through the system of interconnection of registers. The register of the branch shall ensure receipt of such information (Article 3d).

3.22 The language of the documents and particulars is determined by the language rules of the Member State in which a file is opened. However, Article 4 requires Member States to allow for disclosure in any official language of the Community on a voluntary basis. Here again, third parties are protected and they may, in principle, rely on the translations disclosed, even in case of a discrepancy with the documents disclosed in the official language of the register.

3.23 Member States must provide for appropriate penalties, at least in the case of failure to disclose the financial statements required by Article 2(f) and in the case of omission of details prescribed by Article 5 from commercial documents or any company website. This article requires that such documents or websites state the information necessary to identify the register where the company has filed, as well as the legal form of the company, its registered office and, where appropriate, the fact that the company is being wound up. The obligation to provide for appropriate penalties is laid down in Article 7 of the Directive. The Court of Justice in the *Daihatsu* case held that the right to apply for the imposition of a penalty in the event that a company does not publish its annual accounts cannot be restricted to, *inter alia,* the members and creditors of the company.[67]

3.24 The Verband Deutscher Daihatsu-Händler eV – the association of German dealers in Daihatsu motor vehicles – applied to the local court for an order requiring Daihatsu Deutschland GmbH, the general agent responsible for the importation of these motor vehicles, to publish its annual accounts. The German Commercial Code, however, provided that such proceedings could only be initiated by a member or a creditor of the company, or by the works council. The question whether or not this was the correct implementation of Article 2(1)(f) of the First Directive was referred to the ECJ, which ruled as follows:

> Article 6 of the First Council Directive 68/151/EEC (...) must be interpreted as precluding the legislation of a Member State from restricting to members or creditors of a company, the central works council or the company's works council the right to apply for imposition of the penalty provided for by the law of that Member State in the event of failure by a company to fulfil the obligations regarding disclosure of annual accounts laid down by the First Directive.

2 *Validity of Obligations*

3.25 With regard to the validity of obligations entered into by a company, distinction is made between actions carried out in the name of the company before it is formed and acts carried out after the company is formed. In the first case, the company is bound only if it assumes the obligations after its formation. To achieve this binding effect, it is not necessary to enter into a new contract with the other party by novation. If the company does not accept liability, the persons that acted in the name of the company are to be held liable.

3.26 Article 8 of the Directive provides as follows:

> If, before a company being formed has acquired legal personality, action has been carried out in its name and the company does not assume the obligations arising from such action, the persons who acted shall, without limit, be jointly and severally liable therefore, unless otherwise agreed.

67. ECJ 4 Dec. 1997, Case C-97/96, *Verband deutscher Daihatsu-Händler eV v. Daihatsu Deutschland GmbH.*

The ECJ in *Ubbink* [1988] held that national law determines whether acts performed in the name of a company not yet incorporated are to be regarded as having been performed in the name of a company being formed within the meaning of Article 8. In this case, the company was never incorporated and the Dutch Supreme Court referred several questions to the ECJ relating to the nullity of companies. This issue is dealt with in paragraph 3.32.

3.27 Post-formation acts of the company are binding upon it if the company is represented by persons with the authority to do so. In principle, acts carried out by the organs of the company are binding upon it. There are only two exceptions to this hard-and-fast rule. Firstly, the company is not bound by acts carried out by its organs in excess of the powers that the law attributes to them.[68] Secondly, Member States may provide that the company be not bound where the acts of an organ fall outside the objects of the company (ultra vires). Further protection is offered against limitations arising from the articles or stemming from a decision of a competent organ, because the company may never rely on these as against third parties. Nonetheless, Member States may allow the articles to confer a general power to represent the company on a single person or on several persons acting jointly. When duly published, such limitations can be invoked against third parties.

3.28 The rather complicated provisions of Article 10 read as follows:

> 1. Acts done by the organs of the company shall be binding upon it even if those acts are not within the objects of the company, unless such acts exceed the powers that the law confers or allows to be conferred on those organs.
>
> However, Member States may provide that the company shall not be bound where such acts are outside the objects of the company, if it proves that the third party knew that the act was outside those objects or could not in view of the circumstances have been unaware of it; disclosure of the statutes shall not of itself be sufficient proof thereof.
>
> 2. The limits on the powers of the organs of the company, arising under the statutes or from a decision of the competent organs, may not be relied on as against third parties, even if they have been disclosed.
>
> 3. If the national law provides that authority to represent a company may, in derogation from the legal rule governing the subject, be conferred by the statutes on a single person or on several persons acting jointly, that law may provide that such a provision in the statutes may be relied on as against third parties on condition that it relates to the general power of representation; the question whether such a provision can be relied on as against third parties shall be governed by Article 3.

3.29 Article 2 of the 2009 Directive requires that Member States ensure the proper disclosure of provisions concerning the power of representation. Section (d)(i) states that such disclosure contains particulars pertaining to:

> the appointment, termination of office and particulars of the persons who either as a body constituted pursuant to law or as members of any such body are authorised

68. This rule goes back to the German approach to representation Edwards, *EC Company Law*, 35.

> to represent the company in dealings with third parties and in legal proceedings; it must be apparent from the disclosure whether the persons authorised to represent the company may do so alone or must act jointly.

The ECJ held in *Friedrich Haaga* that, according to this provision:

> disclosure must be made not only of the provisions as to representation applicable in the event of appointment of several directors but also, in the event of the appointment of a single director, of the fact that the latter represents the company alone, even if his authority to do so clearly flows from national law.[69]

3.30 Third parties are also protected against irregularities in the appointment of persons, who, as an organ of the company, are authorized to represent it.

Article 9 of the First Directive reads as follows:

> Completion of the formalities of disclosure of the particulars concerning the persons who, as an organ of the company, are authorised to represent it shall constitute a bar to any irregularity in their appointment being relied upon as against third parties unless the company proves that such third parties had knowledge thereof.

3.31 Articles 9 and 10 force Member States to offer solid protection to third parties who rely on acts carried out by the organs of the company. As stated by Edwards, the term 'organ' is not a familiar one in UK company law.[70] In continental legal systems, 'organ' is the generic term for bodies exercising the functions and powers of a company, notably the general meeting of shareholders and the board of directors. Of course, national law has to determine what the organs of a company are, how they are composed and what their functions and powers are. The organs exercise their functions and powers to decide on company matters and to manage and administrate its business. Continental systems generally draw a distinction between decision-making, management and administration, which primarily have an effect on the internal affairs of the company on the one hand, and the power to represent the company toward third parties on the other hand. The organs exercising the 'internal' functions and powers are not necessarily identical or similar to the organs taking care of the 'external' functions and powers. For example, most of the powers of the general meeting of shareholders serve to decide on matters such as raising the company's capital or approving a decision taken by the board of directors. Once the decision has to be carried out, the company must be represented vis-à-vis third parties by the organ(s) designated by national law. The board of directors will have such status, but, in principle, the power of representation will also be vested in the individual directors. According to Article 10(3), national law may provide that the statutes of a company confer the power of representation on a single person or on several persons acting

69. ECJ 12 Nov. 1974, Case 32-74 (*Friedrich Haaga GmbH*).
70. Edwards, *EC Company Law*, 34.

together. In addition, national law may provide that such a provision may be relied on as against third parties but only if the statutes confer the general power of representation on these persons.

3 *Nullity of the Company*

3.32 With respect to the nullity of companies, the directive has a very restrictive character. According to Article 12, nullity must be ordered by decision of a court of law and only on the grounds specified in section (b). Examples of such grounds are that no instrument of constitution has been executed, that the requisite legal formalities have not been complied with or that provisions of national law concerning the minimum amount of capital to be paid up have not been complied with. Article 13 adds that the decision of nullity pronounced by the court may only be relied on as against third parties if it is duly disclosed. Additional protection is offered where Article 15 provides that the nullity must entail the winding up of a company on the same footing as dissolution.

3.33 What is the difference between a company that is null and therefore has to be wound up and a non-existent company? In *Ubbink Isolatie* [1988], a contract was agreed upon in the name of Ubbink Isolatie BV, while the commercial registry had an entry of a partnership Ubbink Isolatie BV i.o. (Ubbink Isolatie, a private limited company in the course of formation). The other party brought proceedings against Ubbink Isolatie BV to terminate that contract and to establish liability thereunder. Ubbink Isolatie BV contended that the other party was wrong to bring its action against Ubbink Isolatie BV because it did not exist. During the proceedings, it became clear that, according to Dutch national law, 'the company has not been constituted because no authentic instrument of constitution within the meaning of Article 11(2) (a) [now Article 12(b)(i) of the 2009 Directive] of the directive was executed or the rules of preventive control, also within the meaning of Article 11(2) (a), were not complied with'. In its preliminary ruling, the ECJ stated that the purpose of the First Directive is not to permit third parties to rely on appearances created by the company's organs or representatives if those appearances do not conform to the information contained in the public register. Consequently, the rules concerning the nullity of companies apply only where third parties have been led to believe, by information published in accordance with section I of the Third Directive (now Directive 2011/35/EU), that a company within the meaning of the First Directive (now Directive 2009/101/EC) exists.[71]

3.34 In *Marleasing* [1990], it was claimed that a company under Spanish law was null, because the contract constituting its formation lacked a cause – it was supposed to be fraudulent – and therefore was void.[72] At the time, Spain had not yet implemented

71. ECJ 20 Sep. 1988, C-136/87 (*Ubbink Isolatie BV v. Dak- en Wandtechniek BV*).
72. *See* paragraph 3.15.

the First Directive. The applicability of national law was questioned, because it was not congruous with the directive. Therefore, the Court of Oviedo asked for a preliminary ruling of the ECJ. The ECJ held that:

> a national court hearing a case which falls within the scope of Directive 68/151 is required to interpret its national law in the light of the wording and the purpose of that directive in order to preclude a declaration of nullity of a public limited company on a ground other than those listed in Article 11 of the directive.[73]

In *Alfred Hirmann v. Immofinanz AG* [2013][74] the ECJ, challenged by a question of the Austrian court Handelsgericht Wien, proceeded to interpret Articles 12 and 13 of Directive 2009/101/EC. The referred case featured the acquisition on the secondary market of shares of a public company on the basis of an inaccurate prospectus, which qualified as an infringement of the company's information obligations. The ECJ stated that Articles 12 and 13 are irrelevant in such circumstances and they must be interpreted in such a way as not to preclude national legislation from providing for the retroactive cancellation of a share purchase contract, leading to the refund of the price paid by the subscriber for the shares.

B Formation and Capital of Public Limited Liability Companies [Second Directive]

3.35 Because the liability of shareholders in a public or private company is limited, it is not surprising that national legislators have tried for a long time to redress abuses. Prior to the adoption and implementation of the 1976 Second Directive, however, the measures taken showed considerable disparities. For example, whereas a permanent minimum capital was obligatory in several Member States, in Belgium and the Netherlands it applied only at the time of incorporation of the company.[75] Thus, in principle, the minimum capital could have been distributed the day after incorporation. In the UK, no minimum capital was prescribed, but, instead, protection was offered by way of disclosure of information concerning the capital of the company.[76] Similar divergences could be observed with most of the topics the Second Directive is dealing with.[77] 'The Capital Directive', as the Second Directive is called, deals exclusively with public companies.[78] In order to ensure protection for both shareholders and creditors of those companies, the directive contains detailed provisions. First, information must be available to enable any interested person to acquaint himself with the composition of the capital of the company. Second, a minimum capital must be subscribed. Third, it aims to maintain the capital by prohibiting any reduction by distribution to the shareholders, where the latter are not entitled to it, and by imposing limits on the

73. ECJ 13 Nov. 1990, C-106/89 (*Marleasing*).
74. ECJ 19 Dec. 2013, C-174/12 (*Alfred Hirmann v. Immofinanz AG*).
75. Schutte-Veenstra, *Harmonisatie van het kapitaalbeschermingsrecht in de EEG*, 16.
76. *Ibid.*, 16–17.
77. *Ibid.*, 23, 35, 54, 79, 110, 162, 181, 192, 196.
78. Second Council Directive of 13 Dec. 1976 (EEC) 77/91, OJ 1977, L 26/1.

company's rights to acquire its own shares. Fourth, it ensures the equal treatment of shareholders in the same position and the protection of creditors in case of alteration of the capital.

3.36 Because the Second Directive has created a rather rigid and costly capital regime, in 2004, the Commission initiated the first step towards its modernization, in order to promote business efficiency and competitiveness without reducing the protection offered to shareholders and creditors.[79] A working group made recommendations on the Simplification of the Legislation on the Internal Market (SLIM) and the report on the regulatory framework for company law was presented by the High Level Group of Company Law Experts.[80] It was recommended to eliminate reporting requirements in some cases (share issuance for non-cash consideration) and to facilitate certain transactions, such as the acquisition of shares by the company itself or by a third party with the company's financial assistance and the streamlining of ownership in a company's share capital. The Commission thereupon proposed to amend the Second Directive, which resulted in the amending Directive 2006/68/EC.

In parallel with this reconsideration process, in 2005, the Commission called for a feasibility study on an alternative to the capital maintenance regime as established by the Second Directive. Alternatives could be, for example, the reinforcement of liabilities in cases of fraudulent trading (e.g., Insolvency Act 1986, section 214) or a solvency requirement, such as that proposed by the High Level Group of Company Law Experts.[81] The feasibility study has been carried out by KPMG. An important finding was that the system of the Second Directive does not constitute a major obstacle to dividend distribution. Since Member States are free to require or allow the preparation of International Financial Reporting Standards (IFRS)-based accounts for dividend distribution purposes, the European Commission concluded not to propose further amendments to the Directive at the time.[82]

In more recent years, however, the Capital Directive was once again the target of revision. The original Directive was, in fact, amended by Directive 2009/109/EC,[83] and later consolidated by Directive 2012/30/EU,[84] which is the recast version currently in force. It provides for a correlation table in Annex III. Besides several formal revisions,

79. Proposal for a directive amending Council Directive 77/91/EEC, Brussels 21 Sep. 2004, Com(2004)final. European Parliament in March 2006 has voted in favour of this proposal, IP/06/312, Brussels 14 Mar. 2006.
80. Commission document COM(2003)final; *Report on a Modern Regulatory Framework for Company Law in Europe*, November 2002.
81. *Report on a Modern Regulatory Framework for Company Law in Europe* (November 2002), 87. *See also* Reinier Kraakman et al., *The Anatomy of Corporate Law: A Comparative and Functional Approach* (New York: Oxford University Press, 2004).
82. KPMG, *Feasibility study on an alternative to the capital maintenance regime established by the Second Company Law Directive 77/91/EEC of 13 Dec. 1976 and an examination of the impact on profit distribution of the new EU-accounting regime*, 2008 http://ec.europa.eu/internal_market/company/capital/index_en.htm (accessed 17 May 2016). Further information: Legal Capital in Europe, Edited by Marcus Lutter, De Grugter Recht, Berlin 2006.
83. Directive 2009/109/EC of 16 Sep. 2009 amending Council Directives 77/91/EEC, 78/855/EEC and 82/891/EEC, and Directive 2005/56/EC as regards reporting and documentation requirements in the case of mergers and divisions. OJ 2009 L 259 14–21.
84. Directive 2012/30/EU of 25 Oct. 2012, OJ 2012 L 315 74–97.

the Recast Directive does not encompass any major substantial modification to the content of the original Capital Directive, as amended over the years. The 2012 version was further amended in 2014[85] to allow for rapid action in urgent situations concerning resolution of credit institutions and investment firms (Article 45(3) was added). The amendments are referred to where appropriate in the next paragraphs, and references are provided in relation to Directive 2012/30/EU.

As a passing note, it is interesting to bear in mind the 2015 Commission proposal,[86] mentioned in paragraph 3.18, that features a merger and codification of six European company law directives and, among these, is the 2012 Directive.

1 *Information*

3.37 The articles of association, or the instrument of incorporation, must, according to Articles 2 and 3 of the directive, always give at least information about, among others:

(i) the amount of subscribed capital, if the company has no authorized capital;
(ii) the amount of authorized capital (if the company has such a capital) and the amount of the capital at the time the company is incorporated and at the time of any change in the authorized capital;
(iii) the nominal value of the shares subscribed and, at least once a year, the number thereof;
(iv) the number of shares subscribed without stating the nominal value, where such shares may be issued under national law;
(v) the nominal value of the shares or, where there is no nominal value, the number of shares issued for a consideration other than in cash, together with the nature of the consideration and the name of the person providing this consideration.

The information under (iii), (iv) and (v) may also appear in a separate document to be published in accordance with the procedures laid down in the national law implementing the First Directive.

2 *Minimum Capital*

3.38 Article 6 of the Directive requires the Member States to maintain a minimum capital for public companies:

85. Directive 2014/59/EU of 15 May 2014 establishing a framework for the recovery and resolution of credit institutions and investment firms and amending Council Directive 82/891/EEC, and Directives 2001/24/EC, 2002/47/EC, 2004/25/EC, 2005/56/EC, 2007/36/EC, 2011/35/EU, 2012/30/EU and 2013/36/EU, and Regulations (EU) No 1093/2010 and (EU) 648/2012, OJ 2014 L 173 190–348.
86. European Commission. *Proposal for a Directive of the European Parliament and of the Council Relating to Certain Aspects of Company Law (Codification)*. COM (2015) 616final.

> 1. The laws of the Member States shall require that, in order that a company may be incorporated or obtain authorisation to commence business, a minimum capital shall be subscribed the amount of which shall be not less than EUR 25,000 [87]

According to a 2008 ECJ judgment[88] it was necessary to amend Article 6 to repeal an existing secondary legal basis, and to confer both on the Parliament and on the Council the competence to examine and revise the minimum capital requirements. This was done within Article 6(3) of the original Directive that is now Article 6(2) of the 2012 Directive.[89]

Article 7 states that the subscribed capital may be formed only of assets capable of economic assessment. However, an undertaking to perform work or supply services may not form part of these assets. Shares may not be issued at a price lower than their nominal value, or, in the absence of a nominal value, their accountable par (Article 8). They must also be paid up at the time the company is incorporated or authorized to commence business, at not less than 25% of their nominal value or their accountable par (Article 9). The same percentage applies for shares issued for consideration in the period subsequent to the incorporation (Article 30, ex Article 26).

3.39 An important requirement, laid down in Article 10, is the independent expert's report on any consideration that is not in cash. It contains a description of each of the assets comprising the consideration and of the methods of valuation. It states whether the values correspond at least to the number and nominal value (or the accountable par) and, where appropriate, to the premium on the shares to be issued for the consideration concerned. The report shall be published in accordance with the requirements of the First Directive (now Directive 2009/101/EC). The 2009 amendment introduced a possibility to dispense companies from certain reporting requirements, in case an independent expert's report in the context of a merger or a division is already protecting the interests of shareholders and creditors. In such a case, the reports can alternatively be drawn up by the same expert(s) (Article 10(5) and Article 31(3)).

To facilitate certain transactions within groups of companies, Member States have the option not to apply this rule where 90% of the nominal value (or of the accountable par) of all the shares is issued to one or more companies for a consideration other than cash and where six other requirements are met. One of these entails that the company or companies furnishing the consideration guarantee(s) the debts of the recipient company up to an amount equal to the nominal value (or the accountable par) of the shares issued for consideration (Article 10(4)(d)).

According to Article 31 (ex Article 27), the requirements for consideration other than cash, in principle apply not only on formation, but also to the issue of shares in

87. In its original version the directive mentioned 'European units of account' but these were replaced by ECUs (European currency units). From 1 Jan. 1999 the currencies of the eleven Member States adopting the single currency were replaced by the euro. Amounts in ECUs therefore are expressed in euros from that date on.
88. ECJ 6 May 2008, *Parliament v. Council* C-133/06.
89. Directive 2012/30/EU of 25 Oct. 2012, OJ 2012 L 315 74–97; recital 14.

any period subsequent to the incorporation. To prevent evasion of the provisions of Article 10 regarding consideration other than in cash, the directive contains special rules regarding post-formation acquisitions. These are necessary because, otherwise, shortly after incorporation, a company can acquire assets owned by the founders of the company against payment in cash and thus avoid valuation and the expert's supervision. Therefore, within at least a two-year period after incorporation or authorization to commence business, the acquisition of assets may be subject to the same provisions as laid down in Article 10 and must be submitted for the approval of the general meeting. This applies where the assets belong to a person or company that has signed the articles or the instrument of incorporation, or, if laid down in the law of a Member State, to a shareholder or other person.[90] The post-formation requirements do not apply to acquisitions effected in the normal course of the company's business, to acquisitions effected at the instance or under the supervision of an administrator or judicial authority, or to stock exchange acquisitions (Article 13, ex Article 11).

Member States may decide not to require an expert report, where transferable securities are contributed as consideration, on the condition that they are valuated at the weighted average price at which they have been traded on one or more regulated markets. The same applies when assets are contributed less than three months after they have already been subject to a fair value opinion by a recognized independent expert or when their value is derived from the statutory accounts of the previous financial year (Article 11, ex Article 10a). In these cases, however, the management or administrative body must submit a declaration for publication containing, *inter alia,* a description of the non-cash consideration (Article 12, ex Article 10b).

3 *The Maintenance of the Capital*

3.40 Distributions to shareholders are not permitted if the net assets as set out in the company's annual accounts would become lower than the amount of the subscribed capital plus those reserves that may not be distributed under statutory law or the articles (undistributable reserves) (Article 17(1), ex Article 15(l)(a)). Moreover, the amount of distribution may not exceed the amount of the profits and sums drawn from reserves available for this purpose, minus any losses brought forward and sums placed in undistributable reserves (Article 17(3), ex Article 15(l)(c)).

Any distribution in violation of Article 17 must be returned by the shareholders who have received it, but only if the company proves that they knew of the irregularity of the distributions or could not, in view of the circumstances, have been unaware of it (Article 18, ex Article 16).

An alternative way of distributing to shareholders is letting the company acquire its own shares from the shareholders.[91] If the law of a Member State permits a company to acquire its own shares, these acquisitions shall be subject to conditions, laid down in Article 21 (ex Article 19 as amended in 2006):

90. These rules are similar to the German *Nachgründung* provisions of § 52 AktG.
91. As might be expected, a company may not subscribe for its own shares (Article 20, ex Article 18).

(a) there has to be authorization by the general meeting;
(b) the acquisition may not have the effect of reducing the net assets below the subscribed capital plus the undistributable reserves; and
(c) only fully paid-up shares may be included in the transaction.

Member States may add certain conditions, as set out in Article 21(1), for example, that the nominal value (or accountable par) of all acquired shares is not allowed to exceed a limit to be determined by the Member States, but that limit may not be lower than 10% of the subscribed capital.

The acceptance by the company of its own shares as security is to be treated as an acquisition of these shares (Article 27, ex Article 24). The general meeting (Article 41(1), ex Article 37(1)) must always decide on the withdrawal of shares acquired by the company itself.

The directive leaves several options open to the Member States to regulate the acquisition of the company's own shares. They may, for example, waive the requisite approval by the general meeting, where the acquisition of the shares is necessary to prevent serious and imminent harm to the company or where they are acquired for distribution to the company's employees or to employees of an associate company (Articles 21(2), ex Article 19(2), and 45(1), ex 41(1)).[92]

The voting rights attached to the shares held by the company itself are to be suspended. If the shares are included among the net assets shown in the balance sheet, an undistributable reserve of the same amount shall be included among the liabilities (Article 24(1)(a) and (b), ex Article 22(1) (a) and (b)).

3.41 To impede the evasion of the restrictions concerning the acquisition of a company's own shares, Article 25 (ex Article 23) regulates financial assistance by the company for the acquisition of its shares by a third party. Where Member States permit a company to advance funds, make loans or provide security with a view to the acquisition of its shares by a third party, it must make such transaction subject to several conditions:

- The transactions shall take place under the responsibility of the administrative or management body at fair market conditions.
- Prior approval of the general meeting is required and the decision must be taken by a majority of not less than two-thirds of the votes attached to the securities or the subscribed capital represented. A report on the transaction must be presented at the general meeting, which also has to be published in accordance with Article 3 of the First Directive (now Directive 2009/101/EC).
- The aggregate financial assistance may not result in the reduction of the net assets below the subscribed capital, plus the undistributable reserves.

3.41a Originally, Article 25 of the Capital Directive prohibited financial assistance, in order to preclude unwanted transactions, but thereby also blocking transactions such

92. *See also* Article 22, ex Article 20.

as management buyouts, which may be for the company's benefit. The acquirer of the shares may need the assets of the target company to secure a loan to finance the buyout. According to the Amending Directive, such assistance may be permitted if certain conditions are met. Article 26 (ex Article 23a) reminds the Member States of the risks involved where members of the administrative or management body are counterparties of the company in a financial assistance transaction. The Member State must ensure that such a transaction does not conflict 'with the company's best interests' (Article 26).

4 *Alteration of the Capital*

3.42 According to Article 29 (ex Article 25), the general meeting has to decide on any increase in capital, unless this power is transferred (limited to a maximum amount and for a maximum period of five years) to another body by the articles, the instrument of incorporation or by the general meeting. Where there are several classes of shares, the decisions of the general meeting shall be subject to a separate vote for each class of shareholder, whose rights are affected by the transaction. Article 33 (ex Article 29) furthers equal treatment of shareholders in the same position, where it provides that the shares must be offered on a pre-emptive basis to shareholders, in proportion to the capital represented by their shares. This pre-emption right, however, may be restricted or withdrawn by the general meeting or by another body, where it is given the power to do so by the articles, the instrument of incorporation or the general meeting. According to Article 44 (ex Article 40), these decisions by the general meeting must be taken by a majority of not less than two-thirds of the votes attached to the securities or the subscribed capital represented. The Member States may, however, require that a simple majority is sufficient when at least half the subscribed capital is represented. If there are several classes of shares and if the increase of capital consists of the issuing of shares in only one of these classes, the Member States are permitted to provide for rules, giving preference to the right of pre-emption to holders of certain classes of shares.

3.43 Any reduction in the subscribed capital, according to Article 34 (ex Article 30), must be subject to a decision of the general meeting acting in accordance with the majority rules of Article 44 (ex Article 40), and this decision must be duly published. Here, again, the directive provides for a separate vote for classes of shareholders whose rights are affected (Article 35, ex Article 31). Creditors whose claims antedate the publication of the decision are entitled to obtain security for claims that have not fallen due by the date of that publication (Article 36, ex Article 32). Member States need not apply Article 36, among other matters, to a reduction in the subscribed capital if its purpose is to offset losses incurred (Article 37, ex Article 33). In any case, the subscribed capital may not be reduced to an amount less than the minimum capital (Article 38, ex Article 34).

3.44 In cases of serious loss of the subscribed capital, a general meeting must be convened to consider whether the company should be wound up or whether any other measure should be taken. The amount of a loss deemed to be serious may not be set by the laws of the Member States at a figure higher than half of the subscribed capital (Article 19, ex Article 17).

5 *Concluding Remarks*

3.45 The Second Directive (now Directive 2012/30/EU) has been criticized for its shortcomings. It lacks effectiveness, for example, where the amount of capital and undistributable reserves at the closing date of the last financial year is decisive for certain distributions and acquisitions. Between that date and the moment of distribution or acquisition, these figures obviously may have changed.[93] Another weakness is the extensive use of minimum provisions ('at least' is a frequently used expression in the directive) and options for the Member States. In certain cases, Member States are free to choose their own solutions, if the subject is of no importance to the protection that the directive aims to offer. For example, the question of ownership of shares that are acquired by the company in violation of the limitations on such acquisitions represents such a 'free question'.[94] Finally, the text of the directive itself sometimes gives rise to different interpretations, or even yields conflicting meanings in the various official languages of the EU.[95]

The Capital Directive may have brought a certain harmonized level of capital requirements for the public company, yet it does not apply to private companies, as they fall outside its scope.

3.45a A request of preliminary ruling referred from the High Court of Ireland is pending before the ECJ with reference to the case *Gerard Dowling, Padraig McManus, Piotr Skoczylas, Scotchstone Capital Fund Limited v. Minister for Finance.*[96] The Irish State had taken over the 'Irish Life' bank to limit the risk of financial contagion. The main question relates to the compliance with the Capital Directive (and the ECJ case law concerning Greek banks[97]) of a Direction Order,[98] deemed necessary by the Minister and thus part of a State plan to fulfil its legal obligations pursuant to the TFEU and the terms of the Irish bailout.[99] The Direction Order has the effect of increasing a company's capital without the consent of the general meeting, thereby allotting new

93. Schutte-Veenstra, *Harmonisatie van het kapitaalbeschermingsrecht in de EEG*, 278.
94. Schutte-Veenstra, *Harmonisatie van het kapitaalbeschermingsrecht in de EEG*, 271. Grundmann, *European Company Law Organization, Finance and Capital Markets*, nr. 335–359.
95. Schutte-Veenstra, *Harmonisatie van het kapitaalbeschermingsrecht in de EEG*, 268–269, according to this author, the last phenomenon concerns, e.g., Art 9(2), 25 and 33 (now Articles 9(2), 29 and 37 of the Recast Directive).
96. Case C-41/15 *Gerard Dowling, Padraig McManus, Piotr Skoczylas, Scotchstone Capital Fund Limited v. Minister for Finance.*
97. http://eulawradar.com/case-c-4115-dowling-the-illegal-takeover-of-a-bank-and-the-irish-bailout/.
98. A court order based on Ireland's 2010 Credit Institutions (Stabilisation) Act.
99. case C-41/15 http://eulawradar.com/case-c-4115-dowling-the-illegal-takeover-of-a-bank-and-the-irish-bailout (accessed 20 May 2016).

shares without offering them pre-emptively to the existing shareholders and lowering the nominal capital of the company's shares through an alteration of the company's memorandum and articles of association.

C Mergers and Divisions of Limited Liability Companies

3.45b The present section deals with three European company law directives in the area of extraordinary operations, namely divisions and mergers. While, at the very beginning, the idea was for the same legislative act to cover both types of activities, at least when they were being carried out within the same national legal system, in the end, domestic mergers were first regulated at the European level in 1978 (Third Directive) and divisions in 1982 (Sixth Directive). As far as CBM's are concerned, it took more time for the supranational legislator to come to the adoption of an adequate framework, which, after over twenty years of debates (mainly pertaining different traditions as to employee participation), led to a first directive proposal in 1985, later withdrawn in 2001. The Tenth Directive was finally adopted in 2005.

As previously mentioned, in December 2015, the European Commission put forward a proposal[100] to codify and merge several existing company law directives, among which all three acts covered by this section are to be found, as well as the First, Second and Eleventh Directives.

D Domestic Mergers of Public Limited Liability Companies [Third Directive]

3.46 The Third or Merger Directive was adopted in 1978 to introduce provisions on mergers into the laws of every Member State.[101] It provided for the coordination of information and protection of the interests of shareholders and creditors, while protection of employees' rights is regulated in accordance with the directive regarding the transfer of undertakings or parts thereof (2001/23/EC).[102] The initial proposal by the Commission included not only mergers, but also divisions, albeit the latter issue has since been made subject of a separate, Sixth Directive (*see* paragraph 3.53).[103] The original Directive was amended several times, most notably, as far as reporting requirements are concerned, in 2007[104] – to fall in line with the 2005 Tenth Directive's solution that provided for an exemption to the requirement of an examination and independent export's report of the draft merger terms in case of merger or division, if

100. European Commission. *Proposal for a Directive of the European Parliament and of the Council Relating to Certain Aspects of Company Law (Codification)*. COM (2015) 616final https://ec.europa.eu/transparency/regdoc/rep/1/2015/EN/1-2015-616-EN-F1-1.PDF.
101. Third Council Directive of 9 Oct. 1978 based on Article 54(3)(g) of the Treaty concerning mergers of public limited liability companies (EEC) 78/855, OJ 1978, L 295.
102. OJ 2001, L 82, replacing the original Directive EEC 77/187.
103. Edwards, *EC Company Law*, 90 *et seq.*
104. Directive 2007/63/EC of 13 Nov. 2007 amending Council Directives 78/855/EEC and 82/891/EEC as regards the requirement of an independent expert's reporto n the occasion of merger and division of public limited liability companies. OJ 2007 L 300 47–48.

all shareholders agree (Article 10(4)).[105] In 2011, the directive was codified, and thus repealed, by Directive 2011/35/EU,[106] which covers protection of shareholders and creditors, and continues to make reference to Directive 2001/23/EC, as far as the protection of rights of employees is concerned in Article 12. Lastly, Directive 2014/59/EU[107] introduced appropriate derogations to allow resolution authorities to take rapid action in case of unsound or failing credit institutions and investment firms (Article 1).

The scope of the Third Directive is limited to public companies. According to Article 2, the directive encompasses two different methods of merger: (1) merger by the acquisition of one or more companies by another company; and (2) merger by the formation of a new company.

1 *Merger by Acquisition*

3.47 Merger by acquisition results when one or more companies are wound up without going into liquidation, while all their assets and liabilities are transferred to another company.[108] In exchange, the shareholders of the acquired company or companies are issued shares of the acquiring company and, if the terms of merger provide so, are paid in cash. The amount may not exceed 10% of the nominal value of the shares, or, where they have no nominal value, the accounting par value of the issued shares (Article 3).

In some Member States, shares may be issued without a nominal value. The accounting par value of a share is obtained by dividing the capital of the company by the number of shares issued. Statutory provisions allowing shares without a nominal value are, for example, paragraph 8(3), AktG (Germany), and Article 453(3), Wetboek van Vennootschappen (Belgium).

2 *Merger by Formation of a New Company*

3.48 Merger by formation of a new company results when several companies are wound up without going into liquidation, and all their assets and liabilities are transferred to the newly incorporated company. In exchange, their shareholders are issued shares in the new company and are paid in cash under the same restrictions applicable to mergers by acquisition (Article 4).

---

105. Amended by Directive 2009/109/EC of 16 Sep. 2009 amending Council Directives 77/91/EEC, 78/855/EEC and 82/891/EEC, and Directive 2005/56/EC as regards reporting and documentation requirements in the case of mergers and divisions. OJ 2009 L 259 14–21.
106. Directive 2011/35/EU of 5 Apr. 2011 concerning mergers of public limited liability companies, OJ 2011, L 110 1-11.
107. Directive 2014/59/EU of 15 May 2014 establishing a framework for the recovery and resolution of credit institutions and investment firms and amending Council Directive 82/891/EEC, and Directives 2001/24/EC, 2002/47/EC, 2004/25/EC, 2005/56/EC, 2007/36/EC, 2011/35/EU, 2012/30/EU and 2013/36/EU, and Regulations (EU) No. 1093/2010 and (EU) 648/2012, OJ 2014, L 173 190–348.
108. *Ibid.*, 97 notes that the concept of 'being wound up without going into liquidation' in English legal language is better expressed by 'being dissolved without being wound up'.

3 *Applicable Rules*

3.49 Essentially, the same rules apply to both types of mergers. The administrative or management bodies of the merging companies must, according to Article 5, draw up the draft terms of the merger in writing. These draft terms must specify, *inter alia*, the share-exchange ratio and the amount of any cash payment, as well as any special advantage granted to independent experts who examine the draft terms or to members of the merging companies' administrative, management, supervisory or controlling bodies. The draft terms must be published in accordance with the Disclosure Directive for each of the merging companies at least one month before the date fixed for the general meeting, which will decide on this matter (Article 6). Companies can derogate from this requirement when the draft terms of the merger are publicly available on their website, free of charge, for a period of at least one month before the general meeting that has to decide on them. Member States can require such publication to be made via the central electronic platform or via any other specific website. (Article 6)

A merger must have, at least, the approval of the general meeting of each involved company. Member States are to establish provisions requiring a majority of not less than two-thirds of the votes attached to the shares or to the subscribed capital present. They may provide, however, that a simple majority be sufficient when at least half of the subscribed capital is present. Moreover, where appropriate, the rules governing amendments to the memorandum and articles of association apply, because the decision taken covers both an approval of the draft merger terms and any proposed amendment to the memorandum or articles of association necessitated by the merger. Where there is more than one class of shares, similar to the Second Directive, a separate vote is exacted from each class of shareholders whose rights are affected by the transaction (Article 7). However, if certain conditions are met, the laws of a Member State need not require the approval of the general meeting of the acquiring company (Article 8).

According to Article 11, all shareholders are entitled to inspect at the registered office, and at least one month before the date fixed for the general meeting, certain documents. Among these are the draft terms of the merger, the financial reports of the merging companies for the preceding three financial years and the management reports of the administrative or management bodies explaining the draft terms of the merger. A report of experts stating whether in their opinion the share-exchange ratio is fair and reasonable must be available. A shareholder is entitled to obtain copies of such documents, in a paper or an electronic format (Article 11(3)). Pursuant to Article 11(4), the same derogation mentioned with reference to Article 6 applies here too, meaning it is possible for companies to make the documents available on their website.

3.50 The laws of the Member States must provide for an adequate system of protection of the interests of creditors of the merging companies, whose claims antedate the publication of the draft terms of merger and are not due at the time of such publication. At the very least, they are entitled to obtain adequate safeguards, where the financial situation of the merging companies makes such safeguards necessary (Article 13). Member States are required to lay down the conditions for such protection, and administrative or judicial solutions must be available to safeguard creditors (Article 13(2)). Where the laws of the Member States do not provide for judicial or administrative preventive supervision of the legality of mergers, the minutes of the general meetings, which decide on the merger and, where appropriate, the merger contract subsequent to such general meetings shall be drawn up and certified in due legal form (Article 16). The laws of the Member States determine the date on which a merger takes effect (Article 17). A merger must be publicized with respect to each of the merging companies, in accordance with the Disclosure Directive (Article 18).

3.51 The protection offered by the Third Directive does not only apply to mergers, but also to operations akin to mergers, but not fully covered by the definitions of Article 3 (merger by acquisition) and Article 4 (merger by formation of a new company). These articles do not allow for a cash payment exceeding 10% of the nominal value of the shares issued by the merger operation. Furthermore, they provide that one or more companies is wound up without going into liquidation. Where Member States allow for a cash payment exceeding the percentage mentioned or permit for merger-like operations without all of the transferring companies thereby ceasing to exist, several provisions of the Third Directive nevertheless apply (Articles 30 and 31). The Third Directive does not cover transactions where only part of the assets is transferred in exchange for shares. Such transactions, however, fall under the ambit of both the Second Directive, because they represent a non-cash contribution, and Directive 2001/23/EC on the safeguarding of employees' rights in the event of transfers undertakings and businesses or part thereof.[109]

3.52 A merger has simultaneous and *ipso jure* legal consequences. In the first place, all the assets and liabilities of any acquired company are transferred. Secondly, the acquired company shareholders become shareholders of the acquiring company. Thirdly, the acquired company ceases to exist (Article 19). Member States may set out provisions of nullification of mergers only under certain restrictive conditions. Notably, court judgment can declare a merger null and void only on the grounds that: (1) there has been no preventive supervision of its legality; (2) it has not been drawn up and certified in due legal form or; (3) it can be shown that the decision of the general meeting is void or voidable under national law (Article 22). This shall not affect nullification of a merger according to the law of a Member State, pronounced following supervision of the merger procedure (Article 22(3)). An example is the supervision of government agencies exerting merger control. Finally, it must be pointed out that the provisions of Chapter V of the directive alleviate the procedural requirements, where the acquiring company holds 90% or more of the shares of the acquired company, thus facilitating intragroup mergers (*see* paragraph 10.26).

109. OJ 2001, L 82.

3.52a In the 2013 ACT case,[110] the ECJ was asked, *inter alia*, to determine whether EU law concerning mergers of companies, notably Article 19 of Directive 2011/35/EU, encompassed:

> a system of transfer of liability for administrative offences to the acquiring company for acts committed by the company being acquired before registration of the merger.

In March 2015, the ECJ ruled that:

> Article 19(1) ... must be interpreted as meaning that a 'merger by acquisition' ... results in the transfer to the acquiring company of the obligation to pay a fine imposed by final decision adopted after the merger by acquisition for infringements of employment law committed by the acquired company prior to that merger.

In any case, the court stated that:

> extinguishing such a liability would run contrary to the very notion of merger by acquisition, as defined in Article 3(1) of Directive 78/855.

and that:

> the category of third parties, whose interests the directive is intended to protect, includes those entities which though not yet creditors or debenture holders at the date of the acquisition may become such post-acquisition as a result of situations predating the acquisition. This is the case, for instance, for infringements of employment law provisions which are found to have been committed in a decision adopted after the merger by acquisition had taken place. ... if such liability were not transferred, a company could use a merger by acquisition as means of escaping the legal consequences of offences it has committed to the detriment of the Member State concerned or other potential interested parties.

E Divisions of Public Limited Liability Companies [Sixth Directive]

3.53 The Sixth Directive concerns divisions, but, as opposed to the Third Directive, it does not require Member States to introduce the division procedure into their legislation.[111] It requires Member States to comply with the directive, if they permit operations to which the directive applies. Divisions are effectuated along the same principles as mergers. A merger is an operation whereby one or more companies are taken over by an acquiring company. The latter can be either one of the merging companies (merger by acquisition) or a newly formed company (merger by formation of a new company). The acquired companies, after being wound up without going into liquidation, transfer all their assets and liabilities to the acquiring company. In exchange, their shareholders are issued shares in the acquiring company. A division,

110. Case C-343/13 *Modelo Continente Hipermercados SA v. Autoridade para as COndições de Trabalho – Centro Local do Lis (ACT)*. Judgment of the Court (Fifth Chamber) 5 Mar. 2015.
111. Sixth Council Directive of 17 Dec. 1982 based on Article 54(3)(g) of the treaty, concerning the divisions of public limited liability companies 82/891/EEC, OJ 1982, L 378.

also referred to as 'scission',[112] is based on the same principles. The main difference is that the company being divided transfers its assets and liabilities to more than one company. Therefore, in the case of divisions, the transfer is effectuated by one company to several others; whereas, for mergers, transfers could be effectuated by either one or more companies, but to one other company only.

3.54 Similar to mergers, in exchange for the transfer of the company's assets and liabilities, shareholders of the company being divided are issued shares in the division. Here, again, division can take place by acquisition (the company being divided transfers all its assets and liabilities to several existing companies, Article 2(1)) or by the formation of new companies (the company being divided transfers all its assets and liabilities to several newly formed companies, Article 21(1)). The rationale behind the adoption of the directive is to avoid the circumvention of the guarantees provided for mergers by offering equivalent protection in the event of a division. In paragraph 3.46, it was noted that the issues covered by the Third and Sixth Directives were initially contained in a single proposal. Therefore, it is not surprising that the provisions of both directives are, in many respects, identical or analogous. The differences originate in the multiplicity of the recipient companies. As a consequence, attention should be drawn to the precise description and allocation of assets and liabilities transferred to each of the recipient companies and the allocation of shares issued in exchange by the recipient companies (Article 3(2)(h)(i)).

3.55 The directive allows Member States to permit a combined method of division, whereby a division by acquisition is combined with a division by formation of one or more new companies (Article 1(3)). Like the Third Directive, the Sixth Directive contains anti-avoidance provisions. The directive applies even where a Member State permits a cash consideration in excess of 10% of the nominal value of the shares issued (Article 24). In the event that a Member State allows for an operation that falls under the description of Article 1, but without the company being divided ceasing to exist, most provisions of the directive apply (Article 25).

3.56 Member States may relieve companies from certain obligations if a division operation is subject to the supervision of a judicial authority. This option only applies where the judicial authority has certain powers, *inter alia,* to call a general meeting of the shareholders of the company being divided, in order to decide on the division (Article 23).[113]

3.56a The Sixth Directive was amended in 2007[114] – to fall in line with the 2005 Tenth Directive's solution that provided for an exemption to the requirement of an independent expert's report of the draft merger terms in case of merger or division, if all

112. *See* Edwards, *EC Company Law,* 91 on the introduction of this word in the English legal language.
113. *See Ibid.,* 101.
114. Directive 2007/63/EC of 13 Nov. 2007 amending Council Directives 78/855/EEC and 82/891/EEC as regards the requirement of an independent expert's reporto n the occasion of merger and división of public limited liability companies. OJ 2007 L 300 47–48.

shareholders agree (Article 10). Further amendments were made in 2009[115] - with notable reference to Article 4 and in relation to the possibility to carry out disclosure requirements online - and, lastly, in 2014.[116]

3.56b Within the framework of the 2012 Action Plan, the 2012 consultation on the future of European Company Law followed. In accordance with the EUROPE 2020 Strategy for Growth, the European Commission put forward its intention to provide for a plan to regulate cross-border divisions, possibly through a modification of the CBM Directive (*see* next section) in the direction of having a unified document pertaining to cross-border restructurings and operations. This could either give birth to a new Directive or only introduce amendments to the Directive on CBM and/or to the Directive on domestic divisions. A study was published in 2013 in relation to the cross-border merger directive (*see* next section), which showed support for further legislative activity in this area, most notably to facilitate cross-border transactions and reduce compliance costs by referring to a more predictable and efficient legal environment.[117] An online public consultation was held in 2014 (*see* next section).

F Cross-Border Mergers of Limited Liability Companies [Tenth Directive]

1 Introduction and Scope

3.57 The Third Directive harmonizes only mergers of domestic companies. Because cross-border mergers (CBM)s were likely to encounter many legislative and administrative difficulties, the Commission put forward a separate draft directive on CBM in 1985. It took twenty years before this Tenth Directive was adopted in 2005, coming into force in 2007. Nevertheless, even prior to that date, according to legal scholars, CBM could be realized based on both the rules of international private law and harmonized national law with regard to mergers. Several CBM have been executed accordingly, though mainly in simple cases where no employees or creditors were involved (*see* paragraph 8.29). This practice was authorized, to a certain extent, by the ECJ in *Sevic* [2005], where it was held that a Member State (Germany) may not refuse to register a merger concluded in 2002 between a company established in that State and one established in another Member State (Luxembourg).[118]

3.57a Sevic Systems AG, a company registered in Germany, and Security Vision Concept SA, registered in Luxembourg, agreed on a merger whereby Sevic would be

115. Directive 2009/109/EC of 16 Sep. 2009 amending Council Directives 77/91/EEC, 78/855/EEC and 82/891/EEC, and Directive 2005/56/EC as regards reporting and documentation requirements in the case of mergers and divisions. OJ 2009 L 259 14–21.
116. Directive 2014/59/EU of 15 May 2014 establishing a framework for the recovery and resolution of credit institutions and investment firms and amending Council Directive 82/891/EEC, and Directives 2001/24/EC, 2002/47/EC, 2004/25/EC, 2005/56/EC, 2007/36/EC, 2011/35/EU, 2012/30/EU and 2013/36/EU, and Regulations (EU) No 1093/2010 and (EU) 648/2012, OJ 2014 L 173 190–348.
117. http://ec.europa.eu/smart-regulation/impact/planned_ia/docs/2015_markt_001_eu_crossborder_cooperation_of_companies_en.pdf (accessed 20 May 2016).
118. Case C-411/03.

the acquiring company. The competent German authority (the Amtsgericht Neuwied) rejected the application for registration in the national commercial register of the merger on the ground that the German law on company transformations provides only for mergers between companies established in Germany.

The ECJ held that:

> 21 (...) a merger such as that at issue in the main proceedings constitutes an effective means of transforming companies in that it makes it possible, within the framework of a single operation, to pursue a particular activity in new forms and without interruption, thereby reducing the complications, times and costs associated with other forms of company consolidation such as those which entail, for example, the dissolution of a company with liquidation of assets and the subsequent formation of a new company with the transfer of assets to the latter.
>
> 22 In so far as, under national rules, recourse to such a means of company transformation is not possible where one of the companies is established in a Member State other than the Federal Republic of Germany, German law establishes a difference in treatment between companies according to the internal or cross-border nature of the merger, which is likely to deter the exercise of the freedom of establishment laid down by the Treaty.
>
> 23 Such a difference in treatment constitutes a restriction within the meaning of Articles 43 EC and 48 EC, which is contrary to the right of establishment and can be permitted only if it pursues a legitimate objective compatible with the Treaty and is justified by imperative reasons in the public interest.

From this, the ECJ ruling followed:

> Articles 43 EC and 48 EC preclude registration in the national commercial register of the merger by dissolution without liquidation of one company and transfer of the whole of its assets to another company from being refused in general in a Member State where one of the two companies is established in another Member State, whereas such registration is possible, on compliance with certain conditions, where the two companies participating in the merger are both established in the territory of the first Member State.

3.57b More recently, another relevant case was lodged before the ECJ: the *KA Finanz AG v. Sparkassen Versicherung AG Vienna Insurance Group* case. The case concerns the 1980 Rome Convention on the law applicable to contractual obligations and its 2008 successor, the so-called Rome I Regulation. It is important to note that both the Convention (*see* Article 1(2)(e)) and the present Rome I Regulation (Article 1(2)(f)) are not applicable to:

> questions governed by the law of companies and other bodies, corporate or unincorporated, such as the creation, by registration or otherwise, legal capacity, internal organisation or winding-up of companies and other bodies, corporate or unincorporated, and the personal liability of officers and members as such for the obligations of the company or body;

The matter at hand relates to the treatment of mergers in relation to conflict of laws. More specifically, it refers to whether the exclusion encompasses: (a) reorganizations such as mergers and divisions, and (b) in connection with reorganizations, the provision of Article 15 of the Third Directive (or of Directive 2011/35/EU, if applicable). That article gives specific rights to holders of securities (other than shares), with special rights attached. Furthermore, the referring court asks whether requirements are to be inferred from European primary law (freedom of establishment, freedom to provide services and free movement of capital and payments) - or, if not, from European secondary law (*inter alia*, the Third and Sixth Company Law Directives) - with reference to the treatment of mergers in relation to conflict of laws. In April 2016,[119] the ECJ stated that:

> the law applicable following a cross-border merger by acquisition to the interpretation of a loan contract taken out by the acquired company, such as the contracts at issue in the main proceedings, to the performance of the obligations under the contract and to how those obligations are extinguished is the law which was applicable to the contract before the merger; the provisions governing the protection of the creditors of the acquired company, in a case such as that at issue in the main proceedings, are those of national law which were applicable to that company.

3.58 The Tenth Directive deals with CBM, hence its frequently used alternative name 'CBM Directive'. The starting point of the Tenth Directive are the rules harmonized by the Third Directive with regard to mergers between companies governed by the same national law.[120] Similar to a merger to which the rules of the Third Directive are applicable, a cross-border merger may also be realized by acquisition or by formation of a new company and the consequences of the cross-border merger are the same as that of a domestic merger.[121] The Tenth Directive provides additional requirements for those aspects of CBM that differ from national mergers, such as the necessary synchronization of the drawing up and certification of documents in due legal form. Once completed, a cross-border merger may not be declared null and void, whereas the Third Directive allows for such declaration of a domestic merger.[122] As opposed to the Third Directive, the scope of the Tenth Directive is not restricted to public companies, but relates to other limited liability companies, though only where the national law permits mergers between such types of companies. Finally, the Tenth Directive deals with the subject of employee participation, a problem that is not relevant for the Third Directive. The drafters of the Tenth Directive, however, in this respect, had the advantage of drawing from the provisions of earlier directives concerning the EWC and the employee participation system of the SE. The provisions of Article 16(2) and (3) of the Tenth Directive are designed to prevent the loss of participation rights arising from a cross-border merger.

119. Case C-483/14 *KA Finanz AG v. Sparkassen Versicherung AG Vienna Insurance Group*. Judgment of the Court (Third Chamber) 7 Apr. 2016.
120. Directive 2005/56/EC of 26 Oct. 2005 on cross-border mergers of limited liability companies, OJ 2005, L 310 (replaced by Directive 2011/35/EU). The original proposal dates from 1984: Proposal for a Tenth Council Directive concerning cross-border mergers of public limited companies (COM(84) 727 final), OJ 1985, C 23.
121. Tenth Directive, Articles 2 and 14.
122. Tenth Directive, Article 17; Third Directive, Article 22.

3.59 Cross-border aspects of employee participation may arise where, for example, a German AG with a co-determined supervisory board merges with an English PLC as the acquiring company. Without additional provisions, the employees of the German undertaking may then lose their participation rights (to co-determinate the supervisory board) because an English company is unlikely to have such a supervisory board, and, under English law, co-determination does not exist at all. Note that, even in Germany, co-determination is of strictly national character, providing rights of participation only to employees of German undertakings. Thus, in the reverse case, where an English PLC would be acquired by a German AG, the employees of the PLC will not gain any co-determination rights. In such a case, conversion of the acquiring company into an SE and negotiating an agreement as provided for by the SE directive can lead to a system in which all employees can participate.

2 *The Essential Provisions*

3.60 The rules applicable to a cross-border merger are, in many respects, the same as those that apply to a domestic merger, in accordance with the Third Directive. Because of the cross-border element, the rules are also similar to those governing the formation of an SE by way of a merger (paragraph 4.18). The law governing the acquiring company determines the date on which a cross-border merger takes effect (Article 12).

3.61 The Tenth Directive's essential provisions are as follows:

- The management or administrative organ of each of the merging companies must draw up common draft terms of the cross-border merger. Among the particulars to be included are: the likely repercussions on employment, the date from which the transactions of the merging companies will be treated as being those of the company resulting from the merger for accounting purposes, the statutes of the resulting company and information on the procedures, by which arrangements for the involvement of employees are determined (Article 5).
- The common draft terms must be published in the national gazette of each of the merging companies and in accordance with the provisions of the First Directive. Publication must be completed at least one month before the date of the general meeting that is to decide on the merger. In comparison with domestic mergers, extra information is required with regard to the arrangements for the exercise of the rights of creditors and minority shareholders (members) (Article 6). In the same article, Directive 2009/109/EC introduced a derogation to the publication requirement, in case the draft terms are published online or via the central electronic platform.[123]

123. For some critical notes on the protection offered: Marieke Wyckaert & Koen Geens, 'Cross-Border Mergers and Minority Protection: An Open-Ended Harmonization', *European Company Law* 5, no. 6 (December 2008): 288–296, Geert T.M.J. Raaijmakers & Thijs P.H. Olthoff, 'Creditor Protection in Cross-Border Mergers: Unfinished Business', *European Company Law* 5, no. 6 (December 2008): 305–308.

- A report on the legal and economic aspects of the merger must be drawn up by the management or administrative organ from each of the merging companies. Such report must be made available to the shareholders (members) and to the employees or their representatives. Where, according to national law, an opinion is received from the employee representatives, that opinion should be appended to the report (Article 7).
- An independent expert report must be made available not less than one month before the general meeting that has to decide on the merger. The report should include at least the same particulars as mentioned by the Third Directive for domestic mergers (Article 8).[124]
- The general meeting of each of the merging companies approve the common draft terms of the merger. It may make the implementation of the merger conditional on express ratification by the general meeting of the arrangements for the participation of employees in the company resulting from the merger (Article 9).[125]
- A certificate must be issued by the competent authority (court, notary or other) conclusively attesting to the proper completion of the pre-merger acts and formalities in each of the Member States concerned (Article 10).
- If a Member State provides for a special procedure to scrutinize and amend the exchange ratio of the shares or to compensate minority shareholders to be effected post-merger, such procedure should only apply if explicitly accepted upon the approval of the merger by the general meeting of the other companies (Article 10(3); *see* paragraph 4.18a for the protection the SE Regulation offers to minority shareholders).
- The legality of the completion of the cross-border merger must be scrutinized by the competent authority of the Member State, where the company resulting from the merger is registered (Article 11).
- Simplified formalities apply where a company is holding all the voting rights of the company or companies being acquired (Article 15) and carries out a cross-border merger by acquisition. Pursuant to a 2009 amendment, Article 15(2) provides that, when the acquiring company holds 90% or more (but not all) voting rights, the reports are required only if either of the national laws governing the companies state so.
- The company resulting from the cross-border merger is subject to the rules for employee participation of the Member State of its registered office (Article 16(1)). These rules, if any, shall not apply where they lead to loss of participation rights for all or a certain part of the employees (Article 16(2)). In such a case, defining the scope and rights of the employee participation system shall be regulated *mutatis mutandis* by rules applicable to the formation of a SE (Article 16(3); *see* paragraphs 4.35 *et seq.*). The cross-border merger may

124. The independent expert's report is not required if all the shareholders of each of the companies involved in the merger have so agreed (Article 8(4)).
125. As under the Third Directive, the laws of a Member State need not require approval of the merger by the general meeting of the acquiring company (Article 9(3)).

not be staged in such a way as to eliminate pre-existing employee participation (Article 16(6)). When the resulting company is operating under an employee participation system, it must ensure that employees' rights are protected in the event of subsequent domestic mergers for a period of three years (Article 16(7)).

3.61a It should be noted here that Directive 2012/17/EU[126] revised the Tenth Directive in two ways, notably by amending Article 13 (regarding the registration of the merger) and by inserting Article 17a, in order to ensure that communication between national registers is carried out via the system of interconnection of central, commercial and companies registers.

3 *Perspectives*

3.62 The Tenth Directive dates from 26 October 2005, and should have been implemented by the Member States by 15 December 2007 (Article 19). Only sixteen Member States transposed the Directive by the 2007 deadline, ten did so in 2008 and four in 2009. The bumpy transposition process was complemented by national technical difficulties, which caused the Directive to be operational in certain Member States only starting from 2012. In September 2014, the European Commission launched an online public consultation on the topic of CBM and divisions, to assess any potential need to change the existing legal framework for such operations. More specifically, two separate issues were the target of the consultation: (a) how to improve the existing framework for CBM, and (b) the possible creation of a framework for cross-border divisions. The consultation ended in February 2015 and included contributions made by a wide variety of respondents, such as public authorities, academia, liberal professions, business organizations, chambers of commerce, trade unions, companies and individuals. A feedback statement was published in October 2015.[127] Interestingly, many respondents favoured the creation of an EU legal framework for all cross-border conversions, encompassing mergers, divisions, transfer of registered office and other possible types of conversion, such as cross-border spin-offs.

3.62a Article 18 called for a review by the Commission five years after the implementation. In 2012, the Directorate-General for the Internal Market and Services commissioned a study on the application of the Cross-border Merger Directive in all EU and European Economic Area (EEA) Member States, with specific reference to five main objectives: (i) to provide a description of the transposition of the Directive, (ii) to report on the scope of the application of national rules in the context of CBM, (iii) to provide an analysis of CBM carried out under the scope of the Directive, (iv) to identify

126. Directive 2012/17/EU of 13 Jun. 2012 amending Council Directive 89/666/EEC and Directives 2005/56/EC and 2009/101/EC as regards the interconnection of central, commercial and companies registers, OJ 2012, L 156, 16 Jun. 2012, 1–9.
127. European Commission. *Feedback statement, Summary of Responses to the Public Consultation on Cross-border Mergers and Divisions*. October 2015 http://ec.europa.eu/internal_market/consultations/2014/cross-border-mergers-divisions/docs/summary-of-responses_en.pdf.

the benefits of the framework, its impact on cross-border mobility, the main problems related to its application and potential gaps or inconsistencies between the Directive and national legislation, (v) to offer a comparison between rules on CBM, their application and national practices. The final report was published in September 2013.[128] According to the study, the Directive has boosted CBM activity and has led to an increase by 173% between 2008 and 2012, notwithstanding the aftermath of the economic crisis and the difficult implementation process. The main benefits of the Directive relate to efficiency gains and savings, mainly stemming from *lower organizational, operational and regulatory costs.*[129]

Nevertheless, major and minor obstacles, pertaining to the five different areas surveyed, are hampering the instrument of cross-border mergers from being fully operational:[130] Among these obstacles are under-harmonization of rules: besides gaps and inconsistencies in the Directive, Member States still have different deadlines and waiting periods, creating delays in the merger procedure.[131] The main driving factors for companies to engage in cross-border mergers are: (i) business advantages stemming from synergies;[132] (ii) reduced organizational costs; (iii) reduced regulatory compliance costs; (iv) tax planning, i.e., finding a favourable tax regime; (v) finding a (more) business-friendly regulatory environment.

G Financial Statements

3.63 Directive 2013/34/EU prescribes what is required from companies and groups of companies in regard to their financial statements, consolidated financial statements and related reports. The 2013 Directive combines much of what was laid down in the pre-existing 'Accounting Directives'. These were the 1978 Fourth Directive, dealing with the annual accounts of companies and its 1983 counterpart on consolidated accounts, the Seventh Directive. In 1984, the Directive on statutory audit completed the threefold framework regarding accounting, auditing and publication requirements. In hindsight, one could speak of an embryonic European accountancy code. From the 1990s onward, however, the internationalization of financial markets and corporate scandals have led to more encompassing and stricter regulation at EU level that certainly goes beyond the initial embryonic stage.

3.63a It took almost ten years to negotiate the Fourth Directive, due to the different approaches of Member States toward accounting and reporting. These approaches varied from liberal and pragmatic to highly prescriptive; from shareholder-oriented

128. *Study on the application of the cross-border merger directive*, Bech-Bruun, September 2013 (Bech-Bruun report). http://ec.europa.eu/internal_market/company/docs/mergers/131007_study-cross-border-merger-directive_en.pdf.
129. Bech-Bruun report, pp. 7–8.
130. Bech-Bruun report, pp. 9–14.
131. The solutions assessed are: (1) full harmonization (deemed as not necessarily feasible), (2) 'fixed menu' (the recommended approach), (3) 'open menu'; additionally, the report advocates for the creation of an online database featuring different rules applicable in different Member States, to help plan cross-border mergers; *see* p. 10.
132. This driver is featured by domestic mergers as well.

information to providing information based on taxation accounting or even from a macroeconomic perspective. Consequently, the rules for valuation and depreciation were very diverse and the Fourth Directive has not removed all the differences.[133]

3.64 In 2007, the European Commission published a Communication, thereby presenting its plan to simplify European rules on accounting and auditing, in order to reduce administrative costs for businesses. This should be achieved mostly through simplification of disclosure requirements for companies and branches and by reduction of the reporting and auditing requirements for small and medium-sized enterprises, in accordance with the 'Think Small First' principle.[134] After several consultations, the Fourth and Seventh Directives were repealed and merged by Directive 2013/34/EU,[135] to be transposed into national legislation by July 2015 and applicable to financial years commencing on or after January 2016. The 2013 Directive also incorporates what was previously covered by Directive 2012/6/EU, exempting 'micro-entities' from publication requirements. Since then, the 2013 Directive is amended by Directive 2014/95/EU to include provisions regarding non-financial statements and diversity information.[136]

3.65 The changes the 2013 Directive brought about were aimed at combining the provisions of the Fourth and Seventh Directive in a single document, together with a more structured layout of the articles. Terminology has also changed, because in the 2013 Directive 'accounts' are called 'financial statements' in line with IFRS (*see* paragraphs 9.01 *et seq.*). The 2013 Directive did not, however, entail a complete conceptual redrafting of what was the core of the Fourth and Seventh Directive. For that matter, the 2013 Directive continues the principles-based approach with an emphasis on the obligation to give a true and fair view of a company's assets and liabilities, financial position and profit or loss.[137] In the sections that follow, the emphasis is on the scope of the 2013 Directive, apart from sections on the importance of general principles and special reports. What details must be included in the financial statements and management reports and how they must be drawn up and published will be dealt with in Chapter 9 of this book. Furthermore, the origins and impact of IFRS and their relation to EU legislation will be set out in that chapter.

3.65a In September 2013, the Republic of Estonia lodged an action of annulment before the ECJ with reference to (i) Article 4(6) and 8; (ii) Article 16(3); and (iii) Article 6(3) of the 2013 Directive on the grounds that they are inconsistent with the principles

133. Commission, *The Fourth Company Law Directive. Implementation by Member States*, 1987, nr. CB-48-87-484-EN-C. Edwards, *EC Company Law*, 117 *et seq.*
134. Commission Communication 'Think Small First – Small Business Act for Europe', adopted in 2008 (revised in February 2011),Brussels 25.6.2008, COM (2008) 394.
135. Directive 2013/34/EU of 26 Jun. 2013 on the annual financial statements, consolidated financial statements and related reports of certain types of undertakings, amending Directive 2006/43/EC and repealing Directives 78/660/EEC and 83/349/EEC, OJ 2013 L 182 19–76.
136. Directive 2014/95/EU of 22 Oct. 2014 amending Directive 2013/34/EU as regards disclosure of non-financial and diversity information by certain large undertakings and groups. OJ 2014 L 330 1–9.
137. Directive 2013/34/EU, Preamble, recital 6 and 9.

of proportionality and subsidiarity and with Article 296 TFEU within the meaning of Article 263 TFEU. In June 2015, the Second Chamber of the ECJ dismissed the action.[138]

1 Scope of Directive 2013/34

3.66 The 2013 Directive applies to several types of 'undertakings'. Firstly, to public and private limited liability companies and limited partnerships with shares. Secondly, it applies to general partnerships and limited partnerships, where the members, in fact, have limited liability, because they are public or private limited liabilities or a comparable form not governed by the law of an EU Member State.[139] Those undertakings are subject to general principles (Articles 6–8) in relation to their annual financial statements and, furthermore, to provisions regarding:

- the balance sheet and the profit and loss account (the financial statements) (Articles 9–14);
- the notes to the financial statements (Articles 15–18);
- the management report, including a corporate governance statement (Articles 19–20).

In addition, the directive applies to a 'group', being a parent undertaking and all of its subsidiary undertakings, in order to create the obligation to draw up financial statements and reports on a consolidated basis (Articles 21–23). In line with the previous sections, the directive features specific provisions for the consolidated financial statements, the notes to these statements and the consolidated management report (Articles 22–29).

3.66a What constitutes a 'group', being a parent undertaking and all of its subsidiaries, according to the definition in Article 2(11), is a rather complicated matter. The requirement to draw up consolidated financial statements and reports rests with the parent undertaking (Article 21). Consequently, the directive further specifies when an undertaking is to be regarded as a parent. The lengthy and complicated definition provided by Article 22 is, in essence, built on two diverging concepts: the group determined by factors of a legal nature or by being an entity according to economic criteria.[140] The first entails that the rights to control be decisive. If a company has a majority of the voting rights in the general meeting of another company (or other legal entity), it should then have a duty to inform its shareholders about this extension of its undertaking. This has been the traditional British and Irish view. By contrast, the economic or Continental view is that it is the financial affairs of an economically integrated entity that should be reflected in the consolidated financial statements. This

138. Case C-508/13 *Republic of Estonia v. European Parliament and Council of the European Union*. Judgement of the Court of 18 Jun. 2015.

139. Article 1.

140. M.P. van Achterberg, *De juridische definitie van het economische verschijnsel concern in het ondernemingsrecht* (diss.) (Deventer: Kluwer, 1989), 151. Edwards, *EC Company Law*, 157 *et seq.*

may lead to a different outcome, because the possession of rights, such as the majority voting rights, does not necessarily signify economic integration. The critical element of whether a group is an economic entity, therefore, is not the power to control, but the control that is actually exercised (effective control). In this view, a group exists if a parent exercises a dominant influence over a subsidiary, regardless of the percentage of the parents' voting rights.

3.66b The diverging concepts were a major issue during the discussions in the drafting process of the Seventh Directive.[141] As a result, both approaches were reflected in the definitions of Article 1 of the Seventh Directive and they are now included in Article 22 of the 2013 Directive. The starting point is the legal approach that initially was preferred by the Commission, because it allows for a more precise definition of the scope of consolidation.[142] The legal approach, as laid down in Article 22(1), purports that an undertaking is to be qualified as a parent undertaking if it has majority voting rights or otherwise the right to appoint or remove the majority of the board members.

More precisely, an undertaking is a parent undertaking if it has, with regard to another undertaking:

(a) the majority of voting rights; or
(b) the right to appoint or remove the majority of board members; or
(c) the right to exercise a dominant influence pursuant to a contract or a provision in the articles of that other undertaking (of which it is a shareholder or member); or
(d) if it has appointed the majority of board members of the other undertaking, solely by the exercise of voting rights or if it controls the majority voting rights, pursuant to an agreement with other shareholders or members.

The economic approach can be found in the second section of Article 22, where it states that:

> Member States may require the parent undertaking to draw up consolidated financial statements if that undertaking has the power to exercise or actually exercises a dominant influence over another undertaking, or, if the parent and subsidiary undertaking are managed on a unified basis by the parent undertaking.
>
> The same applies if unified management happens on the basis of a contract or provisions in the articles of the subsidiary, or where it is due to the fact that the boards of the undertakings concerned have a majority of their members in common (Article 22(7)).

3.66c Further details on how to calculate the required number of voting rights and rights of appointment and removal of board members are laid down in sections 3–5 of Article 22. It is worth mentioning, that the rights of a subsidiary shall be added to those

141. Edwards, *EC Company Law*, 161.
142. Karel Van Hulle *Council Directive (EEC) 83/349* (Seventh Company Law Directive – Consolidated Accounts) in: Butterworths European Law Service – Company (London: Butterworths, 1992).

of the parent undertaking (section 3). Section 6 further determines the scope of consolidation by including subsidiaries 'regardless of where the registered offices of such subsidiary undertakings are situated'.

Notwithstanding their different origins, the legal and economic approaches will, in most cases, lead to the same result. As a rule, the parent undertaking will hold the majority voting rights of a subsidiary and, simultaneously, exercise dominant influence or manage that subsidiary on a unified basis. Furthermore, it should be noted that the function of Article 22 of the 2013 Directive is limited to determining whether an undertaking is a parent undertaking and, consequently, under the obligation to report on a consolidated basis. It has no bearing on other issues, such as the impact the interests of the group as a whole may have vis-à-vis the interests of a subsidiary within the group. These matters will be dealt with in Chapter 10 of the book.

3.66d The 2013 Directive features several refinements as to its scope, notably by discerning between the following categories of undertakings:

- *micro-undertakings*: not exceeding at least two of the following criteria: (a) balance sheet total EUR[143] 350,000, (b) net turnover EUR 700,000, (c) average number of employees: ten (Article 3(1));
- *small undertakings*: not exceeding at least two of the following criteria: (a) balance sheet total EUR 4 million, (b) net turnover EUR 8 million, (c) average number of employees: fifty; Member States may opt for higher thresholds of EUR 6 million and EUR 12 million, respectively (Article 3(2));
- *medium-sized undertakings*: not exceeding at least two of the following criteria: (a) balance sheet total EUR 20 million, (b) net turnover EUR 40 million, (c) average number of employees: 250 (Article 3(3));
- *large undertakings*: exceeding at least two of the following criteria: (a) balance sheet total EUR 20 million, (b) net turnover EUR 40 million, (c) average number of employees: 250 (Article 3(4));

The same thresholds apply to determine whether a group is small, medium-sized or large. The thresholds serve to allow for a differentiated system of simplifications and exemptions to the reporting requirements for micro, small and medium-sized undertakings.[144] Such alleviations do not apply to *'public-interest entities'*. These are listed companies, credit institutions, insurance undertakings and other entities designated, as such, by Member States because of their significant public relevance because of the nature of their business, their size or the number of employees (Article 2(1)(a-d)). Consequently, public-interest entities are treated as large undertakings, regardless of their net turnover, balance sheet total or average number of employees (Article 40).

143. EUR or the equivalent amount in the national currency, Article 3(9).
144. Articles 14 and 36.

2 *General Principles*

3.67 Article 4(3) articulates the overriding character of the general principle that the annual financial statements shall give a true and fair view of the undertaking's assets, liabilities, financial position and profit or loss. Where application of the provisions of the directive is not sufficient to give such a true and fair view, additional information shall be given in the notes to the financial statements. The 2013 Directive formalized several other general accounting principles, which are set out in Article 6. The importance of the general principles is also underlined in paragraph 6 of the Preamble, where it is stated that 'The scope of this Directive should be principles-based and should ensure that it is not possible for an undertaking to exclude itself from that scope by creating a group structure containing multiple layers of undertakings established inside or outside the Union.'

3 *Special Reports and Publication*

3.68 The financial statements of public-interest entities, medium-sized and large undertakings shall be audited by one or more statutory auditors or audit firms approved by Member States to carry out statutory audits on the basis of Directive 2006/43/EC as amended (Articles 34 and 35). Statutory Audit is further discussed in paragraphs 3.70 *et seq.*

3.68a Separate reports on payments to governments and on sustainability and diversity must be drawn up and published. To prevent illegal wood from entering the EU market and to improve the way countries manage their oil, gas and mineral resources, further good governance, large undertakings and public-interest entities must report and publish their payments to governments on an annual basis (Articles 42–45). Furthermore, large undertakings that are public-interest entities having more than 500 employees shall include in the management report a non-financial statement on the impact of their activities. More specifically, the impact on environmental, social and employee matters, respect for human rights, anti-corruption and bribery matters (Article 19a). These matters belong to the wider concept of Corporate Social Responsibility (CSR).[145] Moreover, a description of the diversity policy regarding membership of the board(s) has to be included in the corporate governance statement that companies and limited partnerships mentioned in Annex I are obliged to draw up (Article 20(1)(g).

3.68b The annual financial statements and the management report must be published within 'a reasonable period of time' but not later than twelve months after the balance sheet date (Article 30). Simultaneously, the opinion submitted by the statutory auditor or audit firm must be published (Article 30(1)). Here again, the 2013 Directive

145. Dániel Gergely Szabó and Karsten Engsig Sørensen, New EU Directive on the Disclosure of Non-Financial Information (CSR), *ECFR* 2015, 307–340.

allows for simplifications and exceptions for micro, small and medium-sized undertakings, not being public-interest entities.[146]

4 *Perspectives*

3.69 Because the 2013 Directive contains many options, the results of implementation by the Member States will be far from uniform. Options are mentioned in the Preamble and are offered by many of the provisions, for instance, in Articles 6–8. Undoubtedly, the internationalization of the economy and the capital markets will remain a stimulus for further harmonization. Worth mentioning here is the influence of IFRS, which apply to the financial statements of listed companies in the EU (*see* paragraph 9.06).

H Statutory Audits [Eighth Directive]

3.70 The original audit directive, the Eighth Directive, dates from 1984 and concerns the qualifications of persons entitled to carry out the statutory audits of accounting documents. The aim was to ensure independence and good reputation of auditors, as well as a high level of theoretical knowledge and the ability to apply that knowledge in practice.[147] Since then, the Commission put forward several communications and recommendations, aiming at modernizing and strengthening the statutory audit process for company accounts (financial reporting).[148] Corporate scandals such as Parmalat and Ahold, and the initiatives taken in the United States (SOX 2002) have led to the introduction of a new Directive, which has been amended.

3.71 The first new Directive 2006/43/EC, pursuing a legislative strategy to offer more clarity, was proposed by the Commission in 2004 and approved by EP in 2005.[149] Consequently, the original Eighth Directive was repealed.[150] Two further developments concerning statutory audits date to March 2008 and April 2014. On the one hand, Directive 2008/30/EC[151] adjusted a series of references, the effects of which were

146. Articles 31, 36 and 40.
147. Eight Council Directive of 10 Apr. 1984 on the Approval of persons responsible for carrying out the statutory audits of accounting documents *(EEC) 84/253,* OJ, 1984 L 126. *See also* Van Hulle, *Company Law, Council Directive (EEC) 84/253, Commentary*.
148. Statutory audit in the European Union, the way forward, *OJ* 1998, C 143 of 8 May 1998) (Communication), Recommendation 2001/256/EC on quality assurance for the statutory audit in the European Union: minimum requirements, Recommendation 2002/590/EC – Statutory Auditors' Independence in the EU: A Set of Fundamental Principles, Reinforcing the Statutory audit in the European Union, *OJ* 2003, C 236 of 2 Oct. 2003) (Communication), Preventing and combating corporate and financial malpractice 2004 (Communication).
149. Brussels 30 Sep. 2005, 2004/0065(COD).
150. Directive 2006/43/EC of 17 May 2006 on statutory audits and consolidated accounts, amending Directives 78/660/EEC and 83/349/EEC and repealing Directive 84/253/EEC.
151. Directive 2008/30/EC of 11 Mar. 2008 amending Directive 2006/43/EC on statutory audits of annual accounts and consolidated accounts, as regards the implementing powers conferred on the Commission, *OJ* 2008 L 81 53–56.

mainly technical in nature. On the other hand, Directive 2014/56/EU[152] thoroughly amended the 2006 Directive and provided a link with Regulation 537/2014 on specific requirements regarding statutory audit of public-interest entities. The goal behind the 2014 Directive was to reinforce investor confidence in the financial statements' truth and fairness, by, *inter alia*, (a) increasing transparency, predictability, independence and objectivity with reference to the auditing process, (b) increasing public oversight of statutory auditors, and (c) reinforcing the credibility of audited financial statements of public-interest entities in consideration of their significant public relevance.

Thus, statutory audit in the EU is currently governed by the 2006 Directive, as amended by Directive 2014/56/EU and by Regulation 537/2014 on specific requirements regarding public-interest entities. Both documents entered into force in June 2014 and Member States had to implement new requirements by June 2016.[153]

3.72 The objective of the 2006 Directive is to achieve the application of a single set of international standards for the audit of annual (consolidated) financial statements and reports, where such audit is mandatory according to EU law and/or national law. Accordingly, one speaks of statutory audit. The main issues covered by the 2006 Directive are the educational qualifications of statutory auditors, their registration, professional ethics, independence and objectivity, quality assurance, public oversight over the audit profession and improving cooperation between oversight bodies in the EU.[154] The appointment and dismissal of auditors is also regulated, because it is related to their independence. Therefore, the statutory auditor shall be appointed by the general meeting of the company to be audited and dismissal is restricted to cases where there are 'proper grounds' for it. Diverging opinions on accounting matters, however, is not such a proper ground.[155] Furthermore, the directive requires that Member States ensure that each public-interest entity has an audit committee.[156]

3.72a As stated in Preamble (5), the directive aims at high level, though not full, harmonization of statutory audit requirements. This implies that Member States may impose requirements that are more stringent, unless the directive provides otherwise. The directive facilitates the operation of auditors on an EU-wide basis, because audit qualifications obtained by statutory auditors based on the directive are considered equivalent between the Member States. Consequently, Member States may no longer insist that locally-approved auditors hold a majority of the voting rights in an audit firm.[157] Furthermore, the directive does not itself deal with all issues regarding the statutory audit, but empowers the Commission to provide for, *inter alia*, the adoption of international auditing standards.[158]

152. Directive 2014/56/EU of 16 Apr. 2014 amending Directive 2006/43/EC on statutory audits of annual accounts and consolidated accounts, *OJ* 2014 L 158 196–226.
153. http://ec.europa.eu/finance/auditing/directives/index_en.htm
154. Articles 6–13, 15–20, 21–22, 29, 32–36 Directive 2006/43/EC as amended.
155. Articles 37 and 38 Directive 2006/43/EC as amended. According to Article 38(3) claims can be brought before a national court for the dismissal of a statutory auditor, *inter alia*, by minority shareholders (5%).
156. Article 39 Directive 2006/43/EC as amended.
157. Preamble recital 6 and Article 3(4), Directive 2006/43/EC as amended.
158. Articles 26 and 48a, Directive 2006/43/EC as amended.

3.73 The 2006 Directive requires Member States to designate competent authorities that will be responsible for approving statutory auditors and audit firms (Article 3(2)). An individual may only be approved to carry out a statutory audit if he or she has attained university entrance or an equivalent level, then completed a course of theoretical instruction, undergone practical training and passed an examination of professional competence of a university final or an equivalent examination level, organized or recognized by the Member State concerned (Article 6). The directive is very detailed when it comes to theoretical knowledge to be tested in the examination (Article 8). Member States must establish a procedure for the approval of statutory auditors who have been approved in other Member States, but these procedures may not go beyond an aptitude test or an adaptation period (which may not exceed three years). The test must be conducted in one of the languages permitted by the Member State concerned and only cover knowledge of the laws and regulations of that Member State, insofar these are relevant for the statutory audit (Article 14). Auditors and audit firms must be registered in a public register.[159] Member States must ensure that such register is electronically accessible by the public (Article 15). Member States must further ensure the independence of auditors by not allowing 'any existing or potential conflict of interest or business or other direct or indirect relationship involving the statutory auditor or the audit firm carrying out the statutory audit (...)' (Article 22(1)).

3.74 Member States must ensure that there are effective systems of investigations and sanctions to detect, correct and prevent inadequate execution of the statutory audit (Article 30(1)). Member States must also organize an effective system of public oversight for statutory auditors and shall designate a competent authority responsible for such oversight (Article 32). These systems must be enabled to cooperate at the EU level (Article 33).

3.74a As already mentioned, Regulation 537/2014 requires Member States to introduce stricter requirements regarding the statutory audit of public-interest entities (listed companies, credit institutions and insurance undertakings).[160] Among these is the prohibition for the statutory auditor or audit firm to provide non-audit services to the audited entity or, if the entity is part of a group, to other entities within the group. A long list of non-audit services is specified by the Regulation. Included are, for instance, bookkeeping, the preparation of financial statements, implementation of internal control or risk management procedures in relation to financial information and certain legal services (Article 5(1)). Furthermore, auditors and audit firms must rotate, because their engagement with an audited entity may not exceed ten years (or less, if so determined by a Member State). After expiry of such period, reappointment is not allowed for a period of four years (Article 17). These and other subjects dealt with by the Regulation aim at safeguarding the independence of the statutory auditor. Payment

159. It is possible to derogate to this provision and Article 16 under exceptional circumstances, when and to the extent to it is necessary to mitigate an imminent and significant threat to the personal security of any person (Article 15(1)).

160. Article 3, Regulation (EU) 537/2014, OJ 27.5.2014, L 158/77, refers to Directive 2006/34 for definitions.

for non-audit services may indeed compromise such independence.[161] Mandatory rotation is based on the assumption that auditors will become more trusting of clients over time, lessening their professional scepticism. The requirement that statutory auditors of listed companies rotate already featured in the 2002 US Sarbanes-Oxley Act (section 203). The effects of rotation may, however, be less beneficial than regulators assume.[162]

3.75 Member States must respect the principle of home country regulation and oversight by other Member States (Article 34). In cases of statutory audits of consolidated financial statements, Member States may not impose additional requirements in relation to the statutory auditor or audit firm carrying out a statutory audit of a subsidiary established in another Member State (Article 34(2)). Where securities of a company are traded on a regulated market in a Member State other than the one where the company has its registered office, a similar rule applies. The Member State where the securities are traded may not impose additional requirements in relation to the statutory auditor or audit firm carrying out the statutory audit of the annual or consolidated financial statements of the company (Article 34(3)).

I Branches: Disclosure Requirements [Eleventh Directive]

3.76 The Eleventh Directive concerns the harmonization of disclosure requirements with respect to branches opened in a Member State by certain types of company governed by the law of another State.[163] The opening of a branch, like the creation of a subsidiary, is one of the possibilities open to companies in the exercise of their right of establishment in another Member State. The Eleventh Directive dates from 1989 and was enacted in order to remove disparities between branches and subsidiaries with respect to disclosure requirements. The previous national provisions on documents relating to branches could no longer be justified in light of the coordination of national laws regarding the drawing up, audit and disclosure of documents by companies. To these ends, the directive contains several provisions in cases where a company to which the First Directive applies (public company, private company, limited

161. Domenico Campa & Ray Donnelly (2016) Non-audit services provided to audit clients, independence of mind and independence in appearance: latest evidence from large UK listed companies, *Accounting and Business Research*, 46:4, 422–449, DOI: 10.1080/00014788.2015.1048772. Further, several measures securing the quality of statutory audit are perceived as 'regulatory overreacting': Vivien Beattie, Stella Fearnley & Tony Hines (2013) Perceptions of factors affecting audit quality in the post-SOX UK regulatory environment, *Accounting and Business Research*, 43:1, 56–81, DOI:0.1080/00014788.2012.703079. Christoph van der Elst, 'The European Legislative Framework for Audit Committees', *ECL* 12, no. 1 (2015), pp. 26–33, doubts whether the regulatory framework will lead to the goal the EU is aiming for.

162. Kendall O. Bowlin, Jessen L. Hobson & M. David Piercey, 'The Effects of Auditor Rotation, Professional Skepticism, and Interactions with Managers on Audit Quality', *The Accounting Review*: July 2015 90, no. 4, pp. 1363–1393.

163. Eleventh Council Directive of December 1989 concerning disclosure requirements in respect of branches opened in a Member State by certain types of company governed by the law of another State (EEC) 89/666, *OJ* 1989, L395.

partnership with shares) opens a branch. The documents and particulars with respect to a branch subject to compulsory disclosure are limited to those enumerated in Articles 2 and 3. The Eleventh Directive was amended in 2012 with reference to the system of interconnection of central, commercial and companies registers,[164] along the lines of the changes also made to the First and Tenth Directives. Hence, the documents and particulars concerned by the Directive must be made publicly available through such system, and branches must have a unique identifier comprising the Member State of the register, the domestic register of origin and the branch number in that register (Article 1(3–4)). As previously mentioned, in December 2015, the Commission put forward a proposal for a Directive relating to the codification of parts of European company law,[165] which would encompass the Eleventh Directive as well.

3.77 Among the documents and particulars to be disclosed are the address and the activities of the branch, the name and the legal form of the company and the register, in which the company file is kept. Furthermore, the appointment and termination of office of the persons who are authorized to represent the company and the accounting documents of the company are drawn up, audited and disclosed pursuant to the law of the Member State by which the company is governed (Articles 2 and 3). However, the Member State in which the branch has been opened may stipulate that the accounting documents be published in another official language of the Community and that the translation of such documents ought to be certified (Article 4). Pursuant to Article 5(a), information on any winding-up or insolvency proceedings and on the striking off of the company from the register must be made available through the system of interconnection of registers, if they have legal consequences in the relevant Member State; in turn, the register of the branch must ensure the information is received without delay and free of charge.

3.78 The directive deals with branches of companies from third countries by requiring that similar particulars and documents be disclosed as required for branches of companies from Member States (Articles 7–9). Where the accounting documents are not drawn up in accordance with or in a manner equivalent to the Fourth and Seventh Directives (now Directive 2013/34/EU), a Member State may require that accounting documents relating to branch activities be drawn up or disclosed (Article 9).

3.79 Article 11a relates the processing of personal data required by this Directive to the scope of Directive 95/46/EC on the protection of individuals with regard to the processing of personal data and on the free movement of such data, the so-called Data Protection Directive.

3.80 Each Member State determines who will carry out the disclosure formalities (Article 13). Appropriate penalties must be provided for in the event of failure to disclose the matters set out in the directive (Article 12). The directive does not apply to

164. Directive 2012/17/EU of 13 Jun. 2012, *OJ* 2012, L 156/1.
165. European Commission. *Proposal for a Directive of the European Parliament and of the Council Relating to Certain Aspects of Company Law (Codification)*. COM (2015) 616final, https://ec.europa.eu/transparency/regdoc/rep/1/2015/EN/1-2015-616-EN-F1-1.PDF.

branches opened by certain credit institutions and financial institutions and need not apply to branches opened by insurance companies (Article 14). For these sectors, specific European measures have been projected or already adopted.

J Single-Member Private Limited Liability Companies [Twelfth Directive]

3.81 Traditionally, national laws have regarded companies as a form of cooperation between two or more persons. For instance, the formation of a private company required a minimum of two persons, or, in the case of a public company, sometimes even more.[166] However, if only one person is economically involved, the requirement of multiple shareholderships does not reflect reality.

3.82 In some Member States, it was not illegal for a company to have only one member subsequent to its formation. In the Netherlands, an entrepreneur often formed a company with the help of an assistant, who received one share. This share was transferred to the entrepreneur immediately after the formation was completed. Eventually the Dutch statute was altered and the formation of a company by one person became allowed in 1987. In Germany, the single-member private company arrived on the scene even earlier. The GmbHGesetz was altered in 1980 and since that time has contained several specific provisions for the single-member company.[167] In 1994, Germany also allowed for a single-member AG (often mentioned as the *kleine* AG).[168] In the UK, a single-member company was not illegal, although it could be wound up on that ground and problems were encountered, such as the impossibility to hold an annual general meeting because of the requirement of two members to constitute such a meeting.[169] These problems could be avoided if the single member transferred a share to some other person, who held the share as his nominee. Taking this into account, the special rules for single-member companies were sometimes pointed at as 'little short of farcical, and (...) merely a trap for the unwary'.[170] As national legal systems were becoming more and more accustomed to the concept of single membership, in line with a general tendency to hurdle corporate forms with the task of offering undertakings competitive advantages, European institutions were prompted to tackle the issue at a supranational level.

3.83 The Twelfth Directive has been adopted to eliminate divergences in the legislation of Member States with respect to the single-member company.[171] It requires Member States to allow for the single-member private company, in order to enable the individual entrepreneur to enjoy limited liability by incorporating his business.

166. Grundmann, *European Company Law: Organization, Finance and Capital Markets*, nr. 324.
167. § 1 GmbHG. Karsten Schmidt, *Gesellschaftsrecht*, 4. Auflage (Köln/Berlin/Bonn/ München: Carl Heymanns Verlag, 2002), 1243.
168. AktG § 42; Drucksache 12/6721 (1994).
169. Companies Act 198, s. 366 as before amendments.
170. John Murray, 'New Concepts in Corporate Law', in *Corporate Law, the European Dimension*, eds Philip Bentley et al. (London/Dublin/Edinburgh/Munich: Butterworth, 1991), 19.
171. Twelfth Council Company Law Directive of 21 Dec. 1989 on single-member private limited liability companies (EEC) 89/667, OJ 1990, C 240/7.

Accordingly, its application is confined to private companies, but it also applies to public limited companies if a Member State allows such a company to have a sole member (Article 6.). After its adoption in 1989, the Twelfth Directive was amended several times. The original Directive and the amendments were codified by Directive 2009/102/EC.[172] The new Directive fully preserved the original content from a substantive point of view. It must be noted here that in 2014, the Commission presented a proposal for a Directive on single-member private limited liability companies, the so-called SUP (Societas Unius Personae) proposal, which will be dealt with in Chapter 4 (paragraph 4.47). The proposed SUP, however, will not pre-empt the 2009 Directive, because the SUP only represents a specific form of private limited liability companies.

3.83a According to the 2009 Directive:

- A company may have a sole member when it is formed and when all its shares come to be held by a single person (Article 2(1)).
- Particulars stating that a company has become a single-member company, together with the identity of the sole member, must be filed or registered and publicized (Article 3).
- The sole member shall exercise the powers of the general meeting and decisions taken in this capacity shall be recorded in minutes or drawn up in writing (Article 4).
- Contracts between the sole member and the company as represented by him shall also be recorded in minutes or drawn up in writing. Member States need not apply this to current operations concluded under normal conditions (Article 2).
- Member States may maintain special provisions or sanctions for cases where a natural person is the single member of several companies ('one person group') or where a single-member company is the sole member of a company (Article 5).

3.83b Some Member States offer an alternative for the formation of a single-member company by providing that an entrepreneur may set up an undertaking the liability of which is limited to a sum dedicated to a stated activity. The safeguards laid down for such undertakings must be equivalent to those imposed by the Directive in regard to companies (Article 7). Accordingly, if a Member States allows for this alternative, the sole entrepreneur can separate his personal liability from the one of his business. An example is the French regime laid down in the Commercial Code, Article L526-6 *et seq.* (*l'entrepreneur individuel à responsabilité limitée*).[173]

172. Directive 2009/102/EC of 16 Sep. 2009 in the area of company law on single-member private limited liability companies (codified version), OJ 2009, L 258, 1 Oct. 2009, 20–25.
173. Another example of such an alternative is the 1986 Portuguese legislation concerning the '*estabelecimento mercantil individual de responsabilidade limitada*'.

K Takeover Bids [Thirteenth Directive]

3.84 The most common method of gaining control over a company has always been the takeover, that is, the acquisition of the shares of that company in such quantity, as represents at least a controlling percentage of the voting rights. In its White Paper, which focused on completing the internal market, the Commission announced the harmonization of laws of Member States on takeover and other general bids. The purpose was to create a level playing field for takeovers within the single market. The Commission viewed takeovers in a positive light, insofar as they encourage the selection by market forces of the most competitive companies. Consequently, a proposal for the Thirteenth Directive was launched in order to remove the various obstacles to the aforementioned 'field' for takeover bids.[174] The proposal initiated a lengthy debate, which came to a conclusion only by the 2002 *Report on Issues Related to Takeover Bids* by a High Level Group of Company Law Experts installed by the Commission after the rejection of the draft directive by the EP.[175] The mandate of the group was to review whether and to what extent a level playing field for takeover bids could and should be created. The group assessed the mechanisms and structures under company law, which may frustrate or inhibit takeover bids. It was recommended that two principles should guide the creation of a level playing field. Firstly, shareholder decision-making should be decisive in the event of a takeover bid and, secondly, there must be proportionality between risk-bearing capital and control. The latter principle means that share capital, which has an unlimited right to participate in the profits of the company or in the residue on liquidation, should normally carry rights (voting power) to ultimately control the company in proportion to the risk carried.[176]

3.84a The first proposal for a Thirteenth Directive was launched in 1989 and provoked strong reactions, particularly because it was supposed to open the door to hostile takeovers by blocking certain defensive measures. It was argued that only companies that have to resort to legal defensive measures will be exposed to hostile takeovers as a consequence of the directive, whereas institutional defences, such as crossholdings existing in other Member States, were not covered by the directive.[177] After delivering its first report on issues related to the Thirteenth Directive ('Takeover Directive'), the mandate of the High Level Group was extended by the Commission, in

174. Obstacles to takeover and other general bids. Communication from the Commission lo the Council (COM (88)823 final) and: Amended proposal for a Thirteenth Council Directive on Company Law concerning takeover and other general bids, OJ 1990, C 240/7.
175. Press release IP/01/1237 of 4 Sep. 2001.
176. *Report on Issues Related to Takeover Bids* (Brussels: 10 Jan. 2002), 2–3. *See* http://ec.europa.eu/internal_market/company/docs/modern/report_en.pdf. The Takeover Directive is criticized for being focused on shareholder primacy, thereby neglecting CSR aspects, Beate Sjåfjell, *Towards a Sustainable European Company Law* (Alphen aan den Rijn: Kluwer Law International, 2009).
177. OJ 1989, C 64, 14 Mar. 1989, 8; with explanatory memorandum, Suppl. 3/89 – Bull. EC. J.M.M. Maeijer & K. Geens (eds), *Defensive Measures Against Hostile Takeovers in the Common Market* (Dordrecht/Boston/London: Springer, 1990). K. Byttebier, 'Protective and Defensive Measures Against Hostile Take-Overs', in *Further Perspectives in Financial Integration in Europe*, ed. Eddy Wymeersch (Berlin/New York: 1994), 181.

order to deal with a number of corporate governance issues, which resulted in a second report: *A Modern Regulatory Framework for Company Law in Europe*.[178] The Directive was finally adopted in April 2004[179] as Directive 2004/25/EC. Five years later, it was amended by Regulation (EC) No. 219/2009[180] and, lastly, it was amended in 2014, by Directive 2014/59/EU,[181] the so-called 'Bank Recovery and Resolution Directive' (BRRD).

3.85 Within the scope of the Thirteenth Directive are takeover bids for the securities of companies governed by the laws of Member States, where all or some of those securities are listed on a regulated market. The directive does not apply to takeover bids for securities issued by collective investment companies and the Member States' central banks (Article 1). By implementing the directive, Member States must comply with a set of general principles. These are laid down in Article 3:

(a) all holders of securities of an offeree company of the same class are to be treated equally and if a person acquires control of a company the other holders must be protected;[182]
(b) the addressees of a bid must have sufficient time and information to enable them to reach a properly informed decision on the bid;
(c) the board of an offeree company acts in the interests of the company as a whole and must not deny the holders of securities the opportunity to decide on the merits of the bid;
(d) false markets must not be created in the securities of the offeree company, of the offeror company, or of any other company concerned by the bid;
(e) an offeror must announce a bid only after ensuring that he can fulfil in full any cash consideration if such consideration is offered and after taking all reasonable measures to secure the implementation of a consideration in securities or a combination of cash and securities;[183]
(f) an offeree company must not be hindered in the conduct of its affairs for longer than is reasonable by a bid for its securities.[184]

178. Brussels, 4 Nov. 2002.
179. Directive 2004/25/EC of 21 Apr. 2004 on takeover bids. OJ 2004 L 142 12–23.
180. Regulation (EC) No. 219/2009 of 11 Mar. 2009 adapting a number of instruments subject to the procedure referred to in Article 251 of the Treaty to Council Decision 1999/468/EC with regard to the regulatory procedure with scrutiny. OJ 2009 L 87 109–154.
181. Directive 2014/59/EU of 15 May 2014 establishing a framework for the recovery and resolution of credit institutions and investment firms and amending Council Directive 82/891/EEC, and Directives 2001/24/EC, 2002/47/EC, 2004/25/EC, 2005/56/EC, 2007/36/EC, 2011/35/EU, 2012/30/EU and 2013/36/EU, and Regulations (EU) No 1093/2010 and (EU) 648/2012, OJ 2014 L 173 190–348.
182. The principle of equal treatment of shareholders bans price differentiation in a takeover situation. *See* Rolf Skog & Erik Lidman, *Equal Treatment of Shareholders – Can There Be Too Much of It?*, Nordic & European Company Law LSN Research Paper Series No. 16–15, https://papers.ssrn.com/abstract=2878773 on the principle's background and its negative effect on furthering long-term shareholder engagement as proposed in 2014/0121 (COD).
183. Article 5(5) allows for such consideration.
184. Terminology used is defined by Article 2.

3.86 One of the main provisions of the Thirteenth Directive concerns the mandatory bid. Any person who has acquired a specified percentage of the voting rights in a company, giving that person control of that company, is obliged to make a bid with a view to acquire all the securities of that company at an equitable price (Article 5(1)). The percentage of voting rights representing control of the company shall be determined by the rules of the Member State in which the company has its registered office (Article 5(3)). The decision to launch a bid, whether mandatory or not, must be made public without delay and the supervisory authority of the Member State(s) concerned must be informed. This must be followed, in good time, by the publication of the offer document containing the information necessary for the holders of securities to decide on the bid. The offer document, however, must first be communicated to the supervisory authority (Article 6). Article 6(3) provides for a list of the minimum information that must be encompassed by the offer document. Pursuant to Article 6(4), amended in 2009, the Commission is allowed to modify non-essential elements of the list (and of the Directive itself) in compliance with the regulatory procedure with scrutiny entailed by Article 18(2) and involving the European Securities Committee (ESC) established in 2001 (Article 18(1)).

After the 2014 amendment, a derogation to Article 5(1) of the Directive is provided in case of use of resolution tools, powers and mechanisms, provided for by Title IV of Directive 2014/59/EU (Article 4(5)).

3.86a The mandatory bid is designed to prevent speculative bids and to ensure protection for persons who hold a minority of the shares (securities). Member States are free to establish further instruments for the protection of (minority) holders of securities. They may, for example, require a partial bid in the event that the offeror does not acquire control of the company (Preamble, paragraph 9). The equitable price mentioned in Article 5(1) equals the highest price paid by the offeror for the same securities over a period between six and twelve months before the bid. Member States may authorize the supervisory authority to adjust the price under clearly determined circumstances, such as where market prices of the securities have been affected by exceptional occurrences (Article 5(4)).

3.87 From the moment that the decision to make a bid is made public, the board of the offeree company must obtain prior authority of the general meeting of shareholders before taking any action that may result in the frustration of the bid, with the exception of the seeking of alternative bids (Article 9). The board of the offeree company must publicize a document expressing its opinion on the bid (Article 9(5)).

3.87a The offeree board's opinion should include its views on the effects of implementation of the bid on all company interests, specifically employment. It should also consider the offeror's strategic plans for the company and the likely repercussions on employment and the locations of the company's places of business, as set out in the offer document. At the same time, the board of the offeree company shall communicate that opinion to the representatives of its employees or, where there are no such representatives, to the employees themselves. Where the offeree company board receives, in good time, a separate opinion from the representatives of its employees on the effects of the bid on employment, that opinion is to be appended to the document (Article 9(5)).Where a company has a two-tier board structure, 'board' shall mean both the management board and the supervisory board (Article 9(6)).

3.88 Arrangements predating the bid may also have a frustrating effect. Therefore, Article 11 of the directive provides for a 'breakthrough' on this matter. Restrictions on the transfer of securities stemming from the articles or from contractual arrangements shall not apply vis-à-vis the offeror during the time allowed for acceptance of the bid. Restrictions on voting rights shall not have any effect at the general meeting of shareholders that decides on any defensive measures and multiple voting rights shall carry only one vote at that meeting. Once the offeror holds 75% or more of the capital carrying voting rights, the same applies at the first general meeting, following the closure of the bid called by the offeror in order to amend the articles or to remove or appoint board members. The Member States must determine the terms for the compensation that must be provided for any loss suffered by the holders of the rights set aside by the breakthrough (*see also* Article 12(1)).

3.89 Member States may reserve the right not to require companies having their registered office within their territories to apply the restrictions set by Articles 9 and 11 (Article 12). Consequently, boards of offeree companies are free to use defensive mechanisms after a bid is launched and the breakthrough rule would not apply. Member States opting out must, nevertheless, grant domestic companies the option of applying the aforementioned restrictions. Companies may thus 'opt in' for the basic approach of the directive, which is not to allow for defensive measures after a bid is made public and not to block decisions by the new controlling shareholder. The decision to opt in must be taken at the general meeting of shareholders and must be communicated to the national supervisory authority and to all supervisory authorities of Member States in which the securities of such a company are listed. However, such an 'unprotected' company should not be defenceless against a takeover bid by a 'protected' company. Therefore, Member States may introduce a reciprocity rule by exempting 'opt in' companies from applying the restrictions of Articles 9 and 11 if they become the subject of an offer by a company that does not apply the same articles as they do.[185]

L Proposal for a Directive on the Transfer of the Registered Office [Fourteenth Directive]

3.90 Already by 1997, public consultations made the Commission aware of 'a pressing need' for EU legislation to allow companies to transfer their registered office from one Member State to another without having to be wound up in their home Member State. Winding up in the home Member State and subsequently acquiring legal personality in another Member State is prone to both legal and tax complications.

185. Peter Callens et. al., Country Status Reports on defensive measures against hostile takeovers and the impact of the 13th EC Directive, *ECL* 2004/1.

These can be avoided by enabling the transfer of the registered office, which allows companies to adapt their location and organizational structure by choosing the most appropriate national law.[186] The issue of recognition and retention of legal personality is at the core of European company law and is related to the question concerning the *lex societatis*, i.e., what is the applicable law to a specific company? It is also linked to the incorporation versus real seat theory debate, the latter posing most of the hindrances to cross-border mobility and freedom of establishment.

In the 1988 *Daily Mail* case, the ECJ had held that a transfer of the registered office cannot be based on the right of establishment as laid down in Article 43 EC Treaty (now Article 49 TFEU) without further legislation.[187] Therefore, the Commission in its 2003 company law Action Plan put the drafting of the Fourteenth Directive dealing with seat transfer high on its list of priorities.[188] In 2004, the Commission put forward an outline of a draft for a Fourteenth Directive,[189] according to which, each Member State would be obliged to recognize the right of a company to transfer its registered office, if the proper procedural rules have been complied with.

3.90a What are the main features of the 2004 outline? The decision to transfer the registered office should be taken at the general meeting and must be publicized in advance. The decision should include alterations to the company's articles that are necessary for the company to become registered in the host Member State. Other requirements for registration may apply, for example, that the registered office and the real seat both be in the host Member State. This, of course, will be the case where the host Member State favours the real seat doctrine for domestic companies. The validity of the decisions taken by the general meeting must be supervised by the home Member State, while the host Member State supervises the substantive, formal and national procedural requirements for the company to be recognized as a legal person and to be registered. Supervision by the host Member State may, however, not result in requiring an act of incorporation. Finally, the transfer must be recorded in the registers of both Member States involved. Protection of the rights of minority shareholders and creditors will be similar to those offered by the Third Directive, the Tenth Directive and the SE statute (the SE may transfer its registered office). The transfer should be tax neutral and should have the same effects as a cross-border merger (now Directive 2009/133/EC). The role of employees should be governed by the legislation of the host Member State, unless the employees enjoy more rights in this respect in the home Member State. In such a case, the rights of employees should be maintained or negotiated.

186. Press Release, IP/04/270, Brussels, 26 Feb. 2004.
187. Case 81/87 (*Daily Mail*) [1988] ECR 5483. The ECJ has interpreted Article 43 EC Treaty in such a way as to enable the transfer of the *real seat* (or de facto seat) to a certain extent (*see* paragraphs 2.54 *et seq.*).
188. Communication from the Commission to the Council and the European Parliament – *Modernising Company Law and Enhancing Corporate Governance in the European Union – A Plan to Move Forward*, COM(2003)284.
189. The outline of the draft Fourteenth Directive is part of the 2004 consultation document, www.ec.europa.eu/internal_market/company/seat-transfer/2004-consult_en.htm.

3.91 The short-term priority of action in this field was confirmed by the 2006 consultation and hearing on future priorities for the Action Plan.[190] Despite the urgency perceived by the Commission, the responsible commissioner decided that there was no need for action at EU level, after an impact assessment on the planned directive was published by 2007. It was considered that the effects of the Tenth Directive on CBM were not yet known and that the issue of the transfer of the registered office might be cleared up by the ECJ in the near future.[191] Arguably, the foremost reason prompting these considerations is a perception of lack of political feasibility.[192] However, committees of the EP did not support this coming to a halt and suggested that a directive on the cross-border transfer of the registered office must be put forward in 2009.[193,194]

3.91a Such plans and initiatives were parallel to a series of decisions by the ECJ, which acted as a background for the legislative strategies, the importance of which is highlighted by the legislative vacuum. The cautious approach adopted in the *Daily Mail* case was partially altered in 2008 by the *Cartesio* decision,[195] although arguably with reference to the transfer of the de facto head office.[196] The ECJ prompted a small (even more so because it was made obiter dictum) but relevant shift in perspective: if a company is willing to change its nationality, and such a change is accepted by both the old and the new home Member State, it has the right to do so.[197] Later, in 2012, the *Vale* decision dealt with a company willing to move its registered seat from Italy to Hungary, the latter allowing for conversions of national companies – but not foreign companies. Although the Court reaffirmed the principle, according to which each Member State reserves the right to set the requirements applicable for a valid incorporation and lasting existence of an entity as a national company, this cannot be done at the expense of the principle of equivalence and equal treatment in cases of cross-border conversion. National and foreign companies must be treated equally when it comes to legal means to convert into another company, unless there are overriding considerations of public

190. Directorate-General for Internal Market and Services, *Summary Report on the Consultation on Future Priorities for the Action Plan on Company Law and Corporate Governance*, 34–35, www.ec.europa.eu/internal_market/company/consultation/index_en.htm.
191. According to the *Impact Assessment on the Directive on the Cross-border Transfer of Registered Office*, Commission Staff Working Document, Brussels, 12 Dec. 2007 SEC(2007) 1707. Philippe Pellé, 'Companies Crossing Borders within Europe', *European Company Law* 5, no. 6 (December 2008): 284–287.
192. Vossestein, G.J. 'Transfer of the Registered Office: The European Commission's Decision Not to Submit a Proposal for a Directive' *Utrecht Law Review* 4, no. 1 (2008), p. 58.
193. *Draft Report with recommendations to the Commission on cross-border transfers of company seats*, Committee on Legal Affairs, 17 Oct. 2008, 2008/2196(INI), preceded by the Draft Opinion of the Committee on Economic and Monetary Affairs, 23 Sep. 2008, 2008/2196(INI).
194. See: Vossestein, G.J. 'Transfer of the Registered Office. The European Commission's Decision Not to Submit a Proposal for a Directive' *Utrecht Law Review*, Volume 4 Issue 1, 2008.
195. Decision of 16 Dec. 2008 in case C-210/06, Cartesio, [2008] ECR I-9641.
196. The ECJ did not specifically refer to the real seat in its final ruling statements, along the same line adopted by the phrasing of the referred questions, but it did so in the previous paragraph 119, in accordance with what could be concluded by the facts of the case.
197. for more information concerning the limitations of the Cartesio decision, see: M. Szydlo, 'The Right of Companies to Cross-Border Conversion under the TFEU Rules on Freedom of Establishment' *European Company and Financial Law Review*, 3/2010, 414–443.

interest.[198] However, since secondary legislation is still deficient in this area, Member States have to apply their national law on the procedure. Since conversions do not belong to the sections of company law that are harmonized, this conclusion will not solve the problem on an EU scale. It illustrates the benefit that will be generated by an appropriate and certain supranational legislative framework.[199]

3.92 The EP repeatedly urged the Commission to take action in this area. In February 2012, a Resolution was adopted with the aim of offering recommendations concerning the adoption of a Fourteenth Directive. The Parliament highlighted the importance of offering a legally certain and safe company migration to effectively guarantee freedom of establishment, most notably after the ECJ's *Cartesio* decision. According to the Parliament's view, such legislative instrument should encompass an appropriate solution to the debate concerning the possibility of a separation between a company's registered office and its administrative seat. Furthermore, the transfer should not entail any circumvention of legal, social and fiscal conditions. More recommendations are offered in relation to, *inter alia*, transparency and information rules preceding the transfer decision, the shareholders' meeting's decision itself, and the question of rights of employees.[200]

3.93 In June 2012, the Parliament recalled its request for the adoption of a Fourteenth Directive,[201] and, in February 2013, it published a European Added Value Assessment (EAVA) on the directive.[202] The assessment was basically a call for action by the European Commission to put forward a proposal for a Fourteenth Directive and to provide for clarity, legal certainty, simplicity and transparency, on the grounds that current Member States practice still varies considerably in this area. The assessment outlines the way cross-border mobility (and its associated positive net economic impact) can be enhanced by such legislative program. It concludes that its adoption is inherently needed to grant freedom of establishment to European undertakings and to achieve the completion of the internal market.

3.94 In January 2013, the European Commission launched an online public consultation on the cross-border transfer of registered offices of companies, ending in April

198. For more information regarding the meaning of the principle of mutual recognition in this field, see: C. Behme, The Principle of Mutual Recognition in the European Internal Market with Special Regard to the Cross-Border Mobility of Companies, *European Company and Financial Law Review* 1/2016, 31–54.
199. J.L. Hansen, 'The Vale Decision and the Court's Case Law on the Nationality of Companies', *European Company and Financial Law Review* (1/2013): 1–17.
200. European Parliament. *Resolution of 2 February 2012 with recommendations to the Commission on a 14th company law directive on the cross-border transfer of company seats (2011/2046(INI))*. P7_TA(2012)0019.
201. European Parliament. *Resolution of 14 June 2012 on ' Single Market Act: The Next Step to Growth'*; paragraph 39.
202. Directorate for Impact Assessment and European Added Value, Directorate General for Internal Policies, European Parliament. *European Added Value Assessment. Directive on the cross-border transfer of a company's registered office 14th Company Law Directive*. February 2013. http://www.europarl.europa.eu/RegData/etudes/etudes/join/2013/494460/IPOL-JOIN_ET(2013)494460_EN.pdf (accessed 20 May 2016).

2013. A summary of responses was published in September 2013.[203] The consultation provided for a (partially) unsatisfactory sample of only 28 companies. Another 58 replies were provided by (mostly EU-wide) public and private organizations and centres. This is symbolic of how difficult it may be to get information and data pertaining to this issue, notably because a vast share of the responding companies had not transferred their registered offices in the previous three years and the majority declared they did not need to do so, they would not even consider it or did not have a clear view on the topic. Nevertheless, the overall impression was that a specific EU instrument would contribute to a significant reduction of transfer costs.

3.94a The Commission's wariness to submit further proposals is related to the fact that a supranational involvement in the field of cross-border transfer of the seat is bound to affect two legal areas, whose national character is traditionally important to Member States: board structures and employee participation. Although, eventually, these elements were no obstacle for the Tenth Directive on CBM, at the time of the 2013 consultation, the Commission had reached no decision in relation to legislative action in the field of seat transfer.

III SHAREHOLDERS' RIGHTS DIRECTIVE

3.95 One of the priorities of the 2003 Commission's Action Plan on modernizing company law and enhancing corporate governance was the improvement of the rights of shareholders of companies across the Member States.[204] To this end, the Shareholders Rights Directive was adopted in 2007.[205] The 2012 Action Plan on European company law and corporate governance[206] reiterated and furthered such priority, notably, by making the encouragement of long-term shareholder engagement one of the main concepts covered by the plan.

3.96 Similar to the Thirteenth Directive, the Shareholders Rights Directive applies exclusively to listed companies.[207] More precisely, this directive applies to companies that have their registered office in a Member State and whose shares are admitted for trading on a regulated market situated or operating within a Member State (Article 1(1)). Article 4 states that these companies must ensure equal treatment of

203. European Commission. *Feedback Statement: Summary of Responses to the Public Consultation on Cross-border transfers of registered offices of companies.* September 2003. http://ec.europa.eu/internal_market/consultations/2013/seat-transfer/docs/summary-of-responses_en.pdf (accessed 20 May 2016).
204. Communication from the Commission to the Council and the European Parliament – *Modernising Company Law and Enhancing Corporate Governance in the European Union – A Plan to Move Forward*, COM(2003)0284 final, paragraph 2.1.
205. Directive 2007/36/EC on the exercise of certain rights of shareholders in listed companies, OJ 2007, L 184, to be transposed into Member States' laws by 3 Aug. 2009.
206. European Commission. *Communication from the Commission to the European Parliament, the Council, the European Economic and Social Committee and the Committee of the Regions. Action Plan: European Company law and corporate governance – a modern legal framework for more engaged shareholders and sustainable companies.* COM (2012) 740 final.
207. Note that the Shareholders Rights Directive is not numbered, as the previous company law directives.

shareholders who are in the same position with regard to participation and the exercise of voting rights in the general meeting.[208] Obstacles to cross-border voting should be removed and the use of electronic means should be encouraged.[209] Cross-border investors should benefit from the directive's provisions and the costs for the digital exercise of shareholder rights may be reduced. Therefore:

- the directive pertains to information that has to be provided prior to the general meeting (Article 5);
- the right to put items on the agenda and to table draft resolutions (Article 6);
- the requirements for participation and voting in the general meeting (Article 7);
- participation in the general meeting by electronic means (Article 8);
- the right to ask questions (Article 8) and voting by proxy and by correspondence (Articles 9–12).

3.96a One of the issues that the directive is dealing with is how, and at which moment prior to the general meeting, shareholders can be identified. These rights shall be determined with respect to the shares held by a shareholder on a specified date prior to the general meeting (the record date). The directive allows Member States to set different record dates for companies that have issued bearer shares and for companies that have issued registered shares (Article 7). The directive further ensures that companies will have the option to offer participation in the general meeting by electronic means, notably (a) real-time transmission of the general meeting; and/or (b) real-time two-way communication, enabling shareholders to address the general meeting from a remote location; and/or (c) a mechanism for casting votes, whether before or during the general meeting, without the need to appoint a proxy holder, who is physically present at the meeting (Article 8). Regarding proxy voting, the directive provides that every shareholder shall have the right to appoint any other natural or legal person as a proxy holder to attend, participate and vote at a general meeting in his name. Nevertheless, Member States may put certain limitations to the use of proxies, for example, by limiting the number of proxy holders that may be appointed by one shareholder (Articles 10 and 11).

3.96b Recently, Articles 1 and 5 were amended by Directive 2014/59/EU, the so-called 'BRRD', whose goal was the creation of a framework for the recovery and resolution of (unsound or failing) credit institutions and investment firms, thereby restoring trust in banks after the financial crisis and maintaining financial stability across the EU and EEA. The amending directive introduced the possibility of appropriate derogations to the Shareholder Directive's minimum notice period for general meetings and the content of the notice, when there is a need for a rapid increase of capital and certain conditions are met (Article 1(4)). Shareholders shall retain the

208. *See also* Article 42 of the Second Directive: the laws of the Member State must ensure equal treatment of shareholders with respect to the issues the directive is dealing with.
209. Preamble (1) and (2).

decision-making power, by a majority of two-thirds, as far as the increase and the shortening of the notice period are concerned (Article 5(5)).[210]

3.97 Following a series of informal discussions with various stakeholders[211] and in line with the necessity to overcome certain corporate governance shortcomings with the aim of providing for long-term financing of the European economy,[212] in 2014, the European Commission presented a proposal[213] to revise Directive 2007/36/EC. On the same occasion, it adopted a Recommendation on the quality of corporate governance reporting (based on the 'comply or explain' principle).[214] The goal is to encourage and foster long-term shareholder involvement in publicly listed companies, as well as increasing information transparency. These recommendations serve to restrict the dangerously increasing instances of inadequate monitoring and short-termism, often associated with institutional investors and widely held companies.[215]

3.97a The impact assessment undertaken by the Commission had brought to light five major corporate governance issues:

(1) institutional investors and asset managers were insufficiently and sub-optimally engaged in monitoring their investee companies, which

210. Directive 2014/59/EU of 15 May 2014 establishing a framework for the recovery and resolution of credit institutions and investment firms and amending Council Directive 82/891/EEC, and Directives 2001/24/EC, 2002/47/EC, 2004/25/EC, 2005/56/EC, 2007/36/EC, 2011/35/EU, 2012/30/EU and 2013/36/EU, and Regulations (EU) No 1093/2010 and (EU) 648/2012, OJ 2014 L 173 190–348; recital 124.
211. European Commission. *Summary of the informal discussions concerning the initiative on shareholders engagement*. March 2013 http://ec.europa.eu/internal_market/company/docs/shareholders/120417_summary-initiative-shareholders-engagement_en.pdf.
212. European Commission. *Communication from the European Commission to the European Parliament and the Council on long-term financing of the European economy*, COM(2014) 168 final http://ec.europa.eu/internal_market/finances/docs/financing-growth/long-term/140327-communication_en.pdf
213. European Commission. *Proposal for a Directive of the European Parliament and of the Council amending Directive 2007/36/EC as regards the encouragement of long-term shareholder engagement and Directive 2013/34/EU as regards certain elements of the corporate governance statement*. COM(2014) 213 final. http://eur-lex.europa.eu/resource.html?uri = cellar:59fccf6c-c094-11e3-86f9-01aa75ed71a1.0003.05/DOC_1&format = PDF
214. Commission Recommendation of 9 Apr. 2014 on the quality of corporate governance reporting ('comply or explain'), 2014/208/EU.
215. Roger Barker, 'Ownership Structure and Shareholder Engagement: Reflections on the Role of Institutional Shareholders in the Financial Crisis', In: William Sun, Jim Stewart and David Pollard (eds), *Corporate Governance and the Global Financial Crisis* 1st edition, (Cambridge: Cambridge University Press, 2011); 146. *See also*: European Commission. *Commission Staff Working Document and Impact Assessment accompanying the document 'Proposal for a Directive of the European Parliament and of the Council on amending Directive 2007/36/EC as regards the encouragement of long-term shareholder engagement and Directive 2013/34/EU as regards certain elements of the corporate governance statement and Commission Recommendation on the quality of corporate governance reporting ('comply or explain')*. SWD (2014) 127 final http://eur-lex.europa.eu/legal-content/EN/TXT/PDF/?uri = CELEX:52014SC0127&qid = 1464678335506&from = EN [Accessed: 31 May 2016].

complemented a tendency for short-termism, due to a misalignment of interests of institutional investors, asset managers and companies;
(2) there was an insufficient link between directors' pay and performance, as well as an inappropriate level of disclosure of information in this area and insufficient tools for shareholders to express their opinion;
(3) shareholder oversight on related-party transactions was lacking because of insufficient disclosure obligations and inadequate tools to oppose possible abusive transactions;
(4) proxy advisors were increasingly influential, but insufficiently transparent and independent;
(5) rights flowing from securities were difficult and costly to exercise for investors, especially in cross-border situations, mainly due to lack of investor identification, untimely transmission of information and rights and price discriminations.[216]

3.97b The amending proposal is built around five main objectives:[217]

(1) to increase both level and quality of the engagement of institutional investors[218] and asset managers[219] within their investee companies;
(2) to improve the relationship between pay and performance of company directors, in compliance with the new Capital Requirements Directive and Regulation;[220]
(3) to strengthen shareholders' oversight and transparency on related-party transactions;
(4) to safeguard reliability and quality of advice of proxy advisors;
(5) to foster transmission of cross-border information, such as voting, notably through improved communication across the chain of intermediaries concerning shareholder identification.

216. European Commission. *Proposal for a Directive of the European Parliament and of the Council amending Directive 2007/36/EC as regards the encouragement of long-term shareholder engagement and Directive 2013/34/EU as regards certain elements of the corporate governance statement*. COM(2014) 213 final; pp. 4–5. On 12 May 2015, the European Parliament reported on the proposal and on 14 Mar. 2017, the amended proposal is adopted http://www.europarl.europa.eu/sides/getDoc.do?pubRef=-//EP//TEXT+TA+P8-TA-2017-0067+0–DOC+XML+V0//EN#BKMD-5.
217. European Commission. *Proposal for a Directive of the European Parliament and of the Council amending Directive 2007/36/EC as regards the encouragement of long-term shareholder engagement and Directive 2013/34/EU as regards certain elements of the corporate governance statement*. COM(2014) 213 final; p. 2.
218. defined as insurance companies and pension funds, *see* Article 1 of the amending Directive, introducing Article 2(f).
219. UCITS (Undertakings for Collective Investments in Transferable Securities) and AIFS (Alternative Investment Funds).
220. Directive 2013/36/EU and Regulation (EU) No 575/2013.

3.97c The strategy to achieve these results without imposing disproportionate burdens encompasses the following five actions:[221]

(1) to impose mandatory transparency mechanisms on institutional investors and asset managers concerning their engagement, their voting and certain asset management arrangements' aspects; they are required to develop a publicly available engagement policy, institutional investors must also disclose an investment strategy and asset managers must report on its implementation, notably focusing on assets' medium to long-term performance (Articles 3f, 3g and 3h);
(2) to introduce disclosure on both policy remuneration and individual remunerations, as well as a shareholder vote: establishment of the so-called say-on-pay scheme, i.e., granting shareholders the right to vote[222] on the directors' remuneration policy on a three-year basis (Articles 9a and 9b);
(3) to introduce additional transparency requirements and independent opinions on the most important related-party transactions, combined with a mandatory submission of the most substantial transactions to shareholder approval: under the proposed framework material, transactions with related parties are subject to approval of the shareholders or supervisory board (Article 9c);
(4) to provide for binding disclosure requirements on both the methodology and possible conflicts of interests of proxy advisors:[223] they are required to disclose information on their voting recommendations, notably, on any actual or potential conflict of interest or business relationship that may influence their recommendations (Article 3i);[224]
(5) to set up a framework, in order to allow publicly listed companies to identify their shareholders, which is complemented by a requirement for

221. European Commission. *Proposal for a Directive of the European Parliament and of the Council amending Directive 2007/36/EC as regards the encouragement of long-term shareholder engagement and Directive 2013/34/EU as regards certain elements of the corporate governance statement*. COM(2014) 213 final; pp. 5 and 6.
222. Under the framework of the original proposal Member States were retaining the right to determine whether such vote was advisory or binding, but later on the European Parliament rejected a binding vote.
223. according to the Presidential Compromise Proposal [For later developments *see* Interinstitutional File 2014/0121 (COD), *inter alia* the latest Presidency compromise text, Council of the European Union, 14 Jan. 2015, 5215/15 [Presidential Compromise Proposal] and the Presidency compromise text Brussels, 5 Dec. 2014, 15647/14, the Presidency compromise text Brussels, 10 Nov. 2014, 13758/14], a proxy advisor is defined as '*a legal person that analyses, on a professional basis, the corporate disclosures of listed companies with a view to informing investors' voting decisions by providing research, advice or voting recommendations that relate specifically to the exercise of voting rights*' for an analysis of the current role and influence of proxy advisors *see* https://europeancompanylawexperts.wordpress.com/papers/shareholder-engagement-and-identification-february-2015.
224. For more information concerning the important role proxy advisors play in the corporate governance of listed companies, also in relation with the Commission's proposal, see: A. Gallego Córcoles, 'Proxy Advisors in the Voting Process: Some Considerations for Future Regulation in Europe'. *European Company and Financial Law Review* (1/2016): 106–156.

intermediaries to efficiently and timely transmit shareholders-related information to facilitate the exercise of shareholder rights (Article 3a–3c).

3.98 It remains to be seen whether the proposed amendments will be adopted and will truly hold the potential to solve agency problems caused by frequent misalignments of interests between owners and managers, thus reducing excessively risky conduct and foster active engagement, or if they would hinder engagement, notably in consideration of institutional investors' fiduciary duties towards their investors.[225] Besides the question whether the actions proposed by the Commission are to be assessed as effective to the end of upholding the long-term performance of an undertaking, there is widespread agreement as to the detrimental impact of corporate short-termism on both the companies themselves and the capital market at large. It has been argued that introducing incentives for managers to favour the interests of long-term shareholders – i.e., giving this category of shareholders more power in the company – may actually lead, in time and under some circumstances, to a reduction in the value generated by the undertaking, thus shrinking the so-called economic pie.[226,227]

3.99 Nevertheless, the main issue that was raised in response to the Commission's proposal was that shareholder empowerment alone does not hold the potential to improve corporate governance, thereby providing effective solutions to the underlying causes of corporate short-termism and boosting European sustainable growth.[228] The interests of non-shareholder stakeholders were highlighted as a topic to be taken into consideration in the context of the long-term versus short-term shareholders debate, as well as managerial agency costs.[229,230] Besides suppressing the current shareholder-centric approach to better governance, it was argued that the plan should encompass,

225. Against the idea that shareholders actually own companies: Jo Andrew Johnston, Paige Morrow & Frank Bold, 'Commentary On The Shareholder Rights Directive' *LSN Research Paper Series* No. 15-13, (University of Oslo 2014); p. 1. Further: Roger Barker, Ownership Structure and Shareholder Engagement: Reflections on the Role of Institutional Shareholders in the Financial Crisis, *Corporate Governance and the Global Financial Crisis*, 1st edition (Cambridge University Press, 2011), 144. *See* on shareholder engagement also the paper by a group of European company law experts, via: https://europeancompanylawexperts.wordpress.com/papers/shareholder-engagement-and-identification-february-2015.

226. In support of this view see: J.M. Fried, 'The Uneasy Case for Favoring Long-Term Shareholders', *The Yale Law Journal* 124 (2015): 1554–1627, http://www.yalelawjournal.org/pdf/e.1554.Fried.1627_diuw1qu2.pdf [Accessed 31 May 2016].

227. Against letting short-termism affect corporate law-making: Mark J. Roe, Corporate Short-Termism – In the Boardroom and in the Courtroom, 68 *The Business Lawyer* [2013]; 980. http://www.law.harvard.edu/programs/olin_center/papers/pdf/Roe_760.pdf [Accessed 31 May 2016].

228. Jo Andrew Johnston, Paige Morrow & Frank Bold, Commentary on the Shareholder Rights Directive, *LSN Research Paper Series* No. 15-13, (University of Oslo 2014), p. 1.

229. J.M. Fried, 'The Uneasy Case for Favoring Long-Term Shareholders', *The Yale Law Journal* 124 (2015): 1554–1627, 1564.

230. For more information concerning the concept of shareholder primacy in corporate law: A. Keay, 'Shareholder Primacy in Corporate Law: Can It Survive? Should It Survive?', *European Company and Financial Law Review* (3/2010): 369–413.

inter alia, positive incentives able to promote long-term shareholding and statements of corporate purpose, to the end of prioritizing the long-term interests of the undertaking itself.[231]

3.100 The Commission's proposal and the debates related to it should be seen in the context of a recent shift in the European approach to corporate governance, a change closely related to the financial crisis. It leads to challenging two traditional company law perceptions: (a) that shareholders hold rights, but not obligations, and (b) that they are a homogenous group. Depending on both the nature of the shareholder and specific concrete situations, company law and capital market law, in fact, impose a series of obligations on them, such as financial (the classic duty to pay up the subscribed capital and the mandatory bid), loyalty (in some Member States), the duty not to abuse rights, and disclosure duties.[232] More specifically, institutional investors have been remarkably targeted by several reforms in considerations of their tendency to put pressure on boards to perform in a short-term perspective, even at the expense of increasing leverage and credit risk.[233]

IV CAPITAL MARKETS

3.101 For companies and businesses in general, the functioning of capital markets is essential. As seen in Chapter 5, companies may need to attract loans and other debt financing, as well as equity, and the capital market is supposed to provide these financial means. Notwithstanding their importance for the globalizing economy, capital markets in the EU are, for the greater part, organized along national lines, which contrast with the free movement of capital as being one of the fundamental freedoms of the EU.[234] In previous versions of this book attention was paid to investor protection (first edition) and financial services directives (second edition), but the scope of the EU regarding capital markets has considerably widened since then. In December 2014, the European Council backed the Investment Plan for Europe (the 'Juncker Plan').[235] The plan is aimed at boosting investment, increasing competitiveness and supporting long-term economic growth in the EU. Under the aegis of the Investment Plan, a European fund for strategic investments has been set up and is managed by the EIB.

231. Jo Andrew Johnston, Paige Morrow & Frank Bold, Commentary on the Shareholder Rights Directive, *LSN Research Paper Series* No. 15-13 (University of Oslo 2014), pp. 1 and 2.
232. Hanne Søndergaard Birkmose, 'Shareholders' Duties in European Company Law', *European Company Law* 13, no. 1 (2016): 5–6. For information concerning shareholder's duties, with a focus on Dutch law: Matthijs J. de Jongh, 'Shareholders' Duties to the Company and Fellow Shareholders', *European Company Law* 9, no. 3 (2012): 185–191.
233. Roger Barker, 'Ownership Structure and Shareholder Engagement: Reflections on the Role of Institutional Shareholders in the Financial Crisis, *Corporate Governance and the Global Financial Crisis*, 1st edn (Cambridge University Press, 2011), 147.
234. Green Paper *Building a Capital Markets Union*, Brussels, 18.2.2015, COM(2015) 63 final, p. 4.
235. http://www.consilium.europa.eu/en/policies/investment-plan (accessed April 2016).

Additionally, an investment project portal and an advisory hub for investments were launched.[236] In terms of the internal market, the creation of a CMU is the most ambitious part of the Investment Plan.[237]

3.102 The CMU is meant to reduce fragmentation in the financial markets and increase the supply of capital to businesses, including SMEs, and to investments projects.[238] The path to realization of the CMU is laid out in the Commission's 2015 Action Plan on Building a CMU. It should lead to an integrated CMU by 2019.[239] Among the steps to be taken are the following:

- modernizing the Prospectus Directive (3.106b) in order to make it less costly to raise funds on the capital market;
- implementing measures to support venture capital and equity financing;
- revision of the requirements for bank exposures to risk by calibrating these requirements to the risks involved with investments in infrastructure;
- enhancing the capacity of banks to lend, *inter alia* by revitalizing European securitizations (5.27) to free up capacity on banks' balance sheet;
- standardization of financial instruments such as covered bonds (5.28) and enabling alternative means of financing like peer to peer lending and crowd funding to develop;
- a legislative initiative on business insolvency, including early restructuring and second chance, in order to address the most important barriers to the free flow of capital, building on national regimes that work well.[240]

3.102a As mentioned in paragraph 3.13, in 2016, the Commission launched a proposal for a directive regarding business insolvency.[241] According to the proposal, Member States will be required to install early warning tools in order to signal to debtors and entrepreneurs that urgent action is needed (Article 3). Where there is likelihood of insolvency, debtors must have access to a preventive restructuring framework enabling them to restructure their debts or business and restore their viability (Article 4). During restructuring, debtors should remain in control of their

236. http://www.eib.org/eiah (accessed April 2016).
237. *Action Plan on Building a Capital Markets Union*, Brussels, 30.9.2015 COM(2015) 468 final. Furthermore, the Commission Communication *Capital markets Union Accelerating Reform* COM(2016) 601 final.
238. *See* for the economic analysis the Commission Staff Working Document accompanying the Action Plan, Brussels, 30.9.2015, SWD(2015) 183 final.
239. *Action Plan on Building a Capital Markets Union*, Brussels, 30.9.2015 COM(2015) 468 final, p. 6.
240. *Green Paper Building a Capital Markets Union*, Brussels, 18.2.2015, COM(2015) 63 final. Communication *Unleashing the potential of Crowdfunding in the European Union*, COM (2014) 172. A critical analysis is presented by David Ramos Muñoz, Shadow Banking: The Blind Spot in Banking and Capital Markets Reform, *ECFR* 2016, 157–196.
241. Proposal for a Directive on preventive restructuring frameworks, second chance and measures to increase the efficiency of restructuring, insolvency and discharge procedures and amending Directive 2012/30/EU, Strasbourg, 22.11.2016 COM(2016) 723 final.

assets and day-to-day operations of their business. Several provisions serve this aim and one of these requires Member States to ensure that debtors may benefit from a stay of individual enforcement actions (Article 6). Furthermore, it is proposed that a competent authority can confirm negotiated restructuring plans and that creditors whose rights are affected can vote on the adoption of the plan (Articles 8–15).

3.102b Banks are an essential element of the capital market, especially in the EU, where bank lending traditionally plays a larger role in financing the corporate sector than the issuance of debt securities (5.24). This applies to SMEs particularly and they turned out to be very vulnerable to the tightening of bank lending as a consequence of the financial crisis triggered by the demise of Lehman Brothers in 2008.[242] Because of that and their systemic function for the financial system, corporate governance of banks and other financial institutions had much attention of the EU in the wake of the crisis.[243] According to the Commission's 2010 Green Paper, corporate governance in the financial services sector differs from general corporate governance and should take account of the interests of stakeholders (depositors, savers, life insurance policy holders, etc.), as well as the stability of the financial system.[244] The Green Paper sketches the deficiencies and weaknesses of corporate governance of financial institutions, as exposed by the financial crisis. The loss of confidence in those institutions is, *inter alia*, due to shortcomings in the way of conflicts of interest and risk management were handled by the boards of financial institutions. The Green Paper contains options to respond to those shortcomings and to strengthen the financial services sector. As a consequence, several legislative measures have been taken, among these the 2013 Capital Requirements Directive (CRD IV), setting requirements for the authorization of banks and other financial institutions in relation to their capital, supervision and corporate governance arrangements (Article 88).[245]

3.102c Apart from the measures suggested in the 2010 Green Paper, other legal instruments have been implemented, notably the creation of three European Supervisory Authorities: the European Banking Authority (EBA), the ESMA, and the European

242. *Green Paper Building a Capital Markets Union*, Brussels, 18.2.2015, COM(2015) 63 final, p. 8.
243. All initiatives taken in the aftermath of the financial crisis are summed up in the 2014 Communication titled *A Reformed Financial Sector for Europe*, Brussels, 5.5.2014, COM(2014) 279 final.
244. *Green Paper on Corporate Governance in Financial Institutions and Remuneration Policies*, Brussels, 2.6.2010 COM(2010) 284 final. Also: John Armour et al., Bank Governance, *ECGI Law Working Paper* 316/2016 http://www.ecgi.org/wp/wp_id.php?id=786 (accessed August 2016).
245. Directive 2013/36/EU of 26 Jun. 2013, OJ 2013, L 176/338, establishing together with Regulation (EU) 575/2013 the legal framework governing the access to the activity, the supervisory framework and the prudential rules for credit institutions and investment firms. For an overview of the legislative measures: http://ec.europa.eu/finance/bank/regcapital/legislation-in-force/index_en.htm. The Directive must be viewed in the light of the 'Basel III' rules of December 2010 adopted by the Basel Committee on Banking Supervision (BCBS), setting standards on bank capital adequacy. Furthermore: Klaus J. Hopt, Better Governance of Financial Institutions, *ecgi Law Working Paper No. 207/2013*, available at http://ssrn.com/abstract_id=2212198.

Insurance and Occupational Pensions Authority (EIOPA).[246] In 2013, the Single Supervisory Mechanism is created, which transfers supervisory tasks for 'significant' banks in the euro area and other participating Member States to the ECB.[247] This competence of the ECB is an important pillar of the so-called Banking Union. Another feature of the Banking Union is a mechanism for an integrated and effective decision-making process in case of failure of systemically important credit institutions.[248] (This had an impact on many directives as is shown in previous section of this chapter.)

3.103 As mentioned, the EU had already taken up, at an earlier stage, investor protection and regulation of the financial services market in its mission to abolish restrictions on the freedom of establishment and the provision of services. A coherent policy was set out in the 1999 FSAP, which led to the enacting of important directives.[249] Among the first was the Consolidating (or Listing) Directive 2001/34/EC, consolidating previously enacted rules on the admission of securities to stock exchange listing and on information to be published on those securities.[250] The FSAP was aimed at creating a common legal framework for integrated securities and derivatives markets and a single set of financial statements for listed companies. Consequently, companies have been obliged to prepare their financial statements in accordance with IAS, in order to allow 'fair value accounting' (paragraph 9.17). Most importantly, a four-level approach was established for the execution of the FSAP.[251] Level 1 directives set out the framework principles, whereas level 2 regulations contain implementing measures. Level 3 stands for strengthened cooperation between Member States, national regulators and the Commission by means of committees, such as the ESC and the Committee of European Securities Regulators (CESR). At Level 4, enforcement of Community rules is strengthened by actions taken by the Commission, other EU institutions and market participants.

As from 2003, four 'level 1 directives' have been adopted, partly amending the 2001 Consolidating Directive:

- the 2003 Market Abuse Directive, replaced by the 2014 Market Abuse Regulation;[252]

246. Regulations (EU) 1092/2010,1093/2010, 1094/2010, and 1095/2010 of 24 Nov. 2010, *OJ* of 15 Dec. 2010, L 331, and Regulation (EU) 1096/2010 of 17 Nov. 2010, *OJ* L331/1 of 15.12.2010.
247. Credit institutions are deemed significant if, *inter alia*, the total value of their assets exceeds EUR 30 billion, Article 6(4), Regulation (EU) 1024/2013 of 15 Oct. 2013.
248. The so-called Single Resolution Mechanism (SRM), Directive 2014/59/EU of 15 May 2014, OJ 2014 L 173/190 and Regulation (EU) 806/2014 of 15 Jul. 2014, OJ 2014 L225/1.
249. *Financial Services: Implementing the Framework for Financial Markets: Action Plan*, COM(1999)232, 11 May 1999.
250. Directive 2001/34/EC on the admission of securities to official stock exchange listing and on information to be published on those securities, OJ 2001, L 184, amended several times.
251. As recommended by an EU advisory committee chaired by Mr Lamfalussy: *Final Report of the Committee of Wise Men on the Regulation of European Securities Markets* (Brussels: 15 Feb. 2001).
252. Directive 2003/6/EC of 28 Jan. 2003, OJ 2003, L 96; Regulation (EU) No 596/2014 of 16 Apr. 2014, OJ 2014, L 173/1.

- the 2003 Prospectus Directive, which will be replaced by the Prospectus Regulation;[253]
- the 2004 Markets in Financial Instruments Directive (MiFID) which has been amended several times and is replaced by Directive 2014/65 (MiFID II);[254]
- the 2004 Transparency Directive, amended by Directive 2013/50/EU.[255]

The Market Abuse Regulation covers financial instruments admitted to trading on regulated markets (stock exchanges) or on other trading facilities. The Regulation is aimed at preserving market integrity and curbing of market abuse. Therefore, it contains rules on insider dealing, unlawful disclosure of inside information and market manipulation. The Prospectus Directive relates, *inter alia*, to the admission of securities to listing, which requires prior publication of a prospectus. The Markets in Financial Instruments Directive ensures protection for investors and creates a single passport for investment firms, enabling them to operate across the EU. The Transparency Directive sets out uniform rules for the disclosure of information by issuers of securities throughout the EU. An overview of the measures at the other levels is provided by several documents, especially by regular progress reports.[256] Several Progress Reports have been published since the FSAP was launched. The Commission has monitored the transposition of the FSAP and provides a database with implementing national legislation.[257] The economic impact of the FSAP and the cost of compliance for firms in the financial services sector were evaluated in 2009.[258]

3.103a The *Market Abuse Regulation* defines insider information regarding financial instruments or issuers thereof as:

> information of a precise nature, which has not been made public, relating, directly or indirectly, to one or more issuers or to one or more financial instruments, and which, if it were made public, would be likely to have a significant effect on the prices of those financial instruments or on the price of related derivative financial instruments(Article 7(1)(a)).

(Such definitions apply to information regarding commodity derivatives and emission allowances.) Issuers of financial instruments must draw up an insider list,

253. Directive 2003/71/EC of 4 Nov. 2003 amending Directive 2001/34/EC, OJ 2003, L 345. *See* for the results of the public consultation on the review of the Prospectus Directive: http://ec.europa.eu/finance/consultations/2015/prospectus-directive/index_en.htm (accessed May 2016).
254. Directive 2004/39/EC of 21 Apr. 2004 amending Council Directives 85/611/EEC and 93/6/EEC and Directive 2000/12/EC repealing Council Directive 93/22/EEC, OJ 2004, L 145; Directive 2014/65/EU of 15 May 2014, OJ 2014, L 173/349.
255. Directive 2004/109/EC of 15 Dec. 2004 amending Directive 2001/34/EC, OJ 2004, L 390; Directive 2013/50/EU of 22 Oct. 2013, L 204/13.
256. Retrievable at www.ec.europa.eu/internal_market/finances/actionplan/index_en.htm#documents. For example the Tenth Report, *Turning the Corner, Preparing the challenge of the next phase of European capital market integration* (Brussels, 2 Jun. 2004). *See also* the Commission Staff Working Document, *The Application of the Lamfalussy Process to EU Securities Market Legislation* (Brussels, 15 Nov. 2004), SEC(2004)1459.
257. http://ec.europa.eu/internal_market/finances/actionplan/transposition/index_en.htm (accessed May 2016).
258. http://ec.europa.eu/finance/general-policy/actionplan/index_en.htm (accessed May 2016).

comprising employees who have access to inside information and others, who have such access by performing tasks as advisors, accountants or credit rating agencies (Article 18). Member States must prohibit any person who possesses inside information from using it either by transactions for their own account or for the account of a third party or by disclosing that information or using it for 'tipping' (Articles 8 and 14). In addition, the issuers of financial instruments must inform the public as soon as possible of inside information that directly concerns the issuer (Article 17).

Market manipulation is, *inter alia*, entering into a transaction, placing an order or any other behaviour:

- gives, or is likely to give, false or misleading signals as to the supply of, demand for, or price of, a financial instrument; or
- secures, or is likely to secure, the price of one or several financial instruments at an abnormal or artificial level (Article 12).

Member States must prohibit any person from engaging into market manipulation (Article 15).

Each Member State must designate a single administrative competent authority for the purpose of the Market Abuse Regulation (Article 22). The competent authorities of the Member States shall cooperate with each other and with ESMA (Article 25).

3.103b The requirements for the admission of securities for listing were harmonized by Directive 2001/34/EC (the Listing directive). The *Prospectus Directive* supplements the listing requirements by provisions regarding the drafting, approval and distribution of the prospectus and by introducing a 'single passport' for issuers of securities. The directive covers a wide range of securities of both an equity and non-equity nature (Article 2). Member States may not allow any offer of securities to be made to the public within their territory, without prior publication of a prospectus (some small offers are exempted, Article 3). The information that must be contained by the prospectus is set out in the directive (Article 5). No prospectus may be made public before the competent authority of the home state of the issuer (Article 13) has approved it. The home Member State approval serves as a 'single passport', because it is valid for a public offer or an admission to trading in other Member States (Article 17). In the 2015 Action Plan, the Commission announced the modernization of the Prospectus Directive, with the view to make raising funds less costly and to allow small firms better access to listing. A public consultation on the review of the directive was held early 2015.[259]

3.103c The *Markets in Financial Instruments Directive* (MiFID II) covers undertakings providing investment services to third parties or performing investment activities through the establishment of a branch in the EU (Article 1). For providing these services or performing these activities (on a professional basis), prior authorization in

259. *See* for the results: *Consultation on the Review of the Prospectus Directive*, 18/02-2015 – 13/05/2015, – Feedback statement on the public online consultation, at http://ec.europa.eu/finance/consultations/2015/prospectus-directive/index_en.htm (accessed May 2016).

the home Member State is required. Authorized firms must be registered in the Member States and every authorization must be notified to ESMA. Investment firms having legal personality must have their head office in the same Member State as its registered office. A firm without legal personality must have its head office in the Member State, where it actually carries out its business (Articles 4 and 5). The authorization represents a single passport because it is valid for the entire Community (Article 6). In order to become authorized, capital and organizational requirements must be met and rules and procedures for fair and orderly trading must be established (Articles 15–18). Member States must ensure that the competent authority is enabled to monitor the activities of investment firms.[260] Furthermore, the directive provides for the authorization by Member States of certain systems as a regulated market and for the admission of financial instruments to trading (Articles 44 and 51). Detailed matters, such as the reporting of transactions to the competent authorities, are governed by the *Markets in Financial Instruments Regulation* (MiFIR).[261]

3.103d The *Transparency Directive* (as amended) harmonizes transparency requirements related to information about issuers of listed securities. These issuers should provide for a regular flow of information. The annual financial report must be made public at the latest four months after the end of a financial year and must remain publicly available for at least ten years (Article 4). In addition, a half-year report must cover the first six months and must be published at the latest three months after that period (Article 5). Issuers active in the extractive or logging of primary forest industries have to report yearly on payments made to governments (Article 6). Member States must ensure that the issuer is notified about 'major holdings', being shareholders acquiring or disposing of shares thereby passing certain thresholds (Article 9). The information contained in the notification must be made public by the issuer (Article 12).

260. Articles 24–26 Regulation (EU) No. 600/2014.
261. Regulation (EU) 600/2014 of 15 May 2014, OJ 2014 L 173/84.

CHAPTER 4

Business Organizations under European Union Law

I INTRODUCTION

4.01 The business organizations under European law have already been introduced in paragraph 2.49, as part of the impact of the European Union (EU) on corporate law. In this chapter, the European Economic Interest Grouping (EEIG), the *Societas Europaea* (SE) and the *Societas Cooperativa Europaea* (SCE) are discussed (in that order, *see* paragraphs 4.02, 4.13 and 4.45, respectively). EU law primarily governs all these forms, they may transfer their registered seat from one Member State to another, and their formation requires a cross-border element. Their European character, however, is weakened by frequent referrals made to national law. All these elements are also present in the long-pending proposals for a European Association (EA) and a European Mutual Society (ME or EMS). The withdrawn proposal to introduce a European Private Company (*Societas Privata Europaea* (SPE)) embodied a new approach in this respect. The cross-border element was not a requirement, and the proposed regulation contained an encompassing set of provisions, thereby reducing referrals to national law to a minimum (*see* paragraph 4.48a). As expected, much criticism was raised exactly by these two elements. The SPE, proposed in 2008, is withdrawn in 2013 due to lack of political support (the regulation required unanimous adoption by the Council).[1] The Commission then took an alternative road and proposed the *Societas Unius Personae* (SUP) as part of the 'Europe 2020' strategy. Member States should provide for a *national* company law form that would follow the same rules in all Member States and would have the EU-wide abbreviation 'SUP'.[2] Although the SUP will not be directly

1. Brussels, 2.10.2013, COM(2013) 685 final.
2. Brussels, 9.4.2014, COM/2014/0212 final. For Europa 2020: Brussels 3.3.2010, COM(2010) 2020.

governed by EU law, as was proposed for the SPE, it will serve the same objective of facilitating cross-border activities of companies. Therefore, the SUP will be dealt with in this chapter, paragraph 4.47.

4.01a The technique of referral to national law is often called 'renvoi' and is frequently employed in the regulations dealing with business organizations under EU law. It must be noted that the regulation concerning the EEIG discerns 'internal law' from 'national law', which may require some explanation. The regulation refers to the 'internal law' of the Member State in which the grouping is registered for additional rules concerning the contract for the formation of a grouping, as well as for its internal organization.[3] The internal law does not include the so-called conflict rules and referral to it leaves no doubt that such law applies even if conflict rules should otherwise have referred the matter to another law system.[4] 'National law', including the national rules on conflict of laws, comes into play to determine the status and capacity of natural and legal persons, the consequences of the unlimited joint and several liability of the members, the liquidation of a grouping, insolvency and tax law.[5] Where a State comprises several territorial units with their own rules of law applicable to the matters mentioned, each territorial unit is to be considered as a State.[6] The UK comprises three such territorial units: England and Wales, which share the same legal system, Scotland and Northern Ireland. In this instance, the EEIG Regulation has been implemented by two separate statutory instruments (secondary legislation) for Great Britain (the first two units) and Northern Ireland.[7] The distinction between 'internal law' and 'national law' of the Member States is not elaborated in this book and 'national law' or 'domestic law' are used for both categories instead.[8]

II EUROPEAN ECONOMIC INTEREST GROUPING

4.02 The idea of a supranational business organization was realized for the first time by the introduction of the EEIG. The EEIG is a 'modest' legal form, offering a flexible and light structure for cross-border cooperation. The EEIG is governed by Regulation (EEC) 2137/85, which required the Member States at the time to take appropriate measures to enable the formation of an EEIG by mid-1989.[9] By its nature, the EEIG is a vehicle for cooperation among enterprises in different Member States. Formation of an EEIG requires few formalities and no initial capital has to be contributed. Subsequently, the members have unlimited joint and several liability. A grouping, like a general partnership, has capacities, distinct from its members, to have rights and

3. Article 2.
4. *See* on this Werlauff, *EU Company Law*, 2003, 121.
5. Article 2(1), 24(1), 35(2), 36, 40.
6. Article 2.
7. Anthony G. Hickinbotham & Alec J. Burnside, in *European Economic Interest Grouping*, eds Dirk van Gerven & Carel A.V. Aalders (Deventer/Boston: Kluwer Law and Taxation Publishers, 1990), 254.
8. The distinction made in the EEIG Regulation cannot be found in the SE Regulation as it refers to 'national law', 'national legislation' or 'national provisions'.
9. OJ 1985, L 199.

obligations of all kinds, to make contracts or accomplish other legal acts, and to sue and be sued. It is left to the national law of the Member States to determine whether the EEIG has legal personality.[10] Article 40 of the Regulation secures fiscal transparency, meaning that the profits and losses of a grouping are taxable only in the hands of its members. The purpose of the EEIG must be limited to facilitating or developing the economic activities of its members. Its purpose is not to make profits for itself, and its activities must not be more than ancillary to the economic activities of its members. The structure of the grouping is simple, and there are only two mandatory organs: the members and the manager(s).

4.02a Credit is given to the French for the invention of such an easy-to-operate legal form for cooperation. The *groupement d'intérêt économique* (GIE) was introduced in France in 1967 and has been successful,[11] even in the field of international cooperation. A famous example of the latter is *Airbus*, which was originally formed in 1970 as a GIE by several European aircraft builders. The enterprise developed into what is now Airbus Group SE, registered in the Netherlands and listed on stock exchanges in France, Germany and Spain.[12]

4.03 The European character of the EEIG is secured by the provision that the grouping 'shall be formed upon the terms, in the manner and with the effects laid down in this Regulation', as stated in Article 1. The regulation has precedence over national law and is directly applicable in all Member States. For this reason, the EEIG is supposed to offer 'legal neutrality', placing its members on an equal footing insofar as no one is operating in a more familiar legal environment.[13] However, this is only partially true, because the binding provisions of the regulation do not cover all aspects of the EEIG. The issues dealt with are:

- the conditions governing the constitution of a grouping;
- certain aspects of its internal operation;
- the protection of third parties and members.

Even for these aspects, provisions of national law may complete the regulation. In addition, a number of important matters, such as the consequences of liability and insolvency, are referred completely to national law.

10. Article 1. For example, under German and Italian law the EEIG is not a legal person, Christian Müller-Gugenberger & Peter Schotthöfer, *Die EWIV in Europa. Texte und Erläuterungen aus rechtsvergleichender Sicht*, 1 Auflage (München: Verlagsgruppe Jehle-Rehm, 1995) (*Die EWIV in Europa*), 661 and 686. Commission of the European Communities, EEIG. *The Emergence of a New Form of European Cooperation* (Brussels/Luxembourg: 1993), 16.
11. G. Ripert/R. Roblot, *Traité de Droit Commercial*, par Michel Germain, Tome 1, Volume 2, 18e édition, 2002, no. 2054.
12. On 27 May 2015 at the Annual General Meeting of Shareholders of Airbus Group N.V., the conversion into a European Company was approved with a majority of 99.99%, Annual Report 2015 and Registration Document 2015 of Airbus Group.
13. Communication from the Commission, 97/C 285/10, OJ 1997, C 285, Ch. II.

A Formation and Publication

4.04 Parties intending to form a grouping must conclude a contract and register it in the Member State in which the official address of the EEIG is established.[14] The contract for the formation of the grouping and its internal organization are governed by the national law of the Member State in which its official address is situated.[15] The contract must include the name of the grouping, preceded or followed by the words 'European Economic Interest Grouping' or by the initials 'EEIG'[16] and the official address. In addition, the contract must include the objects for which the grouping is formed, the name of each member of the grouping, as well as other information relating to the members and the duration of the grouping. If the latter provision is absent, it is assumed that the duration is indefinite.[17] If national law provides for the nullity of the grouping, its nullity must be established or declared by judicial decision. However, the court must, where it is possible for the affairs of the grouping to be put in order, allow time to permit that to be done.[18]

4.05 A contract for the formation of a grouping must be filed at the commercial registry, together with several other documents and particulars, notably: notice of the appointment of the manager or managers, their names and other identification particulars required by the law of the Member State in which the register is kept. In addition, notifications that managers may act alone or that they must act jointly must be filed, as well as any information concerning the termination of any manager's appointment.[19] Any grouping establishment situated in a Member State other than that in which its official address is situated must be registered in that other State. This 'secondary' registration is carried out simply by submitting copies of the documents that must be filed for its 'primary' registration, together with, if necessary, a translation conforming with the practice of the registry where the establishment is registered.[20] Upon its primary registration, the EEIG is formed and possesses the juridical capacities described previously.[21] Thus, from that moment on, it may also assume obligations that have arisen out of activities carried out on behalf of the grouping before its

14. Articles 1 and 6.
15. Article 2(1). This provision does not bar the members from agreeing that certain legal relationships underlying the contract such as regarding distribution of costs and insurance shall be governed by the law of another state. *See* on this Werlauff, *EU Company Law*, 2003, 121.
16. The mandatory words or initials should be in the national language. In Danish: *Europæisk økonomisk firmagruppe* (EØFG), Dutch: *Europees Economisch Samenwerkingsverband* (EESV), French: *groupement européen d'intérêt économique* (GEIE), in German: *Europäische wirtschaftliche Interessenvereinigung* (EWIV), in Polish: *Europejskie Zgrupowanie Interesów Gospodarczych*; in Spanish: *agrupación europea de interés económico* (AEIE), in Italian: *Gruppo Europeo di Interesse Economico* (GEIE). The European *European Economic Interest Grouping* 97 Court of Justice has decided that inclusion of other elements may be required by national law, Case C-402/96 (EITO) as of 18 Dec. 1997.
17. Article 5.
18. Article 15.
19. Articles 6, 7, 9 and 39, Commission, EEIG, 73 and 74.
20. Article 10.
21. Article 1.

registration. If the grouping does not assume these obligations, the persons who carried out those activities will bear unlimited joint and several liabilities for them.[22]

4.06 After registration, several particulars must be published in the national gazette, such as the mandatory minimum content of the contract, the number, date and place of registration and almost all of the documents and particulars that have to be filed at the registry.[23] Although publication is not a prerequisite for its existence, it is essential for the functioning of the EEIG in relation to third parties. Pursuant to the First Directive, the documents and particulars that must be published may be relied on by a grouping against third parties under the conditions laid down by the applicable national law.[24] Following the publication in the national gazette, notice that a grouping has been formed should be given to the *Official Journal of the EU.*[25]

4.07 The contract must designate the official address of the EEIG. It must be situated in the EU, either where the grouping has its central administration or where one of the members has its central administration or, in the case of a natural person, the place of his principal activities, provided that the grouping carries on activities there.[26] The second option, thus, makes it legal for an EEIG to conduct its activities by using the infrastructure of one of its members. The official address may be transferred within the EU, as long as the new address fulfils the aforementioned conditions. Such a transfer will result in a change of applicable law, if the address is moved from one Member State to another. In that case, a transfer proposal must be drawn up and filed, and the proposed address must be published. The decision to transfer may only be taken two months after publication and the members must decide on it unanimously. During the two-month period, a competent authority of the Member State in which the EEIG is registered may oppose its transfer, but only on grounds of public interest and if the law of the Member State so provides.[27] If no objection is raised, the transfer may be carried out by registering the EEIG in the transferee state. Until the cancellation of the old address is published, third parties may continue to rely on that address, unless they have actual knowledge of the transfer.[28]

4.08 As already mentioned, the regulation requires the activity of the grouping to be ancillary to the economic activities of its members and its purpose may not be to make profits for itself. Therefore, partners wanting to start a new economic activity that is not

22. Article 9(2).
23. Article 8.
24. Article 25.
25. Articles 8 and 11, The Official Journal of the EU previously was the Official Journal of the EC.
26. Article 12. Note that the EEIG Regulation uses 'Community' where now European Union should be read.
27. Articles 13 and 14. Spain, the UK and Ireland have exercised this option, *Die EWiV in Europa, o.c.*,595, 631, 740 However, it is argued that in other Member States authorities may intervene as well, e.g., to take legal steps to ensure that the grouping complies with tax obligations, Aalders, *European Economic Interest Grouping*, 73, 120, 138, 204, 236, 259.
28. Article 14.

connected with their own activities would have to set up another type of business organization, such as a company. The ancillary role must not be interpreted too narrowly, that is, in the sense of 'accessory' or of 'less importance'.[29] The regulation does not prohibit the EEIG from completely, though temporarily, taking over some of its members' activities. This can be the case for the purposes of performing site work in the construction industry, for example.[30] In accordance with this ancillary character, a grouping may not direct a group, that is, exercise the power of management or supervision over the activities of the members or the activities of another undertaking. Shareholding in another undertaking is allowed only insofar as it is necessary for the achievement of the grouping's objective and if it is done on its members' behalf. The grouping is also prohibited from being a member of another grouping, in order to avoid a complicated chain of liabilities in an international context.[31]

4.08a In addition, two specific prohibitions apply. The grouping may not employ more than 500 persons, a limitation that stems from German law concerning employee representation on the supervisory board (*see* paragraphs 6.24 and 6.31). Without this limitation, employee representation would be obligatory for a grouping employing more than 500 people and having its official address in Germany, as opposed to non-German groupings employing more than 500 people.[32] Secondly, a grouping may not be used by a company for granting loans to the director of that company or for the transfer of property between the company and a director, when those transactions are restricted or controlled under the Member State's laws governing companies.[33] This clause was inserted at the request of the UK and reflects certain sections of the Companies Act (*see* paragraph 6.78). In general, a Member State may impose appropriate sanctions in order to prevent abuse or circumvention of its national laws by a grouping.[34]

4.09 The membership of a grouping may consist of only three categories:

- companies or firms within the meaning of the second paragraph of Article 54 TFEU (ex Article 48 TEC);
- other legal bodies that have been formed in accordance with the law of a Member State and that have their registered or statutory office and central administration in the EU;
- natural persons who carry on a business activity or who provide services in the EU.[35]

In practice, these are not serious limitations, because a wide range of legal entities is included, that is, not only business organizations but also non-profit-making

29. Commission, *EEIG*, 47.
30. Communication from the Commission, 97/C 285/10, OJ 1997, C 285, Ch. II(3).
31. Commission, *EEIG*, 59.
32. Aalders, *European Economic Interest Grouping*, 13.
33. Article 3.
34. Preamble of the regulation.
35. Article 4(1).

organizations and legal bodies governed by public law to the extent that they exercise an economic activity.[36] However, entities formed in accordance with the law of a 'third country', such as a Delaware incorporated company, cannot be members of an EEIG.[37] To participate, they would first have to constitute one of the aforementioned entities in accordance with the law of a Member State.

The cross-border dimension of the grouping is secured by the requirement that the enterprises concerned are situated in at least two different Member States.[38]

4.09a The members of a grouping have unlimited joint and several liability for its debts and other liabilities. New members incur all existing liabilities, unless a clause is added in the formation contract exempting a new member from liabilities that originated prior to his admission.[39] Former members of an EEIG remain liable for five years following their withdrawal for liabilities arising out of the grouping's activities during the period of their membership.[40] Creditors may not proceed against a (former) member for payment before the liquidation of a grouping is concluded, unless they have first requested payment from the grouping and payment has not been made within an appropriate period.[41]

As already mentioned, national law determines the consequences of the liability of members and former members, such as the recourse a member may take on his co-members in case he has paid more than his share.

B Structure

4.10 The mandatory organs of a grouping are the members acting collectively in a general meeting and the manager(s), but the contract for the formation may provide for other organs as well. The members, acting as a body, may make any decision for achieving the objects of the grouping.[42] Each member has one vote. The contract for the formation, however, may give more than one vote to certain members, provided that one single member does not hold majority of the votes.[43] For several decisions, unanimity is always required. For example: to alter the objects of the grouping; to transfer its official address to another Member State; to alter the number of votes allotted to each member; or to decide on the admission of new members. For other decisions, the contract may set forth different rules, but, where it fails to do so, unanimity may also be required.[44] The members have full freedom to organize their

36. Aalders, *European Economic Interest Grouping*, 15.
37. But an 'associate membership' can be created via underlying agreements, Werlauff, *EU Company Law*, 2003, 122.
38. Article 4(2).
39. Article 26(2) and 7 sub j.
40. Article 34.
41. Article 24.
42. Article 16.
43. Article 17(1).
44. Article 17(2) and (3), Article 26(1).

meetings and they can regulate their own methods of decision-making, which may take place, apart from via meetings, by other means, such as postal votes or teleconference.[45]

4.10a The grouping is managed by one or more natural persons, appointed by a contract or by decision of its members. Member States may allow legal persons to be managers, on the condition that such legal persons designate one or more natural persons to represent them. Those persons are liable as if they were the managers of the grouping concerned. The appointment and removal of the managers are determined by the contract for its formation or, failing that, by unanimous decision of the members.[46] Each of the managers may represent the grouping in dealings with third parties and bind the grouping acting on behalf of it. The rules concerning acts not falling within the objects of the grouping or the limitations that can be relied on as against third parties reflect the provisions of the First Directive.[47] The law of the Member State in which the EEIG has its official address governs the liability of the managers towards its members.[48] For this purpose, the general provisions for the duties of managers of legal persons may apply to the managers of an EEIG. As an alternative, Member States may also rely on the provisions pertaining to the partners of a partnership.[49] In addition, special provisions may apply, for instance, in the case of bankruptcy.[50] Towards third parties, the liability of the grouping and/or its managers is, of course, subject to the law applicable according to private international law.[51]

C Involvement of Employees

4.11 As opposed to the SE (and SCE), the EEIG is not subject to special EC legislation concerning the involvement of employees. Consequently, national law governs this matter. It must be noted, however, that community law certainly has a bearing on the role of employees. Due to a 1994 directive, community-scale undertakings may have an obligation to establish a European Works Council (EWC) or an alternative procedure for information and consultation of employees. Dependent on specific circumstances,

45. Commission, *EEIG*, 12.
46. Article 19.
47. Article 20, paragraph 3.18 of this book.
48. Article 2(1).
49. An example of the first is Article 9 Book 2 of the Dutch Civil Code: 'Each officer or managing director shall be responsible to the legal person for the proper performance of the duties assigned to him (...).' An example of the second is Article 144 of the Spanish Commercial which states that 'damage to the Company's interests caused by malice, abuse of power or gross negligence on the part of one of the partners shall result in that partner being liable (...)'.
50. For example Article 138 Book 2 of the Dutch Civil Code, which applies to the EEIG and states that each managing director is liable if the management has 'manifestly performed its duties improperly'. According to a pending reform (nr. 34 491), this provision will be included in Article 9c of Book 2.
51. In case of non-contractual liability, this will normally be the *lex loci delicti*, Werlauff, *EU Company Law*, 2003, 428 and Aalders, *European Economic Interest* Grouping, 45. For jurisdictional matters, *see* Regulation (EU) No. 1215/2012 (Brussels I Regulation). Further: on the law applicable on contractual obligations: Regulation (EC) No. 593/2008 (Rome I) and Regulation (EC) No 864/2007 (Rome II) dealing with the law applicable to non-contractual obligations.

employees of an EEIG or of its members may take part in such councils or procedures. On the national scale, another directive forces Member States to meet minimum requirements for the right to information and consultation of employees.

The involvement of employees is further discussed in Chapter 7.

D Perspectives of the EEIG

4.12 The introduction of the EEIG at community level aims to facilitate cross-border cooperation, especially for Small- and Medium-sized Enterprises (SMEs).[52] This intention is perfectly justified by the global trend to increase intercompany cooperation.[53] The flexibility regarding formation, operation and financing of an EEIG should make this legal form particularly accessible to SMEs.[54] Through cooperation, they are able to match the advantages of large enterprises without any loss of independence. However, international cooperation among SMEs is not as universal as might be expected. Lack of communication between business people operating small enterprises and differences in conditions for doing business from one country to another present obstacles. Legal barriers do not seem to play much of a role here.[55]

By 1997, the European Commission reported that with more than 800 EEIGs being set up, optimum use of this legal form was still not being made. The Commission advised the EEIG for firms wishing to cooperate as a 'consortium' in order to participate in public contracts and programmes financed by public funds.[56] With regard to the sectors of activity in which the members of groupings operate, an earlier survey indicates a predominance in the service sector. There are various types of activities that may be assigned to a grouping. However, it is most frequently used as a means of providing services for its members or third parties, but also for distribution, research and production.[57] The number of EEIGs is constantly growing. By October 2015, about 2,400 EEIGs were founded. A few Member States counted for most of these, notably Belgium (493), Germany (416) and France (311).[58]

52. Communication from the Commission, 97/C 285/10, OJ 1997, C 285, Positive on the perspectives for the EEIG in practice are Gugenberger & Schotthöfer, *Die EWIV in Europa. Texte und Erläuterungen aus rechtsvergleichender Sicht*, nr. 21–25. Note that because the introduction of the EEIG the EU policy has shifted from SMEs to entrepreneurs, Rudy Aernoudt, *European Enterprise Policy: From SME Policy to Entrepreneurship Policy* (Antwerp/Oxford/New York: Intersentia, 2003).
53. S.E. Huyzer et al., *Strategische samenwerking. Orientatie en Implementatie*, 2nd edition (Alphen aan den Rijn/Zaventem: Coopers & Lybrand Dijker Van Dien, 1992), 11.
54. Commission, *EEIG*, 8.
55. Commission, *Panorama of Industry* 1993, 99–106.
56. Participation of European Economic Interest Groupings (EEIGs) in public contracts and programmes financed by public funds, COM(97) 434 final, OJ 1997, C 285.
57. Commission, *EEIG*, 23 and 35. According to Hans Zahorka, a few 'megatrends'are, *inter alia*, the use of the EEIG for IT-based virtual firms and for cooperation between self-employed professionals, EWIV-Konferenz, Frankfurt, 5.11.2004, http://www.libertas-institut.com/de/Praesentationen/HJ_Zahorka.pdf (accessed 11 May 2016).
58. Furthermore: Spain (228), Italy (221), Netherlands (198) and the UK (255). EEIG Statistics from the European EEIG Information Centre (at LIBERTAS – European Institute GmbH), www.ewiv.eu – www.libertas-institut.com (accessed 11 May 2016).

III EUROPEAN COMPANY

4.13 In the context of an integrated market, the Commission proposed, in 1970, the Statute for the European Company, officially named the *Societas Europaea* (SE).[59] The idea was to create a supranational business organization to enable enterprises to restructure their businesses at European level. The original proposal was very ambitious. The Commission suggested that the statute should cover all aspects of modern company law to avoid the application of divergent national laws, but the proposal was substantially amended and weakened in that respect before it was eventually adopted in 2001. As a result, the SE Regulation on the Statute for the SE and the SE Directive supplementing the statute with regard to the involvement of employees entered into force on 8 October 2004.[60] Both the regulation and the directive are based on Article 308 of the EC Treaty (now Article 352 TFEU). Under this provision, the council may take appropriate measures by a unanimous decision, in order to achieve Union objectives where the treaties do not provide the necessary powers thereto.[61]

4.13a The original proposal raised much debate on employee involvement and other issues, such as the law of groups, which were part of the first draft. Therefore, the proposal proved to be 'non-negotiable' and it was substantially amended over the years in order to improve its political credibility.[62] Compared to the original proposal, later proposals were far less comprehensive and referred to national law more often.[63] Eventually, about thirty options were worked in, where Member States may follow patterns of domestic company law. Finally, the provisions concerning employee involvement were removed altogether from the regulation on the statute, in order to form the substance of a separate directive (the SE Directive). In hindsight, it can be said that the lack of an SE did not hamper the internationalization of European business enterprises during the decades when the SE was the subject of debate. The European Commission probably overrated the need for a European business organization at the

59. OJ 1970, C 12411; Supplement to the Bulletin 8-1970 of the European Communities. A preliminary draft was delivered by Pieter Sanders, Pieter Sanders, 'From Conception to Reality', in *The European Company: Developing a Community Law of Corporations: Collected Papers from the Leiden University Unilever Programme 2002*, ed. Jonathan Rickford (Antwerp/ Oxford/New York: Intersentia, 2003), 37–39.
60. Council Regulation (EC) No. 2157/2001 of 8 Oct. 2001 on the Statute for a European company (SE), OJ 2001, L 294, 10 Nov. 2001 P. 0001-0021 *(SE Regulation);* Council Directive 2001/86/ EC of 8 Oct. 2001 supplementing the Statute for a European company with regard to the involvement of employees, OJ 2001, L 294, 10 Nov. 2001 P. 0022-0032. For the introduction in the Member States: Oplustil, Krzysztof and Teichmann, Christoph, *The European Company – all over Europe: A state-by-state account of the introduction of the European Company*, De Gruyter, 2004.
61. The Commission initially proposed to ground the SE Statute on the 'traditional' legal base of Article 44 (ex Article 54). *See* on the legal basis: A. Wehlau, 'The Societas Europaea: A Critique of the Commission's 1991 Amended Proposal', *Common Market Law Review* 29, no. 3 (1992): 473.
62. Jonathan Rickford (ed.), *o.c.*, *The European Company*, 18.
63. Supplement to Bulletin EEC *4175*; OJ 1989, 263/07 and 263/08; OJ 1991, C 176/01 and C 138/08.

instance of the first drafting.[64] Nevertheless, the reactions to the 1997 consultation paper on the SE were rather supportive of the Commission's views.[65]

4.14 Although the SE is not the first type of company of a non-national nature, as can be seen from paragraph 1.02, where reference is made to 'international companies', its introduction is hailed as 'a unique and historic step (...) in European company law'.[66] It opens up new possibilities for the restructuring and internationalization of European businesses. It also offers flexibility, because the SE may transfer its seat across national borders without winding up and according to a procedure set out in the statute. Due to its statute, which takes precedence over national law, the SE may be of help solving the delicate question as to which law will govern in the case of a cross-border acquisition or a joint venture. The SE also acts as a catalyst for further legal developments and its introduction has certainly helped to make the Tenth Directive on cross-border mergers acceptable to the Member States. Even as a draft, the SE already provided a model for other European business organizations to be proposed by the European Commission, such as the SCE.[67]

4.15 An SE is a public limited liability company with capital divided into shares. Upon registration, it obtains legal personality.[68] Access to the SE is primarily reserved for national public limited companies, which, under certain conditions, are even allowed to transform directly into an SE. Private limited companies and other legal bodies are only allowed to participate in the formation of an SE by forming a holding company or a joint subsidiary, respectively.[69] As already mentioned, an important characteristic of the SE is that it may transfer its registered office within the EU without being wound up.[70] Another hallmark is the choice that the SE offers to its founders between a one-tier and a two-tier board structure.[71] In addition, the SE features cross-border employee involvement, for which rules are laid down in the accompanying Directive 2001/86/EC.[72]

64. Thomas Raiser, 'Die Europäische Aktiengesellschaft und die nationalen Aktiengesetze', in *Unternehmen und Unternehmensführung im Recht*, ed. Festschrift fur Johannes Semler zum 70. Geburtstag (Berlin/New York: Walter de Gruyter, 1993), 296.
65. Analysis of Replies to Commission Consultation Paper on Company Law (XV/6013/97). The history of the SE drafts are adequately described by Edwards, *EC Company Law*, 399 *et seq.*
66. Erik Werlauff, *SE – The Law of the European Company* (Copenhagen: DJØF Publishing, 2003), 1.
67. Council Regulation (EC) No. 1435/2003 of 22 Jul. 2003 on the Statute for a European Cooperative Society (SCE), OJ 2003, L 207 and Council Directive 2003/72/EC of 22 Jul. 2003 supplementing the Statute for a European Cooperative Society with regard to the involvement of employees, OJ 2003, L 207. *See also* OJ 1992, C 99 as amended, OJ 1993, C 236.
68. Articles 1 and 16 of Council Regulation (EC) No. 2157/2001 of 8 Oct. 2001 on the Statute for a European company (SE), OJ 2001, L 294, 10 Nov. 2001 P. 0001-0021 (SE Regulation).
69. Article 2.
70. Article 8. This is, generally speaking, not an option for companies under national law may. They may, however, use a cross border conversion which may lead to a similar result but without the legal guidance the SE Regulation offers (*see* 2.65 and 2.65a).
71. Chapter 6 deals with board structures in general.
72. Council Directive 2001/86/EC of 8 Oct. 2001 supplementing the Statute for a European company with regard to the involvement of employees, OJ 2001, L 294, 10 Nov. 2001 P. 0022-0032.

A Applicable Law

4.16 As with the EEIG, the European character of the SE is secured by the rules determining the applicable law. For the SE, Article 9(1) of the SE Regulation ranks the sources of law. Thus, the SE is primarily governed by the regulation itself and, where the regulation expressly authorizes it, its articles of association or statutes.[73] Where matters are not, or not completely, regulated by the SE Regulation, an SE is governed by provisions of the law of the Member State in which the SE has its registered office. In such a case, the national provisions adopted specifically to implement EU measures prevail over other national provisions.[74] Second, national company law may apply, insofar as it relates to public companies. Finally, the articles of the SE may contain additional provisions in the same way as allowed for a domestic public limited company.[75] It is important to note that, for taxation purposes, the SE will be subject to the legislation of the State in which it has its registered office and it will enjoy no more facilities for deduction of losses incurred by establishments abroad than other business organizations.[76]

4.16a As will be seen next, the most important matters covered by the SE Regulation itself are the formation of the SE, the transfer of the registered office, the board structure and the general meeting. The reader who is familiar with the company law directives, as set out in Chapter 3, will feel at home with many details of the SE Regulation, because it contains the essence of the harmonization of company law.[77] Pursuant to the SE Regulation, the statutes of an SE may provide for a number of matters pertaining to the SE's internal organization. Examples include the determination of the board as either one-tier or two-tier (Article 38), the determination of the number of board members (*inter alia,* Article 43(2)) and the fixation of the majority required for a decision by the general meeting to amend the statutes (Article 59(1)).

4.16b The SE Directive must, as any directive, be implemented through appropriate measures by the Member States.[78] The directive ensures that negotiations take place between employee representatives and management on the involvement of employees in the SE. Whenever the negotiations lead to an arrangement that conflicts with the statutes of the SE, the arrangement prevails and the statutes must consequently be amended. The high ranking of this agreement is laid down in Article 12(4) of the SE

73. Wino J.M. van Veen, 'The Law Governing SEs: An Interpretation Based on a Textual Analysis and the Referencing Methodology in the Regulation', *European Company Law* 1, no. 3 (October 2004): 111–116.
74. These implementation measures must be in accordance with the Directives applicable to public companies, Article 9(2). *See* on this: Werlauff, *SE – The Law of the European Company*, 23.
75. Article 9(1c,iii). Where the SE Regulation refers to harmonized law, competition between the law systems of the Member States can hardly occur. Carla Tavares da Costa & Alexandra de Meester Bilreiro, *The European Company Statute* (The Hague/London/New York: Kluwer Law International, 2003), 14.
76. Preamble, Recital 20. Directive 90/434/EEC on the common system of taxation applicable to mergers, divisions, transfers of assets and exchanges of shares concerning companies of different Member States must be amended as to include the SE.
77. Werlauff, *EC Company Law*, 1993, 75.
78. Article 288 TFEU.

Regulation. An example of such a conflict would be an arrangement leading to more seats on the supervisory body than allowed for by the articles (Article 39(4)).

4.16c The highest-ranking provisions of national law are those specifically adopted to implement the SE Regulation and SE Directive. The former attributes the regulation of several matters to the Member States, partly as an option, and partly on mandatory basis. Examples are: the obligation to designate the competent authority to affirm the completion of the formalities for the SE to transfer its registered office (Article 8(8)), the option to require additional publication of the proposal to transfer the registered office (Article 8(2)) and the option to require less than 10% of the subscribed capital for shareholders, in order to demand a general meeting (Article 55(1)).[79] Second in the hierarchy of national law are provisions of company law that are relevant for the public limited liability companies, as specified in Annex I of the SE Regulation. Again, the SE Regulation itself makes several references to the rules of the law of the Member States that are applicable to public limited companies. This way, the SE Regulation invokes harmonized national legislation for issues such as the capital of the SE (Article 5) and the preparation of the annual financial statements (Article 61). However, referrals are also made to non-harmonized provisions of national law, such as for the winding up, liquidation, insolvency and cessation of payments and similar procedures (Article 62).[80] By introducing national provisions that go beyond what is strictly necessary for the SE Regulation's implementation, Member States may try to make the SE an attractive legal form, in order to compete with other Member States for SE incorporations.[81]

4.16d It follows from the ranking as laid down in Article 9 of the SE Regulation that the statutes of the SE might only contain additional provisions with respect to matters not covered by the SE Regulation. The same goes for national law, which is applicable pursuant to the SE Regulation. Therefore, it depends a great deal on the Member State in which the SE has its registered office what additional provisions may be allowed in the statutes of the SE.

B Formation and Publication

4.17 Formation of an SE may be undertaken according to several methods. The first four of these are 'primary' formation methods, in the sense that no pre-existing SE is involved, whereas this would be the case if 'secondary' formation applies. Each of

79. According to Wino Veen, more than forty provisions of the SE Regulation refer to the Member States in this way, 'The Law Governing SEs: An Interpretation Based on a Textual Analysis and the Referencing Methodology in the Regulation', *European Company Law* 1, no. 3 (2004): 113.
80. Referral to the national law for public limited companies is to be found in thirty-three provisions of the SE Regulation, Wino Veen, 'The Law Governing SEs: An Interpretation Based on a Textual Analysis and the Referencing Methodology in the Regulation', *European Company Law* 1, no. 3 (2004): 114.
81. Michel Menjucq, 'Implementation in France of the Regulation on the European Company: A Strategic Interpretation', *European Company Law* 1, no. 3 (October 2004): 117 *et seq.*

these methods is mentioned here, and the relevant provisions of the SE Regulation are highlighted in the next paragraph (4.18). An SE can be formed according to the following methods:

(1) *Formation of an SE by merger* between public limited companies. Those companies have to be formed under the law of a Member State and have their registered offices and head offices within the EU. To secure the cross-border dimension, at least two of them must be governed by the law of different Member States (Article 2(1)). The merger may be carried out as an acquisition by one of the merging companies (the acquiring company), which will take the form of an SE upon the completion of the merger, or by formation of a new company, which will have the form of an SE (Article 17).
(2) *Formation of a holding SE* by public and/or private limited companies. As under (1), the involved companies must have been formed under the law of a Member State and have their registered offices and head offices within the EU. At least two of them must be governed by the law of different Member States or have, for at least two years, a subsidiary company governed by the law of another Member State or a branch situated in another Member State (Article 2(2)).
(3) *Formation of a subsidiary SE* by companies and firms within the meaning of Article 54 TFEU, including other legal bodies governed by public or private law, safe for those that are not profit-making. The same conditions apply as mentioned under (2): the participating companies, firms and other legal bodies must have their registered offices and head offices within the EU. At least two of them must be governed by the laws of different Member States or have, for at least two years, a subsidiary company governed by the law of another Member State or a branch situated in another Member State (Article 2(3)).
(4) *Conversion into an SE* by a public limited company, if that company has a subsidiary company governed by the law of another Member State for at least two years (Article 2(4)).
(5) *Setting up an SE subsidiary* by an SE (Article 3(2)). As this fifth mode implies the pre-existence of an SE, its formation is sometimes referred to as 'secondary' formation.[82] The same applies when an SE participates in the formation of another SE by way of a merger or by creating a holding SE or a subsidiary SE. The regulation facilitates this by stating that an SE, in this respect, shall be regarded as a public limited company governed by the law of the Member State in which it has its registered office. Therefore, apart from the setting up of a subsidiary SE already mentioned here, the following 'secondary' methods can also be exploited.
(6) *Formation of an SE by merger* between an SE and one or more other SEs, or one or more public limited companies. The requirements are the same as

82. Article 3(2) guarantees that the SE subsidiary can be wholly owned.

mentioned under (1), so the participating companies must be formed under the laws of a Member State and have their registered offices and head offices in different Member States within the EU.

(7) *Formation of a holding SE* by an SE with one or more other SEs, or together with one or more public or private companies as mentioned under (2).

(8) *Formation of* a *subsidiary SE* by an SE with one or more other SEs, or with one or more companies or legal bodies as mentioned under (3).

It must be noted here that the formation of an SE cannot be completed by registration before the involvement of employees is settled in accordance with the rules set out in the SE Directive.[83] The involvement of employees is explained in paragraphs 4.35 *et seq.*

4.17a To summarize, the SE is not available to natural persons or companies, firms and other legal bodies without 'cross-frontier credentials'.[84] The restriction is understandable in the light of the introduction of the SE as being 'necessary to attain, in the course of the operation of the common market, one of the objectives of the Community', according to the previous wording of what is now Article 352 TFEU (ex Article 308 TEC). Moreover, the restriction may help curb the circumvention of national law by using the new form where a company under national law is indicated. However, the cross-border dimension seems to be easy to create, because there is no requirement that companies participating in the formation of an SE be independent. The SE Regulation even grants facilities to holding companies merging with wholly owned subsidiaries, as well as with subsidiaries owned for 90% or more.[85] For example, Company A in one Member State may form a subsidiary B in another Member State and after that, both companies may merge into an SE or form an SE by way of a holding company.[86]

4.18 The SE Regulation contains several provisions on the procedure for formation, notably formation by merger and by way of forming a holding company. These provisions are as follows:

- Articles 17–31 on the formation by *merger* are largely similar to those of the Third Directive and the Tenth Directive, which are set out in Chapter 3.[87] Because of the cross-border dimensions of the merger, Member States may provide for its competent authorities to oppose the merger on grounds of public interest.[88] Member States may also adopt provisions to ensure protection for minority shareholders who have opposed the merger.[89]

83. Article 12(2).
84. Rickford, *The European Company, o.c.*, p. 22.
85. Article 31. Note that this article refers to the Third Directive.
86. Rickford, *The European Company, o.c.*, p. 22.
87. Chapter 3, s. II.C. The merger procedure also is dealt with in Ch. 8.
88. Article 19. The grounds mentioned can be, e.g., tax claims, which may be put at risk by the merger.
89. Article 24(2).

- Articles 32–34 govern the formation of an SE as a *holding company*. This is a very different operation, because no company ceases to exist, as is the case with a merger, and the actual decision lies with the shareholders, because they must decide whether they intend to contribute their shares in exchange for shares in the SE to be formed.[90] Nevertheless, the procedure shows strong similarities with the merger procedure. The draft terms for the formation of the holding company shall contain the same particulars and must be approved by the general meeting of each of the companies involved.[91]
- Articles 35 and 36 governing the formation of a *subsidiary SE* do little more than refer to provisions of national law for the formation of a subsidiary of a public limited liability.
- Article 37 deals with the *conversion* (transformation) of a public limited company into an SE. The operation does not result in the winding up of the company or in the creation of a new legal person. The conversion must be approved by the general meeting of the company after, *inter alia*, draft terms of conversion and a report on the implications for both shareholders and employees have been drawn up.

4.18a Essential elements of the merging procedure are:

- approval of the draft terms of the merger by the general meeting of each of the merging companies (Articles 20 and 23);
- publication (Article 21);
- examination of the draft terms of merger by independent experts (Article 22);
- protection of creditors and holders of bonds and securities other than shares (Article 24);
- scrutiny of the legality of pre-merger acts and formalities by the national authorities of the participating companies and by the authority of the Member State in which the SE is to be registered after the completion of the merger and the SE is formed (Articles 25 and 26).

Some Member States provide for a special procedure to scrutinize and amend the share-exchange ratio or a procedure to compensate minority shareholders, without preventing the completion of the merger. Such procedure could favour shareholders of a merging company to the detriment of shareholders of other participating companies, which may not have access to such procedures under their national law. To reach 'equality of arms', Article 25(3) states that such provisions only apply when accepted by the general meeting of those other companies. If accepted, the decision in the procedure becomes binding on the SE and all of its shareholders.[92] The merger takes

90. Article 33(1) and (4).
91. Article 32(2) and (6). The question whether or not a qualified majority is required is discussed by Christoph Teichmann, 'Minderheitenschutz bei Gründung und Sitzverlegung der SE', *ZGR* 3 (2003): 367 *et seq.*
92. A special procedure as mentioned by Article 25(3) is the German Spruchverfahren (paragraphs 5–8 and 9–11 SE-AG, modelled after paragraph 15 Umwandlungsgesetz), Christoph Teichmann,

effect on the date on which the SE is registered (Article 27) and may not be declared null and void thereafter (Article 30). The issue of employee involvement must be dealt with before registration of an SE; *see* paragraphs 4.35 *et seq.* of this chapter.

4.18b The formation of a holding SE differs from the merger procedure, *inter alia*, in relation to the following issues:

- there is no right for the authorities to oppose it on grounds of public interest;
- there is no scrutiny of the legality of the pre-formation formalities;
- the formation depends on decisions taken by individual shareholders, during a period of three months, to contribute their shares and only if more than 50% of the shares of each participating company is contributed (Articles 32 and 33).[93]

4.19 Irrespective of the method of formation, the SE acquires legal personality on the date on which it is registered in the Member State where it has its registered office.[94] For the purpose of its registration, the name of the SE must be preceded or followed by the abbreviation 'SE'.[95] An SE may not be registered until an arrangement for employee involvement has been concluded or, when no arrangement could be reached, until the applicable rules for employee involvement have been otherwise determined in accordance with the SE Directive.[96] The SE's formation and registration are then published in the manner laid down by the laws of each of the Member States concerned, in accordance with the First Directive. In addition, notice of an SE's registration also is published in the *Official Journal of the European Union*.[97]

C The Law Applicable to Formation

4.20 Because companies from different Member States may participate in the formation of an SE, a question may arise as to which law should be applied to the formation. As pointed out before, Article 9 of the SE Regulation gives precedence to the regulation itself, but it does not cover all aspects of the formation procedure. In relation to formation by merger, Article 18 of the SE Regulation states that, for matters not covered, each company involved in the formation is to be governed by the provisions of its domestic law concerning the merger of public companies, as harmonized by the Third Directive. The completion of the merger, however, is subject to the law of the Member State of the proposed registered office of the SE.[98]

'Minderheitenschutz bei Gründung und Sitzverlegung der SE', ZGR 2003, 367 *et seq.*, Christoph H. Seibt, 'Report from Germany', *European Company Law* 1, no. 3 (2004): 131–134.

93. Teichmann, 'Minderheitenschutz bei Gründung und Sitzverlegung der SE', 388 *et seq.*
94. Article 16.
95. Article 11.
96. Article 12(2). Directive 2001/86/EC. *See* paragraph 4.35.
97. Articles 13 and 14.
98. Articles 26 and 15.

4.20a If, for example a Spanish company merges with a French company into a newly formed SE, matters such as decision-making, publication, protection of creditors, scrutiny of the pre-merger acts and formalities and the striking off from the register are governed by Spanish and French law. However, this will not lead to the completion of the merger, because the SE has to be registered and the *ipso iure* consequences have to be determined. Therefore, Article 26, together with Article 15, provides for additional scrutiny of the legality of the merger by the competent authority of the Member State of the proposed registered office of the SE. If the SE formed by the Spanish and French company is to be registered in Belgium, the completion of the merger will be subject to Belgian law.

4.21 One would expect the same approach for the formation of a holding SE, but a provision equivalent to Article 18 is missing in this respect. In any event, however, the procedure preceding the formation of the holding may only be followed according to the rules of the national law of the companies involved. For example, when the general meeting of a Polish public company approves the draft terms of formation of a holding SE to be registered in Germany, Polish law will govern the decision-making on the Polish side, as it would in the case of a merger.[99] Therefore, Article 18 must be read analogously with respect to the formation of a holding SE.

The formation of a subsidiary SE will be governed, like the formation of any subsidiary, by the law of the Member State in which the SE will have its registered office. For the participating companies, national provisions apply to the decision-making on the formation of a subsidiary as it would with regard to the formation of any subsidiary.

D Widening the Range of Participating Companies

4.22 Article 2(5) offers the option for Member States to provide that a company whose head office is not within the EU may, nevertheless, participate in the formation of an SE. Such a company must be formed under the law of a Member State, have its registered office in that state and have a 'real and continuous link with a Member State's economy'. Needless to say, such a company can only be formed and continue its existence under the law of a Member State adhering to the incorporation doctrine.[100] Member States relying on the real seat doctrine will not allow a company registered in that state having its head office elsewhere. Therefore, those Member States will probably not use this option, as opposed to countries with the incorporation doctrine, such as the UK, Sweden and the Netherlands.[101] Companies having their registered

99. Teichmann, 'Minderheitenschutz bei Gründung und Sitzverlegung der SE', 388.
100. Paragraphs 2.65 *et seq.* Note that such company very likely will have its head office in a country that equally applies the incorporation doctrine because only then its legal status there will be secured.
101. The option is used by Statutory Instrument 2004 No. 2326, Part 4 (UK), Lag om Europabolag (SFS 2004:575), paragraph 4 (Sweden) and Article 2, Uitvoeringswet verordening Europese vennootschap (Netherlands).

office outside the EU – irrespective of the place of their head office – may not participate in the formation of an SE. They may become a shareholder of an SE after its formation as a matter of course.

4.22a As a result, a UK registered public limited company having an establishment in England but its head office in the United States may, according to English law, participate in the formation of an SE.[102] The same company may also participate in such formation according to Danish or Dutch law. This means, for example, that a Danish *aktieselskab* may merge with such a company in order to form an SE registered in Denmark. Turning back to the example of the UK company with its head office in the United States, the conclusion must be that such a company could, in principle, not participate in the formation of an SE with a registered office in a Member State that adheres to the real seat requirement.[103]

E Registered Office and Head Office

4.23 The registered office of an SE shall be situated at the place specified in its articles of association ('statutes'). It must be located within the Community in the same Member State as its head office. A Member State may impose on SEs registered in its territory the additional obligation of locating the head office and the registered office in the same place.[104]

4.23a To be acceptable for all Member States, the SE Regulation contained the real seat arrangement of Article 7, but, in the preamble, one reads that such is without prejudice to Member States' laws and does not pre-empt any choices to be made for other Community texts on company law. Nevertheless, the real seat requirement prevents the SE from moving its head office to another Member State and leaving the registered office where it is in order to avoid a change of applicable law.[105] It also limits the converse movement of 'jurisdiction shopping' by the founders of an SE or by way of transfer of the registered seat only. Therefore, the Delaware effect, which is to be expected where the registered office can be chosen regardless of the actual head office, will not have much impact here.[106]

102. Preamble, Recital 23, specifies what is meant by 'a real and continuous link with a Member States' economy'.
103. On the effects of the real seat doctrine in this respect, Hans-Werner Neye & Christoph Teichmann, 'Der Entwurf für das Ausführungsgesetz zur Europäischen Aktiengesellschaft', *Die Aktiengesellschaft,* Heft 4 (2003): 171.
104. Article 7. The stricter requirements – registered office must be the same as the location of the head office – had initially been opted for by e.g., Germany, but have been removed in the course of the company law reform allowing the German GmbH and AG to locate the head office outside Germany.
105. This limitation very probably conflicts with the case law by the European Court of Justice, Eddy Wymeersch, 'Cross-Border Transfer of the Seat of a Company. Recent EU Case Law and the SE Regulation', in *The European Company, o.c.*, ed. Rickford, 88; Erik Werlauff, 'Cross-Border Transfers of SE Companies. Domicile Requirements Contrary to the EC Treaty Right of Establishment', *European Company Law*, no. 3 (October 2004): 121 *et seq.*
106. Werlauff, 'Cross-Border Transfers of SE Companies', 109 *et seq.* and, on the meaning of head office, p. 113 *et seq.*

4.24 In the event that the registered office and the head office of an SE do not coincide, the Member State in which the registered office is located should take appropriate measures to oblige the SE to conform to the prescriptions of the SE Regulation within a specified period. This can be done either by re-establishing its head office in the same Member State as its registered office or by transferring its registered office to the Member State in which the head office is situated.[107] For the latter option, the procedure of Article 8 must be applied. This procedure, resulting in the transfer of the SE, is an important characteristic of the SE. Such transfer does not result in the SE being wound up or in the creation of a new legal person. Crossing the border of a Member State, however, will result in a substantial change of applicable law, because of the regulation's frequent reference to the national law of the registered office.[108] The transfer of an SE is subject to the same rules applicable for the EEIG (*see* paragraph 4.07). The proposal to transfer must be duly published and no decision may be taken for two months after publication. Member States have the option to include a provision that its authorities may oppose the transfer on grounds of public interest.[109]

4.24a Article 8 of the SE Regulation, dealing with the transfer of the SE's seat, is far more detailed than its corresponding provision in the EEIG Regulation. For example, the proposal to transfer an SE must cover: (a) the proposed registered office of the SE; (b) the proposed statutes of the SE, including, where appropriate, its new name; (c) any implication the transfer may have on employee involvement; (d) the proposed transfer timetable; and (e) any rights provided for the protection of shareholders and/or creditors.[110] The transfer to another jurisdiction represents a threat to the creditors of the SE. Although they retain their claims, it may be more difficult to obtain repayment once the SE has crossed borders. Therefore, the SE is to satisfy the interests of creditors and holders of other rights with respect to the SE and ensure that they have been adequately protected, for example, by way of actively informing the creditors in advance or offering them sufficient security upon demand. This protection concerns any liabilities arising prior to the publication of the transfer proposal. A Member State may even extend this protection to liabilities that arise or may arise prior to the transfer.[111]

4.25 The decision on the transfer is taken at the general meeting.[112] It is an option for the Member States to adopt provisions designed to ensure protection for minority shareholders who oppose a transfer. Once the transfer is decided on, their position vis-à-vis the SE may be rather different, because a new set of national rules will be

107. Article 64. Werlauff, 'Cross-Border Transfers of SE Companies', 115 *et seq.*
108. Article 8.
109. The option will be used by most Member States, e.g., UK (Statutory Instrument 2004 No. 2326, Part 4) and the Netherlands (Article 5 Uitvoeringswet verordening Europese vennootschap).
110. Article 8(2).
111. The UK, Statutory Instrument 2004, No. 2326, Part 4 extends the protection to the date of the transfer, the Netherlands, Uitvoeringswet, Article 4 offers an instrument of protection which can be used up to two months after publication but also for liabilities that may arise until the date of the transfer. Germany extends the protection to fifteen days after the publication of the proposal, SEAG, s. 13(2).
112. Article 8(6) and 59.

applicable. Of course, opposing shareholders can sell their shares prior to the transfer, but there may not always be a market available. Therefore, protection may be offered over and above the protection that would apply under national company law.[113] Although Member States tend to rely on existing rules, Germany, for example, has adopted specific provisions in this area.[114]

The transfer procedure has a built-in safety valve because registration in the 'new' Member State can only be effected when a certificate has been submitted by the competent authority of the 'old' Member State, attesting to the completion of the acts and formalities to be accomplished before the transfer.[115] The transfer takes effect from the date of registration of the new office.[116] Upon publication, the new registration may be relied on against third parties. However, they may continue to rely on the old registered office as long as the deletion of the SE's registration in the old Member State has not been publicized, unless there is proof that they were aware of the new registered office.[117]

F Capital

4.26 The capital of an SE and its shares is to be denominated in euro and the subscribed minimum may not be less than EUR 120,000. This minimum is meant to secure that the SE has sufficient assets, without making it too difficult for small and medium-sized undertakings to form SEs.[118] If a Member State requires a greater subscribed capital for domestic companies carrying out certain types of activity, such as financial institutions and insurance companies, the higher amount shall apply to SEs carrying on such activities and having their registered office in that Member State.[119] Member States not having the euro as their currency[120] may subject SEs with registered offices within their territory to the same provisions applicable to public limited companies in relation to their capital. In any case, an SE may express its capital in euro as well.[121] The SE Regulation contains no further provisions in relation to the capital and Article 5 refers all other matters to national law.

G Structure: One-Tier or Two-Tier Board

4.27 The structure of the SE comprises of the general meeting, combined with either the two-tier system with a management organ and a supervisory organ, or the one-tier

113. Article 8(5); Werlauff, 'Cross-Border Transfers of SE Companies', 124.
114. The UK and the Netherlands have not used this option. Under German law, the SE must offer to repurchase the shares of the opposing shareholders (cash out), SEAG, s. 12(2).
115. Article 8(9).
116. Article 8(10).
117. Article 8.
118. Preamble, Recital 13, Articles 1(2) and 4.
119. Article 4(3).
120. Because the third phase of the Economic and Monetary Union (EMU) does not apply.
121. Article 67(1). The national currency/euro conversion rate shall be that for the last day of the month preceding the formation of the SE.

system with an administrative organ only. The statutes of the SE determine the choice between these two systems.[122] A Member State without provisions for one of the systems in relation to public companies should adopt appropriate measures for SEs registered within its territory.[123] In other words, Member States are supposed to facilitate both systems for the SE, but may apply certain rules of their national system, such as provisions concerning the registration of members of the organs, their rights and obligations and conditions for eligibility. Some Member States, such as Germany, having a mandatory two-tier structure for all public companies, have introduced such provisions, thus offering legal certainty and securing equal treatment of SEs and public companies registered within its territory.[124] Others, such as the UK, where company law shows great flexibility for the statutes to allocate powers, have not adopted such additional measures.[125]

4.28 In the two-tier system, the management organ (board) is responsible for managing the SE. Member States may adopt rules providing that one or more members from the management organ are responsible, as managing directors, for the current (day-to-day) management under the same conditions as the directors of domestic public limited companies. The members of the management organ of an SE are appointed and removed by the supervisory organ (board), but these powers may lie with the general meeting if a Member State allows the statutes of the SE to provide for it.[126] The members of the supervisory organ are appointed by the general meeting, but this rule does not affect national law permitting minority shareholders or others to appoint some of the members of a company organ.[127] Moreover, arrangements for employee participation, having a bearing on the composition of the supervisory board, must be taken into account.[128] The supervisory organ oversees the duties performed by the management organ, but may not exercise the power to manage the company.[129]

4.29 In the one-tier system, also called a unitary board system, the administrative organ (board) has the power to manage the SE. Where the responsibilities of management and those responsible for supervision are automatically separated by the two-tier system, these responsibilities must be clearly defined in the one-tier system.[130] Member States may articulate rules providing that one or more managing directors of the

122. Preamble, Recital 14 and Article 38. Both systems were mentioned in paragraph 3.10a in connection with the withdrawn Draft Fifth Directive.
123. Articles 39(5) and 43(4).
124. Sections 20 *et seq.* SEEG. Silja Maul, 'Konzernrecht der deutschen SE – Ausgewählte Fragen zum Vertragskonzern und den faktischen Unternehmensverbindungen', ZGR 5–6 (2003): 743 *et seq.*
125. DTI, Implementation of the European Company Statute, A Consultative Document, October 2003, 3.40. In the Netherlands, the structure regime, a compulsory governance system for sizable companies, does not apply to the SE, Memorie van Toelichting, 29,309 nr 3, p. 3 *et seq.*; further: paragraphs 6.62 *et seq.* According to Klaus Hopt, In: Rickford (ed.), *o.c.*, 52–53, Member States must adopt measures in order to rule out uncertainties.
126. Article 39(2).
127. Articles 40(2) and 47(4).
128. Article 40(2).
129. Article 40(1).
130. Preamble, Recital 14.

one-tier board are responsible for the day-to-day management under the same conditions as for domestic public limited companies.[131] The general meeting appoints and removes the members of the administrative organ unless minority shareholder rights under national law or arrangements for employee participation provide otherwise.[132] Overall, under the one-tier system, the general meeting has direct influence on the election of those persons who are to conduct the company's affairs.

4.30 Several provisions of the regulation are common to the one-tier and two-tier systems (Articles 46–51). Among these are the following:

- members of company organs are not appointed for longer than a six-year period, although reappointment is possible;[133]
- the statutes of the SE may permit a legal person to be a member of one of its organs, provided that the law of the registered office of the SE does not provide otherwise with respect to public limited companies; the legal person must then designate a natural person to exercise its functions on the board;[134]
- the statutes shall list the transactions that require the authorization of the management organ by the supervisory organ (two-tier system) or an express decision by the administrative organ (one-tier system);
- decision-making requires that at least half of the members of an organ are present (or represented) and that decisions are taken by the majority of the members present or represented, unless the regulation or the statutes provide differently;[135]
- members of the SE's organs are liable for loss or damage sustained by the SE as a result of breach, on their part, of the obligations attached to their functions; this liability is governed by the provisions applicable to public companies in the Member State in which the SE has its registered office.[136]

4.30a The SE Regulation obliges the SE to draw up a list of transactions, which require authorization by the supervisory organ or an express decision by the unitary board. Member States may alternatively enact rules providing, though only for the two-tier system, that the supervisory organ designates the transactions subject to its authorization.[137] Member States may also determine certain transactions that must be indicated in the statutes of an SE. Transactions requiring authorization or express decision-making, as a rule, generally consist of major business operations, such as large investments, the setting up, acquisition, disposal or closing down of undertakings, and the raising or granting of loans. Thus, if employee representatives are among

131. Article 43(1). For an example of this option, seethe German implementation act, s. 40(1) *SE – Ausführungsgesetz*.
132. Article 43(3).
133. Article 46.
134. Article 47(1).
135. Article 50(1).
136. Article 51.
137. Germany has used this option, s. 19 SEAG.

the members of the organ concerned, the authorization or deliberation requirement can be viewed as a guarantee of their influence.

H Structure: General Meeting

4.31 The general meeting decides on matters for which it has sole responsibility under the SE Regulation or the SE Directive, as implemented.[138] Besides the appointment of members of the SE's management organ(s), as set out previously, the regulation allocates to the general meeting the decision-making powers concerning the transfer of the SE's registered office, the amendment of its statutes and the conversion of an SE into a public company of national law.[139] Moreover, where an SE is involved in the formation of another SE by way of a merger or in the formation of a holding SE, it follows from the SE Regulation that the general meeting is the body that decides on this matter.[140] Regarding other matters, the general meeting of the SE has the same powers as the general meeting of a domestic public limited company. This is of special importance for the various matters that are almost completely referred to national law, most notably the financial statements (annual accounts) and the winding up of an SE.

4.31a To recapitulate, the following articles of the SE Regulation require a decision of an SE's general meeting:

- Article 8(4): transfer of the SE's registered office.
- Article 23(1): approval of the draft terms of merger, whereby an SE is formed (if an SE is involved in the merger).
- Article 32(6): approval of the draft terms of formation of a holding SE (if an SE is one of the parties involved in such formation).
- Articles 23(2) and 32(6): ratification of the arrangement of employee involvement accompanying the merger or formation of a holding SE (if an SE is involved and its general meeting has reserved the right to ratification).
- Article 40(2), two-tier system: appointment of the members of the supervisory organ (of the management organ, only if the Member State has opted for it, Article 39(2)).[141]
- Article 43(3), one-tier system: appointment of the members of the administrative organ.
- Article 59: amendment of an SE's statutes.
- Article 66(6): approval of the draft terms of conversion of an SE into a public limited company and of the statutes of that company.

138. Article 52.
139. Articles 8(4), 59(1) and 66(6).
140. Article 3(1).
141. Note that Article 39(2) deals with both the appointment and removal of members of the administrative organ where Articles 40(2) and 43(3) only mention appointment (of members of the supervisory organ and the administrative organ, respectively).

4.32 Decisions of the general meeting are taken by a majority of the votes cast, unless the SE Regulation or national law requires otherwise.[142] One of the exceptions concerns the amendment of the articles, where a majority of two-thirds of the votes cast is required. However, Member States may require a simple majority, provided that at least half of the subscribed capital is represented.[143] It is important to note that the votes cast do not include votes attached to shares, in respect of which the shareholder has not taken part in the vote, abstained or returned a blank or spoiled ballot paper.[144] Where an SE has two or more classes of shares, each decision by the general meeting shall be subject to a separate vote by each class of shareholders – if the decision of the general meeting affects their class rights.[145] The SE Regulation contains some provisions on the convening of the general meeting, which normally lies with the organs of the SE, but can also be initiated by minority shareholders.[146] They may also request that additional items be put on the agenda.[147] Insofar as the organization and conduct of the general meeting, as well as the voting procedures, are not covered by these rules, the law of domestic public limited companies applies.[148]

I Financial Statements, Winding Up and Liquidation

4.33 The preparation of financial statements (accounts) and consolidated financial statements (accounts), including the accompanying management report and the auditing and publication of these documents, is governed by national law, harmonized, as a matter of course, by the directives dealing with these matters (paragraphs 3.63 *et seq.*; Chapter 9). Listed SEs, just like other listed companies in the EU, will have to comply with the International Accounting Standards (IAS/IFRS) (*see* Chapter 9).[149]

4.34 As regards winding up, liquidation, insolvency, cessation of payments and similar procedures, an SE shall be governed by the applicable national law, including provisions relating to decision-making by the general meeting on those matters.[150] As opposed to the financial statements, here, the referral concerns national law that has not been harmonized.

4.34a With regard to insolvency, questions of competence and the recognition of foreign insolvency procedures may rise when business enterprises engage in cross-border activities. International insolvency law is characterized by two conflicting principles. On the one hand, the principle of universality requires that all the assets of the debtor are included in one single insolvency process, regardless of the territoriality of the assets and liabilities. The territorial principle, on the other hand, claims that

142. Article 57.
143. Article 59.
144. Article 58.
145. Article 60(1).
146. Articles 54 and 55.
147. Article 56.
148. Article 53.
149. Werlauff, 'Cross-border Transfers of SE Companies', 160.
150. Article 63.

domestic proceedings always remain possible, regardless of any foreign insolvency decree. Because harmonization of substantive insolvency law is difficult, especially with regard to the priority of claims, the Insolvency Regulation 1346/2000 is primarily oriented to cross-border insolvency procedures. After evaluation of the application by the Commission in 2012, a recast Regulation (EU) 2015/848 was adopted.[151] Like its predecessor, the regulation is enacted to ensure that insolvency procedures in one Member State are given legal effect in others, in order to obtain the equal treatment of creditors. According to Article 3 of the regulation, the main insolvency proceedings may be opened in the Member State where the debtor has the Centre of its Main Interests (COMI). The COMI shall be the place where the debtor conducts the administration of its interests on a regular basis and which is ascertainable by third parties. In the absence of proof to the contrary, the place of the registered office shall be presumed to be the centre of its main interests. This presumption does not apply if the registered office has been moved to another Member State within the three-month period prior to the request for the opening of insolvency proceedings. This exception serves to neutralize incentives for forum shopping, which happens when parties transfer assets or judicial proceedings from one Member State to another to obtain a more favourable legal position to the detriment of creditors. Secondary proceedings may be opened in the Member State of the debtor's establishment. The effects of secondary proceedings are limited to the assets located in that state (Article 3(2)). In cases of insolvency of an SE, the real seat requirement, as a rule, will imply that the main proceedings have to be opened before the competent court of the place of the registered seat of the SE.[152]

J Involvement of Employees

4.35 As will be demonstrated in Chapter 7, within the EU, national regimes have always differed considerably within two basic forms of employee involvement.[153] In the first place, there are mechanisms for information and consultation of employees through a representative body, be it a works council or the representatives of trade unions. The second form is called employee participation and encompasses representation of employees at board level or influencing the selection or appointment of board members. Although the first form is widespread within the EU, only some of the Member States have introduced employee participation.[154] It was feared that the formation of an SE could be used for the evasion of national rules, particularly those of the second category. This could be the case, for example, if a German AG should merge with an English Plc in order to form an SE registered in the UK. Consequently, the

151. Regulation (EU) 2015/848 of 20 May 2015, OJ 2015, L 141/19. Denmark has not participated in the adoption of the regulation and is not bound by it, Preamble, Recital 88. The Commission's report is downloadable: http://ec.europa.eu/justice/civil/files/insolvency-report_en.pdf. *See also* Werlauff, 'Cross-Border Transfers of SE Companies', 163 *et seq.*
152. On the meaning of centre of main interests, *see also* ECJ 2 May 2006, C-341/04 (Eurofood).
153. SE Directive, Article 1 defines those forms.
154. The Davignon Report, *Group of Experts on European Systems of Worker Involvement*, Final Report (Brussels, May 1997), Table 1.

German participation system, having no equivalent in the UK, could disappear if no adequate measures are adopted. On the other hand, should EC legislation safeguard all pre-existing rights of employees, the UK might fear the export of the German system of employee participation to an SE registered in England.

4.36 The involvement of employees has been a controversial issue for many years. While the debate was still going on, the directive on the EWC was enacted in 1994 and it has certainly helped pave the way for the introduction of the SE.[155] This directive contains a mechanism for the involvement of employees in undertakings with a community dimension. The mechanism is initiated by the formation of a special negotiating body of employee representatives. This body has the task, together with central management, to negotiate on the scope, composition and functions of the EWC, or an equivalent procedure for information and consultation. Should negotiations fail, Subsidiary Requirements (standard rules), which are annexed in the directive, would apply. The EWC is further discussed in Chapter 7, but it is important to note that this system of negotiations, combined with a fallback on standardized rules, is copied in the SE Directive (Directive 2001/86/EC supplementing the SE Regulation).[156]

4.37 The preamble of the SE Directive explains that the creation of an SE simultaneously implies the necessity to introduce information and consultation procedures at a transnational level, as well as the preservation of existing participation rights within the companies establishing the SE. However, in the latter case, the parties may decide otherwise.[157] Employee rights in force before the establishment of an SE should provide the basis for employee rights of involvement in the established SE, according to the so-called before and after principle. Consequently, that approach applies not only to the initial formation of an SE but also to structural changes in an existing SE.[158]

4.38 The directive extensively regulates the negotiating procedure. The responsibility to take the necessary steps to start negotiations lies with the organs of companies participating in the formation of an SE.[159] As a matter of course, information must be provided. The SE Directive determines that these must take place as soon as possible after publishing the draft terms of merger or creating a holding company or after agreeing a plan to form a subsidiary or to transform into an SE. Information must be given on the identity of the participating companies, the subsidiaries or establishments concerned and the number of their employees.[160] A special negotiating body must be

155. Council Directive 94/45/EC of 22 Sep. 1994 on the establishment of an EWC or a procedure in Community-scale undertakings and community-scale groups of undertakings for the purposes of informing and consulting employees, OJ 1994, L 254.
156. Paul L. Davies, 'Employee Involvement in the European Company', in *The European Company: Developing a Community Law of Corporations: Collected Papers from the Leiden University Unilever Programme 2002*, ed. Jonathan Rickford (Antwerp/Oxford/New York: Intersentia, 2003), 67 *et seq.*; Werlauff, 'Cross-Border Transfers of SE Companies', 133 *et seq.*; Carla Tavares da Costa & Alexandra de Meester Bilreiro, *The European Company Statute* (The Hague/London/New York: Kluwer Law International, 2003), 73 *et seq.*
157. Preamble, Recitals 6 and 7.
158. Preamble, Recital 18.
159. Article 3(1).
160. *Ibid.*

established in accordance with the provisions of the directive. The members of this body must be in proportion to the number of workers employed in each Member State by the participating companies and their relevant subsidiaries or establishments.[161] Once the negotiating body is established, negotiations commence and they may continue for six months. The parties may decide, however, to extend this period for up to one year.[162]

4.39 The negotiating body decides on the outcome of the negotiations. Decisions may be taken by an absolute majority, provided that such majority also represents an absolute majority of employees. Should the results lead to a reduction of participation rights, a qualified majority is required. This varies among the different methods of forming an SE.[163] The negotiating body may also decide not to open negotiations or to terminate negotiations already opened, in order to rely on the rules on information and consultation in force in the Member States where the SE has employees. Here, again, a qualified majority is required.[164] Should the negotiations fail or if the parties so agree, the Standard Rules, which have to be implemented by each Member State, would apply. The Standard Rules are to be found in the Annex to the SE Directive.[165] Included are rules for the composition of the body representing the employees (Part 1 of the Standard Rules), for information and consultation (Part 2) and for participation (Part 3).

4.39a To summarize, the following options have to be taken into account:

(1) the negotiations lead to either (a) an agreement on employee involvement or (b) to an agreement that the Standard Rules apply;
(2) if the negotiations produce no result or the (extended) period for negotiations expires, then the Standard Rules would then apply;
(3) if the negotiating body decides to terminate the negotiations or not to open them at all, then there would be no special employee involvement provisions for the SE, but national legislation will be applicable.[166]

4.40 The Standard Rules limit the competence of the representative body to cross-border issues: 'questions which concern the SE itself and any of its subsidiaries or establishments situated in another Member State or which exceed the powers of the decision-making organs in a single Member State'.[167] Against this background, it might

161. Article 3(2).
162. Article 5.
163. Article 3(4).
164. Article 3(6).
165. The Standard Rules in the Annex to the SE Directive are almost identical to the Subsidiarity Requirements in the Annex to the Directive on the EWC.
166. Several examples are described by Lone L. Hansen, 'Employee Involvement and the Formation of European Company: The Competition Between the Approaches of Different Member States When a European Company Is Formed Through International Merger', *European Company Law*, no. 3 (October 2004): 126 *et seq.*
167. SE Directive, Annex, Part 2(a).

be expected that comparable formulas will constitute parts of agreements on information and consultation. In general, management will not easily agree on more involvement of employees than prescribed by the Standard Rules, while the negotiating body will not be adamant to accept lower standards. Therefore, the negotiations have been described as 'bargaining in the shadow of the law'.[168]

4.41 The Standard Rules apply, as already mentioned, when the parties so agree, when the negotiation period expires without result or when negotiations have never begun due to a decision of the negotiating body.[169] The issue of participation is dealt with in Part 3 of the Standard Rules but these rules will apply only when the following additional criteria are met:

- In the case of a transformation of a public company into an SE, employee participation is relevant where national rules for employee participation apply to the transforming public company.[170] Part 3(a) confirms that all the existing rules 'shall continue to apply to the SE'. There is no option for the negotiating body or management to decide not to have that employee participation for the SE.[171]
- In the case of a merger, if the existing participation rules in one or more participating companies cover at least 25% of all employees involved in the merger, unless the negotiating body decides to lower this threshold.[172]
- For the setting up of a holding SE or a subsidiary SE, the threshold is set at 50% coverage, but here, again, the negotiating body may decide to apply Part 3 even when less than 50% of all employees involved are covered by the pre-existing system(s) of participation.[173]

If there was more than one form of participation within the companies involved in the formation of an SE, the special negotiating body would decide which of those forms must be established in the SE.[174]

Member States may opt out of the application of Part 3 of the Standard Rules in the case of a merger, thus preventing the 'import' of the system of employee participation, as determined by the Annex.[175] The option, if used, will prevent registration of an SE in the case of a merger, unless none of the participating companies is governed by participation rules or an agreement on employee involvement has been concluded, including participation rules.[176]

4.41a The UK has not opted out of the application of Part 3 of the Standard Rules dealing with employee participation. It was argued that, because forming an SE will be

168. *See* Davies, 'Employee Involvement in the European Company', 77.
169. Article 7(1).
170. Article 7(2)(a).
171. Article 3(6), 4(4), Part 3(a).
172. Article 7(2)(b).
173. Article 7(2).
174. *Ibid.*
175. Article 7(3) and Preamble, Recital 9.
176. SE Regulation, Article 12(3). *See* on this option, Rickford (ed.), *o.c.*, p. 28.

entirely voluntary, companies might perceive social benefits by embracing the employee involvement arrangements, including participation at board level, as the case may be. Pointing at evidence from Japanese companies with works councils in Germany, it was assessed that such participation will not slow down the decision-making process within companies.[177]

4.42 Finally, the rules on the involvement of employees in the SE form an 'indissociable complement' to the SE Regulation and must be applied concomitantly.[178] Their application is secured because an SE cannot be registered unless the involvement of employees has been determined. As already pointed out, this requires that an agreement is concluded, that the standard rules apply, or that a valid decision has been taken by the negotiating body to rely on national legislation.[179] Whenever the statutes of the SE conflict with an arrangement for employee involvement, the latter prevails and the statutes must be amended.[180]

4.42a Rules of the SE Directive and of the EWC Directive do not cumulate. Where an SE is an undertaking with community dimension and therefore falls within the ambit of the EWC Directive, the rules from this directive give way to an agreement on employee involvement, but apply where no agreement is concluded.[181] Provisions of national legislation on the participation of employees, other than those implementing the SE Directive, do not apply to an SE. However, the SE Directive does not prejudice other rights concerning the involvement of employees provided for by national legislation.[182]

K Perspectives of the SE

4.43 The SE is supposed to facilitate the restructuring of business enterprises at a European level and to simplify group structures. Therefore, the SE may replace a series of national companies, all working under different rules. In addition, it offers enhanced flexibility, because it can move its registered seat to another Member State. Finally, the SE represents a 'European identity' not associated with companies under national law.[183] On the downside, there is the potentially lengthy negotiating procedure on

177. DTI, Explanatory Memorandum to the European Public Limited-Liability Company Regulations 2004, no. 2326.
178. SE Regulation, Preamble, Recitals 19 and 22.
179. SE Regulation, Article 12(2).
180. SE Regulation, Article 12(4).
181. SE Directive, Article 13(1).
182. SE Directive, Articles 13(2) and (3). *See* on national rules Ch. 9.
183. Most of these pros can be found in the Preamble of the SE Regulation. *See also* Commissioner Frits Bolkestein, 'The New European Company: Opportunity in Diversity', in *The European Company: Developing a Community Law of Corporations: Collected Papers from the Leiden University Unilever Programme 2002*, ed. Jonathan Rickford (Antwerp/Oxford/New York: Intersentia, 2003), 41–42 and Carla Tavares da Costa & Alexandra de Meester Bilreiro, *The European Company Statute* (The Hague/London/New York: Kluwer Law International, 2003), 59.

employee involvement,[184] as well as the manifold references to national law, leaving substantial differences between SEs in the various Member States and the lack of a separate tax regime.[185] How these pros and cons will be perceived in practice and to what extent the SE will be used remains to be seen.[186] By August 2016, the total number of registered SEs was 2,615, which is a huge increase in comparison to the 284 SEs, as mentioned in the 2009 edition of this book.[187] Several large businesses use the legal form of the SE as the top holding company, such as Airbus Group SE, BASF SE and Groupe Eurotunnel SE. The majority of SEs, however, had no employees upon registration, which raises concerns that the obligations under the SE Directive will not be complied with, because they apply to the period of formation of the SE.[188]

4.43a In 2010, the Commission forwarded a report to the Council and the European Parliament on the application of the SE Regulation.[189] The report sums up practical problems related to setting up an SE. These are, for instance, the rather high minimum capital requirement, the lack of the option to form an SE by way of cross-border division and the period of at least two years, during which a company must have had a subsidiary or branch in another Member State in order to convert into an SE or to participate in a cross-border merger.[190] Moreover, further problems are caused by the lack of clarity and the complexity of the SE Statute. Article 2 of the Statute refers to a 'subsidiary', but without providing a proper definition of the term. Another example is Article 18, which, in determining the applicable rules on the formation of an SE by merger, refers to national provisions harmonized by the Third Directive, hence raising

184. The negotiating procedure has proven not to be an impediment to the formation of sizeable SEs, especially in Germany: Jochem Reichert, 'Experience with the SE in Germany', *European Company Law* 5, no. 6 (December 2008): 297–304.
185. Bolkestein, 'The New European Company', 43, mentions initiatives to amend taxation directives as to include the SE (and SCE) resulting in Directive 2003/123/EC amending Directive 90/435/EEC (parent-subsidiary directive) and a Commission proposal of October 2003 to amend the Merger Directive. *See also* the survey on the taxation of the Societas Europaea, International Bureau of Fiscal Documentation 2003, http://europa.eu.int/comm/taxation_customs/taxation/company_tax/developments.htm.
186. *See* for a rather optimistic perspective *Die Aktiengesellschaft*, Heft 4 (2003): 169 *et seq.* as well as Da Costa & De Meester Bilreiro, *The European Company Statute*, 175–178. On issues related to the implementation of the SE Directive: *Communication from the Commission on the Review of Council Directive 2001/86/EC of 8 Oct. 2001 Supplementing the Statute for a European Company with Regard to the Involvement of Employees*, Brussels, 30 Sep. 2008, COM(2008)591(final) and the reports and minutes of the Group of Experts 'SE - European Company' on the implementation of the SE Directive, retrievable at http://ec europa.eu/employment_social/labour_law/documentation_en.htm.
187. Database on http://ecdb.worker-participation.eu/.
188. COM(2008)591(final), 7 and 8. The number of SEs in October 2008 was 284. August 2016, a relatively large number (1,524) of SEs having no employees are registered in the Czech Republic. Perhaps law firms have been setting up 'shelf' or 'UFO' SEs with a view to sell these companies to parties that want to avoid the formation procedure. To compare, Germany has registered 203 SEs without employees.
189. *Report from the Commission to the European Parliament and the Council on the application of Council Regulation 2157/2001 of 8 October 2001 on the Statute for a European Company (SE)*, COM(2010) 676 and the *Accompanying Commission Staff Working Document*, Brussels, 17.11.2010.
SEC(2010) 1391 final.
190. Report COM(2010) 676, paragraph 3.1.

questions about the applicability of other rules of national law, especially those based on the Tenth Directive on cross-border mergers.[191] The Commission announced the plan to propose potential amendments to the SE Statute (and the SE Directive) by 2012. The 2012 Action Plan, however, proposed nothing more than the launch of an information campaign to increase awareness of the SE and the opportunities it offers.[192] In appreciating this campaign, Article 69 of the SE Regulation comes to mind. It requires the Commission, five years after the entry into force of the Regulation at the latest, to analyse in particular the appropriateness of the following:

(a) allowing the location of an SE's head office and registered office in different Member States;
(b) broadening the concept of 'merger' in Article 17(2), in order to also admit other types of merger (such as types of 'merger' – actually divisions – entailed by the Sixth Directive);
(c) revising the jurisdiction clause in Article 8(16), when necessary, because relevant sources of law have been adapted;
(d) allowing more freedom to Member States to accept provisions in the statutes of an SE, even when such provisions are not permitted for national public companies.

IV OTHER EUROPEAN BUSINESS ORGANIZATIONS

4.44 In the wake of the drafts for the SE Statute, the Commission launched proposals for a European Association (EA), a European Cooperative Society (SCE) and a European Mutual Society (EMS) by 1992, to be followed by a proposal for a European Foundation (FE) in 2012. The 1992 proposals were amended in 1993, following the comments of Economic and Social Committee.[193] However, after screening the pending legislative proposals, the Commission withdrew the proposals for an EA and EMS by 2005.[194] The 2012 proposal for the FE was also taken off of the legislative agenda by 2014, due to the failure of the Member States to reach consensus.[195] It must be noted that, among those entities, the EA and the FE are basically not to be regarded as business organizations, as they cannot distribute profits among the members (EA) or, generally, serve other than public benefit interests (FE).

4.44a Withdrawal of a legislative proposal by the European Commission can be challenged. This was illustrated by the Council, supported by several Member States, in seeking the annulment of the Commission's decision to withdraw a proposed

191. Accompanying Document SEC(2010) 1391 final, paragraph 3.1.6.
192. *Action Plan: European company law and corporate governance – a modern legal framework for more engaged shareholders and sustainable companies*, COM(2012) 740 final, paragraph 4.5. Further: http://ec.europa.eu/internal_market/company/societas-europaea/index_en.htm.
193. OJ 1992, C 99 and 1993, C 236 and OJ 1993, C 236.
194. Communication *Outcome of the screening of legislative proposals pending before the Legislator*, Brussels, 27.9.2005, COM(2005) 462 final.
195. The proposal: Brussels, 8.2.2012 COM(2012) 35 final. Withdrawal: Annex 2 to the Commission Work Programme 2015, Strasbourg, 16.12.2014, COM(2014) 910 final.

regulation laying down provisions for macro-financial assistance to third countries. According to the ECJ, the Commission is accorded with legislative initiative by Articles 17(2) TEU and 289 TFEU. Consequently, it is for the Commission to decide whether or not to submit a proposal for a legislative act (under the ordinary legislative procedure). Such power is safeguarded by Article 293(1) TFEU, stating that the Council, when acting upon a proposal by the Commission, may amend that proposal only by acting unanimously and by Article 293(2), granting the Commission the power to alter its proposal, as long as the Council has not acted. If the Commission decides to withdraw its proposal, Article 296 TFEU requires the Commission to state to the Parliament and the Council the reasons for the withdrawal, which, in the event of a challenge, have to be supported by cogent evidence or arguments. The ECJ further explains that Article 296 TFEU implies an assessment of such statement of reasons with regard not only to its wording but also to its context.[196]

4.44b The SCE (and the withdrawn EMS) can be regarded as business organizations for the cooperation of natural persons who act according to principles different from those of other economic subjects. These principles embody the notion of man taking priority over capital by allotting voting rights to persons independent of their share of the capital.[197] Together with foundations and associations, cooperative societies and mutual societies are sometimes referred to as the Social Economy. Unlike capital companies they do not offer investor driven structures, but they spring from the economic and social needs of their members and are generally managed in accordance with the principle of 'one member, one vote'. The importance of this approach was stressed by the UN, declaring 2012 the International Year of Cooperatives.[198] In a comparative study, it was concluded that globalization and other factors urge to rethink the essence of legislation for cooperatives.[199] In 2003, the European Council adopted the SCE Regulation and the ECS Directive.[200] The SCE Regulation applies as of 18 August 2006.

A European Cooperative Society

4.45 The SCE has the status of a legal person and it is a company with its capital divided into shares. The members are only liable up to the amount of their shares, unless the articles impose stricter liability. The purpose of the SCE is to fulfil its

196. ECJ 14 Apr. 2015, C-409/13, dismissing the action by the Council and the Member States.
197. Preamble of the proposed regulation concerning the Statute of the European Cooperative Society as amended and the proposed regulation concerning the Statute of die European Mutual Society as amended.
198. http://social.un.org/coopsyear/ (accessed August 2016).
199. Dante Cracogna, Antonio Fici & Hagen Henrÿ (eds), *International Handbook of Cooperative Law* (Springer-Verlag Berlin Heidelberg, 2013).
200. Council Regulation (EC) No. 1435/2003 of 22 Jul. 2003 on the Statute for a European Cooperative Society (SCE), OJ 2003, L 207 with some corrections by Corrigendum, OJ L 49, 17.2.2007, p. 35 (1435/2003) and Council Directive 2003/72/EC of 22 Jul. 2003 supplementing the Statute for a European Cooperative Society with regard to the involvement of employees, OJ 2003, L 207.

members' needs and to further their business and/or social activities. Unless the articles provide otherwise, the SCE is not allowed to serve non-members.[201] There are no severe restrictions for participating in the formation of an SCE. An SCE may be formed 'from scratch' by five or more natural persons residing in at least two Member States. It may also be formed by one or more natural persons, together with one or more companies, firms and other legal bodies, or by two or more of those companies, firms or legal bodies. The law of at least two different Member States must govern the participating companies, firms and legal bodies. The SCE may also be formed by a merger between cooperatives or by conversion of a cooperative. As with the SE, Member States may provide that a legal body, the head office of which is not in the Community, may participate in the formation of an SCE (*see* paragraph 4.22).[202]

4.46 In many respects, the SCE Regulation is similar to its SE counterpart, for example, regarding the applicable law, the structure of the SCE with the same option between a one-tier and a two-tier system, plus an accompanying directive on the involvement of employees.[203] However, the cooperative nature of the society is reflected by several specific provisions, for example, on the acquisition and loss of membership. The articles may contain certain conditions for membership, such as subscription of a minimum amount of capital.[204] When a member leaves the SCE, he or she may be entitled to repayment of his or her part of the subscribed capital, reduced in proportion to any losses.[205] Another example of expressing the cooperative nature is seen in the 'one member, one vote rule', which is the principle laid down in Article 59(1). However, if the law of the Member State in which the SCE has its registered office so permits, the statutes may provide for multiple votes, though within certain limits, for example, no member may exert more than 30% of the voting rights.[206] Because of its decision-making characteristics, it may not be easy for a cooperative to find investors willing to take shares. Therefore, the articles may allow for members that do not regularly make use of the services of the SCE (non-user members). However, collectively such members may not have more than 25% of total voting rights.[207]

B Single-Member Private Limited Liability Company (SUP)

4.47 As already mentioned in paragraph 4.01, in 2014, the Commission proposed a directive holding a format for single-member private limited liability companies, aiming at a company that follows the same rules in all Member States and has an EU-wide abbreviation - SUP.[208] The overall objective of the proposal was to make it easier for any potential company founder, in particular for SMEs, to set-up companies

201. Article 1 ECS Regulation.
202. Article 2.
203. Articles 8 and 36.
204. Article 14(2).
205. Article 16.
206. Article 59(2).
207. Article 59(3).
208. Proposal for a Directive on single-member private limited liability companies, Brussels, 9.4.2014, COM(2014) 212 final.

abroad. The proposed SUP indeed was to follow the same rules as to online registration by the use of an EU template registration document and articles of association. The proposal further included some basic provisions with regard to the protection of creditors and the division of powers, such as rules for the appointment and removal of directors. In order to facilitate the operation of groups of companies, the proposal stated that instructions issued by the single member to the management body should be binding.[209] The proposal, however, received criticism by the EESC and the Council, after several rounds of discussion, published a much lighter version of the draft directive in May 2015.[210] Most of the rules the Commission planned to harmonize are taken out of the draft, hence these issues will continue to be governed by the diverging national laws for private companies. What remains, essentially, is the mandatory registration online, and even that is not too great an achievement, as the majority of the Member States already allow for online registration.[211]

4.48 The essential provisions of the 2015 SUP proposal are the following

- Several proposed articles provide rules, initially introduced by the Twelfth Directive (replaced by Directive 2009/102/EC), that apply not only to the SUP, but to every single-member company. For instance, the mandatory disclosure of the single member (shareholder) and the obligation to record contracts between the company and the single member are laid down in Articles 3–5. Consequently, Directive 2009/102/EC will be repealed after the proposed directive has entered into force.[212]
- An SUP may be incorporated by an individual or a legal person, or, if a Member State allows for it, by entities without legal personality. Conversion into an SUP by private limited liability companies mentioned in the Annex is also possible (Article 8 and 9). The SUP itself may decide 'at any moment' on its conversion into another company law form, however, the conversion is subject to the conditions laid down by national law (Article 25).
- The registration formalities for those companies that meet the SUP standard shall be governed by national law, but Member States must allow for registration online via a 'national template of registration' (Article 13). To use this facility, the founder has to provide the information specified in Article 11 and also in Article 13. Uniformity is not guaranteed, because, according to section 3 of that article, Member States may decide 'not to request all the information

209. Article 23 of the proposed directive and paragraph 23 of its preamble. On this and other benefits from the original SUP proposal: Pierre-Henri Conac, The Societas Unius Personae (SUP): A 'Passport' for Job Creation and Growth, *ECFR* 2/2015, p. 139 *et seq.*
210. Council of the European Union, Proposal for a Directive of the European Parliament and the Council on single-member private limited liability companies, Brussels 29 May 2015, 9050/15, DRS 41, CODEC 751.
211. Impact Assessment accompanying the proposal for a Directive on single-member private limited liability companies, Brussels, 9.4.2014, SWD(2014) 124 final, p. 29. Further: Christoph Teichmann and Andrea Fröhlich, How to make a Molehill out of a Mountain: The Single-Member Company (SUP) Proposal after Negotiations in the Council http://www.jura.uni-wuerzburg.de/fileadmin/02130100/Teichmann_Froehlich_SUP.pdf (accessed August 2016).
212. But only after two years of that date, Article 29.

from the founder that is listed under paragraph 2'. Other provisions of the proposed directive covering the registration procedure are Article 14, 14a and 14b.

- The first section of Article 14 states that an SUP must be registered in a Member State in which it is to have its registered office and complies with the rules of that Member State. This boils down to subjecting an SUP to the real seat requirement, if that Member State adheres to such system. The Commission's proposal should, in fact, have liberated the SUP by requiring that the 'SUP shall have its registered office and either its central administration or its principal place of business in the Union.'[213]
- The abbreviation SUP will be reserved for companies having the legal form as set out in the directive. The Member State of registration may require SUPs to add to the company name an indication that the company is registered in that Member State (Article 7).
- The SUP shall have only one share and it cannot be split. Where national law allows such a share to be owned by more than one person, those persons shall be regarded as the single member of the SUP (Article 15). This may occur, for instance, where partnerships, not having legal personality, own a share of an SUP.
- The minimum capital is EUR 1 or, where the euro is not the currency, one unit of the Member State's currency. Member States may require the SUP to build up legal reserves as a percentage of the profits of the SUP and/or up to the amount of the minimum share capital required for private limited liability companies listed in Annex I (Article 16).
- Creditor protection is, in principle, left to national law. Article 18(1) states that 'Member States shall ensure the establishment of mechanisms in national law that would prevent SUPs from being unable to pay their debts after making distributions.' According to Article 18, Member States 'may' provide that distributions of dividend are not allowed if a solvency test turns out negative (2(a)) and/or a liquidity test shows that the SUP is unable to pay its debts within six months after the distribution (2(b)).
- Regarding the organization and governance of the SUP, the proposal, again, leaves much to the Member States. They may provide that an SUP has a supervisory board and they may refuse to accept a person to serve as a director if that person is disqualified by another Member State (Article 22). Earlier versions of the proposal included the right of the single member to issue instructions to the management body and the power to act and represent the SUP in relation to third parties. However, these harmonizing provisions were also deleted in the 2015 SUP proposal.[214]

213. Article 10 of the Commission's proposal, Brussels, 9.4.2014, COM(2014) 212 final.
214. For an account of the negotiations on these and other subjects: Christoph Teichmann and Andrea Fröhlich, How to make a Molehill out of a Mountain: The Single-Member Company (SUP) Proposal after Negotiations in the Council http://www.jura.uni-wuerzburg.de/fileadmin/02130100/Teichmann_Froehlich_SUP.pdf (accessed August 2016).

4.48a The 2015 SUP proposal is not only a watered down version of the SUP as envisaged by the Commission but is also a far cry from an earlier plan to introduce a European Private Company (SPE). The idea of an SPE was originally promoted in 1973 by Ms Boucourechliev in a study named *Pour une SARL européenne*.[215] This was to be followed by a comparative study, published by the Commission in 1997.[216] In order to push the idea of the SPE, a draft regulation was proposed by the Paris Chamber of Commerce in 1998.[217] Despite this private initiative, the European Commission did not immediately take action. It viewed the SPE in the larger framework of facilitating SMEs by means of legal, tax and social policy regimes. In its 2003 Action Plan 'Modernising Company Law', the European Commission announced a feasibility study, with the view to presenting a proposal for an SPE statute in the medium term.[218] Eventually, by June 2008, the Commission presented a proposal for a Regulation on the Statute for a European Private Company (the SPE Proposal).[219] The use of a regulation means that SPE legislation would take the same form as that of the other supranational company forms (i.e., the EEIG, the SE and the SCE. However, unlike the SE and SCE, there was no (proposed) accompanying directive on employee involvement for the SPE.[220] The SPE was destined to be a private limited liability company on a European supranational level with the basic features and traditional benefits afforded to the other supranational European forms, such as a procedure for the transfer of the corporate seat within the EU. There is a fair amount of consensus among the various proponents of the SPE that such a simple and flexible corporate form should be specifically geared to SMEs and be subject to uniform law (i.e., ideally with no references to national law).[221] In spite of the obvious benefits an SPE could have for facilitating cross-border cooperation and for the structuring of cross-border operations, the SPE proposal was withdrawn in 2013.[222] Among the impediments for political agreement are those that also weakened the SUP proposal: the real seat requirement versus the liberal incorporation approach and concerns that mandatory employee involvement, especially representation of employees on boards, will be circumvented.

215. Jeanne Boucourechliev, *Pour une SARL européenne* (Paris: PUF, 1973).
216. Propositions pour une société européenne, Étude du centre de recherche sur le droit des affaires de la Chambre de commerce et d'industrie de Paris (CREDA), CCIP-CREDA, 1997.
217. An updated version is published in *European Company Law* 3, no. 6, 279 *et seq.*
218. *Modernising Company Law and Enhancing Corporate Governance in the European Union: A Plan to Move Forward* (Brussels, 21 May 2003), COM(2003) 284 final, 20–21.
219. Presented in June 2008 Commission of the European Communities, 'Proposal for a Council Regulation on the Statute for a European Private Company', {SEC(2008)2098} SEC(2008)2099], Brussels, COM(2008)396/3.
220. Respectively: Council Directive 2001/86/EC of 8 Oct. 2001 supplementing the Statute for the European company with regard to the involvement of employees. OJ 2001, L 294/22; and Council Directive 2003/72/EC of 22 Jul. 2003 supplementing the Statute for a European Cooperative Society with regard to the involvement of employees. OJ 2003, L 207/25. This issue was dealt with rather summarily in Ch. VI of the proposed SPE Regulation.
221. *See* in particular: K-H. Lehne, 'Committee on Legal Affairs', *Report, with Recommendations to the Commission on the European Private Company Statute* (2006/2013(INI) (EN). The report was based on an expert hearing and the statements by Bloemarts, Druzy, Lamandini, Schunk and Teichmann are published in *European Company Law* 3, no. 6 (2006): 265 *et seq.*
222. Brussels, 2.10.2013, COM(2013) 685 final.

CHAPTER 5

Formation and Financing of Companies

I INTRODUCTION

5.01 This chapter aims at analysing the main features with regard to the formation procedure of private and public limited liability companies in the European Union (EU) Member States relevant to this book. In addition, the most essential substantive requirements for formation will be dealt with, as well as liability issues directly connected with the formation of companies. For this purpose, the relevant provisions of the First and Second Directives will be outlined and attention will be drawn, where appropriate, to some of the particularities evident in the different legal systems.[1] Basically, the formation of private and public limited liability companies will be shown to be considerably similar in the relevant Member States. The harmonization programme of the EU, especially through the enactment of, and subsequent amendments to, the First and Second Directives, has certainly contributed to this.

II PUBLIC COMPANIES

A Formation Procedure

5.02 As a rule, a public company can be set up either through its formation or through the transformation of an existing legal entity. In the first case, there are two options: (i) the capital can be subscribed only by the members, resulting in a closely held company; or (ii) the initial capital can also be raised by a public subscription of

1. Although this chapter will deal separately with the formation of public companies and the formation private companies, it is worth mentioning that these two procedures are almost identical in the UK, and quite similar in the Netherlands and in Belgium. The incorporation of a private company in Italy is also largely regulated by the same provisions (namely in respect of incorporation conditions, filing of the deed of incorporation and registration of the company, registration's effects, nullity of the company, founders) by way of references to provisions regarding the public company.

shares, with a view to incorporate it as an open company or a publicly held company. Some jurisdictions, such as Spain or France, provide for this special procedure to form a company (*constitution avec offre au public d'instruments financiers* in French,[2] and *constitución en forma sucesiva por suscripción pública de acciones* in Spanish). Due to the complexity of its requirements, this special procedure has rarely been adopted by those interested in setting up public companies. Nevertheless, it remains the object of regulation in the respective acts.

5.03 The First Directive,[3] applying to both private and public companies, is particularly relevant to the formation of companies. It does not only set standards in relation to the compulsory disclosure of certain documents and particulars but also restricts the grounds on which obligations entered into under the name of the company are not binding – i.e., concerning the validity of obligations – and the situations where the nullity of the company can be ordered. This directive was created with the intention of safeguarding the interests of shareholders and third parties (*see* 3.19 *et seq.*). The Second Directive, also commonly designated as the Capital Directive, is deemed to govern the maintenance and alteration of capital and, most importantly with regard to this chapter, the formation of public or stock companies. This directive's main objective is the protection of the interests of the company's shareholders and creditors (*see* 3.35 *et seq.*).[4]

5.04 Member States are supposed to ensure that companies disclose their instrument of constitution and articles of association ('statutes' according to the First Directive), where they are contained in a different instrument.[5] Accordingly, the instrument of incorporation or the statutes must contain, at the very least, information with regard to:[6]

- the type and name[7] of the company;
- the objects of the company;
- the amount of the subscribed capital, where the company has no authorized capital;
- the amount of the authorized capital, where the company has such capital, and the amount of the subscribed capital at the time the company is incorporated and at the time of any change in the authorized capital;

2. Maurice Cozian, Alain Viandier et Florence Deboissy, *Droit des sociétés*, 28e édition (Paris: LexisNexis, 2015), 295.
3. The original First Directive is replaced by the consolidating Directive 2009/101/EC, *see* 3.18 *et seq.*
4. The original Second Directive is replaced by the consolidating Directive 2012/30/EU, *see* 3.36, and referrals are made to the 2012 directive unless otherwise stated.
5. Article 2(a) First Council Directive 68/151/EEC of 9 Mar. 1968, now: Directive 2009/101/EC of 16 Sep. 2009, OJ 2009, L 258 (*see* 3.18). By Directive 2012/17/EU, OJ 2012, L 156a few provisions are inserted with a view to realise interconnection of central, commercial and companies registers (Articles 2a, 3a-3d, 4a-4e and 7a) (*see* 3.61a).
6. Article 2 Second Council Directive 77/91/EEC of December 1976, now Directive 2012/30/EU of 25 Oct. 2012, OJ 2012 L 315 74-97 (*see* 3.36).
7. The name for a public company shall contain a description which is different from the description required for other types of companies, Article 1(1) Second Directive, now Directive 2012/30/EU.

- in so far as they are not legally determined, the rules governing the number of, and the procedure for appointing, members of the bodies responsible for representing the company with regard to third parties, administration, management, supervision or control of the company and the allocation of powers among those bodies;
- the duration of the company, unless this duration is indefinite.

5.05 In addition, the instrument of incorporation, the articles of association or a separate document published in conformity with the procedure rules stated in Article 3 of the First Directive, must contain the following minimum content:[8]

- the registered office;
- the nominal value and number of the shares subscribed;
- the number of shares subscribed without stating the nominal value, provided that such shares may be issued under national law;
- any special conditions restricting the transfer of shares;
- if there are different classes of shares, the details required in the three points listed above shall be provided with regard to each class, as well as the rights attached to the shares of each class;
- an indication as to the type of shares (registered or bearer shares, where both are allowed according to national law) and any provisions pertaining to the conversion of those shares, unless this procedure is provided by law;
- the amount of the subscribed capital paid up at the time of incorporation;
- the nominal value of the shares or, where there is no nominal value, the number of shares issued for a consideration other than in cash, together with the type of the consideration and the name of the contributor;
- the identity of the natural or legal persons by whom, or in whose name, the statutes or the instrument(s) of incorporation have been signed;
- the full amount, or at least an approximation, of the formation costs payable by, or chargeable to, the company and, where appropriate, also the costs before the company is authorized to start operating;
- any special advantages granted to anyone who has been involved in the formation of the company or, where applicable, in transactions leading to the grant of an authorization to commence business.

Because the Second Directive provides for a minimum to be disclosed, Member States may require other elements to be added to the documents to be disclosed.

5.05a In Germany, the articles of association of the *Aktiengesellschaft* (AG) must also contain provisions stipulating the form that the company's announcements shall

8. Article 3 Second Directive, now Directive 2012/30/EU.

assume, and the indication of the enterprise's objects must include details as to the type of goods and products to be traded and manufactured, when industrial and commercial enterprises are concerned.[9]

5.05b The formation deed of a Spanish *Sociedad Anónima* (SA)[10] also comprises of a statement ensuring the founders' intention to form this type of company; the identity of those who will, at first, manage and represent the company; and the covenants agreed between the members, provided that they are in accordance with the provisions and structural principles of the SA.[11,12] Furthermore, the articles of association should include the commencement date of its operations (provided that it is not prior to the execution date of the incorporation deed, except in cases of transformation); the procedure for shareholder meetings; and an indication as to the completion date of the company's financial year.[13]

5.05c In the UK, the two principal instruments of incorporation are the memorandum and the articles of association. Although the formation process in the UK was not considered to be especially burdensome for persons interested in setting up companies, the Company Law Review Steering Group (hereinafter 'the CLR Steering Group') – a committee charged with the responsibility of developing a consultation process with a view of creating the 'Strategic Framework' for the forthcoming modernization of company law – has proposed some changes of substance with the view to promoting an even 'smoother and more efficient' process. The CLR Steering Group also suggested some improvements with regard to the drafting of certain provisions, with the intention of making them 'simpler and more readily comprehensible'.[14] Many provisions of the Companies Act enacted on 8 November 2006 (hereinafter 'Companies Act 2006'), incorporate the recommendations prepared by the CLR Steering Group. Consequently, following the Companies Act 2006, the shape and scope of the memorandum has changed considerably.[15] In essence, the memorandum of association now serves the purpose of stating the subscribers' intention to establish a company and become members of the company. In the case of a company that is to have a share capital, the memorandum also demonstrates the members' agreement to take at least one share each.[16] Under the UK legal system, the company's constitution comprises not only the

9. § 23, ss 3 and 4 *Aktiengesetz* (German Stock Corporation Act).
10. The SA is essentially regulated by the *Ley de Sociedades de Capital*, as amended. It is also important to refer the Reglamento del Registro Mercantil ('Spanish Commercial Register Regulation'), dealing with the aspects related to the registration of the SA.
11. Article 22 Ley de Sociedades de Capital and Article 114 Spanish Commercial Register Regulation.
12. Article 28 Ley de Sociedades de Capital and Articles 115 *et seq.* Spanish Commercial Register Regulation.
13. Articles 23 (f), 24 and 26 Ley de Sociedades de Capital.
14. Companies Act 2006 – Explanatory Notes, retrievable via http://www.legislation.gov.uk/ukpga/2006/46/notes/contents; and Companies Act 2006, 'Regulatory Impact Assessment', January 2007, retrievable via http://webarchive.nationalarchives.gov.uk/20070603164510/http:/www.dti.gov.uk/files/file29937.pdf.
15. *Ibid.*
16. Section 8 Companies Act 2006 and Companies Act 2006 – Explanatory Notes, p. 6, retrievable via http://www.legislation.gov.uk/ukpga/2006/46/notes/contents.

articles of association, but also some classes of member's resolutions and agreements.[17] The articles of association are deemed to deal with the crucial information regarding the 'internal allocation of powers between directors and members of a company'.[18] It is also possible to (fully or partially) adopt model articles.[19] These model articles are also applied, where necessary, as default articles.[20]

5.05d In Italy, Article 2328(2) of the Civil Code provides for a list of mandatory requirements in relation to the contents of the deed of incorporation. However, in practice, the deed of incorporation of a public company includes more information than what is required by law as a minimum, because it is an established practice to outline the governance structure as well. Usually, two documents are drafted: the *deed of incorporation* and the *statute*, the latter being more analytical and encompassing legal and agreed-upon norms pertaining to the company's functioning. The two documents make up a single contract; the statute is an integral part of the deed of incorporation (Article 2328(3) Civil Code).

5.05e Recently, the EU has been paying more attention to what is called digitalization in company law, as part of the wider policy regarding the Digital Single Market.[21] Digitalization will change the way companies communicate with the state, *inter alia*, regarding the filing of documents and online registration (*see* 4.48). As already mentioned in paragraph 3.19, Directive 2009/101/EU, as amended by Directive 2012/17/EU, requires the interconnection of companies' registers. The Business Registries Interconnection System (BRIS) will be established for this purpose. BRIS will make it easy to access information on EU companies via the e-Justice or other national portals. It will also facilitate electronic communication between registries in relation to cross-border mergers and branches of companies registered in other Member States. The Commission's Implementing Regulation 2015/884 sets technical specifications, standards and procedures for BRIS. Furthermore, digitalization has an impact on how companies communicate with their shareholders and other stakeholders. Companies should be allowed to provide information by electronic means and, on turn, shareholders should be allowed to provide information to companies and to exercise their rights by electronic means.

17. Companies Act 2006 – Explanatory Notes, p. 10, retrievable via http://www.legislation.gov.uk/ukpga/2006/46/notes/contents. Sections 29–30 Companies Act 2006.
18. Companies Act 2006 – Explanatory Notes, p. 6, retrievable via http://www.legislation.gov.uk/ukpga/2006/46/notes/contents. The Companies Act 2006 introduces the possibility to include a 'provision for entrenchment' to make it harder for the members to amend certain provisions of the company's articles. Companies Act 2006, 'Regulatory Impact Assessment', January 2007, p. 39, retrievable via http://webarchive.nationalarchives.gov.uk/20070603164510/http:/www.dti.gov.uk/files/file29937.pdf.
19. Different forms are available for public companies and private companies limited by shares, s. 19 Companies Act 2006.
20. Section 20 Companies Act 2006.
21. http://ec.europa.eu/justice/events/company-law-2015/index_en.htm (accessed April 2017); Opening speech on the Conference on *Company Law in the Digital Age*, Brussels, 2 Oct. 2015 by Commissioner Věra Jourová, *Company Law in the Digital Age* and the *Report on digitalisation in company law* by the Informal Company Law Expert Group (ICLEG), March 2016.

The 2016 report of independent experts includes some thirty recommendations on issues that the Commission should take action on.

5.06 In accordance with the First Directive, the instrument of constitution and the company statutes 'shall be drawn up and certified in due legal form', except in those Member States, whose laws provide for preventive control at the time of formation of a company.[22] The same applies to any amendments made to these documents.

5.06a Most Member States analysed in this chapter regarding the formation of a public limited liability company provide for a mandatory requirement to notarize the instrument of incorporation and/or the statutes.[23] The statutes of a French company, however, must be drawn up in writing before a notary when there is a contribution of a good that is subject to land registration ('*bien soumis à publicité foncière*' – e.g., real estate).[24] The Belgian regime provides for a distinctive rule that requires companies to prepare a financial plan on incorporation for a two-year period, which assures the adequacy of the subscribed capital with a view to the company's ordinary operations under normal circumstances. Consequently, if the company turns out to be insolvent within three years from the date of incorporation, and its capital has been considered by the court to be insufficient to carry out the company's proposed operations during at least two years, the founding members will bear unlimited liability.[25] The notary does not verify this financial plan, but keeps it together with the original articles of association. The UK has no concept of a notarial deed. In addition to the requirements set out in the Second Directive, the English system requires[26] a statement of compliance,[27] which is aimed at replacing the former 'statutory declarations' (legally attested signatures). In Italy, a public company may be set up in two ways:[28] (a) by *contract*; and (b) following the 2003 reform of company law,[29] by *unilateral deed*. In any case, the deed of incorporation must be a public deed; otherwise, the contract/agreement is null and void.[30]

22. Article 10 First Directive: now: Article 11 Directive 2009/101/EC.
23. Article 440 *Wetboek van Vennootschappen* (Belgian Companies Code); § 23 German Stock Corporation Act; Articles 157 and 306 *Kodeks spółek handlowych* (Polish Commercial Companies Code); Article 44 Ley de Sociedades de Capital; Article 64 *Boek 2 Burgerlijk Wetboek* (Book 2 Dutch Civil Code).
24. Maurice Cozian, Alain Viandier et Florence Deboissy, Droit des sociétés, 28e édition (Paris: LexisNexis, 2015), 106. The lists of subscriptions may be registered with a notary but also by other institutions such as the Caisse des dépôts, Article R225-6 *Code de commerce* (French Commercial Code).
25. Articles 440 and 456(4) Belgian Companies Code.
26. It is also worth mentioning that the process of forming a company in the UK is almost identical whether the company is to be private or public.
27. Section 13 Companies Act 2006. This statement does not have to be witnessed and can be submitted either in paper or electronic form. It is, without a doubt, an offence to make a false statement of compliance, s. 1112 Companies Act 2006.
28. G.F. Campobasso, *Diritto Commerciale. 2. Diritto delle Società*. Nona Edizione, UTET Giuridica, Wolters Kluwer Italia S.r.l. 2015; p. 150.
29. Legislative Decree No. 6 of 17 Jan. 2003 'Riforma organica della disciplina delle società di capitali e società cooperative, in attuazione della legge delega 3 ottobre 2001, n. 366', published in the *Official Journal* No. 17 on 22 Jan. 2003 (Supplement No. 8).
30. Articles 2382(2) and 2332(1) Civil Code. The same goes for the preliminary contract, Article 1351 Civil Code.

1 *Registration*

5.07 Generally speaking, after obtaining the deed of incorporation, the incorporators must file an extract of the deed and statutes within a certain timeframe, and where appropriate, also file other documents, with a view to *register* the company into the commercial register. The commercial register should then register the company, provided that all the documents are properly submitted and every legal requirement has been duly complied with.[31] Accordingly, an announcement of the registration must be published in the national gazette, appointed for that purpose by the Member State.

5.08 Member States should ensure that files are opened in a central commercial register or companies register for each of the companies to be registered therein.[32] Member States are also required to facilitate the filing of, *inter alia*, the instrument of constitution and the statutes by electronic means. In addition, they must also ensure that copies of those documents are obtainable from the register 'by paper means or electronic means', at the applicant's choice.[33] The disclosure of the instrument of incorporation and the statutes must be effected by publication in the national gazette, which may be kept in electronic form and it may even be replaced with equally effective means, including a system whereby the information can be accessed through a central electronic platform in chronological order.[34] The instrument of incorporation and the statutes 'shall be drawn up and filed in one of the languages permitted by the language rules applicable in the Member State' in which the file is deemed to be opened.[35]

5.08a In the Member States, various types of institutions keep the companies register and handle the registrations. It can be the (commercial) court, as is the case in Belgium and France; the Chamber of Commerce, as is the case in the Netherlands; or the Registrar of Companies, which is the competent authority in the UK.[36] Registration is essential for the company to come into existence in most of the Member States (*see* 1.09). In the event that no notarial deed is required, registration assumes particular importance. Therefore, in the UK, the Registrar will issue the company with a certificate of incorporation, which is conclusive evidence that all formalities of incorporation have been complied with and that the public company has been registered.[37] In Italy, the notary drafts the deed of incorporation (provided that the respective legal requirements are met) and, at the same time of the filing of the deed and its annexes, he requests the registration of the company in the register of

31. *Inter alia*, tax duties. Francis Lefebvre, *Sociedades Mercantiles 2007*, Ediciones Francis Lefebvre, 2006, p. 77, with regard to the formation of a Spanish SA, Article 31 *et seq.* Ley de Sociedades de Capital. Another example is Article 69 Book 2 Dutch Civil Code.
32. Article 3(1) First Directive; now: Directive 2009/101/EC.
33. Article 3(2) and (3) First Directive; now: Article 3(3) and 3(4) Directive 2009/101/EC.
34. Article 3(4) First Directive; now: Article 3(5) Directive 2009/101/EC.
35. Article 3a First Directive; Article 4 Directive 2009/101/EC.
36. Sections 1060 *et seq.* Companies Act 2006. Further: Articles 67, 68 and 73 Belgian Companies Code, Articles R210-1 *et seq.* French Commercial Code and Annexe a l'ártricle R123-30, § 36 German Stock Corporation Act, Article 3 *Handelsregisterwet* (Netherlands).
37. Sections 14–16 Companies Act 2006.

enterprises. The office of the register of enterprises, before registering the deed of incorporation, conducts a check on the formal regularity of the documents (Article 2330(3) Civil Code). Registration has 'constitutive effectiveness' (*efficacia costitutiva*), meaning that it is the moment when the company acquires legal personality (Article 2331(1) Civil Code).

B Substantive Requirements

5.09 A public company can be formed for any purpose, in accordance with the law, by one or more persons acting as founders/subscribers. In some countries, the participation of more than one person is required for the formation of a public company, as opposed to the private company, which can generally be formed as a single-member company. This requirement, however, seems to be declining, since formation of a single-member public company is allowed in the Netherlands and Poland, for example.[38] Germany dropped the requirement that only five persons can form an AG in 1994, and the UK, in 2006, also enacted rules whereby a single person is able to form a public company (and not just a private company).[39] In France, the minimum number of founders and shareholders required to form an SA is two (however, for the public companies whose shares are admitted to negotiation on a regulated market or on a multilateral system of negotiation, the minimum number of shareholders is still seven).[40] In Spain, the minimum is also set at two for both types of limited liability company (however, it is worth mentioning that the Ley de Sociedades de Capital includes a specific chapter on single-member companies, which applies to public and private limited liability companies).[41] The Belgian Companies Act apparently requires two or more founders.[42] Where national law requires a company to have more than one member, the fact that all shares are held by one member 'shall not lead to the automatic dissolution of the company', according to Article 5 of the Second Directive. In Italy, a public company can be set up by a single member by a unilateral deed (Article 2328(1) C.C.) and, as a general rule, only the company is liable for its obligations.[43]

38. Article 64 (2) Book 2 Dutch Civil Code; and Article 301 Polish Commercial Companies Code.
39. § 2 German Stock Corporation Act as amended by the *Gesetz für kleine Aktiengesellschaften und zur Deregulierung des Aktienrechts*, BGBL 1994 I, 1961 and s. 7 Companies Act 2006, on the recommendation of the Company Law Steering Committee, *see* the Explanatory Notes, *o.c.*, p. 6.
40. The minimum number of shareholders generally applicable used to be of seven, however, the Law no. 2014-1545 of 20 Dec. 2014 in respect of the simplification of the companies' business authorized the French Government to reduce that minimum number of shareholders on SAs. Maurice Cozian, *Alain Viandier et Florence Deboissy, Droit des sociétés*, 28e édition (Paris: LexisNexis, 2015), 296.
41. Article L225-1 French Commercial Code, Article 19 and Articles 12–17 of Ley de Sociedades de Capital.
42. Article 440 Belgian Companies Act, whereas for the private company it is explicitly allowed to have only one founder, Article 211.
43. However, the Italian legislator introduced certain precautions: (i) the single founder has a joint liability, together with those who conducted operations before registration; (ii) there is a stricter framework with reference to contributions, in order to safeguard the actual formation of the company's pool of assets: contributions in kind must always be fully paid-up; if the plurality of

5.10 The capital requirements pertaining to the formation of public limited liability companies are a subject covered by the Second Directive (Articles 6–12). It is important to note that, in Europe, there are different approaches with regard to legal capital and the requirements for its maintenance. This concept was only introduced, for instance, in the UK, due to the implementation of the Second Directive, which, to a certain extent, followed the German model. There is no consensus as to the need to maintain the legal capital regime.

5.10a At the time that the Second Directive was adopted in Europe, the US Model Business Corporation Act was doing away with legal capital and mandatory pre-emption rights, due to their alleged ineffectiveness and burdening effect on corporate activities, with pointless costs.[44] In 2004, a study on the merits of this legal system was published by an interdisciplinary working group of experts led by Jonathan Rickford and supported by the British Accounting Standards Board (ASB) and the Company Law Centre at the British Institute of International Comparative Law (BIICL). According to this study, a legal capital regime is costly, redundant and defective. In practice creditors do not widely rely upon this regime and, according to the report, it tends to produce 'inconsistent results as between companies within Member States and between different Member States within the EU'. Not surprisingly, the group supports the idea that the Second Directive should be repealed.[45,46] According to Rickford, in such a case the UK could still 'rely on fiduciary duties (including the special duty for creditors) and wrongful trading, plus robust liquidation procedures'.[47]

5.10b The opposite conclusion was drawn by the Working Group 'Kapital in Europa' directed by Marcus Lutter. This group of German and other European company law experts carried out a study on the benefits of fixed legal capital and its related specifics.[48] The conclusions achieved by this study, which was published in 2006, are that the concept of fixed legal capital has a useful function, that the EU Commission

shareholders no longer exists, outstanding payments must be made within ninety days; (iii) it is not necessary to refer the single-membership within the company's name, but it must be included in all deeds and correspondence; and (iv) the name, surname, date and place of birth, domicile and citizenship of the single founder, or subsequent different single-member, must be filed with the register by the directors; since failure to comply leads to unlimited liability, this task can be taken on by the single-member.

44. *See* 'European Shadow Financial Regulatory Committee of The Centre for European Policy Studies Statement n. 21'.
45. J. Rickford *et al.*, 'Reforming Capital: Report of the Interdisciplinary Group on Capital Maintenance', *European Business Law Review* 15 (2004); *see also* J. Rickford, 'Legal Approaches to Restricting Distributions to Shareholders: Balance Sheet Tests and Solvency Tests', in *European Business Law Review* 7, (2006): 179.
46. The same position was adopted in 19 Feb. 2007 by the European Shadow Financial Regulatory Committee of The Centre for European Policy Studies, *see* 'European Shadow Financial Regulatory Committee of The Centre for European Policy Studies Statement n.21', *o.c.*
47. J. Rickford, 'Legal Approaches to Restricting Distributions to Shareholders: Balance Sheet Tests and Solvency Tests', *European Business Law Review* 7 (2006): 179.
48. *See* Marcus Lutter (ed.), 'Legal Capital in Europe', *European Company and Financial Law Review*, special volume 1 (2006).

must be convinced as to the benefits of the Second Directive and that there is leeway to amend this Directive with a view to render it even more effective.[49]

1 Capital

5.11 The Second Directive provides that the Member States shall require a minimum share capital to be subscribed for on incorporation.[50] This minimum may be not be less than EUR 25,000[51,52] and Member States have implemented differing amounts for this minimum capital requirement.

5.11a The amounts required as a minimum capital by the Member States dealt with in this book are as follows:

- The minimum share capital that shall be subscribed for on the formation of a public company in Belgium amounts to EUR 61,500.[53]
- The registered share capital required for the formation of the French SA must be at least EUR 37,000.[54,55]
- The minimum share capital stipulated under German Company Law for the formation of an AG is EUR 50,000.[56]
- The share capital set as minimum for the formation of a Dutch NV amounts to EUR 45,000.[57]
- The formation of the Polish public company requires a minimum share capital of PLN 500,000 (approximately EUR 116,220).[58]
- The formation of the Spanish SA requires a minimum share capital of EUR[59] 60,000.
- The minimum amount required in the UK is GBP 50,000 (approximately EUR 58,620).[60]

49. *See* Universität Bonn website, http://www.zew.uni-bonn.de.
50. Some jurisdictions refer to an 'authorised share capital', i.e., a figure that acts as a ceiling on the amount of capital that may be issued (in any case this limit can be augmented through an ordinary resolution). The Companies Act 2006 abolished the requirement to have an initial 'authorised share capital'. *See* Companies Act 2006 – Explanatory Notes, *o.c.* and Companies Act 2006, 'Regulatory Impact Assessment', January 2007, retrievable via http://webarchive.nationalarchives.gov.uk/20070603164510/http:/www.dti.gov.uk/files/file29937.pdf). The Dutch Civil Code, Article 67 (2), states that the authorised [and issued] share capital must amount at least to the minimum capital.
51. Article 6 (1) Second Directive, now Directive 2012/30/EU.
52. Shares cannot be issued at a price below their nominal value, or, in the absence of a nominal value, their accountable par, Article 8 Second Directive, now Directive 2012/30/EU.
53. Articles 439 and 448 Belgian Companies Code.
54. Some activities require a higher minimum share capital, e.g., EUR 450,000 for insurance companies and EUR 225,000 for banks. Maurice Cozian, Alain Viandier et Florence Deboissy, *Droit des sociétés*, 28e édition (Paris: LexisNexis, 2015), 296.
55. Article L224-2 French Commercial Code.
56. Section 7 German Stock Corporation Act.
57. Article 67 (2) Book 2 Dutch Civil Code.
58. Article 308 Polish Commercial Companies Code.
59. Article 4 (2) Ley de Sociedades de Capital.
60. Section 763, 1 Companies Act 2006.

- In Italy, the public company features a minimum capital requirement of EUR 50,000, with the exception of some cases of mandatory higher minimum capital, regulated by special legislation, such as banking and financial companies, asset management companies and investment intermediaries.[61] Such exceptions may, of course, also occur in other Member States.

5.12 The Directive further states that 'shares issued for a consideration must be paid up' at incorporation to at least 25% of their nominal value.[62] Furthermore, 'shareholders may not be released from the obligation to pay up their contributions'.[63] With the exception of France, all jurisdictions analysed set this minimum precisely at 25% of the nominal value of the shares subscribed for. In France, this percentage was set at 50% of the nominal value and the balance must be paid up within five years of incorporation.[64]

5.12a Failure to comply with the national provisions pertaining to the minimum capital to be paid up can trigger the company's nullity by court order (Article 12 (b)(iv) Directive 2009/101/EC). It may not always be clear when such failure occurs, because EU Law does not prescribe a time limit within which the balance amount must be paid.[65]

5.12b In Belgium and the Netherlands, the rules with regard to the minimum share capital go beyond the scope of the directive's requirement, because the minimum share capital prescribed in these two jurisdictions relates not only to the minimum amount to be subscribed for but also to the minimum amount to be paid up at incorporation.[66]

5.13 The Second Directive requires the subscribed capital to only consist of cash or 'assets capable of economic assessment'. To secure the latter's value, any contribution other than in cash must be subjected to an independent expert's report. These requirements and the exceptions allowed to Member States have already been discussed in paragraphs 3.39 and 3.40, to which the reader is referred.

5.13a According to Article 10(2) of the Second Directive, the experts' report should contain 'at least a description of each of the assets comprising the consideration as well as of the methods of valuation used and shall state whether the values arrived at by the application of these methods correspond at least to the number and nominal value or, where there is no nominal value, to the accountable par and, where appropriate, to the

---

61. Until 2014, the minimum capital requirement used to be of EUR 120,000.
62. Article 9 (1) Second Directive, now Directive 2012/30/EU.
63. However, an exemption can be made provided that the rules on capital reduction are observed, Article 12 Second Directive, now Article 14 Directive 2012/30/EU.
64. Article L225-3 French Commercial Code.
65. Erik Werlauff, *EU – Company Law – Common Business Law of 28 States*, 2nd edition (Copenhagen: DJØF Publishing, 2003), 208.
66. Articles 439 and 448 Belgian Companies Code and Article 67(3) and 80(1) Book 2 Dutch Civil Code.

premium on the shares to be issued for them'. The expert is thus required to state whether the value of the assets equals at least the nominal value (or accountable par) of the shares issued in exchange for these assets. Where the nominal value is kept low, it will not be problematic for the expert to meet this requirement, because then the shares will be issued at a premium, which he does not have to include in his statement.

5.13b Because Article 10 represents a minimum level of protection and does not pertain to all details of consideration other than in cash upon formation, legislation in the various Member States regarding this issue is certainly not identical. A few examples may illustrate this. The Belgian Companies Code requires the founders to report after the expert has reported and to explain why they value the non-cash contribution differently (if they do so). The Dutch legislator has provided for the reverse order and requires the expert to report on the description and valuation of the non-cash contribution, as drawn up by the founders.[67] Where the Directive states that any consideration other than in cash must be transferred, in full, to the company within five years of the date of incorporation or the authorization to commence business, Member States may opt for a shorter period. In Poland, the contribution in kind must be fully paid up within one year of registration of the company. In the Netherlands, payment must take place 'without delay' after subscription ('*or after the day on which an additional payment, which may be made through a contribution other than money, must have been received by the Corporation or on which such contribution has been agreed upon*'). However, in Germany, the five-year term has been implemented.[68] In Italy, contributions must be made in cash, if the articles of association do not provide otherwise (Article 2342(1) Civil Code). At least 25% of cash contributions must be deposited with a bank.[69] With reference to non-cash contributions, the framework differs from the one of private companies, and not all assets capable of economic assessment are allowed. It is not possible to confer the performance of work and services (Article 2342(5) Civil Code). It is possible to confer these in other ways, provided that they are not included in the share capital. Contributions in kind and assignment of receivables must be paid in full upon subscription (Article 2342(3) Civil Code). In general, it is possible to confer anything that can be objectively evaluated and that can be immediately made available to the company.[70]

Article 2343 provides for a specific evaluation procedure when it comes to non-cash contributions. The contributor must submit a sworn report (*relazione giurata di stima*) of an expert, appointed by the court of the district of the company's registered office; the report must be attached to the articles of association.

67. Article 444 Belgian Companies Code; Article 94a Book 2 Dutch Civil Code.
68. Article 309(3) Polish Commercial Companies Code, Article 80b(2) Book 2 Dutch Civil Code and § 36a(2) *AktG* (German Stock Corporation Act).
69. G.F. Campobasso, *Diritto Commerciale. 2. Diritto delle Società*. Nona Edizione, UTET Giuridica, Wolters Kluwer Italia S.r.l. 2015; pp. 181–183.
70. G.F. Campobasso, *Diritto Commerciale. 2. Diritto delle Società*. Nona Edizione, UTET Giuridica, Wolters Kluwer Italia S.r.l. 2015; pp. 183–185.

C Pre-incorporation Transactions

5.14 When a company acquires legal personality, it is fully capable of acting in its own name and is regarded to be a separate legal person, distinct from its members and, as a result, confers limited liability to them.[71] However, the process of establishing a company is far from instantaneous, and, therefore, many questions may arise as to the capacity of the company to acquire certain rights or liabilities before the moment of incorporation. The First Directive provides a rule with regard to the so-called pre-incorporation contracts, which has been briefly mentioned in paragraphs 3.25 and 3.26. Pursuant to Article 8 (ex Article 7), if, before a company has acquired legal personality, actions are carried out in the company's name and 'the company does not assume the obligations arising from such action, the persons who acted shall, without limit, be jointly and severally liable therefore', unless agreed otherwise. Accordingly, subsequent to obtaining legal personality, the company may assume liability for pre-incorporation transactions. Article 8 aims at ensuring that third parties contracting with the company always have recourse to a debtor.[72]

5.15 There are diverging opinions concerning the choice of the party on whose behalf an action has to be taken for the Article 8 rule to apply: the company as existing prior to incorporation (which may constitute a partnership under national law), or the future legal person. In any event, as noted by Grundman, the English-language version of the First Directive (containing the phrase 'before a company being formed has acquired legal personality, action has been carried out in its name') points to the application of Article 8 at least in those cases, where action was taken on behalf of the future legal person.[73] Further, the assumption of liability by the company does not necessarily demand the company's consent, even though the English-language version, as well as the German and the French, seems to suggest this interpretation.[74] Although the assumption of liability does not require the consent of the third party (creditor), it seems that there is a presumption that the third party knew he was dealing with a company. Otherwise, the third party cannot be obliged to accept that a company assumes the position of his 'presumed contractual partner'.[75]

5.15a According to Belgian company law, companies are fully incorporated upon the execution of the deed, i.e., they acquire full legal personality before registration.[76] The company can assume liabilities arising from pre-incorporation transactions, provided that these liabilities arose within two years of the filing of the extract of the deed and

71. *See* 1.09 for the moment upon which a company comes into existence.
72. Erik Werlauff, *o.c.*, p. 207.
73. Stefan Grundman, *European Company Law*, 2nd edition (Cambridge-Antwerp-Portland: Intersentia, 2012), 156, according to him, the wording of Article 9(2) of the EEIG Regulation supports this view.
74. Stefan Grundman, *o.c.*, pp. 140–142.
75. Erik Werlauff, *o.c.*, p. 207.
76. Articles 66 and 450 Belgian Companies Code.

articles, and that the ratification of these liabilities is performed within two months of the aforementioned filing.[77] In the case of a public company, it is possible to provide for a distinction between founders, owning altogether at least one-third of the capital, and other subscribers.[78] The latter are not liable for the liabilities connected with the subscription, raising and effective payment of the share capital.[79]

5.15b While the founders of a French SA do not necessarily have to sign a notarial deed, the pre-registered company is formed the moment the contract is signed, though the SA only acquires legal personality upon registration.[80] Persons who have acted on behalf of the company in formation (*société en formation*), before it has acquired full legal personality, are held jointly and severally liable for those acts, except if the company, after having been properly formed and registered, assumes its obligations thereby entered into.[81] Nonetheless, it is worth mentioning that an action on behalf of the future legal person is void under French law; therefore, only actions on behalf of the company prior to registration are legally accepted.[82]

5.15c German Company Law, with regard to the formation of a public company, sets out two essential criteria in the process of establishing a company. The promoters must subscribe to all shares in return for contributions.[83] This subscription has to be recorded by a notary and included in the formation deed. Once all shares are subscribed to, the company is established and a *pre-AG* is considered to be formed.[84] It is 'an independent organisational form which possesses temporary legal capacity and, as such, is liable for legal and statutory obligations'.[85] However, the pre-AG does not hold full legal personality until registration and whoever acts in its name as such is personally liable.[86] Registration provides the company with legal personality, though it is possible to assume rights and liabilities negotiated for it prior to registration.[87]

5.15d The public company in the Netherlands is incorporated upon the notarial deed of incorporation.[88] Prior to its incorporation, legal acts may be performed in the name of the company to be incorporated. Legal acts prior to incorporation are binding upon the company only if it, after its incorporation, expressly or implicitly, ratifies those acts. Persons who perform such legal acts are bound jointly and severally until ratification by the company ('*unless the contrary has been stipulated explicitly in respect of*

77. Article 60 Belgian Companies Code.
78. Article 450 Belgian Companies Code.
79. Article 456 Belgian Companies Code.
80. Article L 210-6 French Commercial Code.
81. Article L 210-6 French Commercial Code.
82. Stefan Grundman, *o.c.*, pp. 140–142.
83. § 29 *AktG* (German Stock Corporation Act).
84. § 29 *AktG* (German Stock Corporation Act).
85. *See* Wirth, Arnold & Greene, *Corporate Law in Germany* (München: Verlag C.H. Beck, 2004), 69 and 74.
86. § 41(1) *AktG* (German Stock Corporation Act).
87. § 41(2) *AktG* (German Stock Corporation Act).
88. Article 64(2) Book 2 Dutch Civil Code.

that juridical act'), but even then they are liable for any loss sustained by a third party as a result of non-performance by the company, provided that they knew or could reasonably have known that the company could not perform its obligations.[89] Upon incorporation, registration must follow. If the directors fail to meet the obligation to register, they are jointly and severally liable for legal acts binding upon the company.[90]

5.15e The incorporation of a Polish public company is similar to the incorporation of an AG. The public company is formed when all of its shares are subscribed to, and from that moment on, there exists a joint-stock company 'in formation'.[91] Accordingly, the company is then able to acquire rights in its own name.[92] After its entry into the register, the public company in formation acquires legal personality and becomes a party to the rights and obligations of the company in formation.[93]

5.15f The Spanish SA acquires legal personality upon registration with the Commercial Registry. Persons acting in the name of the company before its registration are personally liable for the obligations arising thereof. Once registered, the SA assumes liability for several acts and contracts, in the first place, the acts and contracts that were essential to its registration. Furthermore, liability is assumed for pre-incorporation contracts (and other acts) performed by the directors within the powers conferred upon them by the deed and for acts stipulated by a specific mandate granted to the persons designated for that purpose by all the shareholders. Finally, the SA can assume liability for other pre-incorporation contracts (and other acts) provided that the company accepts them within three months.[94]

5.15g In the UK, companies are formed and acquire legal personality upon registration.[95] Prior to registration, the founders of the company may enter into contracts on the proposed company's behalf.[96] Since there is no concept of a pre-registered company structure, a contract on behalf of the company prior to registration must be construed as a contract on behalf of the future legal person or it will be void.[97] Anyone purporting to act for the proposed company, or as an agent for the company, is liable concerning the contract, unless there is an express agreement to the contrary. This provision aims at improving legal certainty of transactions for third parties 'by avoiding the consequences of the contract with the company being a nullity'.[98]

5.15h The 2003 reform of Italian company law provided this topic with a more detailed and analytical framework. Pursuant to Article 2331(2) of the Civil Code, for operations conducted in the company's name before its registration, unlimited and joint liability is imposed on those, who acted on its behalf towards third parties. Most

89. Article 93 Book 2 Dutch Civil Code.
90. Article 69 Book 2 Dutch Civil Code.
91. Article 310 Polish Commercial Companies Code.
92. Article 11(1) Polish Commercial Companies Code.
93. Article 12 Polish Commercial Companies Code.
94. Articles 33, 36, 37 and 38 Ley de Sociedades de Capital.
95. Section 7 Companies Act 2006.
96. Paul Davies, *Gower's Principles of Modern Company Law* (Sweet and Maxwell, 1997), 142.
97. *Ibid.*
98. Paul Davies, *o.c.*, p. 142.

case law applies the same principle to operations conducted before the stipulation of the deed of incorporation. Further, either the single founder or, in case of more than one founder, those who authorized or allowed to operate on its behalf are also jointly and unlimitedly liable towards third parties (Article 2331(2) Civil Code). Issuing shares or offering them to the public before the company is registered is not allowed, unless the incorporation occurs through public subscription (Article 2331(5) Civil Code).

III PRIVATE COMPANIES

A Formation Procedure

5.16 Generally, the formation procedure for private companies is not very different from the procedure for public companies, even though the scope of the Second Directive is limited to public companies. The instruments of incorporation and the articles of a private company contain roughly the same elements that are demanded for public companies and the formalities regarding the execution of the articles are often the same. Thus, the considerations set out above with regard to the documents required for the formation of companies, such as the statement of compliance in the UK, or the financial plan required in Belgium, apply equally to private companies. A notable exception is created by the German Modernisation Act (MoMiG). It provides for model articles of association, which, if used, allow for a simplified formation procedure, meaning that it will be exempted from certifying these articles by notarial deed. Public authentication of the signatures will suffice to identify the shareholders. However, a company formed this way may not have more than three shareholders.[99]

1 *Registration*

5.17 The way private companies are registered is generally similar to the registration of public companies. Nevertheless, a few peculiarities will be mentioned here. All documents required to establish a German private company must be submitted electronically to the court, which then verifies whether the application complies with all requirements.[100] An application may not take place before a quarter of the nominal value on each of the shares has been paid up, representing at least half of the amount of the minimum capital. Non-cash contributions must be at the free disposal of the company before application.[101] To speed up the formation procedure, the requirement

99. § 2(1a) *GmbHG* (German Limited Liability Company Act) inserted by the *Gesetz zur Modernisierung des GmbH-Rechts und zur Bekämpfung von Missbräuchen (*MoMiG*)*, 23 Oct. 2008 (Act to Modernise the Law Governing Private Limited Companies and to Combat Abuses).
100. In accordance with the Act on Electronic Commercial Registers, Registers of Cooperatives and Business Registers, which entered into force in 2007. §§ 7 and 9(c) *GmbHG* (German Limited Liability Company Act).
101. § 7 ss 3 and 8 *GmbHG* (German Limited Liability Company Act).

to enclose certificates of public permits, which may be necessary for certain activities,[102] was repealed by the 2008 revision.[103]

To apply for registration of the Spanish '*Sociedad de Responsabilidad Limitada*', it is also required that public permits have been acquired.[104] It must also be set up through a public deed, which must be registered at the Commercial Register. Upon such registration, the company acquires legal personality.[105]

In the UK, the Companies Act 2006 provides that, among the documents to be provided upon application for registration, there must be a statement of capital and initial shareholdings, regarded as a 'snapshot' of a company's share capital at a specific moment.[106] This requirement is similar to what Article 2 of the Second Company Directive prescribes for public companies.[107]

In France, copies of the articles must be delivered to the registrar of the Commercial Registry (*registre du commerce et des sociétés*), together with the instrument appointing the directors (if not in the articles) and a declaration of compliance with all the procedural requirements. The company will then be registered. No capital can be withdrawn from the company's bank account before the Registry issues a registration certificate (this certificate is called *Récépissé K Bis* or *Extrait K Bis*).[108]

B Substantive Requirements

5.18 In general, a private company may be formed by one or more persons for any legally permissible purpose. However, Member States may still cling to the idea that a company is a legal form for cooperation and therefore, as a rule, may require at least two persons to participate in its formation. Such is the case in Spain, where the statute provides that a private company must be formed by at least two persons,[109] unless it is explicitly formed as a single-member company.[110] The simplified version of the Spanish private limited company, the *Sociedad Limitada Nueva Empresa,* may only be established by individuals and may not have more than five members upon formation.[111] By the same token, the simplified version of the Italian private limited liability company (designated '*società a responsabilità limitata semplificata*') can only be incorporated (by contract or unilateral deed) by individuals, but they are no longer required to be younger than 35 years old. The company's capital must be of at least EUR

102. For example, credit institutions – banks or investment companies – and transport or gaming businesses. *See* Klaus J. Muller., *The GmbH – A Guide to the German Limited Liability Company* (München: Verlag C.H. Beck – Kluwer Law International, 2006), 8.
103. §(1)(6) *GmbHG* (Limited Liability Company Act) is repealed by the *MoMiG*. *See* Federal Ministry of Justice official website, Press release – Berlin, 23 May 2007.
104. Article 84 Spanish Commercial Register Regulation.
105. Article 33 Ley de Sociedades de Capital.
106. Sections 9 and 10 Companies Act 2006. *Companies Act 2006 – Explanatory Notes, o.c.*, pp. 7–8.
107. *Companies Act 2006 – Explanatory Notes, o.c.*, pp. 8, 10.
108. Article L223-8 French Commercial Code.
109. Article 116, *Código Comercial* (Spanish Commercial Code).
110. Article 12 *Ley de Sociedades de Capital*. Also, Article 1 of the Belgian Companies Code stipulates as a starting point plurality of the founders.
111. Article 437 Ley de Sociedades de Capital. More members are allowed, but only after incorporation. This company form is already mentioned in paragraph 2.09a.

1 and the maximum is of EUR 10,000, with only cash contributions are allowed, which must be fully paid up to the management body upon incorporation.

5.18a Domestic laws may also cap the number of members of a private company. For example, in France, the *société a responsabilité limitée* (SARL) may not have more than a hundred members. If the company surpasses this threshold, it will be dissolved within one year, unless during this period the situation is normalized. This can be done either by reducing the number of members or by transforming the company into another form, such as the SA, which allows for the extended amount of members.[112]

5.19 Member States may also place restrictions on the use of the single-member company to prevent abuse, which is feared, in particular, if it would be allowed to set up a cascade of single-member companies, each being the single member of another company. Thus, in France and Poland, a single-member company is not permitted to form another single-member company.[113] In Belgium, the individual who is the single member will be liable for all obligations of any other single-member company formed by him. The same goes for the single-member company that itself forms another single-member company.[114] Dutch law provides a more general rule, also applying to single-member companies, that, where a legal person is appointed as a director of another legal person, the directors of the former legal person are personally joint and severally liable for the obligations arising out of that directorship.[115]

5.19a Another restriction may follow from the regulation of certain industries, requiring that certain operations may only be carried out by public limited companies. For example, in France, the SARL cannot be utilized for insurance, investment and savings companies (*'sociétés d'assurance, de capitalisation et d'épargne'*).[116]

1 Capital

5.20 Since the Second Directive only pertains to public limited liability companies, there are no harmonized European rules for private limited liability companies with regard to legal capital. This leaves considerable room for regulatory competition and, accordingly, jurisdictions with different legal backgrounds provide for varied solutions. Against this background, the UK traditionally follows a liberal approach, according to which no minimum capital is required to incorporate a private company, while Germany preserved its fixed legal capital during the 2006 modernization of its GmbH legislation. The proposal to substantially lower the amount from EUR 25,000 to EUR 10,000 was not approved by the German legislator.[117] It was argued that, even though

112. Article L223-3 French Commercial Code.
113. L223-5 French Commercial Code; Article 151 (2) Polish Commercial Companies Code.
114. Article 212 and 213 Belgian Companies Code.
115. Article 11 Book 2 Dutch Civil Code.
116. Article L223-1(4) French Commercial Code.
117. Michael Beurskens & Ulrich Noack, 'The Reform of German Private Limited Company: Is the GmbH Ready for the 21st Century?', *German Law Journal*, no. 9 (1 Sep. 2008) – Special Edition, retrievable from http://static1.squarespace.com/static/56330ad3e4b0733dcc0c8495/t/56b858251bbee056bdd30b6f/1454921767447/GLJ_Vol_09_No_09_Beurskens.pdf.

capital requirements may not play a fundamental role in protecting creditors' interests, they also function as a threshold to assure credibility and seriousness, thereby preventing the creation of too many unserious businesses. However, there is an exception, as laid down in § 5a GmbHG, facilitating start-ups specifically in the service sector. Reforms of private company law undertaken in other European jurisdictions, namely throughout the last decade, show rather the opposite tendency, i.e., towards lower requirements. For example, minimum capital as a requirement to form a SARL in France was abolished in 2003, as well as the minimum capital requirement to form a BV in the Netherlands, which was abolished in 2012 (following discussions that have been held, at least since 2007, with the aim of simplifying legislation regarding the private company).[118] The trend can be explained by the fear that businesses seem to prefer incorporating abroad, where they would find lower or less restrictive requirements than the ones they would have to comply within their own jurisdictions. Governments have been reconsidering the attractiveness and feasibility of domestic company law since the ECJ liberalized the market for incorporations to a certain extent (*see* paragraph 2.61 *et seq.*). How such a market may function is illustrated by the 'post Centros' significant increase of incorporations in the UK.[119]

5.20a Furthermore, it must be mentioned that the 2008 German reforms introduced the option for entrepreneurs to set up a variation of the GmbH without minimum capital: the *Unternehmergesellschaft (haftungsbeschränkt)* or *UG (haftungsbeschränkt)*, which can be literally translated as 'entrepreneur company (limited liability)'.[120] This variation is geared at meeting the needs of people starting up businesses that only require a modest amount of nominal capital (particularly relevant in the service sector). However, this new form has its limitations, such as considerable restrictions imposed upon the distribution of profits, in order to enable the company to progressively save up or accumulate the minimum nominal capital required for a normal GmbH.

5.20b It follows from the previous paragraphs, that the capital required to form a private company varies from zero, which applies to the Ltd, the SARL, the BV and the UG *(haftungsbeschränkt)*, up to EUR 25,000 for the GmbH.[121] According to Belgian company law, the minimum share capital for a private company amounts to EUR 18,550 and one-third of this amount must actually be paid up at the time of incorporation. In addition, 20% of each contribution in cash shall be paid up and the

118. Act of 18 Jun. 2012, Stb. 2012/299. Hylda Boschma, Loes Lennarts & Hanny Schutte-Veenstra, 'The Reform of Dutch Private Company Laws: New Rules for the Protection of Creditors', *European Business Organization Law Review* 8 (2007): 590–598.
119. Marco Becht, Colin Mayer & Hannes F. Wagner, Where Do Firms Incorporate? (October 2006), CEPR Discussion Paper No. 5875. Available at SSRN: http://ssrn.com/abstract=953820.
120. § 5a *GmbHG* (German Limited Liability Company Act). *Gesetz zur Modernisierung des GmbH-Rechts und zur Bekämpfung van Missbräuchen (MoMIG)*, 23 Oct. 2008, Beurskens/Noack, *o.c.*, p. 1083.
121. § 5 *GmbHG* (German Limited Liability Company Act).

contributions in kind shall be paid up in full.[122] In the Netherlands, the minimum share capital requirement for the formation of a private company (BV), which used to be EUR 18,000, has been abolished in 2012. The articles of association may mention an authorized capital, but that is not mandatory. Further, the articles of association must refer the nominal value of the shares and it can be indicated in any currency.[123]

In Poland, the minimum capital required for the creation of a (private) limited liability company is PLN 50,000 (approximately EUR 11,620)[124] and this amount must be fully paid up (prior to its filing for registration).[125]

For the Spanish SRL, the required capital amount is EUR 3,000 and it must be fully paid up prior to incorporation.[126] Furthermore, the 'Sociedade Limitada Nueva Empresa' not only has to be formed with a minimum capital (EUR 3,000), but only contributions in cash are allowed and capital is maximized at EUR 120,000.[127]

In Italy, although the minimum capital requirement is of EUR 10,000 (Article 2463(2)(4) Civil Code), since 2013, the minimum capital is no longer a condition to incorporation of a company. It can be set up with at least EUR 1 of capital, provided contributions are fully paid up to the directors upon incorporation (Article 2463(4) Civil Code) - in the latter case, the company is a so-called *società a responsabilità limitata a capitale ridotto*.[128] It is worth noting, however, that if the capital is below EUR 10,000, all contributions are to be in cash and must be fully paid up upon incorporation.

5.21 Generally speaking, since the Second Directive does not apply to private companies, the requirements with regard to contributions in kind tend to be less stringent for these types of companies. However, some countries still provide for very similar solutions with respect to contributions in kind in public and in private companies.

5.21a Both Belgian and Dutch law apply similar rules regarding contributions in kind for private companies and for public companies.[129] German and Polish law require that contributions in kind must be specified in the articles and Spanish law requires that they are specified in the incorporation deed or in the deed on the increase of share capital, therefore a report by an independent expert is not required.[130] In the UK, private companies are not subject to requirements such as the valuer's report

122. Articles 214 and 223 Belgian Companies Code. Conversely, pursuant to Articles 223 and 211 Belgian Companies Code, where a private company is constituted by a single founder the minimum amount to be paid up is EUR 12,400.
123. Article 178 Book 2 Dutch Civil Code.
124. The nominal value of each share must be at least 50 zlotys.
125. Article 154 (1), (2) and 163, 2 Polish Commercial Companies Code.
126. Article 4 (1) Ley de Sociedades de Capital.
127. Article 443 Ley de Sociedades de Capital.
128. G.F. Campobasso, *Diritto Commerciale. 2. Diritto delle Società*. Nona Edizione, UTET Giuridica, Wolters Kluwer Italia S.r.l. 2015; p. 556.
129. Articles 218 and 219 Belgian Companies Code, Article 204a Book 2 Dutch Civil Code. There are slight differences, such as the fact that according to Dutch law the description of the non-cash contribution, unlike for public companies, does not have to be attached to the deed.
130. § 5(4) *GmbHG* (German Limited Liability Company Act), Article 158 Polish Commercial Companies Code, Article 63 Ley de Sociedades de Capital.

concerning the adequacy of the consideration (required for public companies). The French Commercial Code requires the memorandum and articles of association to comprise of a valuation of the contribution, which must be drawn up by and under the responsibility of an auditor of the formation proceedings, appointed by unanimous decision of the future members or by a court order. Future members may decide unanimously to give up the use of an auditor, if no contribution in kind exceeds an amount determined by decree and if the value of all contributions in kind not valuated by an auditor does not exceed the amount corresponding to half the capital.[131] As far as contributions in kind are concerned, in the Italian legal system, the framework is simpler in comparison to public companies. They must be paid up in full, but the expert who carries out the evaluation is not mandatorily appointed by a court.[132]

C Pre-incorporation Contracts

5.22 Considering that the First Directive is applicable to both public and private companies, the elements pertaining to the company in formation are generally regulated in the same way as described above with regard to public companies. This applies to the moment of acquisition of legal personality, the liabilities for pre-incorporation contracts and other aspects related to the liability of founders of private companies.

5.22a It must be noted that German Law provides for a distinction between two essential stages before the registration of a GmbH. The first stage is the period starting from the decision of the founders to establish a GmbH, through a preliminary and binding agreement, until the moment when the articles are notarized – pre-formation company (‘*Vorgründungs-gesellschaft*’). During the second stage, the company assumes the legal form of the civil law partnership or, since commercial trade is taken up, the legal form of a general partnership or even limited partnership. Thereof the founders are treated as partners without limited liability. At this point, the company resembles the future GmbH, except for the legal capacity, which only arises upon registration in the commercial register. At the time of registration of the German GmbH in the commercial register, the rights and obligations of the pre-registered GmbH[133] are wholly transferred ‘to the registered GmbH by operation of law’ and the personal (joint and several) liability of the shareholders (who acted on behalf of the company) expires.[134]

131. Article L223-9 French Commercial Code.
132. G.F. Campobasso, *Diritto Commerciale. 2. Diritto delle Società.* Nona Edizione, UTET Giuridica, Wolters Kluwer Italia S.r.l. 2015, 558–560.
133. This means that from this moment on relevant parts of the German Limited Liability Company Act apply to the pre-GmbH, provided that they do not presuppose legal capacity. *See* Wirth, Arnold & Greene, *Corporate Law in Germany* (München: Verlag C.H. Beck, 2004), 5–6.
134. § 11(2) GmbHG (German Limited Liability Company Act). Wirth, Arnold & Greene, *Corporate Law in Germany* (München: Verlag C.H. Beck, 2004), 5 *et seq.*

IV FINANCING OF COMPANIES

A Share Capital

5.23 One of the traditional means utilized to finance companies is share capital (also designated as equity), the other one being loan capital. All capital companies, by definition, have a share capital, which represents a capital fund, contributed to by the members and available to creditors in fulfilment of the company's liabilities to them. Company law provides companies with the power to ensure that this fund is actually contributed to in the first place – raising capital provisions. Furthermore, it may ensure the maintenance of that capital, i.e., the fund is retained by the company for the benefit of its creditors and not returned to the members, to the extent that it may prejudice the interests of creditors. Usually, the company's capital is divided into shares,[135] which can differ with regard to their form and transferability. The share capital is deemed to include: (i) the nominal value of allotted shares; (ii) the amount of any premium paid; and (iii) the capital reserves, which companies are required to retain. The Second Company Law Directive requires Member States to enact rules pertaining to both raising and maintaining share capital of public companies. This Directive also addresses the alteration (increase[136] and reduction) of share capital, including purchase and redemption by a company of its own shares, and the financial assistance provided by a company for the acquisition of its own shares by a third party[137] (*see* paragraphs 3.41 *et seq.*).

5.23a Companies may also issue shares with no-par value, i.e., without nominal value.[138] These shares are issued without the indication of a par value, neither in the company's articles of association nor on the share certificate itself. Among the reasons why some companies issue this type of share is avoidance of liability that companies would have to assume towards shareholders if the share price would fall considerably below the par value of the shares. Further, the issuance of no-par value shares provides companies with more flexibility to set higher or lower prices for potential public offerings.

B Loan Capital

5.24 The loan capital of a company may include loans from a specific lender, such as a bank or a finance company, as well as bonds issued by the company, which are debt

135. In some countries, private companies use a term other than 'shares' to designate each part of the capital. For instance: in Spain, 'participaciones sociales'; in France, 'part social', which correspond to 'parts' or 'quotas'; in Germany, 'Geschäftsanteil'; and in Poland, 'udzialu'.
136. The increase of capital refers to actual addition to the company's capital, thereby excluding the capitalisation of reserves and any premiums, which are considered an accounting exercise.
137. Directive 2006/68/EC mitigated the general prohibition on financial assistance, which was prescribed by the original Article 23 of the Second Directive and this assistance may now be permitted under certain conditions, Articles 25 and 26 Directive 2012/30/EU.
138. For example Article 3(h) Second Directive, now Directive 2012/30/EU.

securities[139] that are supposed to be repaid (normally at a fixed date) and attract interest payments rather than dividends. The company may give the providers of such loan capital security in the form of a charge over part or all the company's assets. There is no harmonization at the European level for this type of funding, therefore national laws assume particular relevance and provide for different solutions, for instance, with regard to the types of bonds that can be issued, or even concerning the procedure that is to be followed by the corporate bodies assigned with the power to decide or approve the issuance of bonds. However, quite often, loan capital is not even regulated under national law.[140]

5.24a The decision of a company's board to attract a loan or to issue debt instruments may be subject to the approval of other corporate bodies. For example, under Dutch legislation, several resolutions of the Board of Directors of sizable companies are subject to the approval of the supervisory board, including the issuance of debt instruments.[141] In Poland, the articles may expand the powers of the supervisory board with the view of binding certain actions of the management board to its consent – a restriction that may, of course, also pertain to acquiring loans.[142] The German Stock Corporation Act also states that the articles of association or the supervisory board shall stipulate that certain types of transactions may only be entered into after receiving the consent of the supervisory board.[143]

5.24b The fact that loan capital is not extensively regulated, let alone harmonized, is, to a certain extent, compensated for by the market. The London based Loan Market Association (LMA) provides for standard loan documentation for syndicated loans (loans offered by a group of lenders) on the primary and secondary markets. Documents, such as standard term sheets, mandate letters, commitment letters and intercreditor agreements, can be used by members of the LMA, thus allowing 'lenders and borrowers to focus on the more important commercial aspects of individual transactions'.[144]

139. Securities are financing instruments which offer evidence of debt or equity and are tradable on the financial markets. For instance: shares, bonds, debentures, notes, options and warrants. These financing instruments can be issued by companies, governments or other organisations. *See* Article 4(18) Directive 2004/39/EC, on markets in financial instruments, usually designated as MIFID. This directive was part of the European Commission's Financial Services Action Plan and aimed essentially at promoting liquidity in the European capital markets, fostering competition in investment services and strengthening investor protection. The international financial crisis was considered to have exposed some areas falling within the scope of the MIFID Directive 2004/39/EU (MiFID I). Against that background, MiFID II is being introduced – *see* paragraphs 3.103c and 5.29 below for further developments in this regard.
140. Erik Werlauff, *o.c.*, p. 225.
141. Articles 164 and 274 Book 2 Dutch Civil Code.
142. Article 384 Polish Commercial Companies Code.
143. Article 111(4) Stock Corporation Act. According to the Article 52 German Limited Liability Company Act, where 'a supervisory board is to be appointed under the articles of association', then Article 111 of the Stock Corporation Act [*inter alia*] applies in conformity, provided that the articles of association do not provide otherwise.
144. http://www.lma.eu.com (accessed April 2017). The LMA covers the 'EMEA' markets (Europe, Middle-East, Africa).

5.25 Generally speaking, loan capital can be divided in various categories and, in the following paragraphs, we will briefly discuss bonds, convertibles and mezzanines. Bonds and convertibles are securities, i.e., they are financing instruments, which offer evidence of debt and are tradable on the financial markets. Mezzanine financing may (partly) consist of securities, such as convertibles, but may also require other instruments.

5.26 A bond is a written and signed promise to pay a certain sum of money on a certain date, or upon the fulfilment of specified conditions. Normally, a company provides collateral for the bonds and the investment is thus not considered risky from the investor's (or bondholder's) point of view. Accordingly, the interest rate is low. In the case of liquidation, bondholders are paid off before shareholders, and their interest payments are given priority to be paid before shareholders' dividends. Conversely, bondholders do not normally share in any capital growth of the company or in any surplus profits.

5.27 Convertibles are usually convertible bonds or convertible preferred shares, which contain an option to convert the security into another form of security, normally common stock, at a fixed price and time. Convertible bonds tend to offer a lower rate of return – compared to ordinary bonds – in exchange for the value of the option to convert the bonds into another form of security. Since these securities, conversion could lead to an increase in the share capital and turn the creditor into a co-owner of the company (thereby causing shareholder dilution). The issuance of such securities is governed by the share capital increase rules laid down in Article 33 (6) of the Second Directive.

5.28 Mezzanine finance is a hybrid and flexible manner of financing that is treated as a cross between debt and shareholder's equity on the balance sheet. Mezzanine capital is regarded as a form of debt, typically a subordinated loan, i.e., subordinated to a senior bank loan. This means that mezzanine creditors[145] can only be paid off after all senior creditors have been paid in full, which increases the risk of non-repayment of the mezzanine loan. In general, this financing instrument does not require collateral. However, where collateral is required, it is also subordinated.[146] Therefore, mezzanine loans are significantly more costly than borrowing from a bank. Usually, the mezzanine creditor requires not only a higher interest rate, but also warrants subscribing for equity, or royalties, in order to partake in the success (or failure) of the borrowing company.[147] The combination of these fixed and variable components allows for flexible pricing. As a result, mezzanine loans can be tailored to meet the specific needs

145. For instance, investment banks or private equity firms and hedge funds. These are new types of institutional investors, normally 'organised as an unregulated investment vehicle' – 'hedge funds' (acting more in the short term) and 'private equity funds' (acting more long-term, between three and five years), Eddy Wymeersch, 'Shareholders in Action: Towards a New Company Paradigm?', *European Company Law* 4, no. 2 (2007): 50–57.
146. If the collateral cannot be subordinated, the mezzanine loan agreement will state that senior lenders have priority on repayment upon execution of the collateral.
147. Marks, Robbins, Fernandez & Funkhouser, *The Handbook of Financing Growth: Strategies and Capital Structure* (Hoboken: John Wiley & Sons, Inc., 2005).

of the borrowing companies and adapted to its expected cash flows. The repayment of the principal is normally due at maturity. Although mezzanine financing is a form of debt, it features on the equity side of the balance sheet, thereby strengthening the company's equity ratio, which may improve its senior lending potential.

5.28a Generally speaking, mezzanine capital is a general term for long-term financing instruments, primarily aimed at supporting growth. Accordingly, it is used, *inter alia,* to finance acquisitions, management buyouts, equipment purchases or business expansion. Due to the additional risks that mezzanine capital involves, it is normally only provided to companies with sound financial records, which generate considerable cash flows and have strong management, all regarded as crucial indications of the company's potential to accomplish success. The European demand for this financing instrument has increased since the beginning of the twenty-first century.[148]

5.28b The Company Law Directives do not specifically mention intermediate financing instruments like the mezzanine. According to Directive 89/299 (on the own funds of credit institutions), banks, mortgage credit companies and other credit institutions may have access to subordinated capital contributions, which, under certain conditions, may be added to the company's equity, provided that the Member States allow for it.[149] Therefore, it can be concluded that the responsibility to assume subordinated capital contributions depends on the national law of a Member State, or, where it is silent, on the terms of the loan agreement.[150]

5.29 As noted above, the international financial crisis illuminated weaknesses in the transparency of the financial markets, which may have harmful socio-economic effects. Some of these areas fell within the scope of the MIFID Directive 2004/39/EU (MiFID I). Against that background, MiFID II is being introduced to strengthen the integrity of the financial system, namely by ensuring and promoting transparency and responsibility, and by improving the functioning of the internal market for financial instruments. MiFID II is generally accompanied by Regulation (EU) No. 600/2014 (MiFIR – i.e., the Markets in Financial Instruments Regulation). The MiFID II Directive and MiFIR are collectively known as 'MiFID II package', and it repeals MiFID I. MiFID II and MiFIR entered into force on 2 July 2014 and must generally apply within Member States by 3 January 2018.

C Securitization

5.30 Securitization is considered an advanced type of factoring or discounting of debts.[151] It consists of a transaction where the owner – originator/seller (typically

148. *Mezzanine Finance, Roundtable between bankers and SMEs*, Enterprise publications, Ref. Ares(2014)78108 – 15/01/2014 and the Commission Communication, *Financing SME Growth – Adding European Value*, Brussels, 29.6.2006 COM(2006) 349 final.
149. Article 4(3) Directive, 89/299. Erik Werlauff, *o.c.*, pp. 248 and 249.
150. *Ibid.*
151. The essential difference between factoring and securitization is that the factoring companies raise their finance mostly from banks, while in securitization the SPVs issue bonds secured on

banks or corporations) – of certain receivables (e.g., home mortgage loans or consumer credit receivables) sells them to a third party, which is a special purpose vehicle (hereinafter 'SPV'), in exchange for a purchase price to be paid upon its sale. The SPV finances the purchase price of the receivables, usually by issuing marketable bonds or, less frequently, by a bank loan, and secures the borrowing precisely on those receivables. The SPV is normally formed as a public company and is a thinly capitalized company, whose shares are held by somebody other than the originator (e.g., by charitable trustees). Thus, the SPV is a different legal entity and not a subsidiary that would have to be consolidated on the originator's balance sheet. Accordingly, the originator cannot be held liable for the SPV's obligations.

Overall, the main effect of securitization is that the originator transfers the risk of non-payment of the receivables to the investors and, in addition, removes the assets and the borrowing from its balance sheet.

This transaction is designated as securitization precisely because the receivables that were non-marketable assets are converted into marketable assets, symbolized by securities (bonds) that the lenders can sell.

5.30a By resorting to securitization, originators try to gain access to extra financial resources and improve their financial ratios.[152] First, securitization can bring about an improved balance sheet for the originator, since it may raise finance from investors without the loan featuring on its balance sheet and can also retain, as a profit, the remainder from the receivables that were sold, thereby improving the return on capital. The cash received by the originator for the receivables can be utilized to pay its liabilities and, once its assets and liabilities are reduced, the financial ratios (such as debt to equity ratio[153]) are improved, thus enhancing the originator's borrowing potential.

Second, the transaction gives rise to an immediate increase of financial means to the originator, whereas, without securitization, there should have been a waiting period for the receivables to be repaid.

Further, the receivables in general are of better quality than the average quality of the originator's total assets, the transaction is secured, and the assets are insulated from the credit of the seller. Consequently, a lower interest rate is involved, thereby offering cheaper finance than the originator would normally obtain from the bond market or banks. Capital raised in this manner can also contribute to widening the company's financial sources, hence diminishing its dependence upon bank loans.

---

the receivables. Moreover, many of the factoring companies are subsidiaries of banks and not single-purpose companies like in securitization. Philip Wood, *The Law and Practice of International Finance Series,* Project Finance, Securitizations and Subordinated Debt', vol. 5 (2007): 111–120.

152. Philip Wood, *o.c.*, pp. 111–120.
153. Also known as 'gearing' or 'leverage'.

D Covered Bonds

5.31 Other financing structures to be considered are covered bonds – known in Germany as *Pfandbrief*[154] – which are debt securities (issued normally by a bank), to be paid 'out of a pool of eligible mortgages',[155] or cash flows from other debt, such as public sector loans. Covered bondholders are entitled to be paid prior to all other creditors. Although similar to the asset-backed securities originating in securitization, they differ in one essential way, i.e., the covered bonds must feature on the issuing bank's consolidated balance sheet. The creation of these structures was aimed at making it easier to finance residential property.[156]

E Off-Balance-Sheet Arrangements

5.32 The securitization carried out by separate companies is considered an example of off-balance-sheet arrangements.[157,158] Normally, these arrangements involve the creation of SPVs (as described above) or, in other situations, involve offshore activities projected with a view to serve, amongst others, economic, legal, tax or accounting purposes. Off-balance-sheet arrangements tend not only to expose a company to benefits but they also may represent risks where the company has accepted to back up the SPV's obligations to investors. Both benefits and risks are relevant for a thorough assessment of the financial position of a company or, where appropriate, for the financial position of a group as a whole. After a series of corporate scandals, such as Enron and Parmalat, regulators in the US and Europe have reacted in such a way as to make risk management one of the most central concerns of board members.[159]

5.32a The United States' Congress responded to Enron and the associated scandals by passing the Sarbanes-Oxley Act (SOX) in July 2002. This Act intended 'to protect investors by improving the accuracy and reliability of corporate disclosures made pursuant to the securities laws'.[160] A controversial provision of SOX is section 404, which requires management to report on the adequacy and effectiveness of the

154. Covered bonds originated in German Law in 1769 under the designation: *Pfandbrief.* Nowadays covered bonds are commonly used throughout Europe.
155. Philip Wood, *o.c.*, p. 130.
156. Philip Wood, *o.c.*, p. 130.
157. Preamble, recital 8 and 9, Directive 2006/46/EC amending the Fourth Directive, the Seventh Directive, Directive 86/635/EEC and Directive 91/674/EEC.
158. Other examples of off-balance-sheet arrangements are: (i) outsourcing; (ii) consignment stock arrangements; (iii) take or pay arrangements; (iv) combined sale and repurchase agreement; (v) operating leasing agreement; (vi) risk and benefit-sharing arrangements; (vii) or obligations arising from a contract like debt factoring; (viii) pledged assets.
159. Corporate scandals and collapses concern, *inter alia*, Enron, WorldCom, Global Crossing and Tyco Parmalat, Vivendi, Skandia and Ahold For details on the Parmalat case *see* Ferrarini & Giudici, 'Financial Scandals and the Role of Private Enforcement: The Parmalat Case', in *After Enron: Improving Corporate Law and Modernising Securities Regulation in Europe and the US*, eds John Armour & Joseph A. McCahery (Oxford: Hart Publishing, 2006), 159 *et seq.*, and John Coffee, 'A Theory of Corporate Scandals: Why the US and Europe Differ', in John Armour & Joseph A. McCahery, *o.c.*, pp. 216–231.
160. Sarbanes-Oxley Act of 2002, 24 Jul. 2002.

company's internal controls over financial reporting through the use of a financial risk assessment - designated as 'top-down risk assessment'. In addition, an external auditor is required to certify and report on management's assessment of the company's internal controls.[161] As a result, the financial community has access to internal control reports.[162] Despite the corporate scandals that emerged during the period of 2007–2009, along with the international financial crisis, which appear to evidence that most of the causes underlying the previous financial collapses have persisted, various authors and financial analysts still consider that the SOX has possibly contributed in order to avoid the emergence of even more scandals caused by inflated financial statements.[163] Against this backdrop, it is also worth mentioning the Dodd-Frank Act of 2010 - even if it focused essentially on the regulation of banks - which includes a sub-title designated 'Strengthening of Corporate Governance'. This was meant to apply to all issuers falling within the scope of the jurisdiction of the Securities Exchange Commission.[164]

5.32b The European response, leading to the amendment of the Fourth and Seventh Directive (annual accounts) and the replacement of the Eighth Directive (statutory audit), embodies, *inter alia*, securing the independence of statutory auditors and requiring boards to report on the internal controls of the company or the group.[165] These issues are dealt with in paragraphs 3.70 *et seq.*, 9.25 *et seq.* and 10.05 of this book. Furthermore, the Commission issued recommendations on an appropriate regime for the remuneration of directors of listed companies and the role of non-executive or supervisory directors and board committees of listed companies.[166] Moreover, on 10 July 2007, the Commission issued a Communication 'on a simplified business environment for companies in the areas of company law, accounting and auditing', which reflects its concerns about the need to reduce administrative burdens to SMEs, especially where the rules provided in the above-mentioned Directives turn out to be excessively cumbersome for them.

161. Wilkins & Gupta, 'Sustaining SOX 404: A Project Management Approach', *Management Accounting Quarterly* 8, no. 2 (Winter 2007).
162. For further reading, *see* Deakin & Konzelmann, 'Corporate Governance after Enron: An Age of Enlightenment', in *After Enron: Improving Corporate Law and Modernising Securities Regulation in Europe and the US*, eds John Armour & Joseph A. McCahery (Oxford: Hart Publishing, 2006), 156.
163. For a comparison of the Enron case with ten corporate scandals that emerged in the 2007–2009 period with a view to assessing if they have resulted from similar causes, *see* Alexandre Di Miceli da Silveira, University of São Paulo (FEA-USP) – School of Economics, Management and Accounting; Alvares Penteado School of Business (Fecap) 14 Aug. 2013, 'The Enron Scandal a Decade Later', Homo Oeconomicus 30(3): 315–347, 2013, retrievable via https://papers.ssrn.com/sol3/papers.cfm?abstract_id=2310114.
164. Sirikanchana, Supawich & Zand, Sharareh, 'The Manner in Which Corporate Law and Financial Regulations Are Made' (2016). Comparative Corporate Governance and Financial Regulation, Paper 6, retrievable via http://scholarship.law.upenn.edu/fisch_2016/6.
165. Klaus Hopt, 'Modern Company and Capital Market Problems: Improving European Corporate Governance After Enron', in John Armour & Joseph A. McCahery, *o.c.*, p. 446. *Board Members on Risk Survey Report 2006*, Ernst & Young, p. 19.
166. Recommendation as of 14 Dec. 2004, OJ 2004, L 385 and Recommendation as of 15 Feb. 2005, OJ 2005 L 52.

5.32c The 'Enron effect' has also given an additional driving force to the application of the International Financial Reporting Standards (IFRS) through the adoption of standards by Commission Regulations (*see* 9.06 *et seq.*). It is important to underline that one of the intentions of the EU Commission, whilst amending the Fourth, Seventh and Eighth Directives, was to approximate the IFRS to the Generally Accepted Accounting Principles (GAAP or US-GAAP),[167] which must be followed by companies willing to be admitted for listing on the Wall Street stock exchanges.[168]

167. The US-GAAP are prepared and reviewed by the Federal Accounting Standard Board (FASB).
168. Menezes Cordeiro, *Direito Europeu das Sociedades* (Almedina, 2005), 398–400.

CHAPTER 6

The Management and Control of Companies under National Law

I INTRODUCTION

6.01 All public and private companies enjoy legal personality and execute their own contracts, employ their own employees and own their own property. However, companies are artificial persons and thus the actual conduct of their activities must, in practice, be carried out by individuals. Although the members of a company are economically involved and are therefore sometimes seen as the owners of that company, in all but the smallest company, it is impracticable for those members to manage the company on a day-to-day basis. Management, therefore, has to be delegated to one or more individuals with power to make binding decisions on all aspects of management. And each national law has to set out a management structure for its companies, entrusting these wide powers to a management body.[1] However, the law must also concern itself with providing a system of checks and balances to ensure that these managers do not abuse their wide powers to the detriment of the members and other stakeholders. This is the area of corporate control or, in modern terms, corporate governance. Such checks often appear in the form of one or more corporate bodies with rights. Examples are the right to require information, to be consulted or informed about day-to-day affairs or the right to consent with certain fundamental proposals (such as an alteration of the company's constitution or a reduction of capital; *see* paragraphs 3.35 *et seq.* and Chapter 5). Perhaps most important is the right to appoint and dismiss the managers, as well as right of taking recourse in order to remedy any wrongs committed by them against the company.

1. On the separation of ownership and management as well as on the related agency problems *see* John Armour, Henry Hansmann & Reinier Kraakman, *The Anatomy of Corporate Law*, 2nd edition (Oxford-New York: Oxford University Press, 2009), 12 *et seq.*, 35 *et seq.*; dealing with the same issues with a focus on closed corporations Gregor Bachmann et al., *Regulating the Closed Corporation* (de Gruyter, Berlin, 2014), 83 *et seq.*

6.01a Several rules regarding corporate governance thus have a statutory character. A typical proponent of those countries regulating corporate governance by mandatory statutory rules is Germany. The German Act of Public Companies (*Aktiengesetz*) consists of numerous rules structuring the management system of a public company, including the strict separation of the management organ and the supervisory board.[2] Listing rules and corporate governance codes can be an alternative to regulating corporate governance without imposing statutory rules on the company. Such codes may deal with a variety of issues like auditor independence, financial reporting and independency of non-executive directors to the agenda setting of the general meeting. An example is the *UK Corporate Governance Code*.[3] It consists of main principles, supporting principles and code provisions. The provisions of the code are not legally binding in a strict sense, but companies listed at the Stock Exchange are expected to 'comply with the Code's provisions most of the time', and to 'give a considered explanation' for departure from the provisions.[4] The *UK Corporate Governance Code* has been complemented by the *UK Stewardship Code*, addressing the responsibilities of institutional investors.[5]

6.02 Different national laws provide different methods of regulating these management and control functions of companies. In part, the method chosen will depend on the size of the company, but much also depends on the political and socioeconomic policies of each country, for example, the different national perceptions as to who should be involved in the control process, particularly the question of employee participation in that process (*see* Chapter 7). For those reasons, it has not yet been proven possible to harmonize the laws of the Member States of the Community in this area, although the draft Fifth Directive, which sought to do so, has been in the Brussels machinery for many years (*see* paragraph 3.10a). The regulation on the SE did not solve the problem either, but rather offered an option to the company itself to have either a one-tier or a two-tier system (*see* paragraphs 4.13 *et seq.*). The European Model Company Act (EMCA) also provides for an optional choice between a one-tier and a two-tier system.[6]

6.03 All legal systems, however, have provisions giving residual control, at least in theory, to the members acting through resolutions in a general meeting. They may have direct control, particularly in private companies, or operate through another controlling agency, such as the supervisory board required for an *Aktiengesellschaft* (AG) in Germany. Such residual majority control by the members raises, in turn, another issue for the law to solve: how to protect minority shareholders from abuse by the majority,

2. From a historical perspective it is worth mentioning, that German corporate law in the nineteenth century evolved from a flexible one-tier system to a mandatory two-tier system (*see* Christoph Teichmann, *Binnenmarktkonformes Gesellschaftsrecht* (De Gruyter, Berlin, 2006), 545 *et seq.*).
3. Retrievable from the Financial Reporting Council's website: www.frc.org.uk. *See also* Brenda Hannigan, *Company Law*, 4th edition (Oxford: Oxford University Press, 2016), 125 *et seq.*
4. This is the so-called 'comply or explain' approach (*see* UK Corporate Governance Code, 5).
5. Also retrievable at: www.frc.org.uk. Brenda Hannigan, *Company Law*, 4th edition (Oxford: Oxford University Press, 2016), 125 *et seq.*
6. Retrievable at http://www.jura.uni-wuerzburg.de/lehrstuehle/teichmann/forschungsprojekte/european_model_company_act/).

particularly if that majority is also acting in a managerial function or is linked to the managers.[7] This chapter is concerned with the legal framework within which all these questions of management and control are governed according to the various national laws. In some countries, the system is very different as between public (*see* paragraph 2.42) and private companies (*see* paragraph 2.40), which are dealt with separately. Out of necessity, many of the detailed rules within each structure, for example, as to the conduct of meetings, are not covered. This chapter proceeds on a country-by-country basis.

II FRANCE: THE SARL

A The Basic Management Structure

6.04 The French *Société à responsabilité limitée* (SARL) is managed by one or more managers (*gérants*), who are under the general policy direction and control of the members of the company. The managers must be individuals, but they are not required be shareholders.[8] The managers are appointed by the articles, or, in subsequent appointments, by members' resolutions in general meetings.[9] Such a resolution must be approved by more than half of the company's shareholders in terms of value. If this majority is not achieved, a second meeting will be called, where the resolution may be approved by a simple majority of the votes cast.[10] The articles can provide for a qualified majority, thereby strengthening the position of the manager within the company.[11] The managers are appointed for the duration of the company, unless the articles provide to the contrary.[12] In practice, only those who are not substantial shareholders in the company are appointed for a fixed term. Those who are appointed for the duration of the company may, however, be removed by majority decision of the members.[13] The articles or members will fix the managers' remuneration, and managers may be given service contracts with the consent of the company's members.[14]

6.05 The managers may act on behalf of the company on all matters, subject to certain restrictions, such as the requirement not to infringe on the company's articles, not to exceed the type of business carried out by the company and not to exceed any special limitations imposed on them by the articles. Such restrictions, in general, will not bind third parties, unless they are *mala fide*, but do provide internal checks on the

7. For an economic analysis *see* Luca Enriques, Henry Hansmann & Reinier Kraakman, *The Anatomy of Corporate Law*, 2nd edition (Oxford-New York: Oxford University Press, 2009), 89 *et seq.*; Gregor Bachmann et al., *Regulating the Closed Corporation* (de Gruyter, Berlin, 2014), 28 *et seq.*
8. Article L223-18(2) French Commercial Code (Code de Commerce).
9. *Ibid.*
10. Article L223-29 French Commercial Code.
11. Yves Guyon, *Droit des Affaires I*, 12th edition (Paris: Economica, 2003), 535.
12. Article L223-18(3) French Commercial Code.
13. Article L223-25 French Commercial Code; Maurice Cozian, Alain Viandier & Florence Deboissy, *Droit des sociétés*, 27th edition (Paris: Lexis Nexis, 2014), 549.
14. Maurice Cozian, Alain Viandier & Florence Deboissy, *Droit des sociétés*, 27th edition (Paris: Lexis Nexis, 2014), 551.

managers' activities[15] and may give rise to a claim of damages by the company. A typical restriction stipulated in the articles could be a provision engaging the manager to ask for the approval of the shareholders before entering into contracts exceeding the normal course of business.[16] If several managers are appointed, each of them will separately have the power to represent the company without any restrictions in relation to third parties.[17] Even the disapproval declared by one manager with regard to an act of another manager will not render the act invalid unless the third party had knowledge of it.

6.05a There are statutory restrictions on the powers of the managers based on the avoidance of conflict between their personal interest and their duties as managers. The company may not lend money to a manager or his immediate family or otherwise guarantee or secure their personal debts.[18] Any contract between a manager and the company must be ratified by the general meeting, failing which, the manager is liable to indemnify the company for any loss caused to it because of the contract.[19] However, ratification is not prescribed if the company contracts with the manager in the ordinary course of its business and under normal conditions.[20]

B Control of the Managers

6.06 The managers are liable to the company for any damage caused to it resulting from any breach of the law relating to SARLs, any infringement of the articles and any negligent or deliberate mismanagement.[21] Because negligence is rather difficult to establish, judgments based on the violation of the law and/or the articles are far more common.[22] If the company does not bring an action against the manager, one or more of the members have a right to bring an action in the company's name, and the damages will be paid to the company.[23] Such a derivative action is called *action sociale.* This minority right cannot be withdrawn or restricted in any way, either by the company's articles or by any resolution of the members.[24] Any such action must, however, be brought within three years of the breach or its revelation (in case it was disguised).[25]

6.07 In addition, the managers can be removed by a resolution approved by the votes of members representing more than half of the share capital and, again, this power cannot be restricted by the company's articles.[26] Although the resolution need not

15. Article L223-18(4) French Commercial Code.
16. Guyon, *Droit des Affaires I,* 12th edition, 542.
17. Article L223-18(6) French Commercial Code.
18. Article L223-21 French Commercial Code.
19. Article L223-19 French Commercial Code.
20. Article L223-20 French Commercial Code.
21. Article L223-22(1) French Commercial Code.
22. Guyon, *Droit des Affaires I,* 12th edition, 546.
23. Article L223-22(3) French Commercial Code.
24. Article L223-22(4) French Commercial Code.
25. Article L223-23 French Commercial Code.
26. Article L223-25(1) French Commercial Code.

specify any reason for the dismissal, the manager can sue the company based on dismissal without a just cause, that is, one not based on mismanagement or incompetence.[27] If the dismissal is not justified, it will, nevertheless, be valid; however, the manager will be entitled to claim damages.[28] If the manager is a shareholder too, he is also entitled to vote. A manager being a major shareholder, therefore, is, in practice, exempt from removal by a vote of the members.[29] Because the power of removal rests with the majority of the shareholders and may be without effect in the case of a manager holding a significant share in the company, the minority shareholders are further protected by the statutory right to apply to the court for the removal of a manager for a legitimate reason, that is, in case of mismanagement or incompetence.[30]

C The Role of the Members

6.08 The members (*associés*) exercise a controlling function in relation to the managers, as detailed previously, and are also empowered to take major decisions, such as those relating to an alteration of the articles. Meetings to approve the accounts and the managers' annual report must be held within six months of the end of the financial year,[31] or upon request from members owning at least a tenth of the shares.[32] Moreover, any shareholder can require the commercial court to designate an agent authorized to convene a meeting, if such shareholder has first given formal notice to the managers and no meeting was convened.[33] Subject to those provisions, the managers may call the meetings and the articles may provide that certain decisions must require such a meeting or a written consultation of the members. The latter takes the form of a registered letter sent to each member, giving the member fifteen days in which to reply with a cast vote.

6.09 The members have certain statutory rights to information. They may inspect the company's documents of the past three years at any time.[34] They may also, prior to a shareholders' meeting, send written questions to the managers, who will be obliged to answer them at the meeting.[35] One or more members representing at least 10% of the company's capital have the right to ask the commercial court to appoint an independent expert who has to report on one or more particular issues of the company's affairs (*opérations de gestion*).[36]

27. Article L223-25(1) French Commercial Code. Diverging views between the director and the majority shareholders on the need to restructure the company are generally not a sufficient justification for the removal of the director (*see* Maurice Cozian, Alain Viandier & Florence Deboissy, *Droit des sociétés*, 27th edition (Paris: Lexis Nexis, 2014), 558).
28. Guyon, *Droit des Affaires I*, 12th edition, 541.
29. *Ibid.*, 540.
30. Article L223-25(2) French Commercial Code.
31. Article L223-26(1) French Commercial Code.
32. Article L223-27(4) French Commercial Code.
33. Article L223-27(5) French Commercial Code.
34. Article L223-26(4) French Commercial Code.
35. Article L223-26(3) French Commercial Code.
36. Article L223-37 French Commercial Code.

6.09a Resolutions may be either ordinary resolutions or extraordinary resolutions, which will be required where either the law or the articles so provide. An ordinary resolution must be passed on the first poll by the holders of the majority of the company's capital or, failing that, if not prohibited by the articles, on the second poll by the simple majority of those present.[37] Weighted voting rights are prohibited, which means that every member has voting rights in relation to his shares.[38] An extraordinary resolution is one approved by holders of at least three-quarters of the share capital, the most important example of which being the alteration of the articles.[39] In certain cases, other specific majorities are required by statute. A unanimous resolution is required for an increase in the individual commitments of the members[40] and for a resolution on the change of the nationality of the company.[41] Such a change is allowed only when the new host country has entered into a special agreement with France, permitting the company to acquire its nationality and to transfer its registered office to the new host country's territory, while retaining its legal personality.[42] Within the European Union, however, companies may also transfer their registered office based on the European freedom of establishment.[43]

III FRANCE: THE SA

A The Alternative Structures

6.10 In France, public companies (*sociétés anonymes* (*SA*)) may adopt one of two management structures. In most cases, this will consist of a single board of directors (*conseil d'administration*). However, companies may also adopt a two-tier board system, having a management board (*directoire*) and a supervisory board (*conseil de surveillance*). Although, in form, these two systems are clearly quite distinct, in effect they still provide comparable distinctions in terms of management and control. The management function of a single board company is, in practice, carried out by the chairman (*président directeur général*) and executive officers, while the other members of the board exercise a controlling function with only a theoretical right to manage. In a two-tier system, the management board manages, whereas the supervisory board controls and their functions are clearly regulated. In both cases, the general meeting possesses an additional controlling function on certain basic issues.

6.10a Later reforms of the unitary board structure called for the separation of the functions of the chairman of the board and the chief executive manager, introducing

37. Article L223-29 French Commercial Code.
38. Article L223-28 French Commercial Code.
39. Article L223-30(2) French Commercial Code. The reform of 2005 also introduced particular quorums for the first and the second convocation of a meeting resolving on an alteration of the articles (*see* Article L223-30 paragraph 3 French Commercial Code).
40. Article L223-30(5) French Commercial Code.
41. Article L223-30(1) French Commercial Code.
42. Article L225-97 French Commercial Code.
43. *See* 2.65 and 2.65a and the case of a French SARL transforming successfully into a German GmbH (Kammergericht Berlin, *GmbH-Rundschau* 2016, 763).

the position of a chief executive (*directeur général*).[44] Thereby, the unitary board moved in the direction of a two-tier system. French authors even talk about a third managing model for the SA called the 'two-headed uniform structure'[45] or the 'mixed structure'.[46] The new structure, nevertheless, remains part of the unitary system and will be considered there.

6.11 The remaining difference between the two forms is that, in the two-tier system, the management and control functions of the two boards and their members are rigidly defined and separated and their liabilities set out accordingly, whereas, in the unitary board system, the distinction can become blurred. There is also a slight difference in the notion of 'control' in the two systems.[47] The non-executive members of a unitary board, when exercising control over the executive members of the board, are following up on the execution of strategic board decisions, which they themselves also have to account for as members of the unitary board. Instead, the supervisory board members in the two-tier system are supervising acts and decisions that they themselves do not have to account for, because the management of the company, including the strategic part of it, is not the purpose of the supervisory organ to which they belong. There are many features in common between these systems, not least the overall duties of all members of all the various boards in areas such as conflict of interest and duty. After examining the system under each alternative structure, this section will consider, in this respect, all the 'directors', that is, members of the board of directors or of the management and supervisory boards.

B The Unitary Board Structure

6.12 The board (*conseil d'administration*) determines the orientation of the company's activities and supervises their implementation.[48] It is therefore the supreme management organ of the company. Subject to the powers expressly attributed to the general meeting and limits imposed by the objectives clause, it deals with all the questions in relation to the proper operation of the company and decides, through its resolutions, on all matters that concern it.[49] Legal acts performed by the board in relation to third parties are binding on the company, even if they are not covered by the object of the company, unless the company proves that a third party actually knew, or should have known, that the act was transgressing the object.[50] The board elects one of its members as president, whose task consists of managing the work of the board.[51]

44. Loi sur les Nouvelles Régulations Économiques n° 2001-420 of 15 May 2001 (NRE).
45. Michel Storck, 'Corporate Governance à la Française – Current Trends', ECFR 1 (2004): 36(43).
46. Guyon, *Droit des Affaires I*, 12th edition, 331.
47. *See* in more detail Christoph Teichmann, *Binnenmarktkonformes Gesellschaftsrecht* (Berlin/New York: De Gruyter, 2006), 572 *et seq.*
48. Article L225-35(1) French Commercial Code.
49. *Ibid.*
50. Article L225-35(2) French Commercial Code.
51. Articles L225-47(1), L225-51 French Commercial Code.

The president is also responsible for the overall management of the company, unless the board nominated a chief executive (*directeur general*) for this task.[52]

6.12a Board members are initially appointed by the articles[53] and subsequently elected by the shareholders.[54] In general, the number of directors must be between three and eighteen.[55] The articles may require that directors must be shareholders of the company.[56] However, they need not be individuals. A corporate director will, in practice, be represented by a permanent human representative on the board. This representative is under the same duties and incurs the same liabilities as if he were a director.[57] If the number of directors falls below three, the board has to immediately convene a general meeting to appoint additional members, in order to meet the minimum number requirement.[58] The board may not, in such circumstances, co-opt replacement directors, although they may do so in other circumstances to replace a director until the end of the former director's term of office, subject to later confirmation at the meeting.[59] The board of large companies listed on a regulated market must consist of at least 40% male and 40% female members.[60] In companies employing a total of more than 1,000 employees, including those working for subsidiaries with their statutory seat in France, or in companies with foreign subsidiaries, if they employ a total of more than 5,000 employees, employees will have at least one representative on the board (*see* paragraphs 7.31 et seq.).

6.13 Directors may not be appointed by the articles for more than three years or by the general meeting for more than six years.[61] Directors can resign or be re-elected without limitations. However, there are age constraints limiting directors aged over 70 to one-third of the board, unless the articles stipulate otherwise.[62] Most importantly, directors can be dismissed at any time by a special resolution of the members, who do not have to justify their decision.[63] This right cannot be limited in any way in the articles and damages will only be awarded if the dismissal took place under damaging circumstances. Directors are allocated a global sum as attendance fees by the meeting and may be paid for special tasks.[64] However, they cannot become employees of the company while they are directors of the company.[65] They can only remain employees under pre-appointment contracts of employment and if the duties of the employment

52. Article L225-51-1(1) French Commercial Code.
53. Article L225-16 French Commercial Code.
54. Article L225-18 French Commercial Code.
55. Article L225-17 French Commercial Code.
56. Article L225-25 French Commercial Code.
57. Article L225-20 French Commercial Code.
58. Article L225-24(2) French Commercial Code.
59. Article L225-24(1), (3) French Commercial Code.
60. Article L225-18-1 French Commercial Code. This applies to listed companies employing at least 500 employees and having an annual turnover or a balance sheet total of at least EUR 50 million.
61. Article L225-18(1) French Commercial Code.
62. Article L225-19 French Commercial Code.
63. Article L225-18(2) French Commercial Code.
64. Article L225-45, Article L 225-46 French Commercial Code.
65. Article L225-44 French Commercial Code.

are clearly separable from the duties of a director.[66] In addition, in general, no director can be a director of more than five companies, including supervisory board membership.[67]

6.14 The board of directors acts collectively through meetings and resolutions on all matters concerning the company, subject to the various matters reserved for the general meeting; although, in practice, it only exercises a general policy management function. It can bind the company to any act, unless it is contrary to the company's objects, and a third party can be proven to have actually known of that fact, or that it should have known it from the circumstances.[68] No internal restrictions (e.g., in the articles) on the powers of the board will affect third parties. The same applies to the power of the chief executive to bind the company in all circumstances.[69] The duties of the board include drawing up an annual inventory of the company's assets and preparing the annual accounts, calling general meetings and, above all, appointing and dismissing the chairman, the chief executive and – upon the proposal of the chief executive[70] – the executive officers, and fixing their remuneration. They are the individuals who actually manage the company on a day-to-day basis.

6.15 The chief executive (*directeur général*) is nominated by the board.[71] The board may nominate its chairman to be the chief executive (*président directeur général*). It follows that the separation of the two functions is not imposed by law, but is subject to the discretion of the unitary board. The choice of the board in favour or against the separation between chairman and chief executive will have to be disclosed. It must be mentioned in the annual report delivered by the board to the general meeting[72] and disclosed in the official journal.[73] The board may remove the chief executive at any time.[74] If the removal is not justified, the chief executive will be entitled to damages. However, a chief executive who is also chairman (*président directeur général*) is not entitled to damages, even if the dismissal was not justified.[75] The chairman of the board and the chief executive must be individuals.[76] A chief executive cannot, except in the case of groups, be the chief executive of more than one company.[77] The number of executive officers (*directeurs généraux délégués*), who can be appointed to assist the chief executive, is restricted to a maximum of five. Their powers are fixed by the board in coordination with the chief executive.[78]

66. Article L225-22 French Commercial Code.
67. Article L225-21 French Commercial Code.
68. Article L225-35(2) French Commercial Code.
69. Article L225-56(2) French Commercial Code.
70. Article L225-53 and Article L225-55(1) French Commercial Code.
71. Article L225-51-1 French Commercial Code.
72. Article 148 D. 1967, *see* Bernard Saintourens, 'Les dispositions du décret du 3 mai 2002 relatives aux organes de direction de la société anonyme', *Revue des sociétés* 120 (2002): 430 (433).
73. Article 299-3 D. 1967, *see* Bernard Saintourens, 'Les dispositions du décret du 3 mai 2002 relatives aux organes de direction de la société anonyme', 430(434).
74. Article L225-55(1) French Commercial Code.
75. Article L225-55(1) French Commercial Code.
76. Article L225-47(1) and Article L225-51-1 French Commercial Code.
77. Article L225-54-1 French Commercial Code.
78. Article L225-56(4) French Commercial Code.

C The Two-Tier Structure

6.16 The two-tier system must be opted for in the company's articles.[79] The company is managed by a management board (*directoire*),[80] which exercises its functions under the control of a supervisory board (*conseil de surveillance*).[81] The management board may consist of two to five individuals, and, in the case of a listed company, up to seven individuals. A company with a capital below EUR 150,000 may have a single executive member. The company is legally represented vis-à-vis third parties by the chairman of the management board. The articles may authorize the supervisory board to attribute the same power to one or more other members of the management board.[82] In practice, there will be a chairman and others who are acting, in effect, as executive officers. The management board assumes many of the functions that are vested in the unitary board in the one-tier structure, such as setting up annual accounts, convening the general meeting and reporting to the general meeting on the state of affairs of the company.[83]

Members of the management board are appointed by the supervisory board for a period of two to six years.[84] They can be removed by a shareholders' resolution or, if provided for in the articles, by the supervisory board.[85] Removal without cause gives rise to a claim for damages. They do not have to be shareholders of the company and are subject to an age limit of 65 years unless otherwise stipulated in the articles.[86] Unlike directors of a unitary board, they may be employees of the company.[87] However, they may not be members of the supervisory board or the management board of another company.[88] The members of the management board act collectively and can bind the company in the same way as the unitary board of directors.[89] In relation to third parties, however, it is the chairman who represents the company, albeit other members can be given a similar power by the supervisory board, if authorized to do so in the articles.[90]

6.17 The function of the supervisory board is solely to supervise the management board.[91] Its basic function consists of exercising retroactive control of the management, instead of actively interfering with management's decisions.[92] This is reflected in the law excluding any liability of the supervisory board members for management

79. Article L225-57 French Commercial Code.
80. Article L225-58 French Commercial Code.
81. Article L225-68 French Commercial Code.
82. Article L225-66 French Commercial Code.
83. *See* Maurice Cozian, Alain Viandier & Florence Deboissy, *Droit des sociétés*, 27th edition (Paris: Lexis Nexis, 2014), 378; Guyon, *Droit des Affaires I*, 12th edition, 382.
84. Article L225-62 French Commercial Code.
85. Article L225-61 French Commercial Code.
86. Article L225-60 French Commercial Code.
87. Maurice Cozian, Alain Viandier & Florence Deboissy, *Droit des sociétés*, 27th edition (Lexis Nexis, Paris, 2014), 375; Guyon, *Droit des Affaires I*, 12th edition, 379.
88. Article L225-67(1) and Article L225-74 French Commercial Code.
89. Article L225-64 French Commercial Code.
90. Article L225-66 French Commercial Code.
91. Article L225-68 French Commercial Code.
92. Maurice Cozian, Alain Viandier & Florence Deboissy, *Droit des sociétés*, 27th edition (Paris: Lexis Nexis, 2014), 379; Guyon, *Droit des Affaires I*, 12th edition, 384.

decisions (*see* paragraph 6.19). However, it is involved in the decision-making process, insofar as its prior approval is required for some important transactions listed in Article L225-68 paragraph 2 *Code de commerce* and others, which may be listed in the articles of the company. Given the legal requirement to obtain approval, the management board will usually involve the supervisory board, or at least its president, much earlier in the decision-making process. The supervisory board may also carry out any checks and controls it considers appropriate[93] and the management board must submit a general report on the affairs of the company to the supervisory board at least three times a year.[94] The supervisory board must provide comments to the general meeting on the report of the management board.

6.17a The number of supervisory board members must be between three and eighteen,[95] and can include employee representatives (*see* paragraph 7.31c). Apart from these employee representatives, the members must be shareholders, who are initially appointed for three years by the articles and subsequently for up to six years, as determined by the articles. In virtually all respects, they are regulated in the same way as the directors in the unitary board structure (*see* paragraph 6.12), so that they can only rarely be employees of the company and can be dismissed at any time by a special resolution of the members. The supervisory board of large companies listed on a regulated market must contain at least 40% female members (or male, as the case may be).[96] The rules on employee representatives being nominated to the unitary board (*see* paragraphs 7.31 et seq.) also apply, *mutatis mutandis*, to the supervisory board.[97]

D Directors' Liability

6.18 All directors, executive officers and members of the supervisory board, who are referred to as directors here, are subject to various statutory controls on their wide powers. In order to avoid conflict between personal interest and corporate duty, there are strict rules on agreements between a director and the company.[98] Loans and guarantees are prohibited and void. This ban extends to immediate family members, but does not apply to banks or to corporate directors within a group. In the latter case, the agreement is subject to the same provisions that apply to other agreements between a company and one of its directors, or between companies with common directors. These agreements are regulated by statute, which also applies if a director is indirectly interested in a transaction with the company. The agreement must be submitted to the board or, in the two-tier structure, to the supervisory board, and approved by them

93. Article L225-68(3) French Commercial Code.
94. Article L225-68(4) French Commercial Code.
95. Article L225-69 French Commercial Code.
96. Article L225-69-1 French Commercial Code. This applies to listed companies employing at least 500 employees and having an annual turnover or a balance sheet total of at least EUR 50 million.
97. *See* Article L225-79-2 French Commercial Code.
98. Article L225-38 *et seq.* (one-tier system) Article L225-86 *et seq.* (two-tier system) French Commercial Code. *See also* Maurice Cozian, Alain Viandier & Florence Deboissy, *Droit des sociétés*, 27th edition (Paris: Lexis Nexis, 2014), 349 *et seq.* (SA), 569 *et seq.* (SARL).

before it is executed. It must be notified by the auditor, reported by him to the general meeting and approved by that meeting. The director concerned cannot vote at any of these meetings. The agreements are valid in relation to third parties once they have been submitted to the board, even if they are then rejected, but, in that case, the company may recover damages from all the directors for any loss caused to the company.

6.19 More generally, the directors are required to act within their statutory powers and in accordance with the articles.[99] They are also required to act in the best interests of the company and not for their own personal gain. The liability of members of the supervisory board is restricted to personal fault, excluding any liability for management decisions.[100] Proof of a specific fault or negligence by a director and consequential loss to the company is required. Damages are the only remedy – there is no remedy for unjust enrichment without loss. Directors are only liable for acts done while they were carrying out their duties as directors. In addition, French law qualifies several forms of self-interested behaviour of directors as a criminal offence. The so-called *abus de biens sociaux* is applied, rather often, in the case of managers making use of the company's assets in a manner that is against the interest of the company.[101] The company may bring actions against directors. In order to protect minority shareholders they may bring derivative actions against the directors in the name of the company if the majority does not wish to do so. The economic incentive of individual shareholders to bring actions against the directors is, however, rather limited, because the damages will have to be paid to the company. The law therefore provides for a collective action procedure, whereby a common representative brings the action in the minority shareholders' names, if these shareholders represent between 0.5% and 5% of the capital, depending on the total amount of capital.[102]

E The Role of the Members

6.20 In theory, the members acting in the general meeting are the supreme body of the company. However, their role is, in effect, one of general control and they cannot interfere with the due exercise of the powers of the executive director or the management board as a whole. Their consent is required for certain transactions, for example, a reduction of capital, and they have residual powers, such as the appointment and dismissal of directors, and the ultimate financial control on the approval of the accounts and reports and the distribution of profits. Meetings may be ordinary or extraordinary. The former are the annual general meeting and other meetings convened to pass ordinary resolutions, for example, for the dismissal of a director. Extraordinary meetings are those required for the passing of a special resolution, for

99. Article L225-251 French Commercial Code.
100. Article L225-257 French Commercial Code.
101. Annie Médina, *Abus de biens sociaux*, Dalloz, Coll. Référence, 2001.
102. Maurice Cozian, Alain Viandier & Florence Deboissy, *Droit des sociétés*, 27th edition (Paris: Lexis Nexis, 2014), 359; Article L225-252 French Commercial Code, complemented by Article R225-169.

example, to alter the articles. The board of directors, the management board or the supervisory board may convene the meetings.[103] Minority shareholders holding a minimum of 5% of the issued capital have a right to petition the court to convene a meeting,[104] and holders of a minimum of 5% may also propose resolutions at any meeting.[105] The latter figure is reduced in the case of large companies.

6.21 The prima facie rule is that each share carries one vote,[106] although the articles can allow those members who have owned shares for more than two years to cast double votes[107] and can limit the number of votes that any member may cast if it applies to all shareholders.[108] Ordinary meetings require a quorum of the holders of one-fifth of the issued voting capital, though, if that is not achieved, it may be convened a second time with no quorum requirements. Resolutions at such meetings require a simple majority of those present.[109] Where a special resolution is required, for example, to alter the articles, an extraordinary meeting must be held. The required quorum this time is the holders of one-quarter of the issued share capital on the first call and one-fifth on the second. The resolution must be passed by a two-third majority of those present.[110] In exercising their votes, majority shareholders must act in the interests of the shareholders as a whole and not to promote their own private interests at the cost of minority shareholders. Otherwise, they may be accused of having abused their majority (*abus de majorité*). The courts may set aside a resolution passed on that basis.[111] This could also apply when a minority consistently blocks a resolution that is necessary for the company's well-being.[112]

IV FRANCE: THE SAS

6.22 In 1994 the French legislator introduced the SAS (*société par actions simplifieé*) as a new legal form in order to offer a simplified structure to French businesses, in particular for the purpose of establishing joint ventures with foreign partners. To a certain extent, its legal framework refers to, on the one hand, the provisions on public companies, insofar as those constitute a body of general company law.[113] On the other hand, it offers more contractual freedom for the articles. The company is represented by a president vis-à-vis third parties, who is appointed in accordance with the

103. Article L225-103 French Commercial Code.
104. Article L225-103(2) French Commercial Code.
105. Article L225-105 French Commercial Code.
106. Article L225-122 French Commercial Code.
107. Article L225-123 French Commercial Code.
108. Article L225-125 French Commercial Code.
109. Article L225-98 French Commercial Code.
110. Article L225-96 French Commercial Code.
111. *See* Maurice Cozian, Alain Viandier & Florence Deboissy, *Droit des sociétés*, 27th edition (Paris: Lexis Nexis, 2014), 235 *et seq.*; Guyon, *Droit des Affaires I*, 12th edition, 498 *et seq.*
112. *See* Maurice Cozian, Alain Viandier & Florence Deboissy, *Droit des sociétés*, 27th edition (Paris: Lexis Nexis, 2014), 236 *et seq.*; Guyon, *Droit des Affaires I*, 12th edition, 499.
113. Article L227-1 French Commercial Code; *see also* Maurice Cozian, Alain Viandier & Florence Deboissy, *Droit des sociétés*, 27th edition (Paris: Lexis Nexis, 2014), 957 *et seq.*; Yves Guyon, *Droit des Affaires I*, 12th edition, 517.

conditions and procedures laid down in the articles.[114] The management structure of the SAS is not regulated by law, but is subject to the articles of the company.[115] Given this scope of contractual freedom, an SAS cannot be listed at the stock exchange.[116] The flexibility of the structure is, however, considered to be the main driver for the great success of the SAS in French corporate law practice.[117]

V GERMANY: THE GMBH

A The Management Structure

6.23 The management of a GmbH is governed by the third part of the GmbHG (*Gesetz betreffend die Gesellschaften mit beschränkter Haftung*). Management is vested in one or more managing directors (*Geschäftsführer*), with general control and certain residual powers being vested in the general meeting, either by the act or by the company's articles. Their position as managing directors gives them the authority to bind the company and, where there is more than one of them, they are joint signatories, unless otherwise provided for by the articles.[118] From a corporate law perspective, the nomination by the shareholders makes the director an organ of the company. From a civil law perspective, there is usually also a service agreement between the director and the company regulating the salary and other issues of his or her internal relationship with the company. Restrictions on their authority in the articles or in the service agreements do not bind third parties, unless the third party knew or had obvious reason to believe that the director was acting outside his authority to the detriment of the company.[119] However, they do have internal effects.[120] Possible consequences of a breach of internal restrictions could be a claim for damages or a removal from the position of the director. Commonly, certain transactions will be stated in the articles as requiring the consent of the members and, if such approval is not obtained, the director will be liable to pay damages and subject to immediate dismissal. Under general commercial law, the managing directors may also appoint one or more other persons who may represent the company (*Prokuristen* and *Handlungsbevollmächtigte*), who must be registered as such. Third parties can assume that they have authority to sign for any transactions that are normal within their competence, as defined by the Commercial Code.[121]

6.24 Whereas usually the only organs of the GmbH are the managing directors and the shareholders meeting, any GmbH may choose to interpose a supervisory board to

114. Article L227-6 French Commercial Code.
115. Article L227-5 French Commercial Code.
116. Article L227-2 French Commercial Code.
117. *See* the collection of articles edited by Pierre-Henri Conac and Isabelle Urbain-Parléani, *La Société par Actions Simplifiée (SAS) – Bilan et Perspectives* (Dalloz, Paris, 2016).
118. Section 35(2) German Limited Liability Companies Act (*GmbHG*).
119. Section 37(2) German Limited Liability Companies Act; BGH, 31 Jan. 1991, *Neue Juristische Wochenschrift* 1991, 1812 (= BGHZ 113, 320).
120. Section 37(1) German Limited Liability Companies Act.
121. Section 49 *Handelsgesetzbuch* (Prokurist), s. 54 *Handelsgesetzbuch* (Handlungsbevollmächtigter).

carry out many of the control functions of the meeting. Such a board is compulsory if the company has more than 500 employees.[122] This compulsory requirement is imposed because of German law's concept of employee participation, which involves the employees, through membership of the supervisory board, in the management structure of companies employing more than 500 employees. The concept of employee participation is discussed in paragraph 7.32. Where a GmbH chooses to have a supervisory board but is not required to do so (i.e., it employs less than 500 employees), most of the powers of that board, its membership and its relationship with the meeting are left to the discretion of the company. The act does refer to the comparable provisions for an AG, unless the articles stipulate otherwise.[123] Where the supervisory board is compulsory due to the regulation of employee participation, the rules applicable to an AG will apply without any choice.

6.25 The managing directors are appointed by the shareholders, unless that function has been assigned to the supervisory board (such assignment is compulsory where the company has more than 2,000 employees).[124] Any change in management must be registered in the Commercial Register.[125] Directors may be dismissed at any time by the members at the general meeting, unless there are restrictions imposed by the articles. If such restrictions are imposed, they must still allow for dismissal based on 'important grounds'.[126] However, such a dismissal will not automatically affect any service agreement that a director may have and which will have to be terminated according to its own terms. These usually contain clauses whereby the parties may terminate the agreement, subject to certain notification periods, or provisions granting the managing director a lump sum payment for termination without observing such periods.

6.26 The managing directors are subject to many duties with respect to their powers of management. In general, they must manage the company with such care as might be expected of an ordinary, prudent businessman.[127] Other duties include those set out in the articles or service agreements, as well as those specified by statute, for example, a duty of confidentiality.[128] To avoid a conflict of interest and duty situation, there is a general rule in German civil law prohibiting contracts in which one partner to the agreement is simultaneously representing the other partner.[129] This is applicable to managing directors of a GmbH as well. Managing directors may be exempted from this restriction by the articles and any such derogation must be registered.[130] It follows that all loans to directors are prohibited, unless the articles allow for self-dealing by the directors. In addition, such loans are always prohibited insofar as the capital actually

122. Section 1 *Drittelbeteiligungsgesetz.*
123. Section 52 German Limited Liability Companies Act.
124. Sections 46 and 52 German Limited Liability Companies Act. *Mitbestimmungsgesetz* 1976.
125. Section 39 German Limited Liability Companies Act.
126. Section 38 German Limited Liability Companies Act.
127. Section 43 German Limited Liability Companies Act.
128. Section 85 German Limited Liability Companies Act.
129. Section 181 *Bürgerliches Gesetzbuch* (German Civil Code).
130. Section 8(4) German Limited Liability Companies Act.

available to the company does not exceed the amount of capital that must be at the disposal of the company according to its articles (*Stammkapital*).[131]

B Shareholder Meetings

6.27 The members of the general meeting exercise general control over the managing directors, including their appointment, dismissal and terms of appointment. They also have specific functions allocated to them, including the approval of the accounts, changes in capital and alteration of the articles.[132] The statute permits shareholders to issue binding instructions to the managers.[133] Resolutions are passed by means of a simple majority, except for alterations of the articles and capital, where a three-quarter majority and notarization are required.[134] Written resolutions are permitted as an alternative to a formal meeting if all shareholders agree to this procedure.[135] There is no legal requirement that other resolutions should be recorded, except if the GmbH is a single-member company.[136]

6.27a Shareholders cannot vote when they have a personal interest in the resolution, except regarding their appointment as directors.[137] The articles may stipulate additional reasons to exclude shareholders from voting.[138] The minority shareholders may be given rights in the articles on top of the rights they have under the GmbHG. In particular, holders of 10% of the capital have the right to demand that a meeting be called, and they are entitled to submit proposals for decision-making at the general meeting.[139] Moreover, every shareholder has extensive powers to obtain information and to inspect the accounts.[140]

VI GERMANY: THE AG

A The Two-Tier Board System

6.28 The AktG requires all AGs to operate with a management board, a supervisory board and the shareholders' meeting. In general, it is the management board's function to manage, the supervisory board's function to control the management board (but not to instruct it on management issues), and the members' function to appoint members of the supervisory board and to approve certain basic transactions, such as alteration of the articles and capital alterations. Employee participation on the supervisory board

131. Section 43a German Limited Liability Companies Act.
132. Section 46 German Limited Liability Companies Act.
133. Section 37(1) German Limited Liability Companies Act.
134. Section 53 German Limited Liability Companies Act.
135. Section 48(2) German Limited Liability Companies Act.
136. Section 48(3) German Limited Liability Companies Act.
137. Section 47(4) German Limited Liability Companies Act.
138. Christoph Teichmann, in: Markus Gehrlein, Manfred Born & Stefan Simon, *GmbH-Gesetz*, 3rd edition (Heymanns, Cologne, 2017) s. 47 nn 48–50.
139. Section 50 German Limited Liability Companies Act.
140. Section 51a and 51b German Limited Liability Companies Act.

is compulsory if the company employs more than 500 employees.[141] There are detailed provisions aimed at resolving some of the conflicts inherent in such a system, for example, as between the shareholder and employee representatives on the supervisory board and between the shareholders' meeting and that board, vis-à-vis the management board.

B The Management Board

6.29 The management board (*Vorstand*) is responsible for the management of the company and for dealing with third parties. It consists of one or more individuals. If the company has capital in excess of EUR 3 million, there must be at least two members (directors).[142] Legal persons cannot be members of the management board.[143] The supervisory board appoints the directors for up to five years and their appointment is renewable.[144] They can be discharged only by the supervisory board, but on limited grounds, that is, for gross breach of duty or incapability,[145] and so are in a stronger position than their counterparts in a GmbH (*see* paragraph 6.25). A vote of no confidence by the shareholders would also constitute good cause for such a dismissal, unless that vote was obviously arbitrary.[146] The directors are not required to own any shares in the company. Any change in the composition of the management board must be registered.[147]

6.30 The management board has the exclusive right to management of the company, including the keeping of accounts and the setting up of a risk management system.[148] It represents the company in relation to third parties.[149] If the management board consists of more than one member, all the members will have to act jointly when representing the company, unless otherwise stipulated in the articles (and disclosed in the commercial register). The supervisory board has no right to interfere in the management of the company, although its consent may be required for certain transactions.[150] Upon refusal, the management board may submit the matter to the general meeting, at which it may be decided to approve the transaction, but only with a three-quarter majority of the votes cast. The managers' powers to bind the company to third parties cannot be restricted, though there can be internal restrictions, such as the need to obtain consent, which, if not complied with, can make the managers liable for damages to the company.[151] The managers are required to report their activities to

141. *See Drittelbeteiligungsgesetz*.
142. Section 76(2) German Stock Corporation Act (AktG).
143. Section 76(3) German Stock Corporation Act.
144. Section 84(1) German Stock Corporation Act.
145. Section 84(3) German Stock Corporation Act.
146. *Ibid.*
147. Section 81 German Stock Corporation Act.
148. Sections 76, 91 German Stock Corporation Act.
149. Section 78 German Stock Corporation Act.
150. Section 111(4) German Stock Corporation Act.
151. Section 82 German Stock Corporation Act.

the supervisory board on a regular basis.[152] To avoid a conflict of interest, the company must be represented by the supervisory board in dealing with the directors.[153] The general standard of care to be taken into account by the directors is that of a diligent and prudent manager, and they have a duty of confidentiality.[154] They are liable if they mismanage the company or act in breach of their duties or in breach of the articles of the company. They will not be liable, however, for management decisions if they had good reason to assume that they were acting on the basis of adequate information for the benefit of the company.[155] This so-called *business judgment rule* does not apply to the obligation to implement a compliance system. A recent judgment confirmed that members of the management board may be liable in cases where they did not establish a compliance system, which could effectively prevent employees from bribing officials in foreign countries.[156] In particular, they cannot compete with the company or obtain credit from it without the consent of the supervisory board.[157] They will not be liable if they acted in conformity with a valid resolution of the company or if the company waives liability, although the latter can only take place after a three-year period and can be vetoed by a 10% minority of the shareholders.[158] If the directors grossly violate their duty of care, creditors who cannot obtain satisfaction from the company are entitled to sue the directors.[159]

C The Supervisory Board

6.31 The main functions of the supervisory board are the appointment and dismissal of the managers, general supervision of the management board and approval of the accounts and other transactions, as set out in the articles.[160] The members of the supervisory board are appointed by the shareholders and, in most cases, also by the employees.[161] If the company employs more than 500 people, one-third of the members must be employee representatives, and this extends to one-half of the members if the company (together with its subsidiaries) employs in excess of 2,000 people. The size of the board varies from three to twenty-one, depending on the size of the company. It is not possible to be a member of both the management and supervisory board at the same time.[162] Members are appointed for renewable periods of four years.[163] They are subject to a comparable duty of care and confidentiality that applies to the directors.[164]

152. Section 90 German Stock Corporation Act.
153. Section 112 German Stock Corporation Act.
154. Section 93(1) German Stock Corporation Act.
155. Section 93(1) 2nd sentence German Stock Corporation Act.
156. Landgericht München, *Zeitschrift für Wirtschaftsrecht* (ZIP) 2014, p. 570. The case concerned a former management board member of Siemens AG.
157. Sections 88 and 89 German Stock Corporation Act.
158. Section 93(4) German Stock Corporation Act.
159. Section 93(5) German Stock Corporation Act.
160. Sections 84 and 111 German Stock Corporation Act.
161. Sections 96 and 101 German Stock Corporation Act.
162. Sections 95 and 105(1) German Stock Corporation Act.
163. Section 102 German Stock Corporation Act.
164. Section 116 German Stock Corporation Act.

In addition to their powers to call for information from the managers, they have, in exceptional cases, the right to call general meetings of the company.[165] The supervisory board is also competent to institute proceedings against the management board for breaches of duty, and, in such cases, inactivity of the supervisory board may constitute a breach of their own duties in relation to the company.[166] The rights and duties of the supervisory board apply equally to all its members, which means that the members nominated by the employees have to take into account the interest of the company in the same way as the members nominated by the shareholders.[167]

D The Role of the Shareholders

6.32 The shareholders at the general meeting are required to, among other matters, appoint and dismiss the members of the supervisory board, appoint the auditors and approve the accounts, consent to the allocation of profits, as determined by the management and supervisory boards, and to effect the alteration of the articles and the company's capital.[168] A three-quarter majority is required for an alteration of the articles.[169] Other resolutions require only a simple majority, unless the articles provide to the contrary.[170] Meetings are usually called by the management board, or, in exceptional cases, at the request of 5% of the shareholders.[171] The agenda must be published when the meeting is called. No additional items may be added onto the agenda after its publication, with the only exception that a minority of 5% of the shareholders (or of shareholders representing EUR 500,000) may require the publication of additional items for the general meeting. It is sufficient if those items are published within ten days after the call.[172] Voting rights are attached to the shares and depend on the amount of shares, or the capital represented by the shares. The articles of an AG not listed at the stock exchange may restrict the maximum number of votes that any shareholder can have.[173] It is, however, not permissible for the articles to introduce the principle of restriction but to leave the actual amount to the managers.[174] A shareholder must not vote on a resolution to be adopted by the general meeting if it relates to his liabilities toward the company.[175]

6.32a Generally, the shareholders are not competent to resolve matters regarding the management of the company.[176] The German Federal Court (*Bundesgerichtshof*) acknowledges, however, the existence of implied powers of the shareholders' meeting

165. Section 111(3) German Stock Corporation Act.
166. Bundesgerichtshof, 21 Apr. 1997, *Neue Juristische Wochenschrift* 1997, 1926 (= BGHZ 135, 244).
167. Bundesgerichtshof, 15 Nov. 1982, *Neue Juristische Wochenschrift* 1983, 991 (= BGHZ 85, 293).
168. Sections 110 and 174 German Stock Corporation Act.
169. Section 179 German Stock Corporation Act.
170. Section 133 German Stock Corporation Act.
171. Sections 121 and 122 German Stock Corporation Act.
172. Section 124(1) German Stock Corporation Act.
173. Section 134(1) German Stock Corporation Act.
174. *See* Hüffer, *Aktiengesetz,* 7th edition (2006), s. 134, n. 7.
175. Section 136 German Stock Corporation Act.
176. Section 119(2) German Stock Corporation Act.

to pass resolutions concerning fundamental management decisions.[177] The landmark decisions are *Holzmüller* and *Gelatine.*[178] In the former case, management decided to transfer roughly 80 % of the company's assets to a wholly owned subsidiary, where the rights attached to the shareholders meeting would obviously be exercised exclusively by the management board of the parent. Coming close to a de facto alteration of the articles, such transaction has to be approved by the shareholders meeting by a three-quarter majority.

6.33 As already noted, a minority of shareholders has the right to ask for a meeting to be convened and to specify items for the agenda of such meetings. They also have other minority rights, including the right of 10 % to apply to the court for a special audit (*Sonderprüfung*), that is, the appointment of auditors to investigate breaches of the law or the articles.[179] A similar minority also has the right to require that, where actions of the directors are being approved, a separate vote must be taken on each director.[180] Every individual shareholder has a right to be given information referring to any item on the agenda during the meeting.[181] If the management board does not sufficiently answer the question, a subsequent resolution may be voidable by the court, the consequence of which is that the right to information is a very important 'weapon' in the hands of minority shareholders.

6.33a Generally, any resolution that is contrary to the Stock Corporation Act or the articles is voidable and may be challenged by each individual shareholder, if he or she has attended the meeting and declared opposition against the resolution.[182] Unlike other jurisdictions, however, individual shareholders have no right to bring a derivative action against the directors for a breach of duty to the company, where the supervisory board and/or the majority of the members do not wish to do so. Instead, 1 % of the members (or shareholders representing a share value of EUR 100,000 in listed companies) can apply for a pre-trial procedure, where the court will assess the merits of the alleged claim.[183] If the court admits the claim for further litigation, the company will have to bear the costs of the procedure, irrespective of the final outcome.

VII POLAND: THE SP.ZO.O.

A The Management Structure

6.34 The Polish private limited company (*spółka z ograniczoną odpowiedzialnością* (*sp.zo.o*)) has one or more directors, who have to be natural persons.[184] A director may

177. *See* Teichmann, *European Company Law* 3, no. 1 (2006): 30.
178. Bundesgerichtshof, 25 Feb. 1982, *Neue Juristische Wochenschrift* 1982, 1703 (= BGHZ 83, 122) and 26 Apr. 2004, *Die Aktiengesellschaft* 2005, 137 (= BGHZ 159, 131).
179. Section 142(2) German Stock Corporation Act.
180. Section 120(1) German Stock Corporation Act.
181. Section 131 German Stock Corporation Act.
182. Sections 243 and 245 German Stock Corporation Act. Hasselbach, Report from Germany, 'Minority Shareholder Protection', *European Company Law* 2, no. 3 (2005): 114.
183. Section 148 German Stock Corporation Act.
184. Article 201 Polish Commercial Companies Code (*Kodeks spółek handlowych*).

be removed by the members at any time, unless otherwise stipulated in the articles.[185] However, in itself, the removal does not affect any claims arising from a separate service agreement. The directors are responsible for the management of the company. In relation to the company and its members, they have to observe restrictions at their own managerial discretion, as contained in the articles or in resolutions of the members.[186] If a director is in conflict of interest, he or she has to refrain from management acts in this respect.[187]

6.34a The directors represent the company in relation to third parties. Internal restrictions on their powers of management do not affect third parties. The act requires at least two directors acting together in order to legally bind the company.[188] Under general Polish Commercial Law, it is also possible to grant a person a particular authority to represent the company (a holder of a commercial power of attorney) – which is similar to the German *'Prokurist'* (*see* paragraph 6.23) – the ambit of the authority being defined in the act.[189] If there is such a representative, they may act together with a director in order to bind the company in relation to third parties. The articles may determine that only one director is authorized to represent the company. Moreover, it is always possible for one director to validly accept legal acts that are directed to the company ('passive' representation as opposed to 'active' representation, which needs two directors, unless otherwise stipulated in the articles). If agreements are to be concluded between the company and the directors, the company is represented either by the supervisory board, if any, or by a special representative authorized by the members.[190] This does not apply if the only shareholder is, simultaneously, the only director, but, in such cases, agreements between the company and the director will have to be notarized.[191]

6.34b A supervisory board may be established voluntarily and is compulsory for big companies (capital exceeding PLN 500,000 and the number of members exceeding twenty-five).[192] The supervisory board must have at least three members to be appointed and dismissed by the members of the company. The articles may subject certain transactions to prior approval by the supervisory board,[193] but, apart from that, the supervisory board may not give binding instructions to the directors regarding the management of the company.[194]

185. Article 203 Polish Commercial Companies Code.
186. Article 207 Polish Commercial Companies Code.
187. Article 209 Polish Commercial Companies Code.
188. Article 205(1) Polish Commercial Companies Code.
189. Articles 1091–1098 Polish Civil Code.
190. Article 210(1) Polish Commercial Companies Code.
191. Article 210(2) Polish Commercial Companies Code.
192. Article 213(2) Polish Commercial Companies Code.
193. Article 220 Polish Commercial Companies Code.
194. Article 219(2) Polish Commercial Companies Code.

B The Role of the Members

6.35 An ordinary shareholders' meeting must be convened within six months of the end of the financial year. It approves the annual accounts and discharges the directors.[195] The members have the power to approve, *inter alia,* the transfer of all the company's assets, or a separately organized part of it, as well as to decide on particular agreements within a group of companies (domination agreement or profit transfer agreement).[196] Moreover, any transaction involving more than twice the amount of the company's capital has to be approved by the members, unless otherwise stipulated in the articles.[197] Subject to the consent of all shareholders, a resolution may be passed in writing.[198] Resolutions usually require a simple majority. A majority of two-thirds of the votes is necessary for altering the articles, as well as for the dissolution of the company, or the transfer of all the assets or a separately organized part of the company.[199]

6.35a Shareholders have an individual right of information, which may be restricted, or even excluded, in the articles in cases where a supervisory board has been established. They are also entitled to claim damages on behalf of the company (*actio pro socio*), if the company fails to do so within a one year period.[200] The minority of shareholders representing at least 5% of the capital has the right to require a shareholders' meeting to be convened or certain items to be added to the meeting's agenda.[201] A minority of shareholders representing at least 10% of the capital may petition the court for the appointment of a special auditor.[202]

VIII POLAND: THE SA

A The Management Structure

6.36 The management structure of the Polish public company (*spółka akcyjna* (*SA*)) follows the two-tier system, with a management board and a supervisory board, and has been influenced by German law in this respect.[203] The management board consists

195. Article 231 Polish Commercial Companies Code.
196. Article 228 Polish Commercial Companies Code.
197. Article 230 Polish Commercial Companies Code.
198. Article 227 Polish Commercial Companies Code.
199. Article 246 Polish Commercial Companies Code.
200. Articles 295 and 296 Polish Commercial Companies Code.
201. Article 236 Polish Commercial Companies Code.
202. Article 223 Polish Commercial Companies Code.
203. *See* Katarzyna Samól, 'One- or Two-Tier Board System? A Comparative Analysis of the British and Polish Systems of Corporate Governance', *European Company Law* 13, no. 2 (2016), 67 *et seq.*; Krzysztof Oplustil & Arkadiusz Radwan, 'Company Law in Poland: Between Autonomous Development and Legal Transplants', in *Private Law in Eastern Europe: Autonomous Developments or Legal Transplants?*, eds Ch. Jessel-Holst et al. (Tübingen: Mohr Siebeck, 2010), 472 *et seq.*; Peter Hommelhoff & Krzysztof Oplustil, 'Deutsche Einflüsse auf das polnische Recht der Kapitalgesellschaften: Vorgesellschaft, Eigenkapitalersatz und dualistische Organstruktur in Aktiengesellschaften', in *Festschrift für Horst Konzen, zum siebzigsten Geburtstag*, eds Barbara Dauner-Lieb et al. (Tübingen: Mohr Siebeck, 2006), 309 *et seq.*

of one or more natural persons who are appointed (for a maximum period of five years) and removed by the supervisory board, unless the articles provide otherwise.[204] In particular, the articles may grant the general meeting the power to appoint members of the management board. In any case, regardless of the manner of the appointment, the members of the management board may also be dismissed or suspended directly by the general meeting.[205] The supervisory board will usually determine the remuneration of the members of the management board in a separate service contract.

6.36a The management board is responsible for the management of the company and represents the company in relation to third parties.[206] Members of the board who have a personal conflict of interest must refrain from the respective management act.[207] Neither the supervisory board nor the shareholders' meeting have the right to give instructions to the management board.[208] The articles – but not the supervisory board itself – may set up a list of transactions that require prior approval of the supervisory board.[209]

6.36b The supervisory board controls the management of the company. The supervisory board must have at least three members, and, in listed companies, at least five members.[210] The members are appointed and dismissed by the shareholders' meeting for a maximum period of five years. Unlike Germany, Poland has no representation of employees at the supervisory board, with the exception of former state-owned and now privatized companies. There is, however, a voting procedure, which allows for a minority of shareholders to appoint members to the supervisory board. A minority of at least 20% of the company's capital may request voting in separate groups.[211] For this purpose, the shareholders may create separate election groups and each group will elect its own representative to the supervisory board. The number of groups results from the division of all shares represented at a given general meeting by the total number of supervisory board members to be elected. Shareholder groups may also merge with other groups in order to elect more members of the supervisory board.[212]

B The Role of the Shareholders

6.37 The competences of the shareholders' meeting are similar to those in the Sp.zo.o., especially in relation to the ordinary meeting and the power to resolve important issues, such as the transfer of the company's assets or a separately organized

204. Article 358(4) Polish Commercial Companies Code.
205. Article 368(4) Polish Commercial Companies Code.
206. Article 368(1) Polish Commercial Companies Code.
207. Article 377 Polish Commercial Companies Code.
208. Article 375(1) Polish Commercial Companies Code.
209. Article 384(1) Polish Commercial Companies Code.
210. Article 385(1) Polish Commercial Companies Code.
211. Article 385 Polish Commercial Companies Code.
212. *See* more on this issue Krzysztof Oplustil & Arkadiusz Radwan, *supra* n. 206, 477 *et seq.*; Artur Fabisch & Krzysztof Oplustil, 'Gruppenwahl der Aufsichtsratsmitglieder: ein besonderes Recht der Minderheitsaktionäre im polnischen Aktienrecht', *Recht der Internationalen Wirtschaft (RIW)*, 2010, no. 2, 823 *et seq.*

part, as well as the alteration of the articles or particular agreements concluded within a group of companies (domination agreement or profit transfer agreement).[213] All these extraordinary resolutions require a majority of three-quarters of the votes.[214] Shareholders may ask the management board for information regarding the topics on the agenda of the meeting.[215] Shareholders representing 5 % of the company's capital may request the general meeting to be convened or additional items to be put on the meeting's agenda.[216] In listed companies, a minority of at least 5 % of the voting rights represented at the meeting may request the appointment of an expert in order to inquire into particular management acts of the company.[217] Resolutions of the meeting may be challenged by individual shareholders on the grounds of a violation of the articles, the interest of the company or the interest of a particular shareholder, or because of an immoral content.[218] Like in the Sp.zo.o., shareholders are entitled to claim damages on behalf of the company (*actio pro socio*) if the company fails to do so within one year.[219]

IX SPAIN: THE SA AND THE SRL

A Management and Representation

6.38 Spanish law does not provide for a two-tier board structure for either the SA or SL. The management and control structures for both types of company are similar in many ways. It has been an objective of recent reforms in Spanish company law to unify the rules applicable to the public company (*sociedad anónima* (*SA*)) and to the private company (*sociedad de responsabilidad limitata* (*SRL*)).[220] Therefore, the law applicable to the SA and the SRL will be set out together in this section.[221] There are only two bodies, the directors and the shareholders. In a public company, if there are more than

213. Article 395 Polish Commercial Companies Code.
214. Article 415(1) Polish Commercial Companies Code.
215. Article 428 Polish Commercial Companies Code.
216. Articles 400 and 401 Polish Commercial Companies Code.
217. Articles 158b *et seq.* Securities Exchange Act.
218. Article 422 Polish Commercial Companies Code.
219. Article 486 Polish Commercial Companies Code.
220. *See* A. Jorge Viera González, 'Closed Capital companies in the Spanish Legislative Evolution: Problems of Legal Policy and Regulatory Interpretation', in *Private Company Law Reform in Europe: The Race for Flexibility*, eds A. Jorge Viera González & Christoph Teichmann (Cizur Menor: Thomson Reuters, 2015), 571 *et seq.*
221. Spanish law on public and private capital companies has been consolidated by Royal Decree 1/2010 introducing the new Act on Capital Companies (*Ley de Sociedades de Capital*). For further references *see Comentario de la Ley de Sociedades de Capital*, coordinated by Angel José Rojo Fernández Rio et al. (Cizur Menor: Thomson Reuters, 2011). Since 2011, the new Act has been reformed several times. For more information see: *Las reformas de la Ley de Sociedades de Capital*, 2nd edition (Cizur Menor: Thomson Reuters, 2012); *Comentario de la reforma del Régimen de las sociedades de capital en materia de gobierno corporativo (Ley 31/2014). Sociedades no cotizadas*, coordinated by Javier Juste Menciá (Cizur Menor, Thomson Reuters, 2015); *Junta general y Consejo de administración en la sociedad cotizada*, coordinated by Fernando Rodriguez Artigas et al., Tomos I and II (Cizur menor: Thomson Reuters, 2016).

two directors, the directors will form a board of directors (*consejo de administración*).[222] In a private company, the structure is more flexible and left to the discretion of the shareholders.[223]

6.39 The directors (*administradores*) could be either natural or legal persons and they need not be shareholders of the company, unless otherwise stipulated in the articles.[224] In cases where a legal person is nominated to be director, it has to designate a natural person acting on its behalf.[225] The directors are appointed by the shareholders, unless the law stipulates otherwise.[226] The directors represent the company vis-à-vis third parties.[227] The power of the board to represent the company is fixed by law for all purposes, which are connected with the company's corporate purpose, as specified in the articles. Third parties are protected, first by the fact that no other restrictions on the powers of the board are binding upon them, and second by the rule that a company will be liable in damages to a bona fide third party, even for transactions outside its corporate purpose.[228]

6.40 The directors' appointment takes effect once the person has accepted the position. Following the acceptance, the resolution making the appointment must be filed for registration within ten days at the Commercial Registry.[229] Appointments of directors in a public company are for a period specified in the articles, not exceeding six years; this period has to be the same for all the directors.[230] In a private company, directors are appointed for an indefinite period of time, unless the articles stipulate otherwise.[231] Within public companies, a system of proportionate voting allows a group of minority shareholders to appoint a board member on their own.[232] All directors can be re-elected once or several times.[233] The activity of the directors is not remunerated, unless the articles stipulate a remuneration system, which may consist of fixed and variable elements.[234] If this is to be a share in the company's earnings in a public company, it must be allocated from the company's net profits after legal requirements for capital reserves have been fulfilled and the shareholders have been paid at least a 4% dividend,[235] whereas in a private company the benefits granted to the directors shall not exceed 10% of the benefits that are distributable to the shareholders.[236] If, in a public company, payment in shares or share options shall be part of the remuneration, it has to be fixed in the articles and specified by a resolution of the

222. Article 210(2) Spanish Act on Capital Companies.
223. Article 210(3) Spanish Act on Capital Companies.
224. Article 212 Spanish Act on Capital Companies.
225. Article 212*bis* Spanish Act on Capital Companies.
226. Article 214(1) Spanish Act on Capital Companies.
227. Article 233 Spanish Act on Capital Companies.
228. Article 234 Spanish Act on Capital Companies.
229. Articles 214 and 215 Spanish Act on Capital Companies.
230. Article 221(2) Spanish Act on Capital Companies.
231. Article 221(1) Spanish Act on Capital Companies.
232. Article 243 Spanish Act on Capital Companies.
233. Article 221 Spanish Act on Capital Companies.
234. Article 217 Spanish Act on Capital Companies.
235. Article 218(3) Spanish Act on Capital Companies.
236. Article 218(2) Spanish Act on Capital Companies.

shareholders.[237] Directors may be dismissed at any time by the shareholders' meeting.[238] The articles of a private company may require a qualified majority for dismissing a director, not exceeding two-thirds of the votes.[239]

6.41 The board, by a two-third majority of the directors, may delegate many of its management functions to one or more managing directors, or an executive committee.[240] However, certain matters cannot be delegated, including the determination of the company's general strategy, the duty to present the accounts and the annual report to the shareholders' meeting.[241]

6.42 Directors are also bound by a duty of loyalty to act in the best interest of the company.[242] The duty of loyalty includes, amongst others, a duty of confidentiality and a duty to abstain from deliberating and voting within the board when a personal interest is involved.[243] Directors are liable for all damages caused by them to the company, its shareholders and its creditors by any infringement of the Act on Capital Companies, the articles or the duty of diligence of directors.[244] The standard of care is that of an orderly businessman and a loyal representative.[245] Directors will not be liable for business decisions if they acted in good faith, without any personal conflict of interest, based on sufficient information and applying an adequate decision-making process.[246] If damage has been caused to the company by directors violating the standard of care, an action may be brought by the company, by the shareholders or even by the creditors.[247] Directors may also be liable for damage to third parties.[248]

B The Role of the Members

6.43 The directors are appointed, dismissed and controlled by the members in the general meeting. The general meeting may issue instructions to the board, regarding the company's management, which is, however, not restricting the power of the directors to represent the company vis-à-vis third parties.[249] Other competences of the general meeting include the approval of the company's annual accounts, the

237. Article 219 Spanish Act on Capital Companies.
238. Article 223(1) Spanish Act on Capital Companies.
239. Article 223(2) Spanish Act on Capital Companies.
240. Article 249 Spanish Act on Capital Companies.
241. Article 249*bis* Spanish Act on Capital Companies.
242. Article 227(1) Spanish Act on Capital Companies.
243. Article 228 Spanish Act on Capital Companies.
244. Article 236 Spanish Act on Capital Companies.
245. Article 225 Spanish Act on Capital Companies.
246. Article 226(1) Spanish Act on Capital Companies.
247. Articles 238–240 Spanish Act on Capital Companies. Regarding the regime on directors' liability, see *La responsabilidad de los administradores de las sociedades mercantiles*, coordinated by Angel José Rojo Fernández Rio, 6th edition (Tirant lo Blanch: Valencia, 2016).
248. Article 241 Spanish Act on Capital Companies. Gaudencio Esteban Velasco, 'La acción individual de responsabilidad', in: *La responsabilidad de los administradores de las sociedades mercantiles*, coordinated by Angel José Rojo Fernández Rio, 6th edition (Tirant lo Blanch: Valencia, 2016), 189 *et seq.*
249. Article 161 Spanish Act on Capital Companies.

modification of the company's articles and the transfer of assets exceeding a value of 25 % of the company's overall assets.[250] In a private company, the general meeting may decide to grant credits, guarantees or other means of financial assistance to its shareholders or directors.[251]

6.44 An ordinary meeting of the members must be held within the first six months of each financial period to review management and approve the accounts and reports of the previous year, as well as to determine the appropriation of the annual profit.[252] Other meetings, known as extraordinary meetings, may be held at any time.[253] Meetings may usually be called by the directors.[254] The directors shall also call a meeting at the request of the holders of at least 5 % in value of the capital, in which case the meeting must be held within two months of the date of the request. In their request, the shareholders must express items to be discussed at the general meeting. By default, a meeting may be called by the Judicial Secretary or the Commercial Register.[255] In a public company, a minority of at least 5 % of the shareholders may request additional topics to be put on the agenda of the meeting.[256]

6.45 Shareholder meetings require prior notice, either on the company's website or by the insertion of an advertisement in the *Official Journal of the Commercial Registry*, and a provincial daily newspaper containing, among other matters, the agenda.[257] For the general meeting of a public company, the convocation may also indicate the date of a second meeting to provide against the failure to obtain a quorum for the first.[258] That second date must be at least twenty-four hours after the first date. These notice provisions cannot be waived, so that, if no second date was fixed and no quorum is obtained, another fifteen days' notice must be given of the second meeting. The minimum quorum requirements for public companies are fixed by law and are 25 % of the holders of capital for a first call, with any number for a second call.[259] These figures are higher for specific resolutions, for example, the alteration of the articles.[260] All resolutions are passed by a majority of those present at the meeting.[261] In a private company, however, the approving majority shall at least represent one-third of the votes, as calculated in relation to the company's capital.[262] In case of an increase or a reduction of the capital, as well as for amendments of the articles, the approving majority shall represent at least one-half of the votes in relation to the company's

250. Article 160 Spanish Act on Capital Companies.
251. Article 162 Spanish Act on Capital Companies.
252. Article 164 Spanish Act on Capital Companies.
253. Article 165 Spanish Act on Capital Companies.
254. Articles 166 and 167 Spanish Act on Capital Companies.
255. Articles 168 and 169 Spanish Act on Capital Companies.
256. Article 172 Spanish Act on Capital Companies.
257. Articles 173 and 174 Spanish Act on Capital Companies.
258. Article 177 Spanish Act on Capital Companies; *see also* Articles 11*bis et seq.* regarding the company's website in general.
259. Article 193 Spanish Act on Capital Companies.
260. Article 194 Spanish Act on Capital Companies.
261. *See* Article 201 Spanish Act on Capital Companies for the public company.
262. Article 198 Spanish Act on Capital Companies.

capital;[263] for other special resolutions – as listed in Article 199 subsection (b) of the Act (such as authorization of directors to compete) – a majority representing two-thirds of the company's capital will be required.

6.46 The articles of a public company can limit the number of votes that any shareholder (including shares owned by a group of companies) may have.[264] The act allows for a 'universal meeting', where all the procedural requirements of convocation are dispensable.[265] The only legal requirement is that all shareholders must be present, in person or by proxy, and that they unanimously agree to hold the meeting. There are no notice requirements. This procedure is useful where the company has a limited number of shareholders.

6.47 Individual shareholders of a private company have a right to information prior to the meeting (written questions) and during the meeting.[266] In a public company, written questions may be sent no later than seven days before the meeting and the board will have until the day of the meeting to gather the required information.[267] During the meeting, shareholders may orally ask questions, which will have to be answered, if possible, during the meeting, or, otherwise, in writing by the directors seven days after the date of the meeting, at the latest.[268] Shareholders owning at least 1% of the share capital in a public company and at least 5% of the share capital in a private company may require that a notary attend a meeting to notarize all resolutions passed there.[269]

6.47a There is another form of minority protection consisting of the right of shareholders to challenge a resolution on the basis of it being contrary to the act, the company's articles or the interests of the company. They may also challenge a resolution if it was adopted in an abusive manner in the interest of the majority and to the unjustifiable detriment of the other shareholders.[270] Shareholders may bring an action to challenge a resolution, as long as they represent at least 1% of the share capital.[271] This quorum may be reduced by the articles. Individual shareholders, even those who do not reach the quorum, are entitled to compensation in cases where they suffered damages by the voidable resolution.[272] Such an action must be brought within one year of the resolution being registered at the Commercial Registry.[273]

263. Article 199 subsection (a) Spanish Act on Capital Companies.
264. Article 188(3) Spanish Act on Capital Companies.
265. Article 178 Spanish Act on Capital Companies.
266. Article 196 Spanish Act on Capital Companies.
267. Article 197(1) Spanish Act on Capital Companies.
268. Article 197(2) Spanish Act on Capital Companies.
269. Article 203(1) Spanish Act on Capital Companies.
270. Article 204 Spanish Act on Capital Companies.
271. Article 206(1) Spanish Act on Capital Companies.
272. Article 206(1) Spanish Act on Capital Companies.
273. Article 205 Spanish Act on Capital Companies.

6.48 The simplified company form (Sociedad Limitada nueva empresa (SLNE)) is mainly subject to the same provisions as the ordinary private company.[274] There are, however, some restrictions which, compared to the ordinary private company, reduce the attractiveness of the SLNE in practice. Only natural persons are allowed to become shareholders of an SLNE and, at the moment of the foundation the company, shall have no more than five shareholders.[275] There is no board of management, which means that, even if several directors are appointed, the provisions governing the board of directors will not apply.[276] Directors must be members and they may be granted remuneration by mere resolution of the members, instead of stipulation in the articles.[277] If the members adopt a resolution on the dismissal of a director, he or she is not allowed to take part in the vote.[278] This provision has been criticized by Spanish authors in the light of the fact that it leads to the strange result that the majority shareholder director may be dismissed by the minority shareholder.[279]

X BELGIUM: THE NV/SA

A The Management Structure

6.49 The structure of the Belgian public company (*naamloze vennootschap* (NV) or *société anonyme* (SA)) contains a unitary board. Consequently, there is management by a board of directors (*conseil d'administration*), with the members in general meeting exercising control and certain residual functions. Each company must have at least three directors, who are appointed initially in the deed of incorporation (but not the articles) or subsequently by the shareholders' meeting.[280] In listed companies, each gender (male or female) must be represented by at least one-third of the board members.[281] Appointments must be for a fixed term not exceeding six years and are renewable, unless the deed provides otherwise. Directors may be dismissed at any time by a simple majority; the articles must not stipulate otherwise. Appointments and dismissals must be officially notified in the *Belgian Official Journal*.[282]

6.50 Directors must not be employees of the company in their capacity as directors, but may be employed by the company in another capacity that is clearly distinct from his or her duties as a director and, in the exercise of which, he or she is under the

274. Article 434 Spanish Act on Capital Companies. *See also* Urbano, Parejo & Garcia-Nieto, Report from Spain, *European Company Law* (on 'Light Vehicle Competition') (2004), 183 *et seq.*
275. Article 437 Spanish Act on Capital Companies.
276. Article 447(1) Spanish Act on Capital Companies.
277. Article 448 Spanish Act on Capital Companies.
278. Article 449(2) Spanish Act on Capital Companies.
279. A. Jorge Viera González, 'Closed Capital Companies in the Spanish Legislative Evolution: Problems of Legal Policy and Regulatory Interpretation', in *Private Company Law Reform in Europe: The Race for Flexibility*, eds A. Jorge Viera González & Christoph Teichmann (Cizur Menor: Thomson Reuters, 2015), 588.
280. Article 518 Belgian Companies Code (*Code des sociétés/Wetboek van Vennootschappen*).
281. Article 518*bis* Belgian Companies Code.
282. Article 74 Belgian Companies Code.

control of another director. Directors can be companies,[283] for example, a controlling company, which must then nominate an individual person as its permanent representative.[284] Other directors, unless otherwise stipulated in the articles, may fill vacancies of a director, occurring during his or her term of appointment. As might be expected, the law requires that such appointment has to be confirmed the first time the general meeting is conducted.[285]

6.51 All powers of management of the company are entrusted by the act to the board of directors.[286] Only those items that are specifically reserved by the act to the general meeting are outside the scope of the directors' powers. The articles may confer the power of representation to one or more directors, and this restriction may be relied on towards third parties.[287] If the articles provide for any additional restrictions on the powers of the directors (e.g., to obtain the consent of the members to a specific transaction) these have no effect towards third parties. However, there is an internal effect, because the directors will be in breach of their duties to the company if they act contrary to such restrictions.

6.52 The statutes may authorize the board to delegate its power of management to an executive committee (*comité de direction*).[288] The general policy of the company and other matters expressly granted to the board in the Companies Code are excluded from such delegation. The executive committee consists of several persons, who may or may not be members of the board. Nomination and remuneration of the members, as well as other issues relevant for the functioning of the committee, are subject to the articles, or, otherwise, to the guidelines given by the board. The appointment of an executive committee must be published and will then be effective in relation to third parties. Day-to-day management may also be delegated to individual persons, who need not to be shareholders, and they will be authorized to represent the company.[289]

6.52a The board of directors is regarded as a collective body, so that all its members must vote on its decisions. Collective decisions may, in exceptional cases, if all the members agree and if the articles allow for that procedure, be taken in writing.[290] This simplified procedure is not applicable to the approval of the annual accounts and to the decision to make use of the power, if attributed by the general meeting, to increase the company's capital. The lack of collective decisions does not affect third parties, but may cause problems concerning the directors' liability to the company for any breach of duty.

283. Article 517 Belgian Companies Code.
284. Article 61(2) Belgian Companies Code.
285. Article 519 Belgian Companies Code.
286. Article 522(1) Belgian Companies Code.
287. Article 522(2) Belgian Companies Code.
288. Article 524*bis* Belgian Companies Code.
289. Articles 525 and 526 Belgian Companies Code.
290. Article 521 Belgian Companies Code.

B Directors' Liability to the Company

6.53 There are provisions aimed at preventing abuse of power by the directors caused by a conflict of their personal interest and their duties to the company. Any director in this position must inform the board of his interest (e.g., in a proposed contract) before the board meeting at which a decision is taken and this must be noted in the minutes and notified to the auditor.[291] The board must submit a report to the next general meeting of the company, setting out the circumstances in which the decision was taken, the conditions to which that decision was made subject and its implications for the company. There must also be a confirmatory report by the auditor. If the company or a third party has suffered damages as a result of the director's interest in the transaction, it may recover the damages from him.[292] Comparable rules apply to managing directors or members of an executive board.[293] The procedure to be observed when a conflict of interest arises does not apply within groups where one company holds more than 95% of the capital of its subsidiary, or where both companies are owned to more than 95% by the same parent company.[294] The rules on conflict of interest do not apply to transactions of day-to-day business if they are subject to normal market conditions.

6.54 In more general terms, the directors (including members of an executive committee or persons to whom the day-to-day management has been delegated) are liable to the company for negligence regarding their management of the company.[295] The standard of care is that of a professional person dealing with a client. It is not clear whether such liability is joint and several. There is additional liability if the directors act contrary to company law or the articles of the company.[296] Liability is then joint and several, but a director will have a defence if he can show that he did not take part in the breach of duty and was unable to prevent its occurrence. Even in such a case, he will not be excused, unless he notified the breach to the general meeting as soon as he became aware of it. The most important personal liability to creditors arises in the event of the company's bankruptcy, if they can be shown to have made an obvious and grave error, which added to the insolvency.[297]

6.54a The general meeting may grant the directors a discharge from liability to the company, if the true state of affairs has been disclosed to the meeting.[298] Decisions to sue the directors on behalf of the company may be taken at the meeting.[299] Minority shareholders representing 1% or more of the total voting rights existing in the company, or at least EUR 1,250,000 of the capital, are entitled to sue the directors and

291. Article 523 Belgian Companies Code. In listed companies, the director may not even take part in any discussions or votes on the relevant measure.
292. Article 529 Belgian Companies Code.
293. Article 524*ter* Belgian Companies Code.
294. Article 523 s. 3 Belgian Companies Code.
295. Article 527 Belgian Companies Code.
296. Article 528 Belgian Companies Code.
297. Article 530 Belgian Companies Code.
298. Article 554 Belgian Companies Code.
299. Article 561 Belgian Companies Code.

then the company bears the cost.[300] If this minority action is defeated, the shareholders concerned may be liable for the costs and for damages suffered by the defendants.[301]

C The Role of the Shareholders

6.55 The general meeting of shareholders may pass resolutions on any issue concerning the affairs of the company.[302] This has, however, only internal effect, given the fact that the management functions are specifically reserved for the board. Any restrictions of the board's powers in the company's constitution will not be effective against third parties.[303] The directors must present a management report at the general meeting and answer questions by the shareholders relating to the report or to any other item on the agenda, unless the information requested may seriously harm the company, its shareholders or employees.[304]

6.56 The general meeting may be convened by the board and the auditors, and must also be convened at the request of a 20% minority of the shareholders.[305] Invitations to all meetings must be officially notified and advertised in both the official journal and a national newspaper, mentioning the agenda at least fifteen days before the meeting; listed companies have to observe a period of thirty days.[306] The ordinary meeting is the annual meeting of the company, which must be held at least once a year, in accordance with the provisions of the articles within six months following the end of each financial year.[307] The functions of such a meeting, which must be called by the directors, are to approve the annual accounts, the auditor's report and the directors' report.[308] The items to be dealt with during the meeting must be specified in the published agenda, and in listed companies, with proposals for the content of the resolution too.[309] Extraordinary meetings are usually held when there is a proposal to alter the articles of association or any other major change to the company's structure or capital.[310] A quorum of the holders of at least 50% of the share capital is required on a first call, although, if no quorum is obtained, a second meeting may be held, at which there is no quorum requirement. Resolutions are normally passed based on a simple majority of those present and voting at the meeting, but for a number of transactions on which the law imposes both quorum and special majority requirements. The majority in favour of the resolution, which is the same at either the first or second meeting, varies from 80% of the votes cast for an alteration of the company's objects clause, to 75% for other

300. Article 562 Belgian Companies Code.
301. Article 567 Belgian Companies Code.
302. Article 531 Belgian Companies Code.
303. Article 522 s. 1 Belgian Companies Code.
304. Articles 95, 96 and 540 Belgian Companies Code, for listed companies the content of the management report is specified in Article 96 s. 2 Belgian Companies Code.
305. Article 532 Belgian Companies Code.
306. Article 533 Belgian Companies Code.
307. Articles 92 and 552 Belgian Companies Code.
308. Article 554 Belgian Companies Code.
309. Article 533 Belgian Companies Code.
310. Article 558 Belgian Companies Code.

amendments of the articles, and down to 25% for a resolution that the company be wound up on the grounds of the loss of three-quarters of the company's capital.[311] If the shares are of equal nominal value, one share grants one vote in the general meeting. Otherwise, the votes depend on the fraction of capital represented by a share.[312] The articles may restrict the number of voting rights of a single shareholder, if such a restriction is equally applicable to all shareholders.[313]

D Representation by the Directors

6.57 The management board has full powers to represent the company vis-à-vis third parties. In addition, the articles may grant the power of representation to one or more directors, acting individually or collectively. Although the articles may limit the power of representation, for example, by excluding a director from representing the company above a certain financial interest, such limitations do not affect third parties, unless the objects of the company are transgressed and it can be shown that the third party actually knew that the transaction was in transgression of the objects, or, given all the circumstances, could not have been unaware of it. The fact that the restriction is contained in the published deed or articles has no evidential effect in this matter.[314]

XI BELGIUM: THE BVBA/SPRL

6.58 The management system of the private company (*besloten vennootschap met bepertke aansprakelijkheid* (BVBA)/ *société privée à responsabilité limitée* (SPRL)) is rather similar to the one described earlier for the NV/SA. Unlike the NV/SA, however, the BVBA/SPRL, under Belgian law, is only required to have one director.[315] Directors are nominated by the members.[316] Each individual director has the authority to bind the company and to make decisions on its behalf, because there is no collective requirement to do so. Restrictions to the power to represent the company contained in the articles are, in general, not effective vis-à-vis third parties.[317] Where more than one signature is required by the articles for the company to be bound, third parties can be affected if they have been officially notified, unless the obligation for two signatures only applies to certain transactions. In such a case, the company cannot rely on the clause. Furthermore, the dismissal of a director must be for a serious reason; the power cannot be exercised at will.[318] Another difference arises through the provision that only shareholders representing 10% of the issued capital may sue the directors, in which case the costs are borne by the company.[319] Finally, the rules on the liability of directors

311. Articles 558, 559 and 633 Belgian Companies Code.
312. Article 541 Belgian Companies Code.
313. Article 544 Belgian Companies Code.
314. Article 526 Belgian Companies Code.
315. Article 255 Belgian Companies Code.
316. Article 256 Belgian Companies Code.
317. Article 257 Belgian Companies Code.
318. Article 256 Belgian Companies Code.
319. Article 290 Belgian Companies Code.

to creditors, where they are adjudged to have committed a breach that contributed to the insolvency of the company, will not apply if the company had an average turnover, excluding Value Added Tax (VAT), of less than EUR 620,000 in the three preceding years and a realized a balance sheet total of less than EUR 370,000 in the last year.[320]

XII THE NETHERLANDS: THE NV AND THE BV

A The Management Structure

6.59 The Dutch public company NV and private company (*besloten vennootschap* (BV)) are governed mainly by identical statutory provisions regarding their management structure. There are three regimes: the first consisting of a management board only, the second being one-tier or two-tier regime on a voluntary basis and the third is the compulsory one-tier or two-tier regime. The first two regimes have a traditional division of powers between management and the members acting in general meeting, whereas the compulsory regime implies a shift of powers to the supervisory board. The compulsory one-tier or two-tier regime, commonly called the structure regime (*structuurregiem),* was introduced in the early 1970s as one of several innovations in Dutch company law. As with the German AG, the structure regime mandates employee participation for the Dutch NV and BV. The structure regime is dealt with in paragraphs 6.62 *et seq.*, whereas employee participation in general is discussed in paragraphs 7.03 et seq. and 7.29.

6.59a As mentioned in paragraph 5.20, in 2007, the Dutch government proposed to simplify the legislation for the BV. Five years later, the revised statute for the BV came into force, effectively ending its twin-ship with the public company.[321] For the BV, capital requirements are almost completely removed and considerably more freedom is allowed to adapt the internal organization of the company to the needs of the founders/shareholders. For instance, the articles may exclude the transferability of shares for a fixed period and allow for the issuance of shares with no voting rights and for directions to the management board to be given by another corporate body.[322] The freedom of establishment as defined by the ECJ has initiated a sort of 'light vehicle competition' between Member States, and the Dutch legislative action is certainly meant to promote the BV as an attractive legal form.[323]

6.60 According to the basic system, day-to-day management is attributed to one or more directors and they are appointed and dismissed by the shareholders at the general

320. Article 265 Belgian Companies Code.
321. Wet van 18 juni 2012, Stb. 2012-299.
322. Articles 195 (3), 228 (5) and 239(4) Book 2 Dutch Civil Code. Due to its greater flexibility, the BV is often called 'Flex-BV', Nicole L. Vreeman, 'Trading the Straightjacket for a Leotard: Introducing the New Dutch B.V. Law', *European Company Law,* no. 6, pp. 305 *et seq.* On the original proposal: Hylda Boschma, Loes Lennarts & Hanny Schutte-Veenstra, 'The Reform of Dutch Private Company Laws: New Rules for the Protection of Creditors', *European Business Organization Law Review* 8 (2007): 590–598.
323. Tom van Duuren, 'The Light Vehicle Competition in Europe: The State of Affairs', *European Company Law* 4 (2004): 153 *et seq.*

meeting.[324] The directors may be individuals as well as legal persons; however, in the latter case, the director's liabilities are also imposed on the directors of that legal person.[325] There are no statutory restrictions regarding the appointment of the directors, but the articles may provide that a director must meet certain requirements. Furthermore, the discretion of the general meeting may be severely restricted by the articles, where they prescribe an appointment to be made from a list of candidates, submitted by those who are entitled to do so by the articles. Often, these are the holders of a special class of shares, the so-called priority shares, and, accordingly, they are entitled to exert a dominant influence on the appointment of management. Although the binding character of such a list of candidates may be overruled by a resolution of the general meeting, it may be a formidable obstacle, because, for such a breakthrough, a two-thirds majority of the votes cast, representing at least 50% of the share capital, is required.[326] If the articles of the BV so provide, one or more directors can be appointed by a meeting of holders of shares of a specific class or type. This way, major shareholders can appoint their 'own' director, although the articles must always allow for each shareholder with the voting right to participate in the appointment of at least one director.[327]

6.60a The main task of the board of directors of the NV or BV is to manage the affairs of the company and the enterprise connected with it, and the board is empowered to represent the company towards third parties.[328] In addition, the power of representation is attributed to every single director, but the articles may disqualify some or even all of the directors from representation and, if properly published, such limitations may be invoked against third parties.[329] A director may be removed by the corporate body that has appointed him at any time. The articles may provide that the general meeting can remove directors via a decision taken by a qualified majority only. The removal of a director also, in principle, terminates the employment (or service) contract under which he may serve the company.[330]

6.61 Any public or private company that is not subject to the compulsory structure regime may opt to establish a supervisory board (two-tier board) or to appoint non-executive directors (one-tier board) by providing for it in the articles.[331] If no supervisory board is established or no non-executives are appointed, the management board must then be supervised by the general meeting. The members of a supervisory board and the non-executive directors must all be individuals. The members of the supervisory board are appointed and dismissed by the shareholders at the general meeting, unless the articles provide for the appointment and dismissal by others, which

324. Articles 132 and 242 Book 2 Dutch Civil Code (*Boek 2 Burgerlijk Wetboek*).
325. Article 11 Book 2 Civil Code.
326. Articles 132(2), 242(2), 133 and 243 Book 2 Civil Code.
327. Article 242(1) Book 2 Civil Code.
328. Articles 129, 130, 239 and 240 Book 2 Civil Code.
329. Article 6 Book 2 Civil Code.
330. Articles 134 and 244 Book 2 Civil Code. Hoge Raad 15 Apr. 2005, NJ (*Nederlandse Jurisprudentie*) 2005/483 (*Bartelink – Ciris*).
331. The one-tier board was facilitated by the 2011 Act regarding the governance of the NV and BV, Wet van 6 juni 2011, Stb. 2011, 275.

is permitted only for a maximum of one-third of the members of the supervisory board. The articles of the BV can also allow for the appointment and dismissal of supervisory board members by the holders of a specific class of shares.[332] According to the statutory provisions, the task of the supervisory board is to supervise, as well as to advise, the board of directors with a view to the interests of both the company and its enterprise.[333]

6.61a The Dutch Corporate Governance Code (2016) applies to companies having their registered office in the Netherlands and a listing on the Amsterdam Stock Exchange. It contains principles and best practice provisions, safeguarding the independence of supervisory board members and non-executive directors. To that end, a supervisor is regarded as independent as long as certain criteria do not apply to him. Among these are: having been an employee or member of the management board in the five years prior to the appointment and having had an important business relationship with the company, or an associated company, in the year prior to the appointment. All members of the supervisory board and all non-executive directors must be independent, with the exception of a minimum of one person. The maximum number of supervisory boards of Dutch listed companies of which an individual may be a member is five. This restriction is laid down in statutory rules of 2012 and[334] it affects all NVs and BVs, not being small or medium-sized (*see* 9.13a), and whether or not they are listed. Persons may not be appointed as a supervisory board member of such a company if they hold more than five supervisory functions with other companies or other legal persons (not being small or medium-sized and governed by Dutch law). For calculation purposes, the chairmanship of a supervisory board or a management board counts as two positions, whereas multiple appointments to boards of companies belonging to the same group shall be counted as one.[335] Restrictions also apply to the members of a management board or executive directors of NVs and BVs. They must not hold appointments as a supervisor with more than two other legal persons and they must not chair the supervisory or management board of another legal person. Again, these provisions are only relevant to companies and other legal persons not being small or medium-sized.[336]

B The Structure Regime

6.62 The structure regime is compulsory for sizable companies. It applies when a company employs, on a regular basis, at least 100 persons. It is then legally obliged to establish a works council and if, according to its balance sheet, the share capital and reserves together are an equal amount, as regularly determined by Royal decree

332. Articles 129a, 140, 142–144, 239a, 250 and 252–254 Book 2 Civil Code.
333. Articles 140(2) and 250(2) Book 2 Civil Code.
334. The aim was to open up the 'old boys network' as it was called by the MP who proposed the amendment resulting in the new provisions of Articles 132a, 142a, 242a and 252a Book 2 Civil Code.
335. Articles 242a and 252a Book 2 Civil Code.
336. Articles 132a and 242a Book 2 Civil Code.

(currently EUR 16,000,000).[337] It should be noted that persons employed by subsidiaries and a works council established by a subsidiary must be taken into account when assessing whether or not these criteria are met. The initial obligation is to disclose, via the Commercial Registry, that the above-mentioned criteria apply to the company. After a three-year period, such a company must establish a supervisory board or appoint non-executive directors. Such a compulsory two-tier or one-tier structure is not only subject to the general rules pointed out above but also governed by special rules with regard to the appointment and removal of its members, as well as to its powers.

6.62a Until 2004, the members of the supervisory board were appointed by co-optation, hence by the supervisory board itself. The board of directors, the shareholders in general meeting and the works council, each were entitled to nominate a person in case of a vacancy. Moreover, both the shareholders in general meeting and the works council had a right of objection once the supervisory board had decided to propose a candidate. In practice, members of the supervisory board were often appointed for a second, or even a third, term and this had raised questions as to the proper functioning of the structure regime and the influence of the shareholders and the works council.[338] A reform in 2004 changed the procedure of appointing the members of the supervisory board. These rules apply, *mutatis mutandis*, to the non-executive directors of the company with a compulsory one-tier board.[339]

6.63 The members of the supervisory board are appointed by the general meeting of shareholders, however, the procedure considerably reduces the actual influence of the shareholders on the composition of the board.[340] The general meeting receives proposals from the supervisory board as to the persons to be appointed and it may only reject such proposal by a majority vote, representing one-third or more of the company's capital. If the general meeting neither appoints the proposed candidates nor expressly rejects them, the supervisory board itself may appoint the proposed members. The procedure encompasses rules for the supervisory board on how to carry out a proposal for the nomination of its members. The supervisory board must allow both the general meeting and the works council to put forward their candidates. For one-third of its members, the supervisory board must follow the proposal of the works council, unless the supervisory board objects to the candidate(s) on the grounds specified in the statute.[341] The position of the general meeting is further weakened by restrictive rules for the dismissal of supervisory board members (or non-executive directors). An individual member of the supervisory board can only be removed by the Enterprise Court and only on limited grounds, *inter alia*, for dereliction of his duties.[342] By a majority vote representing one-third or more of the company's capital, the general

337. Articles 153 and 263 Book 2 Civil Code.
338. A. Dorresteijn, 'Corporate Governance Issues in the Netherlands: The Legal Structure for Large Companies', in *Further Perspectives in Financial Integration in Europe*, ed. Eddy Wymeersch (Berlin/New York: De Gruyter, 1994), 209 *et seq.*
339. Articles 164a and 274a Book 2 Civil Code.
340. *See* Articles 158 and 268 Book 2 Civil Code.
341. Articles 158 and 268 Book 2 Civil Code.
342. Articles 161 and 271 Book 2 Civil Code.

meeting can pass a motion of no confidence that results in the immediate removal of all members of the supervisory board. The management board shall then request the Enterprise Court at the Amsterdam Court of Appeal to temporarily appoint one or more supervisory board members.[343]

6.64 The structure regime confers extended powers to the supervisory board. Apart from the basic tasks and powers of the common supervisory board, it has the right to appoint and dismiss the directors of the company. Moreover, several important resolutions of the management board must be approved by the supervisory board, for example, resolutions concerning the issue of shares and bonds or a lasting cooperation with another legal person.[344]

6.64a The structure regime is mitigated where the company is a subsidiary of an international group.[345] In such a case, the supervisory board does not have the right to appoint and dismiss the directors, in order not to impede central management of such a group. According to case law, however, even under the mitigated structure regime, the majority of the members of the supervisory board of the Dutch subsidiary should be independent, though the board is allowed to convince the court that there are reasons justifying an exemption to this rule.[346] The structure regime is not applicable to subsidiaries of companies that are themselves subject to the structure regime.[347]

C The Duties of Directors

6.65 Directors and members of the supervisory board are, to a great extent, subject to the same duties in performing their tasks and, therefore, we will discuss the duties of directors only. In general, directors are responsible for the proper performance of their duties.[348] They must act in the interests of the company, as well as the enterprise that is carried on by the company.[349] In case of bankruptcy, they may incur liability for the amount of damages to the company, to the extent that these cannot be satisfied out of the liquidation of the assets of the company. This is the case if management has manifestly performed its duties improperly and if it is plausible that this is an important cause of the involuntary liquidation.[350] Special duties may apply when there is a conflict of interest between the company and one or more of its directors.

6.65a Traditionally, conflicts of interest between the company and one or more directors resulted in the loss of representative powers of all directors. Instead, members of the supervisory board had to step in to act for the company. The 2011 Act dealing with governance of companies brought about a significant change in the regulation of

343. Articles 161a and 271a Book 2 Civil Code.
344. Articles 164 and 274 Book 2 Civil Code.
345. Articles 155 and 265 Book 2 Civil Code. Articles 155a and 265a Book 2 Civil Code also mitigate the regime for single-member companies where that member is an individual.
346. Ondernemingskamer (*Enterprise Chamber*) 2 Feb. 1989, NJ 1990, 86 (Kodak).
347. Articles 153(3) and 253(3) Book 2 Civil Code.
348. Article 9 Book 2 Civil Code.
349. Articles 129(5) and 239(5) Book 2 Civil Code.
350. Articles 138 and 248 Book 2 Civil Code.

conflicts of interest. Inspired by the Dutch corporate governance code, the new provisions state that an interested director shall not participate in the deliberation and adoption of resolutions if he has a direct or indirect personal interest therein, which is in conflict with the interests of the company. If, as a result, no management resolution can be adopted, the resolution shall be adopted by the supervisory board. Where there is no supervisory board, the resolution shall be adopted by the general meeting, unless the articles otherwise provide.[351] According to its wording, the statutory provision deals with personal interests only, leaving aside a conflict of duties. In its leading *Bruil* case, the Dutch Supreme Court, however, also regarded – apart from interests of a personal nature – other interests, as possibly relevant where they do not coincide with the interests of the company.[352] In case law, additional rules have been developed. In *Linders v. Hofstee,* a member of the company's supervisory board was holding shares in another company. The company bought these shares of the supervisory board member for a rather high price. Consequently, there were serious doubts whether there had been any serious bargaining, due to the influence that the supervisory board member might have had on the decision to buy the shares. It was held that, when such a conflict of interest arises, the interested member, as well as the board itself, is under a duty to disclose the interests concerned and these interests must be kept strictly separated from the interests of the company. In addition, they must seek the advice of an independent expert, if necessary.[353]

D The Role of the Shareholders

6.66 It follows from the previous paragraphs that the position of the shareholders acting in a general meeting may vary considerably. In any case, however, it is the general meeting that decides on fundamental matters, such as the alteration of the articles, including the objects of the company, the transformation of the company into another legal form and its winding up.[354] For the NV, approval of the general meeting is required for management resolutions relating to 'an important change in the identity or character of the company or the undertaking', such as the transfer of the company's business to a third party.[355] Moreover, as a basic rule for the division of powers, Book 2 Civil Code attributes all those powers not conferred upon another organ of the company to the general meeting of both private and public companies.[356]

6.66a The powers of the general meeting may be limited in a number of ways, first of all, by statutory provisions, if the structure regime applies (*see* paragraph 6.62). Aside from this, the articles of any company may attribute some of the powers of the general

351. Articles 129(6) and 239(6) Book 2 Civil Code.
352. HR 29 Jun. 2007, JOR 2007/169 (Bruil). Confirmed by the Amsterdam Court of Appeal 22 Sep. 2015, ECLI:NL:GHAMS:2015:3914, JOR 2016/117.
353. Enterprise Chamber of the Amsterdam Court of Appeal, 26 May 1983, NJ 1984, 481.
354. Articles 18, 19, 72, 183 Book 2 Civil Code.
355. Article 107a Book 2 Civil Code.
356. Articles 107 and 217 Book 2 Civil Code. Note that this rule is the reverse from rules applying in some other Member States, e.g., s. 119 German Stock Corporation Act (Germany).

meeting to other organs, such as the power to issue shares.[357] The statutes may also require that certain resolutions be proposed or approved by other persons, for example, the holders of priority shares. This is even allowed for decisions to appoint directors, which the articles can subject to a binding nomination that can only be set aside by a qualified majority.[358] In listed companies, however, a simple majority of the votes cast may cancel such nomination in principle.[359] Another frequently used means to reduce the influence of investors is certification of shares. This implies that the shares are held by an intermediate person, often a foundation, which issues certificates of the shares instead. The position of the holders of certificates vis-à-vis the intermediate shareholder is a contractual one, but they enjoy statutory rights in relation to the company, for example, to participate in the general meeting. Their position, therefore, resembles that of the holders of non-voting shares in other countries. Although originally designed to diminish the influence of outsiders, those devices turn out to be defensive measures for the management in case of a hostile takeover (*see* 8.18 *et seq.*).

6.67 The general meeting of shareholders must be held once a year, but the articles may provide for extraordinary meetings to be held in specific cases.[360] Subject to the articles providing otherwise, the board of directors or the supervisory board, upon notice given in a national newspaper or in an announcement by electronic means, convenes a general meeting.[361] The shareholders of the BV must be notified in writing or by electronic means.[362] Upon request, every shareholder can be authorized by the court to convene a compulsory general meeting of shareholders, in the event that the board refuses to do so. Moreover, persons holding shares representing 10% of the issued capital of an NV, or 1% in case of a BV, may petition the court to grant authorization to convene a general meeting, if such a meeting is in their interest.[363] As a rule, the persons convening the meeting set the agenda. Minority shareholders may find protection against abuse by the majority or management by invoking judicial interference with decisions taken by any organ of the company. Such decisions may be void or voidable if they are contrary to the law or the articles, or if some prior mandatory act, such as an approval or a notification, fails. In addition, nullification may also take place if the principles of reasonableness and fairness are violated.[364]

6.68 Minority shareholders, holding a number of shares representing 10% or more of the issued capital, have the right to apply for an inquiry to be made under supervision of the Enterprise Chamber as to the policy and conduct of the business of the company. In case the issued capital of the company exceeds EUR 22.5 million, the required

357. Articles 96 and 206 Book 2 Civil Code.
358. For example, Articles 133 and 243 Book 2 Civil Code.
359. Dutch Corporate Governance Code, Principle IV.1.
360. Articles 108 and 218 Book 2 Civil Code.
361. Articles 109 and 219 Book 2 Civil Code.
362. Article 223 Book 2 Civil Code.
363. Articles 110–112 and 220–222 Book 2 Civil Code.
364. Articles 14 and 15 Book 2 Civil Code.

percentage is 1%.[365] If, by evaluating the report of the inquirers, the Enterprise Chamber concludes that there has been misconduct, the original applicants may seek several remedies, such as the nullification of resolutions, the dismissal of a director or a member of the supervisory board, and even the winding up of the company. The right of inquiry is regularly used and an application may be filed, even if the company is already in a state of bankruptcy. In such a case, however, the main purpose is not to enable recovery of the company but to investigate who is accountable for the disastrous results.[366]

XIII THE UK: PUBLIC AND PRIVATE COMPANIES

A The General Management Structure

6.69 The management and control structure for both public and private companies under UK law is the same. The structure is that of a unitary board with shareholder meetings and minority shareholder protection. Where, under previous acts, much was left to decisions of the courts, using general concepts derived from the common law and equity, the Companies Act 2006 lays down a more extended framework by codifying aspects of the case law, notably regarding the duties of directors.[367] Many details are also a matter for the company's own constitution, which may or may not follow the suggested pattern of the model articles enacted by the Secretary of State.[368] In particular, the powers of the directors depend on the articles because, apart from requiring that certain things, for example, alteration of the articles or reduction of capital shall be done by the members in general meeting, the Act leaves much of the distribution of powers between the board and the general meeting to the articles.

6.69a The company's constitution is defined by section 17 of the Act and includes, besides the articles, the resolutions and agreements that comply with the requirements as set out in section 29 *et seq.* A copy of such a resolution or agreement must be forwarded to the registrar within fifteen days after it is passed or made.

6.70 In practice, the powers of the directors are very wide, and the ability of the shareholders to control them is very limited. In large companies, effective control is often exercised by extra-legal bodies, such as investor protection committees or by codes of practice. For example, such control is imposed by the UK Corporate Governance Code for listed companies, which rely on the presence of non-executive and

365. Articles 344 *et seq.* Book 2 Civil Code. *See* Mieke M. Tuijtel, 'The Dutch Inquiry Proceedings: A Unique Instrument for Minority Protection from a Comparative Law Perspective', *European Company Law* 2, no. 3 (2005): 90 *et seq.*
366. Hoge Raad (*Supreme Court*), 10 Jan. 1990, NJ 1990, 466 (Ogem).
367. For an overview *see* John Birds, 'Reforming United Kingdom Company Law in a European Context: A Long and Winding Road', in *European Company Law in Accelerated Progress*, ed. Bartman (Alphen aan den Rijn: Kluwer Law International, 2006), 10 (18 *et seq.*); Paul Davies & Jonathan Rickford, 'An Introduction to the New UK Companies Act', ECFR 5 (2008): 48 *et seq.*
368. Section 19 Companies Act 2006.

independent directors on the board.[369] Not only the stock exchange but also the City Panel on Take-overs and Mergers has a regulatory role that operates outside the act. In smaller companies, the directors are also often the majority shareholders, which prevents control of abuses by the members' general meeting. Consequently, minority protection provisions play an important role.

B The Directors: Their Appointment, Dismissal and Powers

6.71 Public companies must have two directors, whereas private companies need only have one.[370] The first directors are those named in the statement of directors sent to the registrar upon incorporation of the company;[371] however, all subsequent directors are appointed in accordance with the company's articles. Thus, there are no statutory requirements as to the method of appointment or the length of that appointment. The Model Articles for public companies allow for either shareholders or directors to appoint persons to be directors.[372] A director appointed by the directors shall hold office only until the following annual general meeting, where his appointment has to be confirmed.[373] The act does provide, for public companies, that, in such elections, each director must be voted for individually.[374] A director may, at all times, be removed by ordinary resolution at a meeting of the members, but he is entitled to be heard with respect to the resolution.[375]

6.72 Directors, as such, are not employees of the company and do not receive any remuneration that is not authorized by the company. Such authorization may be delegated to a committee of the board, but only if the correct procedure has not been followed can the payment to a director be attacked. Thus in *Guinness plc v. Saunders* (1990), payments made to a director for his assistance in a takeover battle were recoverable from him, because they had not been authorized by the correct committee.[376] Directors may also be employed by the company under a service contract.[377] The act requires that such contracts be open to inspection by the members.[378] The directors of a listed company must prepare a report on their remuneration for each financial year.[379] As already mentioned, the act also gives the members the right to dismiss a director at any time by an ordinary resolution, despite anything in any agreement between the company and the director.[380] Even that can be circumvented by giving each director weighted voting rights on any such resolution, rendering his position, in

369. The text of the UK Corporate Governance Code is retrievable on the website of the Financial Reporting Council www.frc.org.uk.
370. Section 154 Companies Act 2006.
371. Section 9 (4) (c) Companies Act 2006.
372. Section 20 model articles for public companies.
373. Section 21 model articles for public companies.
374. Section 160 Companies Act 2006.
375. Sections 168 and 169 Companies Act 2006.
376. *Guiness plc v. Saunders* (1990), 2 A. C. 663 (HL).
377. Section 227 Companies Act 2006.
378. Section 228 Companies Act 2006.
379. Sections 420 *et seq.* Companies Act 2006.
380. Section 168 Companies Act 2006.

fact, quite secure, and is thus justifiable in some small private companies.[381] Further, such a dismissal may be in breach of his service agreement and so may be too costly to achieve in practice.[382] The division of management powers between the directors and the general meeting is, subject to certain reserved functions for the meeting, a matter for the company's articles. In practice, these give the directors extensive powers.[383]

6.72a The model articles give the directors authority to manage the business of the company and exercise all the company's powers, subject only to the reserved powers.[384] The courts have consistently interpreted such articles widely in favour of the directors, so that they are not bound by any ordinary resolution of the meeting.[385] The directors' powers can be altered for the future by alteration of the articles in the proper way, although such alterations must not have retrospective effect. The model articles also empower the directors to delegate any of their powers to such persons or committees as they deem fit.[386] In public companies, this usually results in some board members acting as non-executive directors, as a control of the executive directors.[387] However, the Act makes no such distinctions.

6.73 UK law regards directors as being agents of the company, so that they may bind the company to any transaction that is within their authority. Under the UK law of agency, this will mean acts within their actual authority, implied authority (what is usual for an agent of that type to be able to do) and apparent authority (where the agent has been represented as having authority to the third party).[388] Whereas implied authority is a question of law and varies according to the type of director concerned, implied authority of the whole board is quite extensive. Apparent authority is a question of fact as to whether the representation was made. If the directors act contrary to the memorandum or articles, this does not affect the position of a third party dealing with the company in good faith. Good faith is presumed, unless the contrary is proven and the third party is not regarded as acting in bad faith only by reason of his knowing that an act is beyond the powers of the directors under the company's constitution.[389] An act contrary to the articles would be a breach of the director's duty to the members and would require a special resolution of the members to be ratified for internal purposes, because without ratification it would amount to a de facto alteration of the articles.[390]

381. *Bushell v. Faith* (1970) A.C. 1099 (HL). Paul L. Davis, 311E.
382. *See also* s. 215 *et seq.* Companies Act 2006 with respect to payments for loss of office.
383. Brenda Hannigan, *Company Law*, 4th edition (Oxford: Oxford University Press, 2016), 182 *et seq.*
384. Section 3 in both model articles (public companies and private companies).
385. *See* e.g., *Breckland Group Holdings Ltd v. London & Suffolk Properties Ltd* (1989) B.C.L.C. 100.
386. Section 5 in both model articles (public companies and private companies).
387. Brenda Hannigan, *Company Law*, 4 th edition (Oxford University Press, 2016), 128.
388. Brenda Hannigan, *Company Law*, 4 th edition (Oxford: Oxford University Press, 2016), 186 *et seq.*
389. Section 40(2) Companies Act 2006.
390. *See also* s. 40(4) Companies Act 2006: although the act may not affect the position of third parties, a member of the company may be entitled to bring proceedings to restrain the doing of an action that is beyond the powers of the directors.

C The Duties of Directors

6.74 The Companies Act 2006 provides a statutory statement of the directors' general duties to the company, codifying the relevant case law.[391] According to the Explanatory Notes, the general duties 'form a code of conduct, which sets out how directors are expected to behave; it does not tell them in terms what to do. More particularly, the duties address: (i) the possibility that a director may put his own or other interests ahead of those of the company and (ii) the possibility that he may be negligent'.[392] Legal literature, however, draws attention to the fact that the Companies Act 2006 is more than simply a restatement of common law principles, as it clarifies some aspects of uncertainty and sometimes even adopts a different approach than that of common law.[393]

6.74a Sections 170(3) and (4) state that:

> (3) The general duties are based on certain common law rules and equitable principles as they apply in relation to directors and have effect in place of those rules and principles as regards the duties owed to a company by a director.
> (4) The general duties shall be interpreted and applied in the same way as common law rules or equitable principles, and regard shall be had to the corresponding common law rules and equitable principles in interpreting and applying the general duties.

6.75 Directors of UK companies must act in accordance with the company's constitution and only exercise powers for the purposes for which they are conferred.[394] In addition, directors of UK companies are subject to three types of duties: fiduciary duties; the common law duty to exercise reasonable care, skill and diligence; and specific duties, such as the duty to convene the general meeting.[395] These duties are briefly discussed in the paragraphs that follow.

6.76 Being agents, the directors are regarded as being in a fiduciary position vis-à-vis the company and therefore are subject to the range of *fiduciary duties* originally designed by equity for trustees. There are three major aspects of such duties:

- First, directors must exercise their powers of management in a bona fide manner, for the benefit of the company and not for their own personal gain, which is now laid down in section 172 of the act concerning the duty to promote the success of the company. Traditionally, the company, in this

391. Sections 170–177 Companies Act. Paul Davies & Jonathan Rickford, 'An Introduction to the New UK Companies Act', ECFR 5 (2008): 48(61).
392. Companies Act, Explanatory Notes, 45.
393. Paul Davies & Jonathan Rickford, 'An Introduction to the New UK Companies Act', ECFR 5 (2008): 48(63).
394. Section 171 Companies Act 2006.
395. In the Explanatory Notes to Companies Act 2006, 47 it is stated that 'Other duties remain uncodified, such as any duty to consider the interests of creditors in times of threatened insolvency'.

context, was taken to mean the shareholders, but the Act, in section 172, requires them to also have regard to the interests of other stakeholders, notably business partners and the employees.[396] This formula is also known as the 'enlightened shareholder value' approach.[397]

- The second fiduciary duty imposed on directors is that they must make *no unauthorized profit* from a corporate transaction. This duty is partly covered by section 176, which contains the duty not to accept benefits from third parties. The company may recover unauthorized profit, even if it has suffered no loss and could not have made the profit itself.[398] It is an action for an accounting rather than for damages. This duty extends to the use of corporate information and business opportunities, though not to general information acquired as a director.[399] It is a matter of dispute as to whether the board may reject an interest in a transaction on behalf of the company, in order to allow the director to continue free of his fiduciary obligation.
- The third fiduciary duty requires that directors do not place themselves in a position in which their personal interest and duty to the company may conflict. Accordingly, section 175 provides the duty of directors to avoid *conflicts of interest* and section 177 requires them to declare their interest in a proposed transaction or arrangement. Thus, directors must disclose all interests in corporate transactions; otherwise, the transaction will be voidable at the instance of the company.[400] This fiduciary duty is not infringed where the transaction or arrangement has been authorized by independent directors, though for a public company such authorization has to be allowed by the articles.[401]

6.76a There is some dispute as to whether, as part of this fiduciary duty, directors will always be liable if they exercise one of their powers for other than the purpose for which it was designed, even if they derive no personal benefit from the transaction and consider that they are acting bona fide for the benefit of the company.[402] In *Howard Smith Ltd v. Ampol Petroleum Ltd* (1974), the court drew a distinction between ordinary powers of management, where only the bona fide test would be applied, and those that affected the structure of the company (e.g., issuing new shares), where the proper purpose test would be applied.[403] Whereas the bona fide test is a subjective one and may be passed if the court is of the opinion that the director honestly believed that

396. *See also* e.g., *Re DKG Contractors Ltd* (1990) BCC 903, directors were required to make a contribution to the assets of the company.
397. Paul Davies & Jonathan Rickford, 'An Introduction to the New UK Companies Act', ECFR 5 (2008): 48(65).
398. Sec e.g., *Regal (Hastings) Ltd v. Gulliver* (1967) A.C. 134s.
399. Sec e.g., *Island Kexport Finance Ltd v. Umunna* (1986) B.C.L.C. 460.
400. Brenda Hannigan, *Company Law*, 4th edition (Oxford University Press, 2016), 238.
401. Section 175(4)(5) and (6) Companies Act. This duty (partly) applies also to shadow directors, s. 187 Companies Act 2006.
402. *See* Brenda Hannigan, *Company Law*, 4th edition (Oxford University Press, 2016), 201 *et seq.*
403. *Howard Smith Ltd v. Ampol Petroleum Ltd* (1974) A.C. 821.

he was acting in the company's best interests, the proper purpose test is an objective one. In *Howard Smith Ltd v. Ampol Petroleum Ltd,* the court held that issuing shares with the aim of manipulating voting control in favour of one particular shareholder was for an improper purpose, even though the company may have benefited from the capital raised from the sale of shares.

6.77 The second category of duties of directors is the duty originating from common law to take *reasonable care in the management of the company.*[404] This is now expressed by section 173 of the Act, regarding the duty to exercise independent judgment, together with section 174, with respect to the duty to exercise reasonable care, skill and diligence. Directors are liable if they are negligent in managing the company's affairs in the ordinary course of events. The standard of care expected of a director has been equated with that for wrongful trading, that is, both objective, based on the reasonable care, which might be expected from someone in his position, and subjective, based on his skills (*Norman v. Theodore Goddard* (1991)).[405] This is to be distinguished from the older cases, which seemed only to expect the reasonable care based on the director's individual subjective skills.[406] The shift to an objective test may give courts a greater role in judging the negligence of a director.[407]

6.78 In the third place, directors are subject to *specific statutory controls* in specific areas. These additional controls on directors apply to 'shadow directors', that is, those, in accordance with whose directions or instructions, the other directors of the company are accustomed to act.[408] There are controls on substantial property transactions involving directors, loans to directors and payments for loss of office, which all require approval by the members.[409] Of particular importance, is the liability of directors for wrongful trading, introduced by section 214 of the Insolvency Act 1986.[410] This section holds a director personally liable to contribute to the assets of an insolvent company if he knew or ought to have concluded that there was no reasonable prospect that the company would avoid going into insolvent liquidation. However, the court may hold otherwise if the director took every step with a view to minimizing the potential loss to

404. Sections 173 (Duty to exercise independent judgment) and 174 (Duty to exercise reasonable care, skill and diligence) Companies Act 2006.
405. *Norman v. Theodore Goddard* (1991) B.C.L.C. 1028.
406. *See* Paul Davies, *Gower and Davies' Principles of Modern Company Law,* 9th edition (London: Sweet and Maxwell, 2012), 517 *et seq.* on the development of the duties of care and skill.
407. Paul Davies & Jonathan Rickford, 'An Introduction to the New UK Companies Act', ECFR 5 (2008): 48(67).
408. As defined in s. 251 Companies Act 251.
409. Sections 190 *et seq.*, 197 *et seq.*, 215 *et seq.* Companies Act 2006. Section 223 provides that these controls apply to shadow directors.
410. *See* Hans H. Hirt, 'The Wrongful Trading Remedy in UK Law: Classification, Application and Practical Significance', ECFR 1 (2004): 71 *et seq.*; it is debated whether this provision may serve as a model for European lawmaking, *see* Thomas Bachner, 'Wrongful Trading – A New European Model for Creditor Protection?', *EBOR* 5 (2004): 293 *et seq.*; *see also* s. 10.04 of the European Model Company Act (EMCA) proposing a provision that is inspired by the English wrongful trading liability (retrievable at http://www.jura.uni-wuerzburg.de/lehrstuehle/teichmann/forschungsprojekte/european_model_company_act/).

the company's creditors, as he ought to have taken. Section 214 further provides a general test for the conclusions that the director ought to reach and the steps that he ought to take. They must be those, that would be reached or taken by a reasonably diligent person having both: (a) the general knowledge, skill and experience that may reasonably be expected of a person carrying out the same functions as are carried out by that director; and (b) the general knowledge, skill and experience that that particular director has.

6.78a Section 178 of the Companies Act 2006 provides civil consequences of any breach of the general duties, thereby preserving the differences between the equitable principles that apply to the duties of a fiduciary nature, on the one hand, and the duty to exercise reasonable care, skill and diligence, which is not considered to be a fiduciary duty, on the other hand. Where breach of the latter may lead to damages, the consequences of breach of fiduciary duties may also include restoration of the company's property; an account of profits made by the director; and rescission of a contract as to which the director failed to disclose an interest.[411] Consequences of an administrative nature include the investigation of companies and their affairs and disqualification of directors.[412]

D The Members in General Meeting

6.79 Although there are no restrictions in the Act on the powers of the general meeting, in practice, its role is reduced by the articles to those rights expressly reserved to it. The model articles state that the directors may exercise all the powers of the company, unless the articles stipulate otherwise (*supra* paragraph 6.72a). Some transactions are reserved for the members by the Companies Act, such as an amendment of the articles (section 21), a reduction of capital (section 641) and the approval of certain transactions (*supra* paragraph 6.78). The members also have a residual monitoring role that arises from the need for it to approve the accounts and the ultimate power to dismiss (but not necessarily to appoint) the directors. Any decision to ratify conduct by a director amounting to negligence, default, breach of duty or breach of trust, must be taken by the members and, without reliance on the votes in favour of the decision, by the director or any connected person.[413] Any action against a director for breach of duty must similarly be approved by the members, because a wrongful act has been committed against the company, so that, if there is a resolution against such an action, it will not, subject to a very few exceptions, be allowed to proceed. Members may have the option to bring a derivative claim with respect to a cause of action arising from an actual or proposed act or omission involving negligence, default, breach of duty or breach of trust by a director of the company. The Companies Act 2006 restates

411. Explanatory Notes Companies Act 2006, 50.
412. Company Directors Disqualification Act 1986. According to the 1985 Companies Act the Secretary of State may appoint inspectors to carry out investigations and the Companies Act 2006 preserves this power but modifies it by inserting new sections in the 1985 Act, Explanatory Notes, 197 *et seq.*
413. Section 239(4) Companies Act 2006.

the rule in *Foss v. Harbottle* and makes the derivative claim available for breach of the duty to exercise reasonable care, skill and diligence, even if the director has not benefited personally, and it will not be necessary for the applicant to show that the wrongdoing directors control the majority of the company's shares.[414]

6.80 Many sections of the Companies Act 2006 provide rules of a procedural nature with respect to the organization of a general meeting and its decision-making.[415] Public companies are required to hold an annual general meeting each year and other meetings (extraordinary meetings) may be held as prescribed in the articles, usually at the behest of the board.[416] Section 303 allows a 5% minority to request that a meeting be held, the directors then must convene the meeting within twenty-one days from the date of the deposit of the request (section 304(1)). In the case of difficulties in calling a meeting, for example, in obtaining a quorum, the court will do so on terms that it deems fit.[417] An ordinary resolution (a simple majority of those present and voting) is required, unless the articles or the act provide otherwise. Special resolutions are passed by 75% of those present and voting.[418] A special resolution is required for alteration of the articles, for example.[419] Different voting rights as between different shares are allowed, and shareholders may bind themselves to voting agreements. In large companies, most votes are exercised by proxy and, although there are minority protection provisions, in practice, that system favours the board in any dispute.[420]

6.81 Minority shareholders are protected by the renewed conditions for the derivative claim, as already mentioned in paragraph 6.79. Furthermore, any member of the company may petition the court under section 994 of the Companies Act 2006, on the basis that the company's affairs are being conducted in a manner that is unfairly prejudicial to some or all of the members. There has been a large number of decisions as to what could amount to unfairly prejudicial conduct in this context. It has proven to be a wide concept and applies whenever the petitioner's 'legitimate expectations' as a shareholder have been infringed.[421] If the court upholds the petition, it can make any order that it sees fit for providing relief in respect of the matters complained of, including, *inter alia*, an order providing for the purchase of the shares of any members of the company by other members or by the company itself.[422]

---

414. Sections 260 *et seq.* Companies Act 2006 and the Explanatory Notes, 74 *et seq.*
415. Sections 281–300 (resolutions), ss 301–335 (regarding all companies), 336–340B (public companies) and 341–361 (quoted (listed) companies).
416. Sections 302, 303 and 336 Companies Act 2006.
417. Section 306 Companies Act 2006.
418. Sections 281–283 Companies Act 2006.
419. Section 21 Companies Act 2006.
420. As to voting by proxies *see* ss 324 *et seq.* Companies Act 2006.
421. Paul Davies, *Gower and Davies' Principles of Modern Company Law*, 9th edition (London: Sweet and Maxwell, 2012), 719–747; Brenda Hannigan, *Company Law*, 4th edition (Oxford: Oxford University Press, 2016), 482–525.
422. Section 996 Companies Act 2006.

XIV ITALY: THE SPA

A Board Models

6.82 Pursuant to the 2003 reform of Italian company law,[423] *three* systems of management and control are available to the *società per azioni* (SPA), the Italian public company: the traditional, the dualistic and the monistic board model. If the statutes of the company do not explicitly provide otherwise, at the time of incorporation or by a subsequent alteration, the traditional system applies.[424,425]

The traditional system features two boards, both appointed by the general meeting (*assemblea*):

(a) the management body, which may consist either of a sole director (*amministratore unico*)[426] or of a board of directors (*consiglio di amministrazione*);
(b) the committee/board of auditors (*collegio sindacale*).

Now, the board of auditors has the role of internal control, although it used to audit the accounts as well – until 1974 for quoted companies and until 2003 for unquoted public companies.[427] The accounts are now mandatorily audited by an external auditor (*revisore contabile*) or auditing business (*società di revisione*).[428,429]

The dualistic system features German traits and comprises of:

(a) a supervisory board (*consiglio di sorveglianza*), appointed by the general meeting; and
(b) an executive board (*consiglio di gestione*), appointed by the supervisory board.

While the executive board has a very similar framework to the one regulating the board of directors under the traditional model, the supervisory board is entrusted with some powers, which the latter model confers on the general meeting, such as the approval of the budget.[430]

---

423. Legislative Decree No. 6 of 17 Jan. 2003 'Riforma organica della disciplina delle società di capitali e società cooperative, in attuazione della legge delega 3 ottobre 2001, n. 366', published in the Official Journal No. 17 on 22 Jan. 2003 (Supplement No. 8).
424. Article 2380 Italian Civil Code.
425. G.F. Campobasso, *Diritto Commerciale. 2. Diritto delle Società*. Nona Edizione, UTET Giuridica, Wolters Kluwer Italia S.r.l. 2015; pp. 353–354.
426. unless the company is listed on a regulated market, which requires more than one director.
427. Legislative Decree No. 39 of 27 Jan. 2010 provided for a reform in this area, by transposing Directive 2006/43/EC and providing for a single legislative document targeting auditing rules (previously to be found in the Civil Code and in the TUF).
428. Article 2409*bis* Italian Civil Code.
429. G.F. Campobasso, *Diritto Commerciale. 2. Diritto delle Società*. Nona Edizione, UTET Giuridica, Wolters Kluwer Italia S.r.l. 2015; pp. 353–354.
430. G.F. Campobasso, *Diritto Commerciale. 2. Diritto delle Società*. Nona Edizione, UTET Giuridica, Wolters Kluwer Italia S.r.l. 2015; pp. 353–354.

Under the monistic board model, featuring an Anglo-Saxon character, management and control are entrusted, respectively, to the board of directors, appointed by the general meeting, and to the internal audit committee (*comitato per il controllo sulla gestione*), whose members shall hold certain traits of independence and professionalism.[431]

Irrespective of the board model chosen, different corporate governance rules apply to listed public companies on the one hand and to unquoted public companies on the other hand.

The three systems will be explained in detail in the following paragraphs.

1 *The Traditional System*

6.82a Pursuant to Article 2380*bis*, the company's directors, which are not required to be members, have the exclusive responsibility to manage the company and they shall do what is necessary to pursue the company's object. If the management is entrusted to more than one person, which is mandatory for quoted companies,[432] they make up a board of directors,[433] which elects a president, if the general meeting did not provide for this.[434] The number of directors, who, in any case, are not necessarily shareholders,[435] is provided for by the articles of association.[436] If this is allowed by the company's statutes or by the general meeting, the board of directors may delegate some of its powers to an executive committee (made up of members of the board of directors itself) or to one or more of the board's members.[437,438]

The first appointment of directors is made through the articles of association; subsequent appointments are dealt with by the general meeting.[439] When it comes to quoted companies, in order to safeguard minority shareholders, at least one member shall be appointed through the slate voting system (*voto di lista*).[440] All directors of quoted companies must fulfil requirements of reputation (*onorabilità*) – which are laid out for auditors, as well as at least one director[441] – and independency (*amministratore indipendente*), in the sense of being compliant with independence requirements laid out for auditors.[442,443] Article 2383 provides for causes of ineligibility and

431. G.F. Campobasso, *Diritto Commerciale. 2. Diritto delle Società*. Nona Edizione, UTET Giuridica, Wolters Kluwer Italia S.r.l. 2015; pp. 353–354.
432. G.F. Campobasso, *Diritto Commerciale. 2. Diritto delle Società*. Nona Edizione, UTET Giuridica, Wolters Kluwer Italia S.r.l. 2015; p. 368.
433. Article 2380*bis*(3) Italian Civil Code.
434. Article 2380*bis*(5) Italian Civil Code.
435. Article 2380*bis*(2) Italian Civil Code. There is no agreement, however, on the issue of allowing legal persons (or, in more general terms, an entity other than natural persons) to be directors.
436. Article 2380*bis*(4) Italian Civil Code.
437. Article 2381(1 and 2) Italian Civil Code.
438. G.F. Campobasso, *Diritto Commerciale. 2. Diritto delle Società*. Nona Edizione, UTET Giuridica, Wolters Kluwer Italia S.r.l. 2015; pp. 355–356.
439. Article 2383(1) Italian Civil Code.
440. Article 147*ter* Consolidated Law on Finance.
441. Or two directors in case of a board of auditors consisting of more than seven members.
442. Article 148 Consolidated Law on Finance.
443. Article 2387 Italian Civil Code.

incompatibility, and further instances are dealt with by specific legislation. They are appointed for a period of three financial years and can be re-appointed, unless the articles of association state otherwise.[444] The appointments, as well as the terminations, must be disclosed in the register of enterprises.[445] As far as their compensation is concerned, it is generally sanctioned by the articles of association or by the general meeting, and it may (partly or wholly) consist of profit-sharing (*partecipazione agli utili*) or the right to buy future shares at a fixed price, the so-called stock options (*diritto di sottoscrivere a prezzo predeterminato azioni di futura emissione*).[446,447]

6.82b Public companies listed on Italian Stock Exchange (*Borsa Italiana S.p.A.*) may voluntarily decide to abide by the principles enshrined by the *Codice di Autodisciplina* (Code of Self-Regulation), first adopted in 1999 and frequently revised since, lastly in 2011 and 2015, by the *Comitato per la Corporate Governance di Borsa Italiana S.p.A.* (Corporate Governance Committee of the Italian Stock Exchange). The system is built on the 'comply or explain' mechanism and mostly implements European and international concepts of corporate social responsibility.

Directors are entrusted with several tasks, which are mandatory in nature, i.e., they may neither be derogated by the statutes nor by the general meeting. To start with, they make all decisions concerning the company's management, which are not reserved by law to the general meeting: the management power (*potere gestorio*).[448] Secondly, some or all directors hold the general representation power of the company (*potere di rappresentanza*),[449] thereby externally showing the company's will, be it sanctioned by the general meeting or by the management body. Thirdly, they provide impetus to the general meeting's activities and implement their decisions. Furthermore, *inter alia*, they are responsible for what concerns compliance with disclosure requirements, for keeping the books and the accounting records (*tenuta dei libri e delle scritture contabili*), and they annually draw up the draft budget (*progetto di bilancio*) to be approved by the general meeting.[450] Specific provisions provide for safeguards concerning non-compete mechanisms,[451] conflicts of interests or other interests,[452] and related-party transactions of quoted companies.[453]

6.82c In the traditional system, the board of auditors (*collegio sindacale*) is the body entrusted with tasks of internal control and surveillance of the management. More specifically, auditors monitor the organizational, managerial and accounting adequacy

444. Article 2383 Italian Civil Code.
445. Article 2383 Italian Civil Code.
446. Article 2389(1 and 2) Italian Civil Code.
447. G.F. Campobasso, *Diritto Commerciale. 2. Diritto delle Società*. Nona Edizione, UTET Giuridica, Wolters Kluwer Italia S.r.l. 2015; pp. 358–368.
448. Article 2364(5) Italian Civil Code.
449. Article 2384(1) Italian Civil Code.
450. G.F. Campobasso, *Diritto Commerciale. 2. Diritto delle Società*. Nona Edizione, UTET Giuridica, Wolters Kluwer Italia S.r.l. 2015; pp. 354–355.
451. Article 2390 Italian Civil Code.
452. Article 2391 Italian Civil Code.
453. Article 2391*bis* Italian Civil Code. G.F. Campobasso, *Diritto Commerciale. 2. Diritto delle Società*. Nona Edizione, UTET Giuridica, Wolters Kluwer Italia S.r.l. 2015; pp. 371–374.

of the company, as well as its concrete functioning. Their monitoring role may, in some circumstances, allow or compel them to act as substitutes to the general meeting and/or the directors, if the legality of the company's running must be preserved, both in a formal and in a substantive sense.[454] To this end, they hold individual powers of inspection and control.[455] They are entitled to ask for information concerning day-to-day management, specific operations,[456] and they have to be present at the board of directors' meetings, at the general meetings and at the meetings of the executive committee.[457] Nevertheless, auditors may not challenge the directors' choices on the merits. Directors must meet several information obligations to allow the activities of the board of auditors, especially when it comes to quoted companies.[458] Furthermore, companies that do not need to draw up consolidated financial statements may entrust the board of auditors with the task of statutory auditing.[459,460]

6.82d As previously mentioned, the legal framework of the board of auditors has evolved over the years with reference to its duties, and some differences are will now be acknowledged when it comes to its composition in quoted and unquoted companies. In unquoted companies, the board of auditors consists of three *or* five members, which may or not be shareholders, plus two deputies, according to what is provided for by the articles of association.[461] The articles of association of quoted companies, on the other hand, may provide for a different number of members, but there is a minimum of three, plus two deputies. Subsequent appointments are within the competences of the general meeting.[462] A peculiarity was introduced for quoted public companies to provide that one member be appointed by minority shareholders, by making use of the slate voting system (*voto di lista*).[463] Other provisions are in place to provide safeguards as to requirements of professionalism and independence: for unquoted companies, at least one member and one deputy must be chosen amongst statutory auditors (i.e., enlisted in the register of statutory auditors) and the others must also have certain features.[464] For quoted companies, specific further provisions are laid out by a Ministerial Regulation, which also provides for requirements of reputation. Some circumstances determine ineligibility.[465] They are appointed for a period of three financial years and they can be re-appointed.[466] The appointments, as well as their

454. Article 2403(1) Italian Civil Code.
455. Article 2403*bis*(1) Italian Civil Code.
456. Article 2403*bis*(2) Italian Civil Code.
457. Article 2405(1) Italian Civil Code.
458. G.F. Campobasso, *Diritto Commerciale. 2. Diritto delle Società*. Nona Edizione, UTET Giuridica, Wolters Kluwer Italia S.r.l. 2015; pp. 395–405.
459. Articles 2403(2) and 2409*bis*(2) Italian Civil Code.
460. G.F. Campobasso, *Diritto Commerciale. 2. Diritto delle Società*. Nona Edizione, UTET Giuridica, Wolters Kluwer Italia S.r.l. 2015; pp. 395–409.
461. Article 148 Consolidated Law on Finance (TUF, Testo Unico Finanziario); Article 2397(1) Italian Civil Code.
462. Article 2400(1) Italian Civil Code.
463. Article 148(2) Consolidated Law on Finance.
464. Article 2397(2) Italian Civil Code and Article 148(4) Consolidated Law on Finance.
465. Articles 2387 and 2399 Italian Civil Code.
466. Article 2400(1) Italian Civil Code.

terminations, must be disclosed in the register of enterprises.[467] The compensation of the auditors must be pre-determined and is invariable.[468,469]

2 *The Two-Tier System*

6.82e As previously mentioned, the dualistic board model features an executive board (*consiglio di gestione*), whose framework closely resembles one of the board of directors of the traditional system, and a supervisory board (*consiglio di sorveglianza*). The latter is entrusted with both monitoring tasks and steering functions, which, under the traditional model, belong to the general meeting, such as the appointment and dismissal of the executive board's members and the approval of the budget.[470] In addition, the articles of association may further widen the scope of the supervisory board's competences. Hence, the two-tier board system provides for a heightened detachment between shareholders and the company's management.

The executive board's functioning and tasks are vastly regulated through referrals to the board of directors' framework.[471] It must have at least two members and they do not have to be shareholders. At the beginning, they are appointed by the articles of association, and, later on, by the supervisory board, unless the articles entrust the general meeting with this duty.[472] The company and individual shareholders, as well as the supervisory board, may bring action against members of the executive board.[473]

6.82f The supervisory board may comprise both shareholders and non-shareholders, their number is decided within the articles of association and must consist of at least three members.[474] At the time of incorporation they are appointed within the articles, subsequently by the general meeting in its ordinary session.[475] As it goes for the board of auditors, when it comes to quoted companies, at least one member of the supervisory board must be appointed by minority shareholders through the slate voting system (*voto di lista*). Members must comply with requirements of professionalism, reputation and independence, which are laid out by law. At least one member of unquoted companies' supervisory boards must be chosen amongst statutory auditors.[476] When it comes to quoted companies, further requirements are provided for by a Consob[477] Regulation and by a Ministerial Decree.[478] They are appointed for a period of three financial years and they can be re-appointed, unless the articles of association

467. Article 2400(3) Italian Civil Code.
468. Article 2402 Italian Civil Code.
469. G.F. Campobasso, *Diritto Commerciale. 2. Diritto delle Società*. Nona Edizione, UTET Giuridica, Wolters Kluwer Italia S.r.l. 2015; pp. 395–405.
470. Article 2409*terdecies* Italian Civil Code.
471. Articles 2409*novies*(1) and 2409*undecies* Italian Civil Code.
472. Article 2409*novies* Italian Civil Code.
473. Article 2409*decies* Italian Civil Code.
474. Article 2409*duodecies*(1) Italian Civil Code.
475. Article 2409*duodecies*(2) Italian Civil Code.
476. Article 2409*duodecies*(4) Italian Civil Code.
477. CONSOB, *Commissione Nazionale per le Società e la Borsa*: the National Commission for Companies and the Stock Exchange.
478. d.m. Giustizia 30 Mar. 2000, n. 162.

state otherwise.[479] Again, the appointments, as well as their terminations, must be disclosed in the register of enterprises.[480] Some circumstances determine ineligibility.[481] The compensation of the supervisory board members must be pre-determined and is invariable.[482,483]

The primary task of the supervisory board is to monitor the company's management. Other remarkable competences are laid out by Article 2409*terdecies*. Members of the supervisory board shall perform their duties in accordance with requirements of diligence, in accordance with the nature of their role. In case they do not monitor accordingly, when it would have prevented damages to the company, they are jointly liable, together with members of the executive board's members.[484] They may be present at the meetings of the executive board and they must be present during general meetings.[485]

3 The One-Tier System

6.82g Within the framework of the monistic board model, there is no board of auditors and its tasks are performed by an internal audit committee (*comitato per il controllo sulla gestione*).[486] The management body is regulated with reference to provisions concerning the board of directors under the traditional model,[487] but, since internal auditors must be chosen amongst its members, there is a significant difference that must be highlighted: at least one-third of the board of directors are subject to the auditors' requirements of independence, as well as their potential need to comply with other specific provisions, if the articles of association state so.[488] When it comes to quoted companies, an independent director must be appointed through the slate voting system.[489]

6.82h Members of the internal audit committee are appointed by the board of directors, with very similar requirements to the ones already laid out with reference to the board of auditors (traditional system) and the supervisory board (two-tier system).[490] Publicly held companies must appoint at least three internal auditors.[491] Also,

479. Article 2409*duodecies*(3 and 5) Italian Civil Code.
480. Article 2400(3) Italian Civil Code.
481. Article 2409*duodecies* Italian Civil Code.
482. Article 2409*quaterdecies* Italian Civil Code.
483. G.F. Campobasso, *Diritto Commerciale. 2. Diritto delle Società*. Nona Edizione, UTET Giuridica, Wolters Kluwer Italia S.r.l. 2015; pp. 421–423.
484. Article 2409*terdecies*(3) Italian Civil Code.
485. Article 2409*terdecies*(4) Italian Civil Code.
486. Article 2409*sexiesdecies* Italian Civil Code.
487. Article 2409*noviesdecies* Italian Civil Code.
488. Article 2409*septiesdecies*(2) Italian Civil Code.
489. Article 147*ter*(3) Consolidated Law on Finance.
490. Article 2409*octiesdecies*(2 and 3).
491. Article 2409*octiesdecies*(1).

when it comes to their tasks and functioning, they closely resemble the ones entrusted to the board of auditors.[492,493] In general, quoted companies are provided with more specific provisions in this area.[494,495]

B Liability of Directors

6.83 From a civil law point of view, the directors of an Italian public company are liable for their actions in three ways, which are subject to separate provisions:

(a) towards the company;[496]
(b) towards the company's creditors;[497] and
(c) towards individual members and third parties.[498,499]

When it comes to their *liability towards the company* itself, directors shall perform their duties in accordance with the law and the articles, while maintaining the proper diligence required by the nature of their task and their specific skills. They have a general obligation of diligence (*obbligazione di mezzi*), as opposed to a specific-result obligation (*obbligazione di risultato*). They are jointly liable towards the company for damages stemming from failure to comply with these duties, unless it is a duty belonging to the executive committee (*comitato esecutivo*) or being concretely entrusted to one or more directors.[500,501] In any case, however, they are held responsible when they are aware of damaging events, but they do not do what is in their power to oppose their completion or to remove or diminish their damaging consequences.[502,503]

6.83a Action against the directors is brought by the general meeting, even if the company went into liquidation, or by the board of auditors by a two-thirds majority.[504,505] If the company is declared bankrupt, is subject to receivership (*liquidazione coatta amministrativa*) or special administration (*amministrazione straordinaria*), the

492. Article 2409*octiesdecies*(5).
493. Article 2409*octiesdecies*(6).
494. Article 151*ter* Consolidated Law on Finance.
495. G.F. Campobasso, *Diritto Commerciale. 2. Diritto delle Società*. Nona Edizione, UTET Giuridica, Wolters Kluwer Italia S.r.l. 2015; pp. 428–431.
496. Articles 2392–2393 Italian Civil Code.
497. Article 2394 Italian Civil Code.
498. Article 2395 Italian Civil Code.
499. G.F. Campobasso, *Diritto Commerciale. 2. Diritto delle Società*. Nona Edizione, UTET Giuridica, Wolters Kluwer Italia S.r.l. 2015; pp. 381–392.
500. Article 2392(1) Italian Civil Code.
501. Pursuant to Article 2381(6), however, they must act in an informed manner, and they hold a right/duty to ask for information concerning the current management of the company. In any case, directors liable for their *culpa in vigilando*, have a right of recourse (*diritto di regresso*).
502. Article 2392(2) Italian Civil Code.
503. Article 2392(3), however, provides that a non-negligent director may not be held liable when he had his dissent timely noted and he had informed the president of the board of auditors in writing. This means the liability of directors is always a fault-based liability (*responsabilità per colpa*), as opposed to strict liability (*responsabilità oggettiva*).
504. The latter option was introduced by Law 28 Dec. 2005 n. 262.
505. Article 2393 Italian Civil Code.

action is brought by the receiver, the liquidator or the special commissioner.[506] The action may not be brought after five years have passed since the director has stepped down from his office.[507] If the decision against the director(s) is taken by a one-fifth majority of the company's capital, they are automatically removed from their office (*revoca di diritto*);[508] their removal must otherwise be expressly sanctioned. Since renunciation and transaction are allowed,[509] provided the general meeting so explicitly sanctions, mechanisms are in place to protect minority shareholders.[510] It is possible, in fact, for the action to be brought by shareholders representing at least one-fifth of the legal capital or, when it comes to publicly held companies, one-fortieth of the legal capital.[511,512]

6.83b It is important to note that liability of directors is of a contractual nature, as opposed to a non-contractual/tortious one. Hence, when it comes to the burden of proof, plaintiffs must provide proof as to the existence of the damages linked to the directors' failure to comply, and the directors must prove the absence of negligence or the absence of a causal link.[513]

6.84 As previously mentioned, directors may be held *liable towards the company's creditors* as well. This happens when the directors fail to comply with their duties concerning the maintenance of the assets of the company (*obblighi inerenti alla conservazione dell'integrità del patrimonio sociale*).[514] Creditors may bring this action when the company's assets are not sufficient to satisfy their claims,[515] even if the company has renounced its own action.[516] In case of a transaction, the company's creditors may bring avoidance action (*azioni revocatoria*).[517] If the company is declared bankrupt, is subject to receivership (*liquidazione coatta amministrativa*) or special administration (*amministrazione straordinaria*), the action is brought by the receiver, the liquidator or the special commissioner.[518] In accordance with what is provided for when it comes to liability towards the company, plaintiffs do not have to prove the wilful or negligent nature of the directors' misconduct.[519]

506. Article 2394*bis* Italian Civil Code.
507. Article 2393(4) Italian Civil Code.
508. Article 2393(5) Italian Civil Code.
509. Article 2393(6) Italian Civil Code.
510. G.F. Campobasso, *Diritto Commerciale. 2. Diritto delle Società*. Nona Edizione, UTET Giuridica, Wolters Kluwer Italia S.r.l. 2015; p. 384.
511. The articles of association may provide for a lower number (Article 2393*bis*(2)).
512. Article 2393 (6) and Article 2393*bis* Italian Civil Code.
513. G.F. Campobasso, *Diritto Commerciale. 2. Diritto delle Società*. Nona Edizione, UTET Giuridica, Wolters Kluwer Italia S.r.l. 2015; p. 387.
514. The relationship between the creditors' action and the company's one is debated by Italian scholars, as well as the consequences of said relationship [G.F. Campobasso, *Diritto Commerciale. 2. Diritto delle Società*. Nona Edizione, UTET Giuridica, Wolters Kluwer Italia S.r.l. 2015; pp. 389 and 390].
515. Article 2394(2) Italian Civil Code.
516. Article 2394(3) Italian Civil Code.
517. Article 2394(3) Italian Civil Code.
518. Article 2394*bis* Italian Civil Code.
519. G.F. Campobasso, *Diritto Commerciale. 2. Diritto delle Società*. Nona Edizione, UTET Giuridica, Wolters Kluwer Italia S.r.l. 2015; p. 388.

6.85 Directors are furthermore *liable towards individual shareholders and third parties*, in terms of compensation, when these individuals are directly damaged by negligent or wilful misconducts (*atti colposi o dolosi*) of the directors.[520] The direct nature of the damage provides for a restriction on the use of this action, and the burden of proof is often remarkably heavy, because plaintiffs must prove direct causal link between said damage and the director(s)'s misconduct.[521] The related action may not be brought after five years have passed since the damaging misconduct.[522]

C The General Meeting

6.86 The general meeting of shareholders (*assemblea dei soci*) of Italian public companies solely has deliberative tasks (*funzioni deliberative*) and its competences are confined by law to the most important decisions for the company's life, as opposed to the day-to-day management. It is a collective body and operates according to the majority principle, with reference to the legal capital. Provided norms related to the general meeting's functioning are complied with, its decisions are binding on all members, even if they were dissenting or absent.[523,524]

6.86a The general meeting may have both ordinary sessions (*assemblea ordinaria*) and extraordinary sessions (*assemblea straordinaria*),[525] depending on the subject matter to be decided on. Following the 2003 reform of Italian company law, competences of the ordinary session vary depending on the chosen board model, and it is possible for the articles of association to entrust specific subjects (in principle, under the competence of the general meeting in its extraordinary session) to the management board.[526] When it comes to the traditional and the monistic board models, pursuant to Article 2364(1), the general meeting features, *inter alia*, the following tasks: the budget's approval, the appointment and removal of directors, the members of the supervisory board, the president of the board of auditors. It may decide on directors' and auditors' compensation, make decisions concerning their liability, and adopt other decisions, as laid out by law or by the articles of association.[527] Under the dualistic system, on the other hand, general meetings feature fewer competences.[528] The tasks of the general meeting in its extraordinary sessions must be explicitly provided for and include; changes to the company's statutes, appointment, substitution and powers of

520. Article 2395(1) Italian Civil Code.
521. G.F. Campobasso, *Diritto Commerciale. 2. Diritto delle Società*. Nona Edizione, UTET Giuridica, Wolters Kluwer Italia S.r.l. 2015; p. 391.
522. Article 2395(2) Italian Civil Code.
523. Article 2377(1) Italian Civil Code.
524. G.F. Campobasso, *Diritto Commerciale. 2. Diritto delle Società*. Nona Edizione, UTET Giuridica, Wolters Kluwer Italia S.r.l. 2015; p. 307.
525. Article 2363(2) Italian Civil Code.
526. G.F. Campobasso, *Diritto Commerciale. 2. Diritto delle Società*. Nona Edizione, UTET Giuridica, Wolters Kluwer Italia S.r.l. 2015; p. 307.
527. Article 2364(1) Italian Civil Code.
528. G.F. Campobasso, *Diritto Commerciale. 2. Diritto delle Società*. Nona Edizione, UTET Giuridica, Wolters Kluwer Italia S.r.l. 2015; pp. 307 and 308.

liquidators, and every other matter entrusted to it by law.[529] Different quorums are in place for the general meeting to be formed and for it to deliberate, depending on the ordinary or extraordinary nature of the session. There are differences between closely held and publicly held companies. The system of quorums features many complexities[530] and aims at facilitating decision-making, while, at the same time, safeguarding minorities, especially when it comes to extraordinary sessions. To facilitate the decision-making process, less strict quorums are in place when it comes to second convocations.[531,532] In case the company has issued special types of shares or other instruments that entail administrative rights, there are both general sessions and special meetings, depending on categories of shareholders.[533]

6.86b The general meeting of shareholders is usually convened by the management body,[534] which, generally, may do so when the directors *see* fit, although there are some mandatory cases. The general meeting in its ordinary session must be convened at least once a year to approve the budget,[535] or when it is called for by (minority) shareholders representing at least one tenth of the company's capital or one twentieth in publicly held companies.[536,537] The board of auditors must convene the general meeting in several circumstances, most notably when it was a mandatory convocation and directors failed to act or when it comes to severe occurrences. In some other cases, the meeting may also be summoned by a court order.[538,539]

6.86c Two rights are relevant in relation to the general meeting: the right to intervene (*diritto di intervento*) and the right to vote (*diritto di voto*). There is an instrumental relationship between the two, since the right to intervene belongs to those who also hold the right to vote, even if under suspension.[540] Holders of shares with no voting rights attached cannot take part in the general meetings. In any case, members of management and control bodies, preference shareholders' spokespersons (*rappresentanti degli azionisti di risparmio*), as well as representatives of bondholders and other participation instruments' holders, join the meeting. Differences are to be acknowledged between quoted and unquoted companies when it comes to rules to establish the right to intervene in order to avoid or limit speculative behaviour. The matter was

529. Article 2365(1) Italian Civil Code.
530. *See*: G.F. Campobasso, *Diritto Commerciale. 2. Diritto delle Società*. Nona Edizione, UTET Giuridica, Wolters Kluwer Italia S.r.l. 2015; pp. 314–320; as well as Articles 2368–2369 Italian Civil Code.
531. Article 2369 Italian Civil Code.
532. G.F. Campobasso, *Diritto Commerciale. 2. Diritto delle Società*. Nona Edizione, UTET Giuridica, Wolters Kluwer Italia S.r.l. 2015; p. 308.
533. G.F. Campobasso, *Diritto Commerciale. 2. Diritto delle Società*. Nona Edizione, UTET Giuridica, Wolters Kluwer Italia S.r.l. 2015; p. 309.
534. Article 2366(1) Italian Civil Code.
535. Article 2364(2) Italian Civil Code.
536. The articles of association may provide for a lower percentage in both cases.
537. Article 2367(1) Italian Civil Code.
538. Article 2367(2) Italian Civil Code.
539. G.F. Campobasso, *Diritto Commerciale. 2. Diritto delle Società*. Nona Edizione, UTET Giuridica, Wolters Kluwer Italia S.r.l. 2015; pp. 309–311.
540. Article 2370(1) Italian Civil Code.

recently reformed by Legislative Decree 27/2010, which implemented Directive 2007/36/EC (the Shareholders Rights Directive).[541] The company's statutes may allow intervention through means of telecommunication and the casting of votes through electronic means.[542] In this area, quoted companies must comply with specific provisions adopted by the Consob.[543,544,545]

6.86d Shareholders may personally take part in general meetings, but they can also appoint proxies, unless the articles of association of an unquoted company state otherwise.[546] The latter type of participation aims at facilitating small shareholders to take part in the company's life and makes it easier to reach the required majorities when it comes to companies whose shareholders are often absent. It is regulated by Article 2372 of the Civil Code and by some other special provisions in relation to quoted companies.[547] Most provisions pursue the limitation of abuses.[548]

XV ITALY: THE SRL

A The Role of the Members

6.87 The legal framework of the *società a responsabilità limitata* (SRL), the Italian private company, was significantly altered by the 2003 reform of Italian company law,[549] resulting in enhanced flexibility and autonomy when it comes to the statutes' drafting process. In any case, the basic structure is one of the public company, comprising of a general meeting, a management body and a supervisory body. When it comes to the general meeting in private companies (*assemblea dei soci*), however, the range of tasks is wider than in public companies. Article 2479(2) of the Civil Code provides for a series of mandatory competences, which are: the approval of the budget and distribution of profits; the appointment of directors (if the deed of incorporation states so); the appointment of auditors, the president of the board of auditors and of the statutory auditor; the alteration of the company's statutes; the decision-making regarding substantial alterations to the company's object; as well as significant alterations to the members' rights. Furthermore, the general meeting may be entrusted

541. G.F. Campobasso, *Diritto Commerciale. 2. Diritto delle Società*. Nona Edizione, UTET Giuridica, Wolters Kluwer Italia S.r.l. 2015; pp. 325 and 326.
542. Article 2370(4) Italian Civil Code.
543. CONSOB, *Commissione Nazionale per le Società e la Borsa*: the National Commission for Companies and the Stock Exchange.
544. Article 127 Consolidated Law on Finance.
545. G.F. Campobasso, *Diritto Commerciale. 2. Diritto delle Società*. Nona Edizione, UTET Giuridica, Wolters Kluwer Italia S.r.l. 2015; pp. 327 and 328.
546. Article 2372(1) Italian Civil Code.
547. Articles 135*novies*-144 Consolidated Law on Finance.
548. G.F. Campobasso, *Diritto Commerciale. 2. Diritto delle Società*. Nona Edizione, UTET Giuridica, Wolters Kluwer Italia S.r.l. 2015; pp. 328–335.
549. Legislative Decree No. 6 of 17 Jan. 2003 'Riforma organica della disciplina delle società di capitali e società cooperative, in attuazione della legge delega 3 ottobre 2001, n. 366', published in the Official Journal No. 17 on 22 Jan. 2003 (Supplement No. 8).

with other tasks by the articles of association[550] and members may decide on every matter that is presented to them by the managers or by quota-holders representing at least one-third of the legal capital.[551]

6.88 Decisions are taken according to the majority principle, unless the articles of association provide, in relation to certain types of less important decisions, for a faster mechanism.[552] The articles of association determine how the general meeting is convened. If it does not do so, it becomes the task of the managers. Members may appoint proxies, unless the articles prohibit it. The weight of the members' votes is proportional to their participation in the company,[553] and deliberative quorums are higher than they are in the case of public companies.[554] If the articles of association do not state otherwise, decisions are taken in accordance with the majority principle, and the majority must represent at least half of the company's capital.[555,556]

B The Management and Control Structure

6.89 In the articles of association, members may flexibly regulate the allocation of competences between shareholders and directors when it comes to the company's management.[557] If it is not provided for in a different way, the management is entrusted to one or more shareholders that are appointed by the shareholders[558] for an unlimited period of time, but managers are allowed not to be shareholders. There is still legal uncertainty, as well as diverging scholarly opinions, concerning the question of whether a company may be a director of another company. Causes of ineligibility and incompatibility shall be dealt with by the statutes. When the management is entrusted to more than one person, they make up a board of directors and act collectively. However, it is possible for the articles of association to determine that directors are, in most circumstances, not to operate as a board, but rather individually or jointly, through personal companies,[559] with the exception of some matters, which require joint decisions. Directors have the general right to represent the company.[560]

6.90 When it comes to liability of directors, they are jointly liable towards the company for damages stemming from failure to comply with duties stated by law, or by the articles of association, unless they prove there was no negligence and, being aware

550. Article 2479(1) Italian Civil Code.
551. Article 2479(1) Italian Civil Code.
552. Article 2479(3) Italian Civil Code.
553. Article 2479(5).
554. Article 2479*bis*(3) Italian Civil Code.
555. Article 2479(6) Italian Civil Code.
556. G.F. Campobasso, *Diritto Commerciale. 2. Diritto delle Società*. Nona Edizione, UTET Giuridica, Wolters Kluwer Italia S.r.l. 2015; pp. 573–576.
557. Article 2479(1) Italian Civil Code.
558. Article 2475(1) Italian Civil Code.
559. Article 2475(3) Italian Civil Code.
560. Article 2475*bis* Italian Civil Code. G.F. Campobasso, *Diritto Commerciale. 2. Diritto delle Società*. Nona Edizione, UTET Giuridica, Wolters Kluwer Italia S.r.l. 2015; pp. 578–581.

of the damaging effect, they had their dissent noted.[561] An action against directors of private companies may be brought by a single shareholder,[562] but it is also assumed that it may be brought by the company, although the code is silent on this issue.[563] Renunciation and transaction are allowed, unless the deed of incorporation states otherwise. Furthermore, as in public companies, directors of private companies are liable towards single shareholders and third parties directly damaged.[564]

6.91 The articles of association may require the appointment of a supervisory body or of a statutory auditor, and determine their competences and powers. Under certain circumstances, such appointment is mandatory.[565] Non-managing shareholders have a right to be informed by the directors as to the company's activities.[566]

C *Società a Responsabilità Limitata Semplificata* (SRLS)

6.92 The Italian company law system features a simplified version of the private limited liability company, which is a legal entity introduced by Law Decree 1/2012, as later converted by Law Decree 27/2012, and whose framework was simplified by Law Decree 76/2013, as later converted by Law Decree 99/2013. It is provided for by Article 2463*bis* of the Italian Civil Code and it is largely regulated with reference to the legal framework of the ordinary private company.[567]

A ministerial standard template for the public deed of incorporation must be used, pursuant to which a memorandum of association shall be drafted by a notary; such template was adopted by Ministerial Decree 138/2012. The standard clauses of the ministerial template are mandatory,[568] which is a limitation to the flexibility otherwise offered by the ordinary private company's framework.[569]

When this type of private company was first created, only shareholders were allowed to be its directors. Later on, Law Decree 76/2013 permitted the allocation of management duties to people who are not shareholders.[570]

561. Article 2476(1) Italian Civil Code. Those shareholders who willingly decided or authorized the undertaking of damaging acts towards the company, the shareholders or third parties, are jointly liable with the directors (Article 2476(7) Italian Civil Code). These shareholders are acting as *de facto* directors of the company.
562. Article 2476(3) Italian Civil Code.
563. G.F. Campobasso, *Diritto Commerciale. 2. Diritto delle Società*. Nona Edizione, UTET Giuridica, Wolters Kluwer Italia S.r.l. 2015; p. 584.
564. Article 2476(6) Italian Civil Code. G.F. Campobasso, *Diritto Commerciale. 2. Diritto delle Società*. Nona Edizione, UTET Giuridica, Wolters Kluwer Italia S.r.l. 2015; pp. 582–585.
565. Article 2477 Italian Civil Code.
566. Article 2476(2) Italian Civil Code. G.F. Campobasso, *Diritto Commerciale. 2. Diritto delle Società*. Nona Edizione, UTET Giuridica, Wolters Kluwer Italia S.r.l. 2015; pp. 585–587.
567. Article 2463*bis*(6) Italian Civil Code. G.F. Campobasso, *Diritto Commerciale. 2 Diritto delle Società*. Nona Edizione, UTET Giuridica, Wolters Kluwer Italia S.r.l. 2015; pp. 592–593.
568. Article 2463*bis*(3) Italian Civil Code.
569. G.F. Campobasso, *Diritto Commerciale. 2. Diritto delle Società*. Nona Edizione, UTET Giuridica, Wolters Kluwer Italia S.r.l. 2015; pp. 592–593.
570. http://www.altalex.com/documents/altalexpedia/2013/09/13/societa-a-responsabilita-limitata-semplificata.

CHAPTER 7

Involvement of Employees

I INTRODUCTION

7.01 Employees may be involved in the decision-making process within the enterprise (or undertaking) at different levels. The first level of employee involvement starts with informing the employees of corporate decisions. The next rung is that of consultation of the employees prior to any corporate decisions affecting the rights of employees. The highest form of employee involvement is participation at the level of corporate bodies. Such participation comprises involvement in the composition and/or in the decision-making process of these bodies. Employee involvement has developed in a national context in various forms, but the conditions for its functioning have changed due to the internationalization of business enterprises on a European and global scale. That is not to say that existing channels of employee involvement became totally ineffective in the context of a multinational enterprise (MNE). Where the structure of such an enterprise requires a centralized strategy – because goods and services are sent from the company's home country to its subsidiaries elsewhere – employee involvement may retain some impact on the policy of the enterprise. However, the collectivity of the MNE's employees cannot be represented based on national arrangements; hence, only the employee involvement of the company's home country may be able to exert some influence. No such influence remains, however, where MNEs have another structure and develop their strategy within a multi-centred, network-like setting. Such MNEs do not operate from a home country in the traditional sense, but combine local operations with cost price reductions and economies of scale by operations in a global dimension.[1] In general, national procedures for the involvement of employees are not very compatible with the transnational structure of MNEs

1. W.M.G. Allertz, *Grensoverschrijdende organisatie-ontwikkeling en medezeggenschap* (Assen: Van Gorcum 2002). For the structures of MNE's: C.A. Bartlett & S. Ghoshal, *Managing Across Borders: The Transnational Solution* (Boston: Harvard Business School Press, 1989). From the same authors: The Multinational Corporation as an Interorganizational Network, *The Academy of*

and may lead to unequal treatment of employees affected by the decisions of such undertakings.[2] The European Commission already observed, in 1980, that the completion of the internal market was bound to generate a process of internationalization of undertakings, leading to such inconsistency. Against this background, the European Union (EU) has taken several legislative actions in order to ensure the social dimension of the internal market, and some of the most relevant directives are discussed in this chapter. Almost thirty years after its first wake-up call, the Commission, again, put the process of globalization on its Renewed Social Agenda of 2008. The Commission stressed that technological change, globalization and an ageing population are transforming Europe's societies and that EU policies need to keep pace with these trends and help people adapt to changing circumstances.[3]

7.01a In 1980, the Commission proposed a directive concerning information and consultation of employees in undertakings with a complex structure, particularly MNEs.[4] This draft could be regarded as nothing more than complementary to the directives already enacted with regard to collective redundancies and the safeguarding of workers' rights in the event of transfers of undertakings.[5] Nevertheless, the draft was abandoned after a 'heated debate', during which no political agreement could be reached.[6] At the time, the draft directive was strongly opposed both at the governmental and at the managerial levels, which also occurred with the draft Fifth Directive. As Blanpain stated: 'Those proposals are ideologically loaded, touch upon delicate power balances between management and labour (...).'[7] Notwithstanding its political sensitivity, the role of employees is now firmly embedded in Community policy. According to the 1989 Community Charter of the Fundamental Rights of Workers, the involvement of employees must be developed, especially in companies or groups of companies having establishments or subsidiaries in two or more Member States.[8] The European Parliament called on the Commission to adopt a series of measures to guarantee these rights of employees. It urged that there should be a directive 'incorporating in identical forms the rights to information and consultation, and in equivalent forms the right to participation, into the statutes of all companies, irrespective of their legal constitution - limited companies, European companies, cooperatives, mutual benefit companies,

Management Review 15, no. 4 (October 1990): 603–625. John H. Dunning and Sarianna M. Lundan, *Multinational Enterprises and the Global Economy* (Cheltenham: Edward Elger Publishing, 2008).

2. Further on the economic and social context of employee involvement and on industrial relations Javier Calvo et al., *Employee Representatives in an Enlarged Europe*, vol. 1, European Commission, Directorate-General for Employment, Social Affairs and Equal Opportunities, April 2008 (retrieved from http://bookshop.europa.eu), 19 *et seq.*
3. Communication of the Commission: *A Renewed Social Agenda: Opportunities, Access and Solidarity in 21st Century Europe.*
4. OJ 1980, C 297. The draft was called the 'Vredeling-directive', named after the commissioner who was responsible for it.
5. Directive EC 75/129, OJ 1975, L 48 and Directive EC 77/187, OJ 1977, L 61.
6. Roger Blanpain, *Labour Law and Industrial Relations of the European Community* (Deventer/Boston: Kluwer Law and Taxation Publishers, 1991), nr. 334–337.
7. Roger Blanpain, 'Representation of Employees at the Level of the Enterprise and the EEC', *Recht der Arbeit* 2 (1992): 127.
8. Articles 17 and 18 of the Community Charter, adopted on 9 Dec. 1989.

self-management-companies – and also into those of the European Economic Interest Grouping (EEIG)'.[9] Moreover, the Member States, with the exception of the UK, agreed to carry out the Charter on the signing of the 1992 Maastricht Treaty. To carry out this policy, the Commission successfully launched a new proposal for information and consultation of employees in enterprises with a Community dimension, which was to become the European Works Council (EWC) Directive of 1994 (now Directive 2009/38/EC). By 1997, the Amsterdam European Council agreed to incorporate the agreement on social policy in the EC Treaty and the UK accepted the EWC Directive.[10]

7.01b Employees may express their interest in the company's affairs not only via the means of information and consultation but also by becoming shareholders. Several Member States have a tradition of so-called Employee Share Ownership schemes (ESO). In its 2012 Action Plan, the Commission announced its objective to identify and investigate potential obstacles to transnational ESO and to take appropriate action to encourage employee share ownership throughout the EU. A 2014 study revealed that barriers for cross-border employee share ownership arise from differences in regulatory density, application of national legal frameworks or differences in the fiscal treatment of existing schemes. Several policy options are suggested in order to overcome these obstacles.[11]

7.01c This book is mainly concerned with legal issues and, therefore, the possible effects of employee involvement on the performance of the enterprise are not discussed here. Nevertheless, the often controversial nature of the topic may justify pointing out recent findings showing that, in the UK, more responsive management to 'worker voice practices', being any formal mechanism by which workers can communicate their views to the management, will result in improved productivity.[12] According to a survey in the way in which Dutch top-management and works council interact, it seems to make all the difference to the firm's economic position in the sense that a positive attitude of managers towards the works council is positively associated with organizational performance.[13] Apart from this phenomenon, the effects of the presence of a works council on performance depend on factors like whether the organization is in the process of restructuring and, more generally, the fluctuation of the economy.[14]

9. Article 45 Resolution A3-175/90 of 13 Sep. 1990.
10. Directive 97/74/EC of 15 Dec. 1997 extending, to the United Kingdom of Great Britain and Northern Ireland, Directive 94/45/EC, OJ 1997, L 010.
11. *The Promotion of Employee Ownership and Participation*, Final report October 2014, EU, available at http://ec.europa.eu/dgs/internal_market/studies .
12. A. Bryson, A. Charlwood & J. Forth, 'Worker Voice, Managerial Response and Labour Productivity: An Empirical Investigation'. *Industrial Relations Journal* 37, no 5 (2006): 438–455.
13. Annette van den Berg, Yolanda Grift & Arjen van Witteloostuijn, *Works Councils and Organizational Performance: The Role of Top Managers' and Works Councils' Attitudes in Bad Vis-À-Vis Good Times* (Utrecht University, Tjalling C. Koopmans Research Institute), Discussion Paper Series nr. 08-14, 2008, retrievable from http://igitur-archive.library.uu.nl/CTK/2008-1124-201117/UUindex.html.
14. Saraï Sapulete, *Works Council Effectiveness: Determinants and outcomes*, Tjalling C. Koopmans Institute, Utrecht University, February 2013 https://dspace.library.uu.nl/handle/1874/272942.

7.02 Several directives deal with the right of employees to information and consultation. Of an overall character is Directive 2002/14/EC, establishing a general framework for informing and consulting employees.[15] This directive was preceded by much older legislation dealing with information and consultation for specific situations, namely, where an undertaking is transferred or collective redundancies are contemplated.[16] In addition, in 1994, a directive was adopted applying to 'Community-scale undertakings' or 'Community-scale groups of undertakings', covering the issue of information and consultation rights in internationalized enterprises. These undertakings or groups are obliged to establish an EWC or an alternative procedure for information and consultation of employee representatives.[17] It must be noted that the directives mentioned here are part of the EU policy regarding employment and social rights, along with issues such as safety and health requirements for the organization of working time and the posting of workers.[18]

7.03 Being distinct from information and consultation rights, participation of employees connects labour to the inner mechanics of the company's (or other legal entity's) decision-making process. Participation rights are dealt with at the European level by the regulations and directives governing EU business organizations and cross-border mergers. These rules protect existing participation rights when a *Societas Europaea* (SE) or *Societas Cooperativa Europaea* (SCE) is formed or a cross-border merger takes place. There has been no harmonization of national systems of participation, which, of course, is due to the abandonment of the proposed Fifth Directive on the structure of companies (paragraph 3.10a).

7.04 In this chapter we deal with the involvement of employees by outlining the information and consultation rights of the EWC (paragraphs 7.05–7.14), followed by a few notes on the directives that accompany the Statutes of the SE and the SCE (paragraphs 7.15–7.16). The directives harmonizing national information and consultation rights are discussed thereafter and in chronological order (paragraphs 7.17–7.26). The remaining paragraphs of this chapter cover the main characteristics of employee involvement in a number of Member States.

7.04a For the purpose of clarity, it must be noted that this study follows the definition of 'involvement of employees' as stipulated by Article 2(h) of the SE Directive, meaning 'any mechanism, including information, consultation and participation, through which employees' representatives may exercise an influence on decisions to be taken within the company'. This terminology is also used in the directive accompanying the SCE Statute and in the Tenth Directive on cross-border mergers.[19] In earlier legal documents and related literature, however, 'participation of workers' features as a generic term

15. OJ 2002, L 80.
16. Directive 77/187/EEC, OJ 1977, L 61 (now: Directive 2001/23/EC, OJ 2001, L 82) and Directive 75/129/EEC, OJ 1975, L 48 (Directive 98/59/EC, OJ 1998, 225), respectively.
17. Directive 94/45/EC, OJ 1994, L 254.
18. *See* http://ec.europa.eu/employment_social/labour_law/index_en.htm.
19. Article 16 of this directive basically refers to the SE Directive for the issue of participation rights.

and 'co-determination' was used for what is now usually called 'participation'.[20] In legal research, other generic terms may be used, for example, 'employee representation', covering similar issues as 'involvement of employees'.[21]

II INFORMATION AND CONSULTATION: THE EWC, THE SE AND THE SCE

7.05 Directive 2009/38/EC, the replacement of the original 1994 Directive, deals with the establishment of an EWC or a procedure for the purpose of informing and consulting employees applies to Community-scale undertakings or groups of undertakings.[22] The Community-scale is reached where an undertaking has at least 1,000 employees within the Member States and employs a minimum of 150 employees in each Member State (at least two are required). For a group of undertakings, the latter criterion is replaced by a similar requirement: the group must have at least two group undertakings in different Member States, each having no less than 150 employees (Article 2(1)(c)).

7.06 Basically, the Directive represents a stimulus for negotiations because it respects any agreements on transnational information and consultation rights reached before the date of the entry into force of the directive. The Directive, therefore, may be applicable only if no such agreement exists or if, upon its expiration, the parties concerned do not mutually decide on renewal (Article 14). The original 1994 Directive was, indeed, preceded by several initiatives to establish European-wide employee involvement within French MNEs, such as BSN and Thomson. These pioneers were to be followed by the initiatives of employees within several other multinationals, for example, Ford, Volkswagen and Continental Can. They varied from arrangements for joint exchange visits between employee representatives of European plants to a joint information and consultation forum on a group-wide, European level.[23] It is estimated that over 400 arrangements with management had been reached before the 1994 Directive came into force.[24] The primarily contractual nature of the EWC Directive

20. *See* for 'participation' in the general sense e.g., the 1989 *Community Charter of the Fundamental Rights of Workers*. Klaus J. Hopt, 'Labor Representation on Corporate Boards: Impacts and Problems for Corporate Governance and Economic Integration in Europe', *International Review of Law and Economics* 14 (1994): 204 *et seq. See also* Michael Gold, *Direct Communications in European Multinationals: A Case Study Approach* (Dublin: European Foundation, 1994) who discerns 'direct forms of participation' (consultation and delegation at workfloor level) and 'representational forms of participation' (information and consultation via employees' representatives).
21. Calvo et al., *Employee Representatives in an Enlarged Europe*, vol. 1, European Commission, Directorate-General for Employment, Social Affairs and Equal Opportunities, April 2008 (retrieved from http://bookshop.europa.eu), 17.
22. Directive 94/45/EC, OJ 1994, L 254/64 and Directive 2009/38/EC, OJ 2009, L 122.
23. Gold, *Direct Communications in European Multinationals*, (Luxembourg : Office for Official Publications of the European Communities, 1994), 20 *et seq.*, Aldo Dikker & Astrid de Lange, 'Europees Overleg in opmars', *Praktijkblad voor Medezeggenschap* 4 (1994): 8. Michael Gold & Mark Hall, *Report on European-Level Information and Consultation in Multinational Companies*. An Evaluation of Practice (Dublin: 1992).
24. *The Impact of the European Works Councils* (1998), retrieved from www.eurofound.europa.eu /eiro/index.htm (August 2008), the website of the European Industrial Relations Observatory

(negotiations combined with a fallback on standardized rules if no agreement is reached) has been copied by both the SE Directive and the Tenth Directive on cross-border mergers (paragraphs 3.57, 4.36 and 8.35).

7.07 If the Directive applies, the central management is responsible for setting up an EWC or an alternative information and consultation procedure.[25] It may therefore initiate negotiations and is obliged to do so at the written request of no less than 100 employees or their representatives in at least two undertakings or establishments in two different Member States. The directive contains guidelines for the composition of a special negotiating body of employees, so as to ensure that the employees in each of the Member States where there is an establishment or an undertaking are represented.[26] The negotiating body has the task, together with the central management, to determine, by written agreement, the scope, composition, functions and terms of office of the EWC (or of the alternative procedure for information and consultation).[27] Article 6(2) spells out the details that the agreement must determine:

(a) the undertakings of the Community-scale group or the establishments of the Community-scale undertaking which are covered by the agreement;
(b) the composition of the EWC, the number of members, the allocation of seats and the term of office;
(c) the functions and the procedure for information and consultation of the EWC;
(d) the venue, frequency and duration of meetings of the EWC;
(e) where necessary, the composition of the select committee set up within the EWC and rules regarding its functions and procedures;
(f) the financial and material resources to be allocated to the EWC;
(g) the duration of the agreement and the procedure for its renegotiation.

If no agreement can be reached or if the central management and the negotiating body so decide, 'subsidiary' (default) requirements apply, as laid down by the legislation of the Member State in which the central management is situated. Such requirements must at least meet the provisions set out in the Annex to the Directive.[28] Notwithstanding this solid fallback provision, the negotiating body may decide, by at least two-thirds of the votes, not to open negotiations or, alternatively, to terminate negotiations already opened and, as a consequence, the subsidiary requirements would not apply.

(EIRO). A database containing transnational company agreements identified and catalogued by the ILO and the European Commission is published at the Commision's website regarding Employment, Social Affairs & Inclusion (retrieved from http://ec.europa.eu/social/main.jsp?catId=978&langId=en, April 2017).

25. Article 4.
26. Article 5(1 and 2).
27. Article 5(5).
28. Article 7.

7.08 According to the subsidiary requirements in the Annex to the Directive, the competence of the EWC to information and consultation is restricted to matters that concern the Community-scale undertaking or group of undertakings as a whole (Annex, paragraph 1(a)). Other provisions concern, *inter alia*, the composition of the EWC, the right to meet with the central management once a year and the right of the EWC to be assisted by experts of its choice (paragraphs 1, 2 and 5). Where exceptional circumstances occur, affecting the employees' interest to a considerable extent, the EWC has the right to be informed and to meet with management. This applies particularly in the event of relocations, the closure of establishments or undertakings and in the case of collective redundancies (paragraph 3).

7.09 The Member States shall provide for rules to secure that the members of the negotiating body or the EWC are not authorized to reveal information that has expressly been provided to them in confidence. The Member States must additionally provide that the central management is not required to transmit any information, which, by its nature, would be seriously prejudicial to any of the affected undertakings. Members States may make such derogation of the duty of information subject to prior administrative or judicial authorization.[29] The directive further provides for protection of the employee representatives. The members of negotiating bodies, EWCs and employee representatives exercising their functions under the alternative procedure for information and consultation enjoy the same protection and guarantees provided for employee representatives by the national legislation and/or practice in force in their country of employment.[30]

7.10 The Directive may be implemented by the Member States not only by bringing into force the necessary laws, regulations and administrative provisions, but also by ensuring that management and labour representatives introduce the required provisions by way of (collective) agreement. The most common way has been the transposition of the directive into law, although several Member States have consulted social partners before taking legislative measures.[31] The directive does not affect the rights of employees to information and consultation under national law (Article 12(2)). Therefore, its implementation has not had significant influence on existing systems of industrial relations because the EWCs could be fitted into existing arrangements.[32]

7.11 Questions regarding the establishment of an EWC have been referred to the European Court of Justice (ECJ). In *Anker* [2004], the works council of the German subsidiary of the Swiss-based Anker group requested information from its local management with a view to establishing an EWC. According to Article 5 of the German implementing legislation, the central management of a Community-scale group, upon request, must provide information to the employees' representatives on the average number of employees, the distribution of these employees within the Member States,

29. Article 8.
30. Article 10(3).
31. *The Impact of the European Works Councils* (1998), retrieved from www.eurofound.europa.eu/eiro/index.htm (August 2008), the website of the EIRO.
32. *Ibid.*

on the undertakings and establishments and on the structure of the group of companies. The Anker works council requested this information from its local management, which was supposed to forward the request to the central management. The management of the German subsidiary replied that both its parent company, being a Dutch BV, and the Swiss parent company of the group refused to provide the information. The works council then started proceedings at the labour court at Bielefeld (Germany). The court submitted preliminary questions to the ECJ, in particular, as to whether an undertaking in the group, which is regarded as the central management, is obliged to provide information to other group undertakings established in different Member States, when such undertakings received a request for information from the employees' internal representation bodies. The ECJ held that Member States are required to impose on undertakings established within their territory and constituting the central management of a Community-scale group the obligation to supply to another undertaking in the group established in another Member State the essential information for opening negotiations with a view to setting up an EWC. The same applies for the 'deemed central management' of groups, where the actual central management is not situated in the EC, which was the case with Anker. In such a case, the responsibilities of the central management lie with the central management's representative agent in a Member State, the management of the establishment or with the group undertaking employing the greatest number of employees in any one Member State (Article 4(2) EWC Directive). The ECJ stressed that any other interpretation of the obligations by which the central management or deemed management is bound 'would be liable to undermine the useful purpose of the Directive'.[33]

7.12 Two earlier cases already demonstrated the difficulties that employee representatives may encounter when requesting information with a view of establishing an EWC. Similar preliminary questions as in *Anker* were referred to the ECJ in *Kühne & Nagel* [2004] and *Bofrost* [2001]. In the first case, as in *Anker,* the central management of the group was established in Switzerland. The ECJ held that, if the central management refuses to cooperate, the deemed central management, in order to be able to fulfil its obligation to provide information to the employees' representatives, must request the information from the other undertakings of the group, insofar as they are located in the EU. The deemed central management has the right to receive that information from them and the management of each of the other group undertakings must supply the deemed central management with the information concerned, if it is in possession of it or is in a position to obtain it.[34] In *Bofrost* [2001], the information was refused on the basis that none of the undertakings was in the position to effectuate central management. Within the Bofrost group, a special agreement was concluded, intending to establish parity between the various undertakings, so that none would be dominant and that there would be no hierarchy between them. The ECJ held that 'an undertaking which is part of a group of undertakings is required to supply information to the internal workers' representative bodies, even where it has not yet been

33. Case C-349/01 (*ADS Anker*).
34. Case C-440/00 (*Kühne & Nagel*).

established that the management to which the workers' request is addressed is the management of a controlling undertaking within a group of undertakings'.[35]

7.13 The original EWC Directive came into force at a time when industrial relations were all but transnational. Traditionally, the heterogeneity of trade unions' interests and the absence of strategic benefits for employers from collective bargaining in a transnational setting are among the factors impeding the development of transnational industrial relations.[36] The introduction of EWCs can be regarded as a stimulus to the 'Europeanization' of these relations, because they represent new forums for information and consultation.[37] By 2007, approximately 820 EWCs had been established, representing more than 14 million employees. Although this may seem impressive, considerably more companies fall within the scope of the EWC Directive and the total number of employees covered by it has reached 24 million in 2008.[38] In 2008, the Commission launched the proposal for an amending directive, in order to extend the number of EWCs and remove legal uncertainties, as well as to insert clear rules for the interplay between information and consultation rights deriving from different directives.[39] The Commission's proposal got the support of the EP[40] and on 6 May 2009, Directive 2009/38/EC was adopted. Among the amendments the new Directive brought about was a provision on the adaptation of preexisting agreements. The central management is required to initiate negotiations on its own initiative or at the written request of at least 100 employees or other representatives if the structure of the Community-scale undertaking or group of undertakings changes significantly or where there are conflicts between two or more applicable agreements or where agreements lack certain provisions (Article 13).

7.14 The issues covered by the amendments proposed by the Commission and inserted in Directive 2009/38/EC are, *inter alia:*

- arrangements for informing and consulting employees must follow the general principle of effectiveness, but the competence of the EWC (or the equivalent procedure) shall be limited to transnational issues (Article 1(2));
- new definitions are provided for the concepts of information and consultation in order to enable employee representatives to express an opinion on the information provided (Article 2(f) and (g));

35. Case C-62/99 *(Bofrost)*, ruling 1.
36. Wolfgang Lecher et al., *European Works Councils. Developments, Types and Networking* (Aldershot (UK)/Burlington (US): Gower Publishing, 2001), 119.
37. *Ibid.*, 120.
38. Commission Staff Working Document accompanying the proposal for an amending EWC Directive, SEC(2008) 2167.
39. Brussels, 7 Feb. 2008, COM(2008) 419 final. The proposal to amend the EWC Directive was part of the renewed social agenda of the Commission (paragraph 7.01).
40. P6_TC1-COD(2008)0141, Position of the European Parliament adopted at first reading on 16 Dec. 2008 with a view to the adoption of Directive *2009/.../EC* of the European Parliament and of the Council on the establishment of an EWC or a procedure in Community-scale undertakings and Community-scale groups of undertakings for the purposes of informing and consulting employees.

- the ECJ's judgments (*see* paragraphs 7.11 and 7.12) on the obligation of undertakings within a Community-scale group are codified; hence the undertakings are obliged to provide information that is required for commencing negotiations with a view to establishing EWCs, in particular information concerning the structure of the undertaking, the group and its workforce (Articles 4 and 5);
- new and simpler rules for the composition of the special negotiating body are inserted (Article 5);
- the agreement establishing the EWC must arrange a link between information and consultation of the EWC and that of the national representation bodies; where such arrangement fails, Member States must ensure that processes of informing and consulting the EWC and the national bodies start in parallel, in case decisions are likely to lead to substantial changes in the work organization or contractual relations (Article 12(2) and (3)).

7.15 The model of the EWC Directive, giving priority to negotiations with a view of reaching an agreement between the employer and employee representatives in a joint special negotiating body, backed by subsidiary (default) rules where no agreement is reached, was duplicated into the directives accompanying the SE and SCE Statutes. According to the Preamble of the SE Directive, information and consultation procedures at a transnational level should be ensured in all cases of creation of an SE. It should also be defined primarily by means of an agreement between the parties concerned or, in the absence thereof, through the application of a set of subsidiary or standard rules. The standard rules are laid down in Part 2 of the Annex to the SE Directive and define the competence and powers of the representative body set up in the SE. Part 1 of the Annex contains the standard rules for the composition of such a body. The right to information and consultation is modelled after the rights as laid down in the EWC Directive. These issues and the relationship between the EWC Directive and the SE Directive are dealt with in paragraph 4.35 et seq.

7.16 The SCE Directive is similar to the SE Directive in many respects and the same standard rules apply where no agreement on employee involvement is reached. In contrast to the SE, however, the SCE may be established by natural persons or by a single legal entity and natural persons. In the event that these persons or the entity may employ less than fifty employees, or employ fifty or more employees in only one Member State, employee involvement is governed by local rules. For the SCE itself, the provisions of the Member State where the SCE is registered apply, and for its subsidiaries and establishments the provisions of the Member State in which they are situated apply. After the registration of the SCE, however, a request by one-third of the total number of employees of the SCE, its subsidiaries and establishments will suffice to have the basic rules of the directive applied; that is, starting the negotiating procedure on a transnational information and consultation procedure (Article 8).

III INFORMATION AND CONSULTATION: OTHER DIRECTIVES

7.17 The directive on collective redundancies, the directive on protection of employees' rights in the case of a transfer of the undertaking, as well as some directives on safety and health, all contain provisions regarding procedures for information and consultation of employee representatives.[41] However, these directives deal with specific situations, whereas Directive 2002/14/EC establishes a general framework for informing and consulting employees.[42]

7.18 The *Directive on collective redundancies* (1975, amended 1992)[43] applies where dismissals are effected by an employer for reasons not related to the individual workers' concerned. The threshold can be set by the Member States at a certain number of dismissals. One of the options is, for example, to apply the rules where, over a period of ninety days, at least twenty dismissals take place, regardless of the number of workers normally employed in the establishments (Article 1). Information on collective redundancies must be given to employee representatives before the decision is taken and before any notification to the competent authority is given. The employer has the obligation to explain, in writing, *inter alia,* the reason for the redundancies, the number of workers to be made redundant, the number of workers normally employed and the period over which the redundancy is to be effected (Article 2(3)). The employer is obliged to notify the competent authority of the projected collective redundancies (Article 3). The consultation must cover ways and means to avoid or reduce the redundancy and to mitigate its consequences. The employer is also required to consult the employee representatives with a view of reaching an agreement. The collective redundancies may not take effect any earlier than thirty days after notification to the competent authority (Article 4).[44]

7.19 The *directive on the safeguarding of employees' rights in the event of transfers of undertakings* (1977, substituted 2001)[45] applies where economic trends lead to changes in the structure of undertakings and businesses, which result in a change of employer. More precisely, this directive applies where an undertaking, business or part of an undertaking or business is transferred to another employer because of a legal transfer or merger (Article 1(a)). For the sake of clarity, it is stipulated that the provisions apply where there is a transfer of an economic entity that retains its identity, meaning an organized grouping of resources that has the objective of pursuing an economic activity, whether or not that activity is central or ancillary (Article 1(b)). This phrase essentially codifies the extensive case law generated by the ECJ on the concept

41. (EEC) 75/129, OJ 1975, L48; (EEC) *111* 187, OJ 1977, L61; *inter alia* (EEC) 89/391, OJ 1989, L 183.
42. OJ 2002, L 80.
43. *See* the consolidating Directive 98/59/EC, OJ 1998, L 225.
44. Blanpain, *Labour Law and Industrial Relations of the European Community*, nr. 283–293.
45. Directive 77/187/EEC, OJ 1977, L 61, amended by Directive 98/50/EC, 1998, OJ 1998, L 201; both directives are repealed by the consolidating Directive 2001/23/EC, OJ 2001, L 82.

of transfer and the concept of undertaking, or part thereof.[46] The rules set by the directive apply where, and insofar as, the undertaking to be transferred is situated within the EU (Article 1(2)). The directive enables employees to remain employed on the terms and conditions of the existing contract and the transferee becomes the employer (Article 3). The transferor and transferee both must inform the representatives of the employees affected by the transfer about the date of the transfer, the reason behind it, the legal, economic and social implications for the employees and the measures envisaged in relation to the employees. If the transferor or the transferee contemplates measures in relation to his employees, he must consult the employee representatives with a view to reaching an agreement (Article 6). More details of the directive are discussed in paragraph 8.35.

7.20 The so-called *Framework Directive on safety and health* (1989, amended 2007) concerns general measures to improve the safety and health of employees at work.[47] Among other matters, it provides for employee involvement in relation to the enterprise's safety and health policy. According to Article 10, employees must receive all the necessary information concerning the safety and health risks and the measures and activities undertaken in this respect. Article 11(1) requires employers to consult employees and/or their representatives and allow them to take part in discussions on all questions relating to safety and health at work. This includes the right to be consulted and to make proposals. It presupposes a balanced involvement in accordance with national laws and/or practices.[48]

7.21 The *Directive establishing a general framework for informing and consulting employees* (2002) was adopted with the view of consolidating the principle of information and consultation in the EU.[49] It serves to supplement the existing directives discussed in the previous paragraphs and to fill gaps in national laws and practices.

7.22 The adoption of the Directive was stimulated by the *Renault Vilvoorde* case, and some coin the directive the 'Vilvoorde Directive' as a result. The management of Renault announced the closure of the production plant at Vilvoorde (Belgium)[50] without prior consultation of employee representatives. At the same time, Renault appeared to be planning to expand its production capacity in Spain, with the envisaged financial aid of both Spanish authorities and the EC. Making a decision affecting the jobs of more than 3,000 employees without due consultation provoked the furious reactions of trade unions and Belgian authorities alike. It also raised interest at EC level, and the Commissioner announced his intention to assess the legality of Renault's actions in terms of the EWC Directive and the collective redundancies Directive

46. C. de Groot, 'The Council Directive on the Safeguarding of Employees' Rights in the Event of Transfers of Undertakings: An Overview of the Case Law', *Common Market Law Review* 30 (1993): 331–350.
47. (EEC) 89/391, OJ 1989, L 183 and 2007/30/EC, OJ 2007, L 165.
48. These provisions of the 1989 Directive are not amended. Therefore, the old terminology is used: 'participation of workers' (which is equivalent to 'involvement of employees').
49. 2002/14/EC, OJ 2002, L 80.
50. Note that 'Vilvoorde' is also spelled as 'Vilvorde'.

(75/129/EEC).[51] However, Renault had set up a 'European group committee' by voluntary agreement before September 1996 and consequently was exempted from the obligation to renegotiate on the formation of an EWC (which is in accordance with Article 16 of the EWC Directive). The text of this agreement contained no obligation for Renault to order an extraordinary meeting of this committee to consult its members on the closure of Vilvoorde. Confronted with the case, both Belgian and French courts held that information and consultation rights had been violated, notwithstanding the wording of the voluntary agreement. The agreement had to be interpreted in a manner consistent with its preamble, which referred to the EWC Directive and the Community Charter on Fundamental Social Workers' Rights. In terms of the EWC Directive, any decision having a significant effect on the interests of employees must lead to information and consultation of the EWC. The Versailles Court of Appeal held that consultation does not necessarily have to be prior to the decision, but must leave scope for criticism, in order to eventually modify the initial decision.[52] In the wake of 'Vilvoorde', the Belgian legislators enacted stricter rules, in order to prevent any further violation of information and consultation rights.[53]

7.23 In the Member States, employees are traditionally represented by works councils and/or trade union representatives. Their systems regarding the rights to information and consultation may vary considerably.[54] The directive does not show a preference for any of these systems and merely establishes a general framework setting out minimum requirements for the right to information and consultation of employees and/or their representatives. The practical arrangements for this right must be defined and implemented in accordance with national law and industrial relations practices in the Member States in such a way, as to ensure their effectiveness (Article 1). The rules regarding information and consultation apply where undertakings employ at least twenty or fifty employees in one Member State. The threshold can be set at either level by the Member States (Article 3). Information must be provided at such time and in such a way, as to enable employees' representatives to conduct an adequate study and, where necessary, prepare for consultation. Consultation must take place at the appropriate level, *inter alia*, on decisions likely to lead to substantial changes in work organization or in contractual relations, insofar as these decisions are within the scope of the employer's powers. The consultation must take place with a view of reaching an agreement with regard to these changes (Article 4). The Directive provides that rules on the handling of confidential information must be implemented to the extent that employee representatives may be bound by an obligation of confidentiality. If

51. The European Parliament adopted a resolution claiming that these directives had been violated, OJ 1997, C 115.
52. Filip Dorssemont, 'The Renault Saga (revisited)', *European Company Law* 3, no 1 (February 2006): 5 *et seq.* Cases are reported in the *Chroniques de Droit Social* 1997, 325 *et seq.* and 1998, 376 *et seq.* and *Revue de jurisprudence sociale* 1997, nr. 829.
53. Isabelle Schömann, Stefan Clauwaert & Wiebke Warneck, *Information and Consultation in the European Community: Implementation Report of Directive 2002/14/EC*, European Trade Union Institute for Research, Education and Health and Safety (ETUI-REHS) (Brussels, 2006), 7 (retrieved from www.worker-participation.eu, August 2008).
54. Calvo et al., *Employee Representatives in an Enlarged Europe*, 45.

information is harmful to the functioning of the undertaking employer, in cases to be specified, it is not obligatory to disclose information to employees or consult with them (Article 6).

7.24 According to the core provision of the Directive, Article 4, the Member States must ensure that the following rules apply:

> (2) Information and consultation shall cover:
> (a) information on the recent and probable development of the undertaking's or the establishment's activities and economic situation;
> (b) information and consultation on the situation, structure and probable development of employment within the undertaking or establishment and on any anticipatory measures envisaged, in particular where there is a threat to employment;
> (c) information and consultation on decisions likely to lead to substantial changes in work organization or in contractual relations (...);
> (...)
> (4) Consultation shall take place:
> (a) while ensuring that the timing, method and content thereof are appropriate;
> (b) at the relevant level of management and representation, depending on the subject under discussion;
> (c) on the basis of information supplied by the employer in accordance with Article 2(f) of the directive and of the opinion that the employees' representatives are entitled to formulate;
> (d) in such a way as to enable employees' representatives to meet the employer and obtain a response, and the reasons for that response, to any opinion they might formulate;
> (e) with a view to reaching an agreement on decisions within the scope of the employer's powers referred to in paragraph 2(c).

7.25 The directive leaves Member States the option to grant management and labour representatives the freedom to establish, through negotiated agreement, the practical arrangements for informing and consulting employees. Such arrangements may deviate from the provisions of Article 4, but they should be in accordance with the principles laid down in Article 1. This means that their effectiveness must be ensured and that the 'employer and the employees' representatives shall work in the spirit of cooperation and with due regard for their reciprocal rights and obligations, taking into account the interests both of the undertaking or establishment and of the employees'.

7.26 Although the directive should have been implemented no later than 23 March 2005, by October 2007, three Member States were still in the process of transposition.[55] Four Member States had declared that no implementation was necessary, because national legislation and practice were already in line with the provisions of the

55. Luxembourg, Finland and Spain. Edoardo Ales, *Studies on the Implementation of Labour Law Directives in the Enlarged European Union. Directive 2002/14/EC establishing a general framework for informing and consulting employees in the European Community, Synthesis Report* (*Synthesis Report*) (October 2007), retrieved from http://ec.europa.eu/employment_social/labour_law (August 2008), 4.

directive; however, the ECJ has judged differently in two of these cases.[56] Article 10 of the directive contains a transitional provision allowing Member States having no general, permanent and statutory system of information and consultation of employees or employee representation to temporarily limit the application of the implementing national provisions to undertakings and establishments with more than the minimum number of employees, required at the time by Article 3. Only six Member States have profited from this facility.[57] Evaluation of the implementation shows that a series of problems remain. Among these are the lack of clarity with reference to the scope of application of the directive due to the vagueness of the definitions of 'undertaking', 'establishment' and 'employee', and the incomplete transposition of Article 6 on the handling of confidential information.[58]

IV EMPLOYEE INVOLVEMENT WITHIN MEMBER STATES

7.27 In order to illustrate the characteristics of employee involvement at the national level, the following paragraphs briefly explain how this subject is dealt with in a selection of Member States. Although no specific attention is paid to the implementation of the directives that have been dealt with in the previous paragraphs, it is worth mentioning that Member States may incorporate the implementing measures in their national labour codes or by way of introducing separate statutory provisions. For example, the French *Code du travail* deals consecutively with the different forms of employee involvement, that is, by trade unions, delegates of the employees or works councils (including the EWC), upon the formation of an SE or SCE and in the case of a cross-border merger.[59] By way of contrast, the Dutch legislator enacted implementing legislation separately from the Works Council Act (*Wet op de ondernemingsraden*).[60] The latter method, of course, is not very helpful in making the body of rules regarding employee involvement easily accessible.

7.28 In general, Member States still have rather different systems of employee involvement, notwithstanding the effects of the harmonizing directives. First, although they are essential connecting factors for the regulation of employee involvement, it must be noted that the concepts of 'undertaking' and 'establishment' are perhaps too vaguely defined in Directive 2002/14/EC to have any harmonizing impact. Second, in the area of information and consultation, the primary actors may be the works council, being a body of employee representatives, or alternatively, trade union representatives, such as in the UK. These two 'channels' may coexist, partly having separate tasks, but they may also be connected where the membership of the two channels is joined. This may be the case, for example, in France, or where the trade unions have a dominant

56. C-320/06 (regarding Belgium) and C-385/05 (regarding France).
57. Cyprus, Ireland, Italy, Malta, Poland, and the United Kingdom. Ales, *Studies on the Implementation of Labour Law Directives in the Enlarged European Union*, 5.
58. *Ibid.*, 34.
59. *Code du Travail* (*version en vigeur au 5 septembre 2008*, retrievable at www.legifrance.gouv.fr).
60. *Wet rol werknemers bij de Europese vennootschap*, 17 Mar. 2005. Belgium also enacted a separate Act (*Wet betreffende de rol van de werknemers in de Europese Vennootschap*) as of 10 Aug. 2005.

role in setting up works councils, such as in Poland. Third, judicial procedures in cases of conflict between the works council or other employee representatives and the employer may differ considerably. For example, in the Netherlands, such a procedure may result in an injunction, obliging the employer to withdraw his decision, if it is done in a manner conflicting with the statutory consultation rules. However, in France, the employer may be punishable for a criminal offence, though that does not affect the decision taken.

7.29 Finally, when it comes to employee participation at the board level, it must be noted that this is not a common feature in the Member States. According to a study completed in April 2008, such participation can be found in thirteen Member States.[61] Most commonly, employee representatives in these Member States have one-third of the seats on the board, most often the supervisory board.[62] In five other Member States, employee participation is limited to state-owned companies or companies owned by municipalities, and two Member States have extended it to privatized companies.[63] Twelve Member States have no legal arrangements at all for board level participation.[64] Although employee participation has not been harmonized, it has been taken into account in the directives regulating transactions of a cross-border nature (Tenth Directive, SE Directive and SCE Directive).[65]

A Belgium[66]

7.30 In Belgium, the works council was introduced by statute in 1948 and is further regulated by Royal Decrees and collective agreements.[67] The establishment of a works council (*ondernemingsraad/comité d'entreprise*) is mandatory if the employer in an undertaking that employs, on average, fifty persons or more.[68] If this number of persons is employed, a committee on safety and health must be formed as a separate body. Moreover, trade unions may have their representatives at enterprise level, where they may be active with respect to problem solving in the area of social policy. For the works council, lists of candidates are to be proposed by trade unions and they must be

61. Denmark, Finland, Norway and Sweden, Germany, Austria, the Netherlands, Luxembourg, Czech Republic, Slovak Republic, Hungary and Slovenia, *Employee Representatives in an Enlarged Europe*, vol. I, 63.
62. Calvo et al., *Employee Representatives in an Enlarged Europe*, vol. I, 64–65. Swedish legislation, which is not discussed in this book, entitles employees to two permanent representatives and two deputies on the board of directors in companies with at least twenty-five employees. If the company has more than 1,000 employees and operates in at least two different lines of business, the number is three permanent representatives and three deputies.
63. Belgium, Greece, Ireland, Poland and Spain. France and Malta have extended employee participation to privatised companies, *Employee Representatives in an Enlarged Europe*, vol. I, 64.
64. Estonia, Latvia, Lithuania, Cyprus, Romania, Bulgaria, Italy, UK and Portugal. 64.
65. *See* paragraphs 3.87, 4.13 and 4.44.
66. Calvo et al., *Employee Representatives in an Enlarged Europe*, vol. 1, 94–101.
67. Act of 20 Sep. 1948 (as amended) (Wet van 20 Sep. 1948 houdende organisatie van het bedrijfsleven).
68. Article 14 Act of 20 Sep. 1948.

made up in such a manner that different categories of employees are represented.[69] The works council, however, has a mixed membership because the employer or his representatives also have seats, and the meetings of the works council are chaired by or on behalf of the employer.[70] The employees on the works council are elected for a four-year period and are entitled to facilities like education and training.[71] They enjoy protection against deterioration of their position. Termination of their contract is only permitted on limited grounds, such as economic or technical circumstances. The works council has the right to be informed about the financial, economic and social matters of the undertaking. The right to be consulted pertains to social matters and economic aspects, such as the productivity of the enterprise or issues on which advice is asked for.[72] The works council has a right to co-decision regarding certain issues, such as holiday schedules.[73] In cases of conflict, the employer or the employees may submit the question to the court.[74] Belgian law does not provide for employee participation at the board level, except for a few companies owned by the state or by a region.[75]

B France[76]

7.31 The French version of the works council *(comité d' entreprise)* was introduced by statute in 1945. The establishment of a works council is mandatory if fifty or more persons are employed within the enterprise for a period of twelve months, either in succession or not, during the three previous years. In any case, a works council may be created by convention or collective agreement.[77] Elections must be held every four years. Lists of candidates may be submitted by trade unions and they must reflect the different categories of employees.[78] As is the case in *Belgium*, the employer or his representative is a member of the works council and presides at its meetings.[79] The employee members enjoy protection against termination of their contract of employment.[80] The employer has to provide for funds for the financing of the cultural and social activities of the works council and carries the costs of experts that may be consulted by the works council.[81] The works council is entitled to information and must be consulted before major economic decisions are taken, such as mergers and restructurings, although no consultation has to take place in case the employer

69. Article 14, 16 and 20*ter* Act of 20 Sep. 1948.
70. Articles 16 and 22 Act of 20 Sep. 1948.
71. Article 21 Act of 20 Sep. 1948.
72. Article 15 Act of 20 Sep. 1948.
73. *Ibid.*
74. Article 24 Act of 20 Sep. 1948.
75. A.M. Koene & H. Slomp, *Medezeggenschap van werknemers op ondernemingsniveau* (The Hague: Vuga, 1991), 63–96. Calvo et al., *Employee Representatives in an Enlarged Europe*, vol. 1, 94–101.
76. Calvo et al., *Employee Representatives in an Enlarged Europe*, vol. 1, 204–218.
77. Articles L2322-1, L2322-2 and L2322-3 French Labour Code (*Code du travail*).
78. Articles L2324-1, 2324-2, 2324-3 and 2324-4; L 2324-24 French Labour Code.
79. Article L L2324-1 French Labour Code.
80. Articles L2411-1 *et seq.* French Labour Code.
81. Articles L2323-86 and L2325-35 *et seq.* French Labour Code.

launches a public takeover bid.[82] Negligence in performing this duty results in a criminal offence for the employer.[83] The French legislator allows for collective arrangements more favourable for the functioning and competences of the works council, compared to the statutory provisions.[84]

7.31a Where there is a group of undertakings, a group works council has to be established by the dominant undertaking. Its members are designated by the trade unions from their members in the works councils of the undertakings belonging to the group. The group works council has extended information rights at both group level and undertaking level.[85]

Delegated members of the works council have the right to participate at all meetings of the board of directors or the supervisory board of an SA (paragraph 6.10) and may advise on the issues that the board is dealing with. As a rule, there are two members delegated, but where the works council is elected by three categories of personnel, four members are delegated.[86] Although they are entitled to participate in all meetings, delegated members of the works council are not members of the board. The articles of an SA, however, may provide for a limited number of employee representatives to be elected as members of the board of directors or the supervisory board.[87]

7.31b Apart from the works council, delegates of the employees are often elected *(délégués du personnel)*, but they may simultaneously be members of the works council.[88] In undertakings employing less than 200 persons, the employer may decide that the delegates constitute employee representation at the works council.[89] The main task of the delegates is to communicate complaints to the management and the works council.[90] In addition, trade union representatives have the task to further the interests of trade union members among the employees and they may conclude a collective agreement with the employer.[91] Very often, however, the representatives of the trade unions are members of the works council as well. A body that is often created by collective agreements is the 'freedom of expression group'. Employees have a statutory right to freedom of expression regarding their work and working conditions.[92] This is a collective right, the exercise of which has to be acceded to by an agreement with the employer in undertakings where trade unions have representatives.[93]

82. Articles L2323-1, 2323-19, 2323-25 *et seq.* French Labour Code.
83. Articles L2328-1 and 2328-2 French Labour Code.
84. Article L2325-4 French Labour Code.
85. Articles L2331-1 *et seq.*, Article L2332-2 and Article L2332-1 French Labour Code.
86. Article L2323-62.
87. *Code de Commerce,* Article L225 French Labour Code.-27 and 225-79. *See also* Articles L225-23 and 225-71 on the election of employee representatives in case employees are holding more than 3% of the company's capital.
88. The threshold for electing delegates is met if the enterprise has eleven employees or more, Article L2312-1.
89. Article L2326-1 French Labour Code.
90. Article L2313-1 French Labour Code.
91. Articles L2111-1 *et seq.* French Labour Code.
92. Articles L2281-1 *et seq.* French Labour Code.
93. Article L228-5 French Labour Code.

7.31c French law, since 2015, also provides for employee representation on the board of large companies.[94] These rules apply to companies employing a total of more than 1,000 employees, including those working for subsidiaries with their statutory seat in France. They also apply to French companies with foreign subsidiaries, if they employ a total of more than 5,000 employees. In these cases, employees will have at least one representative on the board, if the size of the board is up to twelve members, and two representatives, if the size of the board exceeds twelve members. The nomination procedure shall be determined by the articles of association and can be chosen from four different possibilities regulated by the law (e.g., election by the employees or nomination by the works council).

C Germany[95]

7.32 Germany has a long tradition regarding works councils, because they have been regulated by statute as far back as the first decades of the twentieth century However, the modern form of employee participation is twofold and encompasses not only participation through works councils, but also through employee representation on the supervisory board of big companies (co-determination or *Mitbestimmung). The works council, in principle, deals with affairs on the plant level, such as working conditions, whereas co-determination regards the economic policy of the company at the management supervisory level. Employee representation on the supervisory board is mandatory for certain business organizations, *inter alia,* the public and private companies, if they employ more than 500 persons. In such a case, one-third of the members of the supervisory board are elected by the employees (paragraph 6.28).[96] This rises to one-half if more than 2,000 persons are employed. If between 2,000 and 10,000 persons are employed, the supervisory board must have twelve members, and six of these are reserved for employee representatives, that is, four employees of the company and two trade union representatives. Different figures apply if more persons are employed, and the largest number of supervisory board members (twenty) must be appointed by companies having more than 20,000 employees. Similarly, half of these seats are set aside for employee representatives, of which a part is reserved for trade union representatives.[97] To avoid deadlock, the chairperson has a casting vote. The chairperson has to be elected by the supervisory board with a two-thirds majority, allowing both employees representatives and shareholder representatives on the board to block the appointment. In such a case, however, the shareholder representatives may choose the chairperson. The employee representatives may then choose the vice-chair.[98]

7.32a The co-determination acts apply, *inter alia,* to the AG and GmbH. All members of the supervisory board are equally held to further the interests of the enterprise and

94. *See* Article L225-27-1 French Commercial Code.
95. Calvo et al., *Employee Representatives in an Enlarged Europe*, vol. 1, 228–246.
96. *Gesetz über die Drittelbeteiligung der Arbeitnehmer im Aufsichtsrat* (DrittelbG), s. 1.
97. Sections 1 and 7 *Mitbestimmungsgesetz.* For certain industries, different rules may apply according to the *Montan-Mitbestimmungsgesetz.*
98. Sections 27 and 29 MitbestG.

the legal position of the employee representatives does not differ from that of other members.[99] Companies incorporated in other jurisdictions are not covered by the co-determination acts, even if the workforce is exclusively or mainly located in Germany. Some German businesses have avoided co-determination by incorporating their company in other European jurisdictions. There is a lively academic and political debate in Germany on whether the German legislator should change the co-determination acts in a way that foreign legal entities would also be covered and whether such a rule would be compatible with the European freedom of establishment.[100] From another angle, German co-determination may be in conflict with European law, because only employees working inside Germany are entitled to vote and to be nominated. This issue was referred to the ECJ for a preliminary ruling. According to the ECJ, legislation restricting the right to vote and to stand as a candidate to employees of establishments located in the national territory is not violating EU law, specifically not Article 45 TFEU.[101]

7.32b The establishment of a works council (*Betriebsrat*) is mandatory for every enterprise where more than five persons are employed and when at least three employees or a trade union call for an election assembly.[102] If the employer has established more than one works council, those councils must form a common works council (*Gesamtbetriebsrat*). If the enterprise or undertaking is part of a group, the common works councils may form a group works council (*Konzernbetriebsrat*).[103] Elections must be held every four years within a period of three months, and candidates may be nominated by 5% of the employees, by fifty employees or by trade unions.[104] In contrast to Belgian and French law, the German legislator only allows for employees to be elected as members of the works council.[105] They may not be at a disadvantage because of their membership and enjoy protection against termination of their contract of employment.[106] The works council has the right to be informed and consulted about major decisions of an economic nature as specified in the statute, *inter alia*, the closing down of the enterprise or a merger.[107] The same applies to management decisions regarding social policy and, in some cases, the works council even has a right to co-decision.[108] Conflicts may, and, in some cases, must, be submitted to a conciliation committee provided for by the statute *(Einigungsstelle)*.[109] In addition to

99. Section 25 MitbestG, ss 116 and 93 AktG.
100. *See* C. Teichmann, *Mitbestimmungserstreckung auf Auslandsgesellschaften*, ZIP 2016, 899–907.
101. Case C-566/15. For the academic debate in Germany *see*: H.-J- Hellwig & C. Behme, *Gemeinschaftsrechtliche Probleme der deutschen Unternehmensmitbestimmung*, AG 2009, 261–278; R. Krause, *Zur Bedeutung des Unionsrechts für die unternehmerische Mitbestimmung*, AG 2014, 485–497.
102. Section 1 *Betriebsverfassungsgesetz* (BetrVG).
103. Sections 47, 54 *et seq.* BetrVG.
104. Sections 13 and 14 BetrVG.
105. Section 5 BetrVG.
106. Section 78 BetrVG and s. 15 *Kündigungsschutzgesetz.*
107. Sections 106 and 111 BetrVG.
108. Sections 91 and 99 BetrVG.
109. Section 76 BetrVG.

the works council, there are councils for the representation of employees in management functions (*Sprecherausschüsse*).[110] Moreover, union representatives may be present within the enterprise, but, in practice, they function only within large enterprises.[111]

D The Netherlands[112]

7.33 In the Netherlands, the first statutory regulation of the works council, introduced in 1950, provided for the employer to preside at the council meetings. Since 1979, however, the employer may no longer be a member of the works council. The establishment of a works council (*ondernemingsraad*) is obligatory if fifty or more persons are employed by the enterprise.[113] In smaller enterprises, the employees are entitled to hold a meeting twice a year and to be informed and consulted about major decisions that considerably affect the level of employment.[114] In such a small enterprise, the employer may establish a body of employee representatives, (*personeelsvertegenwoordiging*) having partly the same rights as the works council.[115] Candidates for the works council may be proposed by trade unions and by a minimum number of employees. The works council can determine that there are lists of candidates related to groups or departments within the enterprise. Members are elected for a three-year period.[116] They enjoy certain facilities and are entitled to education and training.[117] They are protected against deterioration of their position as employees and against termination of their contract of employment.[118] If the employer has established more than one works council for the enterprise, or if the enterprise is part of a group of undertakings, the establishment of group councils (*groepsondernemingsraden*) and a central council (*centrale ondernemingsraad*) may be obligatory. The works council is entitled to information, not only concerning economic and social policy but also concerning financial matters.[119] It has to be consulted on major economic and financial decisions, as specified in the statute, such as the closing down or transfer of the enterprise.[120] The works council has a right to co-decision regarding matters of social policy, as specified in the statute, for example, a change in the salary system.[121] The works council is entitled to judicial remedies if the employer does not perform its statutory duties regarding works councils. If the works council has not been properly

110. Sections 1 *et seq. Sprecherausschußgesetz.*
111. Sections 2, 23 and 77 BetrVG. *Employee Representatives in an Enlarged Europe*, vol. 1, 228–229. Von Hoyningen-Huene in *Munchener Handbuch zum Arbeitsrecht*, B and 3, paragraph 294, Rdnr 28–30. On German employee participation in general: Koene & Slomp, *Medezeggenschap van werknemers op* ondernemingsniveau, 97–142.
112. Calvo et al., *Employee Representatives in an Enlarged Europe*, vol. 2, 78–87.
113. Article 2 *Wet op de ondernemingsraden.*
114. Article 35b *Wet op de ondernemingsraden.*
115. Articles 35b–35d WOR.
116. Articles 9–12 *Wet op de ondernemingsraden.*
117. Articles 16–18 *Wet op de ondernemingsraden.*
118. Article 21 *Wet op de ondernemingsraden.*
119. Articles 31–31d *Wet op de ondernemingsraden.*
120. Article 25 *Wet op de ondernemingsraden.*
121. Article 27 *Wet op de ondernemingsraden.*

consulted, the court may order the employer to withdraw its decision. Decisions regarding social policy may be void if taken without the involvement of the works council.[122]

7.33a As is the case in Germany, apart from the works council there is a form of employee participation at the level of the supervisory board of certain business organizations.[123] The Dutch system applies to fairly large public and private companies, that is, companies having a share capital of EUR 16 million and employing at least 100 persons. The members of the supervisory board are appointed according to a rather complicated mechanism, resulting from a statutory review in 2004. Although the members of the supervisory board are appointed by the general meeting upon the proposal of the supervisory board, both the general meeting and the works council may first put forward persons to be appointed as members of the supervisory board. For one-third of the seats, the persons proposed by the works council must be accepted by the supervisory board. The supervisory board may object to the proposed person, but only if he lacks the abilities to carry out his duties, or if the board would be improperly constituted due to that particular appointment. If no agreement can be reached, the supervisory board may request the Enterprise Chamber of the Amsterdam Court of Appeal to decide on the matter.[124] This so-called structure regime system further differs from the German system in that members of the supervisory board may not be employed by the company, its subsidiaries or by the trade union that is involved in collective negotiations with the company.[125] The members of the supervisory board, as a principle, must be independent (*see* paragraph 6.61a). Finally, it must be noted that, *inter alia,* international holding companies are exempted from the structure regime.[126]

E Poland[127]

7.34 Works councils were introduced in Poland in 2006 by the legislation implementing Directive 2002/14/EC. Consequently, every employer who carries out an economic activity and employs fifty people or more is obliged to set up a works council. The implementing legislation contains no definition of 'undertaking' and 'establishment', but connects it to the notion of 'employer'.[128] In enterprises with a trade union, the members of the works council are elected by that union. If more trade unions are represented within the enterprise, each has the right to elect at least one member. However, this may conflict with the restricted number of works council members, for

122. Articles 26 and 27 *Wet op de ondernemingsraden.*
123. Articles 152 *et seq.* (public company) and 262 *et seq.* (private company) Book 2 Dutch Civil Code.
124. Articles 158 and 268 Book 2 DCC.
125. Articles 160 and 270 Book 2 DCC.
126. Articles 153 and 263 Book 2 DCC.
127. Calvo et al., *Employee Representatives in an Enlarged Europe*, vol. 2, 115–123; Jan Czarzasty & Rafal Towalski, 'Information and Consultation Bill Adopted', retrieved from the website of the European industrial relations observatory on-line: www.eurofound.europa.eu/eiro/2006/country/poland.htm.
128. Ales, *Synthesis Report*, 67.

example, only three members where there are 50–250 employees. In such a case, more members can be elected, so that each trade union can exert its election right. The cost of the works council's activities is covered by the trade unions where the members are elected. If no trade union is represented, the members are elected by the employees and candidates can be put forward by ten or twenty employees, depending on the size of the workforce. The members of the works council are protected against termination of their employment contract and/or deterioration of the terms and conditions of their work or payment. The works council must be granted certain facilities and they may use the help of experts. The employer is required to inform and consult the works council on developments regarding the employer's activities and economic situation, the development of employment and on measures likely to lead changes in the organization of work. This obligation of the employer is stated in general terms, similar to Article 4 of the Directive. Requests of works councils to disclose specific documents are often disputed by the employers. A Warsaw court decision, however, obliged the employer to disclose the requested information at the cost of the temporary persons he employed.[129] There is no employee participation in corporate bodies in Poland, except in state-owned enterprises.[130]

F Spain[131]

7.35 Initially, works councils were regulated in Spain in 1947, to function under the presidency of the employer. However, by a 1980 statute, the all-employee works council was introduced.[132] The establishment of a works council (*comité de empresa*) is mandatory if fifty or more persons are employed in the enterprise.[133] In smaller enterprises, delegates of employees (*delegados de personal*) must be elected instead of a works council.[134] If the works council is established, but the enterprise forms part of a group of undertakings, a group council may be formed by way of collective agreement.[135] Candidates for the works council may be proposed by trade unions or by a minimum number of members of the works council. There must be at least two lists to reflect the two categories of employees indicated by the statute, which are, roughly speaking, blue-and white-collar workers.[136] The members of the works council are elected for a period of four years, but their position may be revoked, under certain conditions, by a majority of the employees who elected them.[137] The assistance of an expert is not provided for in the Statute of Workers Rights. The members of the works council may not be treated advantageously or disadvantageously because of their

129. Rafal Towalski, 'Court Ruling Gives Works Council More Extensive Right to Information', 2008, retrieved from www.eurofound.europa.eu/eiro/2008/country/poland.htm (September 2008).
130. Calvo et al., *Employee Representatives in an Enlarged Europe*, vol. 2, 122 and 123.
131. *Ibid.*, 197–208.
132. The statute is amended in 1994, *Boletin Oficial del Estado*, 1994/122.
133. Article 63 Ley del Estatuto de los Trabajadores (ET) (Statute of Workers Rights).
134. Article 62 ET.
135. Article 63 ET (*comité intercentros*).
136. Articles 69 and 71 ET.
137. Article 67 ET.

membership. They enjoy protection against termination of their contract of employment.[138] The works council has a right to be informed about a number of economic and social matters and must be consulted, *inter alia,* regarding plans for a major collective change to working conditions, collective redundancies and generally consulted regarding decisions of the employer that could lead to material changes in the organization of work.[139] The works council may initiate judicial remedies in case the employer does not fulfil its duties with respect to the works council or in those matters, where the works council is entitled to be active. The works council or the employee representatives may participate in the conclusion of collective agreements.[140]

7.35a Parallel to the system of employee representation by works councils or representatives in small enterprises, a trade union committee may be set up and trade union representatives may be appointed. Their position in many respects equals that of the other persons representing employees.[141] In practice, the membership of the works council and the trade union committee often has some overlap.[142]

7.35b Apart from the works council, employees have a right to hold meetings at the premises of the enterprise. Such a meeting may be convened by the delegates of the employees, the works council or by a group of 33% of the employees. The meetings must be used to approve agreements that can affect all employees by a majority of the votes cast.[143]

G The UK[144]

7.36 In the UK, there is no legislation stipulating that employees must be represented at enterprise level. However, where such representation exists, several legal provisions apply providing rights for the representatives. Traditionally, trade unions almost exclusively deal with representation of the employees at enterprise level.[145] Due to the implementation of Directive 2002/14/EC, the employer is under a duty, upon receipt of a valid employee request, to initiate negotiations, in order to reach an agreement on, *inter alia,* the circumstances in which the employer must inform and consult the employees. To facilitate these negotiations, the employer should make arrangements

138. Article 68 ET.
139. Articles 41, 51 and 64 ET. These articles apply equally to the employee representatives in small enterprises, Articles 41(4), 51(4), 62 ET.
140. Article 87 ET.
141. The legal position of the trade unions is for the greatest part regulated by the *Ley Orgánica de Libertad Sindical.*
142. Calvo et al., *Employee Representatives in an Enlarged Europe,* vol. 2, 197–198; Koene & Slomp, *Medezeggenschap van werknemers op ondernemingsniveau* 215–232.
143. Articles 77 *et seq.* and Article 80 ET.
144. Calvo et al., *Employee Representatives in an Enlarged Europe,* vol. 2, 243–254. H. Slomp, 'De Drie Stelsels van arbeidsverhoudingen in West-Europa', *OR- Informatie* 4 (1990).
145. Barbara Kersley et al., *Inside the Workplace* (London: Routledge, 2006), 125, concludes that only 5% of workplaces has stand-alone non-union representation.

for the election or appointment of negotiating representatives.[146] Bodies set up under the terms of the implementing legislation are granted the standard information and consultation rights, as prescribed by the Directive.[147] Such bodies, known as joint consultative committees or works councils, function as a complement to, and sometimes as a substitute for, union representation (which is the dominant form of employee representation). They cover a relatively small number of workplaces.[148]

7.36a The majority of employees is represented at enterprise level by trade union representatives, who are generally known as 'shop stewards'.[149] There are no legal rules on the number of these representatives, nor on the composition of their committees and the method by which they are elected. These matters may vary from union to union.[150] Even where the union is recognized, its representatives have no general right to finance and the use of various resources, though these may be taken care of by a negotiated agreement. The union representatives enjoy protection against dismissal and detrimental treatment. They have information rights that enable them to conduct collective bargaining and they must be informed and consulted in cases of collective redundancies and business transfers.[151]

7.36b Employee involvement as it has developed in the UK does not fit easily into the EU mould. For example, the directive on EWCs revealed a 'representation gap', because unlike most Member States, the UK did not have provisions for national consultation that could function as a platform for effective operation in an EWC.[152]

H Italy

7.37 The main representative bodies of employees are the *rappresentanze sindacali aziendali* (RSAs), who are elected by the workforce as a whole, but are essentially union bodies and unions nominate the candidates. The legislative basis is provided for by the 1970 Workers' Statute, which entrusted workplace representation to trade unions through the RSAs.[153] In 1991, the three main Italian union confederations (CGIL, CISL and UIL) agreed to set up a new structure for the most productive sectors, the *rappresentanze sindacali unitarie* (RSUs). It entails creating a joint committee at company level, of which two-thirds of the members are appointed by all employees,

146. Articles 7, 14 and 16 Information and Consultation of Employees Regulations 2004, Statutory Instrument 2004 No. 3426. It is not expected that many new arrangements will be negotiated, Calvo et al., *Employee Representatives in an Enlarged Europe*, vol. 2, 244. On the effects of EC Directive 2002/14; *see also* Frank Burchill, *Labour Relations*, 3rd edition (New York: Palgrave MacMillan, 2008), 171–175.
147. Articles 18 *et seq.* Information and Consultation of Employees Regulations 2004.
148. According to Kersley et al *Inside the Workplace*, 126 *et seq.*, such committees are present in 14% of the workplaces (in 2004).
149. Other terms are 'union rep' or 'local rep', Calvo et al., *Employee Representatives in an Enlarged Europe*, vol. 2, 245.
150. *Ibid.*, 246.
151. *Ibid.*, 247 and 248.
152. Frank Burchill, *Labour Relations*, 3rd edition, 174.
153. Article 19 of Law 300/1970 *Statuto dei Lavoratori* (the Workers' Statute).

and one-third by the trade unions, which signed the relevant national collective labour contract. The new structure is not implemented in some key sectors, such as banking and insurance, which still make use of the old RSAs. In 2013 and 2014, the rules on trade union representation went through a process of modification by a consolidating law. It lessened the direct impact of appointments by the unions, leading to a system where all members of the RSUs are chosen on the basis of employees' votes.[154] When Italian members of the special negotiating body for the EWC must be appointed, they are appointed by the unions and the RSUs, if any, or by agreements between union and management. The same goes for Italian members of the special negotiating body for the European Company.[155]

7.38 When a workplace has more than fifteen employees, it is possible to set up an RSU. Establishments employing 16–200 persons shall have at least three RSU members, whereas, in case of 201–500 employees, the minimum is six members. In companies with more than 500 employees, there are three extra seats for each 300 additional persons up to 3,000 employees, then three extra seats for each additional 500 employees. These numbers are sanctioned by national agreements, but it is possible to have more favourable thresholds for employee involvement through specific agreements, both at industry and at company level. RSUs solely consist of employees. The manual and non-manual share shall be a reflection of the actual workforce on the basis of separate voting groups, and adequate male to female representation mechanisms are in place.

The RSUs' key function as representatives of trade unions at workplace level is to pursue negotiations with the employers. They must be informed and consulted when it comes to safety and health, use of public funds for industrial restructuring, business transfers and large-scale redundancies, as well as certain issues specified by the industry and company level agreements, such as the company's financial situation. Consultation often happens in a context of joint committees made up of representatives of the management and of the trade unions – a system that aims to be as non-confrontational as possible.[156]

7.39 Directive 2002/14/EC on information and consultation rights was transposed in Italy by Legislative Decree No. 25/2007. This decree applies to undertakings employing at least fifty employees, which means approximately two-thirds of Italian employees fall outside the scope of Legislative Decree No. 25/2007. However, many stakeholders agree that Directive 2002/14/EC has not introduced any major changes, on the grounds that most aspects were already included in collective agreements. The administrative

154. http://www.diritto24.ilsole24ore.com/art/dirittoLavoro/2014-02-11/nuove-regole-rappresentanza-sindacale-120117.php.
155. L. Fulton (2015) Worker representation in Europe. Labour Research Department and ETUI. Produced with the assistance of the SEEurope Network, online publication available at http://www.worker-participation.eu/National-Industrial-Relations.
156. L. Fulton (2015) Worker representation in Europe. Labour Research Department and ETUI. Produced with the assistance of the SEEurope Network, online publication available at http://www.worker-participation.eu/National-Industrial-Relations.

sanctions provided for breaches of information and consultation rights are deemed inadequate and limited, and they consist of fines ranging from EUR 3,000 to EUR 18,000 for each violation.[157]

7.39a Although the 2012 legislation had the potential to create an optional framework of employee participation on the supervisory board for stock companies with more than 300 employees, further legislation has not been introduced. Italian companies are under no obligation to abide by the dualistic corporate governance system.[158] The 2014/2015 reform of labour law, the so-called Jobs Act, does not include any reference to a possible change in this respect.[159]

157. S. Leonardi, 'Employee Participation and Involvement: The Italian Case and Trade Union Issues'. *ETUI*. 2015 [URL: http://www.mitbestimmung.it/wp-content/uploads/2016/01/Allegato-Employee-participation-and-involvement.pdf].
158. Further thoughts on the matter: F. Vella, 'Il governo dell'impresa e il lavoro: vecchi e nuovi paradigmi della partecipazione' in Zoli, C. (a cura di) *Lavoro e impresa: la partecipazione dei lavoratori e le sue forme nel diritto italiano e comparato*. Giappichelli Editore 2015; pp. 101–107.
159. The 2014/2015 reform of labour law, the so-called Jobs Act, does not include any reference to a possible chance in this respect. L. Fulton (2015) Worker representation in Europe. Labour Research Department and ETUI. Produced with the assistance of the SEEurope Network, online publication available at http://www.worker-participation.eu/National-Industrial-Relations.

CHAPTER 8
Cross-Border Cooperation and Acquisitions

I INTRODUCTION

8.01 As a principle, one can discern two extremes on the scale of industrial organization, that is, how economic decisions of business enterprises are coordinated.[1] The first is coordination by the market via contracts to buy or sell, lend or hire, etc. This requires little cooperation between business enterprises, apart from reaching an agreement on the terms of a contract. The other extreme is full integration, where an acquisition of a business, a takeover or a merger has resulted in complete control by one business enterprise over the activities of another enterprise. In such a case, economic decisions are no longer coordinated by market mechanisms, but by the hierarchy within the combined enterprise. In between these two extremes, many forms of cooperation occur. They differ, *inter alia,* due to variations in the duration of the arrangement and the commitment of the parties involved. This chapter begins with some observations on cooperation with a long-term impact, which is termed 'strategic cooperation' (paragraphs 8.02–8.06) and the cross-border dimension of such cooperation (paragraphs 8.07–8.09). The chapter further deals with joint ventures as a form of strategic cooperation, whereby a separate business organization is created (paragraphs 8.10–8.13a). Then cross-border acquisitions are considered in their various forms: acquisition of assets (paragraphs 8.14–8.16), acquisition of shares (paragraphs 8.16–8.27) and mergers and divisions (paragraphs 8.28–8.34). The chapter finally concludes with some remarks concerning the protection of the rights of employees (paragraph 8.35) and European Union (EU) merger control (paragraphs 8.36 *et seq.*).

1. W.G. Shepherd, 'The State of the Industrial Organisation Field', in *Multidisciplinary Economics*, eds P. de Gijsel & H. Schenk (The Netherlands: Springer, 2005), 103–126.

II CROSS-BORDER COOPERATION

A Strategic Cooperation

8.02 Global developments generate incentives for firms to cooperate.[2] Where markets are internationalized, firms are exposed to new competitors. They face massive investments for research and development, which are enhanced by the complexity of modern technology and the need to build cross-border exchanges of knowledge.[3] Furthermore, product cycles are shortened by new innovations, urging businesses to realize a quicker return on investment. These challenges require flexible organization, but, at the same time, only very large enterprises are able to fund the necessary investments.[4] Even these may need their financial resources for other purposes and, therefore, substantial cooperation may be indispensable. It enables firms to share the costs of research and development and to strengthen their position with regard to manufacturing, marketing and distribution.[5] A business enterprise may find itself in the paradoxical situation that it has to cooperate in order to stay competitive.[6]

8.03 The keywords are 'strategic alliances', 'co-makership' and the intention to create a 'partnership in production'. Companies may become 'networked firms'.[7] As a result, the tendency to focus on core competences by contracting out everything else (outsourcing) has been enhanced, as can be seen, for example, within the electronics manufacturing sector.[8]

Note that the same factors furthering cooperation may also lead to concentrations; that is, the reduction of the number of independent enterprises in a market.[9]

---

2. S.E. Huyzer et al., *Strategische samenwerking*, 11; Bernhard Nielsen, 'An Empirical Investigation of the Drivers of International Strategic Alliance Formation', *European Management Journal* 21, no. 3 (June 2003): 301–322; Paul Almeida, Jaeyong Song & Robert M. Grant, 'Are Firms Superior to Alliances and Markets? An Empirical Test of Cross-Border Knowledge Building', *Organisation Science* 13, no. 2 (March 2002 to April 2002): 147–161.
3. *See*, e.g., the aims of the strategic cooperation between Shell and Rosneft, *inter alia*, to share experience and technologies, www.shell.com/home/content/media-en/news_and_library/press_releases/2007.
4. Therefore, some strategic cooperation is aimed at better utilizing capacity and efficiency, for example, in the case of *Austrian Technik and Lufthansa Technik*, Logistics Business Review, www.logistics-business-review.com.
5. Huyzer, *Strategische samenwerking*, 19–25; Bernhard Nielsen, 'An Empirical Investigation of the Drivers of International Strategic Alliance Formation', 301–322.
6. H. Schreuder & A. van Witteloostuijn, 'Strategische allianties: Concurrentie en samenwerking', *Maandblad voor Accountancy en Bedrijfseconomie* 63 (1990): 611.
7. *Strategic Issues for Management in an Integrated European Context*, Open University of the Netherlands, 1994; John Watson, 'Modeling the Relationship Between Networking and Firm Performance', *Journal of Business Venturing* 22, no. 6 (November 2007): 852–874.
8. Financial Times Survey, *Contract electronics manufacture*, 16 Mar. 1993. *See* specifically for the EU: D. Vannoni & L. Rondi, 'Are EU Leading Firms Returning to Core Business? Evidence on Refocusing and Relatedness in a Period of Market Integration', *Review of Industrial Organisation* 27, no. 2 (1 Sep. 2005): 125–145.
9. Schreuder & Van Wittelloostuijn, 'Strategische allianties: Concurrentie en samenwerking', 605–607; Y. Luo, 'A Coopetition Perspective of Global Competition', *Journal of World Business* 42, no. 2 (June 2007): 129–144.

8.04 Where cooperation has a long-term impact on the competitiveness of the companies involved, while retaining their independence and identity, it is generally identified as strategic cooperation.[10] From the viewpoint of the individual companies involved in such an arrangement, the cooperation results in a strategic alliance.

The terms 'strategic alliance' and 'joint venture' are sometimes used interchangeably. As already mentioned in paragraph 8.01, the latter is considered to be a specific form of strategic alliance. Note, that the terminology used in this chapter so far is rather loose. 'Business enterprise', 'enterprise', 'firm' and 'company' are used interchangeably, but at all times meaning an independent economic entity, whatever legal form that entity may be. In EU competition law and policy papers, the alternative term 'undertaking' is frequently used for such entities.

8.05 As a matter of course, the law bears little relation to decisions of firms on whether or not to cooperate. Apart from excluding certain options for cooperation for the sake of competition, the role of the law is restricted to the structuring of cooperation and the enforcement of contracts agreed upon by the parties involved. Legal structuring of cooperation between business enterprises requires the lawyer to pay attention to issues such as:

- limitation of liabilities and risks;
- flexibility, *inter alia:* whether parties may withdraw and new parties be admitted, as well as provisions for narrowing or extending the scope of cooperation;
- the division of profits and losses;
- taxation;
- the financing of the cooperation; and
- the confidential handling of information.

The lawyer can use legal instruments such as:

- contracts;
- partnerships and the European Economic Interest Grouping (EEIG);
- companies (or other legal persons under national or EU law);
- intellectual property rights; or
- arrangements for dispute settlement.

The lawyer should take care to align these instruments with the objectives and scope of the envisaged cooperation.[11]

8.06 Moreover, the lawyer should pay attention to factors that are conditional for the cooperation, such as permissions to be granted by government institutions or local authorities, as well as the consequences for employees, for example, cases involving the transfer of part of an undertaking (paragraph 8.35). Furthermore, lawyers should

10. Huyzer, *Strategische samenwerking*, 29.
11. Rachelle C. Sampson, 'The Role of Lawyers in Strategic Alliances', *Case Western Reserve Law Review* 53, no. 4 (1 Jun. 2003): 909–927.

take into account the external institutional framework. If the cooperation is governed by a jurisdiction with a strong rule of law and an efficient judicial system, less extensive structuring may be needed.[12] Finally, they need to be aware of the paradox, inherent to the choice between contractual solutions on the one hand, and structuring via formation of a legal entity, such as a company, on the other. Parties drafting a contract are free as to the conditions of the contract, but, once the contract is agreed upon, any change will require the consent of each of the parties. By way of contrast, the formation of a legal entity will leave less freedom to the parties, because mandatory statutory provisions may apply. However, these provisions generally allow for decision-making by majority voting (be it simple or qualified majority), thus facilitating future adaptations.[13]

B The Cross-Border Dimension

8.07 The cross-border dimension arises when the companies involved in the cooperation are subject to different jurisdictions, such as if a Plc from the UK agrees on a co-makership with a German GmbH. Contracts between the parties will then generally be deemed to have an international character and, accordingly, conflicts of law may arise.[14] Additionally, it may be questionable which court is competent to hear the case if parties start litigating. Therefore, the complexity of any strategic cooperation is compounded by the cross-border element. A *renegotiation clause* obliging parties to enter into negotiations to adapt the contract in case of hardship may help to prevent litigation in the first place. Besides, complications may be kept to an acceptable level by specific clauses, such as:[15]

- clauses regarding a choice for *alternative dispute resolution (arbitration, mediation):*[16] mediation clauses may serve to settle conflicts on the interpretation of the documents of the contract, even before the commencement of further proceedings in accordance with an arbitration clause;[17]
- choice of applicable law clauses;[18] and
- in the absence of alternative dispute resolution clauses, *choice of forum* clauses, to determine which court of jurisdiction is competent in case of litigation.

12. *Ibid.*, 921.
13. W.J. Slagter, in Huyzer and others, *o.c.*, 82–83.
14. F.J.A. van der Velden, *Commerciële contracten. Internationale aspecten.* (Eindhoven: Euroforum, 1992), 3; Steven R. Salbu, 'Parental Coordination and Conflict in International Joint Ventures: The Use of Contract to Address Legal, Linguistic and Cultural Concerns', *Case Western Reserve Law Review* 43, no. 4 (Summer 93): 1221–1268.
15. *Ibid.*
16. In order to avoid the traditional dispute resolution within courts of jurisdiction.
17. For arbitration, one can resort to several institutions like the International Chamber of Commerce, which often also provide examples of arbitration clauses.
18. Klaus Langefeld-Wirth (ed.), *Joint Ventures im Internationalen Wirtschaftsverkehr Praktiken Und Vertragstechniken Internationaler Gemeinschaftsunternehmen* (Heidelberg: Verlag Recht und Wirtschaft GmbH, 1990).

8.08 If parties to a contract do not opt for alternative dispute resolution, they may have the choice between the judiciary of any national state as to hear their case. In *Powell Duffryn plc v. Wolfgang Petereit* [1992], the European Court of Justice (ECJ) held that a choice of forum clause in a company's articles, pertaining to disputes between the company and its shareholders, is covered by Article 17 of the Brussels Convention on jurisdiction and the enforcements of judgments in civil cases (As of 2001 this subject is governed by Article 23 of Regulation 44/2001, Brussels I Regulation).[19] According to the ECJ, the relationship between a company and its shareholders, as embodied in the articles, is a contractual one and, therefore, a jurisdiction clause qualifies as an agreement under the convention. This applies even to shareholders who voted against the adoption of the clause or who acquired their shares afterwards. By becoming and remaining a shareholder, the shareholder consents to the company's articles and the decisions taken by its organs, regardless of any objections to a certain clause or decision.[20]

8.09 The international character of a cooperation should already be reflected by precautions in the early stages of the negotiations. To avoid ambiguity, the official language of the contract must be determined, in case the parties use different languages.[21] Usually, results of initial negotiations are laid down in a document called a Letter of Intent (often referred to as an LOI), 'heads of agreement' or a 'Memorandum of Understanding' (often referred to as an MOU). To what extent this represents a legally binding document may vary according to the applicable law. English law, for instance, qualifies an agreement to be void for uncertainty, if major terms are left not agreed upon.[22] Under Dutch law, documents such as heads of agreement are prone to legal consequences. They can force the parties to continue negotiations or may even qualify as a contract.[23] Another *caveat* is that a contract to cooperate may qualify as a partnership under the applicable law. Consequently, the relationship between partners, the distribution of profits and losses and their accountability are governed by default statutory rules, implying the risk of liability for debts incurred by the other partners.[24] Finally, cross-border cooperation usually requires the addition of even more prerequisite conditions than domestic cooperation does. Official license or approval may be obtained from national and/or international authorities, such as the European Commission, if EU rules on competition and mergers apply.[25]

---

19. Council Regulation (EC) No. 44/2001 of 22 Dec. 2000 on jurisdiction and the recognition and enforcement of judgments in civil and commercial matters.
20. Case C-214/89, *Common Market Law Review* 1993, 406.
21. Steven R. Salbu, 'Parental Coordination and Conflict in International Joint Ventures', *Case Western Reserve Law Review* 43, no. 4 (1993).
22. Linklaters & Paines, with Christopher Nightingale, *Joint Ventures* (London: Addison Wesley Publishing Company, 1990), 14 Clive M. Schmitthoff, *The Law and Practice of International Trade*, 9th edition (London: Sweet & Maxwell, 1990), 89.
23. *See* for a comparison: Geoffrey Samuel & Jac Rinkes, *Contractual and Non-contractual Obligations in English Law* (Nijmegen: Ars Aequi Libri, 1992), nr. 98 and 99.
24. M.J.G.C. Raaijmakers, *Enkele rechtsvergelijkende beschouwingen over joint ventures* (Deventer: Preadvies Nederlandse Vereniging voor Rechtsvergelijking, 1992), 25.
25. Ekaterina Pannebakker, *Letter of Intent in International Contracting*, dissertation. Rotterdam (Cambridge: Intersentia, 2016).

C Joint Ventures

8.10 The term 'joint venture' is frequently used in economic and legal literature, as well as in legal practice. Although literally every joint activity of business enterprises can be designated as a joint venture, the definition is often narrowed to cooperation, whereby a separate business organization is created. In such a case, the cooperating enterprises supply know-how and/or capital to that entity, but they remain independent outside the scope of the cooperation itself.[26] In this respect, the joint venture differs from the other forms of strategic cooperation, such as contractual agreements, leading to the transfer of technology or co-makership, where no separate entity is formed.

8.11 It follows from the previous paragraph, that a joint venture is defined as a separate enterprise (undertaking) that has been created to structure the cooperation of two or more business enterprises. The choice is between the incorporated joint venture or equity joint venture on the one hand, and the unincorporated joint venture or contractual joint venture on the other hand. The first implies the participation of the joint venture partners in a private or public company, whereas the second is a contractual joint venture, resulting in an entity that most likely will have the form of a partnership.

8.12 The joint venture company may be newly formed, but the partners may also use a company previously owned or acquired by one of them. Likewise, the relationship of joint venture partners may vary considerably. If there are two partners, as a rule, they will each take 50% of the shares and votes of the joint venture company. However, the distribution of profits may deviate from that percentage, where an unequal contribution to the assets of the joint venture has to be compensated for. The management of the joint venture business may be attributed to a mixed board or to one of the partners exclusively. That, however, may give rise to issues inherent to the law of groups of companies, such as mandatory consolidation of the joint venture by the managing partner,[27] thereby considering the joint venture company as a subsidiary of one of its shareholders (however, this is normally *not* the intention of its shareholders).

Contractual joint ventures, as already mentioned, frequently have the partnership form. Although commercial partnerships may have legal personality, especially in continental countries, this feature does not affect the essential personal and contractual character of such a partnership and the same applies to the EEIG. Consequently, the joint venture partners generally enjoy more freedom as to the provisions laid down in the contract or articles, in comparison with the incorporated forms.

Whatever form is chosen, questions may arise as to the seat of the new entity, if the joint venture has a cross-border dimension. The options are to have the entity

26. See, for example, J. Brodley. 'Joint Ventures and Antitrust Policy', *Harvard Law Review* 95 (1982): 1521, 1527-9 and Clive M. Schmitthoff, *The Law and Practice of International Trade*, 9th edition (London: Sweet & Maxwell, 1990), 338, where it is stated that 'The joint venture is a common undertaking created by two or more participants for a specific purpose of commercial, financial or technical nature.'
27. According to Article 1 of the Seventh Directive (as amended).

seated in the country of one of the joint venture partners or in a third country, but, once the choice is made, it may turn out to be rather definite. Member States generally do not allow domestic companies to transfer their registered office to another state, although the transfer of the real seat has been liberated to a great extent by the ECJ (paragraphs 2.61–2.66). As a principle, there are no legal restrictions to the transfer of a joint venture's registered office, if it has the form of a business organization under EU law, notably the EEIG and the *Societas Europaea* (SE).

8.13 Parallel to the formation of a joint venture entity, the partners will often draw up a separate joint venture contract (the JV contract).[28] Such a contract, for instance, may regulate commercial transactions between the partners and the joint venture. It may also cover specific contributions, such as the transfer of technology and intellectual property rights or the supply of employees and goods. In addition, the contract may also relate to the transfer of shares, to pre-emption rights and to the resolution of deadlock situations. Although essential for the joint venture, the articles of a joint venture company very rarely regulate these issues. The main reason is that the articles have to be disclosed, thus making sensitive business information available to competitors if such issues were included. Where the joint venture has an international character, attention should be paid to avoiding divergences between the law governing the legal entity and the law applicable to related contracts. Finally, it should be noted here that a joint venture may have effects on competition, which must be assessed under Articles 101 and 102 Treaty on the Functioning of the European Union (TFEU), and/or the Merger Regulation (paragraphs 8.39 *et seq.*).

8.13a Sophisticated devices are sometimes used for the legal structuring of joint ventures, especially for buyout provisions. An example is the *right of first refusal,* which prohibits parties to sell their stake to a third party before having offered to the joint venture partner(s) to buy it for the price the third party is willing to pay. If the parties do not mind whether they sell their own interest or buy that of the other party, they may resort to clauses, which have been given fancy names by the business and legal community, such as 'auction clauses' or 'envelope clauses', whereby the parties aim at letting the party who is willing and able to pay the highest price for the company, take over the company and carry on its business. This is essentially an option for a party (say, A) to put an end to the cooperation by calling the price for which the other party (B) may buy A's share. B may then decide whether to buy A's share or to sell his own share to A for the same price.

Parties located in different countries and cooperating in contractual or corporate manners should always consider whether:

(1) to apply the national legislation which the Rome I Regulation appoints; or
(2) to agree on a certain country's laws, either one of the parties' country, or a third country (such as English law, or Swiss law); or

28. A.L. Mohr, *Commerciële contracten IX. Samenwerkingscontracien* (Eindhoven: Euroforum, 1992), 16–17.

(3) to agree on a neutral, simple and easily understandable set of common rules, in scholarly books often named *lex mercatoria*, which for all practical purposes would in our times normally be the UNIDROIT Principles (on international commercial contracts).[29]

III ACQUISITIONS

A Methods of Acquisition

8.14 As has been set out in paragraph 8.01, the integration of business enterprises, or parts thereof, goes beyond strategic cooperation. Such integration can be realized, to put it simply, where one business enterprise has acquired the control of another enterprise. There are three different methods of acquiring control (under one common umbrella named M&A: merger and acquisition): the acquisition of a business (often by way of an Asset Purchase Agreement (APA), or a Business Transfer Agreement (BTA)), the acquisition of a company's shares (often by way of a Share Purchase Agreement (SPA)) or the completion of a (legal) merger (i.e., merger according to the rules of the Third or Tenth Directive):

- Acquiring a business means the acquisition of the assets or a separable part of the assets of an undertaking.
- The acquisition of the shares of a company means the acquisition of control of that company and, therefore, also of the business carried out by that company.
- A merger means the winding up of a company without going into liquidation, while all its assets and liabilities are transferred to the acquiring company (paragraphs 3.45b *et seq.*).
- A division means acquiring a part of a company, often in form of a business or a part of a business, by way of dividing the company that owns the business.

8.14a A rather important control question, facilitating the choice of the right method of M&A, would often be: who receives the remuneration for the sale (because an M&A is always some kind of sale)? The answers are that: (a) when acquiring a business, the selling company receives the remuneration, (b) when acquiring a majority, the individual shareholders receive the remuneration, (c) when merging company A and B, with B as the continuing company, the shareholders of A receive the remuneration, and (d) when dividing company A, thereby transferring a part of its assets to company B, the shareholders of A receive the remuneration, just as in a merger (and thereby also contrary to the transfer of business, where the selling company receives the remuneration).

29. Erik Werlauff, *International Contracts – The UNIDROIT Principles as an Alternative to Clauses on Governing Law* (Copenhagen 2013, Ex Tuto Publishing).

8.14b Sometimes, the choice will be dictated by tax considerations.[30] For example, share acquisitions may be more attractive to the seller in countries where the sale of his shares will not be taxed, whereas, in the same country, an asset acquisition will be fully taxed on the gain. The purchaser, however, may prefer the acquisition of the assets if he cannot depreciate the purchase price of shares.[31] However, EU legislator has done all within their power to make tax considerations neutral to the choice. This is done through the merger taxation Directive 2009/133/EC, which aims at making it neutral from a tax perspective, whether to conduct an M&A by way of: (1) merger, (2) division, (3) majority takeover, or (4) business transfer.

8.14c Further, it must be noted that share transactions are generally easier to carry out than asset transactions. Cross-Border Mergers (CBM), on the other hand, can only be executed by a relatively lengthy and costly procedure and are therefore likely to remain the exception, whereas the acquisition of shares will be the rule. However, if the transaction aims at transferring the registered office of the company from one Member State to another, thereby changing the nationality of the company, the international merger as offered in the Tenth Directive (CBM Directive) should be preferred. In that case, a company P in state A can simply establish a subsidiary S in state B, thereafter merging P into its subsidiary S, with S as the acquiring company. The compensation is paid to shareholders of P in the form of shares in S. As a fully accepted tool for migrating a company from state A to state B, this kind of transaction is even recommended by the Commission,[32] as long as the Fourteenth Directive on the transfer of the seat is not adopted by the EU and implemented by the Member States.

8.14d On a national level, the choice of acquisition methods may be influenced by specific rules, such as in the case of France, where favourable taxation regimes traditionally stimulate acquisitions by way of merger. Otherwise, mergers seem to be mostly used for restructuring within a group of companies and the Third Directive allows for a simplified procedure for such situations. The same is provided for by the SE Statute and the CBM Directive in case of a cross-border merger.[33]

8.15 Cross-border acquisitions are likely to meet several regulatory hurdles, such as taxation, exchange control, investment restrictions, stock exchange requirements and merger control.[34] Within the EU, however, a lot has been done to facilitate cross-border

30. Miguel Correia, *Taxation of Corporate Groups* (Kluwer Law International, 2013); Madalina Cotrut (ed.), *International Tax Structures in the BEPS Era: An Analysis of Anti-Abuse Measures*, IBFD Tax Research Series, 2015.
    Peter C. Cussons, 'Structuring for International Taxation', in *Penetrating International Markets: From Sales and Licensing to Subsidiaries and Acquisitions*, eds Dennis Campbell & Fernando Pombo (Deventer/Boston: Kluwer Law and Taxation Publishers, 1991), 175–190.
31. Nigel Carrington & Beatriz Pessoa de Araujo (eds), *Acquiring Companies and Businesses in Europe* (London: Chancery Wiley Law Publications, 1994), 16.
32. Cf. Commissioner Charlie McCreevy's speech on 3 Oct. 2007 in the EU Parliament's Legal Affair Committee, speech No. 07/592.
33. Article 24 Third Directive, Article 15 Tenth Directive and Article 31 SE Statute.
34. Terence E. Cooke, *International Mergers and Acquisitions* (Oxford/New York: Blackwell, 1988); David J. Ben-Daniel & Arthur H. Rosenbloom, *The Handbook of International Mergers & Acquisitions* (Englewood Cliffs, NJ: Prentice Hall, 1990).

transactions. Several operations mergers, divisions, formation of a holding company ('exchange of shares') and business transfer ('transfer of assets') are recognized as combination or takeover methods by directives, such as the Merger Tax Directive 2009/133.[35] Consequently, this has diminished tax complications and related directives, which account for the harmonized taxation of transfer of assets, exchange of shares and mergers (as well as divisions), if companies from two or more Member States are involved. Furthermore, exchange control and investment restrictions, for the most part, have been removed in order to realize free movement of capital.[36] Stock exchange requirements play a role if an acquisition takes place by a public takeover bid, but here harmonization has had its effects too (paragraphs 3.84 *et seq.* and 3.95 *et seq.*). Finally, merger control can be exerted by national authorities, but EU control prevails when mergers have a Community dimension (paragraph 8.36 *et seq.*).

B Acquisition of Assets

8.16 Acquisition of a business through the acquisition of its assets (an asset purchase agreement, APA, or a business transfer agreement, BTA)[37] may have some advantages in comparison with the other methods. It is a flexible method because it does not automatically lead to the acquisition of all the assets of a business, which would happen on a merger and, albeit indirectly, on the acquisition of the shares of a company. Moreover, the purchaser, as a rule, does not automatically incur the liabilities of the acquired business, because the purchaser is only liable if he expressly assumes all or part of those liabilities. However, there may be exceptions for tax liability, and, under German law, the acquirer of a commercial business is liable for the debts of the former owner, unless an agreement to the contrary is registered with the Commercial Registry.[38] Notwithstanding its flexibility, an acquisition of assets may be less attractive due to taxation and the complicated nature of the transfer of assets. There is no universal transfer of title to the purchaser. This means that every single asset has to be transferred in accordance with the applicable rules of national law.[39]

35. Directive 90/434/EEC, OJ 1990,L 225, amended by Directive 2005/19/EC of 17 Feb. 2005 on the common system of taxation applicable to mergers, divisions, transfers of assets and exchanges of shares concerning companies of different Member States, OJ 2005, L 58. Directive 2005/56/EC, OJ 2005, L 310 on cross-border mergers of limited liability companies.
36. Article 63 TFEU.
37. The names, APA resp. BTA, are often applied interchangeably, but there may, for practical reasons, be a slight difference. The APA may refer to a transfer of assets only, i.e., that no transfer takes place of a whole business, regarded as an economic entity having maintained its 'identity', whereas the BTA certainly refers to such transfer of an 'entity'.
38. Paragraph 25 HGB (Commercial Code). Wilhelm Beisel & Hans-Hermann Klump, *Der Unternehmenskauf* (München: C.H. Beck, 2016).
39. Some countries allow for a universal title of transfer of a business, such as in France, Articles 141-1 *et seq. Code de commerce (fonds de commerce).*

C Acquisition of Shares

8.17 Although acquisition of shares may pertain to both privately held and publicly held or listed companies, the following is limited to transactions of shares of listed companies. The acquisition of control of a company, in general, involves the acquisition of a majority of the shares carrying voting rights, which, in most cases, will require a takeover bid. Takeover bids are regulated in order to provide for disclosure, transparency and proper procedures to enable shareholders to decide on the merits of the bid, thus safeguarding the interests of shareholders and securing the proper functioning of the capital market.[40]

8.17a Takeovers may be explained by the pursuance of economies of scale and reduction of agency costs. The first is obvious and also applies to other forms of acquisition, whereas the latter may need some clarification. Agency costs are costs made by the principal to align the agent to the interests of the principal. Within the company, the shareholders, taken together, can be regarded as the principal and the managers as the agents. Shareholders may not, under the various national management structures, direct the managers to pursue particular projects (*see* Chapter 6). Especially where shareholdership is dispersed, they have to rely on their residual powers to monitor the performance of managers. A takeover leads to a concentration of voting power in the hands of the acquirer who then, as the controlling shareholder, is able to replace inefficient managers – a situation that is likely to occur if the takeover is hostile, that is, where the incumbent management is opposing it.[41] Accordingly, the mere threat of a takeover already functions as a disciplinary power.[42] Not surprisingly, this effect is diminished by defensive measures against hostile takeovers. Thus, the agency theory and the related concept of 'market for corporate control' are elements of the wider issue of corporate governance (*see* paragraph 6.01).

8.18 The Takeover Directive 2004/25 was already dealt with in paragraphs 3.96 *et seq.* Here, the emphasis is on the directive's importance for defensive measures regarding hostile takeovers. The most important provisions of the directive dealing with this issue are Articles 9, 10, 11 and 12. Article 9 deals with the 'board neutrality rule' and Article 10 with 'information' about takeover defences. Article 11 deals with 'breakthrough' (i.e., the setting aside) of such defences. Lastly, Article 12 provides the measures that a Member State must or may introduce into its legislation in relation to Articles 10 and 11.

40. *See*, e.g., Preamble paragraphs 1 and 12 of the Directive 2004/25/EC of 21 Apr. 2004 on takeover bids, OJ 2004, L 142 (Takeover Directive).
41. Roberta Romano, 'A Guide to Takeovers: Theory, Evidence and Regulation', in *European Takeovers: Law and Practice*, eds Klaus Hopt & Eddy Wymeersch (London: Butterworths, 1992), 3–10.
42. *See*, e.g., the Bangemann memorandum, COM(88)823 final.

IV TAKEOVER DEFENCES

A The Board Neutrality Rule

8.19 As already mentioned in paragraphs 3.99–101, the directive makes a distinction between pre-bid and post-bid defence measures. Member States must ensure that once the company is subject to a takeover bid, the board refrains from any action that may frustrate the bid, unless it acquires prior authorization of the general meeting. This 'board neutrality rule', laid down in Article 9, concerns post-bid defence measures, such as the issuing of shares to raise the costs of the bid.[43] The directive does not guarantee a level playing field in this respect, because Article 12(2) allows Member States not to apply Article 9, on the condition that they grant companies the option of applying the board neutrality rule. It goes without saying that pre-bid measures are taken prior to the bid and they include restrictions on the transfer of shares, reduction of voting rights, ownership ceilings and shares with differential voting rights (e.g., A and B class shares). They generally either bar the transfer of shares to the offeror or prevent him from exercising control in the general meeting after the takeover has succeeded.

B Information about Takeover Defences

8.20 The directive requires full transparency of all provisions, whether in the articles of association or in contracts, which may impede the takeover of a listed company through a public bid. Article 10 actually contains a catalogue of defences, ranging from different classes of shares (section a) to golden parachute agreements with board members or employees in the case of a takeover bid (section k). All these defences must be disclosed in two ways: (1) whether the interested reader may find them in the articles of association or not, they must be mentioned in the annual report (Article 10(2)); and (2) they must be explained in an explanatory report to the shareholders at the general meeting (Article 10(3)). It does not seem that such measures need to be voted on – and some cannot be voted on, because they will be contained in agreements – but they may be discussed and shareholders can, of course, exercise their membership rights to propose their cancellation. To conclude, the disclosure requirements of Article 10 force companies to draw up a list of their defence measures (if they have any), which may eventually lead to discussion, criticism and proposals for their cancellation.

43. David Kershaw, *Hostile Takeovers and the Non-Frustration Rule: Time for a Re-Evaluation*, LSE Law, Society and Economy Working Papers 19/2016, London School of Economics and Political Science.
    Law Department http://ssrn.com/abstract=2875772, describes the board neutrality rule (non-frustration rule) as a keystone of the UK Takeover Code but suggests that by curbing actions by the target's board, it has adverse effects such as facilitating short-term preferences on the market for corporate control.

8.21 Pre-bid defence measures inserted in articles of associations encompass:

- a reduction of voting rights (voting right ceilings);
- ownership ceilings; and/or
- a division of the share capital into A and B class shares with differential voting rights.

Voting right ceilings are aimed at the *shareholder*, because they limit the shareholder's voting rights in the event of a concentration of shares in that shareholder's possession. Differentiation of voting rights via A and B class shares is aimed at the *share* itself, because the relative weight of the voting rights attached to a given share is defined by the articles of association independently of who owns the share. Limitation of ownership is a limitation on transferability aimed at a shareholder's holding in a given company. A voting right ceiling, and sometimes an ownership ceiling, is typical for many banks. Protection by a division of shares into classes with differential voting rights is typical for many industrial companies, trusts and family-owned companies.

Contractual defence mechanisms include cases, where the company has promised special rights to one or more employees in the event that the company is taken over, for example, in the form of severance pay or a particularly extended termination notice, etc. Other agreements with a third party can include special termination clauses in the event of a takeover. Such agreements can be golden parachutes for the persons who benefit from them. For the company, however, and, thus, for its new owner, they may be poison pills that reduce the company's value and thus impede a takeover.[44]

The (pre-bid) defence measures must be listed in the company's annual report and must be open for discussion at the company's annual general meeting, thus allowing company shareholders to place them under pressure. The Takeover Directive does not contain provisions requiring Member States to set aside voting right ceilings, ownership ceilings or any voting right differentiation.

8.21a The Commission is required by Article 20 to examine the Takeover Directive in the light of the experience acquired in applying it and, if necessary, propose its revision.

C The Breakthrough Rule

8.22 According to Article 11, pre-bid defences may be set aside, albeit on a temporary basis, and, therefore, this article is referred to as the Breakthrough provision. As is the case with Article 9, implementation of Article 11 is not mandatory on the same condition that Member States grant the right to companies to choose whether to apply the Breakthrough rule (Article 12(2)). Companies then may use the option by a decision of the general meeting in accordance with the rules for amending the articles of association. Such a decision is reversible.

44. *See* for many examples of defensive measures: ECL 2004/1.

8.23 Member States may also elect to follow an interesting middle way, which made its entry as a compromise during the directive's prolonged progress through the various instances. This middle way is found in Article 12(3) and is sometimes called the *reciprocity principle.* According to Article 12(3), a Member State can formulate its legislation in such a way that companies that are open to takeover (i.e., companies that comply with Article 9 and/or Article 11) can, nonetheless, rely on defences if they become the target of an offer by a company not complying with Article 9 and/or 11. Such a defence, however, requires authorization by the general meeting, albeit by a decision, which may be taken in advance (Article 12(5)). To put it differently, when a Member State presses the Article 12(3) button, it means that a public company cannot be taken over by a 'closed' company. This solution came in response to critical voices that found it unreasonable that European companies should be open to takeover and be in an 'Article 11 situation', as discussed later, whereas foreign companies, for example, from the United States, would be protected by takeover defences.

8.24 The Breakthrough rule of Article 11 pertains to the following:

- *Restrictions on the transfer of shares* (securities) shall not apply vis-à-vis the offeror during the period in which the bid can be accepted (Article 11(2)).[45] If the offeror acquires 75% of the voting share capital, then the other defences are broken through (Article 11(4)).
- *Restrictions on voting rights* shall not have effect at the general meeting, which decides on post-bid defensive measures (Article 11(3)).
- *No extraordinary rights of shareholders concerning appointment or removal of board members* provided for in the articles shall apply (Article 11(4)).
- *Multiple voting rights* shall carry only one vote at the general meeting, which decides on post-bid defensive measures (Article 11(3)), as well as on the first general meeting following the closure of the bid, called by the offeror in order to amend the articles or to remove or appoint board members (Article 11(4)).

If any shareholder suffers losses by having his or her legal rights reduced, equitable compensation should be provided (Article 11(5)).[46] This will apply, for example, to the lapse of special voting rights of A class shares, where domination of the company has previously been upheld via such shares.[47]

45. An example is the prior consent of the board for the transfer of registered shares, which can be required by the articles of German companies (*Vinkulierte Namensaktien)*, s. 68(2) AktG.
46. *See*, e.g., Article 11 of the German control and Transparency Act, *Gesetz zur Kontrolle und Transparenz im Unternehmensbereich* (BGB, 1998), nr 24.
47. Bernhard Gomard in *Revision & Regnskabsvaesen,* Copenhagen 1993 No. 1 p. 8 ff. and in 'Festskrift til Bertil Bengtsson', 141 ff, and Erik Werlauff in *EU-ret & Menneskeret,* Copenhagen (2001), 208 ff, 'Ownership, Interference in Ownership Requirements Regarding Authority, Predictability, Equality and Proportionality under the European Human Rights Convention' (in Danish); Henrik Zahle in *Juristen*, Copenhagen, 2004, 279 ff.

D Takeover Defences: Conclusion

8.25 One may conclude that the directive provides two recipes for maintaining certain defence mechanisms. The recipe for state legislatures is the reciprocity rule of Article 12(3), mentioned previously. It could be expected that a Member State that decides to implement the Breakthrough rule of Article 11 will also make use of the reciprocity rule, such that a company that is open to breakthrough can only be taken over by another company that is equally open. However, the majority of the Member States have not imposed the Breakthrough rule, and those who did have not provided for the reciprocity option.[48]

The second recipe can be applied at company level and is found in Article 11(6). It diffuses the Breakthrough rule for shares 'where the restrictions on voting rights are compensated for by specific pecuniary advantages'. It appears that it may apply in cases where shares forfeit their voting rights temporarily or permanently, that is, with regard to supernumerary shares above a voting right ceiling (temporary forfeiture) and also to non-voting shares (permanent forfeiture). The latter, of course, cannot occur in jurisdictions, where the issuing of non-voting shares is not permitted.[49] 'Specific pecuniary advantages' must be paid in such cases, or the shares will be activated and gain full voting rights under an Article 11 Breakthrough situation. This is to the effect that a sum must be specified, in order to compensate for the forfeiture of voting rights. Article 11(6) may, therefore, develop its core application in shareholder agreements, reducing voting rights against financial compensation.

8.26 One may observe that the Thirteenth Directive aims at breaking through defences of a legal nature by (temporarily) neutralizing certain provisions in the articles or agreements regarding voting rights and the like. Chances are that a future revision of the directive leaves no options for such defences by public companies. An escape, then, could be to use an alternative legal entity, such as the French SCA, but, of course, only if it has access to listing.[50] What will probably remain as the ultimate defence is a greater level of parallelism between the interests of shareholders and management. This can be achieved by share-based incentive schemes, share accumulation funds associated with the company, cross participation and employee funds as to prevent an uninvited bidder to reach one of the magic capital thresholds (75%, Article 11(4), 90%, Article 15(2)).

8.27 The Commission reported in 2007 that the implementation of the Thirteenth Directive is partly having adverse effects.[51] Although a majority of the Member States have implemented the board neutrality rule, with the exception of one Member State,

48. The breakthrough rule is implemented by the Baltic States only, *Report on the Implementation of the Directive on Takeover Bids* (Brussels, 21 Feb. 2007), SEC(2007) 268, 7 and 12.
49. For example, the Netherlands. Denmark for shares subscribed for after 1973: cf. s. 67(1:19) and s.169(1) of the Danish CA.
50. According to Yann Christin, 'Report from France', *European Company Law* 1 (April 2004): 13–15.
51. *Report on the implementation of the Directive on Takeover Bids*, Commission Staff Working Document (Brussels, 21 Feb. 2007), SEC(2007) 268.

it was not a new concept. Some Member States introduced the reciprocity option, leaving company management, in fact, more options than they had before to take protective measures without the authorization of the general meeting, because such authorization may be given up to eighteen months in advance (Article 12(5)).[52] Moreover, Member States previously having no mandatory board neutrality rule have chosen not to apply the rule and, instead, allow the use of reciprocity.[53]

As for the Breakthrough rule, the vast majority of Member States have not imposed (or are unlikely to impose) the Breakthrough rule, but have made it optional for companies.[54] The Commission rather cynically concludes that 'the main "benefit" of reciprocity seems to be the fact that it gives management new powers to take frustrating action and makes it easier for companies not to apply the Board Neutrality or Breakthrough rules'.[55]

V CROSS-BORDER MERGERS OF COMPANIES

8.28 EU legislation regarding CBM is rather recent. The first legislative act in this respect was the 2001 enactment of the SE Statute, offering the cross-border merger facility as one of the methods available for formation of an SE (paragraphs 4.17 *et seq.*). The Tenth Directive (CBM Directive), adopted a few years later (paragraphs 3.57 *et seq.*), provided for the cross-border merger as a generic instrument for domestic companies, not necessarily leading to the formation of an SE. This directive allows both public and private companies to merge across borders on the condition that they may merge under their national laws.[56] Finally, according to *Sevic* [2005], CBM are permitted based on Articles 49 and 54 of the TFEU, probably even outside the realm of the Tenth Directive and the SE Statute (paragraph 3.57a).

8.29 Before tools such as the SE Statute, *Sevic* and the Tenth Directive came into play, most jurisdictions did not expressly allow for CBM. Nevertheless, some of these mergers were completed based on international private law, that is, by cumulative appliance of the harmonized national merger provisions and the mutual recognition of the results of the operation.[57] A famous example is the Barclays merger of 1993 between the English holding company and its French subsidiary, the English company being the acquiring party.[58]

---

52. France, Greece, Hungary, Portugal and Slovenia, Commission Report SEC(2007) 268, 6.
53. Denmark, Germany and Luxembourg but with the exception of Malta; Belgium, the Netherlands and Poland are expected to follow Denmark, Germany and Luxembourg in this respect, Commission Report SEC(2007) 268, 7.
54. Breakthrough is expected to be imposed only by the Baltic States, Commission Report SEC(2007) 268, 7.
55. Commission Report SEC(2007) 268, 9.
56. Article 4(1)(a) of the Tenth Directive. Most Member States have introduced merger rules for private companies similar to those of the Third Directive (paragraphs 3.46 *et seq.)*, Gerard van Solinge, *Grensoverschrijdende juridische fusie* (Deventer: Kluwer, 1994), Ch. 3.
57. *ibid.*, 204.
58. A. Viandier & J. Caussain, *Chronique, Droit des sociétés*, La semaine Juridique (JCP), ed. G (JurisClasseur, Paris, 1993), I-3715, 461, no. 14.

Although *Sevic* allows for a cross-border merger solely based on the TFEU, it goes without saying that guidance will often be needed on how to deal with creditor protection and the role of employees. The provisions of the Tenth Directive allow for this and, where analogically applied, they even facilitate the completion of other cross-border operations, which, according to *Sevic*, are covered by Articles 49 and 54 of the TFEU, such as divisions or the transfer of the registered seat (paragraph 3.53a).

8.29a In assessing which operations are covered by the TFEU articles guaranteeing the right of establishment, it is important to be aware of the fact that some operations, although theoretically very different, may lead to a similar result. For example, when company P in country A forms a subsidiary in country B and subsequently merges into that subsidiary (merger by absorption), the effect will be the same as if company P had transferred its registered seat to country B.[59] We refer to the example mentioned under 8.14c above, where it was mentioned that company P in state A can simply establish a subsidiary S in state B, thereafter merging P into its subsidiary S, with S as the acquiring company. The compensation is paid to shareholders of P in the form of shares in S. We also mentioned under paragraph 8.14c, that as a fully accepted tool for migrating a company from state A to state B, this kind of transaction is even recommended by the Commission.[60]

8.30 Both the SE Statute and the Tenth Directive refer to provisions of national law for compliance with the formalities of the cross-border merger.[61] Although these provisions are certainly similar, they are not identical, as a consequence of the implementation of the various options offered by the Third Directive to the Member States regarding important issues, such as the decision-making by the general meeting, the way protection is offered to creditors and the date on which the merger takes effect.

8.31 Decision-making is one of the issues that may be treated differently by Member States. According to Article 7 of the Third Directive, a merger requires the approval of the general meeting of each of the merging companies with a majority of not less than two-thirds of the votes. Member States, however, may provide that a simple majority of the votes shall be sufficient when at least half of the subscribed capital is represented. Under national law, the required majority may also be higher. This is the case, for example, in the UK, where the Companies Act 2006 requires a 75% majority.[62] The terms of the merger must be approved by resolution of the general meeting of each of the companies merging; however, Member States may leave the decision of the acquiring company to another organ.[63] The Netherlands have used this option by empowering the board of directors of the acquiring company with the power to decide on the merger, unless otherwise provided by the articles.[64] The Tenth Directive

59. *See also* Commission Staff Working Document Impact assessment on the directive on the cross-border transfer of registered office, Brussels, 12 Dec. 2007, SEC(2007) 1707.
60. Cf. Commissioner Charlie McCreevy's speech on 3 Oct. 2007 in the EU Parliament's Legal Affair Committee, speech No. 07/592.
61. SE Statute, Articles 9 and 18; Tenth Directive, Article 2.
62. Companies Act 2006, s.907.
63. Article 8 Third Directive and Article 9(3) Tenth Directive.
64. Article 331, Book 2 Civil Code (Netherlands).

requires approval by the general meeting of each of the companies to merge but does not specify a majority or quorum (Article 6).

8.32 Furthermore, systems of creditor protection may differ. According to Article 13 of the Third Directive, Member States are required to provide for an adequate system of protection of the interests of creditors of the merging companies, whose claims predate the publication of the draft terms of merger and have not fallen due at the time of such publication. Such creditors are entitled to obtain adequate safeguards, where the financial situation of the merging companies makes such protection necessary and where those creditors do not already have such safeguards. The Tenth Directive ensures that this protection is offered similarly in a cross-border merger (Article 4(2)) and the same is done by the SE Statute (Article 24).[65] Consequently, the system of the Third Directive is proliferated to CBM, allowing for creditor protection a priori or a posteriori. The first enables creditors to require securities of the debtor company, or another company to be merged, from the moment the draft terms of the merger are published, whereas the second offers protection after the merger has already been registered and published. Then, of course, securities can be obtained from the acquiring company only. The Netherlands, Belgium and France have implemented the a priori system. Germany opted for protection a posteriori in the case of a domestic merger, but introduced protection a priori for the cross-border merger.[66] Such divergences may complicate CBM. Not surprisingly, the High Level Group of Company Law Experts, after concluding that Member States show 'a wide diversity of practice (...) in relation to creditor protection in restructuring', recommends harmonization of creditor protection not only for CBM, but also for all kinds of restructuring transactions.[67]

8.33 Even the date on which a cross-border merger takes effect may vary, because this is determined by the law of the Member State, whose jurisdiction the company resulting from the cross-border merger is subject to (Article 12).[68] It can be the date of the registration of the merger with the commercial registry of the acquiring company, or the newly formed company, as is the basic rule in Germany.[69] In France, however, parties enjoy considerable freedom to determine the date in the merger agreement and it may even be retroactive for financial or tax reasons.[70]

65. The provisions differ however, with respect to holders of bonds and securities and/or shares.
66. Article 684 Code of Companies (Belgium), Article 316 Book 2 Civil Code (Netherlands), Article L236-14 Commercial Code (France) and *Umwandlungsgesetz* s. 22 for domestic mergers and s. 122 j(1) for cross-border mergers (Germany). Van Solinge, *Grensoverschrijdende juridische fusie*, 95–146.
67. Report of the High Level Group of Company Law Experts on *a Modern Regulatory Framework for Company Law in Europe* (Brussels, 2002), 113.
68. *See also* Article 17 Third Directive.
69. Umwandlungsgesetz s. 20, Carrington and Pessoa, *Acquiring Companies and Businesses in Europe*, 46. Irrespective of the date on which the merger takes effect, the merging companies may determine another date from which the transactions of the company being acquired shall be treated for accounting purposes as being those of the acquiring company, Third Directive, Article 5(2)(e).
70. This facility pertains only to mergers by absorption, Article L236-4 Commercial Code, Carrington and Pessoa, *Acquiring Companies and Businesses in Europe*, 21. Van Solinge, *Grensoverschrijdende juridische fusie*, 115.

8.34 Due to their cross-border aspects, both the SE Statute and the Tenth Directive contain additional rules for the execution of a merger in comparison to the Third Directive. The issues concerned are, for instance, the information to be included in the draft terms of the merger and the protection of (minority) shareholders (paragraphs 3.88 and 4.18). Typical to the cross-border aspect, the choice of law for pre-merger and post-merger issues, respectively, must be determined. The SE Statute contains rather detailed rules for the formation of an SE by way of a merger and these rules supersede national law. In addition, Article 18 refers to the national law of the companies to be merged, as harmonized by the Third Directive. Likewise, the Tenth Directive in Article 4(2) refers to the provisions and formalities of the national law of the 'merging companies', in particular, those concerning the decision-making process. Further, 'taking into account the cross-border nature of the merger', national provisions apply for the protection of creditors of the merging companies, debenture holders and the holders of securities or shares, as well as of employees, regarding rights other than those governed by Article 16 (which covers employee participation).[71] Finally, it must be noted that both the authorities competent to scrutinize the legality of the completion of the cross-border merger and the negotiation procedure with respect to the involvement of employees are governed by the law of the Member State of the registered office of the company resulting from the cross-border merger.[72]

VI PROTECTION OF RIGHTS OF EMPLOYEES

8.35 To understand to what extent the rights of employees will be protected in the case of a cross-border acquisition, one must discern between the various directives for the protection of these rights on the one hand, and the methods of acquisition on the other hand:

- In the first place, national provisions regarding the *right to information and consultation* of employees or their representatives may apply whatever method of acquisition used. Minimum standards in this respect are set by Directive 2002/14/EC, establishing a general framework for informing and consulting employees in the EU.[73] The directive is meant to prevent serious decisions affecting employees from being taken and made public without adequate procedures having been implemented beforehand to inform and consult the employees or their representatives.[74]
- Where an *acquisition of assets* can be qualified as a transfer of an undertaking (business) or part thereof, the rights of employees are protected by rules

71. Despite the phrase 'taking into account the cross-border nature of the merger', the national law of a Member State protects only interests connected to the company that is governed by that national law.
72. Article 26(1) SE Statute and Article 11(1) Tenth Directive; Article 6 SE Directive and Article 16(3)(d) of the Tenth Directive.
73. Directive 2002/14/EC, establishing a general framework for informing and consulting employees in the European Community, OJ 2002, L 80.
74. Preamble No. 6, Directive 2002/14/EC, OJ 2002, L 80.

prescribed by Directive 2001/23/EC on the safeguarding of employees' rights in the event of transfers of undertakings.[75] Such an event occurs when an undertaking or part thereof is transferred to another employer as a result of a legal transfer or merger. This covers any transfer of an economic entity, which retains its identity, meaning an organized grouping of resources that has the objective of pursuing an economic activity, whether or not that activity is central or ancillary (Article 1). According to the directive, the transferor's rights and obligations arising from employment contracts shall automatically be transferred to the transferee, that is, the company acquiring the business (Article 3). The ECJ held that transactions may fall within the ambit of the directive, if there is a change in the person carrying out the business and incurring the obligations of an employer, 'regardless whether or not ownership of the undertaking is transferred'.[76] Consequently, even a lease agreement may come within the meaning of the directive.[77] The transfer of an undertaking shall not, in itself, constitute grounds for dismissal by the transferor or the transferee. Nevertheless, dismissals may take place for economic, technical or organizational reasons entailing changes in the workforce (Article 4). The protection offered by the directive does not apply if the transferor is the subject of bankruptcy proceedings or any analogous insolvency proceedings (Article 5).[78] Notwithstanding its ample scope, Directive 2001/23/EC is not tailored to cases, where undertakings or parts thereof are transferred across borders. According to Article 1(2), the directive applies to the transfer of undertakings 'situated within the territorial scope of the Treaty'. The criterion for the applicability, therefore, is the place where the undertaking is situated at the date of the transfer, irrespective of the nationality of the transferor and the transferee.[79] However, cross-border transfers are not mentioned in the directive and conflict of laws provisions are missing.[80] Difficulties may arise especially if the transfer of the undertaking implies its relocation to another Member State, or even outside the EU. Against the background of the importance of outsourcing and the increasing mobility of production factors in

---

75. Directive 2001/23/EC relating to the safeguarding of employees' rights in the event of transfers of undertakings, businesses or parts of undertakings or businesses, OJ 2001,L 82 replacing Directive (EEC) 77/187, OJ 1977, L 61.
76. Court of Justice, C-287/86 *Ny Mølle Kro*.
77. C. de Groot, 'The Council Directive on the Safeguarding of Employees' Rights in the Event of Transfers of Undertakings: An Overview of the Case Law', *Common Market Law Review* 30 (1993): 339.
78. The issues mentioned here as well as many others are dealt with in the 2007 Commission Services Working Document, *Memorandum on Rights of Workers in Cases of Transfers of Undertakings*, retrievable from http://ec.europa.eu/employment_social/labour_law/documentation_en.htm.
79. Commission, June 2007, *First phase consultation of social partners under Article 138(2) of the EC Treaty concerning cross-border transfers of undertakings, businesses or parts of undertakings or businesses*, retrievable from http://ec.europa.eu/employment_social/social_dialogue/consultations_en.htm.
80. John McMullen, 'Some Problems and Themes in the Application in Member States of Directive 2001/23/EC on Transfer of Undertakings', *The International Journal of Comparative Labour Law and Industrial Relations* 23, no. 3 (2007): 353.

a globalizing economy, the Commission started exploring the possibility of amending the directive to ensure legal certainty for cross-border transfers of undertakings.[81]

The case decided on by the Hamburg Labour Court illustrates the types of issues that arise when an undertaking is transferred across borders. A German company transferred its English news service, which was part of its activities, to its Irish subsidiary. The employee carrying out the publishing of the news service in Hamburg was dismissed. The employee, however, was willing to move to Cork and successfully brought a claim under German law in the Labour Court of Hamburg. The court held the dismissal notice to be invalid.[82] As McMullen remarks, in this case, only the transferor was sued and, therefore, it does not clarify whether the employee could have enforced his rights against the transferee, which was situated in another Member State.[83]

- In the case of an acquisition by means of a *share transaction,* employment contracts to which the acquired company is a party remain with that company. Although the control of the company changes hands, there is no change in the legal person that is responsible for carrying out the business and that incurs the obligations of an employer. Nevertheless, national laws of the companies concerned may provide for information and consultation rights for the employees or their representatives. Where the acquisition results in a group of companies with a Community dimension ('Community-scale group of undertakings'), an obligation may be triggered for the acquiring company to establish a European Works Council.[84] Directive 2001/23/EC does not cover acquisitions by a transfer of shares, because, in such a case, the identity of the employer remains the same. As a result, employees are not protected by this directive against dismissals that are connected to the transfer of shares.[85] Similarly, the information and consultation rights under Article 7, in the case of a transfer of an undertaking, do not apply to a share transfer, but this may be compensated for by national law.[86]

81. Commission, June 2007, *First phase consultation of social partners under Article 138(2) of the EC Treaty concerning cross-border transfers of undertakings, businesses or parts of undertakings or businesses*, s. 9.
82. Landesarbeitsgericht Hamburg, 22 May 2003, as reported by McMullen, 'Some Problems and Themes in the Application in Member States of Directive 2001/23/EC on Transfer of Undertakings', 353–354.
83. *Ibid.*, 354.
84. Directive 94/45/EC on the establishment of a European Works Council or a procedure in Community-scale undertakings and Community-scale groups of undertakings for the purposes of informing and consulting employees, OJ 1994, L 254.
85. McMullen, 'Some Problems and Themes in the Application in Member States of Directive 2001/23/EC on Transfer of Undertakings', 338.
86. For example, the Dutch Works Council Act, Article 25(1)(a) confers the right of information and consultation in the case of transfer of control of the enterprise or any part thereof. This may include the transfer of control by the acquisition of shares, Roel Fluit, What a US Buyer Should Expect in a Dutch M&A Transaction, *ECL* 2017, 29-42.

- In the case of a *merger*, the automatic transfer of all assets and liabilities as a matter of course pertains to the obligations arising from the contracts between the acquired company and its employees. Nevertheless, the Third Directive in Article 12 explicitly mentions that the protection of the rights of the employees of each of the merging companies has to be regulated in accordance with Directive 2001/23/EC on the safeguarding of employees' rights in the event of transfers of undertakings. The Tenth Directive does not affect employees' rights, other than rights of participation. Therefore, in the case of a cross-border merger, the rights of employees are protected to the same extent as where an (cross-border) asset transaction constitutes the transfer of an undertaking.[87]

Unlike the Third Directive, both the SE Directive and the Tenth Directive provide for additional rules regarding *employee participation* in the company resulting from the cross-border merger. The concept of employee participation used in the Tenth Directive corresponds with participation, as defined in the SE Directive.[88] It points at rights of employee representatives to elect or appoint some or all of the members of the company's supervisory or administrative organ or the right to recommend and/or oppose the appointment of such members. The starting point is that a company resulting from a cross-border merger shall be subject to the rules in force, concerning employee participation, if any, in the Member State in which that company has its registered office (Article 16). If national law does not provide for the same level of participation as operated in one or more of the merging companies, this matter must then be regulated. The SE Statute and the SE Directive contain provisions used for this purpose. Details of employee participation in the SE have been set out in paragraphs 4.35 *et seq*. The same rules and procedures apply for a cross-border merger, according to the Tenth Directive, albeit with some modifications, because the company resulting from a cross-border merger in accordance with the Tenth Directive is subject to national law.[89] The involvement of employees is discussed in Chapter 7.

VII MERGER CONTROL

A The Treaty Provisions

8.36 The TFEU, in Articles 101 *et seq*., provides rules on competition, which is an important area of EU policy. For the subject of cooperation and acquisitions, Articles 101 and 102 TFEU are the most relevant. Article 101 prohibits agreements between undertakings, decisions by associations of undertakings and concerted practices that may affect trade between the Member States and that have as their object competition, or effect the prevention, restriction or distortion of competition in the common market.

87. Tenth Directive, Preamble No. 12.
88. Article 2(k), SE Directive defines employee participation. The concept of employee participation of the Tenth Directive corresponds with this definition because Article 16 refers extensively to the SE Directive.
89. Paragraph 13, Preamble of the Tenth Directive.

This article applies exclusively to *cooperation* between undertakings (business enterprises). An example of illegal conduct infringing Article 101 is a secret agreement (cartel) between competitors, leading to price-fixing and/or market sharing.[90] Article 101 also covers cooperative joint ventures and acquisitions of shareholdings, falling short of a concentration as defined by the Merger Regulation (paragraph 8.39). The prohibition does not apply if the agreement, decision or practice has beneficial effects, such as improvement of products or technical progress if a fair share of these is allowed to the consumers (Article 101(3)).

8.36a Cartels are generally not easily detectable. Therefore, the Commission encourages companies to hand over inside evidence, in exchange for complete or partial immunity for fines.[91] Individuals are also encouraged to report inside knowledge they may have of a cartel to the Commission. They can do this openly or anonymously through a 'whistleblower' tool established in 2017.[92]

8.36b Cooperation between undertakings (businesses) may negatively affect trade, but can also have beneficial effects. Article 101(3) allows for cooperation, if it contributes to improving the production or distribution of goods or to promoting technical or economic progress, while allowing consumers a fair share of the resulting benefit. In its 2011 Communication, the Commission explains how it assesses the effects of so-called horizontal cooperation (agreements between actual or potential competitors).[93] In the same vein, certain categories of vertical agreements and concerted practices are acceptable, if they meet the conditions laid down in Regulation EU 330/2010.[94]

8.37 Behaviour of undertakings, not leading to cooperation, but to *concentration* was originally dealt with under Article 102 (at the time Article 82 EC Treaty), which prohibits any abuse by an undertaking of its dominant position within the common market or in a substantial part thereof. In *Continental Can v. Commission*, the court held that this provision, indeed, had to be applied where a company in a dominant position acquired a competitor, if the acquisition reinforced the acquirer's position.[95] Obviously, this applies only to concentrations, where one of the parties involved already has a dominant position. However, other concentrations may be equally incompatible with the undistorted competition envisaged by the treaty. Therefore, the position of the Commission was reinforced, initially by Regulation 4064/89 (on the

90. *See* the Commission's website:, http://ec.europa.eu/competition/cartels/overview/index_en.html.
91. http://ec.europa.eu/competition/cartels/leniency/leniency.html.
92. http://ec.europa.eu/competition/cartels/whistleblower/index.html.
93. Communication from the Commission, *Guidelines on the applicability of Article 101 of the Treaty on the Functioning of the European Union to horizontal co-operation agreements*, OJ 14.1.2011, C 11/1.
94. Commission Regulation (EU) No. 330/2010 of 20 Apr. 2010 on the application of Article 101(3) of the Treaty on the Functioning of the European Union to categories of vertical agreements and concerted practices. The regulation concerns undertakings operating at a different level of the production or distribution chain.
95. C-6/72, *Continental Can v. Commission* [1973] ECR 215.

control of concentrations between undertakings), which was based on Article 83 (87) and 308 (233) of the EC Treaty.[96] This regulation was replaced by Merger Regulation EC No 139/2004.[97]

8.38 Strengthening the position of the Commission must also be viewed against the background of the objectives of the EU, as embodied in Article 9 of the TFEU. This includes, *inter alia*, the promotion of a high-level employment and the guarantee of adequate social protection. The Commission was of the view that European integration could be furthered by competition and merger control policy.[98]

8.38a The dominant position of an undertaking in the internal market or in a substantial part of it is not, by itself, a concern for the competition authorities. It is the abuse of such position that is declared incompatible with the internal market, insofar as it may affect trade between Member States. Article 102 TFEU further specifies what may, in particular, constitute abuse. Imposing unfair prices or limiting production to the prejudice of consumers are, *inter alia*, mentioned. The growing importance of innovation and high-tech industries has put the effectivity and even the necessity of this part of competition policy under debate.[99]

B The Merger Regulation

8.39 According to Article 3(1) of the 2004 Merger Regulation, a concentration is deemed to arise where a *change of control on a lasting basis* results from:

- a merger of two or more previously independent undertakings or parts of undertakings; or
- the acquisition by one or more undertakings of direct or indirect control of one or more other undertakings (or parts thereof), whether by purchase of securities or assets, by contract or by any other means.

Control is defined in Article 3(2) and 'shall be constituted by rights, contracts or any other means which (...) confer the possibility of exercising decisive influence on an undertaking'. The provision specifies that control is, in particular, realized by

96. Regulation EC 4064/89, OJ 1989, L 395/1 and 1990, L 257/14, amended by Regulation (EEC) 1310/97 OJ 1997, L 180.
97. Regulation EC 139/2004, OJ 2004, L 24.
98. Karel van Miert, cited by Haid, in *Competition, Efficiency and Welfare*, eds Dennis C. Mueller, Alfred Haid & Jurgen Weigand (Boston: Kluwer Academic Publishers, 1999), 167.
99. See, for the original purpose of what is now Article 102, C.S. Rusu, *European Merger Control: The Challenges Raised by 20 Years of Enforcement Experience* (Alphen aan den Rijn: Kluwer Law International, 2010). Furthermore: M.L. Katz & H.A. Shelanski, 'Schumpeterian Competition and Antitrust Policy in High-Tech Markets', *Competition* 2005; P. Ibáñez Colomo, 'Intel and Article 102 TFEU Case Law: Making Sense of a Perpetual Controversy', *LSE Law, Society and Economy Working Papers* 29/2014; N. Petit, 'Intel, Leveraging Rebates and the Goals of Article 102 TFEU' (20 mei 2015), available at SSRN: http://ssrn.com/abstract = 2567628 .

ownership or the right to use the assets of an undertaking, as well as by rights or contracts that confer decisive influence on the composition, voting or decisions of the organs of an undertaking.

8.39a It follows from the previous paragraph that the Merger Regulation covers not only mergers in the strict sense but also all operations that lead to a lasting change in the structure of the undertakings concerned. Unlike company law, whose function is to offer a legal structure for entrepreneurial activities without affecting these activities, the Merger Regulation pertains directly to a specific entrepreneurial activity, namely, the acquisition of control. It does so irrespective of whether control is acquired by legal instruments like mergers, contracts and majority or controlling voting rights or by de facto circumstances, like economic dependence and dominance. As a matter of course, these factual elements of control are especially hard to assess. Not surprisingly, the Merger Regulation gives rise to many questions on how to interpret its provisions. Therefore, the Commission has provided for jurisdictional notices, in order to explain how the most important concepts have to be applied, most recently, in a document called the Consolidated Jurisdictional Notice.[100]

8.40 The scope of the Merger Regulation is limited to concentrations with a *Community dimension*. The powers of national authorities are limited to cases where, failing intervention by the Commission, effective competition is likely to be significantly impeded within the territory of a Member State.[101] Member States are not permitted to apply their national legislation on competition to concentrations with a Community dimension, unless the Merger Regulation makes provisions in that respect. According to Article 9, concentrations with a community dimension may be referred to national authorities when they affect competition in a 'distinct market' within a Member State. The reverse situation – referral to the Commission by Member States – is dealt with by Article 22. Accordingly, Member States may request the Commission to examine a concentration that does not have a Community dimension, if such concentration affects trade between Member States and threatens to significantly affect competition within the territory of the Member State(s) making the request. In general, the Commission has the duty to carry out the procedures set out in the Merger Regulation in 'close and constant liaison' with the competent authorities of the Member States (Article 19).

100. Consolidated Jurisdictional Notice under Council Regulation (EC) No. 139/2004 on the control of concentrations between undertakings, 10 Jul. 2007, OJ 2008, C/95; retrievable from http://ec.europa.eu/competition/mergers/legislation/legislation.html . *See* for merger cases examined by the Commission http://ec.europa.eu/competition/mergers/cases/ .

101. Merger Directive, Preamble, paragraph 18 and Article 21(3). An overview of national competition laws can be found in publications like Peter F.C. Begg, *Corporate Acquisitions and Mergers* (looseleaf) (Aspen Publishers) Baker & McKenzie, *Acquiring Companies and Businesses in Europe*, 5th edition, 2005 and Peter Verloop & Volérie Landes, *Merger Control in Europe*, International Competition Law Series Volume 11 (The Hague: Kluwer Law International, 2003).

8.40a A concentration has a Community dimension where:

Article 1(2):

(a) the combined aggregate worldwide turnover of all the undertakings concerned is more than EUR 5,000 million; and
(b) the aggregate Community-wide turnover of each of at least two of the undertakings concerned is more than EUR 250 million.

Article 1(3):
A concentration below the thresholds of Article 1(2) nevertheless has a Community dimension where:

(a) the combined aggregate worldwide turnover of all the undertakings concerned is more than EUR 2500 million;
(b) in each of at least three Member States, the combined aggregate turnover of all the undertakings concerned is more than EUR 100 million;
(c) in each of at least three Member States included for the purpose of point (b), the aggregate turnover of each of at least two of the undertakings concerned is more than EUR 25 million; and
(d) the aggregate Community-wide turnover of each of at least two of the undertakings concerned is more than EUR 100 million.

Even if the thresholds, as defined by sections 2 or 3, are met, the Community dimension is deemed to be absent, where each of the undertakings concerned achieves more than two-thirds of its aggregate Community-wide turnover within one and the same Member State.

Article 5 further specifies the calculation of turnovers.

1 The First Phase

8.41 *Notification* of a concentration with a Community dimension to the Commission must take place following the conclusion of the agreement, the announcement of the public bid or the acquisition of a controlling interest leading to such concentration (Article 4). Earlier notification is allowed where the undertakings concerned demonstrate to the Commission a good faith intention to conclude an agreement or, in the case of a public bid, where they have publicly announced an intention to make such a bid, Article 4(1). Such intention can be demonstrated by 'letters of intent' or 'heads of agreement'. However, these, by themselves, do not create binding obligations for the parties concerned. It is standard practice for parties to engage in pre-notification discussions with the Commission, even in an earlier stage, to ensure that the intended concentration does not raise too many concerns and that the notification itself contains the essential information. Although concentrations may not be implemented before notification, or until it has been declared compatible with the common market, the Merger Regulation does not prevent the implementation of a public bid but rather restricts the use of the acquired voting rights instead (Article 7(2)).

8.42 The subject matter and content of the information to be provided in the notification is defined by the implementing Regulation (EC) 802/2004.[102] Annexes to this regulation contain forms to be used by parties notifying a concentration. According to the full notification form (Form CO), parties to the concentration must specify 'the nature of the concentration (e.g., merger, acquisition or joint venture), the areas of activity of the notifying parties, the markets on which the concentration will have an impact (including the main affected markets) and the strategic and economic rationale for the concentration'.[103] In describing the nature of the concentration, parties must state, *inter alia,* 'whether the proposed concentration is a full merger, an acquisition of sole or joint control, a contract or other means of conferring direct or indirect control within the meaning of Article 3(2) of the Merger Regulation or the acquisition of joint control in a full-function joint venture within the meaning of Article 3(4) of the Merger Regulation'.[104] In the case of a joint venture, details about the cooperative effects must be provided.[105] Further guidance can be found in the Commission's Best Practices on the conduct of EC merger control proceedings.[106]

8.43 After receiving the notification, the Commission, according to Article 6(1), can make several *decisions* by concluding that the concentration:

(a) does not fall within the scope of the Merger Regulation; or
(b) does not raise serious doubts as to its compatibility with the common market; or
(c) in case it raises serious doubts to initiate proceedings.

These decisions must be taken within twenty-five working days and it is often referred to as the first phase. The period shall be increased up to thirty-five days, where the undertakings concerned offer commitments in order to modify the concentration in such a way as to make it compatible with the common market (Article 10(1)).[107]

In a 2007 notice, the Commission provides guidance on modifications to notified concentrations, including commitments to modify a concentration. The object of such commitments, or 'remedies', as they are more commonly called, is to eliminate the competition concerns identified by the Commission. Such remedies include, for

102. The implementing regulation further contains rules for time-limits, hearings, confidentiality and the terms of reference of hearing officers in competition proceedings. The regulation is amended by Commission Regulation (EC) No. 1033/2008 (Official Journal L 279, 22.10.2008, pp. 3–12) and by Commission Implementing Regulation (EU) No. 1269/2013 of 5 Dec. 2013 (Official Journal OJ L 336, 14.12.2013, pp. 1–36).
103. Section 1, Article 1.1.
104. Section 3, Article 3.1(a).
105. Section 10, Article 10.
106. Article 1, Form CO. The document is provided for by the DG Competition on it's website http://ec.europa.eu/competition/mergers/legislation/legislation.html . On the website a document in pdf, including all relevant legislation, is available and is updated from time to time: *EU Competition Law: Merger Legislation.*
107. The extended period also applies when the undertakings concerned require referral to national authorities, Article 9.

example, divestitures (the commitment to sell a business unit) and granting competitors access to key infrastructures on non-discriminatory terms.[108]

2 *The Second Phase*

8.44 The second phase starts when proceedings have been initiated, because of the serious doubts raised. After investigation, the Commission may decide that the concentration is, nevertheless, declared compatible with the common market (Article 8(1) and (2)). The concentration then has to fulfil the criterion of Article 2(2), meaning that it does not significantly impede effective competition and, where a joint venture is created, that the effects on the coordination of the competitive behaviour of the cooperating undertakings are in accordance with the criteria of Article 101(3) TFEU. During the second phase, modifications may also be made in order to remove the objections of the Commission (Article 8(2)). Where the Commission finds that a concentration would *significantly impede effective competition* in the common market or in a substantial part of it, in particular as a result of the creation or strengthening of a dominant position, it should then be declared incompatible with the common market (Article 8(3) and (4)). Where the Commission finds that such a concentration has already been completed, it may require the dissolution of the merger or the disposal of the acquired assets or shares. Decisions completing the second phase must be taken within ninety days of the date on which the proceedings were initiated and may be extended to 105 days where the undertakings offer commitments to modify the concentration (Article 10(3)).

8.44a The Merger Regulation grants wide powers to the Commission, but also provides for some checks and balances. An Advisory Committee on concentrations (consisting of representatives of the competent authorities of the Member States) must be consulted before any decision is taken by the Commission, *inter alia,* on the (in)compatibility of a concentration with the common market and on the imposition of fines (Article 19(3)). Most of the decisions must be published together with the opinion of the Advisory Committee in the *Official Journal of the European Union* (Article 20).[109] Furthermore, decisions of the Commission may be reviewed by the ECJ (*inter alia:* Articles 16 and 21).

8.45 The Commission has adopted guidelines, describing the analysis for the substantive test as to whether concentrations are compatible with the common market. The *Horizontal Guidelines* deal with mergers between competing or potentially competing firms.[110] Horizontal mergers generally reduce the number of firms active on the relevant market and the primary competition concern over these mergers is that the

108. Commission Notice (2007) on remedies acceptable under Council Regulation (EC) No. 139/2004 and under Commission Regulation (EC) No. 802/2004, retrievable from http://ec.europa.eu/competition/mergers/legislation/legislation.html.
109. The latest case information is to be found at: www.ec.europa.eu/comm/competition/mergers/news.html and/or: ec.europa.eu/comm/competition/mergers/cases
110. Guidelines on the assessment of horizontal mergers under the Council Regulation on the control of concentrations between undertakings, OJ 2004, C 31.

structural changes they create will lead to higher prices in comparison to if the merger would not take place. The Commission's assessment of mergers normally entails a definition of the relevant product and geographic markets, as well as the competitive assessment of the merger. In assessing the competitive effects, the competitive conditions that would result from the notified merger will be compared with the conditions that would have prevailed without the merger. Thereby, the Commission may take account of the likely entry or exit of firms if the merger would not take place when considering what constitutes the relevant comparison.

Vertical and conglomerate concentrations (non-horizontal concentrations) are dealt with by the *Guidelines for merging companies with vertical or conglomerate relationship*.[111] Vertical concentrations involve companies operating at different levels of the supply chain, for example, when a manufacturer merges with one of its distributors. Conglomerate concentrations are mergers or acquisitions of firms that are not in a horizontal relationship (as competitors in the same relevant market) and not operating at different levels of the supply chain. The focus of the guidelines is on mergers between companies that are active in closely related markets, for example, between suppliers of complementary products. According to the guidelines, non-horizontal concentrations are generally less likely to significantly impede effective competition than horizontal mergers, *inter alia,* because they do not imply loss of direct competition as horizontal mergers do. Concerns raised by non-horizontal concentrations are possible 'anti-competitive foreclosure', meaning the hampering or elimination of rivals' access to supplies or markets that may lead to the loss of these companies' abilities to compete. Another concern is that due to the concentration, firms may significantly more likely coordinate their activities to raise prices or otherwise harm effective competition. Pro-competitive effects of non-horizontal concentrations may stem from substantiated efficiencies benefiting consumers.

3 Joint Ventures

8.46 Joint ventures, as has been explained in paragraph 8.10, function to structure the cooperation of business enterprises that remain independent. Therefore, they are not automatically covered by the concentration concept. It makes a difference whether a joint venture originates from the joint acquisition of an existing undertaking or from the creation of a new entity, created by the cooperating partners. The first case clearly constitutes a concentration according to Article 3(1)(b) of the Merger Regulation, where the *acquisition of control by one or more undertakings* is explicitly mentioned. By way of contrast, a joint venture resulting from the creation of a new undertaking will only constitute a concentration if it performs, on a lasting basis, all the functions of an autonomous economic entity (Article 3(4)). Autonomy, in this respect, means that the joint venture must be operationally autonomous, whereas the joint venture partners

111. Guidelines on the assessment of non-horizontal mergers under the Council Regulation on the control of concentrations between undertakings, OJ 2008, C 265.

may direct its strategy.[112] It implies, *inter alia,* that the joint venture has management dedicated to its day-to-day operations and that the joint venture has access to sufficient staff, finance and assets, in order to conduct, on a lasting basis, its business activities within the area provided for in the joint venture agreement.[113]

8.47 To the extent that a joint venture has as its object, or effects, the coordination of the competitive behaviour of undertakings that remain independent, such coordination will be appraised in accordance with the criteria of Article 101(1) and (3) TFEU. In doing so, the Commission must take into account whether the joint venture partners (parent companies) retain activities in the same market, in a market upstream or downstream or in a neighbouring market. Another important aspect is whether the coordination, which is the direct consequence of the joint venture, affords the undertakings concerned to eliminate competition with respect to the relevant products or services (Article 2(4) and (5)).[114] According to Article 101(1) TFEU, agreements between business enterprises (undertakings) leading to the prevention, restriction or distortion of competition within the common market are prohibited. Agreements may be exempted if they contribute to improving the production or distribution of goods or to promoting technical or economic progress, while allowing consumers a fair share of the resulting benefit (Article 101(3)).[115] Although joint ventures are not mentioned as such, both the prohibition and the conditions for exemption pertain to joint ventures. The Commission has provided several examples of joint ventures and other arrangements, which, although falling under the ambit of Article 101(1) TFEU, may be exempted on the grounds of section 3 of that article.[116]

112. Consolidated Jurisdictional Notice, No. 91–93.
113. Consolidated Jurisdictional Notice, No. 94.
114. Further reading: Nicole Tyson, Joint Venture Regulation under European Competition Laws: An update, *European Law Journal* 13, no. 3 (May 2007): 408–423.
115. Even then, certain conditions must be met, Article 81(3) and Communication from the Commission - Notice - Guidelines on the application of Article 81(3) of the Treaty, OJ 2004, C 101, 27 Apr. 2004 0097 - 0118.
116. Guidelines on the application of Article 81(3) of the Treaty, OJ 2004, C 101, 27 Apr. 2004, nr. 38 *et seq.*

CHAPTER 9

Financial Statements and Related Reports

I INTRODUCTION

9.01 The 2013/34/EU Directive (Accounting Directive), consolidating the Fourth and Seventh Directives and concerning the annual financial statements (previously called annual accounts), is discussed in Chapter 3 (paragraphs 3.63 *et seq.*). In addition, the application of International Accounting Standards (IFRS) is mentioned in several paragraphs (notably 3.65a and 3.69). This chapter contains a more detailed analysis of the Accounting Directive and the applicable international standards. First, by way of further introduction, it sets out the scope of the directive (paragraph 9.02) and looks at the background of the international standards (paragraph 9.06). Second, it deals with the general principles that the annual financial statements have to comply with (paragraph 9.11), followed by a more detailed description of the balance sheet (paragraph 9.14), the profit and loss account (paragraph 9.20), the notes to the accounts (paragraph 9.21) and the management report (paragraph 9.23). Third, it sets out the publication of the annual financial statements (paragraph 9.26) and any additional reports by listed companies (paragraph 9.28). The last subjects presented in this chapter are the consolidated financial statements (paragraph 9.29) and the statutory audit (paragraph 9.45).

9.02 The corporate bodies must ensure that the annual financial statements and the consolidated financial statements are drawn up and published in accordance with the requirements of the Accounting Directive and, where applicable, in accordance with the IAS. The annual financial statements must be audited and published in accordance with the First Directive (as amended) and the 2006 Directive on statutory audits (as amended). These directives are set out in Chapter 3. The financial reporting obligations concern public and private limited liability companies, public limited partnerships and certain partnerships and limited partnerships. These are mentioned in Article 1 and further specified in Annexes I and II of the Accounting Directive. Consequently, entities of the 'GmbH & Co. KG' type fall within the scope of the directive and partnerships cannot be used to avoid the requirements of the European Union (EU) accounting norms, nor the publication of essential data concerning its members, where these members have limited liability.[1] To alleviate the administrative burden for entrepreneurs, simplifications and exemptions are allowed for micro-undertakings, small undertakings and medium-sized undertakings. These categories are defined in Article 3, according to their balance sheet total, net turnover and the average number of employees. Finally, as prescribed by the Transparency Directive, listed companies are subject to additional obligations, in order to ensure that information is published on a regular basis to inform investors.

9.03 Each Member State is free to decide on the technical manner in which the requirements of the Accounting Directive are carried out. The Member States may incorporate the accounting rules in specific company legislation (e.g., in their Companies Act or Private Companies Act) or set up a common accounting act governing all relevant company types. Finally, the accounting provisions may be incorporated in an already existing act that is common for the various company types, as Germany did when incorporating the provisions of the original Accounting Directives in sections 264–289 of its *Handelsgesetzbuch* (HGB).

9.03a The Accounting Directive is a minimum directive according to Article 4(5), which means that Member States are free to require undertakings (with the exception of the small ones) to disclose additional information in their annual financial statements. A company may not rely on the fact that other Member States have less stringent accounting requirements or that they do not observe the directive as a ground for not complying with the legal requirements with respect to accounting or the duty to submit financial statements. In the *Blanguernon* case, the court held that the companies must observe the duty to submit financial statements, even if one or more of the other Member States (such as Germany) have failed to implement the directive with respect to minor private companies. In addition, the companies must observe this duty, even if it results in a certain degree of competition distortion to the detriment of those companies.[2]

9.04 Since 2005, EU companies whose securities are offered to the public ('listed companies') must prepare their *consolidated financial statements* in conformity with the IAS adopted by the Commission.[3] By contrast, Member States have the option to allow or require adherence to these standards for the non-consolidated annual financial statements of listed companies. As for non-listed companies, almost all Member States require or permit them to draw up their *consolidated* financial

1. The extension to hybrid entities such as the GmbH & Co happened by the amending Directive 90/605/EEC, OJ 1990, L 317. Germany, where the use of the GmbH & Co was widespread implemented this directive with prolonged hesitation, Claus Luttermann, *ZIP* (2000): 517 *et seq.*
2. ECJ 11 Jan. 1990, C-38/89 (Blanguernon).
3. *EU Accounting Strategy: The Way Ahead*, COM(2000) 359 of 13 Jun. 2000 and Article 5 Regulation EC 1606/2002 on the application of international accounting standards, OJ 2002, L 243.

statements according to the IAS/IFRS, but most do not permit the use of these standards by the companies for their annual financial statements.[4]

9.05 According to Directive 2013/34/EU, as amended by Directive 2014/95/EU, large undertakings and groups must disclose non-financial and diversity information. The initiative for this directive lies with resolutions of the European Parliament on, respectively, 'Corporate Social Responsibility: accountable, transparent and responsible business behaviour and sustainable growth' and 'Corporate Social Responsibility: promoting society's interests and a route to sustainable and inclusive recovery'. The EU legislator is of the opinion that disclosure of non-financial information is vital for managing change towards a sustainable global economy by combining long-term profitability with social justice and environmental protection.[5] The non-financial statement should include, *inter alia*, a brief description of the undertaking's business model and its policies and activities relating to environmental, social and employee matters, as well as respect for human rights, anti-corruption and bribery matters (Article 19a and 29a Directive 2012/34/EU). The non-financial statement is dealt with in section VII of this chapter.

9.05a Scholars and accounting practitioners have developed several instruments to account for the social, economic and environmental value that results from the activities of businesses. Among these are Integrated Reporting (IR) and Social Return on Investment (ROI). IR means that organizations account for both the financial and non-financial effects of value creation. ROI is an investment appraisal technique that is explicitly designed to include social and environmental effects into the assessment of a project.[6] The effects of the obligation to report on Corporate Social Responsibility (CSR) activities are not deemed very significant. On the one hand, this is due to the fact that many organizations already engage in CSR activities and publish such information, and, on the other hand, the minimum harmonization approach not supported by detailed rules and standards.[7]

II THE IAS/IFRS

9.06 A few remarks concerning IAS may be useful. For starters, the aim of the original Accounting Directives was to ensure that information extracted from the accounting materials is reliable and comparable, regardless of the company that an investor or creditor is looking at. However, full comparability was not achieved due to the

4. Report of the Commission, COM(2008) 215 final, 3.
5. Preamble of Directive 2014/95/EU, paragraph 3.
6. Mayra Ortega Maldonado & Michael Corbey, Social Return on Investment (SROI): A Review of the Technique, *MAB, Maandblad voor Accountancy en Bedrijfseconomie* 90 (2016), pp. 80 *et seq.* http://mab-online.nl .
7. John Quinn & Barry Connolly, The Non-financial Information Directive: An Assessment of Its Impact on Corporate Social Responsibility, *ECL* 14, no. 1 (2017): 15–21. See also, Tineke Lambooy, *Corporate Social Responsibility: Legal and Semi-Legal Frameworks Supporting CSR* (Deventer: Kluwer 2010), Chapter 4.6: companies listed in The Netherlands prefer to create an extensive complementary CSR report, based on the GRI Sustainability Reporting Guidelines (2006), rather than to provide detailed non-financial information in their annual accounts.

considerable number of options offered to the Member States by the directives. Additionally, the ECJ could not substantially further harmonization, because not many cases have been lodged with the court.[8] At the same time, IAS were evolving. The Commission initially tried to bridge the gap between these standards and Community law by its Interpretative Communication, concerning certain articles in the Fourth and Seventh Directives.[9] By 1999, however, the Commission in its Communication on Accounting Harmonisation recognized both the shortcomings of the Accounting Directives and the need to set standards that are accepted worldwide.[10] The US GAAP (General Accepted Accounting Principles) were internationally accepted, but they were developed without European input. Therefore, the Commission preferred to cooperate with the IASC in order to further develop the IAS. The IAS are more oriented to value-based (market-based, future-oriented) annual accounts, rather than transaction-based accounts (historical, retrospective).

9.06a The roots of the present IAS/IFRS go back to 1973, when the International Accounting Standards Committee (IASC) was formed. France, Germany, the UK and the Netherlands were among the founding members of the IASC, whereas the Commission had 'a difficult relationship' with the IASC. This changed in 1990, because the Commission then finally became an observer at the IASC board meetings.[11] The current International Accounting Standards Board (IASB) succeeded the IASC by 2001 and adopted all IAS that were in force at the time. From then on, standards adopted by the IASB were referred to as the IFRS. The standards are set according to an extended process that may include public consultation.[12]

9.07 The introduction of IAS/IFRS at the EU level dates back to the 2000 Lisbon European Council's endorsement of the Financial Services Action Plan, in order to create a single financial market in Europe. In the aftermath of the Council, Regulation (EC) 1606/2002, more commonly known as the IAS Regulation, was enacted to empower the Commission to identify and adopt the standards that are to be mandatory.[13]

9.08 Article 6 of the IAS Regulation requires the Commission to act in accordance with the procedure of Council Decision 1999/468/EC for the exercise of its

8. *See* e.g., ECJ 27 Jun. 1996, C-234/94 (Gebrüder von der Wettern GmbH), ECJ 3 May 2005, C-387, C-391/02 and C-403/02 (Berlusconi). Further Cases: C-161/78 (Conradsen), C-275/97 (DE + ES Bauunternehmung GmbH), C-306/99 (BIAO), C-234/94 (Tomberger).
9. Interpretative communication concerning certain Articles of the fourth and seventh Council Directives on accounting, OJ 1998, C 016.
10. 'Accounting Harmonisation: A New Stragey vis-à-vis International Harmonisation', Com 95 (508).
11. Barry J. Epstein with contributions by Abbas Ali Mirza, *IFRS 2006. Interpretation and Application of International Accounting and Financial Reporting Standards (Wiley IFRS 2006)* (Hoboken, NJ: John Wiley & Sons, 2006), 11.
12. More on the background of IFRS can be read in: Paul Pacter, *Pocket Guide to IFRS® Standards: The Global Financial Reporting Language* (London: IFRS Foundation, 2016) (downloadable at http://www.ifrs.org).
13. Regulation (EC) 1606/2002 on the application of international accounting standards, OJ 2002, L 243. *See also* the preceding Commission Recommendation *EU Financial Reporting Strategy: the way forward,* COM(2000) 359 of 13 Jun. 2000.

implementing powers. This procedure is made up of several steps. First, the Commission receives recommendations from an advisory group and the opinion of another group before it decides to propose a standard or an interpretation for endorsement. Then, the Accounting Regulatory Committee (with representatives from the Member States) votes on the endorsement. After confirmation by the European Parliament, the Commission makes the final decision on the adoption of standards.[14]

9.09 According to Recital 9 of the Preamble to the IAS Regulation, IAS (now: IFRS), in order to apply throughout the EU, must meet the basic requirement of the Fourth and Seventh Directives (now: Directive 2013/34/EU) – that is to say that its application results in a true and fair view of the financial position and performance of an enterprise. Furthermore, a standard should be conducive to the European public good and meet basic criteria as to the quality of information required for financial statements to be useful to users. Notwithstanding the wording of this recital, critics state that the EU 'is in effect rubber-stamping laws created by a small, self appointed, private sector body'.[15] Nevertheless, the EU, by adopting international standards, contributes toward a 'global accounting convergence'.[16] It must be noted, however, that even if financial statements are prepared according to IFRS, some requirements of the Accounting Directive still have to be applied.[17]

9.10 Starting with Commission Regulation (EC) 1725/2003, numerous standards have been adopted.[18] In 2015, the Commission published an evaluation of the IAS Regulation. According to the evaluation, IFRS was successful in creating a common accounting language for capital markets and companies were mostly positive about their experience of using IFRS. Investors also largely supported IFRS for improving the transparency and comparability of financial statements. Finally, the criteria that all new IFRS should meet to become EU law were deemed appropriate and most stakeholders considered that the process through which IFRS become part of EU law works well.[19] It is estimated that, on a global scale, more than 50,000 listed companies use IFRS.[20]

---

14. *Report from the Commission on the operation of Regulation (EC) No. 1606/2002 of 19 Jul. 2002 on the application of international accounting standards*, Brussels, 24 Apr. 2008, COM(2008) 215 final, 4.
15. *Wiley IFRS 2006*, 11. *See also* http://ec.europa.eu/finance/company-reporting/committees/arc/index_en.htm .
16. Robert K. Larson & Donna L. Street, 'The Roadmap to Global Accounting Convergence', *The CPA Journal* (October 2006), retrieved August 2008 from www.cpajournal.com.
17. List of requirements above IFRSs when IFRS financial statements are prepared http://ec.europa.eu/finance/company-reporting/standards-interpretations/index_en.htm#related-information (accessed May 2017).
18. (EC) No. 1126/2008 of 3 Nov. 2008 adopting certain international accounting standards in accordance with Regulation (EC) No. 1606/2002 of the European Parliament and of the Council, OJ 2008, L 320. See: www.ec.europa.eu/internal_market/accounting/index_en.htm. IFRS 1 'First Time Adoption of IFRS' guides companies to the application of IFRS: http://ec.europa.eu/internal_market/accounting/docs/consolidated/ifrs1_en.pdf (accessed May 2017).
19. *Evaluation of Regulation (EC) No 1606/2002*, Brussels, 18.6.2015, COM(2015) 301 final.
20. According to www.ifrs.org (accessed May 2017).

III GENERAL PRINCIPLES

9.11 The annual financial statements for a public or private limited liability company consist of a balance sheet, a profit and loss account and notes to the financial statements – together, these documents constitute a 'composite whole', Article 4(1) of the Accounting Directive. The annual financial statements must be drawn up clearly and in a non-complex manner, Article 4(2). They must give a *true and fair view* (i.e., a reliable and accurate view) of the company's assets, liabilities, financial position and result (Article 4(3)). If the application of the directive's provisions does not suffice in giving a true and fair view, additional information must be provided (Article 4(3)) and, in exceptional cases, the application of a provision of the directive has to be departed from in order to give a 'true and fair view' (Article 4(4)).

9.12 The Member States must implement provisions in their national law, ensuring that the annual financial statements are prepared adhering to the general principles laid down in Article 6 of the Directive:

(a) The company is deemed to continue its activities. This principle of a business as a *going concern* implies that the assets may be assessed from the presumption that operating equipment, etc., may continue to be applied for the operation of the company. The value of an active asset may be considerably less if it is to be sold to third parties, that is, a value computed at scrap value.
(b) The accounting policies and measurement bases shall be applied *consistently* from one financial year to the next.
(c) A *prudence principle* must always be observed. Thus, Article 6(1)(c) of the Directive prescribes, *inter alia*, that recognition and measurement shall be 'on a prudent basis and in particular: only profits made on the balance sheet date may be recognised'. Concrete effects of this principle are that only realized profits may be included, that regard must be given to all liabilities and that all negative value adjustments must be included, irrespective of whether the result of the financial year is a profit or a loss.[21]
According to the Preamble of the Directive, it is inevitable that the recognition and measurement of some items in financial statements are based on estimates, judgements and models, rather than exact depictions. 'This is especially true in the case of provisions, which by their nature are more uncertain than most other items in the balance sheet. Estimates should be based on a prudent judgement of the management of the undertaking and calculated on an objective basis, supplemented by experience of similar transactions and, in some cases,

21. *See* ECJ 27 Jun. 1996, C-234/94 (*Tomberger v. Gebrüder von der Wettern GmbH*): it is not contrary to the prudence principle if national law requires from a parent company, whose subsidiary has decided to appropriate profits to its parent, that the profits be entered in the parent company's balance sheet for the financial year in which they were appropriated by the subsidiary, instead of the next financial year in which actual payment has taken place.

even reports from independent experts. The evidence considered should include any additional evidence provided by events after the balance-sheet date.'[22]

(d) The amounts recognised in the balance sheet and the profit and loss account shall be computed on the *accrual basis*. The accrual basis requires recording of transactions in the period in which they actually occur, rather than the period in which the cash flows related to these transactions occur.

(e) The opening balance shall correspond to the closing balance sheet for the preceding financial year.

(f) and (g) The components of asset and liability items shall be valued separately and any set-offs between asset and liability items or between income and expenditure are prohibited. The Directive thus prescribes the *gross principle*.

(h) Items shall be accounted for and presented having regard to the substance of the transaction or arrangement concerned. This points towards the *substance over form principle,* meaning that items should be accounted for with regard to their commercial reality, rather than their legal form. This may be of importance, for instance, in reporting the consequences of lease contracts. Although the lessor remains the owner of the asset leased, the lease may shift all risks and rewards towards the lessee. In such a case, the *lessee* must report on the value of the asset. IFRS 16 specifies how leases must be recognised, measured, presented and disclosed.

(i) The items in the financial statements shall be measured in accordance with the principle of purchase price or production cost.

(j) The requirements regarding recognition, measurement, presentation, disclosure and consolidation need not be complied with when the effect of complying with them is immaterial.

9.13 The provisions of the Accounting Directive apply, in principle, to large companies (undertakings) and large groups. Member States may permit several exemptions for micro-undertakings, small undertakings, small groups, medium-sized undertakings and medium-sized groups, as defined by the Directive. The exemptions allowed for micro-undertakings are substantial and they are enumerated in Article 36. Exemptions for the small- and medium-sized categories are mentioned throughout the Directive, where applicable. For instance, Article 14 sums up the simplifications that small- and medium-sized undertakings may apply to their balance sheets and profit and loss account. In Article 17, the categories differ in regard of the mandatory content of the notes to the annual financial statements.

9.13a A company or group is deemed to be a *large undertaking or large group* if it meets at least two of the three following criteria on the balance sheet date (Article 3(4)):

22. Paragraph 22 Preamble of Directive 2013/34/EU.

- balance sheet total: EUR 20,000,000;
- net turnover: EUR 40,000,000;
- average number of employees during the financial year: 250.

A company is deemed to be a *micro-undertaking* if it meets at least two of the three following criteria on the balance sheet date (Article 3(1)):

- balance sheet total: EUR 350,000;
- net turnover: EUR 700,000;
- average number of employees during the financial year: 10.

A company or group is deemed to be a *small undertaking or small group* if it meets at least two of the three following criteria on the balance sheet date (Article 3(2) and (5)):

- balance sheet total: EUR 4,000,000;
- net turnover: EUR 8,000,000;
- average number of employees during the financial year: 50.

A company or group is deemed to be a *medium-sized undertaking or medium-sized group* if it meets at least two of the three following criteria on the balance sheet date (Article 3(3) and (6)):

- balance sheet total: EUR 20,000,000;
- net turnover: EUR 40,000,000;
- average number of employees during the financial year: 250.

A group, for this purpose, consists of parent and subsidiary undertakings, to be included in a consolidation and which, on a consolidated basis, do not exceed the limits of at least two of the three criteria on the balance sheet date of the parent undertaking.

The figures denoting when a company qualifies for the small size status is revised at five-year intervals (Article 3(13)).

IV BALANCE SHEET

9.14 The Accounting Directive contains detailed rules for the drawing up and presentation of the balance sheet in Articles 9–12 and the Annexes. The company has a choice between a presentation in horizontal format (Annex III) or vertical format (Annex IV). The Member States may prescribe one or the other. If a Member State allows both, the choice is left to the individual company (Article 10).

9.15 A horizontal balance sheet is characterized by an enumeration of the company's assets, followed by an enumeration of the capital, reserves and liabilities.

A vertical balance sheet will state the assets, followed by the debts and will be concluded by a statement and specification of the equity (capital and reserves). Thus, a balance sheet in a vertical format will 'compute' its way to the equity as an end item emerging from the preceding figures.

Companies must comply with the specifications of the Directive when drawing up their statements with regard to both contents and order. However, Members States may permit companies to make even more detailed subdivisions of the items, as long as the prescribed layouts are complied with (Article 9(2)). Some of the items may need to be combined (Article 9(3)). For each item on the balance sheet and profit and loss account, the figure relating to the corresponding item for the preceding financial year must be shown for comparison purposes (Article 9(5)).

9.16 In the following paragraph, the balance sheet according to the Annexes in the Directive is briefly discussed. It must be noted, however, that the Directive offers many options to the Member States and, for that reason, jurisdictions show considerable variations in both presentation and valuation of the balance sheet. In addition, it must be stressed that IFRS differ in many respects from the rules set by the Directive. This is addressed by a few remarks only, which will provide a general idea regarding the nature of these differences.

9.17 According to Annexes III and IV of the Directive, the balance sheet must state as assets:

- *Subscribed, but not paid-up capital,* unless the law of the Member State provides that called-up capital must be shown under 'Capital and reserves' (paragraph A).
- *Formation expenses* must be listed where national law allows such expenses to be shown as assets (paragraph B). Where the state allows the inclusion of such expenses under 'assets', they must be written off within a maximum period of five years; Article 12(11).
- Subsequently, the *fixed assets* of the company must be stated (paragraph C). These will generally include assets intended for use on a continuing basis for the company's operation; Article 12(3). The concept of fixed assets covers intangible assets (e.g., costs of R&D and patents), tangible assets (e.g., land, buildings, equipment) and financial assets (e.g., shares in affiliated companies, investments held as fixed assets).
  In regard to the *valuation* of fixed assets in the balance sheet, it is noted that they must be shown at purchase price or production cost (Article (6(1)(i)). Member States may permit or require that fixed assets are measured at revaluated amounts (Article 7(1)). The amount of the difference between measurement on a purchase price or production cost basis and measurement on a revaluation basis shall be entered in the balance sheet in the revaluation reserve under 'Capital and reserves' (Article 7(2)).
  Where the commercial exploitation of a fixed asset is limited in time, the price or production cost must be reduced by *writing* off the value of such assets systematically over their useful economic lives (Article 12(5)). It must be

noted that the accounting write-off of fixed assets may well deviate from the tax depreciation made, to the extent that an asset depreciates often more rapidly in a tax context than in an accounting context.
Member States may permit or require measurement 'at fair value' for assets that are financial instruments, including derivative financial instruments. Fair value is the market value, if there is a market for the financial instrument or, in case no market can be identified, the value resulting from generally accepted valuation models and techniques that ensure a reasonable approximation of the market value (Article 8(7)).
Under the heading of 'intangible assets', *goodwill* must be shown, if such value was acquired against a valuable consideration. The goodwill mentioned is the amount paid as a specified additional price, in excess of the fair value of demonstrable assets at the purchase stage of a business. Where goodwill is capitalized, it must be written off within a maximum period set by the Member State between five and ten years (Article 12(11)). This is one example out of many, where IFRS take a different approach by not allowing for this method of write-off. The standard of IFRS 36 requires a yearly review of the activated goodwill in order to determine whether it has suffered any impairment. Only if it has, may partial or complete write-off of this asset follows.
The national law determines whether a purchase of goodwill may be deducted or written off in the tax accounts of the undertaking and the extent to which the consideration received for a sale of goodwill is liable to tax.

- The balance sheet's assets must further contain *Current assets* (Annex III, paragraph D: stocks, debtors, investments, cash) and *Prepayments and accrued income* (paragraph E).
  An example of an item to be stated under 'current assets' is the debtors of the company, being the (outstanding) claims of the company. Claims may derive from sales and services rendered (trade debtors), which may consist of claims against associated undertakings, or against undertakings in which the company holds a participating interest (subsidiary companies and associated companies) and must be specified as such. The same applies to subscribed share capital that has been called but has not yet been paid up (unless national law prescribes that such capital be stated under heading A, as previously mentioned) and prepayments and accrued income (unless national law prescribes that it has to be stated under a separate heading, which is under the already mentioned paragraph E).

9.18 So far, both layouts specified in Annex III (horizontal layout) and Annex IV (vertical layout) follow the same pattern. The listing, however, subsequently varies according to whether the balance sheet is made in horizontal form or vertical form:

(a) In horizontal format, an enumeration of capital, reserves and liabilities must follow.

(b) In contrast, the balance sheet in vertical format continues its report of company property matters by stating, under paragraph F, the debts due within one year, followed by the net current assets (paragraph G) and another total in the form of a statement of all the assets, after the deduction of current liabilities paragraph H), and so on.

9.19 Both Annexes sum up the *capital, reserves and liabilities* that have to be mentioned (albeit positioned differently, depending on the horizontal or vertical layout):

- The amount of subscribed capital must be stated, as well as the premium paid at issue, the revaluation reserve (and other reserves) and the profit or loss for the financial year (paragraph A in the horizontal layout).
  The directive does not mention the concept *of subordinated capital (mezzanine)* (*see* paragraph 5.28). Such capital is a loan and may not be entered under equity, but because it is a debt commitment, it must be reflected under 'debts'. A company may find it useful to enter it as a separate item in the balance sheet and provide more information on the terms of the loan, such as currency, rate of interest, and so forth, in the notes of the accounts.
- Under the next item (B), *Provisions*, the company must state, *inter alia*, pensions and similar obligations and provisions for taxation. In general, provisions are 'liabilities, the nature of which is clearly defined and which at the balance sheet date are either likely to be incurred or certain to be incurred, but uncertain as to their amount or as to the date on which they will arise'. (Article 12(12)).
  The IFRS specify detailed rules for the recognition of a provision. According to IAS 37, a provision can only be a present obligation because of a past event, probably leading to a future outflow of resources, the amount of which can be reasonably estimated. These requirements no longer permit vaguely defined reserves, such as restructuring reserves created upon the completion of a merger process. Because only *present* obligations are recognized, future restructuring costs will have to be recognized after the merger.[23]
- *Creditors* are the next heading (C) under liabilities and here, like the debtors in the assets part of the balance sheet, several items have to be separately stated, *inter alia*, debenture loans, amounts owed to credit institutions, trade creditors and amounts owed to affiliated undertakings.
- Following this, *Accruals and deferred income* (D) are stated, unless national law provides for such items to be shown under *Creditors*.

23. Wiley IFRS 2006, *supra* n. 15, 424.

V PROFIT AND LOSS ACCOUNT

9.20 EU law also provides options for the layout of the profit and loss account (Article 13). Member States may prescribe one of the options provided or they may leave the choice among them to the companies themselves. The choice is between a layout based on the nature of expenses (Annex V) and a layout based on the function of expenses (Annex VI):

(1) The first layout starts with the net turnover and operating income and continues, *inter alia*, with expenses for raw materials, staff and value adjustments, all taken together, in order to close with the profit or loss for the financial year.

(2) The second layout also starts with the net turnover, but continues with entries like cost of sales and administrative expenses and ends, as a matter of course, also with the profit or loss for the financial year.

9.20a Among the IFRS adopted by the EU is IAS 1, Presentation of Financial Statements.[24] According to this standard, 'Profit or loss is the total of income less expenses, excluding the components of other comprehensive income.' The total comprehensive income of a company 'is the change in equity during a period resulting from transactions and other events, other than those changes resulting from transactions with owners in their capacity as owners' (IAS 1.7). The profit and loss may be presented in a single statement of profit or loss and other comprehensive income, with profit or loss and other comprehensive income presented in two sections. But it is also allowed to present the profit or loss section in a separate statement of profit or loss. If so, that statement shall immediately precede the statement presenting comprehensive income, which shall begin with profit or loss (IAS 1.10A). Among the items to be presented in the statement regarding profit or loss are:

- revenue, presenting interest revenue separately;
- gains and losses arising from the derecognition of financial assets measured at amortized cost;
- finance costs;
- impairment losses;
- share of the profit or loss of associates and joint ventures accounted for using the equity method;
- tax expense;
- a single amount for the total of discontinued operations.[25]

24. Commission Regulation (EC) No. 1126/2008 (consolidated version) http://eur-lex.europa.eu/legal-content/EN/TXT/PDF/?uri=CELEX:32008R1126&from=EN.
25. IAS 1.81A *et seq.*

VI NOTES ON THE ANNUAL FINANCIAL STATEMENTS

9.21 Together with the balance sheet and profit and loss account, the notes to the financial statements make up a composite whole (Article 4(1)). The notes are thus an integrated component of the annual financial statements. The content of the notes is partly determined by the items and their order in the balance sheet and the profit and loss account. For example, if application of a provision of the Directive is incompatible with the true and fair view requirement, the disapplication of such provision shall be disclosed in the notes, together with an explanation of the reasons for it and of its effect (Article 4(3) and (4)). In the same vein, departures from the prescribed layout of the balance sheet or profit and loss account may be permitted, but the departure and the reasons therefor shall be disclosed in the notes (Article 9(1)). Lastly, value adjustments in respect of financial fixed assets or other fixed assets shall be disclosed separately in the notes if they have not been shown separately in the profit and loss account (Article 12(6)(c)).

9.22 Furthermore, Article 16 lists a large number of matters that must be set out in the notes to the financial statements of *all undertakings*.

Among these matters are:

- the accounting policies adopted;
- detailed information on revaluation of fixed assets and financial instruments;
- the total amount of any financial commitments, guarantees or contingencies that are not included in the balance sheet;
- the amount of advances and credit granted to members of the administrative, managerial and supervisory bodies (note that the extent to which such loans are allowed is a matter for national law).

Article 17 requires additional disclosures for *medium-sized and large undertakings and for public-interest entities* (these are, *inter alia*, listed companies and credit institutions as defined in Article 2(1)).

Among the additional disclosures are:

- more specific information on the valuation of fixed assets and (derivative) financial instruments;
- the name and registered office of each of the undertakings, in which the undertaking, either by itself or through a person acting in his own name, but on the undertaking's behalf, holds a participating interest;
- the nature and business purpose of arrangements that are not included in the balance sheet ('off-balance sheet arrangements'), provided that the risks or benefits arising from such arrangements are material and in so far as the disclosure is necessary for the purposes of assessing the financial position of the undertaking;
- information regarding transactions, which have been entered into with related parties: Members States may permit or require that disclosure is limited, *inter*

alia, to transactions that have not been concluded under normal market conditions and/or that intragroups transactions are exempted from disclosure.

Article 2(3) refers to IFRS (IAS 24) for the meaning of related parties. These are, *inter alia*, close relatives of key management members if they have or can be expected to have significant influence (via the key management member) on the dealings of the company. Although party relationships are a normal feature of commerce and business, transparency regarding transactions with related parties is deemed necessary because they may be effected on different terms (i.e., not at arm's length) than transactions with unrelated parties. It is noted that there seems to be 'particular resistance to reporting certain types of related-party transactions, such as loans to directors, key management personnel, or close members of the executive's families'.[26] Intragroup transactions are also prone to suboptimal conditions. If, for instance, a subsidiary sells goods to its parent at cost price it might not sell on those terms to another customer. Nevertheless, Member States may exempt intragroup transactions if subsidiaries that are party to the transaction are wholly owned (Article 17(1)(r)).

Article 18 requires even more additional disclosures for *large undertakings* and *public-interest entities*.

These additional disclosures concern the following matters:

- the net turnover broken down by categories of activity and into geographical markets, in so far as those categories and markets differ substantially from one another, taking account of the manner in which the sale of products and the provision of services are organized;
- the total fees for the financial year charged by each statutory auditor or audit firm for the statutory audit of the annual financial statements, and the total fees charged by each statutory auditor or audit firm for other assurance, tax advisory and for other non-audit services.

Members States may allow omission of the additional information on the net turnover if disclosure would be seriously prejudicial to the undertaking (Article 18(2)).

VII THE MANAGEMENT REPORT

9.23 According to EU law, the management report is not an integral component of the annual financial statements of the company, but rather constitutes a natural 'addendum' hereto. Although the statements must be submitted in their entirety to the registration authority and made available to the public, Member States may exempt the management report from mandatory publication, provided that a copy of all or part of the report can be easily obtained upon request (Article 30(1)).

The management report must include a fair review of the development and performance of the company's business and its position, including the principal risks and uncertainties it faces. To the extent necessary for understanding of the company's

26. Wiley IFRS 2006, *supra* n. 15, 776.

development, performance or position, both financial and, where appropriate, non-financial key performance indicators must be mentioned. This includes information relating to environmental and employee matters (Article 19(1)).

Further, the management report must describe the following:

(a) the company's likely future development;
(b) the activities in the field of research and development;
(c) the reasons underlying the company's acquisition of its own shares and the number and nominal value of such shares;[27]
(d) the company's existing branches;
(e) in relation to the company's use of financial instruments, the company's financial risk management objectives and policies, and its exposure to price risk, credit risk, liquidity risk and cash flow risk.

9.23a Member States may exempt small companies from the obligation of preparing a management report, as long as they make the mandatory disclosure under Article 24(2) of Directive 2012/30/EU on the acquisition of their own shares in the notes to the annual financial statements (Article 19(3)). Small- and medium-sized companies may be exempted from the obligation to provide non-financial information on the development and performance of their business (Article 19(4)).

9.24 In 2014, Directive 2014/95/EU was enacted in order to oblige public-interest undertakings to provide non-financial information in the management report. Large undertakings that are public-interest entities and have, on average, more than 500 employees shall provide a statement concerning the undertaking's development, performance, position and impact of its activity, relating to, as a minimum, environmental, social and employee matters, respect for human rights, anti-corruption and bribery matters.[28] The information has to be provided 'to the extent necessary for an understanding' of these aspects. The obligation is included in the Accounting Directive, Article 19a(1).

9.24a The obligation to provide non-financial information is further detailed by Article 19a. The policies and risks in relation to the matters mentioned in the previous paragraph (environmental, social and employee matters, etc.) shall be described and the non-financial key performance indicators must be mentioned. If the undertaking does not pursue policies in relation to one or more of those matters, the non-financial statement must provide a clear and reasoned explanation for not doing so. Member States may require that the information in the non-financial statement must be verified by an independent assurance services provider (Article 19a(6)).

27. *See* 24(2) of Directive 2012/30/EU.
28. OJ 2014, L 330, included as Article 19a in the consolidated version of Directive 2013/34/EU http://eur-lex.europa.eu/legal-content/EN/TXT/PDF/?uri=CELEX:02013L0034-20141211&from=EN.

9.24b Articles 41 *et seq.* deal with the report on payments to governments, which is to be drawn up and published by large undertakings and public-interest entities active in the extractive industry or the logging of primary forests. The obligation serves to support the implementation of principles set by the Extractive Industries Transparency Initiative. These undertakings and entities have to prepare and publish a report on payments of EUR 100,000 or more (on an annual basis) made to governments of countries with rich natural resources (Preamble, paragraphs 44 *et seq.*). Member States shall ensure that the members of the responsible bodies of an undertaking will, to the best of their knowledge and ability, draw up and publish the report on payments to governments in accordance with the requirements of Directive 2013/34.

9.25 Another category of non-financial information concerns corporate governance. The obligation to provide information on this subject was introduced by Directive 2006/46/EC[29] and is laid down in Article 20 of the Accounting Directive. The obligation applies to listed companies, in order to enhance the comparability of financial statements and reports throughout the EU.[30] The corporate governance statement of listed companies must include, *inter alia*, a reference to the corporate governance code that the company is subject to, deviations from such a code (in case deviation is allowed by national law) and a description of the company's internal control and risk management systems in relation to the financial reporting process.

9.25a The corporate governance statement must also provide for information required by the Takeover Directive, such as restrictions on voting rights, information on the operation of the shareholder meeting and shareholders' rights and for information on the composition and operation of the administrative, management and supervisory bodies and their committees. Furthermore, a description of the diversity policy on the company's administrative, management and supervisory bodies must be added.[31] Such policy concerns, for instance, age, gender or educational and professional backgrounds. The objectives and results of that diversity policy must be set out. If no such policy is applied, the statement shall contain an explanation as to why this is the case (Article 20). The obligation to report on the diversity policy does not apply to small- or medium-sized listed companies (Article 20(5)).

VIII PUBLICATION OF THE ANNUAL FINANCIAL STATEMENTS

9.26 The responsibility and liability for drawing up and publishing of the annual financial statements is on the members of the administrative, management and supervisory bodies collectively. The same collective duties apply in regard to the management report, the corporate governance statement (if provided separately) and the consolidated version of these documents. Where applicable, the content and publication should happen in accordance with the IAS, adopted in accordance with Regulation (EC) 1606/2002. Publication must take place within a reasonable period of

29. OJ 2006, L 224.
30. Preamble paragraph 13, OJ 2006, L 224.
31. This obligation is introduced by Directive 2014/95/EU.

time, which shall not exceed twelve months (Article 30(1)). Member States must further ensure that a breach of these duties may lead to liability of the members of the corporate bodies (Article 33). Member States have to impose penalties where disclosure requirements are not respected (*see* paragraph 3.23).

9.26a The fact that competitors may inspect their annual accounts may keep businesses from complying with the disclosure requirements. German legislation actually restricted competitors from filing requests to the court in order to impose penalties on a company that does not publish its annual accounts. In *Daihatsu Deutschland GmbH,* the ECJ held that Article 6 of the First Directive precludes the legislation of a Member State from restricting the right to apply for imposition of the penalty to members of the company and its creditors and works council. Daihatsu GmbH failed to submit accounts for publication with the registration authority for several years. The union of German car dealers brought proceedings to gain access to the accounts, but the issue was referred to the ECJ, because German law only granted shareholders and current company creditors the right to sue in this respect. The ECJ emphasized that the Company Law Directives were designed to assist the implementation of the freedom of establishment, as well as to protect third parties. It held that Article 3 of the First Directive confirms the concern of enabling any interested persons to avail themselves of the financial information that should be made available to the public by companies that are in competition with one another. Therefore, a third party, such as the union of Daihatsu dealers, would be entitled to sue and German legislation had to be adapted accordingly.[32]

9.26b In another case, the publishing company Axel Springer AG had filed a request with the local court to impose penalties on a small competitor that was carrying out its business as a GmbH & Co (*see* paragraph 2.46). The small publisher, according to Axel Springer, had to disclose its annual accounts for the year 2000 with the local commercial register. The local court (Landgericht Essen) referred the case to the ECJ on fundamental questions, such as the relationship between the freedom to exercise a trade or profession and the obligation to publish annual accounts without any restriction to the group of persons entitled to inspect these documents. The ECJ ordered that it could not discover any reason to affect the validity of Directive 90/605, which inserted disclosure requirements for limited partnerships into the First Directive.[33] Note that, in this respect, according to Schön, disclosure of the annual accounts has effects on the competitive environment and, therefore, the EU should alleviate the disclosure requirements for closely held companies.[34]

9.27 Where the annual financial statements and the management report are published in full, they must be reproduced in the form and with the text on the basis of

32. ECJ, 4 Dec. 1997, C-97/96 (Daihatsu Deutschland GmbH). Wolfgang Schön, *Corporate Disclosure in a Competitive Environment*, ECGI Working Papers Series in Law, 2006, retrievable from the website of the European Corporate Governance Institute (ECGI), www.ecgi.org.
33. ECJ, 23 Sep. 2004 in Joined Cases C-435/02 and C-103/03 (*Axel Springer AG v. Zeitungsverlag Niederrhein GmbH & Co. Essen KG and Hans-Jürgen Weske*).
34. Schön, *Corporate Disclosure in a Competitive Environment*, 40–41.

which the statutory auditor (or audit firm) has drawn up his opinion. The full text of the audit report shall also be published (Article 32(1)). The publication requirements may be alleviated in different ways:

- Member States may make an exemption for the publication of the management report if such a report is easily obtainable upon request (Article 30(1)).
- The audit report shall not be published if the annual financial statements and the management report are published in an abridged form (Article 32(2)). Abridged versions of the annual financial statements are allowed for micro-undertakings, small- and medium-sized undertakings (Article 31; *see also* paragraphs 9.13 *et seq.*).
- Member States may exempt general partnerships and limited partnerships from the obligation to publish financial statements. However, this exemption does not fully apply in two situations. First, if all partners that have unlimited liability are companies (as mentioned in Annex I) governed by the law of a Member State other than the one whose law governs the partnership and none of these companies publishes the financial statements of the partnership with its own financial statements (Article 30(2)(a)). The second situation that does not allow for exemption of general partnerships from publication requirements happens if all partners that have unlimited liability are companies (undertakings), not governed by the laws of a Member State, but with a legal form comparable to the companies and partnerships mentioned in Article 1 of Directive 2009/101/EC (Article 30(2)(b)). If one of those situations occurs, the partnership must provide that the financial statements are available to the public at its head office (Article 30(2)).

IX REPORTS TO BE PUBLISHED BY LISTED COMPANIES

9.28 For listed companies, the 1982 directive on 'information to be published on a regular basis' (Directive 82/121/EEC) introduced additional rules for the mandatory periodic disclosure of information, including half-yearly reports. This directive was incorporated in Directive 2001/34/EC, which, in turn, has been amended several times.[35] The legislative basis of the additional obligations changed again when provisions regarding the flow of information that listed companies have to provide to financial markets were included in the 2004 Transparency Directive (*see* paragraph 3.103d).[36] Apart from annual financial statements, half-yearly financial reports shall be made public by listed companies, covering the first six months of the financial year (Article 5). The directive applies to listed companies and, in principle, to all other issuers of securities who are admitted to trading on a regulated market in a Member

35. Directive 2001/34/EC on the admission of securities to official stock exchange listings and on information to be published on those securities, OJ 2001, L 184 (amended).
36. Directive 2004/109/EC (as amended), OJ 2004, L 390. References are made to the consolidated version http://eur-lex.europa.eu/legal-content/en/TXT/?uri=CELEX:02004L0109-20131126&qid=1483900264194 .

State (Article 1).[37] Technological developments have a bearing on financial reporting of listed companies. It is envisaged that, from 1 January 2020 onwards, all annual financial reports must have a single electronic format. The European Securities and Markets Authority (ESMA) will draft regulatory technical standards to specify this format and the power is delegated to the Commission to adopt these standards (Article 4(7)).

9.28a The annual financial report to be made public by listed companies (and other issuers of securities) must include the audited financial statements, the management report and the statements made by a company's board members[38] that the financial statements, 'to the best of their knowledge', provide a true and fair view. Furthermore, they have to state that the management report includes a fair review of, *inter alia*, the performance of the business of the company and of the principal risks and uncertainties that the company faces (Article 4(2)). The audit report must be disclosed in full, together with the annual financial report (Article 4(4)). If the company is required to prepare consolidated accounts, the audited financial statements shall comprise these accounts (Article 4(3)).

9.28b The half-yearly financial report includes a condensed set of financial statements, an interim management report and statements, similar to the statements by a company's board members,[39] as already mentioned. With regard to the interim management report, the board members have to state that it includes a fair review of, *inter alia*, important events that occurred during the first six months of the financial year and of the principal risks and uncertainties for the remaining six months (Article 5(2)(4)). If the half-yearly report has been audited, the audit report shall be reproduced in full (Article 5(5)).

9.28c The Directive empowers the European Commission to enact delegated regulations in order to deal with more detailed and technical matters; *see* Article 4(6) and (7) and Article 5(6).[40] In delegated Regulation (EU)2016/1437, the Commission deals with regulatory technical standards on access to regulated information at EU level. It provides that ESMA shall set up a web portal, in order to enable end users to search for regulated information. The portal is called European Electronic Access Point (EEAP) and it will be accessible through ESMA's website (Article 1). In December 2016, ESMA published a statement setting out the digital format, which listed companies must use to report their information from 1 January 2020. *Inline XBRL* is said to be the most

37. Member States may make a few exemptions as described in Articles 1 and 8.
38. Literally: 'the persons responsible within the issuer'. *See also* Article 7 on responsibility and liability.
39. Literally: 'the persons responsible within the issuer'. *See also* Article 7 on responsibility and liability.
40. Commission Delegated Regulation (EU) 2016/1437, OJ 2016 L 234. *See* further http://ec.europa.eu/finance/company-reporting/legal-framework/index_en.htm#legal-acts-other (accessed May 2017).

suitable technology for issuers to report their annual financial reports in a single electronic format, because it enables both machine and human readability.[41]

X CONSOLIDATED FINANCIAL REPORTS

9.29 The provisions of the Seventh Directive on consolidated accounts were originally designed to be an integrated part of the Fourth Directive.[42] However, due to a debate concerning the scope of the consolidation, the Fourth Directive went ahead without provisions on consolidated accounts. In particular, the debate related to the applicability to: (1) certain types of companies; (2) companies in which the parent company has minority holdings; and (3) horizontal groups ('co-ordination groups'), in the sense of companies sharing only management and certain functions.

9.30 The solution eventually adopted was the 'parent company' definition. It presupposes control by the 'parent' of a company body in two forms. One is in the form of control of the majority of the voting rights in the general meeting of the subsidiary. The other is in the power to appoint or dismiss the majority of the members of the administrative, managerial or supervisory bodies of the subsidiary (which is the same as controlling at least one company body of lower rank than the general meeting) (Article 1, Seventh Directive). In general, the main notion of the group concept of the Seventh Directive was that a group exists when at least one of the company bodies of the subsidiary is controlled. It is important to note that EU law contains no mandatory group definition in company law, with the exception of matters relating to accounting.[43] Consequently, Member States may themselves set definitions for group concepts in areas other than in accounting law.

9.30a The group concept is extensively debated in Chapter 10. The decision-making within the EEC regarding this issue in relation to consolidation is described by Diggle and Nobes. They conclude that the first memorandum on consolidation (1970) had several German features, notably a definition of the group based on central control. The first draft of the Seventh Directive was published in 1976, that is, after the accession of the UK, Ireland and Denmark, which, with the Netherlands, supported the so-called Anglo-Saxon accounting method, as opposed to the other Member States at the time that practised the 'continental accounting method'. This eventually led to a different approach in the directive, which was enacted in 1983. The directive proclaims the parent–subsidiary relationship as the starting point, but allows for alternative criteria

41. *Feedback Statement on the Consultation Paper on the Regulatory Technical Standard on the European Single Electronic Format (ESEF)*, 21 Dec. 2016, ESMA/2016/1668.
42. Seventh Directive, 83/349/EEC, OJ 1983, L 193.
43. Reference is made to paragraph 3.86, the Takeover Directive which uses 'control' with a different meaning. Furthermore, 3.89, 'control' as defined in the Merger Regulation.

for the group to be consolidated, among these forms of central control (Article 1).[44] The mixture of approaches is expressed in the second recital of the Preamble to the Seventh Directive:

> [w]hereas, in the determination of the conditions for consolidation, account must be taken not only of cases in which the power of control is based on a majority of voting rights but also of those in which it is based on agreements, where these are permitted; whereas, furthermore, Member States in which the possibility occurs must be permitted to cover cases in which in certain circumstances control has been effectively exercised on the basis of a minority holding; whereas the Member States must be permitted to cover the case of bodies of undertakings in which the undertakings exist on an equal footing with each other.

9.30b The IFRS, of course, also pertain to consolidated reporting. According to IFRS 10, Appendix A, consolidated financial statements are the financial statements of a group, presented as those of a single economic entity. A group is a parent and its subsidiaries. A subsidiary is an entity, including an unincorporated entity, such as a partnership, which is controlled by another entity (known as the parent). Interestingly, the IFRS define control not only in terms of power, but also require that the parent is entitled to variable returns and has the ability to use its power to affect the amount of returns (IFRS 10.6 and 7).

9.31 In line with the predecessing Seventh Directive, the Accounting Directive, in Article 22, deals extensively with the issue of how to identify a parent undertaking (company). This is already explained in paragraph 3.66b. Member States have the option, to a certain extent, to choose one or more of the criteria mentioned in Article 22, to determine which companies are to be regarded as parent undertakings and, as a consequence, have to draw up consolidated financial statements.

9.32 The parent undertaking and its subsidiaries shall be consolidated by the parent undertaking (Article 22). The duty to consolidate is, prima facie, not dependent on the legal form of the parent or subsidiary. The main rule prescribes a duty to prepare consolidated financial statements if the parent undertaking is among the undertakings listed in Annex I: a public limited liability company, a private limited company or a public limited partnership (limited partnership with shares; paragraph 2.47) (Article 21 and Article 1). The same applies for undertakings mentioned in Annex II: a partnership or a limited partnership, in which all members, having unlimited liability, are public or private limited liability companies from an EU Member State or a having a comparable legal form, while being governed by the law of a non-EU State. The duty to prepare consolidated financial statements will lie irrespective of where the registered office of the subsidiary is situated (Article 22(6)). Thus, a company (undertaking) in an EU State is bound to consolidate the financial statements of all its subsidiaries outside the EU.

44. Graham Diggel & Cristopher Nobes, 'European Rule-Making in Accounting: The Seventh Directive as a Case Study', in *International Accounting and Comparative Financial Reporting: Selected Essays of Christopher Nobes* (Cheltenham (UK)/Northampton (MA, USA): Edward Elgar Publishing, 1999), 177 *et seq.*

9.32a Member States may exempt a subsidiary from the obligations of the Directive regarding the content, auditing and publication of the annual financial statements and the management report, if a total number of seven conditions are met. Among these, are that the subsidiary is consolidated and the parent undertaking has declared that it guarantees 'the commitments entered into by the subsidiary undertaking' (Article 37). Note that consolidated statements will aggregate operational and balance sheet figures from a grouping of companies as if they were one single business. The summing up process may cause important information to be lost, with regard to the individual company's result and balance sheet. Therefore, conditions like the guarantee serve to protect the interest of creditors and other interested parties.

9.33 Member States have to exempt small groups from the obligation duty to prepare consolidated financial statements and a consolidated management report. They may allow the same exemption for medium-sized groups, except where an undertaking within the group is a public-interest entity (Article 23(1) and (2)).[45] Furthermore, an (mandatory) exemption is made for a parent company that itself is a subsidiary of another parent company governed by the law of a Member State. Such an intermediate-level company is not required to prepare consolidated financial statements on its own and on its subsidiaries' behalf, if it is wholly owned by its EU-based parent or at least 90% of it is owned with other shareholders, consenting to exempt the intermediate company from preparing consolidated accounts. The exemption is conditional on, *inter alia*, the intermediate-level company being consolidated by a parent company, governed by the law of a Member State or even of a non-EU state (Article 23(4) and (8)). Of course, a non-EU parent company has to draw up the consolidated financial statements in accordance with the Accounting Directive and the IFRS, or in a manner equivalent to these. Article 23(5) offers further options for Member States regarding the exemption of this requirement for intermediate companies. Listed companies at an intermediate level cannot be exempted from the obligation to draw up consolidated financial statements (Article 23(3)).

A Exclusion of Individual Undertakings

9.34 In certain cases, an undertaking need not be included in the consolidation. To start with, an undertaking may be excluded from consolidation, if the information necessary to prepare the consolidated financial statements cannot be obtained without disproportionate expense or undue delay. An exemption can further be made if the shares in a company are held exclusively with a view to their subsequent resale. Another case mentioned in Article 23(9) is where severe long-term restrictions substantially hinder the parent company to exercise its rights regarding the management of the undertaking. This exemption reveals that undertakings, although covered by the definition of a subsidiary, cannot always be deemed to be in a group relationship with the parent company. Finally, undertakings may be excluded on the grounds of

45. In these provisions, the term 'affiliated undertaking' is used, which is defined as undertaking within a group, Article 2(12).

immateriality (Article 28(2)(a)). If all subsidiaries are immaterial for compliance with the Directive, the parent company is exempted from the obligation to consolidate (Article 23(10)).

9.35 Member States may permit a partly owned subsidiary to only be proportionally included in the consolidated accounts (Article 26). This proportional inclusion – which is a practical device, where joint ventures must be included in the annual accounts – also implies that the undertakings owning the rest of the shares in the subsidiary are not included in the consolidation.

B Contents of Consolidated Financial Statements

9.36 The methods that must be applied when drawing up the consolidated financial statements are, to a considerable extent, built upon the provisions for the financial statements of the single undertaking. Article 24 starts by providing that Chapters 2 and 3 of the Directive 'shall apply in respect of consolidated financial statements, taking into account the essential adjustments resulting from the particular characteristics of consolidated financial statements as compared to annual financial statements'. As a consequence, consolidated financial statements consist of a consolidated balance sheet and consolidated profit and loss account, as well as notes to the financial statements, and these documents constitute a composite whole. The consolidated financial statements must give the true and fair view as described in Article 4. As previously explained for the annual financial statements, the requirement of a true and fair view is the overriding principle. It can lead to the necessity of providing further information and, if certain provisions in the Directive are incompatible with the true and fair view principle, the relevant provision must be departed from. The departure must be disclosed and explained in the notes (Article 4(4)).

9.37 When an undertaking is included in the consolidation, all its assets and liabilities are incorporated in full in the consolidated balance sheet, except, of course, where proportional consolidation is allowed (Article 24(2)). The income and expenditure of all the undertakings comprised by the consolidation must also be incorporated in full in the consolidated profit and loss account (Article 24(5)).

9.37a Because the parent company must necessarily have entered the value of its share in the capital of a subsidiary, the amount thus entered must be deducted in connection with the consolidation. As Article 24(3) states: 'The book values of shares in the capital of undertakings included in a consolidation shall be set off against the proportion which they represent of the capital and reserves of those undertakings.' Differences arising from such set-offs must be entered in the consolidated balance sheet as a separate item (Article 24(3)(a)). Where the amount is positive, it shall be shown as 'goodwill' in the consolidated balance sheet (Article 24(3)(c)).

9.38 The consolidated financial statements must show the assets, liabilities, financial positions, profits or losses of the consolidated companies as if they were a single undertaking (Article 24(7)). This is the key provision in the Directive. As regards the balance sheet, it implies that mutual claims and debts between the companies have to be eliminated. For the profit and loss account, it means that expenses and income deriving from transactions between the consolidated undertakings are excluded. However, the latter exclusion will not neutralize profits or losses (deriving from mutual transactions between the consolidated undertakings), which may be included in the book value of assets. Such profits and losses must be neutralized via the consolidation.

9.39 In principle, the consolidated financial statements must be drawn up as on the same date as the annual financial statements of the parent company but exemptions may be allowed (Article 24(8)). The principle of aiming, as far as possible, at the same financial year for undertakings in a group is also present in the tax law of several Member States to avoid time displacements. In accounting law, the fear is usually that profits are brought forward, whereas in tax law, the fear is for profits to be deferred – in both instances, by exploiting the fact that one company terminates its financial year while other companies in the group are still in the middle of their financial year.

9.40 In order to satisfy the key provision of the directive in Article 24 that consolidated financial statements must present the undertakings as a single undertaking, it is necessary that the assets and liabilities in the various undertakings be evaluated using uniform methods (Article 24(10)). However, undertakings comprised in the consolidation may have varying value assessment methods. To offset this, it is necessary that such assets and liabilities be revalued by applying the methods used at the consolidation (Article 24(12)).

9.41 Participating interests in associated undertakings (in which 20% or more of the voting rights is controlled, Article 2(13), which are not included in the consolidation) should, as a main rule, be shown as a separate item in the consolidated balance sheet. How the value of such participation shall be calculated is prescribed by Article 27.

9.42 The notes to the consolidated financial statements are subject to the same provisions as the annual financial statements, taking into account essential adjustments resulting from the characteristics of consolidated financial statements. An example is that, in disclosing related-party transactions, transactions between related parties included in the consolidation shall not be included (Article 28).

9.43 The requirements with respect to the consolidated management report are basically the same as the requirements for the management report of a single undertaking. Of course, essential adjustments may result from the characteristics of consolidated financial statements, which facilitate the assessment of the position of consolidated undertakings as a whole (Article 29).

9.44 The obligation to disclose non-financial information is, again, basically the same as prescribed for single undertakings (*see* paragraph 9.24). The obligation applies to public-interest entities that are parent undertakings of a large group with more than 500 employees (Article 29a). Concerning the payments to governments (*see* paragraph 9.24b), large undertakings and public-interest entities have to draw up a consolidated report (Article 44).

XI AUDIT

9.45 The annual financial statements and the consolidated financial statements must be audited and the auditor must verify that the (consolidated) management report is consistent with the consolidated financial statements (Article 34). What the audit report shall include is set out in the amended Article 28 of Directive 2006/43/EC. There is no duty of having the consolidated accounts audited by the same person who audits the parent company's own annual accounts, though this will often be a more practical solution. *See* for more details about statutory auditors, appointment of auditors and audit committees paragraphs 3.70 *et seq.*

CHAPTER 10

Groups

I INTRODUCTION

10.01 In the preceding chapters of this book, the company has been mainly referred to as an independent legal entity. This is logical, because virtually all company laws – not only in Europe but all over the world – basically consider the company to be a separate legal entity, having its own economic business interests to pursue. Although companies can operate on their own, they frequently do so in group structures. Listed companies often head a group of subsidiaries, but also medium-sized and even small businesses operate in groups. Group structures are created for a number of reasons, ranging from the spreading of risks to facilitating succession (in family-owned businesses). They may be tax driven and they may result from takeovers. Groups of companies, although regarded as exceptional in law, have become the rule, thereby causing a discrepancy between company law and economic reality.

10.02 The various reasons for setting up group structures are summarized in a consultation document by the UK Company Law Review Steering Group (2000):

> The most obvious company law consideration favouring the use of subsidiaries is the scope to readjust the level of limited liability afforded to the group as a whole. For example, by holding valuable assets, such as group freehold properties, in a non-trading subsidiary and placing higher risk activities in a subsidiary with few assets, a parent reduces risk. However, there is a much wider variety of reasons why businesses choose a group structure, *e.g.* tax, ability to buy and sell businesses, managerial organisation of segmented or geographically dispersed businesses, a balance of power in collaborative enterprises, or local regulatory or cultural considerations.[1]

1. Modern Company Law for a Competitive Economy: Completing the Structure, A consultation document from the Company Law Review Steering Group (November 2000), 177.

10.03 In this chapter, groups are further explored, especially how this phenomenon is dealt with in company law. After the next introductory paragraphs, German statutory group law is discussed, because it can be regarded as an autonomous body of law regulating groups of (public) companies, and it illustrates issues that are inherent to any regulation of group relationships. This part of the chapter is followed by a section on European Union (EU) group law. Although the EU legislator was originally inspired by the German example, the EU did not succeed in enacting a body of law comparable to that of Germany. Instead, the EU pursued the piecemeal approach, which is typical for most of the Member States as well. Groups, as a matter of course, can be of a transnational nature and the consequences of this, for the involvement of employees, were discussed in Chapter 7. In this chapter, we focus on issues of international private law that may arise when groups are operating across borders. Finally, definitions of groups and issues of group liability in Member States are briefly discussed.

10.04 Corporate groups consist of legally independent, but economically associated, companies. As a rule, such groups have a single parent company, but, in some cases, 'horizontal groups' with more than one parent company do occur; for example, Unilever and, previously, Eurotunnel.[2] Most groups, however, are vertically organized with a single parent company or holding company at the top, controlling the others, the controlled or subsidiary companies.[3] Another feature of many groups is their multi-layered structure. Consequently, control of a particular subsidiary may be exerted by a sub-holding company and only indirectly by the parent company itself. Whatever the structure of the group may be, the polar elements of legal independence and economic association may create tension at the level of the interests of the different parties concerned. That is, the interests of the subsidiary company - and its minority shareholders (if there are any), creditors and employees - versus the interests of the parent, representing the group as a whole. Where an independent company will develop its own policy to carry on its business successfully, a subsidiary is bound by the policy of the group. Generally, in an independent company, the interests of the various parties involved are more or less concurrent: they all strive for the continuity of that specific company or, at least, have an interest in it. In principle, this bond will be disconnected when the company becomes a subsidiary controlled by its parent and utilized for the group's interests.[4] Because this could give rise to ambiguities and conflicts, a lot of attention has been paid to the possible introduction of a law on groups.

2. In such a case, the parent companies are not dependent on one another but associated on an equal footing and mostly seated in different countries. *See* on such 'bi-national horizontal groups', Koen Byttebier & An Verroken, *Structuring International Cooperation Between Enterprises* (London: Graham & Trotman, 1995) (with diagrams).
3. Corporate groups may also be formed by other legal entities such as cooperatives or even limited partnerships. In this chapter, however, only groups of companies are discussed.
4. Phillip Blumberg, 'The Transformation of Modern Corporation Law: The Law of Corporate Groups', *Connecticut Law Review* 37 no. 3 (2005), Faculty Articles and Papers. 192, http://digitalcommons.uconn.edu/law_papers/192; Cándido Paz-Ares, in *Curso de derecho mercantil I*, Capitulo 55, eds Rodrigo Uría & Aurelio Menéndez (Uniones de empresas y grupos de sociedades); (Madrid: Civitors, 2006); J.E. Antunes, *Liability of Corporate Groups* (Deventer/

10.05 Traditionally, less attention has been given to the shareholders of a parent company, who are left with a rather unsubstantial form of control. The reason, of course, is the fact that the actual business is not carried on by the parent company, but by its subsidiaries and/or sub-subsidiaries. Consequently, the shareholders control a board that is not directly accountable for the business activities of the group, but for the control of the subsidiaries instead. A rather recent countervailing development is that parent companies have to report in their corporate governance statement on the main features of the internal controls and risk management systems for the consolidated undertakings, with those undertakings 'taken as a whole' (Article 29(2)(b), Directive 2013/34/EU).[5] This provision is due to the 2006 amendment of the Seventh Directive that was part of the EU's answer to the strict requirements posed by the Sarbanes-Oxley Act in the United States.[6] It is obvious that this reporting obligation forces parent companies to install group-wide control mechanisms, thereby reinforcing the position of the board and the shareholders of the parent company. However, company law, still being based on the view that a company is an *independent* legal entity, may be an obstacle to effectuate such a rigid control regime. Alternatively, such a regime may lead to liability of the parent company, if the control represents a dominant influence and if it is exerted at the detriment of the subsidiary's creditors (*see* paragraphs 10.09 *et seq.* and 10.34 *et seq.*).[7]

10.06 As already mentioned, the single legal entity is the basic subject of company law whereas incorporated businesses are overwhelmingly carried on by groups of companies. According to Blumberg, this is an institutional weakness that 'in a growing number of areas is being supplemented by a doctrine of enterprise law that focuses on the business enterprise as a whole, not on its fragmented components'.[8] Examples of these 'areas' are, at national level, labour law and tax law. At EU level, the concept of 'undertaking' in competition law must be understood as 'designating an economic unit, even if, in law, that economic unit consists of several persons' (ECJ in *Akzo Nobel*).[9] How to deal with the phenomenon of groups has already been a concern for

---

Boston: Kluwer Law and Taxation Publishers, 1994); Steef Bartman, 'From Autonomy of Interests to Concurrence of Interests in Dutch Group Company Law', *European Company Law* 4, no. 5 (October 2007): 207–210.

5. Note that parent companies of micro-groups and small groups do not have to draw up consolidated financial statements and consolidated management report. Member States have the option to exempt also the parent companies of medium-sized groups, Article 23(1) and (2), Directive 2013/34/EU.
6. Amending Directive 2006/46/EC, OJ 2006, L 224.
7. S.M. Bartman, *Voorbij NV en BV. Over corporate governance en tekort van ons vennootschapsrecht.* Rede uitgesproken bij de aanvaarding van het ambt van hoogleraar in het ondernemingsrecht aan de Universiteit Leiden (Deventer: Kluwer, 2004), 8.
8. Blumberg, o.c., p. 605.
9. ECJ 10 Sep. 2009, Case C-97/08 (Akzo Nobel), paragraph 55, preceded by Case C-217/05 *(Confederación Española de Empresarios de Estaciones de Servicio)*, paragraph 40 and Case 170/83 (*Hydrotherm)*, paragraph 11. Furthermore, it must be noted that at EU level a proposal is launched for harmonization of taxation of cross-border groups: proposal for a Directive on a Common Consolidated Corporate Tax Base is launched, Strasbourg, 25.10.2016, COM(2016) 683 final. Furthermore, the group of companies is a starting point for many rules set by Insolvency Regulation (EU) 2015/848, OJ 2015, L 141.

a long time for national legislators and courts, as well as for the EU. Non-governmental bodies, such as the Organisation for Economic Cooperation and Development (OECD) and legal researchers have also taken up the challenge. Leading German academics have noted that subsidiaries are actually 'satellites'[10] and that the problem was caused by 'nothing but the fact that the management of (...) companies do indeed follow instructions from the head offices of their parent companies'.[11] Although the economic reality of groups was acknowledged, 'they are the centre of very specific and particular juridical problems', even though Germany had set an example in 1965 by introducing a specific body of statutory rules governing the relationships of enterprises forming part of a group *(Konzernrecht)*.[12] The background of some of these problems is that group structures, in fact, create multiple limited liabilities for the shareholders of the parent company. They carry limited liability for the operations of the parent company, but not to the same extent for the business, insofar as it is carried on by a subsidiary, because, in such a case, its risks are confined to that legal entity.[13] Although this feature may contribute to the growth of enterprises because it allows for risk channelling, multinational enterprises, in particular, may also utilize this shield to contend lawsuits generated by risky local activities. The OECD, therefore, enacted guidelines to prevent abuses, such as human rights violations and environmental damage. They are directed at all entities within the group and represent standards of behaviour supplemental to applicable national and international law.[14] Some of these behavioural standards belong to the sphere of 'corporate social responsibility' and are, *inter alia,* aimed at protecting the so-called involuntary creditors (tort victims).[15] Typical company law-related issues raised by group structures include: the protection of minority shareholders and creditors of a subsidiary; intragroup transactions (which may be at the detriment of some group entities); conflicts of interest (e.g., where representatives of the parent company manage the subsidiary); group influence (to what extent is it permissible at the level of a subsidiary); disclosure of group relations (in order to assess the position of a single entity); and the annual accounts (on a consolidated basis). As illustrated in the next paragraphs, German statutory group law primarily deals with these issues.

10. Ernst-Joachim Mestmäcker, *Verwaltung, Konzerngewalt und Rechte der Aktionäre* (Karlsruhe: Müller, 1958), 303.
11. Marcus Lutter, 'The Law of Groups of Companies in Europe: A Challenge for Jurisprudence', *Forum Internationale* 1, no. 1 (1983): 6.
12. *Ibid.*, 6; C.M. Schmitthoff, 'Introduction', in *Groups of Companies,* ed. C.M. Schmitthoff & F. Wooldridge (London: Sweet & Maxwell 1991), xiii.
13. Peter Hommelhoff, Produkthaftung im Konzern, ZIP Zeitschrift für Wirtschaftsrecht (Jahrgang, 1990), 762; Y. Guyon, *Traité des contracts. Les sociétés. Aménagements statutaires et conventions entre associés,* 5th edition (Paris: Impr. Jouve, 2002), 81 *et seq.*; Phillip.I. Blumberg, *The Multinational Challenge to Corporation Law,* (New York – Oxford: Oxford University Press 1993); J.E. Antunes, *Liability of Corporate Groups* (Deventer/Boston: Kluwer Law and Taxation Publishers, 1994).
14. The OECD Guidelines for Multinational Enterprises, 2011 edition. Retrievable at www.oecd.org.
15. Jennifer A. Schwartz, 'Piercing the Corporate Veil of an Alien Parent for Jurisdictional Purposes: A Proposal for a Standard That Comports with Due Process, 2008', *California Law Review* 96, no. 3 (1 Jun. 2008): 731 *et seq.*

II THE LAW OF GROUPS IN GERMANY

10.07 Germany is one of the few countries that actually introduced a statutory law of groups in order to regulate the relationships between the enterprises organized as a group. It formed an important part of the 1965 reform of the German law on public companies. The relevant provisions aim at establishing a balance by providing, on the one hand, a legal framework to determine what constitutes a group and how it may function. On the other hand, they contain rules for the protection of outside minority shareholders and creditors.[16] The underlying assumption is that conflicts between the interests of the distinct companies within a group are inevitable and that they have to be neutralized through the medium of special provisions governing group relations (conflict model).[17]

10.08 The legal framework is based on a definition of associated enterprises *(verbundene Unternehmen)* in the AktG (Stock Corporation Act) 1965, paragraphs 15–19. These definitions are elaborated in paragraphs 291 *et seq.* for public companies (*Aktiengesellschaft* (AG) and KGaA). Associated enterprises are subject to special rules, but this partly depends on the category of association by which they are connected.[18]

Enterprises are regarded as being associated, although not necessarily as a group, if they are connected by one or more of the following elements:

(i) An enterprise has a *majority shareholding* (or majority voting rights) in another enterprise.[19]

(ii) An enterprise exerts a *dominant influence* on another enterprise. The former is then the dominant enterprise *(herrschendes Unternehmen)* and the latter is the dependent enterprise *(abhängiges Unternehmen)*. A dominant influence is presumed if a majority shareholding exists, but it may also be established by factual indications, such as the existence of guidelines on policy making and/or a centralized financing policy.[20]

(iii) Enterprises are subject to *uniform management*. The influence exerted by the dominant enterprise on the dependent enterprises is presumed to lead to uniform management and, consequently, the enterprises, together, constitute a group *(Konzern)*. A group is deemed to be uniformly managed if a control contract *(Beherrschungsvertrag)* has been concluded between the

16. Herbert Wiedemann & Heribert Hirte, 'Konzernrecht', in *50 Jahre Bundesgerichtshof. Festgabe aus der Wissenschaft*, eds Claus-Wilhelm Canaris et al. (München: Verlag C.H. Beck, 2000), 337 *et seq.*
17. G.H.J. Houwen, A.P. Schoonbrood-Wessels & J.A.W. Schreurs, *Aansprakelijkheid in concernverhoudingen* (Deventer: Kluwer, 1993), 54.
18. *See* ss 90, 131, 192 & 319 German Stock Corporation Act *(AktG)*.
19. Sections 15 and 16 German Stock Corporation Act.
20. Sections 15 and 17 German Stock Corporation Act; Volker Emmerich and Matthias Habersack, *Aktien- und GmbH-Konzernrecht*, 8. Auflage (München: C.H. Beck, 2016), commentary to s. 17 AktG, nn. 9–10.

dominant enterprise and the dependent enterprise(s) *(Vertragskonzern)*, or if a dependent enterprise is integrated *(eingegliedert)*.[21]

(iv) If enterprises hold *cross-participations*. This happens where enterprises participate reciprocally for more than 25% in their capital *(wechselseitig beteiligte Unternehmen)*. Such enterprises may simultaneously qualify as dominant or dependent enterprises, if at least one of the criteria mentioned in (ii) and (iii) is applicable.[22]

(v) If enterprises are associated by an *enterprise agreement* (*(Unternehmensvertrag)*. In addition to the control contract, the AktG defines other types of enterprise agreements between associated enterprises (*see* paragraph 10.10).[23]

It should be noted that uniform management *(einheitliche Leitung)* is the factor determining the (non)existence of a group. Although the concept of uniform management is of a factual nature, it may be established by more easily confirmable legal criteria, as mentioned previously: A majority holding leads to the presumption that dominant influence is exerted and that, in turn, leads to the presumption of uniform management.[24]

10.09 The provisions of the AktG dealing with associated enterprises apply when a subsidiary or dependent company has the form of an AG or a KGaA, because the legal form of the controlling enterprise (the parent) is not relevant to the application of the law of groups. However, the parent must be an enterprise in every case, because the German law of groups applies exclusively to *associated enterprises (verbundene Unternehmen)*. Normally, a legal person will own an enterprise, yet a partnership, a sole trader, the state or even a private individual could own it. The central issue then is whether such a person has other - external - business interests to pursue.[25]

A Enterprise Agreements

10.10 The AktG regulates the consequences of group relations on the one hand by providing the terms for so-called enterprise agreements *(Unternehmensverträge)*, of which the control contract is the most important (section 291 AktG). On the other hand, it limits the exertion of control where no enterprise agreement is concluded and

21. Sections 15, 18, 291 and 319 German Stock Corporation Act. *Beherrschungsvertrag* may also be translated as 'domination agreement'.
22. Sections 15 & 19 German Stock Corporation Act.
23. Sections 15, 291 & 292 German Stock Corporation Act.
24. On the factual nature of uniform management, *see* Frank Wooldridge, 'Aspects of the Regulation of Groups of Companies in European Laws', in *European Company Laws: A Comparative Approach*, eds Robert Drury & Peter G. Xuereb (Aldershot: Dartmouth, 1991), 109.
25. The basic decision is *VEBA* (1977) BGHZ, (Entscheidungen des Bundesgerichtshofes in Zivilsachen), 69, 334, ruling that even the state of Germany can qualify as an enterprise in the sense of group law since it pursues business interests in several companies. For enterprises other than the state *see*: *Autokran* (1985) BGHZ, 69, 334; *Video* (1991) BGHZ 115, 187. Volker Emmerich and Matthias Habersack, Aktien- und GmbH-Konzernrecht, 8. Auflage (München: C.H. Beck, 2016), commentary to s. 15 AktG, nn. 6–25.

requires the controlling enterprise (undertaking) to compensate the controlled company for prejudicial transactions it has been forced to conclude (section 311 AktG). Concluding a control contract *(Beherrschungsvertrag)* provides the legal basis for the exertion of control by the controlling company, as well as for the application of rules protecting creditors and minority shareholders of the controlled company (enterprise).[26] The main characteristic of a contractual group is the parent's express power to induce its subsidiary to act for the benefit of the group or a group company, even if that implies acting against the subsidiary's interest. The parent has the right to issue binding instructions to the board of a public company contractually subordinated to it *(Weisungsrecht)*.[27] In order to protect the subsidiary's creditors and outside shareholders, the parent has to compensate the subsidiary's losses and it must offer to the outside shareholders of the subsidiary a guaranteed annual compensation payment as well as the opportunity to withdraw, in exchange for an equitable compensation in cash or in the form of shares in the parent company.[28]

10.11 Other contracts are the profit pooling contract (leading to absorption of both profits and losses by one of the parties), the partial profit transfer contract and the business-leasing contract. These types of contracts are different from the control contract because of their reciprocal character: there should be agreement on a contribution to be made by each of the contracting parties, between which a relation of subordination does not necessarily exist.[29] Agreements regarding profit and loss absorption, as well as control contracts or a combination of these, are often entered into for reasons of taxation, that is, in order to create a tax unity between the companies concerned, leading to taxation of the pooled profits and losses at the level of the dominating company.[30] Any kind of enterprise agreement must be in writing and only becomes effective upon the consent of the members' general meeting, of all parties to the contract. The resolution requires a majority, which must comprise at least 75% of the share capital represented at the passing of the resolution. The registration of the agreement with the Commercial Registry is conditional for the contract to have legal effect.[31]

10.12 The group formed by means of integration of a subsidiary company *(Eingliederung)* could be regarded as a special type of the contractual group. Although an integrated company maintains its legal independency, it functions economically and organizationally as a branch of its parent. Once a company has become integrated, the parent has a general and unrestricted right to issue instructions to the board of that company. The parent is also allowed to dispose of the integrated company's assets and

26. *See* paragraph 10.08 for terminology.
27. Section 308 German Stock Corporation Act.
28. Sections 300–307 German Stock Corporation Act, especially 302, 304 and 305. U. Immenga, 'The Law of Groups in the FRG', in *Groups of Companies in the EEC: A Survey Report to the European Commission on the Law Relating to Corporate Groups in Various Member States*, ed. Eddy Wymeersch with a foreword by G.E. Fitchew (Berlin/New York: Walter de Gruyter, 1993), 104.
29. Section 292 German Stock Corporation Act.
30. Gerhard Wirth, Michael Arnold & Mark Greene, *Corporate Law in Germany*, 144 and 146; U. Immenga, 'The Law of Groups in the FRG', 96.
31. Section 294 German Stock Corporation Act.

profits. As a counterpart, the parent becomes jointly and severally liable for all acts and debts of the integrated company. If all the shares of the subsidiary are held by one person, that sole shareholder will decide on the integration at a formal general meeting. Integration by majority resolution is possible even against the minority's will, when the parent holds at least 95% of the subsidiary's shares. In such a case, minority shareholders must be bought out against an adequate settlement.[32]

10.13 If control is exerted in the absence of a contract, a de facto group is constituted. The way the AktG (sections 311–318) deals with a parent's liabilities in the absence of such a contract reveals that, in German law, a parent enterprise in a contractual group is favoured above a parent in a de facto group. This is not surprising, because, in a de facto group, a parent that has not accepted the same legal commitments as would be the case if a contract was concluded controls the subsidiaries. If such a contract is absent, the parent company may not use its dominant influence to cause the subsidiary (the dependent/controlled AG or KGaA) to enter into disadvantageous transactions, unless the controlling enterprise compensates the subsidiary for it *(Nachteilsausgleich)*.[33] The compensation must take place ultimately by the end of the financial year. Alternatively, it must be stated when and how compensation will follow, a provision that is remotely similar to the 'Rozenblum doctrine' developed in French case law (*see* paragraph 10.17a).[34] The controlling enterprise can, in fact, only avoid compensation by operating at arms' length, if transactions are concluded with its subsidiaries. The management board of a controlled AG (or KGaA) must report each year on the intragroup relations, specifying details of the transactions the company has entered into with the controlling enterprise or at the instruction of that enterprise. The company's auditor examines the report and submits it to the supervisory board, which is then required to report to the general meeting on this issue.[35]

B Groups Involving Private Companies

10.14 The courts have held that a GmbH, by analogy with an AG, can conclude contracts with another enterprise, in order to become associated with that enterprise.[36] In groups based on a control contract, the construction of the right to issue instructions corresponds with the AG rules. The same applies to the parent's obligation to compensate for losses.[37] The analogy ends where de facto dependence exists, because the statutory provisions on the internal structure of the GmbH allow shareholders to issue binding instructions to the management without the prerequisite of a specific contract. Thus, the single or majority shareholder of a GmbH can, in principle, exercise a dominant influence on the company's management (*see* paragraph 6.27). With

32. Sections 319–327 German Stock Corporation Act.
33. Section 311 German Stock Corporation Act.
34. Section 311 German Stock Corporation Act.
35. Sections 312–314 German Stock Corporation Act.
36. Landmark cases in this respect are *Supermarkt* (1988) BGHZ 105, 324 and *Siemens*, BGH ZIP 1992, 395.
37. Immenga, 'The Law of Groups in the FRG', 113–115.

respect to groups, this means that a dominant enterprise can control its GmbH subsidiary without the need for further justification. Nevertheless, enterprise agreements may be concluded for reasons of taxation, that is, to create a tax unity of the parties to the agreement.[38]

10.15 In the case of a de facto group, the outside minority shareholders and creditors are protected, *inter alia,* by the fiduciary duty *(Treuepflicht)* that the majority shareholder owes toward the GmbH and the other shareholders. Breach of this duty when influencing management imposes a liability on the dominant shareholder, and individual shareholders may lodge claims for injunctions and compensation for damages caused by the exerted influence.[39] Creditors' interests should also be taken into account, and there may be circumstances justifying that they bring their actions directly against the dominant shareholder (the parent).[40] Where the parent enterprise exerts a permanent and comprehensive influence on the subsidiary's management, it is mostly impossible to isolate detrimental interventions from harmless ones and to calculate the damage caused. The subsidiary is then managed merely as a branch. This goes beyond simple dependence and, therefore, is called *qualified* de facto *dependence.*[41] The position of a subsidiary then can be compared to the position of a subsidiary controlled by its parent based on a control contract. The predominant view has long been that the protection of outside shareholders and creditors in such a case be modelled on the AktG-provisions, but rather recently, courts seem to rely more on the classic approach of *piercing the corporate veil,* depending on the specific circumstances of the case (*see* paragraphs 10.34 *et seq.*). In light of the new concept of *'existenzvernichtender Eingriff'* (a withdrawal destroying the economic base of the subsidiary) elaborated in the landmark case *Bremer Vulkan,*[42] the concept of the *qualified* de facto dependence has actually been abandoned. Since the *Trihotel* decision in 2007, the *Existenzvernichtungshaftung* is considered a tort-based liability of the shareholder towards the company.[43]

10.16 The German legislative example was not followed by other EU jurisdictions, with a few exceptions, notably Portugal.[44] A planned French reform in this respect has not been successful and even Germany has not extended its statutory *Konzernrecht* to the private company (GmbH).[45] This, of course, is due to difficulties that are inherent to a comprehensive regulation of group relationships. For example, it is difficult to

38. Klaus J. Müller, *The GmbH: A Guide to the German Limited Liability Company* (München: Verlag C.H. Beck, 2006), 144-146.
39. ITT (1975) BGHZ 65, 15; Autokran (1985) BGHZ 95, 330.
40. Tiefbau (1989) BGHZ 107,7. *See also* paragraph 10.35.
41. Autokran (1985) BGHZ 95, 330; Tiefbau *(1989)* BGHZ 107, 7; Video (1991) BGHZ 115, 187.
42. BGHZ 149, 10. Peer Zumbansen, 'Liability Within Corporate Groups (*Bremer Vulkan*) – Federal Court of Justice Attempts the Overhaul', *German Law Journal* 3, no. 1 (1 Jan. 2002), www.germanlawjournal.com.
43. BGHZ 173, 246; confirmed in Gamma (2008) BGHZ 176, 204.
44. In 1986 Portugal inserted a Chapter VI on group law in the Commercial Companies Code (*Código das Sociedades Comerciais*), Cordeiro, *Direito Europeu das Sociedades*, 778 *et seq.* Slovenia also seems to have followed the German example.
45. Lutter, *The Law of Groups of Companies in Europe, o.c.*, ns 18 and 19.

determine the compensation that must be offered for detrimental dominant influence, because such influence is hard to isolate and calculating the damage resulting thereof is equally difficult.[46] Admittedly, national legislators and the EU have dealt with single aspect of groups, notably in the area of consolidated financial statements (*see* Chapter 9), but many issues are still left unsolved. Therefore, Prentice's remark on how English law deals with the group phenomenon still holds for most jurisdictions: 'the principles of company law do not address themselves in any coherent way to the problems to which this form of doing business can and does give rise'.[47] That is not to say that national legislators have been negligent in this respect. As Wymeersch has pointed out, groups show such variety that it is almost impossible to design a comprehensive set of rules. For example, groups may operate within one single jurisdiction, but they may also constitute a multinational enterprise. Subsidiaries may be wholly owned but they may also have minority shareholders and, in the latter case, even be listed (*see* paragraph 10.19).[48] In addition, identifying groups may be less straightforward in some cases because actual control can also be exerted through undisclosed voting agreements, coalition structures (companies linked by cross-shareholdings) and even managerial structures (top managers exercising control without a controlling shareholder coalition).[49] Notwithstanding this variety, legislators have found ways to deal with groups, not only with regard to annual accounts and a few other company law issues but also in related areas, such as financial markets, labour law, insolvency law and tax law.

III EU GROUP LAW

10.17 Group law already aroused the European Commission's interest as a possible subject for harmonization and regulation a long time ago. Articles dealing with group relations were included in the original draft statute for the European company (1970). In 1985, the Commission published a preliminary draft Ninth Directive on the Law of Groups. Support, however, was lukewarm in most Member States and the Commission withdrew the group-related provisions from the *Societas Europaea* (SE) Statute (*see* paragraph 4.13). In 1990, even before its formal submission to the Council of Ministers, the proposal for theNinth Directive was also withdrawn (*see* paragraph 3.10b). Despite this, the Commission did not entirely abandon the project and initiated a study examining the development of the group phenomenon within the Member States. This study was carried out in 1993, suggesting that the Commission might take up the

46. The number of enterprise agreements seems to be limited and their importance in practice is hard to assess, Wiedemann & Hirte, 'Konzernrecht', 369.
47. D.D. Prentice, 'Groups of Companies: The English Experience', in *Groups of Companies in European Law. Legal and Economic Analysis on Multinational Enterprises. Volume II*, ed. Klaus J. Hopt (Berlin/New York: Walter de Gruyter, 1982), 99.
48. Wymeersch, *Do We Need a Law on Groups of Companies?*, 576 *et seq.*
49. Gerard Hertig & Hideki Kanda, 'Creditor Protection', in *The Anatomy of Corporate Law: A Comparative and Functional Approach*, eds Reinier Kraakman et al. (Oxford: Oxford University Press, 2004), 74 *et seq.*

project again, but that did not happen.[50] Instead, in the 1998 Forum Europaeum Konzernrecht, a group of law professors conducted and presented another study containing a proposal for a directive on European group law.[51] An essential element of this proposal was a provision codifying the 'Rozenblum doctrine'. It states that directors of group entities are allowed to follow a group policy, even where it conflicts with the interests of that entity, on the condition that the group is well structured based on a balanced policy and only if the directors of that entity may reasonably assume that the disadvantages will be offset within a reasonable time span.[52]

10.17a The so-called Rozenblum doctrine was formulated by the French Supreme Court *(Cour de cassation)* in the *Rozenblum* case.[53] Mr Rozenblum controlled a number of companies that were not related by a common policy. Nevertheless, assets were transferred from some of these companies to others that were suffering losses. Mr Rozenblum was prosecuted for the criminal act of abuse of a company's assets *(abus de biens sociaux)*. The Supreme Court held that such transfers were only permissible, if the following criterion was met:

> the financial assistance given by the 'de iure' or 'de facto' directors of a company to other group companies in which they held a direct or indirect interest, should be supported by an economic social or financial common interest, to be evaluated in the light of a policy developed with regard to the group as a whole and should not be devoid of any return or disrupt the balance of the mutual obligations of the companies involved, nor exceed the financial capacity of the company that is supporting the burden.[54]

10.18 The next committee to advise on group law was the High Level Group of Company Law Experts, installed by the Commission in 2001 for the purpose of designing a modern regulatory framework for company law. They took the view that the enactment of an autonomous body of law, specifically dealing with groups, was not advisable at the EU level. In other words, a new attempt to bring about the Ninth Company Law Directive on group relations was not recommended. Instead, they suggested that rules to solve problems in some particular areas be introduced: (i) the transparency of a group's structure and relations; (ii) the conflicts between the interests of the group and of its parts; and (iii) the special problems arising from

50. Wymeersch (ed.) with a foreword by G.E. Fitchew, *Groups of Companies in the EEC*.
51. Forum Europaeum Konzernrecht, *Konzernrecht für Europa*, ZGR 4 (1998): 672–772. In 2000, a version was published in English: 'Corporate Group Law for Europe', Forum Europaeum Konzernrecht, Stockholm (Corporate Governance Forum) 2000 and also in the *European Business Organization Law Review* (EBOR) I (2000) 165–264.
52. Forum Europaeum Konzernrecht, *Konzernrecht für Europa*, ZCR 4(1998): 769.
53. Cour de Cassation, Chambre criminelle du 4 février 1985, 84–91.581, *Revue des sociétés* 1985, 648, note Bouloc. For an account on recent developments *see* Pierre-Henri Conac 'Das französische Recht zur Anerkennung des Gruppeninteresses seit der Rozenblum-Entscheidung' in *Corporate Governance im grenzübeschreitenden Konzern*, eds P. Hommelhoff, M. Lutter & C. Teichmann (de Gruyter, Berlin, 2017), 89.
54. Translation quoted from Eddy Wymeersch, 'Conflicts of Interest in Financial Services Groups', Financial Law Institute Working Paper No. 2007-05 (Universiteit Gent, 2008), 4, retrievable from www.papers.ssrn.com.

'pyramid structures'.[55] Regarding the second issue, the High Level Group explicitly promoted the work of the Forum Europaeum Konzernrecht.[56] The Commission accepted the recommendations in its 2003 Company Law Action Plan.[57]

10.19 With respect to the first recommendation, regarding better financial and non-financial information about groups of companies, the Commission pointed out that this matter was already addressed by the application of IAS to consolidated accounts, that such information was to be provided under the Thirteenth Directive and in the annual corporate governance statement (both still proposals at the time). The Commission noted that the scope of these measures is limited to listed companies, but that rules providing for information on group structures if the parent company is not listed should be made a short-term priority.

On the second issue raised by the High Level Group, the Commission endorsed the view that Member States should facilitate the adoption and implementation of a coordinated group policy 'provided that the interests of (...) creditors are effectively protected and that there is a fair balance of burdens and advantages over time for that company's shareholders'. Thus, a framework directive dealing with this issue, especially with the appropriate safeguards, was announced to be presented in the medium term.[58]

The last recommendation concerns pyramid structures. These are chains of holding companies with the ultimate control based on a small total investment, thanks to the extensive use of minority shareholders.[59] This happens, for example, where a minority (49%) of the shares of a family-owned parent company A are listed. If company A then forms a subsidiary B, of which, again, a minority of the shares (49%) are listed, the family will retain control, albeit indirectly, over the operations of B and its subsidiaries, notwithstanding the fact that investment by third parties has doubled.[60] The Commission noted that the requirement of an annual corporate governance statement could improve the information on these structures. The Commission considered it necessary to further examine the risks that are inherent to these structures.[61]

10.20 The results of a 2006 consultation on future priorities for company law are not supportive of the Commission's plans to follow the High Level Group's recommendations. The majority of the respondents showed little enthusiasm for the proposals to create a legal framework for the implementation of a group policy and to curb abusive pyramids. The majority held the view that stricter transparency rules would represent

55. Report of the High Level Group of Company Law Experts on *A Modern Regulatory Framework for Company Law in Europe* (Brussels, 4 Nov. 2002), 94 *et seq.*
56. *Ibid.*, 97.
57. *Modernising Company Law and Enhancing Corporate Governance in the European Union – A Plan to Move Forward* (Brussels, 21 May 2003), COM(2003) 284 final (Company Law Action Plan 2003).
58. *Ibid.*, 19.
59. *Ibid.*, 19.
60. This basically is the ownership structure of Heineken: http://www.theheinekencompany.com /investors/governance/ownership-structure (with diagram).
61. Company Law Action Plan 2003, 19–20.

a better solution.[62] This demonstrates, once more, that the original idea of enacting an autonomous body of group law at EU level is illusory.

10.21 In 2010, the 'Reflection Group on the Future of EU Company Law' was, again, concerned with the topic on the EU level. The results were published in its 2011 report,[63] which deals with three measures on groups. The main approach of the experts regarding European law on groups was the recognition of the group interest. This target was to be achieved by some sort of modified *Rozenblum* doctrine. Moreover, the issues of group transparency and introduction of a 'simplified single-member company template' were discussed. Following the experts' report, the Commission dealt with the topic in its 2012 Action Plan,[64] which announced an initiative on the recognition of the group interest by 2014. Yet, specific results were missing.

10.21a In the meantime, more informal expert groups were established. The *Forum Europaeum on Company Groups*, an association of academics and practitioners from all over Europe, published a proposal to facilitate the management of cross-border company groups in Europe in 2015.[65] Significantly, this proposal distinguishes between two types of subsidiaries, taking into account their size and function. Based on this distinction between the so-called Service Companies and Ordinary Companies, it suggests the introduction of two different frameworks by means of an EU directive. In March 2016, the *Informal Company Law Expert Group* released a report on the information on groups,[66] which was followed by a report concerning the recognition of the interest of the group.[67] The latter discusses three options. Each option sets out different criteria, the observance of which allows the manager of a subsidiary to take into account the group interest. It should be noted, however, that the proposal is restricted (at least in its ambitions for harmonization) to wholly owned subsidiaries. Eventually, another proposal for reforming group law in the EU came about, which was published by the *European Company Law Experts*.[68] Besides confirming the need to recognize the group interest at EU level, this proposal mainly deals with the handling of Related-Party Transactions.

---

62. Directorate General for Internal Market and Services, *Summary Report on the Public Consultation on Future Priorities for the Action Plan on Company Law and Corporate Governance* (Brussels), 22.
63. Reflection Group on the future of EU company law, *Report of the Reflection Group On the Future of EU Company Law*, Brussels, April 2011, http://ec.europa.eu/internal_market/ company/docs /modern/reflectiongroup_report_en.pdf.
64. European company law and corporate governance –. a modern legal framework for more engaged shareholders and sustainable companies, Com(2012) 740/2.
65. Forum Europaeum on Company Groups, *European Company and Financial Law Review* (ECFR) 2015, 299.
66. Informal Company Law Expert Group, *Report on information on groups*, March 2016, http://ec .europa.eu/justice/civil/files/company-law/icleg-report-on-information-of-groups-march-2016 _en.pdf.
67. Informal Company Law Expert Group, *Report on the recognition of the interest of the group*, October 2016, http://ec.europa.eu/justice/civil/files/company-law/icleg_recommendations_ interest_group_final_en.pdf.
68. European Company Law Experts, *A proposal for reforming group law in the European Union – Comparative Observations on the way forward*, https://europeancompanylawexperts.wordpress .com/papers_trashed/reforming-group-law-in-the-eu/.

10.21b An entirely new path is taken by the recently published '*European Model Company Act*' (EMCA), which was released in early 2017. The *EMCA* offers the Member States a model company law that can be enacted in its entirety or just in parts. It aims at harmonizing company law of the Member States by providing a modern, low cost and easy to use alternative to the drafting of national company laws. Chapter 15 of the EMCA deals with groups of companies and combines a *Rozenblum*-inspired approach for recognizing the interest of the group with a liability for *wrongful trading* against the parent.[69]

A The Formation of Groups

10.22 The search for a common approach for the development of group law at EU level is a painstaking and lengthy process, as is illustrated in previous paragraphs. In the meantime, several single issues of group law are, nevertheless, dealt with by a number of directives and by the introduction of business organizations under EU law. As will be set out in this and the following paragraphs, several provisions of EU legislation in the area of company law and employee involvement pertain to the formation or the functioning of groups.[70] To start with, Articles 40 and 54 TFEU are essential for the formation of a group, because they grant companies the *right of secondary establishment*, enabling the formation of cross-border subsidiaries or partnerships (*see* paragraphs 2.54 *et seq.*) According to Article 49, the parent company, having established a subsidiary in another Member State, must not be placed in a weaker position than a parent company from that other Member State.[71] In addition, Directive 2012/30/EU (previously the *Second Directive*) facilitates the formation of a subsidiary because Member States have the option not to apply the requirements for non-cash contributions at the incorporation of a subsidiary (paragraph 3.39). Where the formation (or expansion) of a group is realized through the acquisition of shares of listed companies, the *Transparency Directive* and the *Thirteenth Directive on Takeover Bids* impose obligations on the acquirer. Shareholders – or persons holding (potential) voting rights – should inform issuers of the acquisition or disposition of major holdings in listed companies. The objectives of the Transparency Directive are, *inter alia,* to improve and equalize investor protection throughout the Community and to curb secret takeovers (*see* paragraph 3.103d). The Thirteenth Directive (*see* paragraphs 3.84 *et seq.* and 8.18 *et seq.*) serves similar objectives. The mandatory bid aims at protecting minority shareholders' interests that, according to the theory of conflicting interests, are mostly adversely affected by the fact that the formerly independent company will operate as part of a group. Directive 2009/102/EC (previously the *Twelfth Directive*)

69. For a first analysis *see* Conac, *The Chapter on Groups of Companies of the European Model Company Act (EMCA)*, European Company and Financial Law Review (ECFR) 2016, 301 *et seq.*
70. Erik Werlauff, 'Group and Community – The European Court's Development of an Independent Community Law Concept of the Group and Its Significance for National Company Law', *European Company Law* 4, no. 5 (October 2007): 201–206.
71. Whether or not the foreign company is qualified as a parent company is, of course, determined by the law governing the subsidiary, Werlauff, 'Group and Community – The European Court's Development of an Independent Community Law Concept', 2007, 203.

has to be mentioned here, because it allows for single-member companies. This facilitates the structuring of groups in Member States where no restrictions have been maintained as to the use of single-member companies (*see* paragraph 3.81). Referral should also be made to the proposal for a *Societas Unius Personae* (SUP), which is intended to facilitate the formation of subsidiaries in other EU Member States (paragraph 4.47).

10.23 The *SE Statute* also facilitates the formation of groups, because the methods of formation of an SE may lead to the creation or expansion of a group structure. This applies when an SE is formed as a holding company or a subsidiary (*see* paragraph 4.17 *et seq.*). Here, the accompanying *SE Directive* on the involvement of employees has an ancillary function, because it regulates the transformation from the pre-existing system in place for the involvement of employees to their involvement in the structure emerging upon the formation of an SE (paragraphs 4.35 *et seq.*).[72]

10.23a Similar to the SE, the *Societas Cooperativa Europaea* (SCE) may operate through subsidiaries, hence, it can function as the parent company of a group.[73] The SCE, however, may not function so easily as a subsidiary in group structures, unless the (majority of the) members are entities of the same group.[74] For the involvement of employees of the SCE, reference is made to the remarks made for the SE. Finally, it must be noted that the European Economic Interest Grouping (EEIG), owing to its ancillary nature, cannot act as a parent entity in a group structure. However, companies within a group may structure their cooperation by using the EEIG form (paragraph 4.08).

10.24 The Preamble of the SE Statute states that it is essential to ensure as far as possible that the economic unit and the legal unit of business in the Community coincide. The SE should facilitate the creation and management of companies with a European dimension, free from the obstacles arising from the disparity and the limited territorial application of national company law.[75] This suggests that the SE should function as the parent company of groups operating on a European scale, such as in the case of Allianz SE,[76] or even as a single company, uniting its operations in branches, instead of subsidiaries. Because group structures clearly yield benefits, the latter is very unlikely to happen, unless groups are lured to restructuring at EU level through tax incentives.

72. To secure the proper implementation of the SE Directive it defines some concepts, *inter alia*, that of a subsidiary, meaning an undertaking over which a company exercises a dominant influence as defined in accordance with Articles 3(2)-(7) of the EWC Directive 94/45/EC.
73. Article 1(3) SCE Regulation.
74. The members of the SCE in principle each have one vote (*see* paragraph 4.46).
75. Paragraphs 6 and 7 Preamble SE Statute. In paragraph 4 it is pointed out that the legal framework within which business must be carried on is still based largely on national laws and therefore no longer corresponds to the economic framework Which is 'a considerable obstacle to the creation of groups of companies from different Member States'.
76. Allianz SE is the parent of the Allianz Group https://www.allianz.com/en/about_us/management/corporate-governance/legal-form/.

B The Functioning of Groups

10.25 Several directives contain elements that regulate or facilitate the functioning of groups and two of these are specifically drafted to deal with groups. Hence, the elements that constitute a group falling within their ambit need to be defined. For accounting purposes, the *Accounting Directive* classifies several relationships between 'members of a body of undertakings'. Article 2 contains definitions of 'parent undertaking' and 'subsidiary undertaking' (an undertaking can be considered as synonymous to an enterprise). As explained in paragraphs 3.66a–c, on the one hand, the definitions reflect the legal approach, in which the legal power to control is the central element. On the other hand, they are based on the economic approach, according to which, a group exists from the moment an undertaking actually exercises a dominant influence over another (*see also* paragraphs 9.29 *et seq.*). The Accounting Directive requires the parent undertaking to draw up consolidated financial statements and a consolidated management report for itself and for its subsidiaries. In the *EWC Directive*, the economic approach prevails, because it requires that the controlling undertaking (parent undertaking) actually exercises a dominant influence over another undertaking ('the controlled undertaking'). However, the legal approach has a supportive role because the dominant influence is presumed, without prejudice to proof to the contrary, when an undertaking holds a majority of another undertaking's capital, controls a majority of the votes or when it can appoint more than half of the members of that undertaking's administrative, management or supervisory body. The EWC Directive requires the central management of the controlling undertaking to set up a European Works Council (EWC), or an alternative information and consultation procedure, if the group is defined as having a Community scale. That is, if it employs at least 1,000 persons within the Member States and has at least two subsidiaries in different Member States, each having at least 150 employees (Article 2(1)). The application of the EWC Directive to certain group structures has generated some European Court of Justice (ECJ) case law, as explained in paragraphs 7.11 and 7.12.

10.26 Several other directives contain provisions pertaining to the functioning of groups. These include:

- *Directive 2012/30/EU* (previously *Second Directive:* as mentioned previously, by way of a facility, Member States may waive the independent expert's report on consideration other than in cash upon the formation of a subsidiary (*see* paragraph 3.39)). Article 28 is a rather restrictive provision because it forwards the prohibition for a company to subscribe for its own shares (and the restrictions to acquire such shares) to its subsidiaries.
  To apply this prohibition,[77] Article 28(2) defines the relevant parent-subsidiary relationship in terms of a mixture of the legal and economic group concept. More precisely, it applies to companies in which the parent company holds, even indirectly, a majority of the voting rights or upon which it can

77. The prohibition is inserted in the Second Directive by Directive 92/101/EEC, OJ 1992, L 347.

exercise a dominant influence. Member States may define the cases in which a company is deemed to hold a majority of the voting rights or to be able to exercise a dominant influence. In the latter case, they must, in any event, specify that such influence can be exercised if a company has the right to appoint or dismiss the majority of the directors or if it has control of a majority of the voting rights under an agreement concluded with the other shareholders (Article 28(2)(a)). Notwithstanding the criterion of the dominant influence, it is the legal approach that seemingly prevails. The required specifications are rather similar to those mentioned in the Accounting Directive.

- *Directive 2011/35/EU* (previously the *Third Directive*): in paragraph 3.52, it was mentioned that the merger procedure may be simplified if the acquiring company holds 90% or more of the shares of the acquired company. Article 23 provides for the exceptions. For example, if the acquiring company holds all the shares, entries in the draft terms of the merger may be skipped, as well as the report on the share-exchange ratio and the control by an independent expert. Where the acquiring company holds 90% or more of the shares of the company being acquired, the Member States need not require approval of the merger by the general meeting of the acquiring company.
- *Tenth Directive:* As mentioned in paragraph 3.61, the Tenth Directive allows for similar simplifications as the Third Directive if, in a cross-border merger, the acquiring company holds 90% or more of the shares of the company being acquired (Article 15).
- *Thirteenth Directive (Takeover Directive):* for the application of the rules regarding takeover bids, 'persons acting in concert' constitute natural or legal persons who cooperate with the offeror or the offeree company on the basis of an agreement (Article 2(1)(d)). The person or entity that controls an undertaking, together with that controlled undertaking, are deemed to be persons acting in concert (Article 2(2)). For the criterion of control, reference is made to the definition of Article 87 of Directive 2001/34/EC,[78] now Article 2(1)(f) of the Transparency Directive. The controlled undertaking is defined as any undertaking in which another entity has the power to exercise or actually exercises dominant influence. Furthermore, a controlled undertaking subsists if another entity has majority voting rights, or controls such majority due to an agreement or has the right to appoint or remove a majority of the directors. This is basically the same approach as laid down in the Accounting Directive.

10.27 The functioning of groups is, of course, subject to many other rules of EU origin, which are not discussed in this book. For example, tax treaties between Member States (to prevent double taxation and double non-taxation) may contain rules that facilitate cross-border activities and establishments. The EU has taken initiatives to

78. Directive 2001/34/EC, OJ 2001, L 184 on the admission of securities to official stock exchange listing and on information to be published on those securities. *See* paragraph 3.103.

coordinate taxation issues and has enacted the Anti-Tax Avoidance Directive (EU) 2016/1164.[79] Reference may also be made to rules pertaining to merger control, as discussed in Chapter 8 in relation to joint ventures and mergers as well as takeovers. In determining whether a concentration is deemed to arise, the decisive factor is the acquisition of control. This may be established by legal instruments such as mergers, contracts and majority or controlling voting rights or by de facto circumstances, such as economic dependence and dominance (paragraphs 8.36 *et seq.*).

IV GROUPS OPERATING ACROSS BORDERS

10.28 A parent company may incorporate its foreign activities by forming subsidiaries that are subject to domestic law; that is, the law of the country in which the subsidiaries have their registered seats. By using this right of secondary establishment, the multinational enterprise complies with local company laws and does not give rise to issues as to which law is applicable. However, ECJ case law on the right of establishment (paragraphs 2.61 *et seq.*) has confirmed that foreign activities may be incorporated under the same law to which the parent company is subject, thus unifying the company law rules applicable to the companies belonging to the group. For example, a parent company under Dutch law may incorporate its German operations in a company under Dutch law, having most or all of its activities in Germany, while being registered in the Netherlands.[80] The ECJ has held that, in such a case, the host Member State may not impose additional requirements on the foreign company. Therefore, the internal relations of the company, as well as the liabilities of its directors, are subjected to the law of the Member State of incorporation.[81] Consequently, the position of minority shareholders and even creditors of such a foreign company may differ from that of a company under domestic law, because Dutch company law applies and not German group law.[82]

10.29 In cases of insolvency, the Insolvency Regulation (EU) 2015/848 determines the applicable law through the use of the 'centre of a debtor's main interests' as the

79. Directive (EU) 2016/1164, OJ 2016, L 193. For initiatives regarding company taxation, *see* the Commission's website Company Tax, https://ec.europa.eu/taxation_customs/business/company-tax_en.
80. 'Post Centros', the number of incorporations in the UK has exploded, Becht, Mayer & Wagner, 'Where Do Firms Incorporate?', October 2006, available at SSRN: http://ssrn.com/abstract=953820.
81. Eike Thomas Bicker, *Gläubigerschutz in der grenzüberschreitenden Konzerngesellschaft. Eine international-privatrechtliche Untersuchung am Beispiel der abhängigen englischen Kapitalgesellschaft mit Verwaltungssitz in Deutschland* (Berlin: Duncker & Humblot, 2007), 41–47. Karl A. Hofstetter, *Sachgerechte Haftungsregeln für multinationale Konzerne: Zur zivilrechtlichen Verantwortlichkeit von Muttergesellschaften im Kontext internationaler Märkte* (Tübingen: Mohr Siebeck, 1995), 44 *et seq. See also* instances where environmental harm has led to forum shopping and litigation before civil courts, such as in the disastrous Bhopal and Amoco Cadiz cases, R.M. Davis, 'The Bhopal Litigation', *Journal of the Indian Law Institute* 29, no. 3 (1987): 331–355 and In re Oil Spill of the Amoco Cadiz, 954 F.2d 1279 (7th Cir. 1992); Edward H.P. Brans, *Liability for Damage to Public Natural Resources: Standing, Damage and Damage Assessment* (The Hague-London-New York: Kluwer Law International, 2001).
82. For involuntary creditors, *see* 10.06.

decisive criterion.[83] The Centre of Main Interests (COMI) should correspond to the place where the debtor conducts the administration of his interests on a regular basis and is therefore ascertainable by third parties. For a company, the place of the registered office is presumed to be this centre in the absence of proof to the contrary. In order to curb fraudulent forum shopping, the presumption applies only if the registered office has not been moved to another Member State within a three-month period prior to the request for the opening of insolvency proceedings (Article 3(1)). In *Eurofood*, the ECJ held that rebutting the presumption that the COMI is the place of the registered office requires factors that are objective and ascertainable by third parties. According to the ECJ, this can be the case when the company is not carrying out any business in the territory of the Member State in which it is registered.[84]

10.29a *Eurofood* was a private limited company, registered in Ireland, which was wholly owned by Parmalat SA, a company incorporated in Italy, which has as its main objective the financing of the companies of the Parmalat group. After Parmalat SA became insolvent, the Italian authorities appointed an extraordinary administrator. One month later, the Irish High Court appointed a provisional liquidator for Eurofood, with powers to take possession of all the company's assets and to manage its affairs. After an application was lodged with the District Court in Parma for a declaration that Eurofood was insolvent, this court took the view that Eurofood's centre of main interests was in Italy and that it had international jurisdiction to determine whether Eurofood was insolvent. The Irish High Court had the opposite view as to Eurofood's main centre of interest and refused to recognize the decision handed down by the court of Parma. Finding that Eurofood was insolvent, the High Court made an order for winding up the company. The Italian extraordinary administrator appealed against that judgment and, on this basis, the Irish Supreme Court referred questions to the ECJ for a preliminary ruling.

V LAWS OF THE MEMBER STATES

10.30 With the exception of Germany, none of the laws of the Member States under discussion in this book contains a systematically ordered body of rules governing the relationships between enterprises associated in a group. Nevertheless, they all have regulated ad hoc group matters in company law, taxation law, insolvency law and others. Group concepts have been developed by each Member State over the years and for varying purposes, but the directives and regulations that have been discussed in the previous sections certainly have had some harmonizing effect. In the next paragraphs, some definitions of group concepts in national company laws are briefly considered. This is to be followed by a section on how courts make exceptions to the limited liability character of companies by 'piercing the corporate veil' in order to protect the creditors of group members.

83. Article 3, Regulation (EU) 2015/848, OJ 2015, L 141. Bicker, *o.c.*, 84 *et seq.*
84. ECJ 2 May 2006, C-341/04 (Eurofood).

A Group Concepts

10.31 The Seventh Directive forced the Member States to at least define groups or elements thereof (parent-subsidiary relation) for accounting purposes. Even Germany had to introduce such definitions when implementing the Seventh Directive and these, therefore, largely correspond to the definitions used in other Member States.[85] In general, the hybrid and partly optional character of the definitions provided by the Seventh Directive, currently the Accounting Directive 2013/34/EU, is reflected by national provisions. Basically, exercising actual control, or being able to exercise such control by the parent company or the management of the parent company over its subsidiaries, is the ultimate factor for the obligation to consolidate. Because it is not easy to ascertain such control or management due to the fact that it lies in the domain of economical and organizational facts, Member States prescribe that it is presumed or even deemed to exist where criteria of a legal nature are met.[86] These legal criteria correspond largely with those mentioned by the Accounting Directive (*see* paragraphs 3.66 *et seq.* and 9.29 *et seq.*): notably, the parent having the majority voting rights or the right to appoint or remove a majority of the members of the corporate bodies of the subsidiary. In addition, it is stated that controlling the majority of the voting rights due to an agreement with other shareholders equals the situation where the parent company alone has the majority voting rights.[87] Additionally, it may be stated that the right to exercise a dominant influence on the subsidiary may follow from a contract or a provision in the articles of the subsidiary.[88] Finally, the obligation to consolidate may also be triggered if a parent company has actually appointed the majority of the members of the administrative, management or supervisory board, because of the exercise of voting rights.[89] The last criterion, however, is a mixture of legal and factual conditions, because it includes not only the right to vote, but also the results of the actual voting. For the sake of completeness, it must be added here that all voting rights and rights to appoint or remove director, which can be exerted by a subsidiary undertaking, must be added to those of the parent company.[90] Accordingly, a parent company A, having a wholly owned subsidiary B, is presumed to exert control over company C, where A and B, together, hold the majority of the voting rights in C. Although details of the group concepts in the Member States still differ, as illustrated in the next paragraph, it is nevertheless quite likely that most economically associated

---

85. Consolidated accounts are regulated by ss 290 *et seq.* Commercial Code (HGB).
86. Corresponding with Article 22 of the Accounting Directive: Article L233-16 Commercial Code (France), Article 5 Companies Code (Belgium), Article 290(1) HGB (Germany), Article 42 Commercial Code (Spain); Article 406 Book 2 DCC (Netherlands); Article 1162, Companies Act 2006 (UK).
87. European Commission, *Implementation of the Seventh Directive in EU Member States Summary of findings from a study on the implementation of Seventh Directive 83/349/EEC in the Member States of the European Union, as per* 1 Jan. 1998 http://ec.europa.eu/internal_market/accounting/docs/studies/1998-seventh-dir_en.pdf.
88. (Belgium, France, Germany, Spain and UK).
89. (Belgium, France, Spain).
90. Article 22(3) Directive 2013/34/EU.

enterprises, which, in one Member State, will be called a parent, subsidiary or group, also fall within a similar description in another Member State.

10.32 Notwithstanding the general pattern illustrated in the previous paragraph, the laws of the Member States show differences in terminology and in details of their definitions of groups and parent-subsidiary relationships. Some of these peculiarities follow here. For example, the Belgian Companies Code *(Wetboek van Vennootschappen)* defines control, parent company and subsidiary along the lines of the Accounting Directive. In addition, it also defines a consortium, being companies under unified management *(centrale leiding)* without a parent-subsidiary relationship between them, a concept provided by Article 22(7) of the Accounting Directive, allowing for consolidation requirements for horizontal groups.[91] Such unified management will be presumed, *inter alia,* if the majority of the members of the boards of companies are the same persons.[92] Consolidation is mandatory for each of the companies forming such a consortium.[93] French law provides that a company is deemed to exercise control *(contrôle),* even if it holds less than a majority of the voting rights, but holds more than 40% of these rights and no other shareholder holds a larger fraction.[94] As already mentioned, the German Commercial Code follows the general pattern of the Accounting Directive but, as a matter of course, refers to the control contract *(Beherrschungsvertrag)* as one of the criteria that triggers the obligation to consolidate.[95] In Spanish law, the presumption that control is exercised follows if the majority of the members of the board of the subsidiary are members of the board or senior executives from the parent company or a company controlled by it.[96] This leads to the presumption that the majority of the directors are appointed by the use of voting power, which, in turn, leads to the presumption that control is exerted.

10.33 It must be noted that definitions of groups and parent-subsidiary relationships that serve accounting purposes are sometimes also utilized for other issues of company law. A few examples may illustrate this. Spanish legislation on public companies refers to the definition of a dominant company in the commercial code for the provisions relating to the acquisition by a company of its own shares or the shares of the dominating company.[97] The same applies for the Belgian and Dutch provisions on the acquisition of shares of the parent company by its subsidiary.[98] The French Commercial Code contains provisions regulating remuneration of directors and company officers by referring not only to commitments of the company, but also to commitments

91. Edwards, *EC Company Law,* 170–171.
92. Article 5 Belgian Companies Code defines control, Article 10 defines a consortium.
93. Article 111 Belgian Companies Code.
94. Article L233-3 (II) and L233-16(II)(2) French Commercial Code. For accounting purposes, this criterion leads to the conclusion that a majority of the directors are appointed by the parent company and that conclusion constitutes control *(contrôle exclusif).*
95. Section 290(3) German Commercial Code *(HGB).*
96. Article 42(1)(d) Spanish Commercial Code. Francis Lefebvre, *Sociedades Mercantiles* (Santiago de Compostela/Madrid: Memento Práctico, 2007), nr. 7504.
97. Article 134 Spanish Stock Corporations Act and Article 42 Commercial Code.
98. Article 631 Belgian Companies Code; Article 98d Book 2 Dutch Civil Code.

of the controlling company or controlled companies, as defined in Article L233-16.[99] Although it may seem logical to utilize the basic concepts provided by the Accounting Directive to a larger extent, several other definitions of group relations are also used by Member States, even in the area of company law. This applies, of course, to Germany, where this may be justified by the unique purpose of the *Konzernrecht*. However, other Member States also feature definitions that, although being different from the Accounting Directive's definitions, in essence, do not add much to the understanding of company group relations. For example, in the UK, the concept of 'holding company' is defined in the Companies Act, serving, *inter alia*, the regulation of transactions involving directors and the provisions containing capital requirements.[100] The concept is similar to that of the parent company, except for the factor of dominant influence (and management on a unified basis), but, in practice, such subtleties will very likely be of little importance.[101] The same goes for the Dutch company law distinction between a 'dependent company' and 'subsidiary company'.[102] The two concepts are, however, virtually the same. A company is regarded as being 'dependent' if 50% or more of the issued capital is held by another company. A company is deemed to be a subsidiary if another company holds more than 50% of such capital, provided that such capital holding corresponds proportionally to the voting rights.

B Piercing the Corporate Veil

10.34 As described in paragraphs 10.07 *et seq.*, in German law, the relationships between the members of the group are regulated in order to protect the minority shareholders and creditors of dependent companies. This concept is based on the assumption of a conflict of interests between the parent and the dependent companies. It does not relate to actual damages suffered by a particular shareholder or creditor and protects the assets of the dependent company instead by requiring the parent to compensate for losses incurred by its dominant influence. Most jurisdictions, however, have developed other techniques to protect minority shareholders and creditors. They aim to protect only those shareholders and creditors whose interests are actually damaged by the prejudicial behaviour of the parent company (or other shareholders having a majority interest). Specific statutory provisions of company law and insolvency law may serve to this end. Often, however, such protection is offered by the courts using a technique commonly called 'piercing the corporate veil'. It happens where courts make an exception to the basic rule that a company's shareholders (and directors) are not liable for the debts of the company in order to grant unpaid creditors recourse to the assets of the company's shareholders and/or directors. These inroads at asset partitioning, which are important elements of full legal personality, have a

99. Article L225-42-1 Commercial Code.
100. Articles 1159, 41 and 136 Companies Act 2006.
101. Section 1159 Companies Act 2006.
102. The dependent company is defined by Articles 152 and 262 Book 2 Dutch Civil Code. These provisions serve exclusively for the application of the mandatory supervisory board for sizeable companies. The definition of subsidiary is laid down in Article 24a Book 2 Dutch Civil Code.

casuistic character and are mostly based on general principles or open norms such as the prohibition to abuse one's rights. Hence, there is no set of precise criteria justifying veil piercing in order to establish group liability.[103] As opposed to the German approach, group relationships, even those of a qualified nature, will not establish such liability alone – additional factual situations are required. These represent some sort of abuse of power by the parent to control its subsidiary. To put it differently, no liability is imposed on the parent solely because of its status. This reflects the theoretical approach of concurring interests, which assumes that what is in the interest of the group, is very often in the interest of the separate group members as well.[104]

10.35 A few additional remarks must be made here. In the first place, the protection of persons whose interests are prejudiced by acts of a parent company happens not only in the realm of company law and insolvency law but also in areas that are not discussed in this book, in particular labour law, product liability law and taxation.[105] Second, the divide between German law and other jurisdictions may not be as deep as it seems, because the method of piercing the corporate veil is sometimes applied by German courts to provide additional protection in extreme situations. Moreover, they seem to return to the protection of creditors by using a tort law approach (*existenzvernichtender Eingriff*, *see* above paragraph 10.15). Third, group indebtedness is not restricted to the issues discussed here. It also arises if one company has expressly assumed liability for another company within the group, for example, by guaranteeing the other's debt or by providing security for it.[106] It can be noted that the assumption of liability by the parent for the subsidiary's debts is sometimes made a statutory condition for certain group facilities, such as the subsidiary's exemption from financial reporting requirements (Article 37(3) Directive 2013/34/EU). Fourth, it must be noted that piercing the corporate veil is a concept that goes beyond group liability, because the instrument is also used for establishing liability in the case of a single company, even where its shareholders are individuals.

10.36 Karen Vandekerckhove carried out an impressive comparative study on piercing the corporate veil, and much of what is discussed in this section is based on her findings.[107] To begin with, norms allowing piercing the corporate veil in such circumstances may originate from company law, insolvency law or civil law, depending on the jurisdiction. This complicates the description of the phenomenon of group

103. José Engracia Antunes, *Liability of Corporate Groups* (Deventer/Boston: Kluwer Law and Taxation Publishers, 1994), 486.

104. A thorough analysis of the issues related to group liability within the EU is presented by Erik Werlauff, 'The Debtor Behind the Debtor, the Tortfeaser Behind the Tortfeasor: On Liability for Another Company's Default and Other Debts', *European Company Law* 5, no. 5 (October 2008): 207–219.

105. For example, in Spain a rather generalized recourse to lifting the veil (*levantamiento del velo*) by the courts can be perceived in labour law, Lefebvre, *Sociedades* Mercantiles, nr. 180 and 7502. José Hurtado Cobles, *La doctrina del levantamiento del velo societario en España e Hispanoamericana* (Rústica, Ed. Atelier, 2008), 309.

106. Because the conclusion of a control contract under German law is, as explained above, completely at the option of the dominant enterprise, the liabilities resulting from it can be said to be of a voluntary nature.

107. Karen Vandekerckhove, 'Piercing the Corporate Veil', II, 765.

liability, and the fact that authors do not use consistent terminology is not very helpful either.[108] Following Vandekerckhove, piercing the corporate veil based on statutory provisions is called legal piercing, whereas establishing liability on additional grounds or general principles is called judicial piercing. Legal piercing occurs, for example, where a parent company is a director or a de facto director (shadow director) of its subsidiary, and statutory duties have been violated, such as in the case of mismanagement leading to insolvency. Judicial piercing happens where courts lift the veil of legal personality on grounds such as tortuous behaviour of the parent company or because it has abused the legal personality of the subsidiary to the detriment of its creditors.[109] These issues are dealt with briefly in the next paragraphs.

10.37 Typical situations that may lead to veil piercing are undercapitalization, transfers of assets that endanger the continued existence of the subsidiary and unduly continuing loss-making operations.[110] Although these situations often overlap and the applicable legal instruments may be partly the same, it is worthwhile to report briefly on some of Vandekerckhove's findings. If a subsidiary is undercapitalized, that is, by far not having sufficient financial means (equity) in relation to its operations, the parent company may be liable. In Belgium, this can be based on the statutory rule that the founders of a company may incur liability if the company goes bankrupt within a period of three years after formation. In addition, creditors may have a claim against the founders on grounds of tort in cases not covered by the statutory provisions. This may happen where the founders try to escape liability by using a 'dormant company' that has existed for more than three years.[111] In other Member States, undercapitalization, as such, is not an issue regulated by statutory law.[112] It may, however, be among a set of circumstances giving rise to claims on the grounds of tort, such as in France, Germany and the Netherlands.[113] Statutory provisions regarding mismanagement, although basically leading to the liability of directors, may also apply to the parent company, if it has operated as a de facto director (shadow director).[114] In Germany, the technique of subordinating shareholders' claims is applied in cases where companies are no longer creditworthy and/or have become insolvent. This implies that in cases of insolvency, shareholders' loans are subordinated to the claims of other creditors (section 39 (1)(5) InsO) and may be subject to revocation (*Insolvenzanfechtung*, s. 135

108. Which cases where liability is established should exactly be called veil piercing is debatable, Vandekerckhove, 2007 II, 12-13.
109. It can be discussed whether holding the parent company liable on grounds of tort or abuse should be called veil piercing because in such a case the limited liability of the parent as a shareholder is not ignored but the liability is based on its behaviour as a separate entity instead.
110. Although other situations may also lead to piercing, e.g., in Spain, where this may happen if the assets of two companies are commingled or if companies operate under the same name and from the same address, Cándido Paz-Ares, in *Curso de derecho mercantil I*, Capitulo 22, eds Rodrigo Uría & Aurelio Menéndez 558-560.
111. Vandekerckhove 2007 II, 105-124. Articles 229(5) and 456(4) Belgian Companies Code.
112. *Ibid.*, 124.
113. *Ibid.*, 124-156. Bartman & Dorresteijn, *Van het concern* (Deuenter: Kluwer, 2006,) 231 *et seq.*
114. Vandekerckhove 2007 II, 134-140.

InsO).[115] UK law is very reticent to veil piercing and restricts it to cases of fraud, where the company is used as a mere façade. Manifest undercapitalization may indicate that a subsidiary is used in such a way, but it does not play an important role in this respect.[116] In Spain, courts have not frequently dealt with undercapitalization by lifting the veil. The issue is a matter of creditor protection, rather than group law.[117]

10.38 The parent company may initiate transfers of assets that endanger the continued existence of the subsidiary. They may vary from the distribution of funds of the subsidiary and intragroup transactions on terms that are unfavourable for the subsidiary to right-out asset stripping.[118] (Note that, for accounting purposes, intragroup transactions are covered by the concept of related-party transactions (*see* paragraphs 3.97a–c)). Intragroup transactions with a high-risk profile are especially likely to occur where the parent company uses a central cash management system to finance the operations of the group as a whole. This may even lead to withdrawals destroying the economic base of a subsidiary.[119] Intragroup transactions may, in general, be covered by statutory rules restricting distributions to shareholders, the Actio Pauliana (or similar instruments) or by piercing the corporate veil on grounds of tort or abuse of legal personality.[120] In Belgium and France, the Rozenblum doctrine (*see* paragraph 10.17) serves to evaluate contested transactions.[121] In French case law veil piercing may also occur on the basis of theories on fictitious companies and asset commingling.[122] German law traditionally deals with intragroup transactions by applying its group law. Thus, intragroup transactions may lead to the parent company's obligation to compensate the subsidiary for losses or disadvantages caused by these transactions. If the parent violates this duty, it may be liable toward the subsidiary's creditors. Note that the parent incurs such liability automatically when the subsidiary is integrated (*see* paragraph 10.08). Although other grounds for establishing liability have long been standing in the shadow of the *Konzernrecht*, recent case law of the Supreme Court concerning de facto groups has moved away from it and relied on grounds like tort and abuse, which may lead to piercing the corporate veil.[123] In the Netherlands, most cases

115. Article 39(1)(5) and 135 Insolvency Act *(Insolvenzordnung)*. Until 2008, shareholder loans were re-qualified by the courts as capital (*eigenkapitalersetzendes Gesellschafterdarlehen*), *see* Vandekerckhove 2007 II, 145–153.
116. Vandekerckhove 2007 II, 156–163.
117. Vandekerckhove has not researched Spanish law. *See*: Wymeersch (ed.), *Groups of Companies in the EEC*, Irujo, 'Eine spanische 'Erfindung' im Gesellschaftsrecht: Die 'Sociedada limitada nueva empresa' – die neue unternehmerische GmbH' 139 and Paz-Ares, *o.c.*, 558.
118. Vandekerckhove 2007 II, 179 *et seq.*
119. Matthias Casper, 'Liability of the Managing Director and the Shareholder in the GmbH (Private Limited Company) in Crisis', *German Law Journal* 9, no. 9 (1 Sep. 2008): www.germanlawjournal.com.
120. Vandekerckhove 2007 II, 13.
121. *Ibid.*, 183 and 227 *et seq.*
122. *Ibid.*, 242 and 243.
123. This approach initially assumed an external liability (claims by creditors of the subsidiary): BGHZ 149, 10 *(Bremer Vulkan)*; BGHZ 151, 181 (KBV). In recent jurisdiction, it has been modified into a liability toward the subsidiary (the administrator in bankruptcy): BGHZ 173, 246 *(Trihotel)*; BGHZ 176, 204 *(Gamma)* (decisions are retrievable at http://dejure.org). Further: Article 64 GmbHG; Article 826 BGB; Article 93 Insolvenzordnung.

of veil piercing are based on the tortuous behaviour of the parent company.[124] In the UK, certain intragroup transactions are facilitated because they are exempted from the requirement of shareholder approval. On the other hand, transactions may be barred by the restrictions posed to distributions in kind.[125] In Spain, detrimental intragroup transactions may lead to liability of the parent company and/or the directors of the subsidiary. The directors of the (dominating) parent company may also be liable if they have acted toward the subsidiary as de facto directors.[126]

10.39 Unduly continuing loss-making operations may occur where the economic and financial situation of a company implies that its existence is endangered, unless appropriate action is taken by the directors and/or shareholders to counteract this development. If they, nevertheless, continue the loss-making activities and the company goes bankrupt, they may be liable because they have caused the insolvency and/or damaged creditor's interests. The law dealing with the unjustifiable continuation of loss-making operations may lead to group liability, where the parent company is acting as the director of its subsidiary or as its de facto director. Member States have enacted statutory provisions in order to hold directors and de facto directors of a bankrupt company liable for neglecting their duties. In addition, there might be provisions obliging to convene the general meeting in the event that the net assets of the company have fallen below certain thresholds (e.g., Belgium). The company's directors may have a duty to file for bankruptcy if critical threshold levels or financial ratios are passed (e.g., Poland). Mismanagement (gross negligence) in the period preceding the insolvency proceedings can be a separate ground for liability of directors (e.g., Belgium, France and the Netherlands).[127] Generally, only the administrator, or other authority appointed according to the insolvency procedure, can pursue actions based on these provisions regarding mismanagement. Apart from that, claims by individual creditors may be made based on tort where the parent company has violated standards of care, which may apply when its subsidiary is continuously generating losses.[128] In Germany, statutory provisions relating to mismanagement of directors or to their obligation to file for bankruptcy do not apply to parent companies[129] and claims of creditors based on tort will only be successful in extreme cases.[130] German group law partly deals with the issue because of the obligations and liabilities of the parent company in contractual groups and qualified de facto groups. Where it is beyond doubt that the company's situation has irreversibly deteriorated and insolvency cannot be avoided, any continued activity is, in fact, at the expense of the creditors. In such a

124. For instance, Dutch Supreme Court in *Comsys*, 11 Sep. 2009, NJ 2009, 565. Geert Potjewijd & Janneke van der Kroon, 'Report from the Netherlands', *European Company Law* 4, no. 5 (October 2007): 235–237.
125. Articles 208, 845 and 846 Companies Act 2006. Explanatory Notes to the CA 2006, 174. Vandekerckhove 2007 II, 265 *et seq.*
126. Cándido Paz-Ares, *o.c.*, 560.
127. Articles 265, 332, 333, 633, 634 Belgian Companies Code; Article L651-2, French Commercial Code; Articles 138 and 248 Book 2 Dutch Civil Code.
128. Vandekerckhove 2007 II, 324 *et seq.*, 335 *et seq.*, 348 *et seq.*
129. *Ibid.*, 352.
130. *Ibid.*, 356.

case, the directors and/or shareholders are liable for having aggravated the losses of the company. In the UK, this situation is covered by the concept of wrongful trading, which is the subject of Article 214 Insolvency Act of 1986. Accordingly, directors of a company that has gone insolvent may be liable if they continued to trade while they knew or ought to have known that there was no reasonable prospect that the company would avoid going into insolvent liquidation. The Commission, in its 2003 Company Law Action Plan, proposed the development of a similar rule, but it gained no support in the subsequent consultation on future priorities for the modernization of company law.[131]

10.39a The comprehensive 2013 *Study on Director's Duties and Liability* reveals that Member States employ two main legal strategies to ensure that the creditors' interests are properly taken into account in companies that are on the brink of insolvency. First, the vast majority of Member States provide for a duty for directors to timely file for insolvency. This strategy generally is then buttressed by a liability of directors for depletion of the company's assets, resulting from the delayed insolvency filing. In most Member States this liability can only be enforced by the administrator or liquidator. The second main strategy is a statutory duty to cease trading at a particular point in time when creditors' interests are at risk: the 'wrongful trading' strategy. Although this strategy seems to offer more leeway for directors where they see a realistic chance for the company to trade its way out of its situation, both legal strategies seem to have similar effects on the behaviour expectations towards directors in pre-insolvency situations.[132]

VI CONCLUDING REMARKS

10.40 Jurisdictions have been able to regulate the formation, functioning and dissolution of companies as single legal entities in their Civil Code, Companies Code or Companies Act, but they do not deal with groups of companies (or other entities) in a similar way; that is, through a coherent and comprehensive set of statutory rules. With the exception of Germany, the Member States and the EU have, instead, created solutions for specific situations involving groups, thereby producing a variety of definitions of groups and group relations. The observation, more than two decades ago, by Geoffrey Fitchew that within each State, several definitions are used that adapt the ambit of the rule to the specific needs of the area in question (company law, accounting law, labour law, tax law, etc.) still holds.[133] Even Germany could not avoid the

131. *Modernising Company Law and Enhancing Corporate Governance in the European Union – A Plan to Move Forward* (Brussels) COM(2003) 284 final, 16 and 25. Consultation document, 13, Commission's website Company Law & Corporate Governance, http://ec.europa.eu/internal_market/company/index_en.htm. Thomas Bachner, 'Wrongful Trading: A New European Model for Creditor Protection?', *European Business Organization Law Review (EBOR)* 5, no. 2 (2004): 293–319.
132. *Directors' Duties and Liability in the EU*, prepared for the European Commission DG Markt by: Carsten Gerner-Beuerle, Philipp Paech & Edmund Philipp Schuster (Department of Law, London School of Economics), 2013, pp. 208 *et seq.*
133. Wymeersch (ed.) with a foreword by G.E. Fitchew, *Groups of Companies in the EEC*, o.c.

introduction of definitions and rules regarding groups in addition to its *Konzernrecht*, for example, for financial reporting purposes, for which the element of unified management was abandoned in favour of a control criterion.[134] The good news is that, in company law, the definitions do not differ so much, because the same system is followed in order to get to grips with the issue of group relations. As a rule, legal criteria are formulated that are relatively easy to confirm, leading to presumptions about the existence of dominant influence, unified management or control, because these are the core criteria for the conclusion whether or not a group exists. This applies to the *Konzernrecht*, where majority voting rights lead to a presumption of dominant influence (paragraph 10.08), as well as for the Accounting Directive and the IFRS (*see* paragraphs 9.29 *et seq.*). In addition, definitions introduced for accounting purposes are sometimes used for other purposes, such as for provisions on capital requirements (paragraph 10.33). However, sometimes slightly different concepts regarding group relations are used for non-accounting areas (paragraph 10.33). Using subtle variations of group concepts within a jurisdiction contributes to the complexity of the law and they should be avoided except, of course, where different concepts are essential.

10.41 As to the consequences of the group phenomenon, Germany has acknowledged the inherent risks for minority shareholders and creditors of the group's subsidiaries by providing, in the *Konzernrecht*, a framework for contractual arrangements and for establishing liability of the parent undertaking, with the aim of protecting the interests of the dependent subsidiaries (paragraphs 10.07 *et seq.*). Other Member States and the EU have only dealt with the 'specific needs', as mentioned by Fitchew (*see* previous paragraph). Examples include facilitating provisions regarding mergers or the formation of subsidiaries, obligations such as the drawing up of consolidated accounts, and rules prohibiting certain transactions where subsidiaries are involved, for example, to issue shares to a subsidiary.

10.42 Finally, it can be observed that the courts have been filling the gaps by dealing with cases where the risks of group structures are not, or not completely, covered by legislation. Although jurisdictions are far from similar in this respect, it is very likely that, in extreme cases, courts in different Member States will not adjudicate very differently with respect to the result by piercing the corporate veil and holding the directors of the subsidiary or the parent company liable. Such cases are largely characterized by an accumulation of circumstances and events, such as manifest undercapitalization, harmful intragroup transactions and unduly continuing loss-making operations (*see* paragraphs 10.36–10.39). It should be noted that piercing the corporate veil is a wide concept, covering rather different grounds for establishing liability. Liability may, as is shown in this chapter, be based on the tortuous behaviour of the parent company, its qualification as a de facto director or the abuse of legal personality.

134. Article 290(1) German Commercial Code *(HGB)*.

Bibliography

Armour, John & McCahery, Joseph A. *After Enron: Improving Corporate Law and Modernising Securities Regulation in Europe and the US*. Oxford: Hart Publishing, 2006.

Bartman, Steef M. (ed.). *European Company Law in Accelerated Progress*. European Company Law Series, Volume 1: Alphen aan den Rijn: Kluwer Law International, 2006.

Berle, Adolf & Gardiner C. Means. *The Modern Corporation and Private Property*. With a new introduction by Murray L. Weidenbaum & Mark Jensen. New Brunswick/London: Transaction Publishers, 1991.

Blumberg, Phillip.I. Blumberg. *The Multinational Challenge to Corporation Law*. New York/Oxford: Oxford University Press 1993.

Boucourechliev, Jeanne (direction). *Propositions pour une société fermée européenne*. Luxembourg: Office des publications officielles des Communautés européennes, 1997.

Brans, Edward H.P. *Liability for Damage to Public Natural Resources: Standing, Damage and Damage Assessment*. The Hague/London/New York: Kluwer Law International, 2001.

Buxbaum, Richard M., Gerard Hertig, Alain Hirsch & Klaus J. Hopt (eds). *European Economic and Business Law, Legal and Economic Analyses on Integration and Harmonization*. Berlin/New York: De Gruyter, 1996.

Calvo, Javier, et al. *Employee Representatives in an Enlarged Europe*. Volumes 1 and 2. Brussels: European Commission, Directorate-General for Employment, Social Affairs and Equal Opportunities, 2008 <http://bookshop.europa.eu>.

Dunning, John H & Sarianna M. Lundan. *Multinational Enterprises and the Global Economy*. Cheltenham: Edward Elger Publishing, 2008.

Edwards, Vanessa. *EC Company Law*. Oxford EC Law Library, Oxford: Clarendon Press, 1999.

Emmerich, Volker & Matthias Habersack. *Aktien- und GmbH-Konzernrecht* 8. Auflage München: C.H. Beck, 2016.

Enriques, Luca. *EC Company Law Directives and Regulations: How Trivial are They?*. ECGI – Law Working Paper No. 39/2005.

Epstein, Barry J. with contributions by Ali Mirza, Abbas. IFRS 2006. *Interpretation and Apllication of International Accounting and Financial Reporting Standards*. Somerset, NJ: John Wiley & Sons, 2006.

Fulton, Lionel. *Worker Representation in Europe*. Labour Research Department and ETUI. Produced with the assistance of the SEEurope Network, online publication 2015. available at http://www.worker-participation.eu/National-Industrial-Relations.

Forum Europaeum Konzernrecht, *Corporate Group Law for Europe*. Stockholm: Forum Europaeum Konzernrecht, 2000.

Gerner-Beuerle, Carsten, Philipp Paech & Edmund Philipp Schuster. *Study on Directors' Duties and Liability, Prepared for the European Commission DG Markt*. London School of Economics, April 2013.

Gonzalez, Jorge Viera & Christoph Teichmann (eds.). *Private Company Law Reform in Europe: The Race for Flexibility*, Cizur Menor: Thomson Reuters, 2015.

Grundmann, Stefan. *European Company Law*, 2nd edition. Cambridge/Antwerp/Portland: Intersentia, 2011 High Level Group of Company Law Experts. *A Modern Regulatory Framework for Company Law in Europe*. Brussels, 4 November 2002, < http://ec.europa.eu/internal_market/company/modern/index_en.htm > .

Kraakman, Reinier et al. *The Anatomy of Corporate Law: A Comparative and Functional Approach*. 3rd edition. Oxford: Oxford University Press, 2017.

Lambooy, Tineke. *Corporate Social Responsibility: Legal and Semi-Legal Frameworks Supporting CSR*. Deventer: Kluwer 2010.

Lecher, Wolfgang, et al. *European Works Councils. Developments, Types and Networking*. Aldershot/Burlington: Gower Publishing, 2001.

Luca, Nicola de. *European Company Law: Text, Cases and Materials*. Cambridge: Cambridge University Press, 2017.

Lutter, Marcus (ed.). *Legal Capital in Europe*. European Company and Financial Law Review, Special Volume 1, 2006.

Lutter, Marcus. *Europaisches Unternehmensrecht*. vierte, neubearbeitete Auflage, Berlin/New York: De Gruyter, 1996.

Marks, Robbins, Fernandez & Funkhouser. *The Handbook of Financing Growth: Strategies and Capital Structure*. Hoboken, NJ: John Wiley & Sons, Inc., 2005.

McCahery, Joseph A., Theo Raaijmakers & Erik P.M. Vermeulen. *The Governance of Close Corporations and Partnerships*. Oxford: Oxford University Press, 2004.

Pacter, Paul, *Pocket Guide to IFRS® Standards: The Global Financial Reporting Language*. London: IFRS Foundation, 2016.

Richard M. Buxbaum & Klaus J. Hopt. *Legal Harmonisation and the Business Enterprise*. Berlin/New York: Walter de Gruyter, 1988.

Rickford, Jonathan (ed.). *The European Company: Developing a Community Law of Corporations: Collected Papers from the Leiden University Unilever Programme 2002*. Antwerp/Oxford/New York: Intersentia, 2003.

Rusu, Catalin S. *European Merger Control: The Challenges Raised by 20 Years of Enforcement Experience*. Alphen aan den Rijn: Kluwer Law International, 2010

Sapulete, Saraï. *Works Council Effectiveness: Determinants and Outcomes*. Utrecht: Tjalling C. Koopmans Institute, Utrecht University, 2013.

Sjåfjell, Beate. *Towards a Sustainable European Company Law*. Alphen aan den Rijn: Kluwer Law International, 2009.

Seidl-Hohenveldern, Ignaz. *Corporations in and under International Law.* Cambridge: Grotius Publications, 1987.

Schömann, Isabelle, Stefan Clauwaert & Wiebke Warneck. *Information and Consultation in the European Community. Implementation Report of Directive 2002/14/EC.* Brussels: European Trade Union Institute for Research, Education and Health and Safety (ETUI-REHS), 2006 <www.worker-participation.eu>.

Sun, William, Jim Stewart and David Pollard (eds). *Corporate Governance and the Global Financial Crisis.* 1st edition. Cambridge: Cambridge University Press, 2011.

Tavares da Costa, Carla & Alexandra De Meester Bilreiro. *The European Company Statute.* The Hague/London/New York: Kluwer Law International, 2003.

Teichmann, Christoph. *Binnenmarktkonformes Gesellschaftsrecht.* Berlin/New York: De Gruyter, 2006.

Vandekerckhove, Karen. *Piercing the Corporate Veil: A Transnational Approach.* Alphen aan den Rijn: Kluwer Law International, 2007.

Verloop, Peter & Valérie Landes. *Merger Control in Europe.* International Competition Law Series Vol. 11, The Hague, London, New York: Kluwer Law International, 2003.

Werlauff, Erik. *EU Company Law. Common Business Law of 28 States.* 2nd edn. Copenhagen: DJØF Publishing, 2003.

Werlauff, Erik. *SE – The Law of the European Company.* Copenhagen: DJØF Publishing, 2003.

Werlauff, Erik. *International Contracts – The UNIDROIT Principles as an Alternative to Clauses on Governing Law.* Copenhagen: Ex Tuto Publishing 2013.

Wood, Philip. *Project Finance, Securitisations and Subordinated Debt.* The Law and Practice of International Finance Series, Volume 5, Hong Kong: Thomson/Sweet & Maxwell, 2007.

Table of ECJ Cases

C-2/74 *Reyners v. Belgian State,* **34**

C-161/78 *Advokatradet comme mandataire pour P. Conradsen A/S,* **306**

C-97/08 *Akzo Nobel,* 331

C-6/90 and 9/90 *Andrea Francovich and Danila Bonifaci and Others v. Italian Republic,***46**

C-103/03 *Axel Springer AG v. Zeitungsverlag Niederrhein GmbH & Co. Essen KG and Hans-Jürgen Weske,* 319

C-387 and 391/02 and C-403/02 *Berlusconi et al.,* **306**

C-62/99 *Betriebsrat der bofrost Josef H. Boquoi Deutschland West GmbH & Co. KG v. Bofrost Josef H. Boquoi Deutschland West GmbH & Co. KG,* **253**

C-349/01 *Betriebsrat der Firma ADS Anker GmbH v. ADS Anker GmbH,* **252**

C-306/99 *BIAO v. Finanzamt für Großunternehmen in Hamburg,* **306**

C-38/89 *Blanguernon,* **304**

C-210/06 *Cartesio Oktató és Szolgáltató bt,* **40, 100**

C-212/97 *Centros Ltd v. Erhvervs- og Selskabsstyrelsen,* 36

C-270/83 *Commission v. France,* **33**

C-217/05 *Confederación Española de Empresarios de Estaciones de Servicio,* **331**

C-97/96 *Daihatsu Deutschland GmbH,* **58, 319**

C-275/97 *DE + ES Bauunternehmung GmbH,* **306**

C-341/04 *Eurofood IFSC Ltd,* **140, 347**

C-402/96 *European Information Technology Observatory, Europäische Wirtschaftliche Interessenvereinigung (EITO),* **118**

C-32-74 *Friedrich Haaga GmbH,* **60**

C-41/15 *Gerard Dowling, Padraig McManus, Piotr Skoczylas, Scotchstone Capital Fund Limited v. Minister for Finance,* **69**

C-440/00 *Gesamtbetriebsrat der Kühne & Nagel AG & Co KG v. Kühne & Nagel AG & Co KG,* 209–210, **252**

C-167/01 *Kamer van Koophandel en Fabrieken voor Amsterdam v. Inspire Art Ltd,* **36**

C-566/15 *Konrad Erzberger v. TUI AG,* **264**

C-26/62 *NV Algemene Transport- en Expeditie Onderneming van Gend & Loos v Netherlands Inland Revenue Administration,* **46**

C-287/86 *Ny Mølle Kro,* **292**

C-106/89 *Marleasing SA v. La Comercial Internacional De. Alimentacion SA,* **53, 62**

C-343/13 *Modelo Continente Hipermercados SA v. Autoridade para as COndições de Trabalho – Centro Local do Lis (ACT)*, **74**

C-214/89 *Powell Duffryn plc v. Wolfgang Petereit*, **53**

C-508/13 *Republic of Estonia v. European Parliament and Council of the European Union*, **84**

C-2/74 *Reyners v. Belgian State*, **34**

C-411/03 *Sevic Systems AG*, **76**

C-81/87 *The Queen v. H. M. Treasury and Commissioners of Inland Revenue, ex parte Daily Mail and General Trust plc*. **99**

C-234/94 *Tomberger v. Gebrüder von der Wettern GmbH*, **306, 308**

C-208/00 *Überseering BV v. Nordic Construction Company Baumanagement GmbH NCC)*, **36, 37**

Index

A

Abhängiges Unternehmen, 333
Abridged balance sheet, 320
Abus de bien sociaux, 194, 195, 339
Abus de majorité, 195
Abuse (by parent company), 213, 351–353, 356
Abuse of dominant position, 295–296, 300
Abuse of legal personality, 353, 356
Abuse of power, 213, 351
Accountable par, 65, 67,
Accounting Directives, 82, 303–304, 307, 309, 310, 318, 323, 324, 344, 345, 348–350, 356
Accounting documents, 55, 56, 88, 92
Accounts, 66, 79, 82–85, 87–89, 110, 113, 303–319, 322, 325, 326, 356. *See also* Financial, statements
Accruals, 309, 313
Acquisition of
  assets, 66, 273, 282, 291
  control, 280, 283, 297, 301, 346
  the company's own shares, 67
Actio Pauliana, 353
Actio pro socio, 204, 206
Action sociale, 186
Administradores, 207
Administrative body, 66, *See also* Board; Organ
Administration expenses, 314
Advisory Committee on concentrations, 300
Agency, 11, 33, 107, 184, 225, 283
Agenda (general meeting), 49, 103, 139, 146, 201
Agreement, 9, 10, 15–19, 21–24, 142–144, 173, 175, 193, 197, 204, 225, 249, 250, 268, 270, 277, 287, 295, 334–338
Aktiengesellschaft (AG), 5, 13, 28, 32, 39, 62, 76, 155, 184, 333
Aktieselskab, 133
Alternative bids, 87
Alternative dispute resolution, 276–277
Amministratore unico, 231
Ancillary role (of EEIG), 120
Annual accounts, 66, 125, 255. *See also* Financial, statements
Annual report, 187, 191, 208, 284, 285. *See also* Management, report
Applicable law, 99, 119, 126–127, 133, 134, 148, 276, 277, 346
Appointment, 55, 56, 59, 60, 85, 89, 92, 118, 122, 138, 140, 149, 185, 190, 194, 198–200, 202, 204–207, 211, 212, 217–219, 223–224, 232–236, 239, 241, 243, 263, 266, 269, 270, 286, 294, 327
Arbitration, 276
Arrangement of employee involvement, 138

Articles of association, 64, 70, 72, 126, 133, 149, 154–158, 164, 168, 172–175, 214, 232–242, 263
Assemblea dei soci, 239, 241
Asset(s)
  capable of economic assessment, 65, 163, 164
  co-owned, 16, 222
  partitioning, 350
  pool of, 16, 22
  stripping, 353
Asset purchase agreement (APA), 280, 282
Association, 9, 11, 17, 55, 58, 64, 70, 72, 115, 126, 146, 147, 149, 154–158, 164, 168, 172–175, 214, 232–236, 239, 241–243, 284, 285, 294, 330, 341
Association momentanée, 17
Associés, 187
Audit, 82, 87–91, 180, 202, 232, 236, 316, 320, 321, 327
  firms, 87, 90
  requirements, 89
  statutory, 82, 87–90
Auditing standards, 89
Auditors, 12, 87–91, 173, 180, 194, 201, 204, 213, 214, 231–237, 239–241, 316, 327, 336
  liability 12, 173, 194, 213

B

Balance sheet 3, 67, 84, 86, 87, 109, 176–179, 216, 218, 303, 304, 308–315, 324–326
  abridged, 320
  consolidated, 179, 325, 326
  horizontal, 310
  layout, 83
  vertical, 311
Bankruptcy, 11, 19, 23, 122, 213, 220, 223–292, 354
Bearer shares, 103, 155
Before and after principle, 141
Beherrschungsvertrag, 333, 335, 349
  'beneficial interest' test, 295
Besloten vennootschap met beperkte aansprakelijkheid (BVBA), 27, 215
Betriebsrat, 264
Binding instructions, 198, 203, 336, 355
Blocking effect, 46
Board. *See also* Organ
  administrative, 45, 55, 66–68, 72–74, 79, 113, 136–138, 229, 240, 251, 270, 294, 304, 314, 315, 318, 344, 348
  committees, 180
  executive, 231, 235, 236
  management, 183–243, 316–318
  members, 85, 98, 126, 140, 179, 189–193, 205, 211, 218–220, 225, 236, 263, 284, 286, 321
  neutrality rule, 283, 284, 287, 288
  structure, 12, 48, 98, 102, 125, 126, 188, 189, 193, 206
  supervisory, 28–29, 48, 51, 79, 97, 98, 136–138, 189, 192–205, 217–223, 266, 315, 318, 322, 336, 344, 348
  two-tier, 48, 98, 125, 126, 135–138, 148, 184, 188, 189, 192, 193, 198–199, 216, 217, 219, 235–236
  unitary, 136–137, 188–193, 211, 223
Bonds, 7, 109, 130, 174–179, 220, 240, 330
  covered, 109, 179
Book value, 325, 326
Branch, 4, 10, 32–34, 36–39, 57, 83, 91–93, 113, 128, 145, 157, 317, 337, 343
Breach of duty, 199, 202, 212–213, 229
Breakthrough, 98, 217, 283, 285–288
British Accounting Standards Board (ASB), 161
Brussels Convention, 53, 277

Business
  enterprise, 1, 3, 4, 12, 16, 29, 43, 124, 139, 144, 245, 273–275, 280, 302, 331
  leasing contract, 335
  non-incorporated – organization, 4
  opportunities, 227
  organization, 1, 3–4, 9–41, 43, 51, 81, 115–152, 248, 263, 273, 278, 342
Business organizations under Community law, 3, 51
Business transfer agreement (BTA), 280, 282
Buyout, 68, 177, 279

C

Capital
  alteration, 47, 63, 68–69, 154, 198
  authorized, 5, 64, 154, 172
  companies, 9–12, 24, 25, 27, 30, 38, 147, 174, 208
  Directive (*see* Second Directive)
  maintenance, 47, 63, 66–68, 154, 174
  markets, 5, 13, 26, 27, 31, 50, 51, 88, 107–114, 283, 307,
  minimum, 5, 13, 14, 27, 36–39, 61, 62, 64–66, 68, 135, 145, 148, 150, 162, 163, 168, 170–172
  paid-up, 311
  reduction, 62, 68, 174, 183, 194, 209, 223, 229
  requirements, 12, 14, 22, 27, 47, 65, 69, 105, 110, 145, 150, 161–163, 171, 172, 216, 350, 356
  subordinated, 176, 177, 313
  subscribed, 62, 64–69, 72, 108, 127, 135, 139, 148, 153, 154, 158, 162, 163, 166, 289, 312, 313
Cartel, 295
Central
  administration, 34, 36, 38, 40, 119, 120, 150
  cash management, 353
  management, 36, 141, 220, 250–253, 344
Centrale leiding, 349
Centre of main interests (COMI), 140, 347
Certificate, 5, 20, 51, 80, 135, 159, 169, 174, 222
Cessation of payments, 127, 139
Chamber of Commerce, 38, 15[illegible], 159
Chief executive, 188–191
Civil law, 173, 196, 197, 237, 351
Class shares, 284–286
Co-determination, 79, 249, 263, 264
Codice di Autodisciplina, 233
Co-makership, 274, 276, 278
Commerciante, 10
Co-optation (cooptation), 219
Co-ownership, 17–20, 22
Collegio sindacale, 231, 233
Collective
  agreements, 251, 260–262, 267, 268, 270
  bargaining, 253, 269
  investment companies, 96
  redundancies, 246, 248, 251, 255–257, 268, 269
Comité d'entreprise, 260
Comité de direction, 212
Comité de empresa, 267
Commanditaire vennootschap (CV), 25, 30
Commanditaire vennootschap op aandelen (Com. VA), 30
Commenda, 25
Commercial
  court, 40, 157, 187
  law, 9–11, 34, 196, 203
  registry, 10, 26, 61, 118, 167, 169, 207, 209, 210, 219, 282, 290, 335
Committee of European Securities Regulators (CESR), 111
Common market, 46, 129, 294, 295, 298–300, 302

Communications by the European Commission
A Reformed Financial Sector for Europe, 110A Renewed Social Agenda: Opportunities, Access and Solidarity in 21st Century Europe, 246
Action Plan: European Company law and corporate governance–A Modern Legal Framework for More Engaged Shareholders and Sustainable Companies, 31, 33, 48, 49, 55, 102, 146, 341
Accounting Harmonisation: A New Stragey vis-à-vis International Harmonisation, 306
Better Regulation: Delivering better results for a stronger Union, 48
Capital markets Union Accelerating Reform, 109
EU Financial Reporting Strategy: the Way Forward, 306
Financial Services: Implementing the Framework for Fiancial Markets: Action Plan, 111
Financing SME Growth–Adding European Value, 177
Guidelines on the applicability of Article 101 of the Treaty on the Functioning of the European Union to horizontal co-operation agreements, 295
Guidelines on the application of Art. 81(3) of the Treaty, 302
Interpretative communication concerning certain Articles of the fourth and seventh Council Directives on accounting, 306
Long-term financing of the European economy, 104
Modernising Company Law and Enhancing Corporate Governance in the European Union–A Plan to Move Forward, 49, 99, 102, 151, 340, 355
Obstacles to takeover and other general bids, 95
Outcome of the screening of legislative proposals pending before the Legislator, 146
Participation of European Economic Interest Groupings (EEIGs) in public contracts and programmes financed by public funds, 123
Preventing and combating corporate and financial malpractice, 88
Review of Council Directive 2001/86/EC of 8 October 2001 Supplementing the Statute for a European Company with Regard to the Involvement of Employees, 145
Simplified business environment for companies in the areas of company law, accounting and auditing, 180
Social Business Initiative, 13
Statutory audit in the European Union, the way forward, 88
Think Small First–Small Business Act for Europe, 83
Unleashing the potential of Crowdfunding in the European Union, 109
Community Charter of the Fundamental Rights of Workers, 246, 257
Community dimension (of a concentration), 297–298
Community Interest Company (CIC), 14
Community-scale group of undertakings, 293
Compañia, 20
Companies Registrar, 55, 56, 81, 92, 136, 157, 159
Company
capital, 9–12, 24, 25, 27, 30, 38, 147, 174, 208,

classification of, 6
close, 6, 27
control of, 183–243
cooperative, 5
dependent, 334, 350
dissolution, 23, 77, 160, 204, 355
financing, 3, 153–181, 347
foreign, 34, 35, 38, 100, 286, 346
formation, 37, 39, 153, 154, 168, 173
general meeting, 60, 72, 80, 84, 89, 130, 132, 186, 201, 209, 212, 213, 232, 237, 239, 289–290, 345
in formation, 166, 167, 173
group, 63, 95, 204, 206, 210, 252, 281, 290, 293, 335, 339, 341, 350
holding, 125, 129, 130, 141, 145, 282, 288, 330, 343, 350
integrated, 335–336
intermediate-level, 324
internal relations, 196, 346
international, 2, 125, 161, 280
limited by guarantee, 11
listed, 29, 45, 51, 86, 88, 90, 91, 102, 104, 106, 111, 139, 180, 192, 202, 205, 206, 211, 214, 218, 222–224, 283, 284, 303, 304, 307, 315, 318, 320–322, 324, 329, 340, 342
management structure, 3, 28, 183, 188, 197, 204, 216
meaning of, 9
medium-sized, 86, 218, 310, 317, 318
nullity, 48, 54, 56, 59, 61–62, 154, 163, 167
offeree, 96–98, 345
parent, 7, 40, 50, 202, 213, 252, 302, 322, 324–327, 330–332, 335, 336, 340, 342–344, 346, 348–354, 356,
personal, 9, 27, 242
private, 3, 5–6, 10–15, 26–28, 30, 31, 37, 39, 55, 62, 69, 91, 93, 94, 115, 129, 149, 151, 160, 164, 168–173, 183–185, 206–211, 215–217, 223–230, 241, 243, 263, 266, 288, 304, 336–338
privately held, 283
protected, 98
public, 5–6, 12, 13, 27–31, 47, 48, 55, 62, 64, 69, 71, 78, 91, 93, 126, 131, 132, 136–138, 143, 146, 153–169, 172–174, 178, 184, 188, 195, 204, 206, 207, 209, 210, 216, 221, 224, 225, 227, 230–234, 237, 239, 241–243, 278, 286, 287, 330, 333, 335, 349
publicly held, 154, 236, 238, 240, 283
registration, 4, 38, 159–173
single member, 3, 93–94, 148–152, 160, 169, 170, 198, 341, 343
small, 317
sub-holding, 330
unlimited, 5, 15, 320
unprotected, 98
Company Law Action Plan (Modernising Company Law and Enhancing Corporate Governance), 49, 99, 340, 355
Company Law centre at the British Institute of International Comparative Law (BIICL), 161
Company Law Review Steering Group (CLR), 156, 329
Competent authority, 51, 80, 90, 110, 113, 114, 119, 127, 129, 132, 135, 159, 255, 297, 300
Competition, 39, 43, 46, 51, 170, 216, 275, 277, 279, 294–297, 299–302, 304, 319, 331
Compliance, 57, 69, 76, 77, 82, 97, 105, 112, 158, 168, 169, 200, 233, 289, 325
Concentration, 53, 274, 283, 285, 295–301, 346
conglomerate, 301
nonhorizontal, 301
notification, 298, 299
remedies, 299

vertical, 301
Conflict
of interest, 90, 106, 189, 197, 200, 203, 205, 208, 213, 220, 221, 350
of laws, 77, 78, 116, 292
rules, 116
Conseil d'administration, 188, 189, 211
Conseil de surveillance, 188, 192
Consejo de administración, 207
Consiglio di amministrazione, 231
Consiglio di sorveglianza, 231, 235
Consideration, 33, 50, 63–66, 75, 89, 96, 100, 107, 108, 155, 163, 164, 168, 173, 281, 312, 329, 344
Consolidated financial statements, 82, 84, 85, 89, 91, 193, 234, 303-305, 323–327, 338, 344
Notes, 322–326
Consolidation, 77, 85, 86, 278, 309, 310, 322–326, 349
exclusion, 324–325
proportional, 325
Consortium, 123, 349
Constitución en forma sucesiva por suscripción pública de acciones, 154
Constitution avec offre au public d'instruments financiers, 154
Consultation rights, 248, 249, 253, 257, 269-271, 293
Contract
control, 333–337, 349
joint venture, 278–280
long-term, 273
of employment, 190, 217, 261, 264, 267, 268, 292
pre-incorporation, 165, 167, 173
Contractual defence mechanism, 285
Contribution, 12, 17, 22, 23, 26, 73, 81, 158, 163, 164, 166, 168, 170-173, 177, 278, 279, 335, 342
in kind, 164, 173
Control
change of, 296
contract, 333–337, 349
internal, 90, 180, 231, 233, 318
Control (constituting a group)
Beherrschungsvertrag, 333, 335, 349
centrale leiding, 349
contrôle, 349
Contrôle, 349
Controlling interest, 298
Conventions, 2, 36, 53, 77, 261, 277
Conversion, 32, 40, 41, 79, 81, 100, 101, 128, 130, 138, 148, 149, 155, 176
draft terms, 130, 138
Convertibles, 176
Cooperation
between undertakings (enterprises), 295
cross-border, 3, 32, 123, 151, 273–302
strategic, 273–276, 278, 280,
structuring of, 32, 275
Cooperative society, 2, 30, 34, 146–148
Corporate governance, 3, 27, 48, 50, 55, 84, 87, 96, 102, 104, 107, 108, 110, 180, 183–218, 221, 223, 232, 233, 271, 283, 318, 331, 340
codes, 184, 218, 221, 223, 318
statement, 84, 87, 318, 331, 340
Corporate Social Responsibility, 87, 233, 305, 332
Corporate
groups, 330
law, 1–3, 31, 43, 50, 51, 53, 115, 196
scandals, 27, 82, 179, 180
veil, 337, 347, 350–356
Corporation, 4, 35, 161, 164, 175, 202, 333
Costs
of distribution, 66
of formation, 155
of sales, 314
Court order, 163, 173, 240
Court of Justice of the European Union (CJEU), 52

Creditor protection, 27, 150, 289, 290, 353
Cross-border
  acquisitions, 280–283
  dimension (EEIG), 276–278
  insolvency, 139
  merger, 31, 32, 48, 76–82, 99, 125, 145, 146, 157, 248, 250, 259, 281, 288–291, 294, 345
  transfer (of the seat), 102
Cross-participation, 287, 334
Current assets, 312, 313

D

Day-to-day management, 136–137, 212, 213, 216, 239
Debenture, 74, 291, 313
Decision making, 3, 13–15, 35, 95, 104, 122, 132, 137–139, 142, 148, 193, 198, 208, 230, 240, 241, 245, 248, 276, 289, 291, 322
De facto directors, 339, 352, 354, 356
Defence measures
  post-bid, 284
  pre-bid, 285
Defensive measures, 95, 98, 222, 283, 286
Deferred income, 313
Delegados de personal, 267
Délégués du personnel, 262
Dependence, qualified, 337
Derivative
  action, 186, 194, 202
  claim, 229–230
  financial instruments, 112, 312, 315
Derivatives, 111, 112
Digital Single Market, 157
Directeur général, 188–191
Directives (including proposals)
  access to the activity, the supervisory framework and the prudential rules for credit institutions and investment firms, 110
  Accounting Directive, 82, 303–310, 317, 318, 323, 324, 344, 345, 348–350, 356
  admission of securities to official stock exchange listings and on information to be published on those securities, 111, 320, 345
  Anti-Tax Avoidance Directive, 346
  Bank Recovery and Resolution Directive, 96
  Capital Directive, 62–64, 67, 69, 154
  Capital Requirements Directive (CRD IV), 110
  collective redundancies, 255–257, 268
  Common Consolidated Corporate Tax Base, 50, 331
  Common Corporate Tax Base, 50
  Data Protection Directive, 92
  Eight Directive, 88–91, 180, 181
  Eleventh Directive, 36, 38, 70, 91–93
  encouragement of long-term shareholder engagement, 102
  establishing a general framework for informing and consulting employees, 248, 256, 291
  EWC Directive, 144, 247, 249, 252–254, 256, 257, 344
  Fifth Directive, 48, 49, 184, 246, 248
  First Directive, 21, 32, 48, 49, 54–62, 64, 65, 67, 70, 79, 91, 119, 122, 131, 154, 155, 158, 165, 173, 224, 226, 303, 319
  Fourteenth Directive, 32, 98–102, 281
  Fourth Directive, 15, 47, 52, 56, 82, 83, 322
  Framework on safety and health, 256
  interconnection of central, commercial and companies registers, 55, 56, 81, 92
  Market Abuse Directive, 111
  Markets in financial instruments directive (MIFID), 112, 113, 177
  Merger Directive, 70, 76, 81

Merger Tax Directive, 282
Ninth Directive, 49, 338
Parent-subsidiary Directive, 322, 348, 349
Preventive restructuring, 52
Prospectus Directive, 109, 112, 113
Safeguarding of employees' rights in the event of transfers of undertakings, 73, 255, 292, 294
SCE Directive, 254, 260
Second Directive, 62–69, 72, 73, 153–155, 158, 160–163, 168, 170, 172, 176, 342, 344
SE Directive, 79, 104, 111, 124, 126, 127, 129, 131, 138, 141, 142, 144–146, 211, 228, 248, 250, 254, 255, 260, 294, 303, 343
Seventh Directive, 55, 82, 83, 85, 92, 180, 303, 306, 307, 322, 323, 331, 348
Shareholders Rights Directive, 48, 102–108, 241
Single-member private limited liability companies, 93–94
Sixth Directive, 70, 74–76, 146
Statutory audits and consolidated accounts, 88, 91
Takeover Directive, 95, 283, 285, 318, 345
Tenth Directive, 31, 48, 70, 75–82, 92, 99, 100, 102, 125, 129, 146, 248, 250, 260, 280, 281, 288–291, 294, 345
Third Directive, 61, 70, 71, 73–80, 99, 129, 131, 145, 281, 289–291, 294, 345
Thirteenth Directive, 47, 48, 95–98, 102, 287, 340, 342, 345
Transfer of the Registered Office, 98–102
Transparency Directive, 112, 114, 342, 345
Twelfth Directive, 93–94, 149, 342
Directoire, 188, 192
Director
agreements between–and the company, 193, 203
appointment, 224–225, 232, 241
board of, 60, 175, 188, 189, 191, 192, 195, 207, 211, 212, 217–219, 222, 231, 232, 234–236, 242, 262, 289
dismissal (*see* Appointment)
duties, 31, 220–221, 223, 226–229
duty of care, 200
fiduciary duties–, 161, 226, 229
liablity, 39, 193–194, 212–216, 228, 237–239, 242, 352, 354, 355
powers, 224–225
removal (*see* Appointment)
remuneration, 51, 180, 349
shadow, 228, 352
Disclosure
Directive (*see* First Directive)
requirements, 4, 31, 36, 38, 76, 83, 91–93, 106, 233, 284, 319
Disqualification, of directors, 229
Distribution, 13, 22, 23, 62, 63, 66, 67, 69, 113, 123, 150, 171, 194, 223, 241, 251, 274, 277, 278, 295, 302, 353, 354
Dividend
of profits and losses, 63, 150, 176, 207
to shareholders, 176, 207
Division
of profits and losses, 275
Domestic law, 2, 44, 116, 131, 170, 346
Dominant
enterprise, 333, 334, 337
influence, 85, 86, 217, 331, 333, 334, 336, 338, 344, 345, 348, 350, 356
Domination agreement, 204, 206
Draft terms of formation, 132, 138
Dutch auction clause, 279
Duty (standard) of care, 200, 208, 213, 228
Duty to exercise independent judgment, 228

E

Economic
dependence, 297, 346
integration, 85
EEIG. *See* European Economic Interest Grouping (EEIG)
Effective
competition, 297, 300, 301
control, 85, 223
Eighth Directive, 88–91, 180, 181
Eingliederung, 335
Einheitliche Leitung, 334
Einigungsstelle, 264
Electronic means, 56, 57, 103, 157, 159, 222, 241
Eleventh Directive, 36, 38, 70, 91–93
Employee
representation, 48, 120, 249, 259, 262, 263, 268, 269
representatives, 80, 126, 137–138, 141, 193, 199, 200, 248, 249, 251–257, 259, 260, 262–265, 268, 294
Employee involvement, 3, 124, 125, 131, 134, 138, 140, 142–145, 151, 152, 245–271
Employee participation
import of the system of, 143
pre-existing, 81, 143
Employees
rights, protection of, 71, 291–294
role, 28, 35, 99, 122, 246, 289
safeguarding of rights, 73, 292, 294
Employer, 253–258, 260–262, 264–268, 270, 292, 293
Enterprise
agreements, 334–337
associated, 333, 334
Chamber, 222, 223, 266
controlling, 334–336
micro-class, 3, 4
Entrepreneur, 2–4, 10, 11, 30, 49, 52, 93, 94, 109, 171, 297, 304
Equity
ratio, 177, 178
Establishment, right of, 32–41, 52, 77, 91, 99, 289, 346
Eurofima *(Société européenne pour le financement du materiel ferroviaire),* 2
European Association (EA), 115, 146
European Banking Authority (EBA), 110
European business organizations, 3, 43, 124–125, 146–152
European Central Bank (ECB), 52, 111
European Code of Conduct relating to transactions in transferable securities, 51
European Community (EC), 4, 36–40, 51, 53–55, 77, 79, 96, 99, 122, 124, 141, 247, 252, 256, 296, 299, 306, 307, 318, 320
European Company. *See Societas Europaea* (SE)/European Company
European Cooperative Society (SCE), 1–2, 30, 146–148
European Court of Justice (ECJ), 1, 14, 32–41, 49, 52, 53, 58–61, 65, 69, 74, 76–78, 83, 84, 99, 100, 147, 171, 216, 251, 252, 255, 259, 264, 277, 279, 292, 300, 306, 319, 331, 344, 346, 347. *See also* Judicial decisions
European Currency Units (ECUs), 65
European Economic Area (EEA), 81, 103
European Economic Interest Grouping (EEIG)
abuse of, 120
formation, 116
formation and publication, 118–121
involvement of employees, 122–123
liability of members, 121
membership, 120–121
official address, 118–122
regulation, 116, 117, 119, 120
structure, 121–122

European identity, 144
European Insurance and Occupational Pensions Authority (EIOPA), 110–111
European Judicial Network, 54
European Model Company Act (EMCA), 184, 342
European Private Company, 30, 115, 116, 151, 152. *See also Societas Privata Europaea* (SPE)
European Securities and Markets Authority (ESMA), 50, 110, 113, 114, 321
European Securities Committee (ESC), 97, 111
European Union (EU), 1, 9–41, 43, 44, 48, 52, 115–153, 188, 246, 273, 279, 300, 304, 330
European Works Council (EWC), 31, 50, 78, 122, 141, 142, 144, 247–254, 256, 257, 259, 269, 270, 293, 344
Exchange ratio, 72, 80, 130, 345
Executive officers, 188, 191–193
Existenzvernichtender Eingriff, 337, 351
EXtensible Business Reporting Language (XBRL), 321
Extraordinary
  administrator, 347
  meeting, 194, 195, 209
  resolution, 188, 206
  rights of shareholders, 286

F

Factoring, 177
Fair value, 66, 111, 312
Family-owned business, 329
Fifth Directive, 48, 49, 184, 246, 248
Financial
  assistance, 63, 67, 68, 147, 174, 209, 311, 314, 339
  institutions, 50, 93, 110, 135
  instruments, 109, 112–114, 177, 312, 315, 317
  services, 3, 43, 44, 47, 108, 110–112
  statements, 31, 55, 58, 82–88, 91, 111, 127, 138–140, 180, 234, 303–327, 338, 344
  year, 55, 66, 69, 72, 83, 114, 156, 187, 204, 214, 224, 233–235, 308–311, 313, 314, 316, 320, 321, 326, 336
Financial Services Action Plan (FSAP), 49, 111, 112, 306
Firm name, 4, 17, 19, 21
Firms, networked, 274
First Directive, 21, 32, 48, 49, 54–62, 64, 65, 67, 70, 79, 91, 119, 122, 131, 154, 155, 158, 165, 173, 224, 226, 303, 319
Fiscal transparency, 15, 117
Fixed
  assets, 311–312, 315
  legal capital, 161, 170
Formation expenses, 311
Forum, choice of, 53, 276, 277
Forum Europaeum Konzernrecht, 339, 340
Fourteenth Directive, 32, 98–102, 281
Fourth Directive, 15, 47, 52, 56, 82, 83, 322
Fraudulent trading, 63
Freedom of establishment, 6, 14, 15, 32–34, 38, 39, 41, 44, 46, 49, 77, 78, 99, 101, 111, 188, 216, 264, 319

G

General Accepted Accounting Principles (GAAP), 181, 306
General duties (of director), 226
General meeting, 6, 60, 66–69, 72, 73, 80, 89, 97–99, 103, 126, 130, 134–139, 184–186, 188–194, 196–199, 201, 205, 208, 209, 212–217, 219, 221–226, 229–241, 266, 286, 322
General principles (of accounting), 308

Gérant, 22, 185
Gesamtbetriebsrat, 264
Gesamthandsgemeinschaft, 22
Geschäftsanteil, 174
Geschäftsführer, 196
Gesellschaft, 9, 13, 17, 27
Gesellschaft mit beschränkter Haftung (GmbH), 5, 13, 27–29, 37, 39, 58, 170, 171, 173, 196–199, 263, 276, 303, 319, 336, 337
Gewone commanditaire vennootschap (Comm.V), 25
GmbH & Co. KG, 28, 29, 303, 319
Going concern, 24, 308
Goodwill, 312, 325
Gross
  profit, 309, 311
Group
  community-scale, 248–254, 293
  of companies, 3, 49, 65, 82, 149, 246, 278, 329, 331, 340, 342, 355
  concepts, 322, 344, 347–350, 356
  contractual, 335, 336
  de facto, 336, 337, 339, 353, 354
  formation, 116, 118, 342–343
  functioning, 342, 344–346
  horizontal, 322, 330, 349
  law, 49, 330, 332, 338–346, 353, 354
  liability, 330, 351, 354
  policy, 49, 339, 340
  relations, 332–334, 336, 338, 339, 350, 355, 356
  structures, 87, 144, 329, 332, 340, 343, 344, 356
  of undertakings, 248, 249, 251–253, 262, 265, 267, 293
Groupement d'intérêt économique (GIE), 117
Grouping, 116–123, 255, 324
Guidelines on the application of Art. 81(3) of the Treaty, 302
Guidelines on the assessment of horizontal mergers, 300
Guidelines on the assessment of non-horizontal mergers, 301

H

Handelsregister, 21, 26, 159
Handlungsbevollmächtigter, 196
Harmonization
  of accounting rules, 83
  of financial information, 90
  programme-, 2, 15, 31, 32, 43–114, 153
Head office, 35, 100, 114, 128, 129, 132–134, 146, 148, 320, 332
Heads of agreement, 277, 298
Hedge funds, 176
Herrschendes Unternehmen, 333
High Level Group of Company Law Experts, 63, 95, 290, 339
Holders of securities, 78, 96, 97, 291
Home country regulation, 91

I

IASC Foundation, 306
IAS Regulation, 306, 307
Imprenditore commerciale, 10
Income (in profit and loss account), 314
Incorporation
  certificate of, 5, 159
  doctrine, 34, 35, 39, 132
  of foreign activities, 346
  instrument of, 64, 66, 68, 154, 155, 158, 159
Independent expert, 65, 66, 70, 72, 75, 80, 130, 158, 163, 172, 187, 221, 309, 344, 345
Industrial relations, 251, 253, 257
Information and consultation (of employees), 45, 50, 122, 123, 140, 246–248, 257, 259, 291
Information, financial, 90, 319
Information, non-financial, 305, 317, 318, 326, 340
Insider
  dealing, 51, 112
  information, 112–113

Insolvency, 19, 52, 57, 63, 92, 109, 116, 117, 127, 139, 140, 213, 216, 292, 338, 346, 347, 350–352, 354, 355
Insolvency Regulation, 140, 346–347
Institutional investors, 104–108, 184
Integrated reporting (IR), 305
Intellectual property rights, 275, 279
Interconnection of registers, 56, 57, 92
Interim dividend, 321
Internal market, 31, 43, 45, 50, 81, 95, 101, 109, 177, 246, 296
International Accounting Standards (IAS), 111, 139, 303, 305–307, 313, 314, 316, 318, 340
International Accounting Standards Board (IASB), 306
International Accounting Standards Committee (IASC), 306
International Financial Reporting Standards (IFRS), 63, 83, 88, 139, 181, 303, 305–307, 309, 311–314, 316, 323, 324, 356
International insolvency law, 139
International Tin Council, 11
Intra-group transactions, 316
Intuitu personae, 5
Investigation of companies and their affairs, 229
Investment firms, 64, 71, 103, 112, 114
Investment Plan for Europe (Juncker Plan), 108
Investor protection, 108, 111, 223, 342
Involuntary creditors, 332
Issuers of securities, 112, 113, 320, 321

J

Joint and several liability, 12, 116, 119, 121, 173
Joint-stock companies, 10, 30, 167
Joint venture
  business, 278
  contract, 279
  contractual, 278
  cooperative, 295
  equity, 278
Judicial decisions, 52–54, 118
Jurisdiction (forum) shopping, 140, 347

K

Kaufmann, 10
Kleine AG, 93
Kommanditgesellschaft (KG), 25, 28, 29
Kommanditgesellschaft auf Aktien (KGaA), 5, 29, 333, 334, 336
Konzernbetriebsrat, 264
Konzernrecht, 332, 337, 339, 340, 350, 353, 356

L

Language, 9, 57, 69, 90, 92, 159, 277, 307
Legal
  basis for EU activities, 44
  bodies, 120, 121, 125, 128, 129, 148
  instruments, 46–54, 110, 275, 297, 346, 352
  person-, 3, 4, 11, 12, 20, 22, 24, 29, 34, 52, 99, 103, 116, 122, 130, 134, 137, 147, 149, 155, 165–167, 170, 199, 207, 217, 218, 220, 275, 293, 334, 345
  personality, 4, 11–12, 15–18, 20–24, 26, 28, 33, 34, 58, 98, 99, 114, 117, 125, 131, 149, 150, 160, 165–167, 169, 173, 183, 188, 278, 350, 352, 353, 356
Letter of intent (LOI), 277
Level playing field, 32, 95, 284
Leverage, 108
Lex mercatoria, 280
Limited liability, 11, 15, 20, 24–28, 84, 93, 130, 165, 171, 173, 304, 308, 323, 329, 332, 347
Limited liability company, 13, 125, 160, 243, 308, 323
Limited liability partnership (LLP), 12

Liquidation, 20, 24, 40, 56, 71, 73, 74, 77, 95, 116, 121, 127, 139–140, 161, 176, 220, 228, 237, 280, 355
Listing requirements, 113
Loan capital, 27, 28, 174–177
Loan Market Association (LMA), 175
Loans to directors, 197, 228, 316
Loan, subordinated, 176
Loss-making operations, 352, 354

M

Maatschap, 18
Major holdings, 49, 114, 342
Majority requirements, 214
Management
  body, 67, 68, 72, 149, 151, 170, 183, 231, 233, 236, 240, 241
  buyout, 68, 177
  organ, 135–138, 184, 189
  report, 72, 83, 84, 87, 139, 214, 303, 316–321, 324, 326, 327, 344
  rights (powers), 19, 22, 25, 183, 203, 212
  structure, 3, 15–16, 28, 183, 185–186, 196–198, 202–205, 211–212, 216–218, 223–224, 283
Management and control, 183–243
Managers
  powers, 199
Managing directors, 136, 196–198, 208, 213
Mandatory bid, 97, 108, 342
Market abuse, 111–113
Market Abuse Directive, 111
Market Abuse Regulation, 111–113
Mediation, 276
Member State, host, 39–41, 99, 346
Memorandum
  of association, 55, 156, 243
  of understanding (MOU), 277
Merchant, 10
Merger
  by acquisition, 71, 73, 74, 78, 80
  control, 73, 273–274, 281, 282, 294–302, 346
  cross-border, 31, 32, 48, 76–82, 99, 125, 145, 146, 150, 157, 248, 259, 281, 288–291, 294, 345
  domestic, 70–74, 78–81, 290
  draft terms, 72, 79, 80, 130, 138, 141, 290, 291, 345
  by formation of a new company, 71, 73, 74, 77, 78, 128
  horizontal, 300, 301
  intra-group, 73
  legal consequences, 73, 74
Merger Directive, 70, 76, 81
Merger Regulation, 51, 279, 295–301
Merger Tax Directive, 282
Mezzanine, 176, 177, 313
Micro-entities, 83
MIFID. *See* Directives (including proposals)
Minority
  protection, 210, 224, 230
  rights, 186, 202
  shareholders, 28, 33, 79, 80, 99, 129, 130, 134, 136, 137, 139, 184, 187, 194, 195, 198, 202, 207, 211, 213, 222, 223, 230, 232, 234, 235, 238, 240, 291, 330, 332, 333, 335–338, 340, 342, 346, 350, 356
Mismanagement, 186, 187, 200, 352, 354
Mitbestimmung, 263
Model articles of association, 168
Modernising Company Law and Enhancing Corporate Governance in the European Union–A Plan to Move Forward, 49, 99, 102, 151, 340, 355
Mortgage, 177–179
Multinational enterprise (MNE), 245, 246, 332, 338, 346
Multiple voting rights, 98, 286
Mutual
  claims and debts, 326

obligations, 339
recognition, 31, 44, 288
societies, 115, 146, 147
transactions, 326

N

Naamloze vennootschap (NV), 28, 30, 162, 211–223
Nachteilsausgleich, 336
National
courts, 38, 46, 53, 62
gazette, 56, 79, 119, 159
Negotiating body, 141–144, 250, 251, 254, 270
Negotiations, 30, 126, 141–143, 160, 249, 250, 252–254, 266, 268, 270, 276, 277, 291
Net turnover, 86, 304, 310, 314, 316
Ninth Directive, 49, 338
Nominal value, 64, 65, 67, 71, 73, 75, 155, 163, 164, 168, 172, 174, 215, 317
Non-cash contribution, 73, 164, 168, 342
Non-executive directors, 184, 217–219, 225
Non-financial information, 305, 317, 318, 326, 340
Notarial deed
of incorporation, 4, 158, 159, 166
Notification form (Form CO), 299
Novation, 58

O

Off-balance sheet arrangements, 179–181
Offene Handelsgesellschaft (OHG), 20, 22
Offeror, 96–98, 284, 286, 345
Official Journal, 119, 131, 191, 209, 211, 214, 300
Ondernemingsraad, 260, 265
One person group, 94
One-tier board. *See* Board
Opérations de gestion, 187
Options
share options, 207
stock options, 233
Organ
administrative, 79, 80, 136–138, 294
supervisory, 135–138, 189, 294
Organization for Economic Co-operation and Development (OECD), 50, 332
Originator, 177–178
Outsourcing, 274, 292
Ownership ceiling, 284, 285

P

Parent-subsidiary relationship, 322, 344, 348, 349
Partial profit transfer contract, 335
Participaciones sociales, 174
Participating
companies, 77, 128–133, 141–143, 148
interest, 312, 315, 326
Participation, 23–24, 26, 79, 103, 136, 141–144, 160, 240–242, 245, 246, 248, 249, 260, 278, 294
Partner(s)
general, 17, 24–26, 28–30
liability, 15, 19
limited, 5, 10, 20, 24–26, 28, 29, 55, 84, 87, 173, 303, 319, 320, 323
Partnerschaftsgesellschaft (PartGG), 12
Partnership
assets, 22
civil, 11, 16–18
commercial, 4, 10, 16–18, 278
continuation, 24
contract, 15, 16, 18, 21–24
dissolution, 23, 24
general, 18–20
liability (of partners), 12
limited, 5, 10, 20, 24–26, 28, 29, 55, 84, 87, 173, 303, 319, 320, 323
liquidation, 24
objects, 16, 21, 23
property, 19, 20

silent, 10, 17, 18
Patrimonial regime, 22
Personal companies, 9, 27, 242
Pfandbrief, 179
Piercing the corporate veil, 337, 347, 350–356
Post-formation
acquisitions, 66
acts, 59
Power of attorney, 26, 203
Pre-AG, 166
Pre-emption, right of, 68, 279
Pre-formation company, 131, 173
Pre-incorporation contracts, 167, 173
Preliminary ruling, 37, 38, 52, 53, 61, 62, 69, 264, 347
Prepayments, 312
Président directeur général, 188, 191
Primary establishment, 33–36
Private equity, 176
Private limited (liability) company, 9, 27, 30, 61, 84, 93–94, 125, 128, 148–152, 160, 169, 170, 172, 202, 243, 303, 308, 323, 343
Profit, 4, 10, 11, 13, 14, 17–19, 22, 23, 34, 50, 66, 83, 84, 87, 95, 117, 119, 146, 150, 171, 176, 178, 194, 201, 204, 206, 209, 227, 241, 259, 275, 277, 278, 335, 336
Profit and loss account
consolidated, 325
layout, 314
Profit or loss, 83, 87, 313, 314
Profit pooling contract, 335
Profit transfer agreement, 204, 206
Prokurist, 197, 203
Prospectus, 62, 112, 113
Prospectus Directive, 109, 112, 113
Prospectus Regulation, 112
Provisions (in annual account), 327
Proxy, 103, 105, 106, 210, 230
Proxy advisors, 105, 106
Prudence principle, 308
Prudential framework, 110
Public-interest entities, 86–90, 315–318, 326
Public limited (liability) company, 28, 29, 62–74, 94, 125–128, 130, 133, 135–139, 153, 158, 161, 170, 303, 323
Pyramid structures, 340

Q

Qualified de facto group, 354
Qualified majority, 44, 45, 142, 185, 208, 217, 222, 276
Quorum, 195, 209, 210, 214, 230, 240, 242, 290

R

Rappresentanze sindacali aziendali (RSA), 269, 270
Rappresentanze sindacali unitarie (RSU), 269, 270
Real seat, 35, 36, 39, 40, 99, 132, 133, 140, 150, 152, 279
Reasonable care, skill and diligence (duty to exercise), 226, 228–230
Receivables, 164, 178
Recepisse K bis (or *Extrait K bis*), 169
Reciprocity principle, 286
Recognition of companies, 34, 35, 39
Recognition of foreign insolvency procedures, 139
Recommendations by the Commission
EU Financial Reporting Strategy: the way forward, 36
new approach to business failure and insolvency, 52
quality assurance for the statutory audit in the European Union: minimum requirements, 88
quality of corporate governance reporting ('comply or explain'), 104

regime for the remuneration of directors of listed companies, 180
role of non-executive or supervisory directors of listed companies and on the committees of the (supervisory) board, 51
Statutory Auditors' Independence in the EU: A Set of Fundamental Principles, 88
transfer of SMEs, 24
Registered office, 1, 33–39, 48, 51, 57, 58, 72, 80, 81, 86, 91, 98–102, 114, 125–129, 131–135, 137, 138, 140, 146, 148, 150, 155, 164, 188, 218, 279, 291, 294, 315, 323, 347
Registration. *See* Company
Registre du commerce et des sociétés, 169
Regulation (legal instrument). *See also* European Cooperative Society (SCE); European Economic Interest Grouping (EEIG); Insolvency; *Societas Europaea* (SE)/European Company
adapting a number of instruments subject to the procedure referred to in Article 251 of the Treaty to Council Decision 1999/468/EC with regard to the regulatory procedure with scrutiny, 96
adopting certain international accounting standards ((EC) 1126/2008), 307
application of Article 101(3) of the Treaty on the Functioning of the European Union to categories of vertical agreements and concerted practices, 295
application of international accounting standards ((EC 1606/2002), 51, 318
establishing a European Supervisory Authority (European Banking Authority), 110
European Economic Interest Grouping (EEIG), 2, 30, 45, 116, 117, 119, 120
European Supervisory Authority (European Banking Authority) ((EU) 1093/2010), 64, 71, 76, 96, 104, 110, 111
European Supervisory Authority (European Insurance and Occupational Pensions Authority) ((EU) 1094/2010), 100, 111
European Supervisory Authority (European Securities and Markets Authority) ((EU) 1094/2010), 111
European Union macro-prudential oversight of the financial system and establishing a European Systemic Risk Board ((EU) 1092/2010), 111
implementing Council Regulation (EC) No 139/2004 on the control of concentrations between undertakings ((EC) 802/2004), 296, 297
Insolvency Regulation ((EU) 2015/848), 140, 331, 346, 347
jurisdiction and the recognition and enforcement of judgments in civil and commercial matters, 53
law applicable to contractual obligations (Rome I), 77, 279
law applicable to non-contractual obligations (Rome II), 122
Market Abuse Regulation, 111–113
Markets in Financial Instruments Regulation (MiFIR), 114, 177
Merger Regulation ((EC) 139/2004), 296

prospectus regulation, 112
prudential requirements for credit institutions and investment firms, 64, 71, 103, 110
specific requirements regarding statutory audit of public-interest entities, 89
Statute for a European company (SE), 1, 124, 125
Statute for a European Cooperative Society (SCE), 2, 125, 147, 151
Statute for a European Private Company (SPE Proposal), 151, 152
supplementing Directive 2004/109/EC of the European Parliament and of the Council with regard to regulatory technical standards on access to regulated information at Union level ((EU) 2016/1437), 321
technical specifications and procedures required for the system of interconnection of registers (2015/884), 157
Related parties, 105, 106, 233, 315, 316, 326, 341, 353
Relocation, 40, 251, 292
Renegotiation clause, 276
Renewed Social Agenda, 246
Renvoi, 116
Representation
of employees, 140, 152, 265
power of, 59–61, 212, 215, 217
Reserves, 13, 56, 66, 67, 69, 100, 150, 174, 207, 218, 310–313, 325
Resolution, 22, 64, 71, 96, 97, 101, 103, 157, 175, 184–186, 188–195, 198, 200–204, 206, 207, 209–211, 214, 215, 217, 220, 221, 223–225, 229, 230, 276, 277, 279, 289, 305, 335, 336
Right of first refusal, 279
Risk management, 90, 110, 179, 199, 317, 318, 331
Rozenblum-doctrine, 336

S

Safety and health requirements, 248
Sarbanes-Oxley Act (SOX), 88, 91, 179, 180, 331
SCE Directive, 254, 260
SCE Regulation, 30, 147, 148
Scission, 75
SE. *See Societas Europaea* (SE)/European Company
Secondary
establishment, 33, 39, 342, 346
formation, 127, 128
proceedings (insolvency), 140
registration, 118
Second Directive, 62–70, 72, 73, 153–155, 158, 160–163, 168, 170, 172, 176, 342, 344
Securities
asset-backed, 179
regulation, 43
Securitization, 109, 177–179
SE Directive, 79, 104, 124, 126, 127, 129, 131, 138, 141, 142, 144–146, 248, 250, 254, 260, 294, 343
Self-employed persons, 34, 44
Senior bank loan, 176
Separation of ownership and control, 27
SE Regulation, 80, 111–113, 124, 126–129, 131, 133–135, 137–139, 141, 144–146
SEC. *See Sociedad en comandita* (SEC)
Service contract, 185, 205, 217, 224
Seventh Directive, 55, 82, 83, 85, 92, 180, 303, 306, 307, 322, 323, 331, 348
Share capital, 28, 30, 37, 38, 63, 95, 150, 156, 162–164, 166, 169, 171, 172, 174, 176, 186, 188, 195, 210, 214, 217, 218, 266, 285, 286, 312, 335

Shareholders
  classes of, 68
  equal treatment, 63, 68, 102, 136, 140
  general meeting of, 6, 60, 97, 98, 214, 219, 222, 239–241
  meeting, 101, 187, 196, 198, 199, 201, 202, 204, 205, 208, 211
Shareholdership, dispersed, 7, 93, 283
Shareholders Rights Directive, 48, 102–108, 241
Share purchase agreement (SPA), 28, 231–241, 280
Shares
  acquisition of, 63, 273, 281, 283, 299, 342, 349
  classes of, 68, 139, 155, 284
  supernumerary, 287
  transfer of, 6, 155, 279, 284, 286, 293
  with no-par value, 174
Shop stewards, 269
Short-termism, 104, 105, 107
Siège réel, 35, 36
Simplification of the Legislation on the Internal Market (SLIM), 63
Single European Act, 45
Single-Member Private Limited Liability Company (SUP), 30, 93–94, 148–152
Single passport, 112–114
Six-month report, 114, 187, 204, 209, 321
Sixth Directive, 70, 74–76, 146
SLIM. *See* Simplification of the Legislation on the Internal Market (SLIM)
Small and medium-sized companies, 317
Small and medium-sized enterprises (SMEs), 4, 12, 13, 33, 83, 109, 110, 123, 149, 151, 177, 180
Social enterprise, 13, 14
Social policy, 43, 45, 50, 52, 151, 247, 260, 264–266
Social return on investment, 305
Sociedad anónima (SA), 28, 29, 156, 206
Sociedad civil interna, 17
Sociedad comanditaria por acciones (S. Com. por A.), 29
Sociedad de responsabilidad limitada (SL; SRL), 27, 169
Sociedad en comandita (SEC), 25
Sociedad Limitada Nueva Empresa (SLNE), 13, 169, 211
Sociedad regular colectiva (SC)
  società a responsabilità limitata (SRL), 13, 27, 169, 172, 241, 243
  società a responsabilità limitata a capitale ridotto, 172
  società a responsabilità limitata semplificata, 13, 169, 243
  società in accomandita per azioni (SAPA), 29
  società in accomandita semplice (SAS), 25
  società in nome collettivo (SNC), 20
  società per azioni (SPA), 28, 231, 280
  società semplice, 18
Societas Cooperativa Europaea; European Cooperative Society (SCE)
  applicable law, 148
  formation, 1
  membership, 148
Societas Europaea (SE)/European Company
  annual accounts
  applicable law, 126–127
  board structure, 125, 126
  capital, 135
  conversion, 128, 130, 138
  creditors
  formation and publication, 118–121, 127–131
  general meeting, 138–139
  head office, 133–135
  holding
  involvement of employees, 122–123
  law applicable to formation, 131–132
  liquidation, 139–140
  negotiating procedure, 141, 144
  participating companies, 128, 129, 132–133, 142–144

registered office, 133–135
Standard Rules (on employee involvement), 142–144, 254
Statutes, 1, 30
structure, 121–122
subsidiary, 128–130, 132, 141, 143, 145, 254
transfer of seat
winding up, 132–133, 139–140
Societas leonina, 23
Societas Privata Europaea (SPE), 30, 115, 116, 151, 152
Societas Unius Personae (SUP), 30, 94, 115, 116, 149–152, 343
Société, 9, 27
Société anonyme (SA), 5, 28–30, 32, 76, 156, 160, 162, 166, 167, 170, 188, 189, 204–215, 262, 347
Société à responsabilité limitée (SARL), 5, 14, 27, 29, 170, 171, 185–188
Société coopérative d'intérêt collectif (SCIC), 14
Société en commandité par actions (SCA), 29, 30
Société en commandite simple (SCS), 25
Société en formation, 166
Société en nom collectif (SNC), 20, 22, 23
Société en participation, 17
Société en participation ostensible, 17
Société Internationale de la Moselle, 2
Société par actions simplifiée (SAS), 13, 25, 160, 195–199
Société privée a responsabilité limitée (SPRL), 27, 215
Sole proprietor (trader), 2, 3
Sonderprüfung, 202
SPE. *See Societas Privata Europaea* (SPE)
Special negotiating body, 141, 143, 250, 254, 270
Special purpose vehicle (SPV), 178, 179
Spólka, 27
Spólka akcyjna (SA), 28
Spólka cywilna, 17
Spólka jawna (sp.j.), 29
Spólka komandytowa (sp.k.), 25
Spólka komandytowo-akcynja (SKA), 29
Spólka partnerska (sp.p), 12
Spólka z ograniczona odpowiedzialnocia (sp. z o.o.), 27
Sprecherausschüsse, 265
Stakeholders, 104, 107, 110, 157, 183, 227, 270, 307
Stammkapital, 198
Standard rules, 141–144, 254
State-owned companies, 260
Statutes, 1, 5, 6, 14, 30, 55, 59–61, 79, 93, 99, 124–127, 133, 134, 136–138, 144–148, 151, 154, 155, 157–159, 169, 188, 193, 197, 198, 212, 216, 219, 222, 231–233, 239, 241, 242, 246, 248, 254, 260, 261, 263–265, 267, 269, 281, 288–291, 294, 338, 343
Statutory
auditors, 87, 89–91, 180, 234, 235, 241, 243, 316, 320, 327
controls, 193, 228
instrument, 116
provisions, 71, 216, 218, 221, 259, 262, 276, 336, 350, 352, 354
Stille Gesellschaft, 17
Stille handelsvennootschap, 17
Stock companies, 10, 12, 27–38, 154, 167, 271
Stock exchange requirements, 281, 282. *See also* Listing requirements
Strategic alliance, 274, 275
Structure regime, 216–221, 266
Subsidiarity, 84
Subsidiary
integration of, 335
requirements, 141, 250, 251
Supervisory
board members, 189, 191–193, 205, 218–220, 236, 263

body, 127, 241, 243, 344
directors, 51, 180
Supranational business organization, 116, 124
Sustainable development, 44

T

Takeover
defences, 284–288
hostile, 95, 222, 283
Takeover bid(s), 31, 48, 95–98, 282–284, 342, 345
Takeover Directive, 95, 283, 285, 318, 345
Taxation, 3, 25, 43, 50, 83, 126, 275, 281, 282, 313, 332, 335, 337, 345, 347, 351
Tenth Directive, 31, 48, 70, 75–82, 92, 99, 100, 102, 125, 129, 146, 248, 250, 260, 280, 281, 288–291, 294, 345
Termination of office, 55, 59, 92. *See also* Appointment
Territorial unit, 116
Third Directive, 61, 70–80, 99, 129, 131, 145, 281, 289–291, 294, 345
Third parties, 13, 16, 17, 19, 21, 22, 26, 54–57, 59–61, 63, 67, 74, 113, 117, 119, 122, 123, 135, 140, 151, 154, 155, 165, 167, 168, 174, 178, 186, 189, 191, 192, 194–196, 199, 203, 207, 208, 212–215, 217, 221, 225, 227, 237, 239, 243, 279, 285, 308, 319, 340, 347
Thirteenth Directive, 47, 48, 95–98, 102, 287, 340, 342, 345
Tijdelijke handelsvennootschap, 17
Tipping, 113
Trade union representatives, 257, 259, 262, 263, 268, 269
Trade unions, 81, 140, 253, 256, 259–262, 264–270
Trading companies, 10
Transfer of
the registered office, 33, 35, 48, 98–102, 126, 133, 289
seat, 56, 102, 281
undertaking, 70, 292
Transfer pricing, 50
Transparency Directive, 112, 114, 304, 320, 342, 345
Treaty Establishing the European Community (TEEC), 54
Treaty of Lisbon, 306
Treaty on European Union, 44, 45, 52, 147
Treaty on the Functioning of the European Union, 15, 33, 35, 36, 39–41, 44–46, 51, 52, 54, 69, 84, 99, 120, 124, 128, 129, 147, 264, 279, 288, 289, 294, 296, 300, 302, 342
Treuepflicht, 337
Tribuneaux de commerce, 10
True and fair view, 83, 87, 307, 308, 315, 325
Turnover, 86, 216, 298, 304, 310, 314, 316
Twelfth Directive, 93–94, 149, 342
Two-tier board. *See* Board

U

UG *(haftungsbeschränkt)*, 13, 171
UG *(haftungsbeschränkte Unternehmergesellschaft)*, 13
Ultra vires, 54, 59
Unauthorized profit, 19, 227
Undertaking
community-scale, 122, 248–254, 293
large, 86, 87, 305, 309, 315–318, 326
medium-sized, 86, 88, 135, 304, 309, 310, 320
micro-, 86, 304, 309, 310
parent, 84–86, 310, 323, 324, 326, 344, 356
small, 86, 304, 309, 310
subsidiary, 84–86, 310, 324, 344, 348

Undertakings, parts of, 296
Undistributable reserves, 66, 67, 69
UNIDROIT Principles, 280
Unified basis (management on), 85, 86, 350
Uniform management, 333, 334
Unternehmensverträge, 334
Unternehmergesellschaft (haftungsbeschränkt), 13, 171
US Model Business Corporation Act, 161

V

Validity of obligations, 48, 54, 58–61, 154
Value-added tax (VAT), 3, 216
Value adjustments, 308, 314, 315
Vennootschap met sociaal oogmerk, 14
Vennootschap onder firma, 20, 22
Verbundene Unternehmen, 333, 334
Vertical concentration, 301
Vertragskonzern, 334
Vilvoorde Directive, 256
Vorgründungs-gesellschaft, 173
Vorstand, 199
Voting
  agreement, 230, 338
  cross-border, 103
  by proxy, 103
Voting rights
  differential, 230
  forfeiture, 287
  majority of, 84, 89, 322, 344, 345, 348, 349

W

Warrants, 176
Wechselseitig beteiligte Unternehmen, 334
Weisungsrecht, 335
White Paper on Completing the Internal Market, 31
Winding up, 35, 40, 56, 57, 61, 77, 92, 98, 125, 127, 130, 138–140, 221, 223, 280, 347
Works council, 31, 50, 58, 122, 140, 144, 218, 219, 247, 251, 252, 257, 259–269, 293, 319, 344
Wrongful trading, 161, 228, 342, 355

EUROPEAN COMPANY LAW SERIES

1. Steef M. Bartman (ed.), *European Company Law in Accelerated Progress*, 2006 (ISBN 978-90-411-2529-3).
2. Karen Vandekerckhove, *Piercing The Corporate Veil: A Transnational Approach*, 2007 (ISBN 978-90-411-2591-0).
3. Beate Sjåfjell, *Towards a Sustainable European Company Law: A Normative Analysis of the Objectives of EU Law, with the Takeover Directive as a Test Case*, 2009 (ISBN 978-90-411-2768-6).
4. Cornelis de Groot, *Corporate Governance as a Limited Legal Concept*, 2009 (ISBN 978-90-411-2873-7).
5. Adriaan F.M. Dorresteijn, Christoph Teichmann, Erik Werlauff, Tiago Monteiro & Nadia Pocher, *European Corporate Law*, Third Edition, 2017 (ISBN 978-90-411-8593-8).
6. Gert-Jan Vossestein, *Modernization of European Company Law and Corporate Governance: Some Considerations on its Legal Limits*, 2010 (ISBN 978-90-411-2592-7).
7. Catalin Stefan Rusu, *European Merger Control: The Challenges Raised by Twenty Years of Enforcement Experience*, 2010 (ISBN 978-90-411-3259-8).
8. Sabrina Bruno & Eugenio Ruggiero, *Public Companies and the Role of Shareholders: National Models Towards Global Integration*, 2011 (ISBN 978-90-411-3423-3).
9. Hanne S. Birkmose, Mette Neville & Karsten Engsig Sørensen (eds), *The European Financial Market in Transition*, 2012 (ISBN 978-90-411-3360-1).
10. Hanne S. Birkmose, Mette Neville & Karsten Engsig Sørensen (eds), *Boards of Directors in European Companies: Reshaping and Harmonising Their Organisation and Duties*, 2013 (ISBN 978-90-411-4141-5).
11. Christoph Van der Elst, *Executive Directors' Remuneration in Comparative Corporate Perspective*, 2015 (ISBN 978-90-411-5607-5).
12. Hanne S. Birkmose, *Shareholders' Duties*, 2017 (ISBN 978-90-411-5670-8).

www.ingramcontent.com/pod-product-compliance
Lightning Source LLC
Chambersburg PA
CBHW071237230926
51849CB00001B/136
* 9 7 8 9 0 4 1 1 8 5 9 3 8 *